Per visibilia ad invisibilia

Anthropological, Theological, and Semiotic Studies
on the Liturgy and the Sacraments

Gerard Lukken

collected and edited by

Louis van Tongeren and Charles Caspers

on the occasion of the retirement
of Gerard Lukken from the chair
of liturgy and sacramental theology
in the Theological Faculty Tilburg

Pharos

Kok Pharos Publishing House
Kampen – The Netherlands

Liturgia condenda 2

1. Gerard Lukken & Mark Searle, *Semiotics and Church Architecture*, Kampen, 1993

2. Gerard Lukken, *Per visibilia ad invisibilia*, edited by Louis van Tongeren & Charles Caspers, Kampen, 1994

Liturgia condenda is published by the Liturgical Institute of the Theological Department of Tilburg (NL). The series plans to publish innovative research into the science of liturgy and serves as a forum which will bring together publications produced by researchers of various nationalities. The motto *liturgia condenda* expresses the conviction that research into the various aspects of liturgy can make a critico-normative contribution to the deepening and the renewal of liturgical practice.

The editorial board: Gerard Lukken (Tilburg), Louis van Tongeren (Tilburg), Gerard Rouwhorst (Utrecht), Anton Scheer (Nijmegen), Lambert Leijssen (Louvain), Charles Caspers (secretary – Tilburg).

Liturgisch Instituut
P.O. Box 9130
5000 HC Tilburg
The Netherlands

De uitgever heeft het nodige in het werk gesteld om de rechten te regelen. Mogelijke rechthebbenden worden verzocht schriftelijk contact op te nemen met de uitgever.

CIP-GEGEVENS KONINKLIJKE BIBLIOTHEEK, DEN HAAG

© 1994, Kok Pharos Publishing House.
P.O. Box 5016, 8260 AG Kampen, The Netherlands
Cover Design by Dik Hendriks
ISBN 90 390 0601 6
NUGI 636
Typesetting: Elgraphic bv, Schiedam

All rights reserved. No parts of this publication may be reproduced, stored in a retrieval system, or transmitted, in any form or by any means, electronic, mechanical, photocopying, recording or otherwise, without the prior permission of the publisher.

Contents

Preface   7

Rite and Sign. Gerard Lukken: Some Bio-bibliographical Notes,
by Louis van Tongeren   9

Gerard Lukken: A Bibliography, 1953-1993. Compiled by
Charles Caspers and Louis van Tongeren   23

PART I: Anthropology & Liturgy
1. Liturgy and Secularization   45
2. La crise de la liturgie aux Pays-Bas. Comment donner
   corps au rituel chrétien dans une société sécularisée?   65
3. No Life without Rituals   88
4. Liturgie und Sinnlichkeit. Über die Bedeutung der Leiblichkeit
   in der Liturgie   118
5. Church and Liturgy as Dynamic Sacrament of the Spirit   140
6. Die Taufe: ein unersetzbares Sakrament   158
7. Theology of Baptism after Vatican II. Shifting Accents
   and Lacunae   184
8. This is a Great Mystery. A Theological Reflection on the
   Sacrament of Marriage   196
9. Funérailles et marginalité   205
10. Liturgiewissenschaft und 'Musik der christlichen Liturgie'   224

PART II: Semiotics & Liturgy
11. La liturgie comme lieu théologique irremplaçable.
    Méthodes d'analyse et de vérification théologiques   239
12. Plaidoyer pour une approche intégrale de la liturgie comme
    lieu théologique. Un défi à toute la théologie   256
13. Semiotics of the Ritual. Signification in Rituals as a
    Specific Mediation of Meaning   269
14. Zur theologischen Rezeption der Semiotik von
    Greimas. Widerstände und Mißverständnisse   284
15. Relevance of Semiotic Analysis to the Liturgical Sciences,
    Illustrated in the Light of the Rite of Marriage   299

16. Die Stellung der Frau im Trauungsritus des *Rituale Romanum* und nach Vaticanum II. Von der Unterordnung der Frau zu einer gewissen Gleichwertigkeit von Mann und Frau   311
17. Semiotic Analysis of the Confession at the Beginning of the Eucharist   335
18. Die architektonischen Dimensionen des Rituals   360
19. La sémiotique de l'architecture de l'église en tant que sémiotique du visuel   375

Index of Names   395

Tabula gratulatoria   402

Preface

The liturgy of the Roman Catholic church has seen an irrepressible development in the twentieth century, especially since the Second Vatican Council. Among the countries in which people, inspired by this council, have worked to open new channels in the liturgy, the Netherlands has a prominent place. One of the Dutch pioneers was, and still is, Gerard Lukken. During his many years' working in the field he has made many an effort to provide guidance to those who are celebrating the liturgy in parishes and elsewhere. At the same time he played a leading part in the development of the study of liturgy in the Netherlands. Even if his scholarly publications now and then show a local colour – and how could it be different –: the subjects which he brought up and the original way in which he elaborated them, exceed our national borders easily. Linguistic borders, however, are a different matter. Many of the products of his pen, which have not lost any value or topicality, have been published only in Dutch so far. The announcement of his early retirement therefore seemed to us to be an excellent occasion to collect some of Gerard Lukken's articles and contributions and to publish them in English, German or French. On the third of March 1994 this anthology was presented to Gerard Lukken on the occasion of his official farewell from the Theologisch Faculteit Tilburg, in which he taught since 1967.

Gerard Lukken has practised liturgical study always as a theological discipline and in the theological approach to liturgy he has taken to heart two aspects especially. From the start he has persued the anthropology of the Christian ritual. In the course of time the opening up of the method of semiotics and its operationalizing for and application to liturgical objects became his second special area of attention. These two accents determine the structure of this book in two parts. And the title covers both of them as well. *Per visibilia ad invisibilia* is a slight paraphrase of a word from Saint Augustine in *De civitate Dei* (book X, chapter 14). Each ritual, and especially a sacrament, professes to be the expression of more than it manifests externally. It refers to another reality, which is deeper or higher. Behind the visible an invisible reality hides itself, which can only be evoked and represented by means of the visible. Semiotics is active expressly in the area of tension of the visible and the invisible and searches for the signification which is hidden under complex systems of signs by uncovering the structures of meaning.

Having consulted with the author the editors have chosen the articles and contributions with two criteria in mind. The choice should result in a representative survey of the scholarly work of Gerard Lukken during the past twenty-five years, and the studies included should offer something new for colleagues outside the Netherlands. Some contributions have been shortened or otherwise slightly edited. Occasionally bibliographical material has been added in a note. The result is the present volume, which could never have come into being without the assistance of many people, to whom we would like to express our thanks. First we mention the translators: Ms. G. Merks-Leinen, M.Div., D. Mader, M.Div., W.M. Speelman, M.Div., M. Schneiders, M.Div., and F. Hoppenbrouwers, M.Div. Important bibliographical searches have been carried out by N. Vreeswijk, research assistent of the section Liturgy of the Theologische Faculteit Tilburg, by Ms. E. Duindam-Dekkers, secretary of the Dutch section of the international periodical *Concilium*, and by K. Kok, M.Div., staff member of the Stichting 'Leerhuis en Liturgie' in Amsterdam. Secretarial assistance we received from Ms. S. Luijk-van den Bogert. Of prime importance was our cooperation with Ms. K. De Troyer, M.Div., from our publishers, Kok-Pharos. This publication has been made possible financially by the support of: the Theologische Faculteit Tilburg; the diocese of Breda; the provinces of the religious order and the five religious congregations which participate in the Theologische Faculteit Tilburg, viz. the Dutch Capuchins (O.F.M. Cap.), Sacred Family Missionaries (M.S.F.), Divine Word Missionaries (S.V.D.), Sacred Heart Missionaries (M.S.C.), Montfort Missionaries (S.M.M.) and Sacred Heart Fathers (S.C.J.); the Stichting Liturgisch Oecumenisch Centrum; the Paul de Gruyterstichting; de M. van Wichenstichting; the Radboudstichting.

L. van T.
Ch. C.

Rite and Sign
Gerard Lukken: Some Bio-bibliographical Notes
by Louis van Tongeren

Gerard Maria Lukken was born on February 8, 1933 in the Dutch royal residence, The Hague, as the third child and second son in a family, which would eventually consist of five children.[1] The first years of his life he spent in Rijswijk, near The Hague. The Lukken family moved a number of times, because of the employment of the father, who was working in the textile trade and in home furnishing, a trade which was also known to his mother, who had worked in her youth as a seamstress. Successively they lived in Apeldoorn, Nijmegen, Tilburg, Venlo, and again in Nijmegen. From the last named city Gerard Lukken moved to Sint-Michielsgestel to attend the diocesan preparatory seminary Beekvliet. His mother had insisted that he would receive his secondary education with the Jesuits at their Canisius College in Nijmegen, which Gerard's elder brother already attended. But even at the age of twelve Gerard knew that he did not want to become a Jesuit; a secular priest he was to be. Having finished Beekvliet he went to the seminary of the diocese of 's-Hertogenbosch in Haaren in 1951. On June 15, 1957 Gerard Lukken was ordained a priest by Monsignor Mutsaerts in 's-Hertogenbosch.

The bibliography shows that the time of study at Haaren already yielded the first products of his pen. At that time he did not yet write solid scholarly articles, but contributed smaller contributions on a range of subjects in de *Domklok*, the magazine of the theology students in the seminary (nos. 1-16).[2] During his period in the seminary Gerard Lukken experienced the first changes in the liturgy: the rites for Holy Week were restored, the first altars were relocated to make the celebration of the Mass *facie ad populum* possible, and hesitatingly the vernacular was introduced into the liturgy. Partly as a consequence of the Liturgical

---

* This contribution was translated by M. Schneiders, M.Div.
1 For some biographical facts I owe thanks especially to Mrs. M. Lukken-Spieringhs and to G. Hoogbergen.
2 The numbers in parentheses in this bio-bibliographical description refer to the numbers of the bibliography of Gerard Lukken, which follows. If the publication concerned is also included in this volume of collected studies, this has been indicated by a number in italics, which refers to the order of the contributions in this volume. I do not, however, give exhaustive references to the bibliography. Only those publications which are most prominent in Gerard Lukken's scholarly development are mentioned here.

Movement and – in line with this – the development of liturgical studies during the preceding decades, the teaching of liturgy was changing and being renewed. The seminary did not have a special lecturer for the field of liturgy, which was thought of mainly as a practical and legal subject, taken care of by the president of the seminary. That different, in the beginning mainly historical aspects of the liturgy, came into focus, is clear from the fact that a special lecturer in liturgy was appointed at the end of the fifties. The diocese did not have somebody for the job and asked the Dominican Th. Vismans. To have a man in the near future from the own clergy to teach liturgy in the seminary the diocese sent Gerard Lukken to study in Rome, after he had had some pastoral experience first as a curate in Veghel. After three years of study in Rome, he pursued his studies abroad for two more years in Paris at the Institut Supérieur de Liturgie. In the meantime he had started on a dissertation supervised by the Dutch Jesuit H. Schmidt, who was attached to the Pontificia Università Gregoriana and to the Istituto Liturgico San Anselmo. According to Schmidt the subject chosen for a thesis should not have any practical relevance. He therefore suggested to Gerard Lukken to go into the development of the theology of sin in the liturgy. Having collected an abundance of text material, Gerard Lukken succeeded in convincing Schmidt, that a restriction to the idea of original sin was a sensible thing. The result was a literary-historical study of the theology of original sin in the early-christian baptismal rite and in other texts of the most important (Roman) sacramentaries in the context of patristics. Gerard Lukken successfully defended his thesis (no. 19) in the Theological Faculty of the Pontificia Università Gregoriana on April 14, 1967. It is still considered to be a standard work, of which an English version was published in 1973 (no. 64).

In the mean time Gerard Lukken had returned to the Netherlands in 1964 and was appointed lecturer in liturgy in the diocesan seminary at Haaren. At the same time he became rector of a home for the elderly in nearby Oisterwijk, in which he was expected to reside. This was a rather unusual arrangement, as the lecturers of the seminary as a rule lived in it. There were, however, fears that, as together with him two others were newly appointed as lecturer after studying abroad, several young newcomers might cause unrest, when they would propagate the progressive ideas acquired abroad. Nevertheless liturgical experiments started cautiously, balancing on the boarders of the margins acceptable in those days. Gerard Lukken combined the two positions in Haaren and Oisterwijk until 1967, the year in which he was appointed lecturer in liturgy and theology of the sacraments in the Theological Faculty in Tilburg, which was founded in the same year. On January 1, 1981 his position was transformed into a professorship. The fact that Gerard Lukken had married

Helma (Mat) Spieringhs in 1970 was in those days no impediment for his new appointment.

At about the same time at which the Theological Faculty in Tilburg (TFT) was founded, in 1967, similar Roman Catholic theological colleges were established in Heerlen, Amsterdam and Utrecht. Like the Theological Faculty in Tilburg these were amalgamations of a number of seminaries, both diocesan and of religious orders. Together with the Theological Faculty of the Catholic University of Nijmegen, founded in 1923, these institutions were assigned the tasks to take care of the education of priests in the Netherlands and to raise the standard of theological studies to an academic level.[3] The four new colleges did not, of course, have an established research tradition. And since a lot of time and energy had to be spent in the early years in the forming of an organisation structure and in developing a curriculum, as well as in taking a stand vis-à-vis the ecclesiastical authorities, the distinctive features in scholarly work did not become prominent until some later time. The lecturers had, moreover, to get to know each other, as they were brought together from many different traditions and backgrounds.

In contrast with the lay lecturers, who were paid according to government schemes, those who were priests had to do initially with an upgraded allowance for expenses, until the Department of Education and Research started to support the TFT in 1970. Four years later, in October 1974, the TFT was recognized legally as an academic theological institution. As some seven years had elapsed between the foundation of the TFT and the state recognition, it did not seem expedient that the professors and lecturers would give an inaugural lecture. In its stead a volume was published with which the academic staff presented itself 'between times'.[4] Gerard Lukken provided a contribution for the volume, which he considers to be his inaugural lecture (no. 80 = 81 = *11*).

The new colleges all started shortly after the Second Vatican Council. Thus many of the lecturers were involved in the introduction of the changes which Vatican II had initiated. Many of them were advisors to the bishops, were involved in new ecclesiastical advisory boards, gave courses throughout the country, published thoughtful observations in scholarly journals, but most of all they wrote for a wider readership in newspapers and magazines, mainly on the recent developments in the church. Thus most of the lecturers in liturgy were involved directly from

---

3 See L. WINKELER: *Om kerk en wetenschap. Geschiedenis van de Katholieke Theologische Universiteit Amsterdam en de Katholieke Theologische Universiteit Utrecht 1967-1991* (Utrecht 1992) 11-20.
4 Thus, in Dutch, the title of the volume, H. BERGER a.o. (ed.): *Tussentijds. Theologische Faculteit Tilburg. Bundel opstellen bij gelegenheid van haar erkenning* (Tilburg 1975).

the beginning in the enormous task of liturgical renewal in the Netherlands. From his appointment in Tilburg this is true for Gerard Lukken. Two of his activities in this regard stand out and accentuate this.

In January 1967 Gerard Lukken became a member of the Dutch Commission for the Liturgy (Nederlandse Commissie voor Liturgie, NCL) and took a seat on the executive board. When H. Wegman had to retire because of illness in 1969 he became chairman of the Commission. The Nederlandse Commissie voor Liturgie was installed on December 12, 1963 as the national liturgical commission recommended in the Constitution on the Liturgy of the Second Vatican Council, which, under the supervision of the episcopal conference, had to "regulate pastoral-liturgical action throughout the territory and to promote studies and necessary experiments whenever there is question of adaptations to be proposed to the Apostolic See" (art. 44). In fact the preparation and implementation of liturgical renewal in the Netherlands rested with this Commission.[5] The activities of the Commission extended over different fields. The official liturgical renewal, as it was formulated in Rome, it put into practice. It organized the work of the translation of the new liturgical books and especially invested much energy in the translation of the *Ordinarium Missae*, the eucharistic prayers and the prefaces. Moreover the Commission guided the liturgical centres of experiment and kept contacts with different liturgical institutions and organisations, both national and diocesan.

In 1971 the organisation of policy making in the liturgy was structured differently. The Nationale Raad voor Liturgie (National Council for the Liturgy, NRL) was established, which works under the final responsibility of the episcopal conference. This body was assisted by an Adviesraad (Advisory Council), which consisted of experts. From 1973 until 1977, when the Adviesraad abolished itself, Gerard Lukken was a member. This short survey shows clearly, that Gerard Lukken was involved explicitly in the official policy in the Netherlands as regards liturgical renewal. He was among those who gave shape to the translation of the official liturgical books, to the implementation of liturgical directions and the 'translation' of these for the parishes, and to the counselling of the first, episcopally tolerated, centres of experiment.

---

5 See for the activities and the eventful history of this Commission, J. JOOSSE: *Eucharistische gebeden in Nederland. Een documentaire studie over de ontwikkeling van de vertaalde Romeinse en 'eigen' Nederlandse eucharistische gebeden (1963-1979)* I-II (= TFT-studies 17) (Tilburg 1991) *passim*, and for a survey, esp. 47-59. As there was no bishop among the members of the Nederlandse Commissie voor Liturgie, the composition of this national liturgical commission differed explicitly from what was prescribed in the instruction *Inter oecumenici* from 1964. For Rome this was a thorn in the flesh, IDEM: *Eucharistische gebeden* 48. Perhaps the absence of the bishops from the Commission partly explains the special way in which the liturgical renewal could be moulded in the Netherlands.

An activity of a different nature also points towards Gerard Lukken's involvement in liturgical renewal and the guiding thereof from the second half of the sixties, viz. his membership of the editorial board of the *Werkmap voor liturgie*. This periodical, which first appeared in 1966, intended initially to offer multiform documentation, that is creative materials for the benefit of the local community.[6] The journal wanted to be a kind of platform, in which creative, experimental liturgical texts, songs and outlines of rites could be published for use on a broader basis in the local communities. Very soon, in 1967, Gerard Lukken joined the board of editors, which initially took responsibility for a similar catechetical periodical, the *Werkmap voor de katechese*, as well.

As the services of the new Roman ritual appeared in Dutch during the seventies, the editorial board decided "to devote part of the *Werkmap* to views about the background of these rituals, to evaluate what had been developed so far in local communities, to consider different aspects of the rituals within a wider pastoral scope, and, whenever possible, to offer pastoral-liturgical suggestions and specific material in this context. Another part of the *Werkmap* would, as was usual, provide straightforward and practical material".[7] During the last few years they have elucidated several topical themes from the liturgical practice. Until this day Gerard Lukken is a member of the editorial board of the *Werkmap voor liturgie*. Through the years he has contributed a considerable number of articles for this periodical and he has edited several issues about diverging themes. During the first years of the *Werkmap* Gerard Lukken entered the creative field in providing two drafts for baptismal liturgies (nos. 28 = 194; 72 = 193) and one draft for an ecumenical ritual of marriage (no. 63 = 240), all three for the *Werkmap*. The idea of the editors thus was twofold: to nourish the parishes with fresh material which originated in local communities on the one hand, and on the other to clarify the official liturgy and comment upon it, and to reflect upon topical liturgical issues. The redactional format was clearly made for liturgical practice and took the actual practice at the same time as its main starting-point. They were choosing in such a way for a liturgy 'from below', an option which, as we have already seen, was shared by the official Commission which had to prepare and counsel the liturgical renewal in the Netherlands, the NCL.

The inductive approach would prove to be characteristic through the years for Gerard Lukken. He would evaluate and reflect upon ecclesiastical and liturgical changes from this focus. But he would also start and reason from the same angle in his teaching and in consultation and

---

6 Thus G. Lukken in a short review on the occasion of the fifteenth anniversary of the journal, G. LUKKEN: 1966-1981. Vijftien jaar Werkmap voor liturgie, in *Werkmap voor liturgie* 15 (1981) 389 (= no. 126).
7 LUKKEN: 1966-1981. Vijftien jaar Werkmap voor liturgie 391.

discussion with students and colleagues, both on matters in his field of study and of university organization. Not a preset norm, prescribed from above, is the decisive criterium for Gerard Lukken. He wants to find out what is feasible from the actual situation as it presents itself. As regards the liturgy this means that it is not a uniform, ordained and changeless, and in this sense sacrosanct rite which constitutes the point of reference, but the actual human being who wants to understand the precarious history of his life religiously within salvation history. While this point of view is distinctive for Gerard Lukken as a person and because it goes along with his open character, many will have met him as an amiable and gentle man, who does neither look for conflict nor attract it, a man who is respected everywhere for his thorough knowledge and his balanced judgement.

The approach of the liturgy 'from below' guided Gerard Lukken to describe the liturgy in his first publications within the field of tension of the very far-reaching process of secularization, which took place rapidly from 1960, and especially from 1966 (nos. 30 = 46 = *1*; 31 = 43; 42; 37). In some recent articles he looks back after 25 years at this more or less stormy situation and evaluates it, especially as regards the specific Dutch context, which then received a lot of interest internationally, but was only partially recognisable and understood by many outside the Netherlands (nos. 228 = 241 = *2*; 243). The fast social-cultural changes influenced the religious experience of people. They posed themselves fundamental questions with regard to God, religion, christianity and church, which had an immediate bearing upon liturgy. The untouchable, static, sacred and nearly suprahistorical liturgy became the target of criticism and more and more it was less accepted as self-evident. Instead attention shifted to religious experience and to the actual life of man, which evolves in the dynamic course of history. As a result of this shift the view developed that liturgy takes shape within our contingent history. Divine salvation is not attainable immediately; it needs mediation from man, who is tied to time and place. Man can experience his actual history as being part of salvation history. In the inductive liturgy the transcendent emerges as trans-as-cendence, while it manifests itself as trans-des-cendence in the deductive liturgy.

The questions which secularization evoked, could be accentuated and clarified with the help of anthropology, which had already made its appearance in theology in the preceding decades. From the moment that Gerard Lukken started to teach in Haaren in 1964, he reflected on the question of the purpose, the function and the meaning of ritual generally and of the liturgy in particular within the context of secularization. The study of this problem constitutes one of the two main lines which characterize Gerard Lukken's scholarly work. Anthropological perceptions inspired him here. This did in the beginning raise eyebrows, as he himself indicates in a recent article (no. 244), in which he presents a short survey of the various phases in which and how anthropology permeated the study of liturgy after Vatican II. Shortly before he left the Institut Supérieur de Liturgie in 1964, he writes: "Père Gy, director of the Institut, asked me how I would teach liturgy to students of theology. As I replied that I would start with a treatment of questions like what are rituals, and what is their position in the life of people and of society, he was surprised. Apparently our country saw the anthropological shift in theology earlier than France and other countries".[8] In his lectures and in many of his publications Gerard Lukken has continued an orientation upon the general human data regarding ritual, from which he wants to reflect on the meaning of the sacraments and the liturgy for believing people who live in a more and more secularized world. Especially one concept plays an important role in his conclusion about the function and meaning of rituals and of the liturgy: the liturgical ritual with its symbols, symbolic acts and symbolic language is *irreplaceable* in the religious communication of man with the divine, the transcendent or the mysterious essence of reality. The many articles on this theme, in which various aspects come back regularly, complemented again with some new elements, find their interim conclusion in his books *De onvervangbare weg van de liturgie* (no. 114 = 144) and *Geen leven zonder rituelen. Antropologische beschouwingen met het oog op de christelijke liturgie* (no. 145 = 158 = 188).[9] In line with the anthropological background of the liturgy, he described the mediating role of human corporality and sensory and of the material world especially in his *Liturgie en zintuiglijkheid. Over de betekenis van lichamelijkheid in de liturgie* (no. 218; see in part 4).[10]

Because of the increasing secularization, which caused a greater distance towards the official liturgy for many, and from an inductive approach to the liturgy Gerard Lukken more than once pleaded for the introduction and the drafting of so-called liminary liturgy or of catechumenical celebrations (nos. 129 = 130 = 131 = 9; 228 = 241 = 2; cf. also 96 = 191 = in part 6; 97 = 192 = in part 6; 109 = 238 = in part 8; 228 = 241 = 2; 243). With this he pleads for a more differentiated offer of liturgical services, which is in keeping with the multiform religious situation. New liturgical forms may then be offered to those for whom the official liturgy is too high-church and no longer fits into their more indefinite religious frame of reference. Such rituals would not be asking

---

8 G. LUKKEN: De 'doorbraak' van de antropologie in de christelijke liturgie, in H. DEGEN a.o. (ed.): *Herinneringen aan de toekomst. Pastoraat in de geest van Vaticanum II* (Baarn 1991) 167-168. (= no. 244)
9 In translation: *The irreplaceable way of the liturgy; No life without rituals. Anthropological reflections with an eye to christian liturgy.*
10 In translation: *Liturgy and sensory. On the meaning of corporality in the liturgy.*

too much of people and they could be an intermediate phase, which functions as a transition to the celebration of the official liturgy. In this he mainly has in view baptism, marriage and the funeral.

Apart from his interest in the anthropological foundations and the theological fundamentals of the ritual and the sacraments, Gerard Lukken gave attention to the renewal of methods from the beginning. The literary-historical approach was and is for him not the only one. During his 'classic' education in Rome and Paris he has mastered this method thoroughly, as e.g. his dissertation, which we mentioned before, amply shows. Later he would, however, make less frequent use of this method. Apart from some surveys of (part of) the history of the liturgy (no. 35; chapter 3 of *De onvervangbare weg* and no. 265) he only wrote a few articles which are specifically historical in character (nos. 91 and 226). His interest in the methodological renewal may have been inspired by liturgical renewal. The analysis and theological evaluation of the renewed liturgy demanded in his view specific methods. A mere literary-historical examination was not sufficient, neither for the official liturgical books, of which the Dutch versions were beginning to appear, nor for the experimental liturgy, which was and is taking shape in local communities from the sixties onwards. In his search for new methods Gerard Lukken first applied himself to the method called 'close reading', a way of looking at a text, which does, in his opinion, do it more justice, "starting from the view that each part of a text has (or: should have) a place in a sensible coherent structure".[11] "It is the method of observing reading, as it were with the nose to the text, in which one tries to perceive immediately and specifically. Thus one tries to discover, how the whole is structurally built up, one unravels the texts, classifies and from the details one finds the motives and themes",[12] without for that matter neglecting the historical context and background. In an article which is methodologically more or less a programm, which Gerard Lukken looks upon as his inaugural lecture, he explains and shows how in his view liturgical texts from past and present, both official and experimental, may best be analyzed on the basis of the close reading method, and how they may be confronted with each other for the purpose of verification, examination and assessment (no. 80 = 81 = 11). To provide an example of this approach, he used close reading to analyse thoroughly an experimental modern funeral liturgy written by H. Oosterhuis (no. 82). On the basis of new methodological ideas, which he developed especially in the eighties, he would later modify this model of analysis and verification from 1975.[13]

11 J. OVERSTEEGEN: Analyse en oordeel I, in *Merlijn* 3 (1965) 178.
12 SEMANET (G. LUKKEN, P. DE MAAT, M. RIJKHOFF and N. TROMP): Een methode van semiotische analyse, in *Bijdragen. Tijdschrift voor filosofie en theologie* 40 (1983) 129. (= no. 138)
13 See the postscript to no. *11*.

His interest in new methods received an important impulse in 1976. In that year the catechist G. Hoogbergen took the initiative to study structuralism and structural textual analysis together with some colleagues of the Theologische Faculteit. Gerard Lukken did not initially belong to the group, but he joined it quite soon. The group at first took the name STREX: STRuctural EXegesis. As the participation in the group changed a couple of times in the initial phase, and as they did not intend to work only in the field of exegesis, the name was altered to SEMANET: SEMiotische Analyse door NEderlandse Theologen (Semiotic Analysis by Dutch Theologians). During its first years of existence the group familiarized itself with structuralism and orientated itself by studying authors from different schools of structuralism. Through an article by C. Galland they became acquainted with the semiotics of A. Greimas (1917-1992).[14] And as Greimas presented in his semiotics a homogeneous system of concepts and a consistent set of instruments with which specific analyses could be carried out, SEMANET soon concentrated more and more on this method. This interdisciplinary method, coming from the study of literature, deals with the world of signs, with the systems of signs, which man uses to communicate with reality, and with the analysis of the signification, of the way in which meaning gets shape in specific discourses. Important for the development of SEMANET are the frequent contacts with CADIR: Centre pour l'Analyse du DIscours Religieux, which was established at the Institut Catholique in Lyon. To this Centre are attached exegetes, theologians and philosophers, trained by Greimas, who are trying together to develop semiotics, to operationalize it and to open it up for a larger group of students, pastors and parishioners. The most fertile contacts between SEMANET and CADIR are the joint study weeks, which are held alternately in Lyon and Tilburg. Gerard Lukken soon developed into a great promotor of semiotics and as one of the driving forces of SEMANET, which from 1980 operates as an interuniversity study group, in which lecturers from the Theologische Faculteit Tilburg and from the Katholieke Theologische Universiteit in Utrecht cooperate.

In 1981 the first semiotic publication appeared (no. 123), which is, as are the next few (nos. 137; 138, 139), the result of teamwork: several members of SEMANET act together as author. And also recently Gerard Lukken cooperated in two contributions, which came into being through teamwork (nos. 263; 264). The analyses are done together on the basis of a view which is held in semiotics, i.e. 'two may see more than one', and

---

14 C. GALLAND: An introduction to the method of A.J. Greimas, in M. JOHNSON (ed.): *The New Testament and structuralism* (Pittsburgh 1976) 1-26. See for a description of the development of SEMANET, SEMANET (LUKKEN, DE MAAT, RIJKHOFF and TROMP): Een methode van semiotische analyse, 118-122; SEMANET (G. LUKKEN ed.): *Semiotiek en christelijke uitingsvormen. De semiotiek van A.J. Greimas en de Parijse school toegepast op Bijbel en liturgie* (Hilversum 1987) 15-17.

also because hypotheses emanating from reading, which are shared by several people, gain in power of expression. Very soon, however, the other members of SEMANET could not keep pace with the speed with which Gerard Lukken was analyzing and publishing. But before he publishes an analysis, he nearly always submits it to some of the other members of SEMANET and discusses it with them. In several of his semiotic articles much space is given to present the analysis in detail. The advantage of this is that the reader gets the possibility to perform the process of analysis himself and to make different choices, if so desired. At the same time attention is drawn in this way to details which would not have been mentioned in a more synthetical presentation.

Initially Gerard Lukken concentrated upon the marriage ritual. He did analyses of both the Tridentine and the new, post-Vatican, ritual. These were only circulated privately (nos. 159; 151), although parts of them were published (nos. 152; 163 = 197; 181; 174; 200 = *16*). After having himself analyzed a fairy tale (no. 171) and the confession of guilt (no. 161 = *17*), and after participating with other members of SEMANET in analyses of a liturgical song (nos. 123; 138) and of some biblical pericopes (nos. 137; 139; 172), Gerard Lukken began to broaden the object of his study and analysis. The analysis is no longer limited to textual discourses. The semiotic set of instruments is also made operational for non-lingual discourses. Thus he analyzed a mortuary card as a visual object (nos. 162; 175), concentrated upon architecture (nos. 208 = 247 = *18*; 210 = *19*; 260), gave attention to the lay-out of a text by analyzing not only the form of the content, but especially the form of the expression (nos. 206; 229), and researched the way in which signification and meaning is given and receives shape as such in rituals (nos. 253; 254 = *13*; 255). In order to make semiotics more well-known and more accessible to outsiders it was not sufficient to publish analyses in learned journals. It was also necessary to publish a theoretical exposition of the method in Dutch. For this reason SEMANET published a book (no. 168), which Gerard Lukken edited and in which he provided a description of the basic concepts of Greimassian semiotics (no. 169), which are followed by some analyses with specific applications by some members of SEMANET.

Meanwhile semiotics turned out to encounter much lack of understanding and opposition among experts. Repeatedly the method had to be explained, clarified and defended, even for groups of colleagues, who consider methodological renewal of paramount importance. The complexity and 'wilfulness' of the system of concepts may be blamed for this, but also the fear of established traditions, who feel threatened. Against this lack of understanding and the growing unwillingness to go into the subject Gerard Lukken regularly went to battle, boosted by hearing from colleagues who successfully work in the field of semiotics abroad, who are being invited to as far as Korea to give biblical instruction based on semiotics, as this method is very well suited to introduce large groups into Scripture, or who have, as is the case in Finland, as many as 600 students for an introductory series of lectures on semiotics.

In the beginning Gerard Lukken defended the method of semiotics by pointing to the importance of the method, which may be deduced from the results of the analyses. Even if other methods have already produced important insights regarding an object, semiotics still offers its own results. Having pointed out regularly in the beginning the fruits which semiotic analysis gives, and thus justifying and answering for the rationale of the existence of the method (nos. 163 = 197 = 15; 177 = 178 = 12; 179; 187), Gerard Lukken chose from time to time for a more confronting approach. The objections against the method usually brought forward by outsiders, he parried, trying to refute them repeatedly with much patience (no. 242 = 14). People find the method not accessible enough, because of the difficult, complicated and 'wilful' system of concepts. The opponent, however, does often also use a special set of instruments and abilities which have to be acquired and mastered first, as linguistic knowledge (Latin, Greek, Hebrew, Aramaic), historical textual criticism, philology, and archival research. Semiotics is blamed for being elitist by doing analysis on the square millimetre. That detailed research is fruitful and necessary to attain general understanding, is a common scholarly point of view, for which, however, semiotics is reproached. The study of source material and textual criticism are usually also detailed work. Another reproach striking semiotics is that some people think that it does not offer any new insights; it would merely confirm and repeat in a very complicated way what is already known. This criticism can only apply to the semiotic treatment of objects which have been studied before. And even then the criticism may be questioned, as one may study an object using different methods. Every method approaches an object along its own way (*meta hodos*), looks at it from a perspective which differs from that of other methods. Methods will therefore see different things and see things differently. But above all semiotics gives the possibility to analyse and study different aspects of an object with one and the same set of instruments, as e.g. the text and music of a song as well as their interrelation. A last objection concerns the idea that objects may only be analyzed synchronically. Gerard Lukken has, however, shown that historical objects can also be studied semiotically in their diachrony (no. 226).

Both his offensive and his defensive pleas for semiotics have not resulted in more understanding and less scepticism among colleagues, both theologians and liturgists. There are hardly any colleagues who have familiarized themselves with the method or studied it in depth. In Tilburg semiotics has a place in the curriculum, which albeit a modest one, is nonetheless firm in the liturgy course. As a consequence during the last few years a small number of students have acquired the semiotic method and applied it in their theses. Gerard Lukken did not, however, really gather a following in the field of semiotics; only one semiotic dissertation was finished under his supervision, while a second one is in preparation. Despite the scepticism towards semiotics the Theologische Faculteit Tilburg did show its appreciation of semiotics, and thus indirectly of SEMANET, in giving one of the two honourary doctoral degrees conferred on the occasion of its twentieth anniversary in 1987 to J. Delorme, doyen of CADIR. At this occasion Gerard Lukken delivered a lecture (no. 186 = 196).

Yet the semiotic approach in liturgical studies has radiated modestly from the Netherlands. For the academic year 1988-1989 M. Searle, late associate professor of liturgy in Notre Dame (USA), came to Tilburg especially to study semiotics with Gerard Lukken and SEMANET. A result of this cooperation is the publication of a volume on semiotics and ecclesiastical architecture, which was written by Gerard Lukken and M. Searle (no. 260). The unfortunate early death of Searle in 1992 took away the basis for the further development of cooperation in the field in America. The invitations which Gerard Lukken received and accepted for a lecture on the import of semiotics for liturgical studies at a colloquium in Louvain and for an outline on the same for a German handbook are a sign that people outside the Netherlands are becoming receptive for methodological renewal of liturgical studies through semiotics (nos. 251 = 252; 255). Gerard Lukken is one of the pioneers who introduced Greimassian semiotics to (theological) Holland and he was the one who mainly propagated the method. He himself applied the method to various subjects and with him others whom he supervised. They elaborated the theoretical set of instruments and operationalized it towards different subsectors, especially in the fields of liturgical study, exegesis and catechetics. The passion for semiotics may rightly be styled the second main focus of Gerard Lukken's scholarly work.

When the Theologische Faculteit Tilburg celebrated its quarter-centennial in 1992, Gerard Lukken was one of the four persons who were honoured by the dean at that time, W. Weren, for being with the Faculty for the complete twenty-five years.[15] Gerard Lukken thus is one of the 'old faithful', who have been working continuously in the Faculty since its foundation. Because of a serious illness he had to withdraw for more than a year during 1977 and 1978. In the years in which he was working in the Faculty he has introduced many students into the different aspects

---

15 W. WEREN: *In het zilver. Rede bij de opening van het academisch jaar 1992-1993, uitgesproken op 10 september 1992* (this address, which was not published, is kept in the archives of the TFT).

of liturgical study and the theology of the sacraments and he has guided them in their first steps in practical liturgics. From the beginning of the seventies, when the first students took the degree of *doctorandus*, he supervised the theses for this degree of about thirty students. He also supervised three Ph.D. students. And currently four others are completing their dissertation wholly or partly under his direction.

Of the various administrative posts which Gerard Lukken held in the Faculty, especially his work for the Commissie Wetenschapsbeoefening (the Research Committee) comes to mind. He was a member and the chairman of this committee from 1983 until 1990. It was mainly during his time of office as chairman that the organization of research in the Faculty received a clear structure, that the research projects were brought into tune mutually, and that the participation of Faculty members in larger national research programmes was stimulated. Because of his marriage in 1970 it was impossible for him to fulfil the highest administrative post, that of dean of the Faculty, which he, however, did not regret at all.

Outside the TFT Gerard Lukken has also made himself useful in many fields. His role in the liturgical renewal in the Netherlands has already been discussed here. Furthermore he participated in various commissions and consultative bodies, in which the academic infrastructure of our country is rich. Belonging, as he does, to the second generation of liturgical scholars in the Netherlands, he has, finally, contributed to the development of the rather 'young' field of liturgical studies and to its extension into a full grown discipline. His many articles and contributions in various books and periodicals, such as *Tijdschrift voor liturgie, Questions liturgiques, Werkmap voor liturgie* en *Jaarboek voor liturgie-onderzoek* testify to this effect. He is moreover a member of the editorial board of the two last-named periodicals, of that of the *Werkmap voor liturgie* from 1967, and of that of the *Jaarboek voor liturgie-onderzoek* since its inception in 1985. In addition to this he is since 1970 a member of the editorial board for the liturgical section of the international theological journal *Concilium*. Together with his colleagues he has stimulated and given shape to methodological renewal and the broadening of the object of research. Thus he has contributed to the particular way in which liturgical studies in the Netherlands has found its distinctive features.

A last achievement which is linked closely with the name of Gerard Lukken is the foundation of the *Liturgisch Instituut* (Liturgical Institute) in the TFT. The official opening of this Institute was on December 4, 1992 (no. 261). For more than two years before this date, he had explored and investigated the possibilities and the advisability of a liturgical institute, together with his immediate colleague L. van Tongeren, and later on with the recently recruited coordinator of the new institute, Ch. Caspers. As liturgical studies become more and more a threatened discipline in the

Netherlands, as it is marginalized further and further, Gerard Lukken sees the foundation of a liturgical institute as a possibility to strengthen the field of study, despite the threats. When during the explorations of the prepatory phase the outlines became visible gradually and the realization of the Institute proved to be a real possibility, Gerard Lukken looked upon it as the last task of his active career to give the Institute a solid foundation and to build it firmly. He has tried to gather around the Institute as many people as possible, both those who are working on research in the field of liturgy within the universities and those who are active in it outside. In this way liturgical studies could give itself a clear profile, in the Netherlands as well as abroad. May the well-being and the continued existence of the Liturgisch Instituut be deemed a worthy tribute to its originator, founder and advocate.

Gerard Lukken: A Bibliography, 1953-1993

*Compiled by Charles Caspers
and Louis van Tongeren*

1953
1. God heeft de mensen nodig, in *Domklok. Opinieblad van het theologicum Haaren* 15 (1952-1953) 5 July, 7-8.
2. Bij wie zal de dogmatische preek aanknopen?, in *idem* 16 (1953-1954) 8 November, appendix, 4-8.

1954
3. Maria is een verborgen moeder, in *idem* 16 (1953-1954) 7 February, 1-5.
4. Domus Dei, in *idem* 16 (1953-1954) 30 May, 4-6.
5. Carmel, in *idem* 16 (1953-1954) 20 June, 1-3.
6. Groeiend bestaan, in *idem* 17 (1954-1955) 21 November, 2-4.
7. De monnik, in *idem* 17 (1954-1955) 28 November, 1-2.

1955
8. [With G. Hoogbergen and F. de Mast:] Sein zum Tode, in *idem* 17 (1954-1955) 29 May, special edition, 1-24.
9. Vindicamus, in *idem* 18 (1955-1956) 2 Oktober, 1-5.

1956
10. [With G. Hoogbergen:] Theologen-congres, in *idem* 18 (1955-1956) 5 February, appendix, 1-3.
11. Examenperikelen, in *idem* 18 (1955-1956) 20 May, 12-13.
12. Onder de lamp, in *idem* 18 (1955-1956) 17 June, 14-15.
13. [With G. Hoogbergen and C. Smeulders:] Psalmen voor de zielzorg, in *idem* 18 (1955-1956) 15 July, 1-2.
14. Onder de lamp, in *idem* 18 (1955-1956) 15 July, 12.
15. [With G. Hoogbergen:] Filosofische eschatologie, in *idem* 19 (1956-1957) 1 December, 1-8.

1957
16. Beste Wolfgang, in *idem* 19 (1956-1957) 31 March, 4-6.

1965
17. Docent repliceert, in *idem* 27 (1964-1965) no. 34-35, 1 May 1965, 547-554.
18. [With R. van Hellenberg Hubar a.o.:] Drama en liturgie, in *idem* 588-602.

1966

19. De erfzonde in de Romeinse liturgie. Onderzoek naar de erfzonde in de Romeinse sacramentaria en de oude doopliturgie (Dissertatio ad lauream, Universitas Gregoriana, Rome), Haaren 1966 (photocopied).
20. Liturgievernieuwing, in *Arabesk. Filosoficum Haaren (Noord-Brabant)* 8 (1966) 2 April, 14-16.

[Review of:]
- R. Guardini, *Peilingen van het christelijk denken. Verzamelde studies, 1923-1963* (Tielt 1965), in *Kerk in ontmoeting* 2 (1966) 19-20.

1967

21. Sanctus, in L. Brinkhoff a.o. (ed.), *Liturgisch Woordenboek* II, Roermond 1965-1968, 2506-2512.
22. Zonde, in *idem* 3003-3011.
23. De romeinse canon en de vernieuwing van de liturgie, in *Tijdschrift voor liturgie* 51 (1967) 79-98.

1968

24. [With J. Duin, P. Drijvers, O. Hof, W. Reckman, B. de Roeck and Ph. Stein:] *Uit en Thuis* (series: Mensen, dieren, dingen), Hilversum 1968.
25. [Contributions in the field of 'liturgy' to:] A. Heidt (ed.), *Catholica. Informatiebron voor het katholieke leven* II, Hilversum 1968.
    Lector, in *idem* 1664.
    Liturgische beweging, in *idem* 1710-1716.
    Manipel, in *idem* 1736-1737.
    Octaaf, in *idem* 2067.
    Pateen, in *idem* 2223.
    Pyxis, in *idem* 2366.
    Sacramentsdag, in *idem* 2448.
    Sacristie, in *idem* 2448.
    Stool, in *idem* 2604.
    Superplie, in *idem* 2605.
    Toog, in *idem* 2631.
26. The letters B-E, L-N, R-Z of the rubric 'catholic liturgy', in *Oosthoeks Encyclopedie*, sixth edition (15 vols.), Utrecht 1968-1973.
27. Enkele kanttekeningen over het exorcisme, in *Tijdschrift voor liturgie* 52 (1968) 254-260.
28. [With W. Reckman and Ph. Stein:] De doop van een volwassene, in *Werkmap voor liturgie* 3 (1968) no. 2, 1-35.

1969

29. [With J. Duin, P. Drijvers, O. Hof, W. Reckman, B. de Roeck en Ph. Stein:] *Geschiedenis van meneer Jona* (series: Mensen, dieren, dingen), Hilversum 1969.
30. Liturgie en secularisatie, in J. Bornewasser a.o., *Christelijk bestaan in een seculaire cultuur*, Roermond 1969, 245-282, 337-340.
31. Is er toekomst voor de liturgie? in *Kosmos en oecumene* 3 (1969) 186-201.
32. Experimentele rituelen van de kinderdoop, in *Rond de tafel* 24 (1969) 19-27.
33. Pastoralia, in *Directorium voor de Nederlandse kerkprovincie in het jaar 1970*, Zeist 1969, 97-147.

1970

34. [With J. Duin, P. Drijvers, O. Hof, W. Reckman, B. de Roeck and Ph. Stein:] *Zo noem ik de dieren mijn vrienden* (series: Mensen, dieren, dingen), Hilversum 1970.
35. *Eucharistie. Enkele notities over liturgie en theologie van het Avondmaal*, Tilburg 1970 (photo-copied).
36. De ontwikkeling van de liturgiewetenschap sedert de praeconciliaire periode, in A. Hollaardt (ed.), *Liturgisch woordenboek, supplement. Liturgische oriëntatie na Vaticanum II*, Roermond 1970, 11-13.
37. De ontwikkeling van de liturgiewetenschap sinds Vaticanum II, in *idem* 19-24.
38. De kinderdoop. Enkele niet-officiële doaprituelen, in *idem* 45-47.
39. De volwassenendoop. Een niet-officieel ritueel, in *idem* 48.
40. De ziekenzalving, in *idem* 56-59.
41. De ziekenzalving. Niet-officiële rituelen, in *idem* 59-61.
42. Liturgy and secularisation, in *Questions liturgiques* 51 (1970) 227-244.
43. Czy liturgia ma pryszriesci?, in *Ruch biblyny i liturgicny* 23 (1970) 112-127 Polish translation of no. 31.
44. Primitief gedoe, in *Katholieke missiën* 91 (1970) 39-42.
45. Pastoralia, in *Directorium voor de Nederlandse kerkprovincie in het jaar 1971*, Zeist 1970, 1-67.

[Reviews of:]
- *Jaarboek voor de eredienst van de Nederlandse Hervormde Kerk, 1967-1968* (Den Haag 1967), in *Tijdschrift voor theologie* 10 (1970) 107.
- Th. Maas-Ewerd, *Liturgie und Pfarrei. Einfluß der liturgischen Erneuerung auf Leben und Verständnis der Pfarrei im deutschen Sprachgebiet* (Paderborn 1969), in *idem* 327-328.
- A. Roguet, *Table ouverte. La messe aujourd'hui* (Doornik 1969), in *idem* 327.
- H. Wegman, *Het paasoktaaf in het Missale Romanum en zijn geschiedenis* (Assen 1968), in *idem* 86-87.

1971

46. Liturgia e secolarizzazione, in J. Bornewasser a.o., *Cultura secolarizzata e autenticità christiana*, Torino 1971, 200-230. Italian translation of no. 30.
47. [Contributions to:] *Dabar. De lezingen en tussenzangen van de zon- en feestdagen op geluidsband, met schriftelijk commentaar*, Nijmegen-Haarlem-Bussum, 1970-1971, no. 2, 1-7; no. 8, 1-13; no. 9, 1-12.
48. Dooprituelen na Vaticanum II, in *Schrift* 3 (1971) 34-38.
49. Laat het geloof één zijn onder verscheiden praktijken, in *Ons geestelijk leven* 48 (1971) 66-80.
50. Zo moeilijk is het nu ook weer niet, in *Analecta van het bisdom 's-Hertogenbosch* 11 (1971) 54-56.

1972

51. [Co-editor of:] *Liturgie rond het ziekbed. Vademecum voor pastores en allen die belast zijn met de zorg voor zieken*, Hilversum 1972.
52. [Texts] in *idem* 151-152; 184-185.
53. [With A. Scheer and H. Wegman:] *Orde van dienst voor de viering van Pasen*, publikatie van de Nationale Raad voor Liturgie, Utrecht 1972 (photo-copied).
54. *De wordingsgeschiedenis van de Liturgische Bibliotheek*, Tilburg 1972 (brochure).
55. Bijdrage voor Open Kerk, in *Open Kerk. De situatie in de Nederlandse kerkprovincie*, Heemstede 1972, 30-33.
56. [With A. Scheer:] Alternatieve paasviering, in *Tijdschrift voor liturgie* 56 (1972) 134-137.
57. Opening van de Liturgische Bibliotheek te Tilburg, in *idem* 160.
58. De rol van voorganger en gemeente in het eucharistisch gebed, in *idem* 272-283.
59. De Amsterdamse Dominicuskerk en de romeinse liturgie, in *G en Sertjes* 8 (1972) no. 5, 3.
60. Gevaarlijke liturgie, in *Ons geestelijk leven* 49 (1972) 177-181.
61. Jongerenkorendag in Heelsum. Overpeinzingen van een jurylid, in *Over en weer in het aartsbisdom Utrecht* 2 (1972) 3.
62. De liturgie van de ziekenzalving, in *Rond de Tafel* 27 (1972) 113-116.
63. [With W. Reckman:] Oekumenische huwelijksviering. Een ontwerp ten dienste van de kerken, in *Werkmap voor liturgie* 6 (1972) no. 3, 2-30.

[Reviews of:]
- L. Braeckmans, *Confession et communion au Moyen Age et au Concile de Trente* (Gembloux 1971), in *Tijdschrift voor theologie* 12 (1972) 253.

- H. Hilgenfeld, *Mittelalterlich-traditionelle Elemente in Luthers Abendmahlsschriften* (Zürich 1971), in *idem* 253-254.
- J. Jungmann, *Messe im Gottesvolk. Ein nachkonziliarer Durchblick durch Misarum Sollemnia* (Freiburg-Basel-Wien 1970), in *idem* 12 (1972) 122.
- F. Mann, *Das Abendmahl beim jungen Luther* (München 1971), in *idem* 106.
- K. Müller (ed.), *Gottesdienst in einem säkularisierten Zeitalter. Eine Konsultation de Kommission für Glauben und Kirchenverfassung des Ökumenischen Rates der Kirchen* (Trier-Kassel 1971), in *idem* 363.
- P. van Hooijdonk and H. Wegman, *Zij breken hetzelfde brood. Een kritische wegwijzer bij de viering van de eucharistie op basis van een liturgiehistorische en -sociologische analyse* (Amersfoort 1972); review titled: Een belangrijke hulp bij de evaluatie van liturgische diensten, in *Inzet. Werkboek voor liturgiegroepen* 2 (1972) [section:] Nieuw, 4-6.

1973

64. *Original Sin in the Roman liturgy. Research into the theology of Original Sin in the Roman sacramentaria and the early baptismal liturgy*, Leiden 1973.
    Revised English translation of no. 19.
65. [With Th. van Eupen and H. Knaapen:] Kritisch verslag van de plenaire discussie, in *Richtingen in de kerk* (= Annalen van het Thijmgenootschap 61, no. 1), Baarn 1973, 167-180.
66. Liturgie, Rooms-Katholiek, in *Supplement* of *Oosthoeks Encyclopedie*, sixth edition (vol. 16), Utrecht 1973.
67. Preekschema en voorbeden, in *Enkele elementen voor het samenstellen van een liturgie rond het thema 'Kerk van de grond'*, Zeist 1973, 10-13.
68. In de liturgie voltrekt zich het geloof op onvervangbare wijze, in *Concilium* 9 (1973) no. 2, 7-20.
69. De aktieve deelname van de gemeente aan het eucharistisch gebed, in *Rond de Tafel* 28 (1973) 129-142.
70. Empirisch onderzoek naar de liturgie in Nederland, in *Theologie en pastoraat* 69 (1973) 73-81.
71. De kinderdoop in de kerk van vandaag, in *Werkmap voor liturgie* 7 (1973) no. 2, 5-20.
72. Een viering van de kinderdoop (zonder eucharistie), in *idem* 21-30.
73. De prefaties voor de veertigdagentijd, in *Getuigenis. Tijdschrift voor liturgisch-bijbelse katechese* 17 (1973) 142-146.
74. De weekendliturgie in Nederland, in *G en Sertjes* 9 (1973) no. 3, 2.
75. Kerstliturgie in het licht van Pasen, in *De Bazuin* 56 (1973) no. 63, 6-7.

[Reviews of:]
- P. van Hooijdonk and H. Wegman, *Zij breken hetzelfde brood. Een kritische wegwijzer bij de viering van de eucharistie op basis van een liturgiehistorische en -sociologische analyse* (Amersfoort 1972), in *Tijdschrift voor theologie* 13 (1973) 115-116.
- W. Rordorf, *Sabbat und Sonntag in der Alten Kirche* (Zürich 1972), in *idem* 231.
- *De weekendliturgie, vormgeving, spreiding, organisatie en ruimte* ('s-Gravenhage 1972), in *idem* 115.

1974

76. De weekendliturgie. Recente empirische onderzoekingen, in *Tijdschrift voor liturgie* 58 (1974) 17-36.
77. Uitvaart van een kind. Elementen, in *Werkmap voor liturgie* 8 (1974) 39-55.
78. Missaal van de beheerste kerk, in *De Tijd* (29 January 1974) 8.

[Reviews of:]
- A. Härdelin, *Aquae et vini mysterium. Geheimnis der Erlösung und Geheimnis der Kirche im Spiegel der mittelalterlichen Auslegung des gemischten Kelches* (Münster 1973), in *Tijdschrift voor theologie* 14 (1974) 203.
- H. Reifenberg (ed.), *Hauseucharistie. Gedanken und Modellen* (München 1973), in *idem* 202-203.

1975

79. [With H. Berger, W. Goddijn and A. Smits editor of:] *Tussentijds. Theologische Faculteit Tilburg. Bundel opstellen bij gelegenheid van haar erkenning*, Tilburg 1975.
80. De liturgie als onvervangbare vindplaats voor de theologie. Methoden van theologische analyse en verificatie, in *idem* 317-332.
81. La liturgie comme lieu théologique irremplaçable. Méthodes d'analyse et de vérification théologiques, in *Questions liturgiques* 56 (1975) 97-112.
    French translation of no. 80.
82. Een dodenliturgie van Huub Oosterhuis. Theologische analyse en toetsing, in *Tijdschrift voor liturgie* 59 (1975) 310-350.
83. Kerstmis, Pasen en Pinksteren in een overgangstijd, in *Inzet. Werkboek voor liturgiegroepen* 4 (1975) 86-89.
84. De Werkmap voor liturgie, in *De liturgiekrant. Actuele informatie voor werkers in de liturgie* (1975) no. 3, 6.
85. Vijf en veertig jaar Bron van christelijken geest, in *idem* no. 5, 1-3.

[Reviews of:]
- J. Amougou-Atangana, *Ein Sakrament des Geistempfangs? Zum Verhältnis von Taufe und Firmung* (Freiburg-Basel-Wien 1974), in *Tijdschrift voor theologie* 15 (1975) 339.
- Fr. Schupp, *Glaube - Kultur - Symbol. Versuch einer kritischen Theorie Sakramentaler Praxis* (Düsseldorf 1974), in *idem* 459.

1976
86. Beoordeling van 31 eucharistische gebeden, eucharistisch gebed 15 en 22, in H. Wegman (ed.), *Goed of niet goed? Het eucharistisch gebed in Nederland*, Hilversum 1976, 92-94, 120-122.
87. The letters A-E, L-N, R-Z of the rubric 'catholic liturgy', in *De Grote Oosthoek. Encyclopedie en woordenboek*, seventh edition (20 vols.), Utrecht 1976-1981.
88. Zij die geloven haasten niet, in *Praktische theologie* 3 (1976) 180-187.
89. Vorm geven aan de gevoelens van dit barre moment, in *Inzet. Werkboek voor liturgiegroepen* 5 (1976) no. 2, 21-24.
90. [Rubric 'De bisschop geeft het woord':] Het huis van gebed, in *Bisdomblad voor het diocees Den Bosch* 54 (1976) no. 48, 3.

[Reviews of:]
- B. Moreton, *The eighth-century Gelasian Sacramentary. A study in tradition* (London 1976), in *Tijdschrift voor theologie* 16 (1976) 448.
- J. Vuijst, *Gemeente van onderen. Een vinger aan de pols* (Baarn 1974), in *Praktische theologie* 3 (1976) 120.

1977
91. Was bedeutet 'benedicere'?, in *Liturgisches Jahrbuch* 27 (1977) 5-27.
92. [With A. van Rijen:] Empirische godsdienstwetenschappen en theologie, in *Praktische theologie* 4 (1977) 193-199.
93. Een dodenliturgie van Huub Oosterhuis. Theologische analyse en toetsing, in *Werkmap voor liturgie* 11 (1977) 359-386.
    Summary of no. 82 by H. Keiren.
94. [Editor of:] De toekomst van de kinderdoop, in *idem* 11 (1977) 81-241.
95. Inleiding, in *idem* 83-84.
96. De doopvoorbereiding, in *idem* 85-92.
97. De doop. Een onvervangbaar sacrament, in *idem* 166-203.
98. Literatuur, in *idem* 238-241.

[Reviews of:]
- G. Blond a.o., *L'Eucharistie des premiers chrétiens* (Paris 1976), in *Tijdschrift voor theologie* 17 (1977) 87-88.
- J. Steiner, *Liturgiereform in der Aufklärungszeit. Eine Darstellung am Beispiel Vitus Anton Winters* (Freiburg-Basel-Wien 1976), in *idem* 90-91.

- B. Weiß, *Themenschlüßel zum Meßbuch. Eine pastoralliturgische Arbeitshilfe* (Einsiedeln etc. 1976), in *idem* 212-213.

1978

99. De taak van de kerk bij de huwelijkssluiting. Een reformatorische visie vanuit katholieke gezichtshoek bezien, in *Praktische theologie* 5 (1978) 255-260.
100. [Editor of:] Dit geheim is groot. Over de pastoraal-liturgische begeleiding van het huwelijk, part I, in *Werkmap voor liturgie* 12 (1978) 331-390.
101. Inleiding, in *idem* 334-335.
102. De nieuwe Romeinse huwelijksliturgie, in *idem* 337-367.
103. De geschiedenis in vogelvlucht, in *idem* 369-373.
104. 'Dit geheim is groot'. Theologische bezinning op het sacrament van het huwelijk, in *idem* 375-390.
105. Het kind dat als een bron in de woestijn begraven werd, in *P.V.-Blad Katholieke Hogeschool Tilburg* 10 (1978) Christmas special, 13-16.
106. [Interview:] Rome heeft duivel nog niet verbrand, in *Algemeen Dagblad* (29 April 1978) 21.

1979

107. [Editor of:] Dit geheim is groot. Over de pastoraal-liturgische begeleiding van het huwelijk, part II and III, in *Werkmap voor liturgie* 13 (1979) 1-168.
108. Huwelijksliturgieën in 'gestencilde boekjes'. Een onderzoek van A. Scheer, in *idem* 61-66.
109. Voorbereiding op de huwelijksliturgie, in *idem* 79-83.
110. [With J. Meijer and J. de Wolf:] Literatuur, in *idem* 161-167.
111. Kwetsbaarheid, strijd, tederheid, in *Beeld van genade. Feestgave voor de Zoete Lieve Vrouwe van Den Bosch bij gelegenheid van het 125e herdenkingsjaar van de terugkeer van het genadebeeld*, Hilversum 1979, 234-240.
112. Het eucharistisch gebed in Nederland. Een oecumenische voorhoede, in *Kosmos en oekumene* 13 (1979) 89-91.
113. De waarachtige kinderdoop. Groei naar een meervoudige praktijk, in *Tijdschrift voor het gezin* 97 (1979) no. 1, 11-13.

[Review of:]
- H. Vorgrimler, *Buße und Krankensalbung* (= Handbuch der Dogmengeschichte IV/3) (Freiburg-Basel-Wien 1978), in *Tijdschrift voor theologie* 19 (1979) 316.

1980

114. De onvervangbare weg van de liturgie, Hilversum 1980.
115. The rubric 'liturgy', in *De Grote Oosthoek. Encyclopedie en woordenboek*, seventh edition (vols. 16-20), Utrecht 1980-1981.
116. Kernvragen rond de christelijke dodenliturgie, in *Tijdschrift voor liturgie* 64 (1980) 146-164.
117. [Editor with A. Blijlevens of:] De Ziekenliturgie. Over de pastoraalliturgische begeleiding van zieken, part I, in *Werkmap voor liturgie* 14 (1980) 293-406.
118. Inleiding, in *idem* 296-297.
119. Anker en vissen, in *Faculteitsblad Theologische Faculteit Tilburg en participerende instellingen* 1 (1980-1981) no. 2, 28-29.
120. Het kind dat als een bron in de woestijn begraven werd, in *Commercium* 4 (1980) no. 10, 1.
Same article: no. 105.

[Reviews of:]
- J. Hermans, *Benedictus XIV en de liturgie. Een bijdrage tot de liturgiegeschiedenis van de Moderne Tijd* (Brugge-Boxtel 1979), in *Tijdschrift voor theologie* 20 (1980) 203-204.
- H. Henrix (ed.), *Jüdische Liturgie. Geschichte – Struktur – Wesen* (Freiburg-Basel-Wien 1979), in *idem* 326.

1981

121. Sacramenten en belangrijke levensmomenten, in R. Hoste-Van Bockel a.o. (ed.), *Van heinde en verre*, Tilburg 1981, 140-147.
122. The rubric 'liturgy', in *Supplement* of *De Grote Oosthoek. Encyclopedie en woordenboek*, seventh edition, Utrecht 1981.
123. [With P. de Maat, M. Rijkhoff and N. Tromp:] Le Seigneur m'a vu. Analyse sémiotique d'un chant liturgique, in *Sémiotique et Bible* 5 (1981) 24-44.
124. [Editor with A. Blijlevens of:] De ziekenliturgie. Over de pastoraalliturgische begeleiding van zieken, part II and III, in *Werkmap voor liturgie* 15 (1981) 1-280.
125. [With A. Blijlevens:] Literatuur, in *idem* 276-280.
126. 1966-1981. Vijftien jaar Werkmap voor liturgie, in *idem* 15 (1981) 389-392.
127. Het woord in de liturgie, in *Inzet. Werkboek voor liturgiegroepen* 10 (1981) no. 3, 4-12.
128. Déze uitvaartliturgie, in *Tegenwoordig* 36 (1981) 103-107.

[Reviews of:]
- J. Finkenzeller, *Die Lehre von den Sakramenten im allgemeinen von der Schrift bis zur Scholastik* (= Handbuch der Dogmengeschichte IV/1A) (Freiburg-Basel-Wien 1980), in *Tijdschrift voor theologie* 21 (1981) 201.

- A. Adam and R. Berger, *Pastoralliturgisches Handlexikon* (Freiburg-Basel-Wien 1980), in *idem* 216.

1982
129. Uitvaartliturgie en randkerkelijkheid, in J. Lescrauwaet a.o., *Met huisgenoten of als met vreemdelingen? Pastoraal-liturgische benadering van randkerkelijken* (= Nike-reeks 3), Leuven 1982, 115-142.
130. Funérailles et marginalité, in C. Traets a.o., *Liturgie et marginalité*, Louvain 1982, 67-84.
French translation of no. 129.
131. Funérailles et marginalité, in *Questions liturgiques* 63 (1982) 143-160.
French translation of no. 129.
132. Liturgiewetenschap en 'muziek van de christelijke liturgie', in *Tijdschrift voor liturgie* 66 (1982) 111-122.
133. [Editor with A. Blijlevens of:] De doop van volwassenen, part I, in *Werkmap voor liturgie* 16 (1982) 75-231.
134. Inleiding, in *idem* 77-78.
135. [Editor with A. Blijlevens of:] De doop van volwassenen, part II, in *idem* 331-387.
136. Dopen: privé of in de gemeenschap?, in *Inzet. Werkboek voor liturgiegroepen* 11 (1982) no. 3, 13-15.

[Reviews of:]
- J. Ambaum, *Glaubenszeichen. Schillebeeckx' Auffassung von den Sakramenten* (Regensburg 1980), in *Tijdschrift voor theologie* 22 (1982) 101.
- *Archiv für Liturgiewissenschaft* 23/1 (Regensburg 1981), in *idem* 338-339.
- H.J. Auf der Maur a.o. (ed.), *Fides sacramenti – sacramentum fidei. Studies in honour of Pieter Smulders* (Assen 1981), in *idem* 426.
- A. Lorenzer, *Das Konzil der Buchhalter. Die Zerstörung der Sinnlichkeit – Eine Religionskritik* (Frankfurt am Main 1981), in *idem* 215.

1983
137. [With P. de Maat, M. Rijkhoff and N. Tromp:] Mattheus 2 – Een semiotische analyse, in B. Hes a.o. (ed.), *Reflecties op Schrift*, Averbode-Apeldoorn 1983, 65-100.
138. [With P. de Maat, M. Rijkhoff and N. Tromp:] Een methode van semiotische analyse, in *Bijdragen. Tijdschrift voor filosofie en theologie* 44 (1983) 118-165.
139. [With P. de Maat, M. Rijkhoff and N. Tromp:] Hoe krijgt Mc 2,15-17 (NBG 1951) betekenis? Analyse van de narratieve syntaxis van het oppervlakteniveau, in *idem* 194-207.
140. Liturgie en zintuiglijkheid, in *Reliëf. Tijdschrift voor religieuzen* 51 (1983) 241-245.

141. [Editor with A. Blijlevens of:] De doop van volwassenen, part III, in *Werkmap voor liturgie* 17 (1983) 81-200.
142. [With A. Blijlevens:] Litteratuur, in *idem* 196-200.
143. Persoonlijke voorkeur, in *Werkschrift voor leerhuis en liturgie* 4 (1983) no. 1, 147-148.

[Reviews of:]
- R. Cantalamessa, *Ostern in der Alten Kirche* (Bern-Frankfurt am Main-Las Vegas 1981), in *Tijdschrift voor theologie* 23 (1983) 99.
- *Doop, eucharistie en ambt. Verklaring van de Commissie voor Geloof en Kerkorde van de Wereldraad van Kerken* (Amersfoort-Voorburg [1982]), in *idem* 320.
- J. Finkenzeller, *Die Lehre von den Sakramenten im allgemeinen. Von der Reformation bis zur Gegenwart* (= Handbuch der Dogmengeschichte IV/1B) (Freiburg-Basel-Wien 1982), in *idem* 186.
- A. Houssiau a.o., *Le baptême. Entrée dans l'existence chrétienne* (Bruxelles 1983), in *idem* 449.
- R. Volp (ed.), *Zeichen. Semiotik in Theologie und Gottesdienst* (München-Mainz 1982), in *idem* 194.

1984
144. *De onvervangbare weg van de liturgie*, Hilversum 1984.
    Second revised edition of no. 114.
145. *Geen leven zonder rituelen. Antropologische beschouwingen met het oog op de christelijke liturgie* (= Tweede serie Geestelijke Volksgezondheid 2-24), Baarn 1984.
146. [Co-editor of:] *Liturgie rond het ziekbed. Vademecum voor pastores en allen die belast zijn met de zorg voor zieken*, Hilversum 1984.
    Revised fifth edition no. 51.
147. [Cooperation:] *Liturgische trefwoordenlijst*, Nijmegen 1984.
148. Liturgie van de kinderdoop tussen bevestiging en evangelische uitdaging, in *Praktische theologie* 11 (1984) 459-466.
149. Strijd en ritueel, in *Lijnen* 1 (1984) no. 1, 48-55.
150. Literaire criteria voor liturgische gezangen, in *Werkmap voor liturgie* 18 (1984) 63-73.

[Review of:]
- B. Neunheuser, *Taufe und Firmung* (= Handbuch der Dogmengeschichte IV/2) (Freiburg-Basel-Wien 1983^2), in *Tijdschrift voor theologie* 24 (1984) 70-71.

1985
151. *Analyse van de nieuwe Romeinse huwelijksliturgie. De huwelijkssluiting zonder de eucharistieviering* I-II, Tilburg 1985 (photocopied).

152. Het binnengaan in de kerk in de Romeinse huwelijksliturgie. Een semiotische analyse, in *Jaarboek voor liturgie-onderzoek* 1 (1985) 69-89.
153. Liturgie en stilte, in *Lijnen* 2 (1985) no. 1, 38-42.
154. Liturgie voor heel de mens, in *Reliëf. Tijdschrift voor religieuzen* 53 (1985) 257-264.
155. Sacrosanctum Concilium, in *Een-twee-een. Informatiebulletin van de Dienst Pers en Publiciteit van het Secretariaat van het Rooms-Katholiek kerkgenootschap in Nederland* 13 (1985) 625-626.
156. [With A. Blijlevens:] Litteratuurlijst [to 'Nieuwe vragen rond dodenliturgie'], in *Werkmap voor liturgie* 19 (1985) 73-74.
157. [With H. Wegman:] De viering van Pasen, in *idem* 353-363.

[Review of:]
- F. Nocke, *Wort und Geste. Zum Verständnis der Sakramente* (München 1985), in *Tijdschrift voor theologie* 25 (1985) 430.

1986

158. Geen leven zonder rituelen. Antropologische beschouwingen met het oog op de christelijke liturgie, Hilversum 1986.
Second edition of no. 145.
159. *Analyse van de "Ritus celebrandi matrimonii sacramentum" van het Rituale Romanum*, Tilburg 1986 (photo-copied).
160. Romero herdenken. Liturgie van binnenuit, in *Oscar Romero*, Oosterhout 1986, 25-26.
161. Semiotische analyse van de schuldbelijdenis aan het begin van de eucharistieviering, in *Bijdragen. Tijdschrift voor filosofie en theologie* 47 (1986) 290-317.
162. Semiotische analyse van een bidprentje, in *Jaarboek voor liturgie-onderzoek* 2 (1986) 12-21.
163. Relevantie van de semiotische analyse-methode voor de liturgiewetenschap, in *idem* 32-48.
164. Liturgie als religieuze en gelovige expressie van wat ons overkomt, in *Speling* 38 (1986) no. 2, 51-58.
165. Het nieuwe zegeningenboek, in *Werkmap voor liturgie* 20 (1986) 44-49.
166. Een goede dienst, in *idem* 153-156.

[Reviews of:]
- H. van der Laan, *Het vormenspel der liturgie* (Leiden 1985), in *Tijdschrift voor theologie* 26 (1986) 98.
- S. Schmid-Kaiser, *Aktive Teilnahme: Kriterium gottesdienstlichen Handelns und Feierns. Zu den Elementen eines Schlüßelbegriffes in Geschichte und Gegenwart des 20. Jahrhunderts* (Bern-Frankfurt am Main-New York 1985), in *idem* 197-198.

1987

167. *Mijn genade is u genoeg (2 Kor. 11, 9). Herdenkingsrede ter nagedachtenis aan prof. dr. H.M.M. Boeracker (1934-1987) op 11-2-1987*, Tilburg 1987.
168. [Editor with SEMANET of:] *Semiotiek en christelijke uitingsvormen. De semiotiek van A.J. Greimas en de Parijse school toegepast op Bijbel en liturgie*, Hilversum 1987.
169. De semiotiek van de Parijse school, in *idem* 8-54.
170. Analyses. Inleiding. De praktijk van de semiotische analyse, in *idem* 56-58.
171. Het sprookje 'De koning der vissen', in *idem* 59-74.
172. [With N. Tromp:] Marcus 3,1-6, in *idem* 75-86.
173. [With K. Joosse and P. de Maat:] Een complex semiotisch object, in *idem* 151-155.
174. De nieuwe Romeinse huwelijksliturgie, in *idem* 155-208.
175. Een bidprentje, in *idem* 255-276.
176. Literatuur, in *idem* 277-282.
177. Pleidooi voor een integralere benadering van de liturgie als theologische vindplaats. Een uitdaging voor heel de theologie, in W. Logister a.o. (ed.), *Twintig jaar ontwikkelingen in de theologie. Tendensen en perspectieven*, Kampen 1987, 194-204.
178. Plaidoyer pour une approche integrale de la liturgie comme lieu théologique. Un défi à toute la théologie, in *Questions liturgiques* 68 (1987) 242-255.
    French translation of no. 177.
179. Semiotics and the study of liturgy, in W. Vos and G. Wainwright (ed.), *Gratias Agamus. An ecumenical collection of essays on the liturgy and its implications. On the occasion of the twenty fifth anniversary of Studia liturgica (1962-1987)* (= Studia liturgica 17), Rotterdam 1987, 108-117.
180. De noodzaak van rituelen in het persoonlijke en maatschappelijke leven, in L. Leijssen (ed.), *De mens leeft niet van brood alleen. Leven van symbolen en sacramenten. Verslagboek van de Vliebergh-Sencie-Leergang, afdeling Catechese, August 1986* (= Nike-reeks 16) Leuven-Amersfoort 1987, 35-53.
181. Semiotische analyse van de huwelijkssluiting in het post-tridentijnse Rituale Romanum, in *Jaarboek voor liturgie-onderzoek* 3 (1987) 41-85.
182. Relaties als grondpatroon van de liturgie, in *Speling* 39 (1987) no. 4, 70-75.
183. De voorganger in het spanningsveld van de liturgie, in *Tijdschrift voor liturgie* 71 (1987) 259-278.
184. Riten en symbolen, in *Kruispunt. Maandblad voor mensen in ontmoeting* 23 (1987) no. 11, 11-16.

185. Het gemengde huwelijk van moslim en christen, in *Werkmap voor liturgie* 21 (1987) 295-300.
186. Laudatio bij gelegenheid van het eredoctoraat van J. Delorme, in *Kohelet. Faculteitsblad van de Theologische Faculteit Tilburg* 4 (1987) no. 5, 25-27.
187. Semanet. Semiotische Analyse door Nederlandse Theologen, in *idem* 19-20, 30.

[Reviews of:]
- F.-J. Bode, *Gemeinschaft mit dem lebendigen Gott. Die Lehre von der Eucharistie bei Matthias Joseph Scheeben* (Paderborn 1986), in *Tijdschrift voor theologie* 27 (1987) 211.
- E. Nübold, *Entstehung und Bewertung der neuen Perikopenordnung der Römischen Ritus für die Meßfeier an Sonn- und Festtagen* (Paderborn 1986), in *idem* 324-325.

1988

188. *Geen leven zonder rituelen. Antropologische beschouwingen met het oog op de christelijke liturgie*, Hilversum 1988.
Third edition of no. 145.
189. [With A. Blijlevens and W. Boelens editor of:] *Dopen met water en geest. Doopliturgieën, elementen voor vieringen en achtergrondbeschouwingen uit 20 jaar werkmap Liturgie (1966-1985)*, Hilversum 1988.
190. De kinderdoop in de kerk van vandaag, in *idem* 11-22.
Same contribution: no. 71.
191. De doopvoorbereiding, in *idem* 23-29.
Same contribution: no. 96.
192. De doop. Een onvervangbaar sacrament, in *idem* 91-110.
Same contribution: no. 97.
193. Een viering van de kinderdoop (zonder eucharistie), in *idem* 153-162.
Same contribution: no. 72.
194. [With W. Reckman and Ph. Stein:] De doop van een volwassene, in *idem* 263-278.
Same contribution: no. 28.
195. Ritueel en menselijke identiteit, in A. de Ruijter a.o., *Totems en trends. Over de zin van identificatiesymbolen*, Hilversum 1988, 20-34, 78-93.
196. Laudatio Jean Delorme, in M. Beelaerts (ed.), *Documentatie bij de lezingencyclus Semiotiek mei-juni 1988*, Nijmegen 1988.
Same contribution: no. 186.
197. Relevantie van de semiotische analyse-methode voor de liturgiewetenschap, in *idem*.
Same contribution: no. 163.

198. Bibliografie semiotiek, in *idem*.
     Same contribution: no. 176.
199. Voorwoord, in H. Vrijdag, *Zonder beelden sprak hij niet tot hen. Nieuwe symbolen en riten in de liturgie*. I. *Kerkelijk jaar*, Hilversum 1988, 9-10.
200. De plaats van de vrouw in het huwelijksritueel van het Rituale Romanum en van Vaticanum II. Van ondergeschiktheid van de vrouw naar een zekere evenwaardigheid van man en vrouw, in *Jaarboek voor liturgie-onderzoek* 4 (1988) 67-89.
201. Het Genootschap voor Liturgiestudie in een nieuw spanningsveld, in *idem* 91-105.
202. Bij de vieringen, [in A. Brugman a.o., Vrouw en Liturgie,] in *Werkmap voor liturgie* 22 (1988) 189-190.
203. Solidariteit, in *Bisdomblad Breda* 2 (1988) no. 9-10, 17.

[Reviews of:]
- R. Berger a.o., *Gestalt des Gottesdienstes. Sprachliche und nichtsprachliche Ausdrucksformen* (= Gottesdienst der Kirche. Handbuch der Liturgiewissenschaft III) (Regensburg 1987), in *Tijdschrift voor theologie* 28 (1988) 194-195.
- O. Herlyn, *Theologie der Gottesdienstgestaltung* (Neukirchen-Vluyn 1988), in *idem* 322.
- M. Lawler, *Symbol and sacrament. A contemporary sacramental theology* (New York 1987), in *idem* 417.
- L. Leijssen (ed.), *De Heilige Geest en de liturgie. Verslagboek van het zevende liturgiecolloquium te Leuven, november 1985* (Leuven-Amersfoort 1985), in *idem* 98.

1989

204. [Editor with A. Blijlevens and W. Boelens of:] *Op dood en leven*. I. *Avondwake*, Hilversum 1989.
205. Voorwoord, in *idem* 7.
206. *Mon âme exalte la gloire de Dieu* (Workpaper meeting Semanet – Cadir, 26-29 June 1989), Tilburg 1989.
207. Het zegel van de faculteit, in *Werken, gedichten en verhalen. Theologische Faculteit Tilburg*, Tilburg 1989, 5-7.
208. Die architektonischen Dimensionen des Rituals, in *Liturgisches Jahrbuch* 39 (1989) 19-36.
209. Studieweek Semanet – Cadir over semiotiek en christelijke uitingsvormen, in *Jaarboek voor Liturgie-onderzoek* 5 (1989) 133-135.
210. De semiotiek van de kerkruimte als semiotiek van het visuele, in *idem* 275-299.
211. Studieweek over semiotiek en christelijke uitingsvormen, in *Tijdschrift voor theologie* 29 (1989) 391-392.

212. Op weg naar eenheid bij de maaltijd des Heren, in *Tijdschrift voor liturgie* 73 (1989) 215-221.
213. De theologie van het doopsel na Vaticanum II. Accentverschuivingen en lacunes, in *idem* 338-348.
214. De maaltijd des Heren, in *Kosmos en Oekumene* 23 (1989) 85-88.
215. De constituering van het subject in het ritueel discours, in *Versus. Tijdschrift voor film en opvoeringskunsten* 4 (1989) no. 2, 34-42.
216. Zoeken naar nieuwe overgangsrituelen, in *Opstap. Werkschrift voor geloofsvorming* 9 (1989) 89-94.
217. Een kwart eeuw liturgievernieuwing, in *De Bazuin* 72 (1989) no. 1, 10-11.

[Reviews of:]
- A. Adam, *Het liturgisch jaar - vieren en beleven. Zijn geschiedenis en betekenis in de liturgievernieuwing* (Turnhout 1987), in *Tijdschrift voor theologie* 29 (1989) 191.
- E. Aman, *Lebensaustausch zwischen Gott und Mensch. Zum Liturgieverständnis Johannes Pinsks* (Regensburg 1988), in *idem* 295-296.
- T. Maas-Ewerd (ed.), *Lebt unser Gottesdienst? Die bleibende Aufgabe der Liturgiereform* (Freiburg-Basel-Wien 1988), in *idem* 190-191.
- F. Senn (ed.), *New eucharistic prayers. An ecumenical study of their development and structure* (New York 1987), in *idem* 78.

1990
218. *Liturgie en zintuiglijkheid. Over de betekenis van lichamelijkheid in de liturgie*, Hilversum 1990.
219. [Editor with A. Blijlevens and W. Boelens of:] *Op dood en leven*. II. *Uitvaartliturgie*, Hilversum 1990.
220. Voorwoord, in *idem* 7.
221. Elementen voor de uitvaart van een kind, in *idem* 108-123.
Same contribution: no. 77.
222. Een dodenliturgie van Huub Oosterhuis. Theologische analyse en toetsing, in *idem* 230-257.
Same contribution: no. 93.
223. [Editor with A. Blijlevens and W. Boelens of:] *Op dood en leven*. III. *Crematie*, Hilversum 1990.
224. Voorwoord, in *idem* 2-3.
225. Literatuurlijst, in *idem* 305-306.
226. Les transformations du rôle liturgique du peuple. La contribution de la sémiotique à l'histoire de la liturgie, in Ch. Caspers and M. Schneiders (ed.), *Omnes circumadstantes. Contributions towards a history of the role of the people in the liturgy*, Kampen 1990, 15-30.
227. Huidige vragen. Illustratie en concretisering (= Leereenheid 5), in A. Blijlevens (ed.), *Liturgiewetenschap* I, Kampen 1990, 55-68.

228. La crise de la liturgie aux Pays-Bas. Comment donner corps au rituel chrétien dans une société secularisée?, in *Recherches de science religieuse* 78 (1990) 485-511.
229. Un chant liturgique néerlandais analysé comme objet syncrétique, in *Jaarboek voor liturgie-onderzoek* 6 (1990) 135-154.
230. Zoeken naar nieuwe overgangsrituelen, in *Werkmap voor liturgie* 24 (1990) 159-166.
Same article: no. 216.
231. Het heilige kan niet zonder rituelen, in *Voorlopig. Maandelijks commentaar bij maatschappij en kerk* 22 (1990) no. 4, 4-6 (section of *Hervormd Nederland* 46 (1990) no. 17).

[Reviews of:]
- W. Barnard and P. van 't Riet, *De slip van een joodse man vastgrijpen. Christelijke eredienst in het spoor van de joodse Jezus* (Kampen 1989), in *De Bazuin* 73 (1990) no. 11, Recensie-katern, 5.
- L. Leijssen (ed.), *Over het vormsel. Oorsprong, geschiedenis en huidige pastoraal* (Leuven-Amersfoort 1989), in *idem* 5.
- B. Kleinheyer, *Sacramentliche Feiern. I. Die Feiern der Eingliederung in die Kirche* (= Gottesdienst der Kirche. Handbuch der Liturgiewissenschaft VII/1) (Regensburg 1989), in *Tijdschrift voor theologie* 30 (1990) 106.
- W. Pannenberg (ed.), *Lehrverurteilungen - kirchentrennend? III. Materialien zur Lehre von den Sakramenten und vom kirchlichen Amt* (Freiburg-Göttingen 1990), in *idem* 317-318.
- G. Ruhbach a.o., *Meditation und Gottesdienst* (Göttingen 1989), in *idem* 422.
- K. Schlemmer (ed.), *Gottesdienst - Weg zur Einheit. Impulse für die Oekumene* (Freiburg-Basel-Wien 1989), in *idem* 421-422.

1991
232. [Editor with A. Blijlevens of:] *In goede en kwade dagen. Beschouwingen over huwelijksliturgie en modellen van huwelijksvieringen uit 20 jaar Werkmap liturgie (1966-1985)*, Baarn 1991.
233. Voorwoord, in *idem* 9.
234. De nieuwe Romeinse huwelijksliturgie, in *idem* 13-40.
Same contribution: no. 102.
235. De geschiedenis in vogelvlucht, in *idem* 41-43.
Same contribution: no. 103.
236. 'Dit geheim is groot'. Theologische bezinning op het sacrament van het huwelijk, in *idem* 44-53.
Same contribution: no. 104.
237. Huwelijksliturgieën in 'gestencilde boekjes'. Een onderzoek van A. Scheer, in *idem* 104-107.
Same contribution: no. 108.

238. Voorbereiding op de huwelijksliturgie, in *idem* 115-118.
    Same contribution: no. 109.
239. [With J. Meijer and J. de Wolf:] Literatuur, in *idem* 183-189.
    Same contribution: no. 110.
240. [With W. Reckman:] Oekumenische huwelijksviering. Een ontwerp ten dienste van de kerken, in *idem* 244-265.
    Same contribution: no. 63.
241. La crise de la liturgie aux Pays-Bas. Comment donner corps au rituel chrétien dans une société sécularisée, in J. Moignt (ed.), *Enjeux du rite dans la modernité*, Paris 1991, 143-169.
    Same contribution: no. 228.
242. De receptie van de Greimassiaanse semiotiek bij theologen. Weerstanden en misverstanden, in P. Beentjes, J. Maas and T. Wever (ed.), *'Gelukkig de mens'. Opstellen over Psalmen, exegese en semiotiek*, Kampen 1991, 121-135.
243. De wisselwerking tussen (katholieke) liturgie en cultuur in Nederland sinds Vaticanum II, in H. Boon-Schilling (ed.), *Liturgievernieuwing in een veranderende wereld. Terugblik en toekomstperspectief* (= Mededelingen Prof. Dr. G. van der Leeuw-Stichting 66), Amsterdam 1991, 27-39.
244. De 'doorbraak' van de antropologie in de liturgie, in H. Degen a.o. (ed.), *Herinneringen aan de toekomst. Pastoraat in de geest van Vaticanum II*, Baarn 1991, 167-176.
245. Wegen uit de hedendaagse crisis van het ritueel (= Leereenheid 10), in A. Blijlevens (ed.), *Liturgiewetenschap* II, Kampen 1991, 59-71.
246. Het belang van het niet-verbale in het ritueel (= Leereenheid 11), in *idem* 72-82.
247. Les dimensions architectoniques du rituel, in *Sémiotique et Bible* 16 (1991) no. 61, 5-21.
    French translation of no. 208.
248. De onvervangbare weg van het ritueel, in *Brabantia. Brabants tijdschrift voor kunst en cultuur* 40 (1991) 17-20.
249. Ritueel en ruimte, in *Werkmap voor liturgie* 25 (1991) 132-140.
250. Een blik op de toekomst. Werkmap liturgie bestaat 25 jaar, in *idem* 260-263.

[Reviews of:]
- Byzantijns Liturgikon (Tilburg-Zagreb 1991), in *De Bazuin* 74 (1991) no. 33, Recensie-katern, 5-6.
- H. Wegman, *Riten en mythen. Liturgie in de geschiedenis van het christendom* (Kampen 1991), in *idem* 6.
- B. Kranemann, *Die Krankensalbung in der Zeit der Aufklärung. Ritualien und pastoralliturgische Studien im deutschen Sprachgebiet* (Münster 1990), in *Tijdschrift voor theologie* 31 (1991) 200-201.

1992

251. Liturgie en taal. Een semiotische benadering, in L. Leijssen (ed.), *Liturgie en taal. Verslagboek van het tiende liturgiecolloquium van het Liturgisch Instituut van de K.U. Leuven – oktober 1991*, Leuven-Amersfoort 1992, 55-78.
252. Liturgy and language. An approach from semiotics, in *Questions liturgiques* 73 (1992) 36-52.
English translation of no. 251.
253. Zingeving langs de weg van de semiotiek, in B. Vedder a.o. (ed.), *Zin tussen vraag en aanbod. Theologische en wijsgerige beschouwingen over zin*, Tilburg 1992, 123-125.
254. Semiotiek van het ritueel. De betekenisvormgeving in rituelen als een eigen bemiddeling van zin, in *idem* 142-157.
255. Die Bedeutung der Semiotik Greimas' und der Pariser Schule für die Liturgiewissenschaft, in W. Engemann and R. Volp (ed.), *Gib mir ein Zeichen. Zur Bedeutung der Semiotik für theologische Praxis- und Denkmodelle* (= Arbeiten zur Praktischen Theologie 1), Berlin-New York 1992, 187-206.
256. De preek als lichamelijk gebeuren, in *Kerugma* 35 (1991-1992) no. 6, 69-77.
257. [With Ch. Caspers:] Liturgisch Instituut in Tilburg, in *De Roerom* 7 (1992) no. 2, 16.
258. Stoten wij op een muur of is er daarachter meer?, in *Voorlopig. Maandelijks commentaar bij maatschappij en kerk* 24 (1992) no. 8, 7-8 (section of *Hervormd Nederland* 48 (1992) no. 34).
259. Inleiding bij het artikel van Jean Delorme, in *Qohelet. Theologische Faculteit Tilburg* 2 (1992) no. 6, 10.

[Reviews of:]
- B. Groen, *Ter genezing van ziel en lichaam. De viering van het oliesel in de Grieks-Orthodoxe Kerk* (Kampen 1991), in *De Bazuin* 75 (1992) no. 4, Recensie-katern, 5.
- B. Böcker a.o. (ed.), *Nova et vetera. 25 jaar Vereniging voor Latijnse Liturgie* (Kampen 1992), in *idem* no. 38, Recensie-katern, 6.
- H. Erharter and H.-M. Rauter (ed.), *Liturgie zwischen Mystik und Politik. Österreichische Pastoraltagung, 27. bis 29. Dezember 1990* (Wien 1991), in *Tijdschrift voor theologie* 32 (1992) 212.
- G. Heimbrock and H. Boudewijnse (ed.), *Current studies on rituals. Perspectives for the psychology of religion* (Amsterdam 1990), in *idem* 117-118.

1993

260. [With M. Searle:] *Semiotics and Church Architecture. Applying the Semiotics of A.J. Greimas and the Paris School to the analysis of church buildings* (= Liturgia condenda 1), Kampen 1993.

261. *Ontwikkelingen in de liturgiewetenschap. Balans en perspectief.* Toespraak gehouden bij gelegenheid van de opening van het Liturgisch Instituut te Tilburg, 4 december 1992 (= Liturgie in perspectief 1), Heeswijk-Dinther 1993.
262. [Editor with A. Blijlevens and J. de Wit of:] *Liturgie met zieken. Beschouwingen over ziekenliturgie en modellen van liturgie met zieken uit twintig jaar Werkmap Liturgie (1966-1985)* I-II, Baarn 1993.
263. [With J. Joosse and J. Maas:] La résurrection du fils de la veuve (Luc 7, 11-17), in L. Panier (ed.) *Le temps de la lecture. Exégèse biblique et sémotique* (= Lectio divina 155), Paris 1993, 254-264.
264. [With SEMANET:] Epilogue aux analyses de la résurrection du fils de la veuve (1 Rois 17, 17-24 et Luc 7, 11-17), in *idem* 264-266.
265. Op weg naar eenheid in verscheidenheid. Modellen van gemeenschapsvorming rond brood en beker, in E. Henau and F. Jespers (ed.), *Liturgie en kerkopbouw*, Baarn 1993, 92-104.
266. De ontwikkeling van de liturgie in de afgelopen honderd jaar, in *Tijdschrift voor liturgie* 77 (1993) 130-139.
267. [With L. van Tongeren:] Een lofwaardig handboek over vocale muziek in de rooms-katholieke eredienst, in *Gregoriusblad* 117 (1993) 221-228.

[Reviews of:]
- R. Hempelmann, *Sakrament als Ort der Vermittlung des Heils. Sakramententheologie im evangelisch-katholischen Dialog* (Göttingen 1992), in *Tijdschrift voor theologie* 33 (1993) 200.
- R. Ahlers, L. Gerosa and L. Müller (ed.), *Ecclesia a sacramentis. Theologische Erwägungen zum Sakramentenrecht* (Paderborn 1992), in *idem* 215.
- J. Meyer zu Schlochtern, *Sakrament Kirche. Wirken Gottes im Handeln der Menschen* (Freiburg-Basel-Wien 1992), in *idem* 308-309.
- D.N. Power, *The Eucharistic Mystery. Revitalizing the Tradition.* (Dublin 1992), in *idem* 427-428.
- R. Meßner and R. Kaczynski, *Sakramentliche Feiern. I/1. Feiern der Umkehr und Versöhnung, Feier der Krankensalbung* (= Gottesdienst der Kirche. Handbuch der Liturgiewissenschaft VII/2) (Regensburg 1992); in *idem* 428.
- L. Bertsch (ed.), *Der neue Meßritus in Zaire: Ein Beispiel kontextueller Liturgie* (= Theologie der Dritten Welt 18) (Freiburg-Basel-Wien 1993), in *idem* 428.

PART I

Anthropology & Liturgy

1. Liturgy and Secularization

1. AN OUTLINE OF THE SITUATION

In today's church, the faithful are assailed by many doubts and uncertainties. Many ask themselves, what is happening to the Catholic church that stood so unshakable in the world for so many centuries? It has suddenly become so restless. Among the previously so concordant Catholics a confusion of tongues like that at the Tower of Babel has suddenly arisen, in which the voices of other Christian churches, other religions and humanists can also be heard. The discussions concentrate on the content of faith and Christian ethics, but liturgy is also up for discussion. Not only the laity, but also the priests who have always considered the liturgy as the most central service of their office, are from time to time tossed to and fro between hope and despair.

It indeed looks chaotic, and the appearances are contradictory. Since the Second Vatican Council, Rome has repeatedly and tirelessly emphasized that in the liturgy no one may go his own way on his own authority. At the same time, it appears that everyone is going ahead and doing just that. New eucharistic prayers appear regularly, people compose services for baptism and the anointing of the sick, the orisons of the Roman liturgy are replaced by popular religious poems or by self-composed texts, and people celebrate without paraments on certain occasions. Throughout the field of liturgy, one can speak of liturgical creativity on one's own initiative. At the same time, in certain places some have again begun using the Latin liturgy, and others will retain plainsong, cost what it may, out of protest at all those beat-masses in which secular music is admitted to the church service. Finally, there is a group who ask the question of what people of our time can still get from sacramental services. They would deprive the priest not only of his alb and chasuble, but also of the altar and temple in which he serves.

Already shortly after the second Vatican Council warning sounds were coming from F. van der Meer, who until then had been a front-runner in liturgical renewal. He wrote in *De Tijd* of February 12, 1965:

---

* Shortened translation of Liturgie en secularisatie, in J. BORNEWASSER a.o.: *Christelijk bestaan in een seculaire cultuur* (Roermond 1969) 245-282, 337-340. Translated by D. Mader, M.Div.

> No one believes that the authorities have really allowed so many experimental sites. The feckless go ahead anyway (...) With flags flying, a part of our concerned clergy have rushed out of our Latin cathedral (...) "It's not quite reached that pass", a young Englishman told me, "but here it's getting like the Church of England: evangelical here, Low Church there, High Church somewhere else, and one thing is clear: most pastors would be right at home in the Low Countries".

For Van der Meer then it was chiefly an issue of the introduction of the vernacular. But since then things have developed further: not only has creativity increased, but there is also what could be called, in the words of Pope Paul VI in his April 1967 message to the post-Conciliar council for liturgy (Consilium):[1]

> An even greater source of anguish is a widening movement toward a liturgy, if it can be called that, which is rashly described as 'desacralized' (...) we cannot hide (...) our feeling that the above-mentioned tendency poses the danger of a spiritual ruin.

In fact, in his message the Pope brought into the open the issue that is being wrestled with to this very day with regard to liturgy: secularization. The question is perhaps more, however, whether people would not be able to evaluate this phenomenon – also in regard to liturgy – more positively. In my opinion, the secularization process can widen our field of vision and give us a key that gives us some fundamental insight into the contradictory and confusing phenomena and opinions confronting us. In any case, we will proceed farther in this way than when we remain fixed on specific issues, such as the question of whether the use of paraments must be maintained or not.[2]

2. THE CATHEDRAL OF THE LAST CENTURIES

Van der Meer called up the image of the Latin cathedral from out of which a part of our concerned clergy were rushing. Anyone who will

---

1 *Documents on the liturgy, 1963-1979. Conciliar, papal and curial texts* (Collegeville (MN) 1982) 229.
2 In connection with liturgy, the literature about secularization is still rather limited. One should refer to H. MANDERS: Desacralisering van de liturgie, oriëntatiepunten van het liturgisch experiment in Nederland, in *Tijdschrift voor theologie en zielzorg* (1966) 129-143; R. VAN EYDEN: Religieloos geloof volgens Dietrich Bonhoeffer, in *Tijdschrift voor liturgie* 51 (1967) 342-355; E. SCHILLEBEECKX: Wereldlijke eredienst en kerkelijke liturgie, in *Tijdschrift voor theologie* 7 (1967) 288-302; P. VANBERGEN: La crise de la liturgie, in *Paroisse et liturgie* 49 (1967) 463-471, 642-659, 739-763 and 50 (1968) 157-160, 239-241; Liturgie in de stad van de mens, in *Tijdschrift voor liturgie* 52 (1968) 1-104. In regard to the issue of secularizing liturgy, the report *The Worship of God in a Secularized World*, approved by the fourth assembly of the World Council of Churches, Uppsala, July 4-20, 1968, is of vital importance.

obtain insight into the issues of liturgy and secularization will first have to comprehend how this Latin Cathedral, in which so many were at home for so long, functioned.

It was a tall building that rose triumphantly above the houses, pointing up toward heaven: a sanctuary on firm foundations. Whoever wanted to enter into contact with God crossed the threshold of that sanctuary and left the world behind, because the church building was *the* place of the Holy God. It was also, first and foremost, the domain of the priest. He prayed and meditated there, and therefore tried to shut out all worldly diversions. He had his own regular place there; he also had his own accustomed path for reading his breviary. It was beyond comprehension that during the church service he would sit in the midst of the people. That was because the priest was the one who performed the liturgy, the holy ritual handed down to us, in the sight of the people. Its celebration was reserved for him alone, the consecrated one, the neo-myst (i.e., literally the newly dedicated one). He esteemed it his duty to do this daily, even if the people were not present, even if at a side altar. The priest belonged entirely to another world, the world of the church building, of untouchable, god-like mystery. Therefore the priest himself was inviolate and untouchable. Until not long ago, on every first Friday of the month people prayed for 'rehabilitation for all indignities towards the priestly office'. Whoever undertook something serious against a priest ran the risk of committing sacrilege and being excommunicated. The priest was not like the people: a man who dressed differently, without wife, without children. In the mind of the people, his celibate status was (and still is) strongly connected with his liturgical function. The laity played no active role in the liturgy; they might not touch the consecrated objects. Only the priest knew how the liturgy must be performed. Years of training were necessary to learn to master the complicated ritual of the liturgy. The clergyman was a specialist in this. Until Vatican II, from the moment he entered the sacristy until he returned to it, the priest was second by second a prisoner in a web of rules, right down to the different towels which he had to use to dry his hands before and after the mass. If something went wrong during the performance of the rubrics, another set of rules came into play. In the *Tractatus de defectibus missae* the priest could look up what he had to do if he by mistake forgot the words of the consecration, or if in error the wine ampul contained water and he discovered this just before the communion. In the official Vatican edition one could find casuistry reminiscent of the middle ages: there one could read what had to happen if the wine froze over during the mass, or if the host suddenly vanished *vento aut miraculo*, through the wind or other wonder. Our liturgy was regulated to the smallest detail; one could say it was top-heavy with ritual. And that ritual was untouchable, even by the priest himself.

Recently many began to realize that the tradition was often less venerable than they had thought, and that such a detailed regulation of the liturgy had grown up only in the last few centuries. This was primarily the work of the Congregation of Rites, established in 1588, under whom the regulation of the liturgy was further expanded. One also had to admit that the social life of the last centuries also came to suffer from an exaggerated growth of rites and rules, of which Victorian etiquette was only one example. However, the influence of life on the liturgy itself remained limited. The consequence was that the liturgy increasingly became a world to which people were strangers, a purely clerical affair that stood outside of life and outside of the existing culture, which went its own way. Liturgy and world, church service and real life became completely estranged from each other.

This led also to the rising isolation of the priest himself. In the early middle ages, in the West a vision of the office appeared in which the priesthood came to be regarded in close or nearly exclusive relation to the liturgy, and in particular to the celebration of the mass. The Counter-Reformation sharpened this accent, which corresponded with:[3]

> the pious and folkloristic accouterments of the 'first mass' as well as the clothing in which a priest was buried: chalice and stole displayed on the first triumphal arch and on his gravestone, the two extremes of the priestly life. Finally, men of our own century began to depict Christ himself clad in a stole and chasuble.

The priest was seen as the one who, in the liturgy, mediated between the divine world and this world which must be sanctified: the man, clad with liturgical power, through whose word and gesture God comes to be present.

Yet within the Cathedral of the last centuries there were attempts to break through this estrangement and clericalization of the liturgy. The most radical was certainly that of the Reformers in the sixteenth century: their plea for Scripture, their respect for the intelligibility of the Biblical word, their desire to use the language of the people in the liturgy and their stress on faith were in part directed at breaking down the distance between liturgy and the faithful and integrating liturgy and life. Alas, it was the Council of Trent (1545-1563) that, second only to Vatican II, was most intensively busy with liturgical matters, and it did not succeed in complying with the justified wishes of the reformers. For the liturgy, the result was that after the Tridentine Council only a responsible restoration, and not a real renewal, took place: the disintegrating elements from the Middle Ages were removed and the old liturgy was restored as

---

3 J. LESCRAUWAET: De celebrant in de eucharistie, in *Ons geestelijk leven* 44 (1967) 131.

responsibly as possible. So a perfect structure came to exist, that, in the spirit of Renaissance culture, must be maintained through uniform laws and rules. The people, however, did not feel at home in this structure, and during the church service went their own way, to experience their faith in forms that were in part determined by influences from the actual cultural order or by reactions to it (the baroque, enlightenment or romantic movements). It was these which shaped the milieu of the 'priestly' liturgy.

Both Protestants and Catholics entered a period of 'hardening' after Trent; on the Catholic side people lapsed into ritualism, while on the Protestant side liturgy disintegrated even further through a quite imbalanced emphasis on word and faith. Yet even in this period one finds brave attempts to breach the walls. In the Anglican Church, at the end of the sixteenth century, some tried to sail between Scylla and Charybdis: under the influence of a Christian humanism they became attentive to the most authentic traditions of Christendom. From these they gained the conviction that the liturgy should be the business of the believing congregation. The original Christian elan would have to come to such an expression in the liturgy that all of the congregation would actively take part in it. They opened the choral prayer to the congregation, who henceforth in the course of the church year could listen to the whole of the Scripture, and they encouraged the real participation of the faithful in the Lord's Supper. On the Catholic side, in the seventeenth century attempts were made to bridge over the chasm between the liturgy and the people. The involvement of the people in the liturgy was encouraged by translations.[4] In France, translations of the Roman missal appeared from Voissin (1660) and Pellisson (1679), and Le Tourneux published his books *La meilleure manière d'entendre la messe* (1680) and *Carême chrétien* (1682). But this movement, which undoubtedly would have led to further renewal, ran into great difficulties, in which both the controversy around Jansenism and political factors played a role. Already in 1661 Voissin's missal was condemned by the bull of Alexander VII as a rash attempt to attack the sublimity of the inviolable holy rites and to explain the truth of the Holy Mysteries to the people.[5] All further movements for liturgical renewal in the eighteenth and nineteenth centuries were doomed. Thus, for example, Pius IX expressly forbade the translation of the missal into the vernacular on three occasions (1851, 1854 and 1858). The growing conviction was that liturgy was by definition a mystery from which the people must keep their distance.

4 L. BOUYER: *La vie de la liturgie* (= Lex Orandi 20) (Paris 1956) 71 ss.
5 Cf. E. CATANEO: *Introduzione alla storia della liturgia occidentale* (= Liturgica 2) (Roma 1962) 158. Alexander VII: "quidam perditionis filii (...) ad eam vesaniam nuper pervenerint (...) ut missale (...) ad gallicam vulgarem linguam convertere (...) Ausi fuerint, et ita sacrosancti ritus majestatem, latinis vocibus comprehensam, dejicere et proterere, ac sacrorum mysteriorum dignitatem vulgo exponere, temerario conatu tentaverint".

In 1710, in his book *Du secret des mystères*, Vallemont gave the following account of the sacred, and thus of liturgy: the sacred is untouchable, or in other words, it must at any cost remain inviolate, and this is only possible if people abandon every attempt to transpose it into living and understandable practice. One finds here, in pointed terms, what was more and more to become the weakness of the liturgy in the Cathedral over the last centuries: the sacred was surrounded with countless taboos, a region apart from the profane; in its totality, it was separated, isolated from all else that existed. This is a development that often is seen in the history of religions, but can certainly not be called typically Christian.[6] It would be unjust to venture the opinion that the religious experience of the faithful in the Cathedral in the last centuries has not been authentic; one often encounters real devotion. Perhaps it could even be argued that the whole of the liturgy contributed to this by symbolizing God as completely untouchable, the Other, the Holy. But equally it cannot be denied that this liturgical experience contained a large degree of estrangement, estrangement from the reality in which we live, from the world, and from the totality of the people's existence.

3. SECULARIZATION

Particularly in the first half of the twentieth century, a movement for liturgical renewal got underway, that achieved its breakthrough in the second Vatican Council. Some are inclined to consider the Constitution *De Sacra Liturgia* of Vatican II (December 4, 1963) as its definitive conclusion: the decisions of the Council have only to be worked out and put in practice in order to effect a real renewal. The opposite, however, appears to be the case. The Constitution *De Sacra Liturgia* called up new, fundamental and really unexpected questions. They all revolve around the relation between the sacred and the profane, between liturgy and the world in which we live. More and more there is the growing conviction, as formulated by Van Baaren, the historian of religion, that one cannot separate liturgy from the larger complex of which it is a part, namely the social-cultural order and religious experience.[7] That is precisely the reason that the Cathedral, that stood there so impregnable, was suddenly shaken to its foundations when its doors were opened to the world, and with it, the new culture. Everywhere cracks are appearing, and, except for a small group of faithful who day by day become smaller, it seems to be impossible to keep the old structure standing, whatever the cost. Most

---

6 Cf. A. NIJK: *Secularisatie. Over het gebruik van een woord* (Rotterdam 1968) 292-293.
7 Th. VAN BAAREN: Cultus en ritus. Een godsdiensthistorische beschouwing, in *Tijdschrift voor liturgie* 51 (1967) 138-139.

have rushed out of the old Cathedral, but at the same time they have discovered, or are discovering, how exposed they stand as believers in the middle of the world. That is true for all of God's people, but the experience is perhaps sharpest for those who hold offices in the church. On all sides one is confronted by the process of secularization.

I use the word secularization with some trepidation. It is a catchword by which many approach the contemporary religious crisis, and everyone is inclined to give the concept their own nuance. The question has even been asked recently, whether the concept of secularization really gives sufficient access to the heart of the process of chance which we are experiencing: Nijk believes that theories of secularization hinder us from clearly distinguishing the most painful aspects of the religious crisis.[8] Yet I would want to maintain the word as a category which indicates the process of social-cultural change from a closed, sacred society to an open, non-sacred society, in which the immediate repercussions of this process on religious life and experience are the primary focus of consideration.[9] To this extent I follow the authors cited. However, I would certainly qualify this by excepting the valuable elements raised by Nijk, which, in a description of secularization, have the consequence of expressly raising the question of its cognitive aspects, namely the issue of agnosticism.

However, it seems to me that indicating in a more concrete way how people in a secularized culture think and act, and what their questions are, is more important than arriving at a definition of the concept of secularization. In a secularized culture, people proceed from the experience that we have come of age, and as free beings must bear responsibility for ourselves. Such a person places trust in human capacity. Where this is yet lacking, it is assumed that in the future people will move ahead. In an era of space exploration and heart transplants this trust rises considerably. As free people they feel responsible for the cultivation and humanization of the world. They feel it is their commission to make the world liveable for all people. The world itself evolves according to its own laws and forces, and supernatural powers cannot randomly be introduced into the process. In this sense, wonder has departed from life. People refuse to see God as the supplement to human incapacity. For people in a secularized world, God is no longer the solution for all sorts of problems which they themselves cannot solve; God does not fill the voids left by human ignorance and impotence, does not directly and, as it were, vertically,

---

8 NIJK: *Secularisatie*, especially 57-79, 326 ss.
9 It is of importance here to note the correction to, and the progress in the description of the concept of secularization as it is discussed in the following contribution: La crise de la liturgie aux Pays-Bas, 70-71. There secularization is no longer discussed in terms of a process of change from a 'sacred' to a 'non-sacred' society, principally because the concepts of 'sacred' and 'not sacred' are not essential for the description of the concept of secularization.

intervene from time to time. If God were to do that, then religion would estrange humans from themselves, from their own responsibility.

This is the experience that at the moment is also breaking through into the lives of the faithful. The consequence of all this is that God steadily recedes from our reach, outside the reach of our experience and understanding. People have become afraid of the very word God, precisely because it is so quickly used as an escape from the world, from our own responsibility. And in fact it must be admitted that in the old image of God, He was often seen as filling in the holes in our imperfect image of the world, and to that extent God existed by the grace of, and was dependent on our ignorance of the world. This is the accusation that the humanists correctly make toward Christians. We once regularly used the adage, 'Man proposes, God disposes'. Now many are asking, if that is true, what is left for us? If everything has already been ordained by God, what is left of our commission and our responsibility? This is not a new question, and it was once answered in terms of a motto displayed in the Frisian Museum in Leeuwarden, 'God provides for the fowls of the air, but they must learn to fly'. In other words, we as humans have to do our best. But this old question now returns more sharply, and thus we have the inclination to put paid to the 'God disposes', precisely because hidden within it is the danger that we will use it to escape from reality and the responsibility for our own life and that of others. We are increasingly come to the realization that "no divine intervention and no divine interference will put a stop to endless war (...) but we ourselves are responsible and must make peace".[10] As a consequence of secularization, God has become a question. It is difficult for many to get an impression of Him. Schillebeeckx remarks that God is the enormous question of our time, "an unspoken question which believers and unbelievers alike touch upon in their daily conversation, in the newspaper, in literature, in radio and television discussions. Now that people no longer feel secure in their conceptions of divinity, God is the topic of daily conversation".[11]

Implicit in Schillebeeckx's description is the attitude of the faithful: the express affirmation of God, who passes all understanding. One can ask, however, whether for many people in the midst of the process of socio-cultural change that is secularization, the mirror of the divine world has not become more blurred. Schlette has pointed out that as a result of secularization there is a growing realization of the limitation and inadequacy of models of religious and spiritual interpretation.[12] In this connec-

---

10 H. OOSTERHUIS: Een priester na zijn dertigste jaar, in H. BOGERS a.o. (ed.): *Over de priester. Essays en interviews* (Utrecht s.a.) 234.
11 E. SCHILLEBEECKX: Het nieuwe mens- en Godsbeeld in conflict met het religieuze leven, in *Tijdschrift voor theologie* 7 (1967) 9.
12 H. SCHLETTE: *Christen als Humanisten* (München 1967) 84 ss.

tion, he speaks of an "agnosticism of aporia", of not knowing where to begin, which those on all sides can recognize and that is typified by the judgment in Plato's *Sophist*, "earlier we knew for certain, but now we sit imprisoned in aporia".[13] Our era has outlived both the old theism and the old atheism. In their place has arisen the consciousness of God's absence and the conviction that it is impossible for people to give an answer to metaphysical questions once and for all. It is characteristic of all metaphysics that it is never 'finished' and must always be prepared to begin moving forward again. In any case, an agnosticism of aporia means the breakdown of a metaphysics and theology that were all too self-confident and certain of themselves. An agnosticism of aporia as a consequence of the secularization process is so widespread among both believers and unbelievers that Schlette characterized it as "that basis of communication between persons" in modern society.[14] It seems to me that this observation has consequences of ultimate importance. It implies that those who do not take the experience of an agnosticism of aporia with sufficient seriousness run the risk of removing themselves from the real world in which we live, and no longer being understood by the majority. It is precisely here that the central problem for Christian theology and the proclamation of the Christian churches lies. One will have to recognize that the shifts in the social-cultural order that have taken place and are yet taking place have radical consequences for the Christian worldview, for after all this order functions as the social infrastructure of this worldview, and forms its "plausibility structure", that is, the structure in which it maintains its credibility.[15] By secularization, the cognitive situation has been so changed that when the standard Christian formulas and formulations are spoken in this moment of time, they will as such communicate something other than they did four hundred or nine hundred years ago. When the church does not recognize this problem, or out of self-defense it identifies itself more strongly than before with the traditional definition of reality and defends that with all means that come to hand, it destroys the credibility of Christianity for modern man before it begins. The reactions to the confession of faith proclaimed by Paul VI at the close of the 'year of faith' and in the encyclical *Humanae vitae* bear eloquent witness to this. If church will stand in the middle of the world, it will have to have the courage to experience the agnosticism of aporia for itself: it must dare to enter into the darkness in order to recover the light in a new way. The tragedy of the Catholic Church today is precisely that the tension around the Christian definition of reality (sometimes desig-

---

13 *Soph.* 344a. Cf. G. MARTIN: *Allgemeine Metaphysik, ihre Probleme und ihre Methode* (Berlin 1965) 331-332.
14 SCHLETTE: *Christen als Humanisten* 111.
15 NIJK: *Secularisatie* 302-325.

nated as ideological conflict) runs so high. Does the conflict in the Church not ultimately exist in the fact that some judge the process of change that constitutes secularization from above, from on high, out of their traditional frame of thought, while others are prepared to enter into the void and, standing in the communal experience of the new situation, listen once again to the message from Israel and the New Testament and seek a faithful and Christian way out of it, without precisely knowing what the outcome will be? The latter is certainly the way of the Gospel, that of a self-risking service to others that seeks the ground under its feet. It is clear that people in our time are not reaching out to each other by repeating old doctrines, to argue over them or to so carefully avoid new questions. If Christianity persists in doing this, there is the danger that it will compromise itself to its very heart for those around it today. There is no room for fear and trembling about a new era. The question which challenges the church is whether it really has a message for the world today. Or does it only have glad tidings for the dead or those who still draw their life from a dead culture? There is sufficient reason to speak of this being a decisive moment for the church. It must dare to formulate the core of the message of God, religion and Christianity anew, and that means the end of conventional Christendom.

4. THE LITURGY IN CRISIS: THE END, OR A NEW BEGINNING?

If one accepts that liturgy can not be separated from the larger complex of which it is a part, that is, religious experience and culture, then it becomes clear how deep the crisis surrounding Christian liturgy is. Are we to speak of the end of the conventional liturgy, or the end of liturgy altogether?

Radical God-is-dead theologians see liturgy as an impossible task in our time. W. Hamilton, one of the most moderate of the group, writes, "I do not see how preaching, worship, prayer, ordination, the sacraments can be taken seriously by the radical theologian".[16] Altizer remarks, "The contemporary theologian should not imagine that he is simply the servant of an ancient faith and cultus, for that faith and cultus has almost disappeared from view (...)".[17] In reply it could be said that these theologians primarily come out of circles that have long borne a strongly non-liturgical stamp, and turned almost exclusively in the direction of Christian ethics for some time. Moreover, one could point to a strong liturgical movement in all Christian churches. On the other hand, it would be too simple for us to think that such answers have saved us from

---

16 W. HAMILTON: American theology, radicalism and the death of God, in T. ALTIZER and W. HAMILTON: *Radical theology and the death of God* (New York etc. 1966) 7.
17 T. ALTIZER: *The Gospel of christian atheism* (London 1967) 27.

the issues that the radical theologians raise. Even in the churches where people are most intensively busy with liturgy, it appears that there is, at the same time, a crisis. A growing number of the faithful approach the liturgy only with difficulty, as witnessed by the fact that statistics for congregational participation continue their steady decline. These people find their experience of religion in concrete service to their fellow man. One can even note that among Catholic clergy the performance of the liturgy is declining, and has been called into question by some radicals. Are we to speak of the end of conventional liturgy, or of the end of liturgy altogether?

That the conventional liturgy is in serious trouble cannot be denied. Since the introduction of the vernacular, people have experienced the breakdown in communication between liturgy and contemporary understandings of life all the more sharply. In the answer from the Belgian Conference of Bishops to questions from Rome regarding the progress of liturgical reform, we can read:[18]

> The present renewal shows more clearly than ever that a great distance exists between contemporary culture on the one side and the gestures and language of the Roman liturgy on the other (...) The reform is wrongly based on mentality and forms that were valid in the seventh century, but which one cannot take as a sufficient point of departure for life in 1967. In all translations and adaptations, people experience all the more that the Roman liturgy is not suitable.

In their answer, the Dutch bishops wrote:

> The experience of faith is ever more directed (sometimes rather exclusively) toward the practice of the Christian message, and people increasingly try (though on Old Testament grounds) to 'see' God in human vicissitudes and in history. That less favorable tendencies, primarily secularism, are also at work is clear, only their influence (...) is difficult to determine.

Repeatedly the report observes that for the majority there is still far too little that could be called real renewal.[19]

It seems important to me to indicate in greater depth why the conventional liturgy does not come across. Through interaction with the new culture, people have difficulty with elements from the previous culture, especially if these are as strongly colored with feudalism as the bishop's

---

[18] Relationes super reformationis liturgicae progressionem: Belgium, in *Notitiae* 41 (1968) 253-254.
[19] *Antwoord van de Nederlandse bisschoppen aan A. Bugnini c.m. over de gevolgen van de hervorming van de liturgie, juni 1968*, in *Katholiek Archief* 23 (1968) 932-939.

miter, the forms of investiture at an ordination, the slap on the face in confirmation, etc. But that is not all. As a consequence of secularization, it is hard for people to imagine that one can seriously speak of a separate place where God, by means of the priest, directly and immediately can penetrate our world. This is experienced as all the more implausible as this separate place of liturgy becomes isolated from life itself, as in the Cathedral of the past centuries. People have difficulty with any ritual that calls on help from divine powers as a supplement and that all too much seeks its point of departure where the potential of human intervention falls short or reaches its limit. Thus it is only with difficulty that people can accept a ritual for the sick, which expresses that healing is to be effected by religious means which medicine does not have – or does not yet have – in its reach. People do not think that way any more, either about God or about sickness.[20]

Van Baaren tells us that for the Gurage, a tribe in Ethiopia, the main staff of life is the Ensete plant, a sort of banana. In view of the tremendous meaning this plant has for the Gurage, one would expect that the planting and cultivation of this crop would be accompanied with a rich ritual. However, this is not the case. Its production is exclusively a matter for agriculture, and no religious act at all is involved.[21] Can we not conclude from this that liturgy does not arise, or disappears, as people are able to carry responsibility for themselves? This would mean that secularization poses the question of the meaning of ritual in the most radical way. I think that this is indeed the case, and that one cannot avoid this fundamental question, neither by all too easily rejecting any potential for liturgy, nor by taking flight into a false answer based on the image of conventional liturgy. One can formulate the fundamental question as follows: Can the rite help us to again find God, whom we have lost? In other words, can liturgy contribute to breaking through the crisis in experiencing God that is the consequence of secularization? I hope to demonstrate that liturgy has an essential function in doing so.

If there is one thing that is clear today, it is this: people are passionately seeking the deeper meaning of humanity, of the world and what happens in it, and they will not withdraw from this search. I find this most touchingly expressed in a letter from a lay person to his spiritual guide, which G. Winter reproduces in his book *The new creation as Metropolis*:[22]

> Recently I have been mulling a problem over in my mind. A problem that may not have an answer. In fact it may not really be a problem at all.

---

20 R. CALLEWAERT: De begeleiding van de liturgische vernieuwing, in *Tijdschrift voor liturgie* 51 (1967) 130-131.
21 VAN BAAREN: Cultus en ritus 139-140.
22 G. WINTER: *The new creation as Metropolis* (New York 1963) 94-96.

> None the less I have attempted to dicuss the problem feeling with others, and as good many things are, it was hard to seriously express in words, the feeling you were attempting to convey. It's even harder to lay down the self erected barriers of society and seriously give vent to your very personal feelings; and thus my discussions were on the light side but a feeling was conveyed.
>
> Basically the problem centers around a feeling of unfulfillment – if there is such a word. Many of us have reached an age where the children are no longer very young and demanding. Our incomes while not high are reasonable and we've learned to live within them. We have the stoves, refrigerators, washing machines, homes, cars, etc., that our standard of living requires. Our job, while interesting, no longer takes one hundred per cent of our available time and we realize we're in all probability, not going to be President, Senator, or a personage of State or National importance.
>
> Now we have time to stop running after the elusive target. We can walk at a brisk pace, but we can walk. We have the precious commodity of time but we are unfulfilled. In former years a man would carve a home, with his hands, out of the woods. He had a feeling, an intangible feeling, of accomplishment. Today this is not done. The man of yesteryear would leave his mark for the generations that came after him. Today man earns money and buys his needs and a basic unfulfillment comes into being.
>
> It's true we leave our children and they reflect parental influence. In our employment we try and do more than is required, because of an honest interest and desire to be worthy of our hire. We have many acquaintances and a lesser number of friends. But this is not sufficient to give the feeling of accomplishment or fulfillment that is necessary.
>
> Perhaps this letter does not properly reflect its true meaning. It is not intended as a letter of complaint or of dis-satisfaction. It is intended to pose a question as to what a man can do; and how he goes about doing it; to acquire a feeling that what he is doing, or should be doing, is for a purpose, a worthy purpose that will give him the quiet satisfaction of knowing that he has done something, or is doing something, that is unselfishly worth while?

It is clear that this letter is not unusual. These are live questions for very many people. Anyone who is mature is sharply confronted by his or her own responsibility, both individual and collective. More than ever, there is a rising consciousness that we live in a world of communications breakdown, between the rich and poor, between east and west, among different races, among Christians, even among Christians within one and the same church. We experience tension and conflict that we have absolutely no way to control. All of this sharpens the demand to know the meaning of life, the world and history. People demand an ultimate meaning, that for which all else must be offered up. In this demand for the source of meaning, people refuse to accept God as the one who can complete human failings; they do not accept him as a slogan, as an unanswerable argument, an empty concept, a separate province of life, a refuge when we have reached our limits. People want to retain their responsibility and at the same time demand the ultimate meaning, the final reality.

One can approach this question in a cognitive, intellectual way. One can seek an answer in philosophy or theology. I would not wish to cast doubt on the worth of this cognitive approach, but the question remains whether precisely such a one-sided approach is of any further help to people today. It appears that we are far too blind to another way of seeking ultimate reality, including Christian reality, namely the way of the rite. Nijk has done us a great service by pointing this out.[23] He views the cognitive path as entirely secondary, and even as completely impossible at the moment. In this, he has possibly gone to the other extreme: one can argue with his hypothesis, that rite is the real origin of religion. But that does not mean that one should not take to heart his critique of the extreme one-sidedness in attempts to break through the contemporary crisis in religion by elevating the question of truth to too central a position.

What perspectives, then, can the way of ritual offer? The letter cited by Winter concentrates on the question of what anyone can do now and how it must be done, in order for anyone to have the feeling that what is done, or must be done, is good for something, is somehow important, to obtain the satisfaction that something has been done – if something is to be done – that is in an unselfish way worth the trouble. The writer of the letter is not asking for an answer about truth; he is searching for the value of his actions. How can I act, so that it is finally meaningful? One could say that his demand for meaningful action bears the 'acute' character of those persons who are conscious of their own freedom and responsibility and lack a frame of reference. It is exactly this that makes this letter so characteristic of what so many are experiencing at this moment. Precisely: and Nijk points out that it is exactly those in these acute situations who can discover the fundamental and ultimate characteristics of acting and ritual. People reach the point where they realize that they 'have-to-act-without-knowing-how'. The one thing that initially can be done is to just do something. Discovering how one can act meaningfully by simply doing is a matter of hindsight, of finding out for which action the feeling of 'having-to-act-without-knowing-how' is replaced by the feeling of 'this is it', or 'this is the goal'. Apparently in the past people have been able to identify such actions, and the realization that 'this is it' which goes with these actions has been so radical that they have repeated these actions with great devotion. This is the origin of ritual: people repeat an action

---

23 NIJK: *Secularisatie*, especially 256-339. See also: A. NIJK: Het primaat van de praxis, in *De toekomst van christendom en cultuur* (Baarn 1968) 84-99.

once it is found, because in that action they encounter a reality that makes the act worth doing. One could say that in this way people can discover reality that for them is ultimately relevant, and which they can consider the 'final reality'. Thus this final reality is grasped precisely within the actuality of the act. It is known, as it were, through the act itself, just as a dancer portrays a 'reality' and only knows this reality in the action of its being portrayed, through his reactions to it and his effort to give this reality form in dance.

It is clear that people can not simply identify this 'final reality', about which we have been speaking, with God or the God of salvation. Perhaps the term 'final realities' would be better. It does, however, seem plausible that one here at least does encounter an infrastructure of religious acts. In other words, in this manner people can come in contact with Ultimate Reality, with the final ground of their being, with God, whom they serve and at the same time who is the impetus to new actions, and brings them to further engagement. The latter is also characteristic of this way, because the ground that people find in action in the Final Reality does not fully answer the groundlessness of their actions; in other words, the Final Reality is dynamic, is also future.

The way of (ritual) action is thus a possible way to God, and it could be asked if people should not travel down it more often. When, in respect to the question of God, we limit ourselves all too much to the cognitive sector, and only reflect and speak about God, we unavoidably and continuously come face to face with the question of whether He really exists, or is purely a projection spun out of our own thoughts – exactly the sort of questions that dominate people's thoughts today. It could be precisely acting and rites that will enable us to break through an important part of the crisis in religion, because they carry the potential of a 'immediate' knowledge of God. It is exactly in their free and responsible acting that people find themselves faced with a proposition that they do not know how to begin to solve. This is true for believers and unbelievers alike. One must accept this aporia of action and move experimentally in a new direction full of questions and uncertainties. One must bear the emptiness and, in that sense, radicalize the religious crisis in order to arrive at renewed and meaningful action, at new rites. It would be the way that leads to new life, and finally to the God of all life.

Schlette spoke of the agnosticism of aporia as "that basis of communication between persons". I would not want to limit this basis of interpersonal communication to the cognitive level, but expand it. It also lies in the acute demand for acting meaningfully while not knowing how. The demand for decent actions comes from all sides, and is valid for all: communists, humanists, for the world religions, for the churches. Humanity, experimenting, seeks a way, and from time to time an experience of 'this is it' breaks through; from this, and by this process, rites and symbols arise.

But in this, it is not always easy to make out if the rites of our time stand within the infrastructure of religious actions or if they go further and are signs of what Metz terms an 'inarticulate faith', or an attempt to rise above the religious crisis. One can not always approach the question by asking whether God is expressly mentioned. It may be much more revealing when there is a silence about God than when endless words are wasted on him. One can speak of an action directed toward God as the ultimate reality, even if that happens 'around the emptiness'. In any case, one can also affirm that in the secularized culture one can speak in the broadest sense of a liturgical act, and that believers are all too quickly inclined to label this ritual act as secularism or (what is really intended) atheism. It is, after all, always a matter of attempts to achieve a meaningful experience of existence, the world and history: it is a search for answers to questions for which people have found no purely intellectual answers. One must see that these liturgical actions stand open on all sides, and offer a real possibility for a new shape for Christian liturgy.

Christian liturgy, after all, is not connected to any one culture. The actual ritual of the Christian liturgy thus cannot be considered as absolutely autonomous or static. This means that the form of Christian liturgy may not be foreign to the forms of experience in our time. It must possess all the characteristics of a modern anthropology. Only then will Christian liturgy be able to contribute to people today being able to more immediately recover the God of salvation, and will it be revealed to them how Jesus of Nazareth is the beginning and the end, the alpha and omega, the consistency of human existence. It seems improbable, when one formulates it that way. We stand, then, at the very first steps of the process. The breakdown between the 'ceremonial dress' of the church and contemporary experience of existence still predominates.[24] The churchly liturgy is still too much a world apart from the ritual acts of secularized society, which are precisely what offer numerous possibilities to arrive at a new, faithful devotion.[25] Where people try to make the connection, one constantly hears the complaint that the liturgy is too verbal. It appears from this that these efforts are still going in too strongly an abstract, intellectual direction. This transforms the celebration of the liturgy into a lesson, a lecture in theology, instruction and pedantry, which are precisely

---

24 Cf. H. WEGMAN: De kerk in ceremonieel tenue, in P. VAN HOOIJDONK, W. VELDHUIS and H. WEGMAN (ed.): *Osmose. Gedachten over leven in kerk en wereld* (Utrecht 1966) 286-309.

25 In connection with this also compare B. BRO: Man and the sacraments. The anthropological substructure of the christian sacraments, in *Concilium* 4 (1968) no. 1, 18-26. Bro writes (p. 22): "It seems to me that current pastoral efforts have contended themselves with vague general ideas and have not followed through with their efforts. Too often they have misconstrued the real substructures of sacramental life and have focused on facile, seductive abstractions".

what must be opened up: revealing, but also concealing.²⁶ There is no way that one can get a corner on ultimate reality.

The Christian liturgy is always still too much an escape out of this world into the past, or to another, alien world, and one encounters too little real creativity. Possibly this is because believers are not daring enough to bear the emptiness which is 'that basis of communication between persons', of 'having-to-act-without-knowing-how', and consequently true experiments are not forthcoming. Only when the faithful dare to endure the unbearable load of 'having-to-act-without-knowing-how', which arises as a consequence of the new sociocultural structure, will they discover that there stands in the middle of this world One whom we do not know, who is, was and will be, who died and rose again. The kingdom of God is in your midst: in other words, it is here, in this world, not above it or outside it. Liturgy will again become credible when it fulfills the condition of becoming integrated into human existence. The Gospel invites us to experiment, acting in the world itself. Jesus of Nazareth never placed God on high as an attempt to escape. He stood in the middle of the complications of his time and cast his lot with people, for all who were defenseless, for sinners and publicans and the outcasts. Defenseless and powerless, without respect, he died, not between two candlesticks, but between two murderers. His life is proclaimed to us in the Gospel as ultimately meaningful, as a human existence that to the end achieved perfection, in self-expending devotion to Ultimate Reality. The life of Jesus of Nazareth spotlighted how thoroughly God is the ground of human life, so much so that the Gospels tell us that this son of man was really the Son of God. For Christians, this inexhaustible man, this Jesus of Nazareth, this happening, is the most eloquent image of God.²⁷

His story must go on. But how? Even Christians are confronted by the aporia of action in the new culture. Their frame of reference is less detailed than they would often want. The deep meaning of the *Ecce homo*, the 'Behold the man', is revealed to them only experimentally, and they can come to devotion to the God of salvation as the ultimate reality. In that they cannot isolate themselves from 'that basis of communication between persons'. It is characteristic that precisely where the evangelical readiness to act grows, as a matter of course the rites of the new and familiar culture are absorbed by Christians. I am thinking, for instance, of the Poor People's March on Washington, singing spirituals as they marched, which seems to be a new form of the processional. The cortege bearing the body of Dr. Martin Luther King in a farmer's wagon drawn by two mules is an

---

26 The eucharistic prayers composed by the Italian theologians Berti and Calabuig form the most characteristic example. Cf. *Paroisse et liturgie* 49 (1967) 431-435 and 50 (1968) 76-78, 371-373.
27 Cf. the description of OOSTERHUIS: *Een priester na zijn dertigste jaar* 228-229.

eloquent rite of devotion that reminds one of the passage of the suffering servant of YHWH to the land of the living and righteous.

In the new order, divisions among Christians are unbearable; separate liturgical acts are increasingly experienced as contradictions of themselves. It is obvious that theologians must busy themselves with questions of orthodoxy, of the church and its offices. However, they must realize that they must be generous and cautious in their conclusions, and that "the churches undermines itself if it forces experimenting groups to take on the form of sects",[28] as has so often happened in the history of the church. One must understand that Christian liturgy is more a matter of life itself than a matter for someone behind a desk, the Congregation of the Faith, or a church institute. Moreover, one must acknowledge that the new liturgy has more need of poets than of Doctors of Liturgical Studies. This is all the more true now that sociocultural shifts have made Christians conscious that they must act, and that they must not give the world a stone when it asks for bread. It is a matter of people today being able to come in a faithful way to the final and ultimate salvific reality toward which they have looked so longingly.

One can expect that the new form of the liturgy shall proceed more from the direction of the life of the original community. In the Acts of the Apostles, it is written of the early Christians, "they broke bread from house to house" (Acts 2:46; KJV). There was no separate worship service, and certainly no specific church building. It was a characteristic of Christianity that the idea of privileged, sacred places was broken through. People celebrated the eucharist in the profane space of their own homes; the distinction between the profane and sacred spheres was given up.

> The fact that churches were built on the sites of, and as the equivalent of heathen temples was a result of the evolution of Christianity into a religion, into a closed, finished, dogmatic system (...) Like the temple in Jerusalem, like all religious monuments, the church building was a symbol of the sacralization of the world by a power above and beyond the world (...) Through the church building, the sacred (...) was again placed in a separate location.[29]

Even though one must admit that in the Christian conception of the church building something of the informal atmosphere of the faith of the first centuries has lived on, and the conviction is still maintained that what is most important is what happens within the individual,[30] it will be

---

28 *Der Priester in einer säkularisierten Welt* (= Akten des 3. internationalen Kongresses zu Luzern, 18-22 September 1967), in *Informationsblatt des Instituts für europäische Priesterhilfe* 2 (1968) nos 1-2, 115.
29 G. BEKAERT: *In een of ander huis, kerkbouw op een keerpunt* (Tielt-Den Haag 1967) 22-23.
30 BEKAERT: *In een of ander huis* 23-24.

sufficiently evident from the description that I gave of the Cathedral of the last few centuries that the church building itself made its contribution to the estrangement of the deep Christian sense from reality in its totality. The church building must be just like 'any other house', or be like 'a shelter from the storm': in other words, it must in itself raise up the ordinary into the sacred.[31] A separate building is not necessary, per se. It only has meaning in so far as it serves people by enabling them to experience and develop their reality at its deepest dimension. Christians can celebrate their liturgy in the church building, and at the same time the building can be used for other purposes, in the service of the whole community.

In the future, the meaning of church offices will more and more consist of service to the community of the faithful and to the world, in imitation of Jesus of Nazareth. People will no longer consider the priest as a sacred person who, on the ground of his ordination itself, stands closer to God. He will not longer be the one who is surrounded by the taboo of the divine world, who is at a distance from the community, with his back to them and with upturned face, performing the ritual. The sacralizing of the image of the priest, which led to an imbalanced and exaggerated coupling of the office and liturgical service as the exclusive right of the priest, will be broken down. The New Testament speaks of the sanctification of the whole of God's people, in which all are brothers and sisters and in which one group in particular place themselves in service to the Lord for the sake of all. The task of those who hold office is *diakonia* in the broadest sense: being a servant in word and deed in the interpretation of the Gospel, letting the purity of the message of Israel and the of the church through the centuries come through. The *diakonia* of the office holders does not lie in their liturgical function, pure and simple, however important this *diakonia* also is. Moreover, the liturgical function is not the exclusive right of the priest. There is more and more discussion about the necessity of including the laity. The very notion of 'including', however, shows how difficult it will be to break down the clericalization of the liturgy. Liturgy is by definition the business of the whole community, and the one who holds the office is in their service. The degree to which we are under the sway of an all too 'priestly' liturgy can be seen from the fact that repeatedly, whenever one allocates liturgical functions to the community of the faithful, it is felt to be an appropriation of the priestly office. It appears sufficiently clear from the history of the church that one may not too absolutely and rigidly draw boundaries between the tasks

---

31 BEKAERT: *In een of ander huis* 30 ss; H. BLANKESTEIJN and W. OVERBOSCH: *Een hut om in te schuilen, kerken van nu en morgen* (Baarn s.a.); F. DEBUYST: Quelques réflexions critiques sur l'architecture religieuse actuelle, in *Paroisse et liturgie* 50 (1968) 126-134.

and powers of the priests and laity. In the past, laymen baptized, administered unction to the sick, and there was what could be called lay confession. From that one can conclude that there is more 'free play' in the community's celebration of the liturgy than has often been thought.

M. Eliade, the Romanian scholar of comparative religion, wrote regarding human liturgical acts, "In order to be able to live in the world, man must find it".[32] It is a characteristic of any liturgy that it gives people ground under their feet: they order their lives, share in its significance, and thereby make it more liveable. Liturgy is like poetry in the prose of daily life. It is *re-creatio*, relief for people, and at the same time a new creation for them. Liturgy is the act of people at play. But it is a serious play, in which they may not deceive themselves with make-believe worlds or those things that are taken for granted. This is equally true for the Christian liturgy. It may not flee into the make-believe world of false gods and certainties, any more than it may become a game around questions which real life does not ask any more, or never did ask.

I have previously indicated how, precisely as a consequence of secularization, numerous new questions about life have arisen, and how people of faith find themselves confronted with an aporia, which could be broken through in an entirely characteristic way by ritual. When Christians take the new questions seriously, they will come to a true renewal of Christian liturgy. It would appear that this new liturgy will be less stable than the liturgy of the Cathedral of past centuries. It will bear the stamp of the faithful, who, in this changed and changing world, continually ask how they can act true to the Gospel. In doing so, Christians can fall back on the infrastructure of ritual acts that exist on all sides in secularized culture, and will try to break it open to Christian reality, thereby realizing that *docta ignorantia* can be as Christlike as the absolute certainty of God's presence. Just crying out for the God of Salvation can open up the believer to the unfathomable ultimate reality, to what is inexpressible: the God of Jesus Christ, who is now and, even more, is future and promise. In the new liturgy the eschatological dimension will be shaped in an entirely characteristic way: not as a flight out of this world, or as a flight to a utopian future, but as an appeal to people to take upon themselves the creation of the world, in Jesus' name. The shape of Christian liturgy could again be *re-creatio*: relief, that recreates the faithful in a new way and places them in the world. In this way it will also be a model of the greater offer of salvation: it will bring salvation to people, make whole, heal, bring them to act out the Gospel. This will not happen in spite of the liturgy, but in it and through it. For Christians too, the rite is a way along which the ultimate reality will only be poured out if they will perform it with faith and devotion.

---

32 M. ELIADE: *Das Heilige und das Profane* (Hamburg 1957) 13.

2. La crise de la liturgie aux Pays-Bas
Comment donner corps au rituel chrétien dans une société sécularisée?

En 1946 la Fédération des Associations Liturgiques aux Pays-Bas a organisé un congrès international à Maastricht. On voulait faire l'inventaire du Mouvement Liturgique et donner le signal de départ à de nouvelles activités.[1] On s'était aperçu qu'il avait été question d'un point culminant dans la participation liturgique pendant la deuxième guerre mondiale. Mais lorsqu'après la guerre la vie se normalisait, les pratiques liturgiques devenaient problématiques. La fréquence de l'assistance à la messe diminuait d'une façon inquiétante. Et on estimait que la distance établie entre liturgie et peuple en était la cause. Donc il s'avérait nécessaire de faire descendre la liturgie de son piédestal et de la faire plus proche du peuple. En ce temps-là on ne pouvait pas deviner qu'on ne recueillerait les fruits mûrs du Mouvement Liturgique qu'après deux décennies. On peut constater qu'aux Pays-Bas la Constitution de Vatican II concernant la Liturgie (1963) était accueillie cordialement et que beaucoup de gens comptaient sur une reprise de la participation à la liturgie. Mais la Constitution conciliaire n'a pas pu retourner en sens inverse la tendance descendante qui avait commencé avant Vatican II. Au contraire, en 1966 encore 64,4 % des catholiques participaient à la liturgie du week-end; en 1988 cette participation tombait à 15,9 %. La courbe descendante ne s'est pas encore arrêtée. Quant au baptême et au mariage il est vrai que les chiffres sont plus élevés, mais la tendance descendante continue également. En 1960, 45,2 % de toutes les naissances aux Pays-Bas étaient baptisées et en 1988, 27,3 %. Quant au mariage de deux catholiques les chiffres sont: en 1970, 90 % et en 1985, 69 %. L'assistance à la messe de Pâques est encore relativement élevée: en 1988, 35,7 %. Une exception intéressante concerne les funérailles, la confirmation et la première communion: la participation à ces rituels n'est relativement pas diminuée. En 1988 le chiffre des funérailles revenait encore à 96 %.[2]

Dans cette contribution je me propose de traiter de la crise de la liturgie catholique aux Pays-Bas après Vatican II et de son contexte. En outre

---

* *Recherches de science religieuse* 78 (1990) 485-511.
1 G. LUKKEN: *De onvervangbare weg van de liturgie* (Hilversum 1984²) 125.
2 P. STOUTHARD et G. VAN TILLO (éd.): *Katholiek Nederland na 1945* (Baarn 1985); G. LUKKEN: De weekendliturgie. Recente empirische onderzoekingen, dans *Tijdschrift voor liturgie* 58 (1974) 17-36; *Kerkelijke documentatie* 1-2-1 15 (1987) 725-761; *Kerkelijke documentatie* 1-2-1 17 (1989) 581-610.

j'entends indiquer comment on a réfléchi à cette crise et quelles issues on a cherchées. Enfin je ferai le bilan.[3]

1. LA CRISE DU RITUEL AUX PAYS-BAS

1.1. La crise du rituel en général

Des mots comme rite et rituel recevaient une connotation négative aux Pays-Bas surtout depuis les années soixante. On commençait à considérer les rituels comme des cadres purement stéréotypés: ils aboutissent facilement à un comportement malhonnête et hypocrite; ils cachent les différences d'opinions et les conflicts. Le psychothérapeute néerlandais O. van der Hart, qui lui-même pratique des rituels dans sa psychothérapie, signale une tendance à tenir les rituels pour dépourvus de sens et à considérer le comportement rituel d'un oeil critique.[4]

La crise des rites dans la société néerlandaise est aussi évidente à d'autres égards. Les rituels d'ouverture et de clôture d'autrefois sont souvent abandonnés depuis les années soixante ou ceux qui y participent sont peu nombreux. On peut penser à l'ouverture de l'année académique pendant laquelle on organise des réunions. Le passage de la semaine de travail au week-end se déroule à pas feutrés. C'est la même chose pour le changement des saisons. Certaines personnes ont des problèmes avec toutes sortes de commémorations: avec des fêtes nationales et des célébrations comme le *dies natalis* de l'université; dans notre université à Tilburg on continue tout simplement les cours et les réunions pendant la session académique. On a encore des rites de passage, qui visent plus loin. Les rituels de puberté qui marquent l'entrée dans l'adolescence font absolument défaut. Le processus du passage s'accomplit sans bruit comme s'il était question d'un changement de vitesse automatique. Aussi, selon O. van der Hart, on trouve de temps en temps des difficultés de détachement entre parents et enfants, tellement compliquées qu'il y a besoin de psychothérapie.[5] Le rituel du mariage est de plus en plus remplacé par la cohabitation, qui n'est accompagnée que de peu d'éléments rituels. Les rituels de naissance sont habituellement assez maigres. Et les rituels autour de la mort et de l'enterrement vont vraiment mal. Il arrive de plus en plus qu'on enterre ou incinère les défunts en silence. Le sociologue néerlandais Zijderveld parle d'une société-*staccato*; il veut dire que la vie

---

3 Quelques éléments ont été élaborés dans G. LUKKEN: *Geen leven zonder rituelen* (Hilversum 1988³).
4 O. VAN DER HART: *Rituelen in psychotherapie. Overgang en bestendiging* (Deventer 1984²).
5 VAN DER HART: *Rituelen* 25, 86, 89-92, 137-138.

dans notre société avance souvent par secousses faute d'actions rituelles. C'est comme si nous sautions à cloche-pied d'une époque à l'autre, parce que nous ne disposons pas de rites de passage pour franchir les seuils nombreux de notre vie.

De l'autre côté il faut constater aussi que de nouveaux rituels sont nés précisément depuis les années soixante. Souvent ce sont des rituels de protestation: grèves de la faim, marches de la paix, occupations de locaux, s'enchaîner à la grille d'une centrale nucléaire, des tribunaux, veilles et cetera. Les hippies connaissaient de nombreux rituels. Le mouvement féministe s'est intéressé explicitement aux rituels. Les historiens leur accordent plus d'intérêt. Et depuis les années quatre-vingt on connaît de nombreuses nouvelles classifications de *lifestyle* et des rituels qui les accompagnent (pensez par example aux rituels des *yuppies*). Pourtant j'ai l'impression que le côté négatif est dominant, puisque, d'une part, souvent les rituels font simplement défaut et que, d'autre part, beaucoup de nouveaux rituels sont tellement passagers qu'on peut se demander s'ils sont de vrais rituels.

1.2. La crise du rituel catholique

Dans les années soixante les catholiques des Pays-Bas étaient confrontés à une donnée paradoxale: lorsque le Mouvement Liturgique devenait du fait de Vatican II une affaire de toute l'Eglise, précisément à ce moment-là la liturgie était plongée dans une crise profonde. Inspirés par le concile, ils quittaient le bâtiment de la vieille cathédrale dans laquelle le sacré avait une place explicite et où la présence divine était tangible. Mais arrivés en dehors de ces frontières, ils découvraient combien ils étaient gênés. Dans l'ordre socio-culturel beaucoup de rites étaient en train de disparaître sans qu'ils fussent remplacés par d'autres. Et précisément parce que, à ce moment-là, on prenait conscience qu'on ne peut pas détacher la liturgie de l'ensemble de l'ordre socio-culturel, le rituel chrétien était plongé dans une crise profonde. L'assistance à la messe diminuait de plus en plus, la participation aux grands rituels chrétiens de passage manifestait une courbe descendante. Les rituels qui stabilisent la vie étaient aussi impliqués dans la crise: la participation à la messe pendant la semaine, la prière du matin et du soir, la prière avant et après le repas, la visite de l'église pendant la journée, et cetera.

1.3. Esquisse du contexte de la crise

Jusqu'aux années soixante aux Pays-Bas on trouvait une société très modérée et traditionelle. Les Eglises y jouaient un rôle important. Elles étaient debout comme des colonnes fixes et imprégnaient tous les segments de la société jusqu'aux organisations séculières. Beaucoup de gens s'étonnent du compartimentage de la radio-diffusion néerlandaise d'aujourd'hui: une diffusion catholique, plusieurs protestantes, une autre socialiste, mais cela n'est qu'un reste du compartimentage d'autrefois. Vers les années soixante, le passage agité de ce pays très peuplé à une société urbaine et industrialisée atteignait un point culminant. Et soudain les colonnes immuables se mirent à chanceler.[6] Quant aux laïques ou personnes sans appartenance ecclésiale: les premiers chiffres dont on dispose sont de l'an 1879. Cette année-la, ils étaient une catégorie négligeable de 0,3 %. En 1960 leur nombre atteignait 21 %, en 1966, 33 %; en 1979, 42 %; en 1985, 47 %; en 1987, 49 %. Entre 1900 et 1960 ce procès de déchristianisation se manifestait surtout dans l'Eglise Réformée. Depuis 1960 il est apparu aussi dans l'Eglise catholique: en 1960, 37 % des Néerlandais étaient catholiques; à présent, le chiffre est de 28 % à 29 %. On peut constater que ce processus s'est accéléré depuis 1960 et qu'il y a maintenant à peu près autant de personnes dans l'Eglise qu'en dehors.[7] Aux Pays-Bas l'appartenance à l'Eglise aujourd'hui n'est pas du tout un automatisme; il s'agit plus qu'ailleurs vraiment d'un choix. Cette situation a pour contrepartie une grande participation active des membres de l'Eglise. Quant aux tendances parmi les catholiques: en 1981 le sociologue de religion G. van Tillo distinguait entre les catholiques cinq groupes: les orthodoxes sévères (environ 10 %), les orthodoxes (environ 20 %), les orthodoxes libéraux (30 %), les libéraux (environ 30 %) et les catholiques marginaux (environ 10 %).[8] En 1985 un autre sociologue de la religion H. Hilhorst parlait d'environ 20 % de catholiques traditionels ou conservateurs versus environ 15 % de catholiques progressistes et critiques; entre les deux on trouve un groupe du milieu de 65 %. Sa conclusion est qu'il faut parler d'une Eglise essentiellement pluriforme.[9]

La sécularisation s'est donc imposée dans les années soixante tout à coup d'une façon choquante. Les Pays-Bas devenaient brusquement un pays sécularisé. Ces développements se déroulaient aussi bien dans la

---

6 J. THURLINGS: *De wankele zuil. Nederlandse katholieken tussen assimilatie en pluralisme* (Nijmegen-Amersfoort 1971); T. DUFFHUES, A. FELLING et J. ROES: *Bewegende patronen* (Baarn 1985); O. SCHREUDER: Katholieken in beweging, dans STOUTHARD et VAN TILLO: *Katholiek Nederland* 101-113.
7 H. DE LOOR et J. PETERS: Een vergelijkende sociologische analyse van de katholieke en de hervormde kerk sedert 1945, dans STOUTHARD et VAN TILLO: *Katholiek Nederland* 144-168; H. HILHORST: De godsdienstsociologie op zoek naar nieuwe vormen van religie, dans IDEM: 114-130; O. SCHREUDER: De religieuze traditie in de jaren tachtig, dans O. SCHREUDER et L. VAN SNIPPENBURG (éd.): *Religie in de Nederlandse samenleving. De vergeten factor* (Baarn 1990) 17-41; J. PETERS: Religie in meervoud. De drie grote confessies, dans IDEM: 42-45.
8 G. VAN TILLO: Roomsen worden weer katholiek. Impasse of doorgangsfase van het Nederlands katholicisme, dans W. GODDIJN e.a.: *Hebben de kerken nog toekomst? Commentaar op het onderzoek 'Opnieuw God in Nederland'* (Baarn 1981) 123.
9 HILHORST: De godsdienstsociologie 121.

société que dans l'Eglise, beaucoup plus vite que par exemple en Belgique qui connaît pour une partie la même région linguistique. Les catholiques qui, jusqu'à ce moment, formaient un bloc très fermé et ultramontain, étaient fortement confrontés avec le problème de la sécularisation. Plus qu'ailleurs ils ont appris ce problème à leurs dépens. Peut-être est-ce aussi lié avec le fait que les courants et réflexions spirituels du dehors pénètrent très vite dans la société néerlandaise et y sont incorporés. Il s'agit d'un petit pays doté d'une communication intense, dans lequel on est obligé d'apprendre plusieurs langues. Selon le sociologue de religion O. Schreuder, ce changement brusque était préparé déjà dans les années cinquante par le renouveau des intellectuels catholiques, par la nouvelle stratégie pastorale et par la critique de la morale matrimoniale classique: ces facteurs constituaient une matière explosive de la radicalité des développements aux Pays-Bas, au début des années soixante, qui faisait du bruit dans le monde.[10] Quoi qu'il en soit, un livre comme *Honest to God* de J. Robinson[11] exerçait une grande influence sur beaucoup de gens, et c'était la même chose quant à la théologie de la mort de Dieu. Ces développements menaient partout au sentiment d'un grand vide. La question se posait avec acuité de savoir si l'on pouvait encore célébrer la liturgie dans une société sécularisée. On lisait ce que Hamilton écrivait: "Je ne comprends pas comment la prédication, le culte, la prière puissent être pris au sérieux par le théologien radical".[12] Et on était confronté avec Altizer qui écrit: "Le théologue moderne ne doit pas penser qu'elle n'est plus simplement que le serviteur d'une foi ancienne et d'un culte ancien, parce que la foi et le culte sont presque totalement privés d'intérêt".[13]

En outre, une grande influence était exercée aux Pays-Bas à la fin des années soixante par la sociologie critique de l'Ecole de Frankfurt et par la théologie politique. La révolte parisienne de 1968 et son idéologie étaient reprises très vite partout aux Pays-Bas. Quant à la théologie politique, plusieurs théologiens néerlandais avaient étudié auprès de J.B. Metz à Münster, mais ils étaient partisans d'une théologie plus radicale que celle de leur maître. Et ils posaient la question de la pertinence de la liturgie d'une façon insistante, également quant aux formes liturgiques renouvelées: La liturgie ne sert-elle pas de couverture à des dissensions politiques? Ne fonctionne-t-elle pas comme un bandeau face aux problèmes réels? Evidemment, elle peut protester, et plaider pour la justice et la paix. Mais

---

10 SCHREUDER: Katholieken in beweging 101-113.
11 J. ROBINSON: *Honest to God* (London 1963).
12 W. HAMILTON: American theology, radicalism and the death of God, dans T. ALTIZER et W. HAMILTON: *Radical theology and the death of God* (Indianapolis-New York-Kansas City 1966) 7.
13 T. ALTIZER: *The gospel of christian atheism* (London 1967) 27. Oeuvres postérieures d'ALTIZER: History as Apocalypse, dans M. TAYLOR: *Deconstruction and theology* (New York 1982) 147-177 and IDEM: *History as Apocalypse* (Albany 1985).

dans ce cas-là n'est-elle pas plutôt une protestation romantique et un plaidoyer romantique? Enfin la liturgie ne peut pas changer réellement les structures de la société et de l'Eglise. La liturgie et l'art recouvrent les blessures, le plus souvent prématurément, du manteau de l'amour. La liturgie n'a qu'une fonction marginale dans la société. Cette critique résonnait surtout dans le périodique *Tegenspraak* qui était alors le porte-parole de la théologie politique dans notre pays.[14]

1.4. La réflexion sur la crise

La crise signalée posait des questions vraiment nouvelles aux théologiens et surtout aux liturgistes. La question n'était plus comment on peut diminuer la distance entre la liturgie et le peuple, mais plus radicalement celle du sens de la liturgie même. Dans ce contexte les centres pastoraux organisaient partout dans notre pays des cours pour les pasteurs et les laïcs, qui avaient pour thème la sécularisation. Dans ces cours aussi le thème de la liturgie dans une société sécularisée était traité. On constatait que la sécularisation n'avait pas comme conséquence la fin de la liturgie tout court, mais seulement de la liturgie conventionnelle et qu'il était nécessaire de chercher de nouveau chemins. Je suis conscient du fait que le concept de sécularisation n'est pas utilisé d'une façon uniforme. En général on l'emploie pour décrire la diminution de l'intérêt envers une autre réalité décisive, impliquant concrètement la diminution de la religiosité, la réduction de l'influence de la religion et l'adaptation de la religion.[15] Un élément essentiel de la sécularisation est le processus social qui se manifeste partout dans notre société et qui en soi n'implique pas une tendance anti-religieuse ou anti-ecclésiastique. C'est l'évolution d'une société close et statique vers une société ouverte et dynamique. On est tenté d'ajouter qu'il s'agit aussi du passage d'une société sacrée et religieuse vers une société non-sacrée et a-religieuse. Mais il n'est pas nécessaire de relier les adjectifs 'clos' et 'statique' avec le sacré et le religieux, et les adjectifs 'ouvert' et 'dynamique' avec le non-sacré et l'a-religieux. Selon moi la clef de la sécularisation réside dans la donnée que notre culture caractérise plus le monde comme *saeculum* que comme *kosmos*.[16] Quand on désigne le monde avec le mot grec *kosmos*, on le voit surtout comme un ordre

---

14 *Tegenspraak* 1 (1969-1970) (no. 1) 16, 28, 35-37; (no. 4) 18-23, 39-40, 61. Aussi B. VON ONNA: *Kritischer Katholizismus* (Hamburg 1969) 31 ss.; L. DULLAART: Macht en dienst van de liturgie, dans *Dwang, dwaling en bedrog. Formulieren van onenigheid* (Baarn 1971) 75-84.
15 Cf. J. BERKELMANS: Secularisatie: wat doen de kerken ermee?, dans *Informatiebulletin 1-2-1* 18 (1990) 379-381.
16 Cf. M. PLATTEL et C. RIJK: Het geseculariseerd mens- en wereldbeeld in verband met het godsdienstig verschijnsel, dans *Werkmap Katholieke Studentendagen 1969* (Tilburg 1968).

spatial et statique. Mais quand on le désigne avec le mot latin *saeculum*, on accentue davantage la dynamique de l'histoire. Dans la culture grecque et romaine on considérait le monde surtout comme *kosmos*, tandis que pour les juifs le monde était surtout histoire, *saeculum*. Dans la culture chrétienne les deux concepts se rencontraient et la tension entre les deux se développait au profit du concept *kosmos*. Dans la vision cosmique du monde Dieu est vécu comme le premier ordonnateur, la force motrice immobile et la loi éternelle, et l'homme y est dépendant de la *nature* comme d'un ordre objectif en tout ce qu'il fait. Dans cet ordre objectif il est question d'un système théologique et éthique qui est immuable et qui est au-delà de l'histoire. Le séculier reçoit alors une signification péjorative comme ce qui n'est que transitoire, instable, temporel, corporel, contrairement au religieux perçu comme immuable, durable, incorporel et spirituel: et c'est à ce domaine que la liturgie appartient. Elle est une donnée intangible, constituée 'd'en haut' par Dieu lui-même et par ceux qui sont le plus proches du monde divin: les ecclésiastiques, qui sont plus spirituels. Le sacré devient un contraire de l'histoire; il est isolé de l'histoire comme quelque chose de supra-historique. Alors que, dans la vision du monde comme *saeculum*, le concept de l'histoire – et avec ce concept le transitoire, l'instable et le dynamique – est spécifié d'une manière propre. On n'accepte plus que le sacré soit isolé de l'histoire d'une façon dualiste. Vivre dans la dynamique de l'histoire ou, avec d'autres mots, dans le monde du travail, de la famille, du mariage, et cetera, n'est plus nécessairement lié au non-sacré. Donc, dans cette vision du monde, le sacré ne se perd pas, mais il va fonctionner d'une autre façon: en liaison avec la dynamique de la tension entre le passé, le présent et l'avenir et avec la responsabilité humaine. Désormais le sacré n'est pas purement fixe. Nous le cherchons, comme la terre sous nos pieds et comme la main qui nous tient.

Ainsi la sécularisation implique la fin d'une liturgie qui se meut trop dans un espace et un temps isolés, à côté de notre monde. La liturgie ne peut plus être un pas au-dessus du monde. Elle doit reconnaître l'homme et le monde dans leur réalité créée et historique. Ce qui est important, c'est que le Dieu du salut soit trouvé en Christ à l'intérieur de l'histoire, dans le *hic et nunc*. Et la communauté des fidèles pour sa part doit découvrir ce Dieu du salut chaque fois de nouveau à l'intérieur de l'histoire. Il est clair que dans la vision sécularisée la liturgie est pleinement plongée dans la dynamique de la tension entre passé, présent et avenir. Aussi n'est-il pas étonnant que cette nouvelle vision l'anamnèse, un concept-clé de la liturgie, a reçu une place centrale. Car il indique la mémoire des événements salutaires du passé dans le *hic et nunc* et leur tension vers l'avenir.

Tout cela a des conséquences pour la forme concrète de la liturgie: les textes, les rites, les vêtements liturgiques et l'architecture. Cela ne veut pas dire que toutes ces choses doivent devenir aussi banales et quotidiennes que possible. La mise en forme du sacré dans une langue propre, des actions propres, un propre espace reste nécessaire. Mais il s'agit de ce propre dans la dynamique de l'histoire. Et cela s'applique aussi au ministère sacerdotal. Ce ministère n'est plus quelque chose de sacré isolé de la communauté chrétienne située dans l'histoire contingente. Désormais il s'agit d'un être à la tête de la communauté comme un serviteur et de la fonction sacerdotale liturgique intégrée dans les fonctions kérygmatiques, pastorales et diaconales.

Il est évident que tous les gens aux Pays-Bas n'ont pas intégré la sécularisation dans leur réflexion de cette manière. Il y en a qui s'enfuient en arrière et qui s'enferment dans leur ancien cloisonnement ultramontain. Surtout, par le choc des événements, une forte polarisation surgissait, qui continue aujourd'hui.

1.5. La recherche d'un *way of life*

Aux Pays-Bas la réflexion ne se bornait point du tout à la théorie. C'était une réflexion sur une praxis liturgique qui avait comme fin la recherche d'un *way of life*. Peut-être précisément cela est-il une chose typiquement néerlandaise. L'histoire néerlandaise est dominée déjà depuis des siècles par une vision qui se concentre sur l'orthopraxis et sur l'engagement dans la vie quotidienne.[17] Les théologiens néerlandais sont, comme les peintres néerlandais, surtout intéressés par le paysage plat et la vie domestique, avec leur propre perspective de lumière et d'ombre. Ils sont intéressés par l'agir ordinaire de chaque jour dans ce monde et par la perception de l'homme aux prises avec ses questions et problèmes concrets. On peut penser aux tableaux et portraits de Rembrandt, Vermeer et Hals. Aussi la question du faire rituel était-elle surtout une question concrète: comment peut-on prier *hic et nunc*, dans une culture sécularisée, dans la petite et grande histoire des hommes et comment les chrétiens peuvent-ils agir rituellement d'une manière qui ait un sens véritable?

Déjà avant Vatican II existaient des centres d'expériences liturgiques comme le 'Werkgroep voor Volkstaalliturgie' à Amsterdam (H. Oosterhuis – B. Huijbers), le 'Boskapel' à Nimègue, le 'Pleingroep' à la Haye et le 'Maastrichtse jeugdmis'. Dans ces centres on visait des célébrations acceptables comme telles. Les évêques néerlandais avaient l'intention de leur donner une place dans l'ensemble du renouvellement liturgique.[18] En 1965

---

17 E. ZAHN: *Regenten, rebellen en reformatoren. Een visie op Nederland en de Nederlanders* (Amsterdam 1990).
18 T. GOVAART: Het liturgisch experiment in Nederland. Informaties en inzichten, dans *Tijdschrift voor liturgie* 50 (1966) 331-342; H. OOSTERHUIS: *Twee of drie. Nederlandse kerkgeschiedenis sinds bisschop Bekkers* (Baarn 1980) 11.

ils cherchaient un contact sur cette question avec Rome. Tout cela conduisit à la visite aux Pays-Bas d'A. Bugnini, secrétaire du Conseil post-conciliaire de la liturgie. Après cette visite de Bugnini les évêques communiquaient qu'ils appréciaient les centres nommés d'expérimentation, et ils annonçaient qu'ils voulaient fonder un Centre pour le Renouvellement de la Liturgie. Mais ce centre n'a jamais été érigé. Après ce temps-là les évêques n'ont plus jamais prononcé leur appréciation d'une façon aussi explicite. On peut considérer ce fait comme un indice significatif de l'histoire émouvante du rituel chrétien aux Pays-Bas après Vatican II. La recherche d'un *way of life* passionnait la base de l'Eglise de plus en plus et la stratégie liturgique épiscopale tombait dans une zone de tension pénible avec le centre de l'Eglise catholique. La question d'un rituel chrétien authentique dans une société sécularisée se maintenait en tout ce qu'elle comportait de véhément et d'urgent. On était convaincu que la liturgie et l'ordre socio-culturel s'étaient aliénés l'un de l'autre de plus en plus et que cette aliénation n'était pas neutralisée par les nouveaux livres liturgiques officiels. Mais les évêques n'avaient pas de marge suffisante d'action. Au contraire, en 1970 et 1971, Rome intervenait de manière forte par la nomination de deux évêques qui considéraient la recherche d'un nouveau *way of life* comme un abrutissement liturgique. Par les nominations d'évêques après 1980 cette tendance sera renforcée. La largeur d'esprit de l'époque du cardinal Alfrink était transformée en réserve et en esprit fermé. Et ceux qui étaient partisans d'une fuite en arrière, se sentaient confirmés.

Du fait de ces développements une certaine route à deux voies s'est ouverte dans la liturgie: les livres liturgiques officiels étaient édités d'une telle manière que même les adaptations exigées par les *editiones typicae* n'avaient pas lieu. Sur ce point ils sont vraiment différents des éditions des autres pays. Ce n'est que les années dernières qu'il y a eu un certain renversement. A côté de cela, il y avait une large évolution à la base. Par certains cette avancée a été décrite comme un retour funeste à l'état sauvage et comme une expérience sans issue. La liturgie devenait un point de cristallisation dans la polarisation. Pourtant une recherche de l'Institut catholique social-ecclésiastique (Kaski) constatait en 1972 que le renouvellement liturgique aux Pays-Bas n'était pas du tout une affaire de sauvages. Au contraire, presque partout, il s'agissait du prototype romain de la liturgie et, à l'intérieur de ce prototype, il se faisait une recherche de nouveaux chemins.[19]

Comme je l'ai dit, cette recherche était une affaire typiquement néerlandaise. Mais, de l'autre côté, je veux souligner que les Pays-Bas étaient le point de cristallisation d'un problème beaucoup plus large de l'Europe occidentale, déjà esquissé en 1973 par Bugnini, secrétaire de la Congréga-

---

19 *De weekendliturgie* (Den Haag 1972)(= Kaski-rapport no 323).

tion pour le Culte Divin, comme le problème du devoir urgent de l'adaptation de la liturgie au caractère et aux traditions des différents peuples: parce que la liturgie doit naître spontanément de leur coeur et ne peut pas rester étrangère à leur culture et leur mentalité.[20] Vraisemblablement, en écrivant cela, il pensait à l'inculturation tant dans la culture de l'Europe occidentale que dans les autres cultures. En tout cas depuis ce temps-là l'intérêt pour l'inculturation s'est augmenté.[21] Seulement a-t-on trouvé suffisamment le *way of life*? La liturgie officielle ne s'est-elle pas arrêtée trop au début du chemin qu'il faudrait suivre pour l'intégrer vraiment dans notre culture?

2. LES CHEMINS CONCRETS

Quels sont les chemins prospectés à la base aux Pays-Bas après Vatican II? Je vais les esquisser à l'aide des thèmes: liturgie du seuil, liturgie modeste, liturgie inductive, liturgie socialement pertinente, donner corps à de nouveaux rites de passage, redécouverte du non-verbal et répétition et créativité. Il est impossible de traiter tous ces thèmes d'une façon détaillée. Mais cela n'est pas nécessaire. Il suffit de donner une idée de la façon dont on cherche et on a cherché une liturgie viable dans une société sécularisée.[22]

2.1. Liturgie du seuil

Après Vatican II l'Eglise catholique aux Pays-Bas était confrontée assez brusquement avec la donnée que beaucoup de gens ne participaient plus à la liturgie et quittaient l'Eglise institutionelle. En même temps on pouvait constater que beaucoup de gens, dans le vide qui était né, se mettaient à la recherche d'un mystère qui dépasse le rationnel et le fonctionnel. La plupart des gens persistent dans la conviction qu'il y a, d'une façon ou d'une

---

20 A. BUGNINI: Progresso nell'ordine, dans *Osservatore Romano* (12 décembre 1973).
21 Cf. par exemple no. 179 (1989) de *La maison-Dieu* sur "L'inculturation".
22 Quant au matériel concret je me limite à l'indication des périodiques comme *Inzet*, *Werkcahiers voor vieringen met kinderen*, *Servicemap voor jongerenliturgie*, *Werkboek weekendliturgie*, *Werkschrift voor leerhuis en liturgie*, les livres nombreux de H. Oosterhuis (cf. K. KOK: *De vleugels van een lied. Over de liturgische poëzie van Huub Oosterhuis* (Baarn 1990)) et *Werkmap voor liturgie*. Dans ce dernier périodique depuis 1977 on peut trouver de listes de rituels nés à la base et leur discussion. Comparez aussi les éditions documentaires du *Werkmap voor liturgie* qui sont en train d'être publiées et L. DAMEN: *Uit goede bron. Literatuurlijst van liturgisch materiaal en achtergrondinformatie* (Breda 1987) (= Liturgische handreikingen 13). En outre il y a plusieurs livres de chants; une liste dans Nationale Raad voor Liturgie: *Directorium voor de Nederlandse Kerkprovincie in het jaar 1990* (Zeist 1989) 122.

autre, quelque chose de plus entre le ciel et la terre.[23] Et ils parlent de ce qui nous dépasse, de la dimension de la profondeur, de la réalité vraie, du sens final de la vie, du fait que la vie a malgré tout pourtant un sens profond mystérieux. Il s'agit ici de ce qu'A. Vergote indique comme 'le pré-religieux' et qui, chez W. Veldhuis, E. Mertens, J. van der Lans et O. Steggink, est nommé 'le religieux'.[24] En partant de cette expérience, on ne dira plus si facilement que l'action rituelle n'exerce d'influence sur la réalité que par des moyens déficients. Au contraire: on peut découvrir de nouveau dans cette expérience le sens d'une praxis rituelle authentique. Dans ce cas-là il ne s'agit pas de pouvoir et de domination, mais de l'adoption d'une réalité qui nous dépasse. Le rituel nous fait vivre un mystère et un avenir plus grands que nous-mêmes.

Eh bien, ces expériences et expressions du (pré-)religieux ne sont pas l'origine de la foi, mais elles forment l'espace et la terre nourricières qui peuvent être remplis par la révélation.[25] Elles semblent plus indispensables depuis le changement brusque de la sécularisation afin que le *disclosure* de la révélation soit possible. L'expérience du (pré-)religieux – qui peut aussi être indiqué comme 'la spiritualité commune'[26] – appartient aux *prae-ambula fidei*, c'est-à-dire au stade préliminaire de la foi dans lequel ou dans le prolongement duquel l'acte de foi peut être éveillé. Cet éveil de la foi en un Dieu personnel qui se révèle à moi, n'arrive pas en vertu de ces *prae-ambula fidei*, mais grâce au *lumen fidei* qui saisit le croyant.

L'expression du (pré-)religieux est essentiellement importante dans la liturgie de notre culture. On a besoin d'une expression religieuse qui traduise le (pré-)religieux d'une façon authentique. Autant qu'on pouvait parler sur la nécessité d'une liturgie du catéchuménat dans l'Eglise ancienne, autant peut-on accentuer la nécessité d'une liturgie du seuil dans notre culture. Cette liturgie du seuil peut être une totalité autonome, par exemple une célébration de la naissance qui ouvre les participants au mystère final. Mais elle peut être aussi un *counseling* explicite vers l'expression de la foi. Quoi qu'il en soit, il semble qu'aux points d'articulation de la vie on ait vraiment besoin de célébrations (pré-)religieuses à côté des sacrements. On pourrait se demander si c'est la tâche des pasteurs chrétiens de donner corps à de telles célébrations. On peut y répondre par une autre question: quand les pasteurs chrétiens ne le font pas, qui se chargera de cette tâche? L'Eglise n'est pas seulement là pour ceux qui sont dedans. Et l'Eglise catholique a toujours adhéré à l'adage *gratia supponit naturam*.

---

23 HILHORST: De godsdienstsociologie 114-130.
24 LUKKEN: *De onvervangbare weg* 37-38; O. STEGGINK: Het traditionele jargon is gaan schuiven, dans *Speling* 38 (1986) no. 1, 32-42.
25 STEGGINK: Het traditionele jargon 38.
26 STEGGINK: Het traditionele jargon 35.

Quand la liturgie du seuil invite et est orientée à l'expression liturgique de la foi, cette liturgie peut y être liée étroitement: comme *counseling* vers la liturgie de la foi ou comme contrepoint. Cette liaison peut avoir lieu d'une façon très spéciale: ainsi il y a des chants d'H. Oosterhuis qui ont un double-fond; on peut les chanter comme une expression du (pré-)religieux, mais aussi – grâce au contexte immédiat et objectif ou au contexte vécu – comme une expression de la foi chrétienne. On peut penser à des textes comme: "En ce cas-là encore je m'accroche à toi / si tu veux ou non / sans conditions. / Je crierai: sauve-moi / ou quelque chose comme: / aime-moi"[27] et: "Que nous nous remplissions avec l'air de la vie / et crions: finalement nés".[28] On peut trouver un autre exemple dans la commémoration à Amsterdam le 21 mars 1982 de quatre journalistes néerlandais, assassinés à San Salvador, faite dans l'église de 'Mozes en Aäron'. A la fin de la célébration le pasteur dit:[29]

> Quand je vous invite au service des prières, je suis conscient d'exprimer une invitation qui sera entendue de très différentes manières. Je sais qu'il y en a beaucoup parmi nous pour qui la prière est une affaire curieuse. Pour qui des mots comme Dieu et foi sont des mots curieux. Pourtant je vous invite, parce que je crois qu'il est possible d'entrer en terre sainte avec des sentiments divers et avec des opinions diverses, où il ne s'agit pas de déclarations ni de la majorité ni du pouvoir ni d'avoir raison, mais d'un respect profond de l'un pour l'autre.
> Et nous prononçons encore une fois ces noms: Koos Koster, Jan Kuiper, Joop Willemsen, Hans ter Laag.
> Et nous pensons, et nous prions, et nous croyons que ces noms ne sont pas effacés, parce que ce n'est pas la violence qui a le dernier mot, mais l'espoir qui fait vivre.
> Nous pensons et nous nous sentons unis avec leur famille, dans notre impuissance, dans notre fureur, dans notre tristesse. Dieu, nous ne le comprenons pas. Pourquoi, pourquoi les avez-vous quittés? Pourquoi, hommes, nous quittons-nous les uns les autres? Pourquoi nous brimons-nous les uns les autres...? Pourquoi estimons-nous 'l'avoir' (la propriété) plus important que 'l'être'? Pourquoi nous approprions-nous ce monde au lieu d'y jouer...? Nous sommes furieux et indignés profondément parce que la violence semble nous battre toujours de nouveau et que les faibles semblent contraints de perdre toujours. Dieu, nous ne le supportons pas. Parce que Jésus a dit qu'il nous faut nous lever et ne pas perdre courage. Alors, nous voici... Amis, levons-nous et sortons de ce lieu-ci. Le monde nous attend. Nous n'améliorerons pas ce monde jusqu'à la fin. Mais nous

---

27 H. OOSTERHUIS: *Zien-soms even. Fragmenten over God. Een voorlees-boek* (Bilthoven 1972) 33.
28 H. OOSTERHUIS: Dat wij volstromen, dans *Liturgische gezangen voor de viering van de eucharistie* (Hilversum 1975) no. 182.
29 Ikon: *Herdenkingsdienst bij de dood van Koos Koster, Jan Kuiper, Joop Willemsen, Hans ter Laag, 21 maart 1979* 33.

ferons ce dont nous ne voulons pas nous abstenir. Au nom de Dieu, faites-le conséquemment. Amen.

2.2. Liturgie modeste

Depuis le changement de la sécularisation, la liturgie comme expression explicite de la foi est devenue plus prudente et plus modeste. Au lieu d'une liturgie qui est une sorte de miroir du monde divin, désormais, il s'agit plutôt d'une liturgie qui essaie chaque fois de trouver Dieu, ici et maintenant, au milieu de nos péripéties, comme notre plus profond fondement et notre perspective ultime. Dieu est cherché de bas en haut et cela s'accomplit par et dans Jésus de Nazareth et ce qui est advenu en lui. La christologie d'en haut est devenue une christologie d'en bas: Jésus et son histoire unique est l'accès au Dieu trinitaire. Ce qui dans la théologie d'aujourd'hui est exprimé réflexivement, est vécu et s'accomplit dans la liturgie nouvelle d'une façon actuelle et sensible. Il faut lire par exemple les prières eucharistiques d'H. Oosterhuis et les comparer avec le canon romain classique.

Contrairement au Seigneur à la fois sévère et clément de la liturgie classique romaine, contrairement au *Pantokrator* byzantin qui domine toute l'abside, et contrairement au Dieu féodal du moyen-âge, maintenant, il y a dans la liturgie le Dieu attentif à l'humanité qui est en route avec son peuple. Ce Dieu, compatissant à ceux qui souffrent, se manifeste dans la liturgie et cela, non en plénitude, mais 'en passant' et 'parfois/brièvement'.[30] Ainsi il nous précède aussi chaque fois de nouveau: comme un ordre de marche vers un nouveau monde.

Dans le prolongement de ce contexte se fait jour la conscience croissante que le Dieu de la liturgie chrétienne est souvent encore trop dominant et trop masculin. Le féminisme a souligné que la langue des symboles et l'action symbolique ne sont pas du tout innocentes. Il faut y ajouter que le Dieu masculin a une répercussion sur toute la liturgie dans laquelle il semble souvent que toute l'humanité serait masculine. De ce point de vue dans les pays anglophones la traduction liturgique officielle a été corrigée. Mais une telle correction n'est pas suffisante. Une transformation plus radicale sera nécessaire. Ce nouveau courant se fait jour surtout dans des textes nouvellement créés dans lesquels on s'adresse à Dieu avec les anciennes images bibliques comme coeur, entrailles, souffle et lumière. Dans un chant eucharistique de M. de Groot le Christ est glorifié comme "l'homme qui nous nourrit avec son corps comme une mère et nous faire boire (...)".[31] Un bon exemple est le chant sur Sara, dans lequel

---

[30] Cf. les livres de H. OOSTERHUIS: *In het voorbijgaan* (Utrecht 1968) et *Zien-soms even* (Bilthoven 1972).
[31] W. VAN HILTEN e.a. (éd.): *Eva's lied. 42 nieuwe liederen, ontstaan binnen de feministische theologie* (Kampen 1984) 31.

on trouve ces phrases: "Elle est une femme renommée. / Elle est une femme qui supporte des peuples / (...) Matriarche Sara, étoile sur notre route dans laquelle la gloire d'Israël s'est manifestée".[32] Et une question cruciale dans ce contexte est celle de l'admission de la femme au sacerdoce.

2.3. Liturgie inductive

Avant Vatican II la messe de *Requiem* était une liturgie impressionnante. Les funérailles en latin étaient une solennité monumentale préformée, accomplie sans acception de personne. On pouvait l'accomplir malgré les changements de l'histoire de ce monde et des invidus et malgré les différentes circonstances de la mort individuelle. L'uniformité et l'a-historicité du rituel n'étaient pas expérimentées comme une charge. C'était une liturgie qui cadrait avec la vision cosmique du monde.

On peut caractériser cette liturgie comme une liturgie déductive c'est-à-dire une liturgie d'en haut; le général est appliqué au particulier. La transcendance est exprimée comme une transcendance de haut en bas: une 'trans-*de*-scendance'; la ligne descendante était accentuée. Ce caractère déductif s'était renforcé à mesure que la liturgie était fixée comme pendant les quatre derniers siècles.

A l'opposé de cette liturgie déductive, se trouve celle que je voudrais caractériser comme une liturgie inductive.[33] Celle-ci procède d'une façon inverse. Il ne s'agit plus de la messe de *Requiem*, mais de *ces* funérailles. La liturgie inductive commence là où sont les gens et pas de l'autre côté. Il s'agit de ces gens qui sont confrontés avec ce défunt. Les proches parents et le défunt ont leur propre histoire. L'aide pastorale doit s'en rendre compte. Le pasteur n'est pas dans le dialogue pastoral *face à*, mais *auprès* de ceux qui sont confrontés avec la mort. Il doit commencer chaque fois de nouveau, cherchant le mot et le geste adéquats. La liturgie s'accomplit dans le contexte de ce faire pastoral inductif. Aussi le pasteur doit opérer d'une façon inductive. Il doit disposer les proches parents afin qu'ils puissent assumer leur souffrance. Il s'agit d'une libération au nom de l'Evangile, dans la lumière de la foi chrétienne. Cet Evangile est servi par authenticité et on lui fait tort quand on prêche seulement *das reine Evangelium*.[34] Ainsi on cherche à donner corps à une liturgie adéquate, c'est-à-dire reliée à cette situation. Du particulier on va au général, d'ici à l'autre côté. La transcendance est découverte et dévoilée peu à peu en partant de

---

32 M. DE GROOT: Lied van Sara: Zij is een vrouw van Naam, dans *Werkschrift voor leerhuis en liturgie* 4 (1983) no. 1, 114.
33 Cf. G. LUKKEN: Funérailles et marginalité (= no. 9 dans ce livre).
34 J. BOMMER: Die Verkündigungsaufgabe der Kasualien Taufe, Hochzeit und Beërdigung, dans J. FURGER e.a.: *Liturgie als Verkündigung* (= Theologische Berichte 16) (Zürich-Einsiedeln-Köln 1977) 195.

l'*hic et nunc*. Il y a une ligne ascendante: de la trans-*a*-scendance. En partant de l'unique, on reprend ce qui a été déjà accompli souvent. Car il s'agit aussi, dans la liturgie inductive, d'un rituel dans lequel le moment de répétition est essentiel. Seulement la répétition est moins littérale; elle s'accomplit d'une façon plus libre et créative. Cette liturgie inductive se lie mieux avec notre situation sociale et culturelle que la liturgie déductive. Car il s'opère dans notre société une grande différenciation et l'accent est mis sur le *saeculum*, sur l'histoire individuelle et commune. Il ne faut pas isoler la liturgie de ce contexte. Elle a sa place dans la dynamique de l'histoire. Histoire veut dire: des événements qui sont chaque fois différents et uniques et qui demandent leur propre éclairage et perspective. On ne peut les transfigurer et transfinaliser qu'en commençant ici et maintenant. Ainsi pendant les funérailles de mon jeune collègue, professeur d'Ancien Testament, nous avons mis sur le cercueil sa bible en hébreu, couverte de taches de doigts. Elle était ouverte à l'endroit du texte d'Isaïe 42, 1-4 qu'il avait choisi lui-même comme lecture pour ses funérailles et qui exprimait ce qu'il estimait de grande importance. C'est un simple exemple, parce qu'il y a beaucoup d'éléments – souvent très petits – dans lesquels on peut marquer qu'il s'agit de ce défunt-ci et de ces proches parents-ci: la parole d'accueil, les oraisons, le porter du cercueil par la famille et les amis, la distribution des rôles, et cetera. Il s'agit de la célébration du mystère pascal ici et maintenant à ce moment-ci. On peut en rendre compte sans que cette liturgie se replie sur elle-même. Il n'est absolument pas question de l'expression la plus individuelle de l'émotion la plus individuelle.

Une telle liturgie est vraiment liée au pastoral le plus large. Elle en est une partie intégrale. Il n'y a pas d'expression liturgique sans une préparation pastorale et sans les soins pastoraux qui suivent nécessairement. Enfin une liturgie inductive implique également que la liturgie est une partie de l'éventualité sociale et qu'elle a des conséquences éthiques dans la société.

2.4. Liturgie socialement pertinente

Depuis le changement brusque de la sécularisation aux Pays-Bas il y a une forte aspiration à enlever la liturgie au climat du secteur privé. Eh bien, la sécularisation est précisément un processus qui a pour effet de séparer les principaux espaces de la vie publique de l'influence religieuse et du contrôle ecclésiastique. Alors que veut-on? Il est clair qu'on n'a pas l'intention de créer une liturgie qui soit reconnue par la société moderne; encore moins veut-on stipuler une situation monopolistique pour la liturgie. Dans une société sécularisée le temps des cloches de l'église qui le dimanche sonnent pour tous et le temps d'une large reconnaissance sociale sont passés. On y trouve une société ouverte et très différenciée avec beaucoup de courants spirituels et une grande tolérance. Dans cette société pourtant la liturgie aussi veut être socialement pertinente. Elle doit l'être pour ceux qui y participent au regard de toutes les situations de leur vie et de toutes les questions fondamentales du moment. Une telle liturgie peut donner plus d'espoir à la vie; et elle doit rendre le chemin plus accessible, ce qui est impossible sans engagement. Cela vaut également quand on célèbre les sacrements. Ainsi le baptême exprime aussi l'orientation vers le royaume de justice, le mariage l'engagement pour les autres, et les funérailles la perspective du pays où il est fait droit aux pauvres et où les puissants n'ont plus droit de cité. Et la célébration de l'eucharistie de chaque semaine ne peut pas négliger le fait qu'elle a pour archétype le repas de Jésus avec les plublicains et les pécheurs. Une telle liturgie socialement pertinente mène à la thématisation de l'engagement, c'est-à-dire à une liturgie politique. On en trouve les premières ébauches à la fin des années soixante (D. Sölle) et depuis ce temps ce type de liturgie chez nous a pris beaucoup de formes: de la prière politique du soir jusqu'au jeûne pour la paix à la veillée franciscaine contre les armes nucléaires à Woensdrecht. Elle exorcise les puissances de la pollution, de la mort et de la destruction. Et elle cherche explicitement – d'une façon rituelle – les chemins d'une nouvelle société, en vertu d'une autre distribution des biens et d'une autre hiérarchie des valeurs. La liturgie politique intègre en elle la 'grande' histoire et elle est capable de s'intégrer à son tour sans se forcer, par exemple, dans la liturgie de la semaine sainte. Ainsi dans une liturgie du vendredi saint on trouve la parole d'accueil suivante:[35]

> Nous nous rassemblons ici pour la mémoire de la mort de Jésus de Nazareth (...) Condamné à mort par le gouverneur romain Ponce Pilate, il a été exécuté comme un esclave révolté (...) On a répandu, en lien avec l'évangile de la résurrection, la fable que le peuple juif est coupable de la mort de Jésus et qu'il a été rejeté par Dieu. Dans notre siècle on a vu et entendu comment, avec la collaboration de beaucoup de chrétiens, des millions de juifs ont été emportés, maltraités, affamés dans les camps, rassemblés dans des chambres à gaz. A l'heure actuelle nous commémorons tous ces assassinés du peuple juif, soeurs et frères de Jésus de Nazareth, abattus comme lui, – voyez comme ils étaient 'envoyés à l'abattoir' et étaient 'muets devant leurs tondeurs'. Que cette commémoration puisse empêcher qu'on injurie et persécute jamais des juifs parce qu'ils sont juifs. Et que personne de nous ne prête jamais l'oreille à cette fable. Et que tous ceux qui prétendent être disciples de Jésus comprennent et reconnaissant qu'ils ont reçu d'Israël le nom de Dieu: 'Dieu de la liberation, Dieu des vivants, Lui tout seul'.

---

35 H. OOSTERHUIS: *Israël, volhard in hem. Een dienst voor Goede Vrijdag. Orde van dienst* (Hilversum 1986).

2.5. Donner corps à de nouveaux rites de passage

Cette question est d'abord liée à celle qui a été traitée au § 2.1. Dans la société sécularisée les rites classiques de passage sont en crise. Pensons aux rituels de la naissance, de la puberté, du mariage et de la mort. De vrais rituels de passage, d'une certaine profondeur, font défaut. Quand les grands rituels religieux de passage de la tradition n'ont plus lieu, normalement ils ne sont remplacés que par la visite à la naissance, l'invitation d'hôtes quand on va cohabiter, le dérailleur automatique à l'époque de la puberté et les funérailles en silence sans assistance de personne. Ici la nouvelle liturgie peut combler des lacunes dans notre société, soit comme expression de la religiosité commune, soit comme expression explicite de la foi chrétienne.

Il y a un deuxième domaine où l'on cherche un *way of life* aux Pays-Bas ces dernières années. De nouvelles lacunes profondes sont apparues dans notre vie pour lesquelles on n'a pas connu de rituels de passage dans le passé. Il s'agit de passages qui ne se trouvent pas ou qui, du moins, ne se produisent pas à ce degré en d'autres cultures. On peut signaler: la crise du divorce, du chômage, de l'incapacité de travail, l'abandon de la maison familiale par les enfants tandis que les parents restent seuls à un âge encore jeune, le passage à la retraite, le départ pour la maison de retraite. Je suis convaincu qu'il est extrêmement important de chercher des rituels qui donnent du sens à ces passages. Il est impossible d'inventer ces rituels derrière son bureau. Ils doivent naître dans la vie même. Mais on peut formuler les conditions susceptibles de favoriser la naissance de ces rituels.

D'abord il me semble important de réaliser la définition des rites de passage par A. van Gennep.[36] Il ne s'agit pas seulement de deux éléments, du passage de la phase antérieure à la nouvelle. Il y a toujours trois phases: a) la séparation par laquelle on quitte la position sociale antérieure, b) la période intermédiaire durant laquelle on exprime et rend supportable l'ambiguïté de sa position d'une façon rituelle, c) l'intégration dans le groupe social par laquelle on entre d'une façon rituelle dans sa nouvelle position. Suivant un rituel spécial un des éléments peut être plus accentué, par exemple la séparation dans le rituel des morts, l'intégration dans le mariage et la période de transition dans le noviciat et les fiançailles.

Deuxième donnée: les rituels de passage ont une certaine durée. Dans notre société on tend à les isoler de leur contexte et à les réduire à un événement qui s'accomplit dans un court espace de temps, par exemple en

---

36 A. VAN GENNEP: *Les rites de passage* (Paris-La Haye 1969; 1re éd. 1909). Cf. J. HAMELINE: Relire van Gennep... Les rites de passage, dans *La maison-Dieu* no. 112 (1972) 133-143.

une heure. Le baptême et le mariage ne durent que trois quarts d'heure ou une heure. Mais les rituels de passage sont toujours emboîtés dans un contexte beaucoup plus large et ce contexte également est plein de rituels. Dans l'Eglise ancienne avant le baptême il y avait de nombreuses sessions rituelles.

Troisième donnée: s'il est vrai que les rites de passage sont enchâssés dans un contexte plus large, il n'empêche que, dans notre culture, ce contexte rituel est souvent beaucoup plus maigre et dans un certain sens plus caché qu'autrefois. C'est lié au fait que l'expérience du sens commence d'une façon inductive, au milieu de l'histoire, plus que dans des cultures antérieures. On ne peut pas simplement s'inspirer de modèles fixes. Ce fait est encore renforcé par la pluriformité des expériences, qui oblige, chaque fois de nouveau, à chercher les mots et gestes adéquats. Plus qu'autrefois il est nécessaire d'articuler les rites de passage dans le contexte d'une assistance humaine ou/et de l'ensemble du pastorat. Le passage du seuil a également besoin de l'assistance du pastorat individuel et du groupe. Et ce pastorat, selon moi, n'est pas encore prêt suffisamment à signifier les moments rituels dans le processus pastoral et à les développer. Ainsi on pourrait accomplir un rituel quand on ferme le cercueil,[37] poser une icône chez le défunt, et cetera. Sans doute il y a moins de moments rituels qu'autrefois, ils sont moins évidents et moins fixes, mais ils restent d'une grande importance comme cadre plus large d'un rite de passage plus concentré.

Il n'y a pas beaucoup d'exemples de ces nouveaux rituels de passage. Depuis quelque temps on peut surtout signaler des rituels de divorce, qui achèvent tout un processus souvent très douloureux, qui connaît sans doute plusieurs moments rituels. A vrai dire, la prononciation du divorce par le juge est une sorte de rite de passage. Mais on peut se demander si cette base rituelle séculière est assez forte pour l'expérience d'un rite de passage. En tout cas il arrive souvent que le rituel n'a pas accompli le passage et que le psychothérapeute insère dans son soutien des moments rituels comme d'écrire une lettre d'adieu, de jeter l'anneau dans la mer, et cetera. Mais tout cela reçoit une nouvelle dimension quand cela s'accomplit dans le contexte du pastorat. Le pasteur protestant néerlandais R. Nieuwkoop remarque que l'Eglise n'a pas seulement une tâche quand les hommes se perdent dans la mort, mais également quand ils se perdent dans la vie.[38] Dans ce cas l'Eglise a la charge de dresser la carte du désert et de chercher par quel chemin aller vers le pays promis. Cela peut se faire dans un dialogue pastoral et individuel. Ce contact est déjà plus qu'indi-

---

[37] *Nouveau Rituel des funérailles. Prières pour les défunts à la maison et au cimetière* II (Tours 1972) no 240.
[38] R. NIEUWKOOP: *De drempel over. Het gebruik van (overgangs)rituelen in het pastoraat* (Den Haag 1986) 142.

viduel du fait que le pasteur représente la dimension publique. Quand il constate qu'il est meilleur de se séparer, cela peut prendre le caractère d'une notification qui implique un moment public rituel. Ce moment rituel peut prendre corps selon les circonstances dans des prières et des rites de pénitence, de pardon et de nouvel espoir. Viennent les moments rituels déjà nommés, comme l'écriture d'une lettre d'adieu, peut-être d'une autre adressée à des amis.[39] Il y a eu aussi ces dernières années des publications dans lesquelles le passage du divorce est accompli d'une façon rituelle plus ou moins publique et concentrée.[40] Dans ce cas une réunion se fait en présence du pasteur et éventuellement des témoins du mariage et des enfants. Selon les circonstances, la famille, des amis ou des représentants de la communauté sont présents. Dans cette réunion s'accomplit un rituel, qui achève publiquement une phase et ouvre une phase nouvelle. C'est un rituel de passage dans lequel les expériences du moment sont exprimées: les sentiments du manque et éventuellement des fautes et la nouvelle perspective de l'avenir. Dans le cadre de cette contribution je ne peux pas développer cet exemple.

Je peux m'imaginer que d'aucuns auront des doutes sur un tel rituel. Je voudrais leur dire deux choses. D'abord, il s'agit d'un problème réel et sérieux, d'une nouvelle situation de passage pour laquelle n'existe jusqu'à maintenant aucun rituel. C'est la vie qui doit montrer si un tel rituel est réalisable. Ensuite, les rituels mentionnés ont leur origine dans des Eglises protestantes. Je sais que dans l'Eglise catholique il y a la difficulté que le divorce, au sens juridique propre, est impossible. Quand bien même on l'accepte, la question reste: que faire quand le divorce est accompli? En outre un tel rituel serait possible quand le tribunal ecclésiastique a prononcé une invalidation. Enfin, ces rituels de divorce peuvent avoir une fonction d'exemple, ils remplissent les conditions mentionnées et peuvent inspirer la création d'autres rites de passage.

2.6. Redécouverte du non-verbal

Ces dernières années, dans notre pays, s'est exprimée la forte conviction que la restauration de la liturgie s'est faite au détriment de beaucoup de chaleur et d'éléments sensoriels. Par rapport à la liturgie officielle on se pose avec A. Nocent cette question. La restauration récente de la liturgie, souvent inspirée par un retour aux lignes sobres du passé et de l'antiquité, n'est-elle pas allée trop loin dans son retour à cet aristocratisme intellec-

---

39 NIEUWKOOP: *De drempel over* 144-145.
40 W. KLOPPENBURG: *Trouwring of oorbel?* (Hilversum 1985) 10-12 (traduction néerlandaise du rituel *Recognition of Divorce* de J. WESTERHOFF et W. WILLIMON de 1980); S. DE VRIES: Gescheiden wegen, dans IDEM: *Op liefde gebouwd* (Delft 1987) 85-91; IDEM: Een kring van getuigen. De helende mogelijkheden van een liturgie bij echtscheiding, dans *De Bazuin* 70 (1987) no. 35, 12-13.

tuel caractéristique du génie romain de l'antiquité? Quand on parcourt les rituels des différents sacrements, la célébration de l'eucharistie, l'année liturgique, il n'est pas difficile de se rendre compte de l'intention évidente d'être sobre et d'omettre, parfois d'une façon assez radicale, tout ce qui n'est pas fonctionnel.[41] La liturgie nouvelle dénote une certaine pauvreté quant à l'élément non-verbal. Cela vaut aussi de la liturgie née à la base, on peut également y trouver les traits d'un certain intellectualisme et d'une pauvreté rituelle. Maintenant, on est plus sensible aux nombreux éléments qui contribuent à un rituel complet: l'authenticité des gestes et des actes symboliques, les mouvements, un juste aménagement de l'espace, l'éclairage, les vêtements, l'approvisionnement en éléments visuels, images, statues, fleurs, cierges, couleurs, le silence, le chant, le parfum, la mise en scène. La publication néerlandaise de H. Vrijdag est intéressante de ce point de vue:[42] dans sa position de programmateur d'émissions liturgiques à la radio il rassemblait ce qu'il trouvait à la base. La récolte est plus grande que prévu. Ses livres donnent de l'espoir, car il s'agit d'éléments vraiment essentiels pour un rituel authentique.

2.7. Répétition et créativité

Une vision statique de la liturgie n'éprouve pas le besoin de créativité, la reprise des rituels suffit. La créativité se réduit au dévouement avec lequel on accomplit le rituel et aux accents personnels inévitablement mis par l'individu. Dans une vision dynamique de la liturgie le rituel sans créativité est un rituel inanimé, il a besoin de créativité pour conserver sa force symbolique. On est conscient de la possibilité de la naissance de nouveaux rituels, du fait qu'ils ne peuvent être répétés comme rituels qu'après leur naissance. A côté de ces nouveaux rituels, notre culture manifeste le besoin d'une assez grande créativité dans les rituels déjà existants.

3. BILAN

Récemment le liturgiste néerlandais J. Hermans publiait le livre *De liturgievernieuwing in Nederland* (Le renouvellement de la liturgie aux Pays-Bas).[43] Sa vision est très négative et se rattache aux opinions que j'ai signalées auparavant. Selon lui aux Pays-Bas il y a eu une destruction du

---

41 A. NOCENT: Gestes, symboles et parole dans la liturgie contemporaine occidentale, dans *Concilium* 152 (1980) 31-32.
42 H. VRIJDAG: *Zonder beelden sprak Hij niet tot hen. Nieuwe symbolen en riten in de liturgie* I-III (Hilversum 1988-1989 et Baarn 1991). Cf. aussi G. LUKKEN: *Liturgie en zintuiglijkheid. Over de betekenis van lichamelijkheid in de liturgie* (Hilversum 1990), traduit partiellement dans no. 4 de ce livre.
43 J. HERMANS: *De liturgievernieuwing in Nederland* (Brugge-Den Bosch 1990).

rituel chrétien, et cela sciemment. Ce sont surtout les spécialistes de la liturgie qui ont contribué à cette destruction. Je peux m'imaginer que cette publication, qui sera certainement traduite, renforcera au centre de l'Eglise et aussi en d'autres Eglises locales l'impression qu'il s'est fait aux Pays-Bas une dé-ritualisation volontaire, un mouvement contre le rite ou, au moins, une déviation par rapport au rite chrétien. Moi-même et mes collègues liturgistes néerlandais avons une autre vision. Nous avouons qu'il y a une crise du rituel, mais nous entendons ce mot *crise* selon son origine grecque, comme un 'choix'. En effet, il est de plus en plus question d'une disparition de la liturgie conventionnelle. Mais en même temps apparaît une nouvelle vitalité des rites chrétiens à mesure qu'on prend au serieux l'inculturation de ce rituel dans notre culture sécularisée. Et après coup il apparaît que ce qui était éprouvé comme une lacune ou comme une discontinuité est plutôt une forme plus digne de foi qui ne contredit point du tout la tradition. Même dans la société sécularisée comme telle on trouve un renouvellement des rites. Un bon exemple est le rituel usité aux Pays-Bas au jour de l'anniversaire de la reine. Auparavant il y avait un défilé devant le palais de Soestdijk. Chez beaucoup prévalait l'opinion que ce rituel était dépassé. Quand Béatrix devint reine, elle abolit ce rituel. Le jour de l'anniversaire de la reine, elle rend visite à deux villes ou villages des Pays-Bas et cette visite est liée à une manifestation socio-culturelle des habitants. Cela cadre avec le nouveau modèle des nombreuses visites de travail qu'elle fait dans le pays pendant l'année et qui ont remplacé le couper de ruban d'autrefois. Le nouveau rituel est plus digne de foi et articulé à la société néerlandaise, qui a été sécularisée aussi quant à la royauté. Dans cette société où beaucoup de rituels ont disparu, de nouveaux naissent. On peut même constater que l'Alliance humaniste, qui est un mouvement 'spirituel' assez fort aux Pays-Bas et qui a depuis l'année dernière sa propre université, revient sur son aversion contre le rituel. Elle commence à s'intéresser au rituel, ce qui est important puisque l'université humaniste forme des conseillers spirituels humanistes qui sont reconnus dans les prisons et les hôpitaux. D'autre part il faut constater que dans la société sécularisée les rituels sont menacés: souvent, c'est le système économique qui les prend à son service; on peut penser à des rituels tels que le carnaval et la mode, mais aussi au rituel des funérailles. Dans ce cas ils sont déterminés par les valeurs de consommation, la possession, la prestation, en un mot, 'l'avoir', et non pas par les valeurs intégrantes de 'l'être'.[44]

Les nouveaux rituels chrétiens sont des rituels qui invitent. Ils manifestent plutôt la face d'une Eglise modeste et servante. Et ils sont articulés à la nouvelle société. En outre ils sont tolérants envers les vieux rituels tra-

---

44 G. LUKKEN: Ritueel en menselijke identiteit, dans A. DE RUIJTER e.a.: *Totems en trends. Over de zin van identificatiesymbolen* (Hilversum 1988) 33-34.

ditionnels: la messe latine, le pèlerinage, le chemin de la Croix, et cetera. Même ces rituels peuvent être intégrés dans les nouveaux rituels. On parle d'une *invented tradition*, c'est-à-dire d'une réponse rituelle aux situations nouvelles sous la forme d'un renvoi à une vieille situation.[45] L'évaluation de la situation rituelle aux Pays-Bas dépend donc – comme on dit chez nous – des lunettes qu'on se campe sur le nez. Récemment G. Hutschemaekers a montré que la gamme bigarrée des descriptions, souvent contradictoires, des changements historiques dans les névroses n'admet que cette conclusion: les jugements d'une augmentation des névroses relèvent davantage de la vision pessimiste de la société chez les spécialistes que de l'état des patients eux-mêmes.[46] La même remarque vaut pour les rites. Le pessimisme est révélateur de certains spécialistes plus que des rites eux-mêmes. Maintenant comme avant, l'accès au sacré n'est possible que par des rituels, mais tant le sacré que les rituels se sont mis en mouvement.

Une évaluation récente de la situation liturgique aux Pays-Bas, 25 ans après la *Constitution de la Liturgie*, était assez positive.[47] Mais cela ne signifie pas qu'on ne peut pas découvrir des aspects négatifs dans ce développement. A juste titre on a reproché aux nouveaux rituels d'être de temps en temps trop verbaux et de s'accomplir trop *High-Brow*. J'ai déjà remarqué qu'on accorde aujourd'hui heureusement une plus grande attention au non-dit. Autre reproche: les nouveaux rituels se passent parfois de la dimension mystique; on ne réalise pas suffisamment que la liturgie est aussi un espace prédonné dans lequel il faut entrer. Enfin il faut avouer qu'ils sont fragiles; ils exigent plus qu'autrefois une bonne expression verbale et corporelle; on a découvert que la sacramentalité est liée à des choses humaines très élémentaires. On peut vraiment parler de la grandeur et de la misère du rite.

Le renouvellement rituel a sa propre herméneutique. Dans chaque inculturation de la liturgie chrétienne il y a tension entre le propre de la foi chrétienne et la forme rituelle avec son caractère déterminé historique. Il est nécessaire de reconnaître cette tension continuellement et de ne pas la résoudre au profit d'une des dimensions en particulier. La provocation de la tension rituelle, c'est qu'on peut faire des exposés théoriques sur cette question, mais qu'en fin de compte c'est toujours la pratique-même, le

---

45 E. HOBSBAWM et T. RANGER (éd.): *The invention of tradition* (Cambridge 1983); P. POST: Verzonnen verleden: volksreligiositeit en de parochieliturgie, dans *Kerugma* 33 (1989-1990) no. 4, 70-78.
46 G. HUTSCHEMAEKERS: *Neurosen in Nederland. Vijfentachtig jaar psychisch en maatschappelijk onbehagen* (Nijmegen 1990).
47 Symposium: Vernieuwing voorbij...? bij gelegenheid van 25 jaar *Constitutie over de heilige liturgie*, dans *Tijdschrift voor liturgie* 74 (1990) 201-251.

way of life, qui doit indiquer le chemin. C'est la conséquence de la donnée primordiale que les rituels ne peuvent pas être conçus, mais qu'ils naissent. Donc l'herméneutique rituelle a ses propres exigences. La question première pour chaque rituel chrétien est d'examiner s'il ouvre un accès vrai au Seigneur ressuscité en tant que premier-né des morts, ici et maintenant, et s'il peut de cette façon être salutaire. Il faut qu'on vérifie continuellement cette question dans la pratique et dans cette vérification les Eglises locales ont leur propre responsabilité en dialogue avec le centre de l'Eglise. Donc il n'est pas question de canoniser les nouveaux rituels *a priori*. L'évaluation continue du 'bien ou non-bien' est nécessaire.

Il est remarquable que beaucoup de gens qui se sont plus ou moins éloignés de l'Eglise, se reconnaissent dans les nouveaux rites chrétiens quand ils y sont confrontés à l'occasion de Noël, de Pâques, du baptême, du mariage ou des funérailles. Surtout à l'occasion des funérailles: la plupart des chrétiens néerlandais (96%) participent à ce rituel, ce qui est remarquable quand on réalise que, précisément, les rituels autour de la mort vont mal dans notre société sécularisée. L'Eglise a vraiment sauvegardé ces rites. Cela implique aussi que les rites chrétiens peuvent être pertinents pour la culture sécularisée comme telle. Bien que le renouvellement du rituel n'ait pas mené à une courbe ascendante dans la participation liturgique, l'Eglise aux Pays-Bas a un visage qui est, quant aux rites, reconnaissable et invitant. Et ce visage n'est pas en contradiction avec la liturgie officielle, mais peut y être intégré.

3. No Life without Rituals

People have many ways of getting on with each other and the world around them. One very special way is communication that moves along the lines of symbolism. In the first section, we will try to steep ourselves in this process, and subsequently ascertain what rituals are in this context (section 2), and what vital role they play in human existence (section 3).

1. SYMBOLISM

Recently a colleague died after a relatively short, incurable illness. He was still young. For several years he had been a member of our faculty teaching Old Testament. He was a capable teacher and a likeable man. At his funeral service, the coffin containing his body was simply laid on the ground at the front of the church, with a paschal candle burning nearby. On top of the coffin lay his own well-thumbed Hebrew Bible, laid open to Isaiah 42:1-4, the messianic text concerning the servant of the Lord, who will not cry out or lift up his voice, or make it heard in the street, who will not break the bruised reed nor quench the dimly burning wick, but will faithfully bring forth justice on the earth. It was a text that had been particularly dear to him, and it had been his express wish that it should be read aloud at his funeral. This we did, using a translation which he himself had made.

Having his coffin carried in by students and faculty, our gathering around his body, the reading from Isaiah 42, the open Hebrew Bible on the coffin, the singing of psalms that he had so loved, the sermon, the breaking of the bread, the prayers: all the celebration rested on our need to symbolize, and thus fulfill as much as possible the wishes he had previously expressed.

It could have been done other ways; we might have buried him even more simply and in silence, the minimum that is necessary in these circumstances. But we did more. As people, we can interact in many ways with each other and the events which break over us, but symbolism is a very specific manner. In it, we use *things* in such a way that the perspec-

---

* *Geen leven zonder rituelen. Antropologische beschouwingen met het oog op de christelijke liturgie* (= Tweede serie Geestelijke Volksgezondheid 2-24) (Baarn 1984) 9-18, 21-33, 35-45, 97-100. Translated by D. Mader, M.Div.

tive is sprung and something breaks open. We use *words* that call up something of a deeper reality. And we *act* in a particular, loaded manner, so as to be able to open up space and admit something of a more distant horizon. Thus, three elements play a role in symbolism: things, words and acts. These elements can also be designated as symbols, symbolic language, and symbolic acts. It is important to look more closely at these various elements.

1.1. Symbols

What is a symbol? Actually, it is an everyday thing that you encounter in your immediate environment. In our dead colleague's room we found his well-thumbed Hebrew Bible. Through placing it in a specific context, this book suddenly took on a particular expressiveness. It revealed something specific: the life and work of a dear person, his daily encounter with the Old Testament, his fondness for a particular passage that was a motto for his life, his encounters with students, his amiableness and meekness, his faith, his early death, his hope for the future and for the kingdom of righteousness, and so much more... It is not easy to express it all in words. In the symbol, the limited receives an infinite amplitude, almost a universality. The symbol has multiple meanings. It functions as a bridge across boundaries. It refers to a deeper reality, a farther horizon, a wider landscape. More immediately, something of that other is really present in the thing which symbolizes.

Thus the reference does not come from outside, from somewhere else: not from a book, nor a commentary, nor from a prior explanation, as is the case for allegory. The Middle Ages was the high point for allegory. As examples, the twelve months of the year referred to the twelve apostles, the four seasons to the four evangelists, and the whole year to Christ himself. When silence fell three times during the mass, it was a sign of the three days Christ lay in the tomb. The walnut signified Christ: the nutmeat was his divine nature, the fleshy outer skin his human nature, and the woody shell between them the cross. J. Huizinga remarks that a poem like Olivier de la Marche's *Le parement et triumphe des dames* stands on the lowest step of symbolism in the Middle Ages. In it, each item of a woman's clothing is compared to a virtue: her shoes are care and diligence, the stockings perseverance, the garter determination, the blouse modesty, and the corset chastity.[1] It is clear that this allegory does not operate at the level of direct perception, but on an intellectual explanation. One could speak of a certain randomness. Yet if the

---

1 J. HUIZINGA: *The waning of the Middle Ages. A study of the forms of life, thought, and art in France and the Netherlands in the fourteenth and fifteenth centuries* (Harmondsworth 1979; first published 1924) 201.

explanations take hold, allegories can eventually become symbols. People consider the five incense grains on the paschal candle as a symbol of the wounds of Christ.

Thus, in a symbol the thing speaks for itself. In the context of our colleague's funeral, the Hebrew Bible inevitably called up something specific and sweeping. One could speak of a direct, non-rational or incomprehensible communication with another reality. Thus symbols can not be invented, and when using them you need not reflect on them. The perception is intuitive and touches the whole person, at the level of feelings and the senses. Symbols do not rest on agreements. In one way or another, the thing that is a symbol refers to itself, because it participates in the reality to which it refers. Goethe formulated it aptly: the symbol is the thing without being the thing, and yet is the thing.[2]

Thus the symbol brings together, unites and gives continuity to what is dispersed. It brings past and future together in the present. It helps one not to react incoherently. In and through the symbol we try to communicate with the land from which we came and with the ground under our feet, but also with the land of our future possibilities. In symbols, our origins and the future toward which we orient ourselves become interwoven with each other in the present.[3]

Thus a symbol is clearly to be distinguished from a sign. A sign is just as much of a reference to another reality. But this reference takes place through a rational process. It does rest on agreement. It is clear, unambiguous, efficient and utile. A thing which is a sign does not refer to itself; it does not participate in that to which it refers. One can think of a traffic sign, crosswalk markings, or a contract. These have no purpose of their own, and do not call us to stop, muse or meditate, as would be the case with a photo that is dear to one. Signs pass the reference through. They are a sort of springboard to another reality, which has nothing to do with the sign as such. If they are no longer clear enough, they are altered by agreement. One must learn signs intellectually. Anyone who drives a car must simply know traffic signs by heart. Understanding, knowledge and learning belong with signs.

It is true for all things, that they are not merely what they superficially appear to be, but in one way or another are more, and so can become symbols. That is true of the hand, the eye, the foot, the body, a flower, the cross, the gallows, bread and wine, a table, a house, a chair, a child, man, woman, color, light, space, etc. The Brazilian theologian L. Boff tells us how a perfectly everyday object can become a symbol. He has just come to Munich to study. It is August, a beautiful summer, two o'clock

---

2 Cited in T. TODOROV: *Théories du symbole* (Paris 1977) 239.
3 W. JETTER: *Symbol und Ritual. Anthropologische Elemente im Gottesdienst* (Göttingen 1978) 68-69.

in the afternoon. The first letter from home arrives. Someone has written! Then the news breaks on him: his father has died, aged 54. One of the mainstays of his life is gone. The next day he discovers a yellowed cigarette butt in the envelope: the last cigarette his father smoked, just before his fatal heart attack. They have sent it to him. From that time on, Boff preserved it in his desk as a keepsake. The color of the cigarette, the aroma of the south-Brazilian tobacco, immediately call to mind his father.[4] Thus the simplest thing can become a symbol, and a symbol can involve all the sense organs, even smell. Indeed, odors can be very compelling symbols. The smell of the cigarette butt is simply part of the symbol and the way it is perceived. Its odor can suddenly call up memories of the home where one grew up and one's native land. Bachelard remarks that the smell of a wet raincoat can bring back bygone school years: you smell the month of October and the school corridors where you once walked.[5]

Our culture has difficulty with perceiving symbols. We are inclined, rather, to look at the sober facts and to take things literally. Our world has become, before all else, a field for research.[6] For us, the moon is a landscape of rocks and craters. The world around us is no longer self-evidently laden with an 'other' reality. It consists of factual data which one can investigate in their regularity. Our way of approaching the world is also strongly influenced by our behavior as consumers. We look to the utility and the profitability of all things. In the advertising which pours out over us daily, always harder and more blatantly than before, this perspective on things does not vary. Or, if it does vary, it is only in one direction: that of the product to be acquired and possessed. The ideal image of young men and women, propagated by television, is that of two persons whose life is realized primarily through consumer goods.[7] Of course, we can not do without the sensory organ which concentrates on the sign. It can also be directed toward humanization. But it is disastrous whenever it becomes so overgrown that its more integral functions of recognition are neglected. Then we degrade ourselves beneath our human level. In perceiving a symbol, it is a matter of a sensory organ reaching into the depths and touching the whole of the person. It is the function of recognition possessed by the child, the poet, or an adult in real, concrete life, and also the religious person. An open mind is necessary for this organ of recognition to function. We must arrive at a certain naivety and simplicity. Because this naivety and simplicity have departed our culture

---

4 L. BOFF: *Kleine Sakramentenlehre* (Düsseldorf 1976) 27-29.
5 G. BACHELARD: *La poétique de la rêverie* (Paris 1971) 119.
6 H. FORTMANN: Primitive man. The poet and the believer, in *Concilium* 47 (1969) 21 ss.; see also IDEM: *Heel de mens* (Bilthoven 1972) 261 ss.
7 D. SÖLLE: The repression of the existential element, or why so many people become conservative, in *Concilium* 17 (1981) no. 1, 69-75.

through the critical approaches of science, one must speak of reaching a second naivety and simplicity. Anyone who perceives symbols has decidedly not devalued research, science and technique. They have merely put them in their proper place.

1.2. Symbolic acts

Deeds and acts differ.[8] A *deed* is purely transaction, with an eye to a tangible result. A deed is good, if it produces the right result. Deeds must be useful. They are aimed at actually changing things, situations and structures. Thus deeds are always unambiguous. One makes a definite product. One sells the product for an established price. Or one pulls the trigger of a gun and the sparrow falls on the roof. Sport in the West is a chain of deeds. It is aimed at getting results, at ever improving performances.

An *act which is a sign* thus is more like a deed. It is subordinate to something outside itself, to which it refers. Thus, the actions of a traffic policeman are directed toward keeping traffic flowing efficiently. That is the case for clear, unambiguous actions that in absolutely no sense are an end in themselves. They refer to, and function as a springboard for, something else. One could add to the list signing a contract, carrying out a rule, and running a meeting efficiently.

A *symbolic act* is in itself laden with meaning. In one way or another it shares in the reality which it calls up. Thus, Japanese archery is not so much aimed at results as at providing one with access to a spiritual path. It is a matter of contact with one's deepest self, concentration, directing oneself toward the one true goal. Other actions in sport can also become authentic human expressions laden with meaning: one can think of harmonious actions performed in dressage, ice-dancing, or on the balance beam, which could become symbolic acts. The accent can shift, so that the perspective springs open. This takes place in a most affective way in modern art, when a performance artist's own actions become a work of art, in and through which the reality of the artwork is revealed.

Human symbolic acts can also have multiple meanings. In his book *Op weg naar het einde*, G.K. van het Reve writes of the appalling trip from Amsterdam to London: it is the stupidest route that exists on earth. Having elaborated on this for three-quarters of a page, he adds:[9]

> I would hope that after this, it is sufficiently clear to you that I travel to get somewhere, and by no means for the pleasure of the trip itself. If God for

---

8 C. VERHOEVEN: *Rondom de leegte* (Utrecht 1967) 11 ss.
9 G.K. van het REVE: *Op weg naar het einde* (Amsterdam 1963) 68-69.

> once is going to be 'all in all', it seems to me that must imply that everyone will be within walking distance, so that, in a way of speaking, you never have to go anywhere any more. That will be the most amazing thing yet that we, in giving up our separation from Him, will get to see: the Kingdom of God will look surprisingly like a village, not much bigger than Schoorl: calm weather; make small talk; man smokes pipe at the back door; watches the clouds go by. Peace, no quarrels: there is already so much trouble in the world. As I said.

This text is full of shifts in perspective. The meaningless trip turns out to be experienced as an eschatological journey, as a way to a new, peaceful world, which radiates warmth.

Compared with symbols, symbolic acts appear to have some peculiarities. Where a symbol relates to things outside us, in all symbolic actions people themselves are at issue: their own actions fulfill the symbolic function as bridges. But immediately the following must be added: the human body itself, the human eye, hand, foot, etc., can function as a symbol. Consequently, the symbol outside the person can never exercise its symbolic function free from human acts; the symbol is always taken up in the human act of symbolization.

Finally, it is possible that one and the same human action at the same time is both a symbol and a sign. Thus enacting a law or chairing a meeting may be actions that are signs, but when at the same time the exercise of authority is emphasized by ceremonial dress or an act of obeisance, the same act also becomes, at the same time, a symbolic act. I will return to this point in section 1.4.

1.3. Symbolic language

In language, the distinction between term and word or symbolic language corresponds to that between sign and symbol, and between acts which are signs and symbolic acts.

A term is unambiguous. Terms are really stripped down words: artificial products that arise through high-handed approaches to and the overmastering of reality. One could also say that a term is a stiff and lifeless word, with only one meaning. It refers to a splinter of reality that is approached in an ordered way. One can speak of a good term, one that does as much as possible with the least possible difficulty, that is, which refers to its piece of reality with maximum clarity. Terms are, just as little as signs, something with which one can linger. They have purely the function of a springboard: you use them as quickly as possible in order to hear or perceive that to which they point. One can also change terms if they no longer fulfill their function. Their realm is knowledge and science, and they have no call on a person as a whole. One finds examples of terms primarily in the exact sciences. The reality about which these sciences speak can easily be abstracted, without misunderstanding. International exchange is very possible. This is made yet easier by the fact that terms are often simply taken over from the language in which they arose: one can think of terms such as x-ray, manager, scriptgirl, or deacon. The newscaster also moves in the realm of terms. There facts are dealt with in a businesslike manner, in clear language. The number of victims in a disaster or battle is announced without emotion, and more pleasing news is given the same distant treatment. It is a question of exactness.

Symbolic language is different. When words are used as symbolic expression, they call up whole worlds. For instance, the words father, mother, and light are ambiguous. They can not be clearly defined. One can pause over them. One uses them with commitment and feeling. They uncover and reveal a deeper reality. They do not separate, but connect. Symbolic language always is opening up new horizons.

In this connection, the original meaning of the word 'say' is revealing.[10] Words that express 'say' regularly also have a meaning associated with 'light'. To say something originally means to bring something to light. 'Say' is related to the word 'see', and originally meant to let something come to light, to let it be seen. The Greek *phemi* (to say) is related to *phaino* (to bring to light, to appear) and also to *phoos* (light). The Latin *dicere* (to say) is related to the Greek *deiknumi* and the German *zeigen* (let see, illuminate). In other words, it turns out from the derivation of words that at least one of the characteristics, and perhaps one of the most fundamental characteristics of the word is that that which is put into words steps into the light. The word hauls things out of their obscurity. It reveals, and brings them to light. It is not random, but has to do with reality itself, and takes part in it. In words, in symbolic language, it is a matter of shining through, of making reality transparent, opening it up into deep perspective. Gusdorf writes, "The word reveals the most intimate nature of the thing".[11] One could also say, 'Speak, and I shall see'.

Our world could not operate without the language of terms. We need that sort of language in order to have dominion in the world. Without the language of terms no trade would be possible, no economic exchange, no scientific research. The language of terms is as important for our welfare as traffic signs are for transit. But it is equally true that this language is insufficient if one "wants to lift up his heart and say what is hidden and ineffable within him. If it is a matter of life and death, of God and man, this first language, this manner of speaking, is not only inadequate, but

---

10 H. SCHMIDT: Language and its function in christian worship, in *Studia liturgica* 8 (1971-1972) 9.
11 G. GUSDORF: *La parole* (Paris 1968⁶) 11.

indeed dangerous".[12] Then symbolic language is needed, a language "more defenseless and modest than the first, the language of what can not actually be said".[13] This language does not describe historically checkable facts, but speaks out the hidden sense – or, it may be feared, nonsense – of our existence. It is not a matter of the impersonal, objectifying descriptive speech of the exact sciences. What is expressed here is not to be spoken *about*; it is speech in which we ourselves are very strongly involved: confession, proclamation, explanation. It is a matter of speech that treats something deeply and brings it about.[14]

Symbolic language does not have to be high and exalted. It can be very simple and direct. Is this not the case with young children's prattle? Their speech is like a babbling brook. The world that surrounds them must be put into words: the cows and the flowers and the car that drives by. Things reveal themselves in this way.[15] This simple speech can also be found in adults. Fortmann describes how he once took a two hour bus ride from London to Canterbury. Behind him sat two women:[16]

> Their conversation lasted two hours, or, subtracting the time for catching their breath, an hour and three-quarters. I could not understand anything more of their dialect than a thousand times 'yes' and five hundred times 'Oh dear'! But it was none the less impressive for that. A waterfall is the only fitting comparison. There is ground to suspect that the whole neighborhood and both families to cousins thrice removed formed the subject (...).

Fortmann points to the innocence and benevolence of this conversation. He reserves the term 'high-level speech' for those conversations that are really self-revealing.

Symbolic language is important not only in the religious realm: it first puts its roots down at the interpersonal level.

> May I conclude that there is a lot of loneliness? That many people have no one with whom they can get off their chest the things deep in their heart, things that preoccupy them day and night? That the real questions seldom are answered and an endless series of personal feelings remain locked inside? (...) It is (...) really a *rare* privilege to be able to speak about the things of the soul – by which I mean not only religious things, though they are included.[17]

---

12 H. OOSTERHUIS: *In het voorbijgaan* (Utrecht 1968) 237; cf. IDEM: *Open your hearts* (New York 1971) 104.
13 OOSTERHUIS: *In het voorbijgaan* 237-238; cf. IDEM: *Open your hearts* 104.
14 W. LUIJPEN: 'De erwtensoep is klaar'. Een filosofische beschouwing over de geloofsakt, in *Streven* 22 (1969) 510-526.
15 FORTMANN: *Heel de mens* 73.
16 FORTMANN: *Heel de mens* 74.
17 FORTMANN: *Heel de mens* 73.

Much has been written about narrative theology. Practicing it is more difficult. How can it happen, as long as the anthropological basis is missing, so long as one's own life story and that of the other remain hidden and secret?

1.4. Double meanings

In contrast to the realm of the sign, the act which is a sign, and the term, stands the realm of the symbol, symbolic acts and symbolic language. They are different ways of relating to reality. These two ways of communication are not interchangeable. One must not confuse them.[18]

The difference between the two realms reveals itself clearly when one places myth next to a scientific report. If one gives a scientific explanation about the origins of the world, it is entirely different than when that origin is told in myth. The book of Genesis occupies an entirely different sphere than a science text. In the latter one finds terms and language which functions as signs; in the former there is symbolic language. Anyone who reads the creation account in Genesis as a scientific explanation has gotten off on the wrong foot.

And yet, it is possible for both realms to be present at the same time, without losing their individuality and without exchanging roles. Thus the symbolic pole can stand in the realm of terms, signs and acts which are signs. When, for instance, someone gives a scientific lecture, he moves in the realm of terms, signs and acts which are signs. But at the same time, one could speak of the symbolic realm, for he appeals to his listeners to take him seriously as a scientist, to recognize him as such and identify with him. An inaugural address certainly aims at the latter too. So, too, it could be that when someone asks a question after a lecture in order to get further information, he really wants to let himself be heard: I am here, recognize me, identify with me.

Often one can speak of double meanings. Really, in practice, meaning can function at two levels. Sometimes these gradually merge, and another time the emphasis will lie on one or the other. When I say, 'Nice weather', I am reporting a fact. But the emphasis undoubtedly lies on symbolic communication; I am really saying 'I'm here: speak with me'. The worst thing that could happen is for the other to deliberately not answer what I've said; my presence, my selfhood is ignored. Thus the strong reaction: you could have at least answered!

Many variants are possible in the relation between the two realms; thus a maximum of information can go together with a pronounced accent on the symbolic pole. This is certainly the case when someone says to bring

---

18 L. CHAUVET: *Du symbolique au symbole. Essai sur les sacrements* (= Rites et symboles 9) (Paris 1979) 61 ss.

them a particular document, and gives some precise information; at the same time it is being said that the other person is subordinate. On the other hand, in the realm of the symbol, symbolic acts and symbolic language one can speak of a cognitive pole. One could even say that that pole regularly plays a part; one can almost always speak of what could be called 'catechetical implications', because when this notional process occurs above all at the realm of symbols, the accent does not lie strictly on intellectual knowledge. If something has been reported, then it happens in such a way that it functions as a means of recognition. Thus it is not a matter of knowing science or theology as such. If this is the case, then the symbolic realm changes into that of the sign, the term, and the act as sign. This is also true for liturgy.

2. RITUAL

Rituals play a large role in every person's life and in every society. Thus, in answer to the question of what rituals are, one can say that in any ritual symbol, symbolic acts and symbolic language come together. But that answer is not sufficient. What characterizes ritual? We shall now look into that.

2.1. Repetition

Symbolization is a human activity. It is connected with the fundamental quality of humanity, and with the specific human potential for dealing with reality in a very particular way. When we speak of symbolization, the emphasis lies on human activity, on human creativity and expression. But in dealing with reality, no human being starts from scratch all over again. He is not a Robinson Crusoe, but lives with others and can fall back on their creativity. And many have already gone before who, through symbolization, have created an entrance into reality. No person enters the world like Adam on the day of his creation. There are already very many previous givens. These begin with one's name: one does not choose it oneself, but it is given by one's parents, and they, in turn, in doing so were dependent on certain customs or trends. What is true of one's name is also true for one's actions and speech. However creatively one engages in symbolization, in fact it is always part of a greater whole in which one is joined. One can never escape the world in which one is taken up, shaped by previous generations.

Indeed, the characteristic of ritual is the accent on this aspect of being previously given. Symbol, symbolic acts and symbolic language come together in ritual, but in such a way that the emphasis lies on their nature as previously given, on their derivative state, on repetition. Repetition is essential for all ritual.

Before I go deeper into that point, a clarification of terms is necessary. We often also use the word rite. In a strict sense, this word refers only to repeated symbolic acts. But often, the word is used in a broad sense, and has the same meaning as the word ritual. Thus the total of all the rituals of the different Orthodox churches is taken up in the expression 'Eastern rites'. The words ritual and rite sometimes here will be used interchangeably.

What A. Nijk has written about the origin of the rite[19] can help clarify our insight into the repetitive aspect of ritual. According to his hypothesis, rites arose in the first instance from no other cause than the consciousness of a lacunae, a hiatus, an undefined realization of 'having-to-act-without-knowing-how'. This realization contained within itself the want of 'something' that would make the action worthwhile. A second moment must have followed this realization, because it is clear that one is not brought to action simply by the feeling of 'having-to-act-without-knowing-how'. The only thing that one can initially do is, to do something, experimentally. That is the only way in which one can determine how to act meaningfully, by doing something to discover which act replaces the realization of 'having-to-act-without-knowing-how' with the realization of 'this is it'. Evidently individuals and peoples have been able to find such actions, into which they packed their deepest reality. And evidently the realization that 'this is it', or 'this is the ultimate' or 'this is ultimately Him' was so radical that they have repeated these actions with great devotion. Thus rites arose.

Nijk speaks only of actions, and thus rites in the strict sense, but one can assume that the same is true of the whole composed of symbol, symbolic act and symbolic language, that is, ritual in the strict sense of the word. In regard to symbolic language, the repetition involves words that 'made sense' and therefore were repeated. They became formulae.

Now, one can understand the deeper reality which is dealt with in Nijk's hypothesis very profoundly. One is then undoubtedly touching upon central rituals, for instance, those dealing with death. But ritual also opens out much more broadly. Everyday life is full of rituals. From morning to night, life runs according to rituals. That begins when one rises: getting up always takes place according to a very strict repetition: washing one's face, dressing, opening the curtains. Then there is the breakfast table: people always sit in the same place, wait to begin until everyone is there, pass the food around, tell what has happened. Sometimes the rituals are individual. Someone recently said to me, "after breakfast I always stop to think what I am going to do for the day, how I will go about it". Someone else told me about the little boy across the

---

19 A. NIJK: *Secularisatie. Over het gebruik van een woord* (Rotterdam 1968) 256-339.

street, who, as he left for school, always turned around at least five times and called out to his mother "See y'all later!", while she continued to stand outside until he reached the corner. Still another once told me he had a friend who has a very laborious, step-by-step procedure for filling and lighting his pipe in moments when he feels really good. In the evening there are many rituals of reading the newspaper, watching the news, closing the curtains, getting the children into bed. Particularly the last is often a detailed ritual. A mother told of her two-and-a-half year old son:[20]

> Every evening after I have kissed him and held his hand I also have to kiss the doll he sleeps with, and shake both its hands, and then do the same with the four feet of a stuffed horse that lies at the foot of the bed. Once I've done that, he sits up once more and asks that I give him one more kiss and say good night one last time.

The clothing we wear, in all its variants, is permeated with ritual: clothing for children and adults, for man and woman or unisex; we dress according to the latest fashion,[21] or consciously deviate from it in protest, but even this protest becomes a ritual conduct. The clothing of clergy, professionals and the military forms a peculiar variant, each having all of their own differences and distinctions: epaulets, stars, buttons, ribbons, colors.[22] Then there are rituals of greeting. A speaker is greeted and introduced according to an established pattern. When people greet each other in company, a number of stereotyped actions are always performed: men close their suit coat, straighten their clothing, make sure their hair is in place, stand to shake hands or give a kiss of greeting, sit in the place indicated, drink a cup of coffee or tea, and so forth. And there are still more: birthday rituals, the rituals of Christmas and New Year, those for dedicating a building, the start of a school year, in sports, at protest rallies, etc.[23]

It is clear that in the case of these everyday rituals it can not be a matter of repeated contact with the very deepest levels of reality. Rather, one could here speak of meaningful communication with others and with the world around us. This meaningful communication is only possible thanks to ritual. If one were to exclude that, there would be an empty space.

20 H. WERNER: *Einführung in die Entwicklungspsychologie* (München 1953) 302-303.
21 R. BARTHES: *Le système de la mode* (Paris 1967).
22 Cf. J. MAERTENS: *Ritologiques IV. Dans la peau des autres. Essai d'anthropologie des inscriptions vestimentaires* (Paris 1978).
23 Anyone wishing an overview of the wealth of human ritual should read MAERTENS: *Ritologiques* I-V (Paris 1978); I. *Le dessin sur la peau. Essai d'anthropologie des inscriptions tégumentaires*; II. *Le corps sexionné. Essai d'anthropologie des inscriptions génitales*; III. *Le masque et le miroir. Essai d'anthropologie des revêtements faciaux*; IV. *Dans la peau des autres. Essai d'anthropologie des inscriptions vestimentaires*; V. *Le jeu du mort. Essai d'anthropologie des inscriptions du cadavre*.

These small social gaps are only prevented by repeating what once was created as a meaningful complex of actions and has been accepted as such.[24] If people repeatedly had to begin again from scratch, it would make life unbearable. One can imagine in the everyday situations mentioned, repeatedly encountering the sense of 'having-to-act-without-knowing-how'. Then life would be full of lacunae and proceed only by fits and starts. We would become very tense and dead tired. Rituals are directed precisely at making progress in life possible when it threatens to seize up. They are necessary to maintain the continuity and coherence of existence. Even where people wish to free themselves of ritual, there quickly arise other latent but established patterns of action. People simply can not live without a sort of 'Ordinary'.

The aspect of repetition, that is essential for ritual, should not allow us to forget that ritual is always a matter of symbol, symbolic act and symbolic language. Thus, what we have said with regard to symbol, symbolic acts and symbolic language is also true for ritual. Rituals are not entities of signs. Thus in and through ritual we actually take part in the reality that is called up through the ritual, are really taken up in the far-reaching sense of what is performed in and through ritual.[25] In one way or another, all ritual itself shares in that reality. In itself, it carries something of the meaning that it calls up. While we stride along in a protest march, the perspective springs open. We do not walk simply to get somewhere; it is not a matter of a purely purposeful and efficient action. Our walking is a 'loaded' action, it truly takes strides forward. We carry signs and banners and repeatedly chant the same slogans. In doing so we declare that the nuclear arms race is a dead end. Thus, the accent shifts in the direction of symbolism. Such rituals function as bridges across boundaries. No further explanation is necessary. They speak for themselves. We are involved as whole persons. We can express ourselves in what we do repeatedly.

2.2. Some characteristics

We can somewhat further expand our consideration of ritual. Ritual is particularly characterized by several properties that deserve separate attention.

---

24 Cf. also A. HAHN: Kultische und säkulare Riten und Zeremonien in soziologischer Sicht, in A. HAHN a.o.: *Anthropologie des Kults. Die Bedeutung des Kults für das Überleben des Menschen* (Freiburg 1977) 51 ss. and 67 ss. Hahn also sees the lacunae created by 'having-to-act-without-knowing-how' as a criterion for the rite. However, the distinction which he makes between rite and ceremony seems to me to be rather artificial. What he calls a ceremony is, in my view, an integrating part of ritual.

25 I emphatically say 'in and through ritual'; thus ritual is not only preparation for this participation. See G. LUKKEN: *De onvervangbare weg van de liturgie* (Hilversum 1980) 22-33.

2.2.1. Palliative and channeling function

From the foregoing, it appears that rituals function to provide a sort of relief.[26] They relieve us of having in each case to discover anew how to proceed and constantly have to confer with others. This is also true for faith. Thanks to rituals, the believer need not repeatedly seek the way again in every new situation or life's difficulty. Rituals are thus a help in new life experiences. In this way, ritual shields the most personal and intimate side of a person's life. This naturally also contains a risk. It can lead to a superficiality and segregation of personal expression. In ritual, one can also, in a way of speaking, creep away from oneself. As rituals become older, time can begin to function as an ally in the further corrosion of the ritual: it becomes an inadequate expression of what troubles us.

Immediately connected with the function of ritual as relief is the function of ritual in channeling the strong emotions that come with any crisis situation. In the case of another's death, ritual fills the lacunae and prevents a blind, random explosion of feelings. It helps one to react sensibly in this situation and actively seek an answer, before reaching the point of complete personality disorganization.[27] In this, one must realize that the good ritual does not make one immune to anger, grief and doubt, that it does not repress existing conflicts and does not function purely as a sort of lightening rod to lead emotions away. What ritual does is to structure the tension that comes out of the conflict, with all the emotions that accompany it. Thus it is not a matter of repression, but of processing and channeling the emotions, of steering and shaping them.[28] This does not only involve feelings of pain, grief and rage, but equally overwhelming feelings of happiness, joy and awe. It can also happen that people can not express their feelings about positive occurrences, or do not know how to do so. One can think, for instance, of the overwhelming feelings that accompany the birth of a child. These feelings too must be processed and directed. Ritual makes it possible to express them in actions and absorb them. Rituals are thus equally important on joyous occasions; there too they help us across the border and do justice to our emotional life.

2.2.2. Mediating function with the past

In one way or another, rituals always carry with them the past from which they come.[29] Rituals are already there; they are ready for us when

---

26 JETTER: *Symbol und Ritual* 54-55.
27 HAHN: *Kultische und säkulare Riten* 67-68. Cf. also IDEM: *Religion und der Verlust der Sinngebung. Identitätsprobleme in der modernen Gesellschaft* (Frankfurt 1974) 72 ss.
28 F. TENBRUCK: Geschichtserfahrung und Religion in der heutigen Gesellschaft, in *Spricht Gott in der Geschichte* (Freiburg 1972) 85.
29 JETTER: *Symbol und Ritual* 96-97.

we arrive. They have something of the familiarity of our childhood home and the mother church. Even new rituals reflect the past: are there not many similarities between peace marches and old prayer processions? I find what J. Ebbers wrote characteristic:[30]

> When I read and heard accounts of therapeutic rituals, the stories seemed to make sense. (...) Even now, if I develop a ritual with a client, I often see before me images of earlier church services: the many candles and flowers, and praying people out of Purgatory on All Souls' Day. Sometimes I can nearly smell the odor of incense when I think back to the requiem masses where I served as acolyte.

Rituals play an impressive role as a mediator with the past. They remind us in a very personal way of where we have come from and, on that basis, give us confidence for the future. In the history of the churches, liturgies have always been the most enduring and effective mediators of belief. In this way, rituals guarantee our continuity with the past. Undoubtedly, however, the fact that rituals sometimes obstinately and wrongly offer resistance against renewal is connected with this quality. It can also happen that they continue to lead a life of their own when they are no longer functional. This is true of the changing of the guard at Buckingham Palace, for scores of rituals in high society and the diplomatic service, for the Pope's Swiss Guards, and for all sorts of national customs. They become folklore and protocol. As such, they then receive a new symbolic value.

2.2.3. *Ethical function*

What is symbolized in ritual refers to a deeper reality. In that sense, ritual is a window through which one, so to speak, perceives unsuspected perspectives and enters into something of that other reality in life.

But symbolization does not stop there. What ritual symbolizes also penetrates life itself. Ritual thus also has an import for non-ritual actions. It can help us to better come to terms with the dark, frightening, angry and impenetrable in life.[31] However, it can also be an impulse setting us to work in a human community. When one can speak of a full-grown and authentic ritual, then something of that which is experienced in and through the ritual almost of its own accord also permeates life itself. The ritual really need not repeatedly or expressly have to say anything that professes this connection with life; this connection is simply inherent in a good ritual. Thus ritual influences our ethical acts. It must not be dis-

---

30 J. EBBERS: *Een bevrijding van knellende banden*, in O. VAN DER HART a.o.: *Afscheidsrituelen in psychotherapie* (Baarn 1981) 44.
31 JETTER: *Symbol und Ritual* 101.

torted into an ethic, but will have everything to do with ethics even as it remains itself. Where a division occurs between ritual and ethics, ritual should be revised, or it has been performed with too little devotion.

2.2.4. *Invocatory function*

When we symbolize, the perspective springs open. There is, so to speak, a 'transfinalisation': things, acts and words change meaning, they get a new sense, full of import. A watch that I inherited from my father and that I now have on the mantlepiece is in no visible way distinguishable from other watches, but through the fact that he wore it, it has been transmuted. It has gotten another meaning and has become a symbol of his life, of how he dealt with time. It also calls up his relation to his grandchildren: how he sometimes held the watch by their ear in order to let them listen to its soft ticking.

But symbolism can happen in entirely different ways. It can reverse a chance of nature. This is the case when it is directed toward opening up perspectives in order to dispel evil. This aspect too is indispensable in human ritual. We can not live life without invoking and exorcising. There is continual occasion for this. Despite all progress, the natural environment is still always a threat to us. We still experience destructive floods. Hurricanes cause great destruction. Volcanic eruptions cost thousands of lives. We are dependent on the weather; ultimately we have no control over it. Not all diseases are under our control, and certainly not death itself.[32] Then there are power structures, that are more powerful than we would want. How many are ruthlessly oppressed? How will we hold back the arms race?

The sense of invocation and exorcism today appears to be, that through them the nature of negative powers can be changed. We deprive the mystery of evil of its terrifying power by expressing in a ritual way that this does not have the last word. We call evil by its name in order to banish it.[33] We suffer in our powerlessness, but at the same time express our conviction that this can not and may not be our future. As Christians, we do this in the realization that in God's name, in Jesus' name, evil can not and may not have the last word. Oosterhuis tells the following story about the birth of his son: "My son Tjeerd-Pieter was born on Christmas Eve, 1971. I immediately gave his a kiss on his forehead and said, 'You are Tjeerd-Pieter David and bogeys don't exist'".[34] This is exorcism speaking.

---

[32] Cf. A. GREELEY: Mislukking en buitenwereld, in *Concilium* 12 (1976) no 3, 35-36.
[33] G. LUKKEN: Enkele kanttekeningen over het exorcisme, in *Tijdschrift voor liturgie* 52 (1968) 259-260.
[34] N. BERGKAMP and H. OOSTERHUIS: Een lijk verbranden is vreselijk, in *De Gelderlander* (Saturday 21. October 1972) 4.

Ritual invocation is thus in no way something that only is at home in primitive cultures. After it has been subjected to criticism by our culture, it remains possible and even necessary, in a second innocence. At the launch of the first Atlas rocket at Cape Kennedy, all the technicians shouted "Go, Atlas, go!", constantly repeating it as a litany. Even there, where only technical control can set things in motion, people suddenly realized that there are powers that we do not control, but must invoke.[35]

2.2.5. Expressive function

Rituals are givens passed on to us. Yet at the same time, and necessarily, they are expressive of ourselves. That expressiveness is of essential importance. If we could not discover anything of ourselves in ritual, it would remain external to us and inert. However, ritual helps us precisely in giving a face to what we experience and helping us understand ourselves. As it does so, we need ritual because in keeping our experiences only in our inner self, they would never become a part of us. They would remain uncertain, unstable, searching, sealed in themselves. Ritual helps us really experience that which has happened to us.[36] Thus ritual is an expression of our selves and what preoccupies us.

The expressive function of rituals is valid not only for the more central rituals, but also for everyday rituals. In the latter, who we are, how we deal with one another and what our world image is also comes to the fore. Our everyday rituals collectively form a great ritual book. To study it is very fascinating, because it brings our selves to light in relevant ways.[37]

Ritual can be an expression of our self, even when it is rehearsed literally. Then it is a matter of performing it with true devotion, and not just formally or by rote, because, according to the rules, that is how it must be. But because ritual is also an expression of those who perform it, that automatically brings with it the fact that variants appear in the ritual. This breathes life into the established framework. That happens, first and foremost, because these persons are involved in the ritual, which automatically leads to their personal accents in its performance. Consequently, certain parts of the ritual as such can be more open and variable. One could think, for instance, of the sermon in the Christian liturgy; even in the absolutely regulated liturgy between Trent and Vatican II, this variable remains present.[38] Another possibility is that new elements will be brought into the ritual. For instance, we laid a Hebrew

---

35 Cf. HAHN: *Kultische und säkulare Riten* 62.
36 Cf. A. ULEYN: Drie idealen waardoor groepen zich laten leiden, in *Speling* 27 (1975) 95; A. VERGOTE: *Het huis is nooit af. Gedachten over mens en religie* (Antwerpen-Utrecht 1974) 121.
37 JETTER: *Symbol und Ritual* 116-117.
38 Cf. JETTER: *Symbol und Ritual* 257 ss.

Bible on the coffin, because it was this particular funeral. To the degree that the singularity of a ritual is emphasized, more new and individual elements will be present. Finally, there is the possibility of an entirely new ritual.

The new within a ritual may not, however, reach the point at which the repetitive aspect entirely disappears. This is true objectively, for the ritual as such. But it is also true for the experience of those taking part: for some, the familiar thread is lost more quickly than for others. A field of tension which one must always acknowledge arises here. But one must not forget – and I underscore this once again – that new rituals can arise.

Finally, it must be remarked that in ritual, creativity is always commanded. In literally rehearsing a ritual, this is commanded by the creativity in the attitude of devotion with which the ritual is performed, and through which personal accents will appear. In the rise of a new ritual, this is primarily expressed in the newly created forms themselves, that must be performed with devotion. Between these two extremes, many variants are possible.

2.2.6. Condensation

In ritual, the normal and everyday is accentuated and stylized, so that the perspective on it can alter. Ritual condenses reality. It sets it somewhat apart, and in a certain sense lifts the thing, act or word out of the realm of the ordinary. The contours become more sharply accentuated. The pace is restrained in order to stride ahead. One stays still, creates a private space, keeps distance. One can speak of a certain effect of estrangement with regard to what was actually expected. So to speak, ritual focuses attention on itself in a peculiar way in order to be able in and through that to reach the undefinable reality that it will call up. The condensation thus does not take place for its own sake, but on behalf of the symbolism: only thus can the participation in the farther reaching, other world be achieved.

2.2.7. Social function

Ritual is not purely directed toward the I. To be sure, ritual can be expressive of one's self, but as such it is just as much directed toward the other. In ritual one expresses oneself in a way recognizable to oneself. But this is done within a structure of communicative acts that has been handed down to one, and can be recognized by others. The ritual is, as it were, a call to the other to communicate with me. It awakens collectivity. By definition, rituals have a social function. That is true for the I and for the Thou that will communicate with each other. It is also true for the small group and the larger community. As the I together with the other finds identity in and through ritual, so the members of a group or larger community, precisely as members of that group or community, find their identity in and through ritual. The community needs ritual precisely in order to be a community. Without ritual the community would disintegrate. They realize themselves in and through ritual. Without the structure of communicative acts in and through which it expresses and at the same time repeatedly encounters its particular face, a community simply could not exist. You can not imagine a political party without programmatic and more or less festive party gatherings, that constitute or affirm and strengthen it. If one studies the rituals of a community, one will come to realize how vital the social function of ritual is. A community better instructs one about itself by its celebrations than by an investigation of its internal structures or its ways of interacting. One could try to find out about the views on marriage of, say, a Zambian by interviewing him (or her), but one could immerse oneself much more deeply in the Zambian culture when one merely studied a Zambian wedding feast, or took part in it.

The social function of ritual reaches still further. Precisely because the moment in which it is repeated is essential for ritual, it brings us, precisely because of the fact that it has been handed down to us, into contact in a vital way with generations before us, with the past of our own community. The social function of ritual thus also extends to those who have preceded us. And does it not also touch in another way on the future of our community: is ritual not preserved, renewed and handed on for the sake of those who will come after us?

2.3. Strength and weakness

In our society, the words rite and ritual rather often have a negative connotation. People put up resistance against rituals or are offended by them, because by definition rituals have to do with the purely formulaic and stereotypical. They cover up and conceal. They lead to dishonest and hypocritical behavior. Rituals deal with an unreal world, or they are directed at maintaining power.

Here one runs up against the dual nature of ritual. Precisely that which is the power of ritual can also be its weakness. The palliative function can also lead to superficiality and escapism. It may be that ritual, rather than channeling feelings, only formalizes and covers them up. Rituals can be fatally stubborn and resist adaptation, precisely when this is necessary. They can be means of propping up the existing order. Rituals can become so isolated that they lose touch with everyday life and ethical acts. They then communicate with a purely vertical reality, without taking into account the horizontal dynamic of that which the depth of reality hands on. The condensation of ritual can degenerate into ritual narcissism. The invocational character can deteriorate into pure magic and superstition. In the social dimension, ritual can also run off the rails. One has only to think of the initiation rituals of Nazism and fascism, the rituals of mass demonstrations and military parades, of the bread and circuses of the Roman Empire. One realizes that this last phenomenon can equally appear in Christianity, when ritual is taken into the service of purely institutional, centralizing interests or certain ideological dogmatisms.

The weakness of ritual springs just as much to the eye when one imagines the deviations involved with the moment of repetition that is so essential. Through these characteristics rituals can easily deteriorate into pure routine and the ordinary, when they are performed without any devotion or creativity. This can be the case in the secular rituals of burial or marriage at the city clerk's office, but it is equally well a possibility in every religious ritual.

It can also happen that ritual comes too much to serve the interests of something other. Then it is lowered to being a sign that, so to speak, must be passed as quickly as possible. This is the case when a ritual is only performed because it has to be, as when some Christians only go to church on Sunday because they must. The Sunday church visit then becomes a sign of good conduct. But ordinary rituals of getting on with others can also be performed purely because they are required. One thinks of certain rules of etiquette that have been strongly formalized. They are performed in what one might say was an entirely 'empty' way. I must, however, note that sometimes such a strongly formalized and 'empty' repetition receives again a symbolic character. This can appear in the case of protocol: by sticking to it in a very precise and formal way, one can take part in that private world that is protected and delimited by protocol. Military exercises like marching, standing at attention and presenting arms, precisely because of their formal and mandatory character, suggest discipline, strength and power.

Now that religious rituals are no longer so strongly prescribed, another possibility through which rituals can decline into bodies of signs reveals itself. The ritual can be put into the service of a certain ethical or political strategy. Such a subordination misunderstands the basic character of ritual.

Rituals can also become compulsive actions at the moment of repetition. When I have forgotten to lock the door of my car several times, the inclination can arise to perform this action even if it is certain that I have locked the car. Religious rituals also lend themselves to compulsive actions: for instance, those with excessive scruples may repeatedly confess their sins and receive absolution.

In connection with the theme of the strength and weakness of ritual, I finally want to report a remark that F. Sierksma, the scholar of comparative religions, made during a discussion. He noted that in the animal world, both hypertrophy and atrophy of rituals can be found. From this, it would seem that this phenomenon can also appear among people. One could think of individuals, but also of various cultural eras. One might ask if during the centuries before Vatican II one might not speak of ritual hypertrophy in the church. In that period, a considerable amount of training was necessary in order to learn to command the complicated ritual of the liturgy. The weakness of ritual can also, thus, express itself in hypertrophy. But we must be cautious about all too quickly judging this as hypertrophy from the perspective of our own culture, which is characterized rather by an atrophy of ritual.

Whatever the case, ritual can be used in a negative way, and undoubtedly the negative connotations of words like rite and ritual is connected to this. But the trend of this word usage is difficult to defend. It ignores the other side of the coin: the considerable power of ritual, which we have previously discussed. To unilaterally judge ritual as negative is as inconsistent as calling all human actions bad because crime is also possible.

2.4. Rites of passage

Both the lacunae created by 'having-to-act-without-knowing-how' and repetition are essentially connected with ritual. Ritual makes it possible for us to fall back on a complex of actions that are, so to speak, a bridge thrown over the void. Ritual makes it possible to cross over from one situation to another. In that sense, any ritual could be called a rite of passage.

The term 'rite of passage', first used by A. van Gennep, has however a more precise meaning.[39] It refers to rituals that are concerned with the transition from one phase of life to another: the birth of a child, the beginning of a course of study (be it primary school, high school or college), first love, engagement, marriage, the novitiate, entering a religious order, ordination, beginning a major journey, farewells, old age, burial. There are also 'cosmic' transitions: the passage of the seasons, New Year's, entering a new century. One might be inclined to think that there are two elements in these rites of passage: the phase left, and the phase entered. However, according to Van Gennep there are always three phases in a rite of passage: the detachment, in which the individual is in a ritual way separated from the earlier social position; the intermediate stage (*période de marge*), in which the ambiguity of the individual's position is ritually expressed and made bearable; and the integration into the

---

[39] A. VAN GENNEP: *Les rites de passage* (Paris-La Haye 1969; first edition 1909); cf. J. HAMELINE: Relire van Gennep... Les rites de passage, in *La maison-Dieu* 112 (1972) 133-143.

new group, in which the entry into the new position is ritually celebrated. Van Gennep indicates that a particular accent can be placed upon any one of these three elements. For instance, in rituals concerning death, it is the detachment; in marriage, the integration; in engagements and the novitiate, the intermediate stage.[40]

As a collective ritual, a rite of passage is only possible when the transition between social positions which fulfills it from the point of view of the society ends in a rather predictable way. Rituals that are valid for the whole of the community presuppose a certain consistency in situation among different individuals: despite the fact that for one particular individual it will be a one-time occurrence, the situation is still considered a repetition within the larger community. In a certain sense, the ritual must be possible irrespective of the individuals.[41]

Our society doesn't seem to know what to do with existing rites of passage. There is discussion of a great multiplicity, by which the collectivity of ritual is broken through. At the same time, we are challenged by new voids which must be filled by actions which must ease the transition from one situation to another – for instance, when a man and woman begin a relationship without marriage, or the beginning of a homosexual relationship; when children leave home, leaving behind the still reasonably young parents together; the transition to living alone after divorce; entering a period of unemployment, perhaps without prospects.

2.5. Religious and Christian dimension

The deeper reality toward which ritual is oriented can remain purely within this world. For instance, funeral rituals can be oriented toward parting from the dead, channeling feelings, getting through the period between the death and integration into, and the processing of, the new social status as widow or widower. Ritual can concern purely human values, that remain within this world: the experience of peace, reconciliation, security, trust, and justice.

But ritual can reach beyond that. At the beginning of the 1970's, one of the largest peace marches ever took place: the protest march on Washington, against the Vietnam War. Forty thousand people, each with a sign with the name of a dead soldier on their chest, marched past the White House. There they shouted the name of the dead soldier, sang about the disappearance of young men and women, and about peace. In a sort of intercession, they prayed for the end of the terrible war, and for money no longer to be spent on weapons, but on the struggle against poverty. They laid the names in a coffin and marched to the national

---

40 VAN GENNEP: *Les rites de passage* 13-15.
41 HAHN: *Kultische und säkulare Riten* 70-72.

cemetery to bury them, led by seven drummers with black-shrouded drums and the widow of one of the dead soldiers. During the event, reporters asked participants about their experience. One woman said this was the most religious experience she had participated in over the past years. Characteristically, the Dutch subtitles on the program left out the word 'religious'. Whatever the case, what for one person is a radical human experience, can have a great religious import for another.

The same is true for the peace and protest marches held subsequently. Very ordinary rituals can call up religious experiences. One could even say that it is precisely rituals that contribute to religious experience. "Rituals are the mother tongue of religion".[42] If you go back to the source, possibly the distinction between religious and non-religious ritual behavior is purely artificial. The etymological root *rta*, that goes far back in Indo-European languages, makes one think of a yet undifferentiated world of experience, in which the divine and human worlds are connected. In one way or another, everything had a religious dimension, and, conversely, nothing was specifically religious.[43] In our culture we have been taught to make the distinction. But the fact remains that there is a hidden meaning present in human rituals, through which they have a religious import when seen from a particular point of view. It is also true that it is precisely rituals that are able to awaken religious experience. This is connected with the revelatory character of ritual. Symbolic communication has characteristics that one could call 'meta-communicative', to use Habermas's term.[44] Precisely because of these qualities, ritual is the language that pre-eminently fits religion, and conversely, ritual is first and foremost a religious phenomenon.

It would be going too far afield here to treat the question of what precisely is being indicated by the word 'religious'. It is sufficient to establish that in the experience of the religious we are dealing with values that in some unknown way are distributed above humans themselves. People experience a greater, a majestic but unapproachable dimension of existence. It involves the experience of the absolute. Thus the experience does not have to be oriented toward an approachable person in order to be denoted as religious. It is true, however, that religious experience comes to its fullest development when the transcendent, absolute reality also is given a name.

In most religions the transcendent, absolute reality is identified as a personal Thou, as Someone over and against us, who addresses us and

---

42 JETTER: *Symbol und Ritual* 93.
43 JETTER: *Symbol und Ritual* 93-94.
44 Legitimationsprobleme der Religion. Treffen Jürgen Habermas, Arbeitskreis "Theologie und Politik", in H. BAHR e.a.: *Religionsgespräche. Zur gesellschaftlichen Rolle der Religion* (Darmstadt 1975) 29.

toward whom we can direct ourselves. Here we touch upon the Christian dimension of ritual.

Christian ritual is oriented toward the revelation of a God who has shown Himself in history, first in Israel, but particularly in one of that nation, Jesus of Nazareth, who chose the side of the poor and the weak, who was ignominiously executed, and has become the first-born from the dead. According to the Christian faith, in Him we are saved. Christians believe that He gives the world, history and life its ultimate meaning. All Christian ritual is directed toward Jesus of Nazareth, in whom God, full of compassion, regards humankind, and in whom He is constantly at work for us. In and through this person, it is possible to approach God.

In Christian ritual the cross also stands as a central presentative symbol of what has happened in Jesus of Nazareth. In the East, people find the icon, with its infinitely varied representations in which the Christ-figure is none the less always central, to be a presentative symbol of what Christian ritual is aiming at. I use the word 'presentative' here with deliberation.[45] It means that Christian ritual does not purely look back to the past as past, but to that past as being contemporary and present in our tangible world and history. This all occurs in the field of tension present in symbolism. In other words, one can speak of a comprehensive presence in and through tangible ritual, but this presence is not such that it coincides with the ritualized; one can also speak of a nonpresence that compels further acts and a look toward the future. Presentative ritual thus gives real ground underfoot, but at the same time is a marching-order toward the future.

In Christian ritual we encounter a symbolism in which one can speak of an inversion of values (*Umwertung aller Werte*). One does not realize this, when one sees the cross only at the apex of church towers, as a decoration on the vestments of a person of authority or as a frequently hung wall ornament. The subversive character of the cross only forces itself upon one when realizes it is an instrument of torture. The cross is like the gallows, the guillotine, the garrote, the firing squad, the electric chair, the gas chamber. In Christian ritual, the central figure is the man of sorrows, his eyes glazed in death. The oppressed in today's world rightly depict him with deep wounds and infinite sorrow in his eyes, as one cast aside. It was because of his suffering and death that God has exalted him and given him a name that is greater than any other name (Phil. 2:9). This executed man lives by God.[46]

---

45 For an explanation of the term 'presentative', see part 3 of the next contribution (no. 4).
46 It is not possible to go more deeply into the Christian dimension of ritual here. Readers are referred to my book *De onvervangbare weg van de liturgie* 41-100. About the uniqueness of Jesus of Nazareth, see f.i. H. OOSTERHUIS and P. HOOGEVEEN: *God is ieder ogenblik nieuw. Gesprekken met Edward Schillebeeckx* (=Annalen van het Thijmgenootschap 70, no. 2) (Baarn 1982) 38-50 and 65-74.

According to the Constitution on the Liturgy, of the Second Vatican Council, "there is hardly any proper use of material things that cannot (...) be directed toward human sanctification and the praise of God" (Art. 61). Thus, the Constitution takes all human symbolization with utmost seriousness. At its heart, virtually all human ritual can be expressive of Christian reality. One can thus speak of a deep coherence between human and Christian ritual. Christian ritual has a strong and indispensable anthropological basis, that coincides with the fact that in Jesus of Nazareth God has become a partner in our human history in such an intimate way. Any weakening in the anthropological basis of Christian ritual damages the unique character of this ritual. The fully human face of the liturgy in no way whatsoever competes with its Christian character. On the contrary, only a really human ritual can represent the Christian reality. This is expressed in a striking way in the classical axiom that can be normative for all liturgical ministry and creativity: the sacraments are there for the sake of humans (*sacramenta propter homines*).

Thus, Christian ritual is closely connected with human life itself, and with the full extent of this life: from birth to death and from morning to evening. There is no season, no day, no hour in which it could not occur. All that a human life brings with it, the deeply radical and the everyday, can have a place in Christian ritual, and thus can be taken up in the perspective of the mystery of Jesus of Nazareth, who was executed and who lives. In the perspective of the cross, an inversion of values that permeates all human life has its place. "One can only talk about revolution if the extraordinary becomes the everyday", is the slogan painted on a building in Cuba.[47] Christian ritual is really just as subversive.

3. FINDING SALVATION AND HEALING

In our communication with reality, rituals play a very familiar role. They give us access to reality that comes only in this way, and in no other. This has important consequences. In particular, it means that without rituals a part of reality remains veiled for us. It is impossible to gain access to that part of reality in any other way, because it is only uncovered through ritual. In one way or another ritual is itself a part of that reality, because it participates in it. Thus rituals are irreplaceable. You can not do without them, under penalty of losing contact with reality and impoverishing human experience.

Perhaps the comparison with a work of art can make this clearer. You can try to convert a work of art into concepts, but the reality represented in the art work reaches further. You can only reach that through the

---

47 Quotation in M. MARTIN: *Fest und Alltag* (Stuttgart 1973) 36.

mediation of the artwork itself. You can not translate a work of art. When you try to tell someone about it and call it up in words, it is necessarily impoverished. The unique character of the mediation is thus far from accidental. An artwork is, after all, itself the carrier, participant and representation of what it calls up. There is thus no other immediate communication possible with the reality that the artwork represents.[48] So also in and through ritual we gain an access to reality that is entirely in a class of its own and irreplaceable.

When rituals are not performed, the experience of reality is lost, and this loss is all the more radical because it involves the impoverishment of an experience of reality that touches human existence as such. Rituals, after all, involve precisely the mystery of human reality: our persons, our relations with others and with the world. They touch that reality which is not to be grasped and which can not be authenticated, the transcendent reality where the religious also finds its point of contact.

Rituals are not about that controllable reality which is the business of technique and the empirical sciences. When the faithful pray to be freed from illness or saved from disasters, or for fertile fields, some might say they are using the wrong means for dealing with reality. But rituals are not about technical causality or a manageable communication with reality. There is an alternative. In and through ritual people let go of their own capacities. They permit the reality which surpasses them its own existence. They seek access to the divine source, to the transcendent secret of existence, to the renewing power of mystery. They express hope that the future shall be greater. Rituals are the praxis of faith and hope, not of might and control.[49] They have to do with a most basic fact of human experience regarding ourselves, society and the world. Rituals are thus a key to human existence and to the ground that bears it. They shed light in the vicissitudes of this life. They are comprehensive and powerful. This comprehensiveness and power remain hidden from outsiders who ask for proof. Rituals only reveal themselves *in actu*, to those who perform the rituals with devotion.

It is, then, a matter of the deeper roots of existence. Severing contact with these roots leads to a constricted consciousness, to chaos and dispersion, to the bisection of human existence. Ritual is precisely directed toward neutralizing that dispersion and making people whole. Rituals heal and mend people.

In a striking way, F. Buitendijk describes how indispensable symbolic language is for public mental health.[50] How a child is spoken to in the first

---

48 L. KOLAKOWSKI: *Geist und Ungeist christlicher Traditionen* (Stuttgart 1971) 90-91.
49 R. SCHAEFFLER: Kultisches Handeln. Die Frage nach Proben seiner Bewahrung und nach Kriterien seiner Legitimation, in HAHN: *Kultische und säkulare Riten* 40-42.
50 F. BUITENDIJK: Taal en samenleven, in *Taal en gezondheid* (= Serie Geestelijke Volksgezondheid 40) (Utrecht 1969) 9 ss.

years of its life, and how it begins to speak, is of decisive importance. In this process, first of all, the mother plays a major role. In how the child approaches the mother, her presence in expression, countenance, gesture and voice, lie the question and the expectation of an answer, an answer that meets an original desire for community and contact with reality. Through her presence, the mother allows the world to be present for the child. Initially in this process the mother is the only speaker and the child follows everything attentively. The child does not do this purely as a spectator, who wants to establish facts empirically and wants to see the world described in unambiguous language. No, it is a matter of words and names that pave the way to life itself, to total reality. The child learns to speak in this way: it learns to give a name to the world, because it can enter in to contact with it in a human way. In this process, in which the child learns to speak, it is thus a matter of symbolic language: it is about words, not merely terms. It is a matter of dialogue, in which initially the mother speaks and 'brings things to light' for the child. The child gradually enters into this process, becomes active and joins in the revelation. The time comes when it begins to ask all kinds of questions: what is this, what is that? Everything must get a name and be revealed. In this way the child grows into a mentally healthy person.

As long as the process runs in the way just described, the climate will be right for the child's healthy growth. But when the child is only spoken to with terms, frustrations arise. When a child receives no answers to questions about deeper reality, the threat of deep-seated disorders arises. When, for instance, a child asks where someone goes after death, and only gets a superficial-descriptive answer on the order of 'after his death grandpa is buried in the ground', mischief is sown. One could thus say that a child is in all respects under the influence of language. One must take into account what is broken when a child is only spoken to with terms, in impersonal language. This leads to an impoverished consciousness, loneliness, frustration, fear. The child can no longer find contact with life and with reality. One expressive way that this surfaces is in stammering and stuttering.

What is true for symbolic language is also true for symbols and symbolic acts. For a person's mental health, not only symbolic language but also symbols and symbolic acts are indispensable. Symbols and symbolic acts appear equally basic in so far as they function as a sort of irreplaceable foundation with respect to symbolic language.[51]

After these considerations, it is not difficult to see that rituals are indispensable for the mental well-being of individuals and society. After all, it is precisely in rituals that symbolic language, symbols and symbolic acts

---

51 For a further explication one may refer to part 3 of the next contribution (no. 4) in which the corporeality of the non-verbal is discussed.

come together. Moreover, I must emphasize that merely the coming together of symbolic language, symbol and symbolic act as such, is not sufficient. It is clear from the foregoing that there must be a balanced confluence of the three.

Thus, when a society lacks rituals, it loses contact with the fullness of reality. Then people come into conflict, and there is a danger to mental health. Without ritual, there is no life. Rituals simply are a part of the equipment of a healthy human being and a healthy society. Martin makes this point more sharply in regard to the rituals of celebration. When celebration is lacking, people become *untergesund*; one can speak of a *sub-sanitas*, which leads to apathy, a reduction of experience and emotionality, a narrowing of horizons. The characteristic of all true celebration is that it is marked by *Übergesundheit* (*super-sanitas*): one can speak of openness, renewal of consciousness, the presence of spirit and self-awareness.[52]

The Christian life, too, can not be without rituals. They are indispensable and irreplaceable for contact with the Christian reality. Without rituals, access to the deeper Christian reality ultimately remains closed off and the Christian community becomes imbalanced. The Constitution on the Liturgy of Vatican II portrayed liturgy as "the summit toward which the activity of the Church is directed; at the same time it is the fount from which all the Church's power flows" (Art. 10). With that, the irreplaceable role of liturgy is underscored. Rituals have their own structural role. No other activity can be substituted for it. When it is not performed, this rebounds on other sectors of Christian life such as proclamation and service to the world. Proclamation then easily deteriorates into the announcement of truths and the promotion of orthodox doctrine. The symbolic character of the Christian confession of faith (the *symbolon*) disappears into forgetfulness. Service to the world deteriorates into activism that lacks a ground of inspiration; what Christians accomplish in this world is ultimately a gift of God, and takes place in hope of a future kingdom of righteousness and love, that we alone can never bring about. Without rituals the Christian life and community become thoroughly vexed. One of the functions of liturgy is precisely that we, in the words of the Roman preface, 'find salvation and healing'. Salvation and healing: that is a familiar theme in the classic Roman liturgy.

Particularly in the second and third centuries there developed in the ancient church a conception of salvation in which the figure of the Christ as physician took the central place. That development was connected with the worship of Aesculapius, the pagan savior and healer, which had spread throughout the Roman empire. In a certain sense, the influence of

---

52 MARTIN: *Fest und Alltag* 24-28, 77.

Aesculapius has reached into our own time: the red snake twined around a staff that serves as a sign of recognition in the health professions is borrowed from the cult of Aesculapius. Against Aesculapius, Christians proposed the Christ as the true healer. Harnack remarks that the gospel came into the world as a message of well-being for all people, and that the Christians of the first centuries considered the church as a great institute for well-being, a hospital for humankind, in which all the church's activities served as means of healing.[53] In the fourth and fifth centuries the terminology of medical salvation had become a cliche, but Augustine recalibrated these terms by connecting them with words involving *salus*, in which the medical meaning has always reverberated. This created an interference in our reception: the words with 'salv-' got a more concrete content through the medical terms, and the medical word group got greater Christian depth through the salvation terminology.[54]

Thus, when the traditional Roman liturgy often speaks about the actual performance of our 'salvation' or our 'healing' in and through the liturgy, that has a comprehensive meaning. Both words deal with the health of the whole of persons. Oosterhuis correctly translated the word *salutare*, that appears in the fixed introductory formula of all Roman prefaces, as 'in order to find salvation and healing'. That is in the spirit of the old liturgy. In the Christian liturgy, it is not an issue of a purely esoteric and elusive salvation, separate from persons. It is an issue of a salvation that permeates the person. One can speak of salvific healing or healing salvation, because Christian ritual touches persons to the depths of their tangible existence and creates integrity within them. It has to do with our psychic health. Fortmann remarks that religion in the ancient world never made a distinction between the health that it expected from surrender to the divinity and that which we today call psychic health. It is a matter of restoring inner unity, the healing of rifts within the person.[55] Christian ritual is still today directed toward this restoration of inner unity.

The above has important consequences for the relation between Christian liturgy and the anthropology of ritual. One can not speak of competition between them. What we said about the wholesomeness of

---

53 A. HARNACK: *Medizinisches aus der ältesten Kirchengeschichte* (= Texte und Untersuchungen 8) (Leipzig 1892); later on re-edited and inserted in his book *Mission und Ausbreitung des Christentums in den ersten drei Jahrhunderten* I. *Die Mission im Wort und Tat* (Leipzig 1906²) 87-107. Cf. M. ELLEBRACHT: *Remarks on the vocabulary of the ancient orations in the Missale Romanum* (= Latinas christianorum primaeva 18) (Nijmegen 1963) 178 and P. EYKENBOOM: *Het Christus-Medicusmotief in de preken van Augustinus* (Assen 1960) xvi-xix.
54 EYKENBOOM: *Het Christus-Medicusmotief*.
55 H. FORTMANN: *Als ziende de onzienlijke* III B. *Geloof en geestelijke gezondheid* (Hilversum 1968) 88.

ritual in general and about the wholesomeness of Christian ritual makes deep inroads in each other. The anthropology of ritual is necessarily the basis for Christian ritual. In that sense it is also true that the grace of nature presupposes (*gratia supponit naturam*). But it is equally true that truly Christian rituals can contribute to a more humane life and a more humane society.

4. Liturgie und Sinnlichkeit
Über die Bedeutung der Leiblichkeit in der Liturgie

Seit den sechziger Jahren kann man in der Theologie von einer anthropologischen Wende sprechen – das heißt von einer Wende zum Menschen hin. In der Theologie geht es um ein Sprechen über Gott, worauf auch das aus dem Griechischen stammende Wort verweist. Die Theologie konzentriert sich also auf Gott. Aber schon 1925 bemerkte der protestantische Theologe R. Bultmann: "will man von Gott reden, so muß man offenbar *von sich selbst reden*".[1] So verwies er auf die enge Verbundenheit zwischen dem Sprechen über Gott und dem Sprechen über den Menschen. Man kann nicht über Gott sprechen, ohne über den Menschen zu sprechen. Unser Sprechen über Gott ist immer menschliches Sprechen. Es ist bedingt durch die Raumgebundenheit unseres leib-geistigen Daseins und auch durch unsere Bindung an die Zeit: unser Sein in der Geschichte. Diese Erkenntnis ist tief in die Theologie unserer Zeit eingedrungen. 1966 sagte der große Theologe K. Rahner, daß seine Theologie sich sicher auf Gott bezieht, daß er aber ebenso davon überzeugt ist, daß wir nichts über Gott sagen können, ohne auch zugleich über den Menschen zu sprechen und umgekehrt.[2] Und ein Jahr später nannte er die Anthropologie 'den umgreifenden Ort aller Theologie'.[3] Diese anthropologische Wende vollzog sich auch in der christlichen Liturgie. Vor allem seit den sechziger Jahren schenkte die Liturgiewissenschaft dem Platz des Menschen mit all seinen Schattierungen immer mehr Aufmerksamkeit. Dabei rückt die Betonung des Eigenwertes der menschlichen Leiblichkeit ins Zentrum. Hierauf möchte ich zuerst eingehen. Dann will ich mich sowohl mit der Leiblichkeit des Verbalen als des Nicht-Verbalen befassen.

---

* *Liturgie en zintuiglijkheid. Over de betekenis van lichamelijkheid in de liturgie* (Hilversum 1990) 7-35. Übersetzt von G. Merks-Leinen, M.A.
1 R. BULTMANN: Welchen Sinn hat es, von Gott zu reden?, in IDEM: *Glauben und Verstehen. Gesammelte Aufsätze* I (Tübingen 1966⁶) 28.
2 K. RAHNER: *Schriften zur Theologie* VIII (Einsiedeln 1967) 43.
3 K. RAHNER: Grundsätzliche Überlegungen zur Anthropologie und Protologie im Rahmen der Theologie, in J. FEINER und M. LÖHRER (Hrsg.): *Mysterium Salutis. Grundriß heilsgeschichtlicher Dogmatik* II (Einsiedeln 1967) 406.

1. DIE LITURGIE IN EINEM GANZ NEUEN LICHT DURCH DIE BETONUNG DER LEIBLICHKEIT

Die anthropologische Wende brachte die Wiederentdeckung des Menschen als leib-geistige Einheit mit sich.[4] Eine lange Periode des Dualismus wurde überwunden. Man hatte, unter dem Einfluß der griechischen Anthropologie, Leib und Seele zu sehr als getrennte Einheiten aufgefaßt, wobei die Betonung auf der Seele lag, auf dem geistigen Element, im Gegensatz zum leiblichen Element. Wohl ist es so, daß die Kirche in ihrer Lehre immer die Einheit von Leib und Seele verteidigt hat; die griechische Anthropologie führte jedoch zur Unterbewertung des Leibes. Wenn es im Buch der Weisheit 9,15 heißt, daß der sterbliche Leib eine Last für die Seele ist und daß das irdische Zelt den Geist beim Denken behindert, dann ist diese Aussage ohne den griechischen Einfluß unmöglich. Ausgehend von dieser Anthropologie wurde die Religion zuallererst zu einer Sache des Geistes. Das Leibliche stand als das nur Vergängliche, das nur Wechselhafte, das nur Zeitliche dem wahrhaft Religiösen als dem Nicht-Leiblichen, dem Geistigen, dem Unvergänglichen und Beständigen gegenüber. Die Liturgie gehörte zur Welt des Geistigen. Wohl sprach man von Vermittlung zwischen Leib und Materie; diese Vermittlung wurde aber nach dem Jahr 1000 und vor allem in der Zeit nach dem Konzil von Trient (1545-1563) immer flüchtiger, immer mehr eine Randerscheinung, immer mehr stilisiert, formalisiert und verrechtlicht. Man denke an die sehr stark vergeistigten und formalisierten Gebärden und Bewegungen und an die sozusagen verwässerten Symbole: vom Untertauchen im Taufwasser blieb nur noch das Ausgießen einiger Wasserstrahlen über den Kopf des Täuflings übrig; das eucharistische Brot war kein echtes Brot mehr, sondern nur eine dünne, ungesäuerte, runde Hostie; und die sakramentale Salbung bestand nur noch aus einem Kreuzzeichen auf dem Körper mit einem kleinen Wattebausch, getränkt mit geruchlosem Öl. Auch wenn die Kirche die Lehre vom Körper als dem Gefängnis der Seele verwarf, so erfuhr man praktisch doch den Leib als Hindernis auf dem Weg zum Heil. Und dann spreche ich noch nicht von der Reformation, die in den Sakramenten eher eine Hilfe für die menschliche Schwachheit sah. Ich gehe hier nicht weiter darauf ein, wie bedrohend diese Betrachtungsweise des Leiblichen für die Liturgie als solche war. Es scheint mir besser, positiv zu arbeiten und die Frage zu stellen: Welche Erneuerung brachte der wiedergewonnene Aspekt der Leiblichkeit für die Betrachtungsweise der Liturgie?

Man könnte sagen, daß das heutige Bild vom Menschen gut zum ursprünglichen, semitischen Menschenbild der Schrift paßt. Biblisches Sprechen über den Menschen klingt sehr körperlich, so sehr sogar, daß menschliche Gefühle dem Herzen, der Leber, den Nieren und dem Fleisch

---

4 A. VERHEUL: *Inleiding tot de liturgie. Haar theologische achtergrond* (Roermond 1962).

zugeordnet werden; auch unsere Erkenntnisse und freien Entscheidungen werden dem Herzen, den Nieren und dem Fleisch zuerkannt. Auch in der heutigen Anthropologie sieht man die enge Verwobenheit von Körper und Geist. Um es plastisch auszudrücken: Man ist davon überzeugt, daß die Aktivität unseres Geistes in den Gebärden unseres Körpers und vor allem in unseren Gesichtszügen zum Ausdruck kommt; dies gilt schon für das Lachen des kleinen Kindes, das den klassischen römischen Schriftsteller Vergil in Rührung versetzte, bis zum Majestätischen der Totenmaske.

Weil wir Menschen nicht reiner, unkörperlicher Geist sind, können wir nicht von unserer Leiblichkeit absehen. Wir können diesem Leben, dieser Welt nur Sinn geben als leibliche Menschen aus Fleisch und Blut, mit Händen und Füßen, mit Gefühlen und Leidenschaften. Und auch das Heil erreicht uns nicht außerhalb unserer Leiblichkeit. Ich zitiere einen Text des Kirchenvaters Tertullian aus dem dritten Jahrhundert:[5]

> Der Leib ist der Angelpunkt des Seelenheiles. Wenn Gott sich die Seele zu eigen macht, so ist es der Leib, der mitwirkt, daß die Seele sein eigen werden kann. Denn der Leib wird bei der Taufe abgewaschen, damit die Seele von ihren Flecken rein werde; der Leib wird gesalbt, damit die Seele geheiligt werde. Der Leib wird [bei der Firmung] bezeichnet, damit die Seele gefestigt werde; der Leib wird durch die Handauflegung beschattet, damit auch die Seele durch den Geist erleuchtet werde. Der Leib genießt [bei der Eucharistie] das Fleisch und Blut Christi, damit auch die Seele aus Gott genährt werde. Was so durch die Arbeit verbunden ist, kann auch bei stattfindender Belohnung nicht getrennt werden.

Tertullian formuliert zwar das ein oder andere im Rahmen der griechischen Anthropologie; es ist aber deutlich, daß er den Wert der Leiblichkeit und ihren unverzichtbaren und eigenen Platz in der Liturgie hoch einschätzt. Gott ist nicht direkt erreichbar, und das Heil kommt zu uns nur über unsere Leiblichkeit und ihre unmittelbare Verlängerung: die natürliche, materielle Welt. Dies nun ist zunächst ein anthopologisches, unausweichliches Faktum; aber es hat durch die Inkarnation selbst auch weiterreichende theologische Dimensionen bekommen. Denn Gott hat sich uns zutiefst in der Leiblichkeit seines Sohnes und durch sie nahegebracht. Ich gehe auf beide Punkte, den anthropologischen und den theologischen, näher ein.

1.1. Das anthropologische Faktum

Wir können das, was uns übersteigt, nur über unsere Leiblichkeit errei-

---

5 TERTULLIAN: *Liber de resurrectione carnis*, in J.-P. MIGNE: *Patrologia latina* II (Paris 1878) 852 (caput 8). Zitat aus *Texte der Kirchenväter. Eine Auswahl nach Themen geordnet* I. Zusammengestellt und herausgegeben von A. HEILMANN unter wissenschaftlicher Mitarbeit von H. KRAFT (München 1963) 356.

chen. Dies muß man jedoch richtig verstehen. Wenn ich sage: Man erreicht das uns Übersteigende nur über die Leiblichkeit, dann verstehe ich das 'über' nicht so, als ob unser Körper nur ein Instrument wäre. Wir können nämlich im Hinblick auf unsere Umgebung auf rein instrumentale Weise handeln: Mit unserer Leiblichkeit und durch sie können wir die Erde bearbeiten und die Dinge für uns einrichten. Die leiblich-instrumentale Vermittlung ist wichtig. Sie ermöglicht es uns, am Leben zu bleiben: Sie verschafft uns Wohlstand; man denke nur an die Technik, die Möglichkeiten der Ernährungsproduktion, die Raumfahrt und die Medizin. Diese instrumentale Vermittling der Leiblichkeit hat jedoch eine beschränkte Reichweite. Ich kann einen viel größeren Raum erreichen, wenn die Leiblichkeit und die Dinge, die mich umgeben, auf symbolische Weise vermitteln. Der Körper und die Dinge, die mich umgeben, können nämlich Ausdruck einer tieferen Welt werden, und sie können den Kontakt mit dieser tieferen Welt auch verwirklichen und vollziehen. Ich meine, daß der Kultur- und Religionspsychologe H. Fortmann dies an Hand des *Wortes* als leibliche Vermittlung auf sehr ansprechende Weise deutlich macht. Er erzählt die Geschichte von dem taubstummen Mädchen Helen Keller, wie sie Miss Sullivan, die Helen begleitete und den Schritt zum Menschlichen hin vollziehen ließ, beschrieben hat:[6]

> Das Mädchen kannte schon sehr bald zwanzig Wörter. Und doch hatten für sie die Dinge noch keinen Namen. Sie befand sich noch auf dem Niveau des 'Zeichens'. Helen verwechselte die Wörter 'Becher' und 'Wasser', weil sie beide mit Trinken assoziierte. Da geschah das Folgende. "Während ich pumpte, ließ ich Helen ihren Becher unter den Wasserstrahl halten. Während das kalte Wasser herausströmte und den Becher füllte, buchstabierte ich 'W-a-s-s-e-r' in Helens Hand. Daß das Wort so unmittelbar dem Gewahrwerden des kalten Wassers, das über ihre Hand strömte, folgte, schien sie zu überraschen. Sie ließ den Becher fallen und stand da wie angewurzelt. Ein Leuchten kam über ihr Gesicht. Sie buchstabierte verschiedene Male hintereinander 'Wasser'. Dann ließ sie sich auf den Boden fallen und fragte nach seinem Namen, sie zeigte auf die Pumpe und auf den Zaun, drehte sich dann plötzlich um und fragte nach meinem Namen ... In wenigen Stunden hatte sie ihrem Wortschatz dreißig Wörter hinzugefügt". Helen erzählt es später selbst so: "Ich stand still, meine ganze Aufmerksamkeit auf ihre Finger gerichtet. Plötzlich überkam mich ein verschwommenes Bewußtsein, wie von etwas, das ich vergessen hatte, eine Erschütterung, wie von einem Gedanken, der wiederkam. Und so wurde mir irgendwie das Geheimnis der Sprache geoffenbart. Ich wußte jetzt, was 'W-a-s-s-e-r' bedeutete: das herrlich Kühle, das über meine Hand strömte. Das lebendige Wort ließ meine Seele erwachen, gab ihr Licht, Hoffnung und Freude und machte sie frei".

---

6 H. FORTMANN: *Inleiding tot de cultuurpsychologie* I (Bilthoven 1971) 94-95.

Anfänglich also gab Helen den Dingen keinen eigentlichen Namen. Die Wörter standen noch auf dem Niveau eines Zeichen-Instrumentes. Und dann kam plötzlich der Augenblick, der ihr das Mysterium der Sprache offenbarte: das Wort als ein reiches Symbol; als etwas, das mehr ist als ein Instrument oder ein Etikett: das Wort als Offenbarung einer tiefreichenden Wirklichkeit.

Dasselbe nun kann mit körperlichen Bewegungen geschehen: Ich kann mich bücken, um etwas aufzuheben: eine rein instrumentelle Handlung. Aber mein Bücken kann auch der Ausdruck meiner Ehrfurcht und meines Gefühls der Abhängigkeit von der mich übersteigenden Wirklichkeit sein: eine reiche Symbolhandlung. Ich kann Wasser holen, um zu waschen; ich kann aber auch so mit Wasser umgehen, daß es ein reiches Symbol wird für Chaos, Untergang, Tod und Leben, Aufstehen und Auferstehung. Übrigens war die Entdeckung der Sprache durch Helen mit der Erfahrung dieser Art Symbolhandlungen verbunden: Sie fühlte das Wasser, sie fiel auf die Erde, sie zeigte auf die Wasserpumpe und das Gitter; dies sind keine instrumentellen, sondern symbolische Handlungen.

Die Symbolsprache, das Symbol und die Symbolhandlungen nun haben sozusagen zwei Seiten: Einerseits sind sie Ausdruck einer anderen Wirklichkeit, die sie wachrufen. Andererseits gilt, daß durch die Symbolsprache, das Symbol und die Symbolhandlung sich die tiefere Wirklichkeit mir offenbart, daß sie zu mir kommt. Es gibt eine Bewegung von mir weg und eine Bewegung auf mich zu. Aber in beiden Fällen vollzieht sich diese Bewegung über die Leiblichkeit der Symbolisierung.

Der Religionspsychologe A. Vergote hat darauf hingewiesen, wie sehr in der heutigen Anthropologie, vor allem in der Sprachwissenschaft und in der Psychologie, der symbolische Ausdruck ein zentrales Faktum ist.[7] In Symbolsprache, Symbol und Symbolhandlung drückt der Mensch sich aus, und nur auf diese Weise kann er seine Menschlichkeit voll zur Geltung bringen. Wenn wir nicht ausdrücken, was wir erleben oder denken, dann gehen die Eindrücke an uns vorbei: Sie werden nicht zu einem lebenswichtigen Teil unserer Person. Sie bleiben innen, unsicher, schwankend, suchend. Erst wenn wir sie ausdrücken, kommen sie zu sich selbst, und es kommt der eigentliche Kontakt in der Tiefe zustande. Erst wenn man dem Wort Wasser echten Ausdruck verleiht, offenbart sich das Wasser in seinem ganzen Reichtum. Erst wenn man auf die Erde fällt, erfährt man, was 'Erde' ist. Und die Liebe kommt nicht richtig zustande, sie verwirklicht sich nicht, wenn sie rein innerlich bleibt. Die Liebe muß sich vollziehen, in Wort und Gebärde. Dieses anthropologische Gesetz nun gilt genauso für den Glauben.[8] Der Glaube ist nichts rein Innerliches. Er

---

7 A. VERGOTE: *Het huis is nooit af. Gedachten over mens en religie* (Antwerpen-Utrecht 1974) 111 ff.
8 G. LUKKEN: In der Liturgie wird der Glaube auf unersetzbare Weise Wirklichkeit, in

kommt erst richtig zustande, wenn er sich äußert. Der symbolische Ausdruck ist für den Glauben unersetzlich. Es gibt keinen authentischen Glauben ohne Glaubensbekenntnis. Nicht für nichts wird das Glaubensbekenntnis von alters her das *Symbolon*, das Symbol genannt. Gerade durch das leibliche, liturgisch gesprochene Wort kann von einem tatsächlich vollzogenen Glauben die Rede sein. Und dasselbe gilt für die leibliche, liturgische Symbolhandlung, das sich Beugen, das sich Hinknien, das Vollziehen des Kreuzzeichens usw.: So kann der Glaube zu sich selbst kommen und sich auf authentische Weise verwirklichen. Der Glaube vollzieht sich also auf konzentrierte und unersetzliche Weise in der Leiblichkeit und durch die Leiblichkeit unseres Symbolisierens: durch unsere Symbolsprache, durch unser Umgehen mit den Dingen als Symbole und durch unsere Symbolhandlungen. Der Glaube ist in Bezug auf Gott eine Befindlichkeit, die nur im symbolischen Ausdruck im wirkenden Wort und in der wirkenden Gebärde aktuell wird. Das bedeutet, daß eine Religion nur da wirklich wirksam ist, wo und in dem Maße ihr symbolischer Ausdruck wirksam ist. Und dieser symbolische Ausdruck ist nur wirksam, wenn er ein vollwertiger Ausdruck und Vollzug der menschlichen Leiblichkeit und unseres leiblichen Umgangs mit den Dingen ist. Die vollwertige Leiblichkeit ist für wahrhaftiges Symbolisieren notwendig. Und dabei ist es immer so, daß der Leib selbst das erste Medium dieses symbolischen Ausdrucks ist: Man denke an Wort und Gebärde. Aber mit unserer Leiblichkeit ist ebenso der symbolische Ausdruck mit Hilfe materieller Dinge, wie dem Geben eines Geschenks oder dem Entzünden einer Kerze, verbunden: Unsere Umgebung, das heißt die uns umgebenden materiellen Objekte, sind sozusagen unsere verlängerte Leiblichkeit.[9]

Wenn die Liturgie an Terrain verloren und sich vom menschlichen Leben entfernt hat, so deshalb, weil sie oft nicht die ganze authentische Leiblichkeit des symbolisierenden Sich-Ausdrückens bewiesen hat. Die Liturgie kann ein so wesentliches, anthropologisches Faktum nicht ungestraft vernachlässigen. Dies berührt die theologische Wirklichkeit selbst. Verarmter symbolischer Ausdruck, sowohl des Wortes als auch der Gebärde, macht das Göttliche nun einmal weniger zugänglich; er verdunkelt die Erscheinung des Göttlichen. Eine solche Verarmung kann dazu führen, daß allerlei zweitrangige Riten entstehen, die die Kernriten überdecken. Man vereinheitlicht und macht aus dem Symbol eine Allegorie, ein Zeichen, das zunächst einmal erklärt werden muß. So sagt man z.B. im Mittelalter, daß die dreimalige Stille während der Messe ein Zeichen für die drei Tage ist, während derer Christus im Grab ruhte. Es ist klar, daß

Concilium 9 (1972) Nr. 2, 86-93; IDEM: *De onvervangbare weg van de liturgie* (Hilversum 1984[2]); IDEM: *Geen leven zonder rituelen. Antropologische beschouwingen met het oog op de christelijke liturgie* (Hilversum 1988[3]).
9 VERGOTE: *Het huis is nooit af* 122 ff.

bei einer solchen Allegorie nicht die Rede von einer direkten symbolischen Wahrnehmung ist; man versteht sie erst nach einer verstandesmäßigen Auslegung. Ein verarmter symbolischer Ausdruck führt auch dazu, daß man die Liturgie formal bis in alle Details regelt und aus ihr eine ethische Pflicht macht. So verliert die Liturgie ihre Wurzeln und wird lebensfremd.

Schließlich will ich noch auf das wichtige anthropologische Faktum hinweisen, daß wir Menschen gerade durch unsere Leiblichlkeit an Raum und Zeit gebunden sind. Dies impliziert, daß auch die Vermittlung durch die Leiblichkeit an dieser raum-zeitlichen Gebundenheit teilhat. Hiermit hängt zusammen, daß, bei aller struktureller Übereinstimmung, doch von einer großen Varietät in der Symbolsprache, den Symbolen und der Symbolhandlung die Rede ist, je nach Raum und Zeit des Geschehens. So ist Wasser immer und überall dasselbe Symbol, jedoch nur in gewissem Sinn. Die Art, in der Menschen das Wasser betrachten, erleben und deuten, verändert sich immer wieder. Das Wasser wird von wechselnden sozial-kulturellen Hintergründen her und von wechselnden geographischen Situationen her wahrgenommen. In einem tropischen Land und in einer primitiven Kultur betrachtet man Wasser anders, als wenn man – wie viele Niederländer – da wohnt, wo eigentlich die Fische wohnen müßten: unter dem Meeresspiegel, auf Land, das dem Meer abgewonnen ist. So betrachten auch die Eskimos den Schnee anders als wir; das wird schon deutlich an der Vielzahl der Wörter, die sie für Schnee haben. Sogar Natursymbole sind demnach geschichtliche, an Raum und Zeit gebundene Fakten, die innerhalb stets wechselnder Kontexte und Strukturen bestehen. So erhielt das Ursymbol – Christus als das Licht – in der griechisch-römischen Kultur, die von Christus als 'aufgehender Sonne' und 'Morgenstern' sprach, eine eigene Farbe. Wegen unserer Leiblichkeit und um des authentischen Symbolisierens willen muß die Liturgie immer wieder in neuen Kulturen Gestalt bekommen. Wenn man dieses Faktum verwahrlost, verursacht man unnötige Hindernisse in der Bewegung des Menschen zum Göttlichen und des Göttlichen zum Menschen hin.

1.2. Das christliche Faktum

Das anthropologische Faktum hat durch die Inkarnation eine tiefere theologische Dimension erhalten. Gott hat sich in seiner Tiefe selbst erschlossen, indem er die menschliche Leiblichkeit angenommen hat. Seitdem ist der fundamentale Ort der Leiblichkeit als unersetzlicher Weg zum Göttlichen hin sozusagen radikalisiert. Der Zugang zum Gott des Jesus aus Nazareth und das Erscheinen seines Gottes ist für uns nur über den Weg der Leiblichkeit möglich, und zwar zuerst über den Weg der Leiblichkeit des Jesus von Nazareth selbst. Er ist dann auch – so Papst Leo der Große im 5. Jahrhundert – das erste und größte Sakrament.[10] In diesem Begriff Sa-

---

10 LEO DER GROSSE: *Die Lehrschreiben des heiligen Papstes Leo des Großen über die*

krament – der mit dem griechischen Begriff 'Mysterium' (*mystèrion*) identisch ist – liegt beschlossen, daß es eine unverbrüchliche Verbindung zwischen dem Leiblichen, Sichtbaren, Vollmenschlichen auf der einen Seite und dem Geistlichen, Unsichtbaren und Göttlichen auf der anderen Seite gibt. Man stößt hier auf eine die christliche Heilsgeschichte bestimmende Struktur. Kern christlicher Sichtweise ist, daß Gott uns in unserer Leiblichkeit durch seinen Sohn aufgesucht hat, durch den – so Patriarch Athanasius im 4. Jahrhundert – die '*mystèrion*-Struktur' des Heilsplanes definitiv feststeht.[11] Die sakramentale Struktur setzt sich dann auch in der Kirche fort, die selbst auch in ihrer ganzen Fülle Sakrament genannt wird und die diese Sakramentalität vor allem dort realisiert, wo sie sich in Symbolsprache, Symbol und Symbolhandlung ausdrückt: kurz, in ihrer Liturgie. Um anzudeuten, wie wesentlich die sakramentale Struktur für die Kirche ist, vergleicht der Theologe M. Scheeben im 19. Jahrhundert die Kirche mit einem wachsenden Baum: Ein solcher Baum kann nicht von seiner eigenen Wurzel abweichen. So kann auch die Kirche nicht von ihrem sakramentalen Ursprung abweichen.[12] Die christliche Liturgie kann also unmöglich an der anthropologischen Basis vorbei, nach der die Leiblichkeit Vermittlung des Göttlichen ist. Man muß sogar sagen, daß alles, was die anthropologische Basis in sich enthält, in der christlichen Liturgie radikalisiert wird. Dies bedeutet auch – ich kehre es jetzt um – daß dem Christentum radikal Schaden zugefügt wird, wenn man der anthropologischen Basis der Liturgie nicht gerecht wird: Die Liturgie darf also nie die Gesetze der Leiblichkeit vernachlässigen und auf diese Weise entmenschlicht werden. Radikalisierung bedeutet auch, daß die Liturgie von ihrem Wesen her für ein Eingehen in alle geographischen und historischen Situationen offensteht. Die christliche Liturgie ist wesentlich kulturbestimmt, und sie muß eigentlich so sein, daß kein Volk und keine Zeit sie als etwas Lebensfremdes in der eigenen Kultur erfahren. Dies ist natürlich nicht unproblematisch, vor allem, wenn man sich klar macht, daß das Christentum seine eigene Identität und Tradition nicht vernachlässigen darf. Der Übergang der Liturgie von der einen Kultur und Kulturperiode in eine andere ist daher auch von vielen Spannungen und von Zögern begleitet. Diese Übergänge sind kompliziert, weil einerseits die eigene christliche Identität der Vergangenheit ganz in die leibliche Kulturbestimmtheit der Tradition eingebettet ist und andererseits die christliche Identität nur glaubwürdig bleibt, wenn sie auf neue ebensosehr kulturbe-

Menschwerdung Christi, aus dem Lateinischen übertragen und eingeleitet von L. WINTERSWYL (= Zeugen des Wortes 9) (Freiburg im Breisgau 1938).
11 ATHANASIUS: *Contra Apollinarium, liber secundus*, in J.-P. MIGNE: *Patrologia graeca* XXVI (Paris 1887) 1133 B.
12 M. SCHEEBEN: *Die Mysterien des Christentums. Wesen, Bedeutung und Zusammenhang derselben nach der in ihrem übernatürlichen Charakter gegebenen Perspektive dargestellt* (= Gesammelte Schriften II) (Freiburg i. Br. 1941) 465.

stimmte biblische Ausdrucksmöglichkeiten, trotz aller Risikos, eingeht. Die christliche Radikalisierung des anthropologischen Faktums führt allerdings noch weiter. Ich habe gerade gesagt, daß von einer Radikalisierung auf Grund der Inkarnation die Rede ist. Wir dürfen aber nicht vergessen, daß es sich bei der Inkarnation keineswegs um ein statisches Faktum handelt. Die Menschwerdung Jesu ist in seinem Leben und durch sein Leben und schließlich durch den Tod hindurch zur Vollendung gekommen. Er ist von den Toten auferstanden. Seit seiner Auferstehung ist bei Ihm die Rede von einer neuen leiblichen Seinsweise: Seine Leiblichkeit ist vollkommen durchdrungen vom Geist. Seit Pfingsten läßt Er, der neue Adam, uns Anteil haben an seinem Lebensatem. Nach der Apostelgeschichte (Apg 2,2-4) kam vom Himmel her ein Brausen, wie wenn ein heftiger Sturm daherfährt. Und es erschienen ihnen Zungen wie von Feuer. Alle wurden mit dem Heiligen Geist erfüllt. Der Durchbruch des Geistes in der Leiblichkeit Jesu bedeutet eine weitere Radikalisierung auch für die Leiblichkeit der Kirche. Ihre Leiblichkeit ist keine reine Fortsetzung der Leiblichkeit der Inkarnation, sondern sie hat ihren Grund in der auferstandenen Leiblichkeit des Herrn, die ganz vom Geist durchdrungen ist. Geist bedeutet unzerstörbares Leben, warmer Lebensatem, Bewegung. Er erfüllt die menschliche Leiblichkeit von innen her und erhellt unser Herz und unsere Sinne. So dringt der Geist in die menschliche Sensibilität und Affektivität ein und macht die menschliche Leiblichkeit transparent und beweglich. Seine Dynamik ist nicht hartherzig, nicht männlich tyrannisch, nicht ideologisch. Im Gegenteil: Der Geist ist wie eine sanfte Brise, eine feurige Zunge, ist innere Freiheit und Wärme. Und dieser Geist ist es, der die Kirche in ihrer Leiblichkeit zum Sakrament macht. Unter dem Einfluß dieses Geistes wird das kirchliche Symbolisieren, wie es in der Liturgie geschieht, dynamisiert. Gerade durch den Geist und in ihm erhält das leibliche Handeln der Kirche und, als Fortsetzung davon, ihr Umgehen mit der materiellen Welt eine neue, verschobene Perspektive. Sie reicht tiefer, ist zielsicherer und transparenter. Es wird sozusagen etwas vom Schleier über der neuen, zukünftigen Welt gelüftet. Es ist natürlich so, daß man nicht von einer vollkommenen Transparenz des Geistes in unserer Leiblichkeit, so wie sie beim Herrn der Fall ist, sprechen kann. Es ist die Rede von einem 'schon' und 'noch nicht'. Auffallend ist dabei, daß je nach Kulturperiode und Kulturgebiet die Akzente verschieden gesetzt werden. So betont die Ostkirche stark das 'schon jetzt' Anwesendsein des Geistes. Der Geist erfüllt die liturgische Wirklichkeit so sehr, daß man von einer himmlischen Liturgie spricht, die hier auf der Erde vollzogen wird. In diesem Licht funktionieren auch die Urelemente Wasser, Erde, Luft und Feuer in ihrer vollen materiellen Gestalt als Träger der göttlichen, 'geistigen' Wirklichkeit. Im Gegensatz zum Osten schenkte der Westen dem Geist immer schon viel weniger Aufmerksamkeit. Wahrscheinlich hängt dies damit zusammen, daß der Westen im allgemeinen und vor allem in unserer Zeit mehr das 'noch nicht' Dasein der neuen Welt betont. Wenn von Sehen gesprochen wird, dann nur von 'manchmal/für einen Augenblick Sehen';[13] es ist eher die Rede von der urchristlichen Sehnsucht des *Maranatha*, der Erwartung eines Geschehens, das schließlich erst im allerletzten Augenblick der individuellen und gemeinschaftlichen Geschichte eintreten wird. Doch gilt auch für die Kirche des Westens, daß seit der Auferstehung Christi der Geist ihr liturgisches Handeln durchdringt. Sie sollte sich dessen noch mehr bewußt sein. Es würde die Kirche in ihrem leiblichen Handeln bescheidener, beweglicher und dynamischer machen. Die Belebung des Geistes braucht nicht auf Kosten eines eigenen Akzentes zu gehen: Mit Paulus können wir erfahren, daß es nur um die 'Erstlingsfrucht des Geistes' geht, sodaß wir auf die vollkommene Erlösung unseres Leibes noch warten müssen (Röm 8,23). Wie dem auch sei: Das leibliche Erleben in der Liturgie kann nicht vom Kommen des Geistes in unser leibliches, menschliches Sein und vom Dasein des Geistes in ihm losgelöst werden. Durch den Geist und in ihm kann unsere Leiblichkeit auf eine wahrhaftigere und würdigere Weise Mittlerin zur neuen Welt hin sein, und so können auch die materiellen Dinge reiner und sicherer zum transfigurierenden Fenster der endgültigen christlichen Wirklichkeit werden. Es geht also in der Liturgie um die menschliche Leiblichkeit als eine durch den Geist Jesu beseelte Wirklichkeit.

2. DIE LEIBLICHKEIT DES WORTES

Der Religionspsychologe A. Vergote stellt zwischen Wort und Gebärde einen gewissen Gegensatz fest; und zwar stellt er nur die Gebärde auf die Seite des Leiblichen und bringt sie damit in eine Gegenposition zum Wort. Vergote sagt:[14]

> Sicherlich erfüllt die Sprache dieselben Funktionen eines Bindegliedes. Aber wenn die Sprache uns auch die grundlegenden Bedeutungsinhalte vorlegt, die es gestatten, die Existenz in ihrer Symbolwirklichkeit zu erfassen und sie auf den letzten Sinn zu beziehen, also auf die 'Religion', so kann sie doch selbst den Existenzvollzug im Symbol nur realisieren, wenn sie mittels des Ritus in unser konkretes Sein herabsteigt, in unser Verhalten, das darin besteht, daß wir lebendiger Leib sind. Außerhalb des Ritus bleibt die symbolische Sprache leer, wie es die Sprache eines Schizophrenen ist, der die Worte behandelt als wären sie wirkliche Dinge. Das gesprochene Wort muß sich füllen mit der existentiellen Dichte des Leibes.

---

[13] Wörtliche Übersetzung des Titels *Zien – soms even* von H. OOSTERHUIS; im Deutschen erschienen als *Weiter sehen als wir sind* (Wien 1973).
[14] A. VERGOTE: Symbolische Gebärden und Handlungen in der Liturgie, in: *Concilium* 8 (1971) Nr. 2, 98.

Was Vergote hier suggeriert, geschieht vielfach. Das Verbale wird als etwas Unleibliches gesehen und das Nicht-Verbale als etwas Leibliches. Ich verstehe wohl, was Vergote meint: Er will – und zwar zu Recht – die Bedeutung der Leiblichkeit des Nicht-Verbalen betonen. Meiner Meinung nach spricht er hier aber zu undifferenziert über das Verbale als solches, als ob es unleiblich wäre. Theologisch stößt man hier auf die Gegenüberstellung von Wort und Sakrament. Damit meint man den Gegensatz zwischen rein verbaler Verkündigung des christlichen Heilsgeschehens und seinem rituellen Vollzug (einschließlich der dabei gebrauchten Worte). Man kann hier konkret an die Gegenüberstellung von Kanzel, Lesepult und Alter oder Taufbecken denken. Auch diese Gegenüberstellung zwischen Wort und Sakrament wird meiner Meinung nach nicht immer sehr differenziert gehandhabt, insofern nämlich das Wort als etwas Unleibliches betrachtet wird und das Sakrament als etwas Leibliches. Die Reformatorische Kirche wird daher auch oft gekennzeichnet als Kirche des Wortes: eine Kirche, die nicht hinreichend akzeptiert, daß der Weg zu Gott über das Leibliche führt; als solche steht sie dann der katholischen Kirche gegenüber, als der Kirche des Sakramentes, die dem Leiblichen als Weg zum Göttlichen einen zu großen Wert zuerkennt. Ich bin daher der Meinung, daß Korrekturen und Differenzierungen nötig sind. Denn man muß sagen, daß auch das Wort leiblich ist.

Zunächst kann man darauf hinweisen, daß für Vergote selbst das Wort an sich nicht etwas rein Geistiges oder Innerliches ist.[15] Es ist eine *Verleiblichung*, und zwar eine Verleiblichung, die notwendig ist, wenn wir unser Innerliches, unseren Geist als solchen aktualisieren und realisieren wollen. Manchmal hat man zu Unrecht die Vorstellung, als ob im Menschen zuerst die Gedanken da seien und danach die Sprache zustandekäme, die die vorhergehenden Gedanken nur versprachliche. Das ist jedoch nicht richtig. Es ist nämlich so, daß zuerst die Ideen gebildet werden und diese dann in Worte gefaßt werden. Die Sprachwissenschaft hat gezeigt, daß die Sprache weder reine Begleitung des Denkens ist, noch ein reines Transportmittel, durch das der schon vorhandene subjektive Inhalt mitgeteilt wird. Nein, das Sprechen selbst ist der Akt, der das Denken ermöglicht. Ohne Sprache, ohne Wörter können wir nicht denken. Mindestens ist Denken ein innerliches Sprechen. Das ist das Äußerste. Wie dem auch sei, ein Gedanke kommt erst zustande, wenn wir ihn ausdrücken. Was Vergote sagt, läßt sich noch durch einige Fakten ergänzen, und dies macht deutlich, daß das Wort sehr leiblich ist.

Das Wort kommt aus der Person und ist *verbunden mit der Person*, die spricht. Das gesprochene Wort hat immer Anteil an der einmaligen Leib-

---

15 VERGOTE: *Het huis is nooit af* 120.

lichkeit dessen, der spricht. Jeder hat beim Sprechen seine eigene Stimmlage und seine eigene Klangfarbe. Gerade daran kann man den anderen erkennen. Man erkennt eine Person im Radio an ihrer Stimme.

Das Wort ist auch sehr eng mit dem eigenen *Lebensatem* verbunden. Das Atemholen durchdringt es. Und damit auch die Art des Atemholens: Es kann ruhig sein, gehetzt, inspiriert, engagiert, kurzatmig, abgeschnitten usw.

Das Sprechen wird auch von den *leiblichen Bewegungen* des Mundes begleitet. Das ist sichtbar. Nach diesem Prinzip lesen taube Menschen vom Mund ab. Wir artikulieren alle auf verschiedene Weise. Die Klänge werden auf leibliche Weise geformt. Außerdem werden sie vom Mienenspiel begleitet. In diesem Zusammenhang ist interessant, was J. Wijngaards sagt: "Es ist erstaunlich, wieviele Lektoren über die Liebe Gottes mit einem grimmigen und toternsten Gesichtsausdruck lesen können".[16] Das Wort ist unlöslich mit den Gebärden und mit der ganzen Mimik des Körpers verbunden. Sehr eindringlich zeigen dies die Gebetshaltungen: Christen beten stehend oder kniend, mit gefalteten oder ausgestreckten Händen. Wenn Juden an der Klagemauer beten, bewegen sie sich ständig hin und her. Und die Islamiten knien und beugen sich tief nach vorne.

Das Wort wird auch unbedingt durch die *Zeit* bestimmt, durch den Augenblick, in dem es gesprochen wird. Das Wort macht notwendigerweise Geschichte mit allen dazugehörenden Verleiblichungen. Es kann sein, daß Menschen an einer bestimmten Gestalt des Wortes aus der Vergangenheit hängen, z.B. an der Luther-Bibel oder an der lateinischen Liturgie.

Das Wort wird auch notwendigerweise durch den *Raum*, in dem es gesprochen wird, bestimmt. Es ist an den Ort gebunden, an dem wir uns leiblich befinden. Es wird von einer hohen Kanzel oder von einem Katheder aus gesprochen, mitten zwischen oder gegenüber anderen usw. Das Wort wird vor allem auch durch verschiedene geographische Landschaften bestimmt. Man denke an die verschiedenen Arten, wie Niederländer und Flamen dieselben Wörter aussprechen, an Dialekte, an verschiedene Sprachen. Diese sind so leiblich, daß man von einem französischen Tonfall und einem französischen Stand des Mundes spricht, für den es schwer ist, die Mimik des Englischen zu lernen. Der Franzose, der von Haus aus den englischen 'th'-Klang nicht kennt, ist geneigt, ihn wie 's' auszusprechen, das er wohl kennt. Sprachen lernen ist, wie auch immer, nichts rein Verstandesmäßiges, sondern auch etwas sehr Leibliches. Das Wort ist

---

16 J. WIJNGAARDS: *Bijbel voorlezen in de liturgie. Dán goed en verstaanbaar* (Boxtel 1974) 66.

also viel leiblicher als wir gemeinhin denken, und es ist, gerade durch seine Leiblichkeit, sehr kulturbestimmt.

Die Kulturbestimmtheit der Sprache geht sogar so weit, daß jede Sprache in sich selbst, in ihrer inneren Struktur, eine Analyse der Welt, die dieser Sprache eigen ist, enthält. Wenn man also eine Sprache lernt, dann lernt und erwirbt man eine *partikulare Sicht* der Welt, für die die Sprache einen sehr authentischen Filter bildet. So werden z.B. die Logik und das Denken der Griechen im allgemeinen gestützt und getragen durch die grammatischen Kategorien der griechischen Sprache. Dies führt dazu, daß die Griechen abstrakter über Gott sprechen als die Juden. Während in der Schrift Gott als Vater, Sohn und Geist bezeichnet wird und als solcher eng mit der faktischen Heilsgeschichte verbunden ist, wird in dem stark durch das griechische Denken beeinflußten christlichen Glaubensbekenntnis der Sohn als eingeborener Sohn Gottes bestimmt, der 'geboren' ist, 'nicht geschaffen, eines Wesens mit dem Vater', und der Geist ist der, 'der vom Vater und vom Sohn ausgeht'. In diesem Zusammenhang ist auch die Feststellung des Exegeten J. Holman interessant, daß die griechische Übersetzung von Psalm 139 die expressiven Bilder und konkreten mythischen Elemente des ursprünglich hebräischen Textes entfernt hat.[17] Dies hängt zweifellos mit der Kulturbestimmtheit der griechischen Sprache zusammen. Es ist daher auch die Frage, ob nicht bei Übersetzungen notwendigerweise etwas vom Ursprünglichen verloren geht. Es ist nun einmal unmöglich, die klassischen römischen Orationen so zu übersetzen, daß ihr eigenes Anliegen des Kurz und Bündigen, der großen Genauigkeit und des ausgewogenen Rhythmus – das, was Augustinus mit *mysteria breva, sed magna* (große Geheimnisse, aber sehr knapp formuliert) bezeichnet[18] – erhalten bleibt. Als Beispiel diene das folgende Gebet aus dem alten Sacramentarium Veronense, das wörtlich übersetzt heißt:[19]

---

17 J. HOLMAN: Psalm 139 een palimpsest?, in *Schrift* Nr. 124 (1989) 148-157. Siehe auch J. HOLMAN: A semiotic analysis of Psalm CXXXVIII (LXX), in A. VAN DER WOUDE: *In quest of the past. Studies on Israelite religion, literature and prophetism. Papers read at the Joint British-Dutch Old Testament Conference, held at Elspeet 1988* (= Oudtestamentische studiën 26) (Leiden 1990) 84-100; J. HOLMAN: Psalm 139 (TM) and Psalm 138 (LXX). A Semiotic Comparison, in K.-D. SCHUNCK und M. AUGUSTIN (Hrsg.): *Goldene Äpfel in silbernen Schalen. Collected Communications to the XIIIth Congress of the International Organization for the Study of the Old Testament, Leuven 1989* (Frankfurt am Main-Berlin-Bern 1992) 113-121.
18 AUGUSTINUS: Sermo IX, in IDEM: *Sermones de Vetere Testamento* (= Corpus christianorum, series latina 41) Hrsg. C. LAMBOT (Turnhout 1961) 100-151.
19 *Veronense* 1031: "Presta, domine, quaesumus, ut temporalibus non destituamur auxiliis, quos alimoniis pascis aeternis", in L.C. MOHLBERG (Hrsg.): *Sacramentarium Veronense (Cod. Bibl. Capit. Veron. LXXXV [80]* (= Rerum ecclesiasticarum documenta. Series maior. Fontes 1) (Romae 1955-1956) 131.

Herr, Du nährst uns mit himmlischen Speisen,
laß uns daher auch nicht ohne zeitliche Hilfe.

Ein solcher Text ist für unsere Kultur viel zu kurz und knapp. Wenn der Text ausgesprochen wird, ist er gesagt, bevor er noch zu uns durchgedrungen ist. Wir brauchen hierfür viel mehr Worte. So könnte man dieses Gebet für unsere Kultur z.B. folgendermaßen übersetzen (wobei ich gleichzeitig anmerken möchte, daß immer mehr Frauen in unserer Kultur es mit der einseitig männlichen Bezeichnung Gottes als dem 'Herrn' schwer haben):

Du, der du der Ursprung allen Lebens bist,
bei dieser Mahlzeit nährst du uns mit Brot und Wein:
Zeichen für unser Leben über den Tod hinaus;
wir bitten dich, der du uns so zu Hilfe kommst,
erhalte und behüte auch unser verletzliches zeitliches Dasein.

Es ist sicher deutlich, daß auch hier geschieht, was ich allgemein über die Notwendigkeit, daß das Christentum auf die verschiedenen Kulturen eingehen muß, gesagt habe. Dabei stößt man unvermeidlich auf komplizierte Fragen mit Bezug auf die Übersetzung der Gebetssprache aus der christlichen Tradition, wobei man – wenn man rein wörtlich übersetzt – wohl der alten Kultur gerecht wird, nicht aber der eigenen Kultur. Müßte der Reichtum der alten Gebete, die jetzt in das Römische Meßbuch und in die neuen Riten aufgenommen sind, nicht viel kreativer als bisher übersetzt werden? Wie dem auch sei: Die gestellten Fragen betreffen zutiefst die Leiblichkeit des Wortes und damit die Glaubwürdigkeit und den erlebbaren Zugang zum Gott des Heiles und der Offenbarung.

Aus dem Vorhergehenden ist deutlich geworden, daß es um die Leiblichkeit der *Symbolsprache* geht. Es geht nicht um die Sprache als Instrument. Als solche wird die Sprache in den positiven Wissenschaften gebraucht und überall da, wo es um technische und genau umschriebene Begriffe geht, wie Strukturregelung, Röntgenapparatur, Drucker usw. Diese Begriffssprache steht unserer Leiblichkeit viel ferner und ist daher auch selbst viel weniger leiblich. In der Liturgie geht es dagegen um das, was die *zweite Sprache* genannt wird, die Sprache der Phantasie. Diese Sprache berührt den Menschen in seiner ganzen Sinnlichkeit. Es geht um Wörter, die eigentlich mehr sind als Wörter, da sie eine unaussprechliche Tiefe berühren und dadurch dem Nicht-Verbalen ganz nahe sind und so auch die anderen Sinne anrühren, wie z.B. das Auge. In diesem Zusammenhang spricht man wohl von *ikonischem Sprachgebrauch*, der der Wirklichkeit sehr ähnlich ist. Man sieht es sozusagen vor sich. Wenn Thatcher als die 'eiserne Lady' bezeichnet wird, dann sieht man sie vor sich. Ein gutes Beispiel für ikonischen Sprachgebrauch ist der folgende Abschnitt aus einer Buchbesprechung von K. Fens über *Honderd jaar monnikenleven in Koningshoeven*.[20] Er schreibt:[21]

> 1981 bestand die Trappisten-Abtei Onze Lieve Vrouw von Koningshoeven 100 Jahre; sie ist eine der größten Abteien in West-Europa. Es wohnen jetzt noch 35 Mönche dort, und wer das Jubiläum-Foto ansieht, kann sehen, daß die Haare der meisten so weiß wie ihre Kutten sind. Kurz vor dem Krieg waren es noch 150 oder so ähnlich. Aber viele zogen weg, und es kam beinahe niemand hinzu: Die Geschichte eines solchen Klosters wird dann zur Kirchengeschichte im kleinen. Natürlich starben sehr viele, die gehörten aber weiter dazu: Jede Abtei hat ein Schatten-Kloster auf dem Friedhof. Nur ist jetzt beinahe überall das zweite größer als das erste. Macarius, Palamon, Nivan also, was sagen die Namen auf den schließlich auch noch uniformen Kreuzen? Eine Ewigkeit von Beten. Wofür stehen die noch Lebenden? Für dasselbe, denke ich ...

Im Vorhergehenden ging es immer um das Wort als gesprochene Sprache. Gerade als solches ist das Wort ganz eng mit der menschlichen Person und ihrer leiblichen Existenz verbunden. Es gibt aber auch das *geschriebene Wort*. Das geschriebene Wort ist eigentlich eine graphische Transkription des gesprochenen Wortes. Diese Verbindung zwischen dem gesprochenen und geschriebenen Wort ist in manchen Sprachen enger als bei uns. So liest man im Arabischen z.B. das Geschriebene laut vor, so daß die Bewegung, der Rhythmus und der Atem des Geschriebenen rekonstruiert werden können; nur dann ist der Text verständlich.[22] Als solches jedoch ist das geschriebene Wort weniger mit unserer Leiblichkeit verbunden als das gesprochene. Daher versucht man in Erzählungen den Kontakt mit dem geschriebenen Wort immer wieder durch Dialoge, die zwischen Anführungszeichen stehen und das gesprochene Wort imitieren, wachzurufen. Auch tut man dies, indem man im Text die ganze leibliche Situation beschreibt und wachruft: den Tonfall, die Klangfarbe der Stimme, das Sprechtempo usw.

In der Liturgie nun geht es immer um das gesprochene Wort, die gesprochene Symbolsprache. Dies ist beim Gebet so, bei der Lesung, bei der Predigt. Wohl ist das Wort oft schon schriftlich in den liturgischen Büchern festgelegt. Auch wenn man von diesem geschriebenen Wort ausgeht, so geht es doch nicht um das geschriebene Wort als geschriebenes Wort, noch auch um die Sprache als geschriebene Sprache, sondern um die Worte und die Sprache als einst ausgesprochene und jetzt aufs neue

---

20 A. TERSTEGGE: *Honderd jaar monnikenleven in Koningshoeven* (Tilburg 1984).
21 A.L. BOOM (= K. FENS): Monnikenleven, in *De Tijd* (4. Januar 1985) 35.
22 P. VAN DEN HEUVEL: *Parole mot silence. Pour une poétique de l'énonciation* (Mayenne 1985) 47.

auf kreative Weise zu sprechende. Beim Beten der Psalmen in der Liturgie geht es nicht um das Lesen eines geschriebenen Textes: Lesen und Studieren des Textes ist Sache des Exegeten, und dies ist ein ziemlich unbiblisches Geschehen, es sei denn, er tut es wie die Araber. Aber in der Liturgie geht es, wie auch immer, um das aufs neue Sprechen, um das Beten des Psalms hier und jetzt. Der, der den Psalmtext in Augenschein nimmt, macht sich den Text auch dadurch zu eigen, daß er ihn ausspricht. So bekommt der Text 'Tiefe', Leiblichkeit und wird zum Gebet. Der geschriebene Text muß durch meinen Atem, meine Intonation, in diesem Raum und dieser Zeit, in dieser Gebetshaltung usw. gesprochen werden. Ich muß den Text also leiblich zu einem Stück meiner selbst machen. Und wenn es durch den Geist inspirierte Worte sind – und das sind nicht nur die Worte der Schrift, sondern auch die uns überlieferten liturgischen Worte –, dann können sie auch in mir den Geist wecken, unter der Bedingung, daß ich sie, in meiner Leiblichkeit, auf authentische Weise aussprechen kann. Man findet oft die Bezeichnung Gebet-'Bücher'; aber Gebetbücher sind nicht zum Lesen da; es sind Drehbücher, Szenarien, die sagen, wie man beten muß und kann. Dasselbe gilt für die Erzählungen aus der Schrift. Sie sind zu allererst dazu da, neu, mitten in der Gemeinde, erzählt zu werden, als gesprochene Erzählungen. Sie müssen wie lebendige Geschichten klingen und erzählt werden, durch unseren Atem getragen. Es ist wichtig, daß dabei auf wahrhaftige Weise gesprochen wird. Ein guter verbaler Ausdruck spielt keineswegs eine untergeordnete Rolle: Er ist notwendig, um ganz und gar menschlich und mit Achtung vor der Leiblichkeit des Wortes sprechen zu können.

In der Bibel kennt man die literarische Gattung der Briefe: Man denke z.B. an die Paulusbriefe. Nun sind Briefe eigentlich dazu bestimmt gelesen zu werden. In der Liturgie erklingen sie jedoch öffentlich, inmitten der Gemeinde, als gesprochenes Wort. Die Briefe werden 'vorgelesen'. Nur dann sind sie als liturgisches Wort wirksam und gültig. Das gesprochene Wort steht in der Liturgie so zentral, daß sogar die 'Lesungen' im strengsten Sinne des Wortes in der Liturgie als gesprochenes Wort, auf lebendige Weise erklingen. So wird deutlich, wie sehr das Wort in der Liturgie leiblich ist und leiblich bleibt. Auch die Reformation hat die Leiblichkeit des Wortes immer respektiert.

Bis jetzt ging es immer um das liturgische Wort in seiner Eigenart. Dieses Wort hat, wie deutlich geworden ist, ziemlich viele leibliche Aspekte. Im folgenden Abschnitt will ich auf die Leiblichkeit des Nicht-Verbalen eingehen. Vorher möchte ich aber noch auf zwei Grenzfälle hinweisen, in denen einerseits das Wort in seiner Eigenart bestehen bleibt, andererseits das Nicht-Verbale besonders stark betont wird. Dies geschieht bei den Litaneien. Sie können zu einem rein akustischen, interrelationalen Geschehen werden, das eine Gemeinschaft mit dem Göttlichen in Kontakt bringt und hält. Auch erhält das Nicht-Verbale eine starke Betonung, wenn in

Gesängen die Melodie den Text beherrscht. Dies kann auch bei Gesängen in einer fremden Sprache, die man nicht versteht, geschehen.

3. DIE LEIBLICHKEIT DES NICHT-VERBALEN

Wenn man auch keine absolute Gegensätzlichkeit zwischen dem Verbalen und dem Nicht-Verbalen aufbauen darf, so kann man doch etwas zugespitzter über das Nicht-Verbale, gerade im Zusammenhang mit dem Thema 'Liturgie und Leiblichkeit', sprechen. Der neuen Liturgie wird oft vorgeworfen, sie sei so verbal geworden. Und tatsächlich, in unserer Kultur gibt doch oft das Wort – trotz des großen Einflusses des Visuellen – den Ton an. Dies führt dazu, daß auch in Riten das Wort vielfach beherrschend ist, auf Kosten des Nicht-Verbalen. Wenn auch das Wort unersetzliche leibliche Aspekte hat, so kann es doch geschehen, daß die Liturgie es am Leiblichen fehlen läßt, indem sie das Nicht-Verbale als solches zu sehr vernachlässigt. Dies geschah z.B. in der reformatorischen Liturgie, die vor allem eine Liturgie des Wortes war. Und die katholische Liturgie wurde besonders nach dem Zweiten Vatikanischen Konzil mit diesem Problem konfrontiert. Dies war etwas Neues. Denn vor dem Vatikanum II spielte in der katholischen Liturgie das Wort eine untergeordnete Rolle. Es war sogar so, daß die Liturgie auf Latein gefeiert wurde, das praktisch niemand mehr verstand: So war das Wort zum Nicht-Wort geworden: non-verbal. Die Eigenart des Wortes wiederherzustellen, war notwendig, sowohl aus anthropologischen, als aus christlichen Motiven heraus. Aus dem Vorhergehenden ist genügend deutlich geworden, wie wichtig und unersetzlich die authentische Symbol-Sprache für den Vollzug der Glaubenstat ist. Die Frage ist aber, ob die neue Würdigung des Wortes nicht zu sehr nach einer Seite hin durchgeschlagen ist. Ist hier vielleicht die Rede von einer Überreaktion?

1981 erschien das Buch *Das Konzil der Buchhalter* des bekannten deutschen Psychoanalytikers A. Lorenzer.[23] Die These Lorenzers kann ich am besten charakterisieren, indem ich den Einband seines Buches beschreibe. Der Umschlag ist ganz schwarz. Die einzigen ansprechenden Farben sieht man auf der Abbildung vorne auf dem Buch: ein Grab mit zwei Kränzen, einer um das Kreuz auf dem Grab und einer, der das Grab bedeckt. Über dieser Abbildung steht der Buchtitel und darunter der herausfordernde Untertitel: *Die Zerstörung der Sinnlichkeit*. Mit anderen Worten: Das Zweite Vatikanische Konzil hat durch seine Liturgieerneuerung die menschliche Sinnlichkeit vernichtet. Zweifellos ist der Vorwurf von Lorenzer zu absolut. Er hat wahrscheinlich in einer starken Idealisierung der

---

23 A. LORENZER: *Das Konzil der Buchhalter. Die Zerstörung der Sinnlichkeit. Eine Religionskritik* (Frankfurt am Main 1981).

Liturgie des Mittelalters und der Gegenreformation seinen Ursprung. Trotzdem fordert uns das Buch heraus, uns auf die menschliche Sinnlichkeit und ihre Funktion in unserem menschlichen Dasein tiefer zu besinnen.

Innerhalb der Symbolik kann man zwischen der sogenannten präsentativen und der diskursiven Symbolik unterscheiden. Den Unterschied zwischen beiden kann ich am besten mit einem konkreten Beispiel illustrieren. Wenn man Menschen fragt, einen Gegenstand mitzubringen, an dem sie besonders hängen, dann bringt jeder sicher etwas anderes mit: einen Ring, eine Uhr, ein Foto... Es kann alles Mögliche sein. Aber gleichzeitig ist es so, daß ein solcher Gegenstand für die betreffende Person in einem Augenblick sehr viel bedeutet. In einem Gegenstand kann das ganze Leben offenbar werden. Ein liebgewordener Gegenstand kann so in einer Sekunde voneinander Geschiedenes heraufbeschwören. In dem Gegenstand und durch ihn ist dann auf einmal unendlich viel 'präsent'. Es handelt sich um 'präsentative' Symbolik. Dies geschieht bei allen nicht streng-verbalen Weisen des symbolischen Ausdrucks. Bei der präsentativen Symbolik geht es um die sinnliche Symbolik des Visuellen, des Raumes, des Lichtes, der Farbe, der Gebärden, der Bewegungen, des Tanzes, der Verzierung, der Kleidung, des Duftes, der Musik, und – ich sagte schon, daß kein absoluter Gegensatz zum Wort besteht – des Auditiven, der Intonation, der Klangfarbe und Tonhöhe der Stimme. Auch diese letzten Elemente können in einem einzigen Augenblick jemanden in seiner Einmaligkeit heraufbeschwören. Auch im gesprochenen Wort gibt es also präsentative Symbolik. In ihrer Totalität ist diese präsentative Symbolik jedoch nur im Nicht-Verbalen als solchem anwesend. Das Typische für die präsentative Symbolik ist also, daß hier nicht die Rede ist von Aufeinanderfolge, sondern von Gleichzeitigkeit. So geschieht die Wahrnehmung eines Fotos nicht dadurch, daß man seine verschiedenen Bestandteile, wie Farbe, Licht, Schatten, in einer bestimmten Reihenfolge hintereinander wachruft. Es handelt sich vielmehr um eine Total-Wahrnehmung.

Neben der präsentativen Symbolik steht die diskursive Symbolik der Sprache, des Wortes als solchem. Bei der diskursiven Symbolik ist die Wahrnehmung nur durch Aufeinanderfolge möglich. 'Diskursiv' kommt vom lateinischen Wort *discurrere* und bedeutet 'durchlaufen'. Wenn wir ein Textganzes als Diskurs bezeichnen, dann geht es um das Ganze als Aufeinanderfolge von Elementen. Eine Geschichte, ein Gebet und eine Lesung durchläuft man. Sie werden linear wahrgenommen. Sprache als solche ist wesentlich diskursiv: Die Bedeutungseinheiten kommen nacheinander. Man liest Wort für Wort und Zeile für Zeile. Und man spricht und hört ein Wort nach dem anderen. Erst wenn das Ganze gesagt oder gelesen ist, ist die Wahrnehmung vollständig und die Botschaft mitgeteilt.

Durch die präsentative Symbolik nun hat unser Umgang mit der Welt eine stark sinnliche Basis. Die präsentative Symbolik spielt eine primäre und unverzichtbare Rolle im menschlichen Leben. Lorenzer verweist darauf, daß die präsentative Symbolik von fundamentaler Bedeutung ist und daß sie der diskursiven Symbolik der Sprache vorausgeht.[24] Sie ist die Basis, von der aus sich die menschliche Entwicklung vollzieht. Bevor ein Kind sprechen kann, sind bereits unzählige sinnliche Interaktionen zwischen Mutter und Kind geschehen. Diese wirken auf das Kind zurück und rufen stets wieder Reaktionen von seiten des Kindes wach. Auch die Ausweitung des kindlichen Aktionsradius zur Welt außerhalb der Mutter hin hat ihre Basis in den sinnlichen Interaktionsformen. Dabei spielen nicht nur die Gegenstände aus der Spielzeugwelt des Kindes eine große Rolle, sondern auch die Ausweitung seiner Welt durch die Kleidungsstükke, den Hausrat, den Wohnraum, die Treppe, den Garten, die Straße, den Wald usw., in der Form, in der das Kind sie antrifft: als durch andere Menschen geformt.

Wenn das Kind zu sprechen anfängt, bedeutet dies eine beachtliche Bewußtseinszunahme. Es kann jetzt durchdacht handeln. Durch die Sprache bekommt das Kind einen Spielplatz, der unabhängig von den wirklichen und konkreten Situationen betreten und benutzt werden kann. Gerade durch die Sprache können wir uns Situationen vorstellen, die nicht sinnlich hier und jetzt präsent sind. Die Sprache macht es uns möglich, über Situationen aus der Vergangenheit zu sprechen, *als ob* sie gegenwärtig seien. Wenn wir über Napoleon sprechen, dann erwartet niemand, daß der Kaiser sich hier und jetzt mitten unter uns befindet. Und wir können über eine lebende Person in ihrer Abwesenheit sprechen. Wenn sie dann unerwarteter Weise hereinkommt, so zeigen wir dies durch eine Gebärde oder durch eine Veränderung in der Mimik. Und das Kind kann durch die Sprache nach einem Spielzeug fragen, das sich woanders befindet. Es kann nach dem Kuscheltier fragen, das noch in seinem Bettchen liegt.

Der Sprachgewinn bedeutet allerdings auf die ein oder andere Weise auch einen bestimmten Verlust. Während das Kind vorher ganz in der Situation des Augenblicks aufgehen und, ohne nachzudenken, spontan auf Situationen reagieren konnte, wird diese Unbefangenheit jetzt in ansehnlichem Maße beschränkt. Gerade diese Unbefangenheit macht den Charme des Kindes aus: Wenn das Kind hereinkommt, lacht die ganze Familie.

Einerseits handelt es sich also um eine Zunahme an Bewußtsein durch die Sprache. Andererseits muß man aber festhalten, daß die Tiefenschicht des Ich gerade durch stark sinnliche Elemente und den damit verbundenen Emotionen gebildet wird. In diesen sinnlichen Elementen geht es um fühlbare Vorstellungen und Bilder, die die Basis unseres menschli-

---

24 LORENZER: *Das Konzil der Buchhalter* 85-94.

chen sinnlichen Daseins bilden. Die Außenwelt rückt uns gerade dadurch sehr dicht auf den Leib. Wir müssen uns dessen bewußt sein, daß das, was wir mit der Sprache benennen, nur ein Bruchteil dessen ist, was wir leiblich erfahren und erleben und daß unser Sprechen ohne diese leibliche Basis dürr und leblos würde. In der präsentativen Symbolik geht es also um eine unverzichtbare Schicht unserer Subjektivität. Man könnte sagen, daß sie die Basis unseres 'Ich' berührt.

Hieraus folgt, daß man nicht ungestraft die präsentative Symbolik und die entsprechenden sinnlich-symbolischen Interaktionsformen vernachlässigen kann. Wenn dies doch geschieht, so führt es zur Desorientierung des Ich. Vielleicht kann ich diese Desorientierung am besten auf folgende Weise nachvollziehbar machen. Wenn jemand in ein Zimmer kommt, in dem er sich täglich aufhält, und plötzlich sieht, daß nichts mehr an seinem Platz steht, fühlt er sich vollkommen desorientiert. In diesem Augenblick wird deutlich, wie sehr das Ich durch die räumlich-symbolischen Interaktionsformen getragen wird. Und was für den Raum gilt, gilt auch für das Licht, die Farbe, die Kleidung, die Bewegung usw.

Im menschlichen Leben spielt also die präsentative Symbolik eine ziemlich zentrale Vermittlerrolle. Wir erinnern uns an die Vergangenheit oft gerade über die präsentativen Symbole und Symbolhandlungen. Man hört eine Melodie, die in einem bestimmten Augenblick des Lebens eine wichtige Rolle gespielt hat, und auf einmal hat man das ganze Geschehen wieder vor Augen. Du empfindest einen bestimmten Geruch, und plötzlich erinnerst du dich an den Geruch des nassen Regencapes, das du früher als Kind trugst, und damit an das ganze Schulgeschehen von damals, an einem regnerischen Tag. Es handelt sich hier um den sogenannten *restringierten Code*: Ganz wenig kann auf einmal ganz viel wachrufen, und dieser restringierte Code steht im Gegensatz zum *elaborierten Code* der Sprache. Man braucht sehr viele Wörter, um dasselbe zu beschreiben. Gerade durch den restringierten Code sind Riten im allgemeinen von einfacher Struktur und können von allen Mitgliedern einer Gemeinschaft erfaßt werden. Man braucht sicher nicht ein Intellektueller zu sein, um diesen Code zu verstehen. Man muß sogar sagen, daß zu viel Intellektualität das Verständnis des restringierten Code unmöglich macht. Ein treffendes Beispiel hierfür findet sich bei O. van der Hart, wo er das Zusammenstoßen zwischen dem restringierten und dem elaborierten Code schildert:[25]

> Alice kam aus einem akademischen Milieu, wo dies (nämlich das Intellektualisieren) in extremem Maße der Fall war. Wenn ihr Mann ihr als Zeichen seiner Zuneigung einen Kuß gab oder sie umarmte, 'sagte' ihr das

25 O. VAN DER HART: *Rituelen in psychotherapie. Overgang en bestendiging* (Deventer 1984²) 51.

nichts. Nein, sie war erst davon überzeugt, daß er sie liebte, wenn er das ausführlich in Worte gekleidet hatte. Das konnte er nicht, er fühlte sich immer mehr blockiert. Die Folge war, daß er immer weniger zeigte, daß er sie liebte und daß sie Streit bekamen über die Frage, ob er sie doch noch liebte.

Die präsentative Symbolik hat durch ihren restringierten Code einen breiten Aktionsradius. Zu Recht bemerkt Augustinus, daß die Sakramente ein sanftes Joch und eine leichte Last sind, nicht schwer zu erfüllen, doch tief an Bedeutung.[26] Dies bedeutet aber keineswegs, daß das, was mitgeteilt wird, auch einfach ist. Gerade in all seiner Einfachheit ist die präsentative Symbolik tiefsinnig und reich an Bedeutung.

Die Bedeutung der präsentativen Symbolik wird auf eindringliche Weise deutlich, wenn man sich klar macht, was geschieht, wenn sie sich in negativem Sinn auswirkt. Dies führt zu negativen Störungen. Lorenzer nennt als markantes Beispiel einen Film über eine Mutter, die ihrem Kind die Brust reicht.[27] Es geht um ein Kind, das an ernsthaften Trinkstörungen leidet. Eine genaue Analyse zeigt, daß die Mutter dem Kind die Brustwarze anbietet, sie aber in dem Moment, in dem das Kind mit seinen Lippen anfangen will zu saugen, wieder zurückzieht. Wenn dann der Trinkreflex aufhört, schiebt sie die Brustwarze wieder zwischen die Lippen des Kindes. So wird die Kommunikation dauernd gestört. Es tritt eine wesentliche Störung in den symbolischen Interaktionsformen auf. Man könnte es mit den Rillen auf einer Schallplatte vergleichen. Man bekommt sie nicht wieder weg. Das Basisvertrauen kann wirklich auf so elementare Weise gestört werden, daß sehr viele neue präsentative Interaktionsformen nötig sind, um die eingekerbten negativen Rillen auszubessern und den Mangel auszugleichen.

Wenn die präsentativen Interaktionsformen also in negativer Gestalt auftreten, wird die Art und Weise, in der die menschliche Leiblichkeit beim Symbolisieren funktioniert, fundamental gestört. Und dies geschieht auch, wenn die präsentativen Interaktionsformen einfach ganz fehlen und man sich rein mit der diskursiven Symbolik begnügt. Für den erwachsenen menschlichen Umgang mit anderen und mit der Welt reicht nun einmal die diskursive Symbolik nicht aus. Sie muß mit der präsentativen Symbolik in Kontakt bleiben. Menschlich gesehen ist die präsentative Symbolik also eine unersetzliche Basis und Vorbedingung für die diskursive Symbolik.

Auch dieses anthropologische Faktum wird durch die Inkarnation und die auferstandene Leiblichkeit des Herrn *radikalisiert*. Dies bedeutet, daß der Glaube nur zustandekommt, wenn wir ihn sowohl durch die verbale

---

26 AUGUSTINUS: *Epistola* 54, caput 1/1, in J.-P. MIGNE: *Patrologia latina* XXXIII (Paris 1865) 200.
27 LORENZER: *Das Konzil der Buchhalter* 153.

als auch die nicht-verbale Symbolik zum Ausdruck bringen. Auch die nicht-verbalen Elemente sind für den Ausdruck unverzichtbar, mehr noch: Sie bilden die unverzichtbare Basis jeder Liturgie und gehen den verbalen Elementen vorauf. Mit anderen Worten: In der Liturgie muß auch etwas zu sehen sein, zu berühren, zu riechen; es müssen auch räumliche Erfahrung und Bewegung da sein. Die primären Interaktionsformen sind die Basis für die Interaktionsformen der diskursiven Sprache. Das bedeutet, daß die Liturgie etwas wesentlich anderes ist als Katechese, auch wenn sie katechetische Implikationen hat. Es bedeutet auch, daß der Ausdruck des Glaubens in der Liturgie sehr viel reicher ist als in der Lehre. Wer in der Liturgie nur die Lehre sucht oder nur eine Bestätigung der Lehre, unterliegt demselben Mißverständnis wie der Junge, der dem Mädchen in einem elaborierten Code seine Liebe erweist, während es doch um den restringierten Code geht. Die Liturgie kann und darf sich nicht mit Worten begnügen; und wo es um Worte geht, müssen sie mit dem Nicht-Verbalen verbunden bleiben. Unser Glaube vollzieht sich nicht nur in der Sprache des Glaubensbekenntnisses und des Gebetes, sondern auch und sogar sehr primär durch unsere Handlungen, unsere Bewegung im Raum, unser Aufstehen und Niederknien, unser Anfassen, unser Sehen der Bilder, unser die Salbe und den Weihrauch Riechen usw. Man kann mit Worten beten, aber ebenso indem man sich in den lebendigen Raum der eigenen Leiblichkeit versinken läßt.[28]

---

28 VERGOTE: *Het huis is nooit af* 94-95.

5. Church and Liturgy as Dynamic Sacrament of the Spirit

In contemporary sacramental theology, words like 'sacrament' and 'sacramental' are no longer used exclusively for the historic seven Sacraments. We have gotten used to a broader usage for the word *sacramentum* which goes back to the oldest Christian tradition, and has been rediscovered in our day. Words like 'sacrament' and 'sacramental' are principally used to connote the relation between the human and the divine, between the seen and the unseen. This is a relation in which the tension can not be resolved in favor of one side or the other; the tension always remains present. In this sense, one can speak of sacramental sacred history that begins with the history of Israel in the Old Testament, and reaches its high point in the New Testament in Jesus of Nazareth, and is continued in and through the sacramental form of the church, and particularly in a concentrated way in the liturgy.[1]

1. SACRAMENTAL SACRED HISTORY AFTER THE DEPARTURE OF THE LORD

In the Christian vision, Jesus of Nazareth is the high point in a sacramental sacred history that begins with Israel. In one way or another, all the sacraments come together in him. It is this belief in Jesus as irreplaceable sacrament that binds Christians together. The Eastern church offers us a striking example of how completely the history of Christians is dominated by the sacramental form of the Lord Jesus: one sees his icon everywhere, because he is the visible form of the invisible God (Col. 1: 15). In him, God appears to us, and he is continuously involved with us. But the Lord has ascended, and dwells with the Father. How can sacred history go any further, now that he has disappeared from sight? Is the visible part of sacramental sacred history now limited to continually looking back to his form in the past, to that sacrament that is gone like a flash in the night?

**De onvervangbare weg van de liturgie* (Hilversum 1984²) 47-57, 80-84, 151-152, 155-156. Translated by D. Mader, M.Div.

1 The various aspects are comprehensively discussed in G. LUKKEN: *De onvervangbare weg van de liturgie* (Hilversum, 1984²). In this essay, one aspect which is rather often neglected is primarily singled out for attention: the church and liturgy as dynamic sacrament of the Holy Spirit.

The answer is that is in every case there is more than a backward glance. Jesus has been made Lord (Acts 2:36). The visible reality of our world and our history henceforth refers to him. In the words of R. Guardini, "The human is that being who henceforth lives from the vicissitudes of the Christ".[2] Or as P. Claudel said:[3]

> What the drama of the cosmos and human nature, what human history in its breadth and the history of each one of us in particular is about, is this: they only become meaningful as they function in and imitate the great drama of redemption (...) There is no action in our normal everyday life that, in one way or another, does not participate in, and is not an imitation of the great drama of our salvation.

It is in the nature of every person to not view the world and life as a flat reality, but as a prospect opening to wider vistas. Now, there is a mystery that simply goes beyond us. We try to name that going beyond. It has to do with abundance, light, life, love, loyalty, eternity. The religions call that mystery that exceeds and yet penetrates all things 'God'. Now, since Jesus' departure to the Father our history no longer refers to abundance, light, etc., in general, and also not merely to God, but to the God of Abraham, Isaac and Jacob, who revealed himself as the God in covenant with his people, and ultimately to Jesus of Nazareth, in whom God appeared to us in the fullness of time. In other words, the staggering perspective of our history also now comes together in him.

Is it really that clear? Is it really so close by us that it is easy to descry? In a certain sense it is. As the old adage has it, *anima naturaliter christiana*, people in a state of nature are Christian. The basic intuition of that saying has not been superseded.

1.1. The church's particular role

Yet at the same time it is true that in our general history the visibility of the invisible Lord remains very veiled and dark. As, after Jesus' departure one could no longer speak of visibility, we would then have to make do with the sacramentality of sacred history. You search for an increase in the visibility, so to speak.

Anyone who examines history from Jesus' departure until our day soon notes a phenomenon that deserves special discussion. It appears that in history there was more happening than that here and there individuals confessed Jesus of Nazareth as a unique way to salvation and organized their lives around that fact. One could, and can, speak of a clearer line:

---

2 R. GUARDINI: *Der Herr. Betrachtungen über die Person und das Leben Jesu Christi* (Würzburg 1940⁴) 259.
3 P. CLAUDEL: *Toi qui es-tu? (Tu quis es?)* (Paris 1936) 50-51.

down through the various centuries and cultures there is a human community in motion, centered around belief in Jesus. In a special way, this community calls upon Jesus as Lord of history. You could speak of the church as mediator. Without the mediation of the church there would perhaps be a handful of specialized historians who would know something about a certain Jesus of Nazareth, but humanity as such would know him no more. "It is through the movement that Jesus called into life that we are still confronted by Jesus of Nazareth today".[4] Whatever else one may say about the church, the truth remains that the church is entirely indispensable, and that without the church the person of Jesus would quickly slip into oblivion.[5] The history of the church, in East and West alike, with all its changes of fortune, reveals him more concretely than general history does. In and through the church, Jesus steps out of the mists, the contours of his form become clear, and we discover his identity. In and through the church he is expressed in human terms, and works concretely in history. That is not to say that outside of the movement of the church no trace of him can be found. Nor, in saying this, is any judgement made about moral characteristics for the history at its largest. What it in fact means is this: anyone who seeks a continuation of sacramental sacred history after the departure of Jesus, finds this first and foremost in the church that began after Jesus' departure and continues to this very day.

That sacramental sacred history continues in and through the church is also open to anthropological influence. Do people not need each other to discover the deepest levels of life? Should the same not be true to discover that things and history are in tension with the Lord? People can not do without the light of community; it is against their nature to have to discover everything as individuals. Only with and for others do you learn to see depth perspectives. Humans are simply both symbolic and social beings. So the church of the past and the present teaches us who Jesus of Nazareth is. In and through the church he approaches us as the irreplaceable way to God and to salvation for all humankind. He is revealed in and through the circle of those whom he has collected around himself as the new people of God. We learn to know him, and deepen our knowledge of him in the community of those who believe and live out that belief.

1.2. The church as sacrament

We have just used phrases and expressions like 'in and through the church

---

4 E. SCHILLEBEECKX: *Jezus, het verhaal van een levende* (Bilthoven 1974) 14.
5 So Marcel Légaut in an interview, see L. TER STEEG: Marcel Légaut, de hoogleraar die boer werd, in *Studio* (22-28 April 1978) 8.

the Lord steps out of the mists', have said he is revealed, takes shape, is expressed, unveiled, approaches us. But one must understand these clearly. These do not imply a complete visibility, a complete unveiling. He does not show himself in the church face to face. The church is moving toward that moment. The Lord is concretely present in his new people of God, but he must yet come in order to perfect all things. In the new people of God, the salvific is celebrated: one can really speak of a community of righteousness and love; the kingdom of God breaks through here in a tangible way. But at the same time, the community looks toward the full dominion of God over the human realm in the future; only in the future shall the kingdom of God be complete and shall the God of salvation be the all-in-all. Thus one could say that in the church there is the field of tension that is so typical of *sacramentum*, the tension between the seen and the unseen, the certainly and the not yet, between present and future. Thus the church can rightfully be called 'sacrament', as it was called in its earliest days. One can cite the Old Gelasian Sacramentary (*Gelasianum Vetus*), that speaks of the church as a miraculous sacrament.[6] This formulation is found again in article five of the Constitution on the Liturgy: "For it was from the side of Christ as he slept the sleep of death upon the cross that there came forth the sublime sacrament of the whole Church".[7] When the Constitution on the Liturgy was put together in 1963, it was the first time that the church had been designated as a sacrament in an official document in many centuries. This was an important step. Why? That shall subsequently become clear.

1.3. Developments since the twelfth century

The designation of the church as sacrament can be found from the early church until the twelfth century.[8] But then the concept disappears, and 'sacrament' persists only in a narrow and specialized way, to be used for

---

6 L.C. MOHLBERG: *Liber Sacramentorum Romanae Aeclesiae Ordinis Anni Circuli* (= Rerum ecclesiasticarum documenta, series maior, fontes 4) (Rome 1960) 70 (no. 432). Cf. AUGUSTINUS: *Enarrationes in Psalmos CI-CL* (= Corpus Christianorum, Series Latina 40) (Turnhout 1956) 1991 (Psalm 138:2).
7 *Documents on the liturgy, 1963-1979. Conciliar, papal, and curial texts* (Collegeville (Minnesota) 1982) 5.
8 With regard to the church as sacrament see L. BOFF: *Die Kirche als Sakrament im Horizont der Welterfahrung. Versuch einer Legitimation und einer strukturfunktionalistischen Grundlegung der Kirche im Anschluß an das II. Vatikanische Konzil* (= Konfessionskundliche und Kontroverstheologische Studien 28) (Paderborn 1972); IDEM: *Kleine Sakramentenlehre* (Düsseldorf 1976); Y. CONGAR: *Un peuple messianique. L'église, sacrement du salut; salut et libération* (Paris 1975) 11-98; O. SEMMELROTH: Die Kirche als Sakrament des Heiles, in J. FEINER and M. LÖHRER (ed.): *Mysterium Salutis. Grundriß heilsgeschichtlicher Dogmatik* IV/1 (Einsiedeln-Zürich-Köln 1972) 309-356; H. DÖRING a.o.: *Sakramentalität der Kirche* (Paderborn 1983).

the seven sacraments. By this approach of the church, people lost sight of the sacramental field of tension. It was resolved in favor of an over-accentuation of the visible aspects. To put it simply and pointedly, people began to look at the church as if it reflected the final shape of sacred reality in all respects. Particularly from late Scholasticism, the emphasis lay on the church as institution, organized in a strongly legalistic fashion. This persisted into nineteenth century theology, and it hung on in the official church until well into the twentieth century. Even in our time this view continues to make itself felt in some circles.

Ecclesiology now became the cherished field of legal experts. To an increasing degree, the emphasis was laid on central authority. The Pope, as the deputy of Christ on earth, is the one who leads the church. But even more, as it were, he came to be looked upon as the personification of the church. Thus in 1302, Aegidius Romanus, pupil of the great Thomas Aquinas, could suggest that the Pope in Rome could be called 'the church', and in the same year Pope Boniface VIII laid out the practical consequences of this theory in his *Unam Sanctam*, proclaiming that all power in both the church and society sprang from the papacy.[9]

Through the controversy with the Reformation, which primarily emphasized the invisible church, the accent on the external aspects of the church received extra stimulus. Bellarminus (d. 1621) described the church as the community of people, bound together by the same belief and the same sacraments, under the guidance of legitimate leaders, and first of all, the one vicar of Christ on earth, the Pope in Rome. A further pronouncement by this same Bellarminus, that the church is equally as visible as the Roman people, the kingdom of France or the Venetian Republic, is well known.[10] Even more revealing is his opinion that someone, in order to be a part of the true church, need have absolutely no inner virtue, so long as he confesses faith outwardly.[11] Gradually the church came to be seen as an independent and fully complete society next to the state: a visible, perfect society (*societas perfecta*), with all the legal characteristics of such a society, under the rule of the Pope as an absolute monarch, who exercised his authority through the bishops (who, until recently, were preferably chosen from the ranks of the church's legal specialists!).

9 A. WEILER: *Deus in terris. Middeleeuwse wortels van de totalitaire ideologie* (Hilversum 1965) 20-21.
10 ROBERTUS BELLARMINUS: *Disputationum de controversiis christianae fidei adversus huius temporis haereticos opus* II (Ingolstadii 1605).
11 Y. CONGAR: *L'église de S. Augustin à l'époque moderne* (Paris 1970) 372-373. Cf. P. HUIZING and B. WILLEMS: Sacramentele grondslag van het kerkrecht, in *Tijdschrift voor theologie* 16 (1976) 246-247.

One meets this view of the church in the First Vatican Council (1870). The church is seen as, first and foremost, the worldwide assembly of all believers who, under obedience to the Pope in Rome, confess the true doctrine of Christ. The church becomes, as it were, a pyramid. At the top stands the Pope, who has universal jurisdiction. A part of this authority is delegated to the bishops, who in a certain sense represent him. The bishops in turn hand down a part of their authority to the priests. The laity form the base of the pyramid.

1.4. Rediscovery

The first figure to again speak of the church as sacrament was Thomassinus (d. 1695).[12] He did so in connection with the church fathers. But his approach was forgotten, as has happened often in history. Something new comes to the surface, but only a long time later comes to fruition. In this case, Thomassinus's influence on later theology was blocked by the Enlightenment and the eighteenth century developments that were consequent on that great revolution.

The next name that surfaces is interesting: the poet Goethe (1749-1832). He called the church 'the great, general sacrament'. This vision is connected with his epistemology, based entirely on his understanding of symbols. In theology itself the idea again surfaces in the nineteenth century, and is then speedily taken up by a number of theologians. The first to whom one can refer is the Viennese theologian A. Günther in 1834. Thereafter names like H. Klee, J. Kuhn, F. Pilgram, J. Möhler and F. Probst follow. The church was even designated as sacrament by theologians from the neo-scholastic school. It was thus no longer a matter for just one movement in theology. One could say that since M. Scheeben, the greatest German theologian of the nineteenth century (d. 1888), it has gradually gained strength as one of the most striking designations for the many-sided reality that is the church. It was a common property for theologians in the twentieth century, and since the 1950's has been taken up systematically as a key concept in theology by K. Rahner, E. Schillebeeckx, O. Semmelroth, P. Smulders, C. Vagaggini, B. Willems and A. Winkelhofer.

The designation was expressly taken up by Vatican II, and since then has become one of the most widely used designations for the church. We have seen how it came to the fore in the Constitution on the Liturgy, the first document they produced.[13] The first chapter of the Dogmatic Constitution on the Church, *Lumen gentium*, carries the title 'De Ecclesiae

---

12 BOFF: *Die Kirche als Sakrament* 112.
13 *Constitution on the Liturgy* no. 5 and no. 26, in *Documents on the liturgy* 5, respectively 10.

Mysterio'. In the commentary it is pointed out that this expression is intended biblically, and that it is indicative of the point of confluence of the transcendental-divine and the mundane-visible. In other words, the term has regained its ancient Christian meaning. In the first article of this Constitution it is stated: "The church is, so to speak, the sacrament in Christ, that is, the symbol and instrument of the most profound union with God and the unity of all humanity".[14] The text formulates it carefully: the church is, so to speak, sacrament. Some among the conciliar fathers were afraid that the use of the word 'sacrament' for the church would sow confusion, as if there were an eighth sacrament. For the same reason, the meaning of the word 'sacrament' is immediately clarified in the text. However, in other places in *Lumen gentium*, and in other council documents, the designation returns without further qualification.[15]

The text just cited reflects in a clear way what the Council wanted to say about the church. When the church is designated as sacrament, it is a matter of the church being a sign and an instrument, or in other words, what people would designate as a symbol, something that calls up and mediates another reality. Moreover, in a suggestive way this text expresses that the church in question is not a church turned inward, but that it is a church which does not receive salvation in a narcissistic way, but which itself is and must be salutary for the world. In regard to the church, the designation as sacrament indicates the unity between its own existence and its mission.[16] The church is the people of God, who are the bearers of Christian sacred history. But this Christian sacred history rises above this people of God. It reaches further, because it is a universal history, intended for all humanity and for the whole cosmos. The church has, in all modesty, a mission for all; it must be of service to and for all peoples. It also has an unmistakable mission in regard to the cosmos. There is an ecology, a care for the environment, that must also be at its heart.

As a sacrament of salvation the church carries no small responsibility. And it can not be denied that for many it is only with great difficulty that this symbolic shape of the church can be discovered. For many, at present the church has become un-meaningful. This is undoubtedly connected with the fact that the pronouncement cited often is not in agreement with the structures and the conduct of the church. When the church pretends to be a real symbol of 'the most profound union with God and the unity

---

14 Cf. *Documents on the liturgy* 29-30.
15 Dogmatic Constitution on the Church *Lumen gentium* no. 9 and no. 48; Pastoral Constitution on the Church in the world of this era *Gaudium et spes* no. 42 and no. 45; Decree on the Church's missionary activity *Ad gentes divinitus*, no. 1 and no. 5 (cf. *Documents on the liturgy* 65-66).
16 CONGAR: *Un peuple messianique* 7 and 76-77.

of all humanity', our day rightly poses rather challenging and critical questions to it. Is the humanity of our God really clearly visible in the church? On the other hand, people must realize that Jesus himself was only illuminated for those who gave themselves over to him. For those who stood outside the circle of disciples, Jesus was and is a dubious symbol, ambiguous and even annoying. This is, in one way or another, also true for the church in its symbolic form as a sacrament of salvation.[17]

1.5. Here and now

In connection with the understanding of the church as sacrament, it is important to point to yet another shift in the view of the church. In the period in which thinking about the sacraments with regard to the church disappeared into the background, all attention shifted to the universal church. But since Vatican II, the emphasis has been on the local church, without excluding the existence of the universal church. In other words, the church is not first and foremost 'the Christians' or 'the Catholics'. Nor is the church first and foremost the whole of all believers including the Pope and bishops, everywhere and in all times, in all that it does. The church is also not there, purely because of the fact that it was once established and appointed and thereafter, as it were, statically kept its footing. No, the church is first of all an occurrence, something that takes place and is repeatedly performed again.[18] That is not something vague, something general and abstract. It is the here and now. The church takes place, first and foremost, locally:[19]

> This Church of Christ is truly present in all lawful, local congregations of the faithful, which, united with their pastors, are themselves called Churches in the New Testament. (...) In them the faithful are gathered together by the preaching of Christ's Gospel and the mystery of the Lord's Supper is celebrated, so that 'by the food and blood of the Lord's body the whole brotherhood is joined together'. (...) In these communities, though frequently small or poor or living in isolation, Christ is present and the power of his presence gathers together one, holy, catholic, and apostolic Church.

In other words, the center of gravity for the concept of the church lies in the local church community, and more, in particular, in its liturgical life. 'Church' does not primarily refer to a hyper-organization of functionaries

---

17 CONGAR: *Un peuple messianique* 84-86.
18 Cf. HUIZING and WILLEMS: *Sacramentele grondslag* 248; H. KÜNG: *De kerk* (Hilversum 1967) especially 98.
19 Dogmatic Constitution on the Church *Lumen gentium* no. 26, in *Documents on the liturgy* 33-34.

that is distant from and stands over the concrete community that gathers together. It is, rather, primarily what happens at the base. The new image of the church, that is at home in the oldest Christian traditions and is confirmed by Vatican II, begins from God's people, who live in countless local communities. The Pope, bishops and priests also belong to the people of God. The local church comes first; the universal church emerges from it. At the same time, it must also be said that the local church is not the whole church. First of all, there must be openness to other local churches. The local churches are, each in their own way, called to service in the building up of one body. Those who are called to offices stand before the local church but, with an eye to the connectedness of the churches, they have an special function and responsibility. They must guard the connectedness with other local churches, the priest with regard to other communities, the bishop with other diocesan churches, and in particular with the bishop in Rome, the successor to Peter, who forms the center of the *communio* and is the chairman of the churches' bond of love.

1.6. An important fact

There is still much confusion about the word 'church'. It is used with all sorts of meanings: for a church building, for Rome with all its administrative bodies, for the whole of bishops and priests, for the believers who faithfully carry out the guidelines from the top, for the simple believers at the base, for the 'church' of the poor, of the saints, and such. In conversations, considerable confusion is possible. Is it not always important when speaking with each other to know from which understanding of church people are proceeding?

I believe that the shifts which have been sketched here are inevitably of importance for a good understanding of sacred history, precisely as they are for sacramental sacred history. If the Lord comes to us in visible form, that is, after all, not far off and not high above us. It is close by and in our midst, here and now, locally, at the base. That is where sacramental sacred history is also going on. It is there, so to speak, that the God of Jesus himself continues to set forth his original plan of salvation. It is there that he is constantly busy with us, and is ineffably close to us, human in our midst, in order that among us, and for the whole world, peace and righteousness will come to pass. 'Your kingdom come': that is the daily prayer of the Christian communities and therefore their daily praxis must also be directed to that end.

All sorts of images are used for the church, such as, for instance, the body of Christ, the people of God, the bride of Christ, a mother, a house. Each image has its own nuances. But the word sacrament is the most suitable for designating the complex reality of the church as such. It was in that spirit that Vatican II confirmed its use. Rahner remarks that this concept is of tremendously great importance in the consciousness of the church of today and tomorrow.[20] For us, it can point out a new way for the church. Thanks to the concept of sacrament, we can discover the tension between the seen and the unseen. We no longer have to stare blindly at the purely external, legalistic aspect of the church, even if this understanding of the church does not entirely disappear and will always be defended by some. Proceeding from the key word *sacramentum* you can again see in the church the tension between the certainly and the not yet, between always present and yet to be realized, between a church of saints and a church of sinners. It is the art of faith to maintain this tension, without breaking it down, either to the purely visible, or to the purely spiritual side. The church does not hang above the world, but stands within the world and within history, without being swallowed up in it. There is no culture that is alien to it, but at the same time, it can not be fully identified with any culture. The church is not intended exclusively for a limited elite or an ethnic group, but for all peoples, races and languages, without coinciding with any of them. A good insight into the meaning of sacrament, applied to the church, can thus preserve us from both extremes: from a false spirituality and from a false institutionalism; from an exclusive emphasis on charisma and from identifying the church with churchly institutions and bureaus that are so certain they know where the bounds of the church lie.

This means that the concept of sacrament as applied to the church is not a matter of secondary importance. M. Scheeben remarks:[21]

> If Christianity is simply sacramental through and through, down to its foundations (...) then anything which is constructed entirely on that foundation must also naturally bear a sacramental character; (...) otherwise the structure would not be consistent with its foundation, and the tree which has grown up would deviate from the idea and tendency of its own root.

Thus, it goes to the very heart of Christianity. Therefore it is of the greatest importance to continue exploration within the field of tension of the church as sacrament. That is a creative happening. It is never finished, and demands a watchful and critical outlook. If the church is sacrament, then it must also really be a symbol of that to which it points, it must in

---

20 K. RAHNER: Das neue Bild der Kirche, in *Schriften zur Theologie* VIII (Zürich-Einsiedeln-Köln 1968) 338.
21 M. SCHEEBEN: *Die Mysterien des Christentums. Wesen, Bedeutung und Zusammenhang derselben nach der in ihrem übernatürlichen Charakter gegebenen Perspective dargestellt* (= Gesammelte Schriften 2) (Freiburg im Breisgau 1941) 465.

one way or another evoke the 'Jesus thing'.[22] Then the church must refer to the reality that it is, but at the same time is not, and must yet become real in the church. When the church is so involved in Jesus' work, then it shall have to place values like salvation, liberation, communication without domination, solidarity with the poor, resistance against oppressive powers and service high on its agenda, beginning this very day. It will have to be, in Congar's words, a messianic people of God, or, in other words, bearers of hope and liberation and a better future.[23] As is characteristic of Christian messianism, it must be directed toward the present, but at the same time expect its definitive salvation from the future. That is also what Jesus, the Messiah, did. Whatever the case, the church must continually be involved in this in order to become a good sacrament; otherwise it will be unfaithful to itself.

1.7. Dynamic embodiment: the risen Lord

The being of the church as sacrament thus must be interpreted in a sufficiently dynamic way. This demands further explanation. For a long time, people have looked rather solidly on the incarnation of Christ as the basic model for the church.[24] Just as in Christ the divine and the human were inseparably bound together with each other, so also the visible church is an unbreakable unity of the divine and the human. The church is thus regarded as the continuation of the incarnation, as the temporary extension of Jesus Christ.

The basic intuition behind this vision is correct: in this way the sacramental structure of salvation, that most tangibly came to light in the incarnation of Christ, is emphasized. God also still meets us now in and through ourselves, in and through our human connectedness with the world. But it is also true that this incarnational model has its limitations. It easily leads to a rather static understanding of the church. In an imbalanced way it emphasizes the church as already all-embracing, as already full of grace. In a way of speaking, the only remaining task of the church is handing out this grace; within history, the church would only have to shift its accent, according to various situations. The church is seen as a closed entity. It knows its precise dimensions and determines the exact boundaries of its membership. The risk of this vision is that the church will too much conduct itself in this world as having 'arrived'. There is too little space for real movement toward the future. After all, the church must always make itself concrete again within time, and thus it is an

---

22 W. BARTHOLOMÄUS: Communications in the Church. Aspects of a theological theme, in *Concilium* 14 (1978) no. 1, 95-110.
23 CONGAR: *Un peuple messianique* 90-98.
24 BOFF: *Die Kirche als Sakrament* 351 ss.

ecclesia semper reformanda, a church that must be constantly renewing itself.

Theologically, it is also necessary to supplement and correct the incarnational model. Correct, because in the model of the church people too easily identify themselves completely with Christ himself, while the church is really another embodiment of God's grace rather than of Jesus' own corporeality. And supplement, because the church is the becoming visible of the incarnation that ended in glorification. In other words, the church is the becoming visible of the Lord who has ascended to heaven. The glorified body of Christ henceforth fulfills the function that it had in his earthly life. Because his glorified body is invisible for us, there is the church, as sacrament of the glorified Lord. The church is first and foremost a continuation of the heavenly Christ, and precisely as such it has the function of his earthly body. One can find this shift of perspective in theologians such as E. Schillebeeckx and J. Alfaro.[25] For them, what matters is the church as sacrament of the heavenly Christ. The Lord has a new way of existing, now that he, in his humanity, is taken up into the glory of the Father. The incarnate is fulfilled by the Spirit. It is this Lord, fulfilled by the Spirit, who is and will be revealed in the earthly church. The church is sacrament, because and as it brings this Lord to light. It is sacrament, thanks to the Spirit which the Lord after his resurrection has poured out upon it. When people draw out all the possible consequences of this vision, it will lead to a much more dynamic view of the church.

The initiatives of Schillebeeckx and Alfaro have been further developed, particularly in the last few years. Thus Boff points out that people must not use the closed corporeality of Jesus within this world as a point of departure, but his corporeality that has been fulfilled through the Spirit.[26] Henceforth, the Lord has a heavenly, a spiritual body (I Cor. 15: 44ff). His corporeality knows no bounds, one can speak of perfect expansiveness and openness, without the boundaries of space and time, Jew or gentile, race or nation. The Lord, fulfilled by the Spirit, is now boundlessly at work in the world. His Spirit is dynamic and creative. His Spirit blows where it will (John 3:7), and is a Spirit of freedom (II Cor. 3:17). This heavenly Lord in his spiritual existence becomes visible in the sacrament that is the church.

The church is only the sacrament of salvation because the Lord has made it alive through his Spirit. Ecclesiology demands pneumatology.[27] Thus,

---

25 E. SCHILLEBEECKX: *Christ, the sacrament of encounter with God* (London-New York 1963). J. ALFARO: Cristo, Sacramento de Dio Padre. La Iglesia, Sacramento de Cristo glorificado, in *Gregorianum* 58 (1967) 5-28. Cf. BOFF: *Die Kirche als Sakrament* 358-360.
26 BOFF: *Die Kirche als Sakrament* 361-375.
27 CONGAR: *Un peuple messianique* 40 ss.

in everything that is performed in and through the church as a sacrament of salvation, in one way or another an epiklesis, i.e., an invocation of the Spirit, is necessary. Thus the church is a continuation of Jesus' action in the Spirit. It rests on the Lord who is the Spirit (II Cor. 3:17) so much that one could, with W. Kasper, call it a "sacrament of the Spirit".[28] This vision is also given impetus by Vatican II; in article 48 of the Dogmatic Constitution *Lumen gentium* it is said that Christ has poured out his Spirit over his apostles and in doing so has constituted his body, the church, as a universal sacrament of salvation.

One still encounters incarnation ecclesiology in many contemporary theologians. In them, one realizes that this ecclesiology is sometimes present in a concealed way, for instance when, in respect to the church, they emphasize an aspect such as the epiphany, the manifestation of the Lord, more than the instrumentality of salvation. However that may be, the consequence of the contemporary vision that is based on Vatican II is the realization that the church's purpose is not within the church itself. Nor is its purpose to dominate the world. No, the church is for the world. It renders service to the world. An ecclesiology grafted on to the Spirit makes the church modest, more modest than it often manifests itself. Perhaps what Karl Rahner called an 'incapability to be poor' – and one must understand that poverty as not only material – is the foremost reason why the church lacks the power to reach out, and has difficulty carrying on sacramental sacred history in all freedom in regard to acquired institutional and cultural forms. The servant church is ever again summoned to new decisions. Is the church – and that first and foremost means the local church that is close to everyone – ready to be the sacrament in the Spirit of the Lord that, without dominating, will stand with all, because all are to be saved?

2. CHURCH, LITURGY AND THE HOLY SPIRIT

After his resurrection, Paul characterized Jesus as the new and definitive Adam. The risen Lord makes history into real sacred history. "The first man Adam became a living being; the last [*eschatos*] Adam became a lifegiving Spirit" (I Cor. 15:45, RSV). As the "first-born among many brethren" (Rom. 8:29, RSV) and the "first-born of all creation" (Col. 1: 15, RSV), the Lord breathes a new and definitive breath of life, which is called the Holy Spirit.[29]

---

28 W. KASPER: Die Kirche als Sakrament des Geistes, in W. KASPER and G. SAUTER: *Kirche – Ort des Geistes* (Freiburg 1976) 41.
29 J. LESCRAUWAET: Zonder 'Maranatha' geen ecclesiologie, in H. BERGER a.o. (ed.): *Tussentijds. Theologische Faculteit te Tilburg. Bundel opstellen bij gelegenheid van haar erkenning* (Tilburg 1975) 19-20.

Since his resurrection, the Lord has withdrawn from our sight. And yet he has not done so, precisely because of the his Spirit. Since Pentecost the Lord, as the new Adam, has shared his life's breath with us. Out of heaven came a sound like the rush of a mighty wind, and fiery tongues appeared, and they were all filled with the Holy Spirit (Acts 2:2-4). On the birthday of the church, Peter referred to what his hearers, thanks to the Spirit, could "hear and see" of the Lord in the first church (Acts 2:32-33). It is a matter of tangibility and visibility, characteristics of all the sacraments. The Spirit reveals Jesus to our eyes and ears as the Lord of history, and certainly in the church, that we can properly call the sacrament of the heavenly Lord.

Previous to this then was there no mention of the gifts of the Spirit? There certainly was! The same Spirit worked in the lives of people before and after the Christ. But after Jesus' return to the Father a tremendous expansion and enrichment took place in the work of the Spirit. Scripture uses words for this that suggest that the Holy Spirit was given then for the first time (John 7:39).[30] What the prophet Joel had predicted was fulfilled on Pentecost (Acts 2:17-18, RSV): "I will pour out my Spirit on all flesh (...) yea, and on my menservants and maidservants in those days I will pour out my Spirit". The Spirit now broke straight through all social barriers and privileges. The church was there for all races, nations and tongues, without distinctions of rank or class or sex. Through the Spirit who was sent, the Lord was revealed in his new, heavenly existence. Also through the Spirit, sacred history remained a sacramental sacred history after Jesus departure. Through the Spirit the church was born as the universal sacrament of salvation. Or, in other words, the church is the sacrament of the Spirit.

One would do well to let what has been said here sink in. The Holy Spirit and the sacramental form of the church are inextricably connected with each other. It is the Spirit who, in and through the visible community of the church, and through its actions, reminds us of the Lord, the one who now remains among us and also is the one who shall come (Rev. 1:4, 1:8, 4:8). All of sacred history is encompassed. Even though the Lord is now revealed in the visible church, precisely by way of the sacramentality of the church one can also speak of the 'not yet': therefore the church also continually prays in and through the Spirit for fulfillment in the future: "Come, Lord Jesus, come!"[31]

It can not be denied that, in contradistinction to the Eastern church, the Western church has difficulty with the Holy Spirit. To many, the Spirit appears so far away. Some have spoken of a "forgetfulness of the Spirit".[32] When we hear the word 'spirit' we think of something fleeting,

---

30 C. TSIRPANTIS: Pneumatology in the eastern Church, in *Diakonia* 13 (1978) 20.
31 LESCRAUWAET: Zonder 'Maranatha' geen ecclesiologie 22-23.
32 KASPER: *Die Kirche als Sakrament des Geistes* 15 and 21.

elusive, bloodless, something abstract. 'Spirit' easily is interpreted as non-vital, as that which has nothing to do with corporeality. However, the realization is breaking through to some in our time that in the Scripture the concept of 'spirit' has to do precisely with concreteness and warm-bloodedness. In the charismatic movement that is the case in a pronounced way. It is being discovered anew that the Holy Spirit indeed has something to do with vital movement and the warmth of the breath of life. The Spirit is dynamic, and this dynamic is not hard-handed, that of masculine tyranny, of ideology. The Spirit is the soft breeze, the fiery tongue, inner freedom that creates warmth and flexibility. The Jewish Christians in the ancient church were even convinced that the Spirit was feminine.[33] She/he is the one who most deeply stirs us. In the prayers of the church we call it the grace of the Holy Spirit that enlightens our heart and our senses.[34] She/he permeates our sensibility and our affectivity. The Holy Spirit has to do with our deepest self, with our intimacy. In the context in which we are speaking here, one can say that the Holy Spirit has to do with the 'heart' of the church itself. The Spirit is the dynamic power that makes the church the sacrament of the heavenly Lord.

Up to this point I have spoken of the church as sacrament in the broad meaning of the word. However, if the Spirit and the church are inextricably bound together with each other as sacrament, this is certainly no less valid for the liturgy, that point where the church, in her sacramental form, is most intensely developed. The Holy Spirit and liturgy are also inextricably connected with each other. In other terms, without the Holy Spirit one could not speak of a Christian liturgy. I want to go further into this, and roughly sketch out the relation of the Spirit and liturgy. This is all the more important because in the West one once rather spoke about liturgy without even mentioning the Holy Ghost. In 1956, Pius XII characterized the Liturgical Movement as a movement of the Holy Spirit in the church.[35] All through the twentieth century there was discussion of a movement that wanted to place the liturgy again in the center of the church, where it is properly at home. It was a movement that resulted in the Constitution on the Liturgy at Vatican II (1963). After saying that, it is not difficult to agree with the words of Pius XII.

But the work of the Holy Spirit with regard to the liturgy reaches further. The Spirit is the origin of all concrete liturgy.[36] When the Holy Spirit rained down on the apostles, they proclaimed God's great deeds of

---

33 G. QUISPEL: The birth of the Child, in *Eranos* 40 (1971) 304-305.
34 Cf. M. ANDRIEU: *Le pontifical romain au moyen âge* III. *Le pontifical de Guillaume Durand* (= Studi e testi 88) (Città del Vaticano 1940) 376, "Spiritus Sancti gratia illuminet sensus et corda nostra".
35 Speech to the Congress of Assissi, in *Acta Apostolicae Sedis* 48 (1956) 712.
36 See J. MULDERS: H. Geest, in L. BRINKHOFF a.o. (ed.): *Liturgisch Woordenboek* I (Roermond 1958-1962) 804-807.

salvation (Acts 2:11). The same was true for the heathen, if the Spirit possessed them (Acts 10:46). Christians must address one another in psalms and hymns and songs inspired by the Spirit (Eph. 5:19). Thanks to the Spirit we can address God as our Father (Gal. 4:6, Rom. 8:15). Indeed, once we did not know how we should pray: it is the Spirit who intercedes for us with sighs too deep for words (Rom. 8:26). These texts reach beyond the liturgy, but likewise it is true that one may not in the least exclude their application to liturgy. In I Cor. 12:3 and Phil. 2:11 Paul is probably speaking expressly about liturgy: only through the Holy Spirit can we confess "Jesus is the Lord", possibly referring to a liturgical formula that touches the core of our faith.

Strikingly, Mulders remarks:[37]

> Because the Holy Spirit, existing as a Person, is 'we' for the Father and Son (compare John 14:23), the church experiences its unity with Him in a way that agrees with the special place of the Spirit in the Trinity, namely that as Body, as a entity, as a 'we'-in-Christ, it rises up to Christ and the Father. One should read Augustine's splendid exposition: Sermo ad populum 71, especially the chapters 18 and 19.[38] In this way, the plural that we find in all liturgical prayers ("let *us* pray") refers not only, on its face, to the joint action of all the participants in the liturgical act, but finds its deepest ground in the fact that the church receives its unity, its being as 'we', from the Holy Ghost. Thus the Holy Spirit can truly be called continuous.

It is open to discussion as to whether one indeed can come to this conclusion from the 'we' of liturgical texts, but quite aside from that, it seems to me that the intuition that liturgical community prayer is always connected with the Holy Spirit in this way is correct. It is the Holy Spirit who has stood at the origin of the Christian liturgy from its beginning, from rebirth by water and the Spirit. In and through the Holy Spirit, the affairs of creation are proclaimed, confessed, sung, prayed for, handled and dealt with in liturgy. Or in other words, in and through the Spirit our history and our world gain a new and staggering perspective in the liturgy. For the Christian, the symbols, words and symbolic actions have a new dimension: in and through the Spirit they become expressions in the perspective of Christian sacred history and involve the Christ, the original sacrament, who was, is, and shall come.

Lescrauwaet remarks that the Holy Spirit is nowhere other than in the living person who has faith. The Spirit does not float in the space in which we move, and does not go through the centuries in the form of books and things.[39] That appears to me to say too little, certainly with

---

37 MULDERS: H. Geest 806-807.
38 J.-P. MIGNE: *Patrologia Latina* XXXVIII (Paris 1841) 461-463.
39 J. LESCRAUWAET: Gij, geestelijke mensen, in *Ons Geestelijk Leven* 55 (1978) 7.

regard to liturgy. The question arises, how does the Spirit relate to the material world?[40] In the first verses of the Bible it is said that the spirit of God floated above the waters (Gen. 1:2). He is thus present in the cosmos. The spirit of God brings matter to life and renews the earth (Ps. 104: 30; compare Ezek. 37:10). One might say there was an overflow of material symbols, in and through which the presence and power of the Spirit was revealed, with the emphatic appearance on Pentecost: a noise like that of a mighty rushing wind, fire that divided itself into tongues, foreign languages (Acts 2:2-4; compare John 3:8, 20:22). In the Wisdom of Solomon it is written, "The Spirit of the Lord fills the world" (Wisdom 1:7). Is this not all the more true since Christ has sent the Spirit? Certainly: and the liturgy does speak of the 'we' of Spirit and believers, who confess, pray, sing and place things in a new perspective and within a new dimension of symbolic acts. Then it can not be otherwise than that the liturgical texts, music and rites bear the stamp of the Spirit. They are co-inspired by the Spirit. Thanks to the 'we', the liturgy becomes like the window in a gothic cathedral: one sees this world, but in such a new dimension that one sees the ultimate Christian reality. In a figure of speech, they are 'spiritual', transfigured windows that look out into what is going on in Christian sacred history. A corner of the veil is lifted. The ultimate meaning of past, present and future comes toward us: "I am the Alpha and the Omega, the first and the last, the beginning and the end" (Rev. 22:12, RSV). In liturgy, it is the Spirit who keeps the tension alive, through which we look toward the day in which the whole cosmos will get a new aspect: that God may be all in all (I Cor. 15:28). The texts and rites of the liturgy are eschatological realities in and through the Spirit. In the eucharist the Spirit most completely fulfills the liturgical reality. The East has come to the most penetrating expression of this in the eucharistic epiklesis. The high point of the eucharistic prayer is the epiklesis, in which the Holy Spirit is invoked over the gifts, in order that the Spirit may make the bread and wine into the body and blood of Christ. In the bread and wine, fulfilled by the Holy Spirit, the Lord himself is among us and makes us into a new community.[41]

When the liturgy bears the stamp of the Spirit this much, people will have to have respect for the rituals that are created in the Christian community. It is already, then, in another degree than the Scripture itself, involving inspired texts and rites that unveil the Christian reality in an intense way and can arouse true faith. But immediately it must be added,

---

40 Cf. Y. KREKHOVETSKY: The Holy Spirit and icons, in *Diakonia* 13 (1978) 3-16.
41 With regard to epiklesis, see: J. MEIJER: 'Zend uw Geest over ons...'. Enkele opmerkingen over de epiklese, in H. WEGMAN (ed.): *Goed of niet goed* II. *Het eucharistisch gebed in Nederland* (Hilversum 1978) 177-185. With regard to Spirit and liturgy, also see I. OÑATIBIA: *Por una mayor recuperación de la dimensión pneumatologica de los sacramentos*, in *Phase* 16 (1976) 425-439.

that we would be unfaithful to the Spirit if we would limit ourselves to this respect. After all, the Spirit is breath, wind and fire, full of vitality. The Spirit ever again moves the Christian community to a new, living liturgy. The church of the twentieth century has to seek the expression of this staggering perspective, not apart from the past, but certainly in its own way. In that respect there is a growing consciousness in our time that the Spirit does not only stir the hierarchy, but all the faithful. The active participation of the laity in the liturgy must not be limited to repetition. It is a matter of the creativity of all. Don't blow the Spirit out!

This 'Don't blow the Spirit out!' reaches still further. Beginning with the experience that the Spirit fulfills the liturgical community and also makes the objects into eschatological realities, we look not only to the ultimate new human community and the new heaven and earth, but we also are given impetus to an effort at actualization: liturgy that really is inspired by the Spirit inspires us to a new praxis, both in relation to other people and in relation to the world, the environment.

6. Die Taufe: ein unersetzbares Sakrament

Im alten holländischen Katechismus begann der Abschnitt über die Taufe folgendermaßen:
– 'Welches ist das erste und notwendigste Sakrament?'
Antwort: Das erste und notwendigste Sakrament ist die Taufe.
– 'Warum ist die Taufe das erste Sakrament?'
Antwort: Die Taufe ist das erste Sakrament, weil wir vor der Taufe kein anderes Sakrament empfangen können.
– 'Warum ist die Taufe das notwendigste Sakrament?'
Antwort: Die Taufe ist das notwendigste Sakrament, weil niemand ohne die Taufe selig werden kann.
Nur wenige Katholiken hatten es schwer mit diesen Fragen und Antworten. Heutzutage ist das anders. Die Taufe hat ihre Selbstverständlichkeit verloren. Wer heute behauptet, die Taufe sei ein notwendiges Sakrament, stößt nicht auf allgemeine Zustimmung. Und doch ist gerade dies mit der Überschrift dieses Artikels gemeint. In dieser 'kleinen Tauftheologie' möchte ich Schritt für Schritt deutlich und nachvollziehbar machen, welchen unersetzbaren Platz die Taufe im christlichen Glaubensleben einnimmt.

1. NATÜRLICHE SAKRAMENTALITÄT

In 1976 schrieb der brasilianische Theologe L. Boff:[1]

> Heutzutage wissen viele Menschen nicht mehr, was ein Sakrament ist. Die Alten dagegen wußten es genau. Auch ich habe lange dazu gebraucht, das zu verstehen: Fünf Jahre lang habe ich täglich viele Stunden studiert, was in allen christlichen Sprachen – von den Tagen der Bibel bis heute – über das Sakrament geschrieben worden ist. Es war dies eine wahre geistige Schlacht, aus der 552 gedruckte und als Buch veröffentlichte Seiten entstanden.[2] Aber dies ist nicht das vorrangige Ergebnis. Nach so vielen Mü-

---

* *Dopen met water en geest. Doopliturgieën, elementen voor vieringen en achtergrondbeschouwingen uit 20 jaar werkmap Liturgie (1966-1985)* (Hilversum 1988) 15-16, 18-19, 21-22, 24-29, 91-110. Übersetzt von G. Merks-Leinen, M.A.
1 L. BOFF: *Kleine Sakramentenlehre* (Düsseldorf 1976) 21-22.
2 L. BOFF: *Die Kirche als Sakrament im Horizont der Welterfahrung. Versuch einer Legitimation und einer strukturfunktionalistischen Grundlegung der Kirche im Anschluß an das II. Vatikanische Konzil* (= Konfessionskundliche und Kontroverstheologische Studien 28) (Paderborn 1972).

hen, Zornausbrüchen, Freuden, Flüchen und Segnungen entdeckte ich, was schon immer entdeckt war. Ich erfuhr etwas handgreiflich Einleuchtendes. Sakrament ist das, was immer schon lebte und was alle Menschen erleben, was ich aber nicht wußte und was nur wenige wissen. Ich begann, die Landschaft der Dinge in Augenschein zu nehmen, die schon immer vor meiner Nase lagen. Jeder Tag steckt voller Sakramente. In den Tiefenschichten des Alltäglichen gedeihen lebendige, erlebte und wirkliche Sakramente. Sakramente sind der Trinkbecher in unserer Familie, Mutters Polenta, der letzte Stummel einer Strohzigarette, den Vater hinterließ und den ich liebevoll aufbewahre, der alte Arbeitstisch, eine dicke Weihnachtskerze, die Blumenvase auf dem Tisch, ein Stück des Gebirgszuges, der alte steinige Weg, das alte elterliche Haus ... All diese Dinge sind nicht einfach mehr Sachen. Menschen sind sie geworden. Sie sprechen zu uns, und wir sind in der Lage, ihre Stimme und ihre Botschaft zu vernehmen. Sie besitzen Innenleben und Herz, Sakramente sind sie geworden. Mit anderen Worten: sie sind Zeichen, die eine andere von ihnen zu unterscheidende, in ihnen aber präsente Wirklichkeit enthalten, darstellen, an sie erinnern, sie sichtbar machen und vermitteln.

Moderne Menschen leben zwar umgeben von Sakramenten, verfügen aber nicht über den offenen und entsprechend geschärften Blick, der notwendig ist, um sie reflektiert wahrzunehmen. Dinge werden als Dinge gesehen, das heißt: nur von außen betrachtet. Wer sie aber von innen her anschaut, entdeckt eine Spalte, durch die ein höheres Licht in sie hineinfällt. Das Licht beleuchtet die Dinge, macht sie transparent und durchsichtig.

Boff spricht über die natürliche Sakramentalität unserer Welt. Wenn hierfür das Gefühl fehlt, ist es unmöglich, den Sinn der christlichen Sakramente zu erfahren. Man muß davon loskommen, nur die reinen Fakten wahrzunehmen und alles nur wörtlich zu nehmen. Wir müssen lernen, perspektivisch zu sehen. Dafür sind besondere Talente erforderlich. Eigentlich ist es ganz einfach und menschlich. Für alle Dinge gilt, daß sie nicht nur sind, was ich oberflächlich an ihnen wahrnehme, sondern daß sie auf die ein oder andere Weise mehr sind und so zum Sakrament werden können. Das gilt für die Hand, den Körper, für Wasser, Brot und Wein, für Tisch und Stuhl, für das Kind, den Mann, die Frau usw. Und was für die Dinge gilt, gilt auch für das menschliche Handeln. 'Handeln' kann ich sachlich betrachten; dann habe ich den Nutzen, den es bringt, im Auge. Dann geht es um das Resultat. Aber im Handeln kann sich auch Tiefe offenbaren. Das Hochheben der Hand kann zum Ballen der Faust werden aus Protest gegen Mißstände; mein Laufen kann zu einem Fortschreiten werden, in dem ich das Leben als geheimnisvollen Weg erfahre usw. Beim Begräbnis von Martin Luther King wurde sein Leichnam auf eine Bauernkarre gelegt, gezogen von zwei Eseln. Diese Handlung verwies weiter als nur auf das Wegbringen des Leichnams. Sie wurde zum Sakrament des Auszugs des leidenden Dieners JHWHS ins Land der Lebenden. Hier vollzog sich die sakramentale Handlung des Begräbnisses.

Bei Dingen und Handlungen kann man also eine Perspektive entdecken, die in die Tiefe verschoben ist. In diesen Fällen vollzieht sich etwas Sakramentales. Eigentlich werden diese Dinge und Handlungen immer durch Worte begleitet, die diese 'sich verschiebende Perspektive' auch benennen. In diesem Zusammenhang ist es interessant anzumerken, daß in verschiedenen europäischen Sprachen die Wörter, die 'sagen' ausdrücken, häufig auch die Bedeutung von 'Licht' haben. Etwas sagen bedeutet ursprünglich: etwas ans Licht bringen. Das Wort in seiner ganz ursprünglichen Bedeutung ist also sakramental. Es holt die Dinge aus ihrer Verborgenheit. Es enthüllt und bringt ans Licht. Das Wort durch-lichtet die Wirklichkeit und gibt Perspektive. Daher der Ausdruck: 'Sprich, so werde ich sehen.'

F. Buitendijk hat darauf hingewiesen, wie wichtig im menschlichen Leben von Anfang an das Wort ist.[3] Indem das Kind sich seiner Mutter zuwendet, stellt es eine Frage und erwartet eine Antwort. Durch seine Gebärden, seine Stimme, seinen Gesichtsausdruck wendet sich das Kind ihrem Dasein zu und verlangt eine Antwort, die seinem ursprünglichen Verlangen nach Gemeinschaft und Kontakt mit der Wirklichkeit entgegenkommt. Durch ihr Dasein bewirkt die Mutter das Dasein der Welt für das Kind. Dabei ist am Anfang die Mutter die einzige, die spricht, während das Kind alles andächtig verfolgt. Das Kind tut dies nicht wie jemand, der die Fakten unzweideutig beschrieben haben möchte. Nein, es geht um die Worte und Namen, die einen Weg bahnen zum Leben selbst, in die Tiefe. So lernt das Kind sprechen und der Welt einen Namen geben. Die Worte der Mutter sind 'Sakramente', die für das Kind die Dinge ans Licht bringen: 'Sprich, so werde ich sehen'. Allmählich beginnt das Kind auch selbst zu sprechen und mit-zu-enthüllen; und auch seine Worte können 'Sakramente' werden für andere.

2. DER INNERSTE KREIS DER NATÜRLICHEN SAKRAMENTALITÄT

Im Sakrament geht es also um Dinge, Handlungen und Wörter in ihrer Tiefen-Dimension. Je nach der Ausrichtung des Ganzen spricht man von einer bestimmten sakramentalen Handlung oder von einem bestimmten Ritus. So kann man z.B. von einem Abend- und Morgenritus, einem Begräbnisritus, Taufritus, Weihnachtsritus usw. sprechen.

Am stärksten ist das Bedürfnis, das Leben sakramental zu erleuchten, dann, wenn man an einem existentiellen Scheideweg des Lebens steht. Vor allem Geburt, feierlicher Eintritt in die Gemeinschaft der Erwachsenen (Initiation), Essen und Trinken, ein Bruch im Leben, Krankheit und

---

3 F. BUITENDIJK: Taal en samenleven, in *Taal en gezondheid* (Utrecht 1969) 9 ff.

Tod, Berufung zu religiöser Leitung und Heirat sind mit sakramentalem Inhalt beladen. In diesen elementaren Lebenslagen konzentrieren wir uns am stärksten auf eine End-Perspektive. Obwohl alle tief-menschlichen Ereignisse sakramental sind, ist hier die sakramentale Verdichtung am größten. Wir stoßen hier auf den innersten Kreis der natürlichen Sakramentalität.

3. DIE BESONDERE PERSPEKTIVE DER CHRISTLICHEN SAKRAMENTALITÄT

Wie wir gerade beschrieben haben, geht es beim Sakrament immer um eine spezifische Weise des Kontaktes mit der Wirklichkeit. Von Natur ist jeder Mensch ein *animal symbolicum*: ein Wesen, das die Welt nicht als platte Wirklichkeit, sondern als Sakrament einer höheren Wirklichkeit betrachtet. Mit der natürlichen Sakramentalität und durch sie kommt in unser Leben das Geheimnis, das uns übersteigt. Diesem Geheimnis versuchen wir, einen Namen zu geben. Es hat mit Fülle, Licht, Liebe, Treue, Ewigkeit zu tun. Die Religionen haben das alles durchdringende Geheimnis 'Gott' genannt. Die Christen fühlen sich am nächsten mit der Art verwandt, in der die Juden dem Geheimnis einen Namen gegeben haben. Oder besser: Gott selbst hat dem jüdischen Volk den Namen des Geheimnisses auf überraschende Weise enthüllt. Der, der sich den Juden in dieser Welt enthüllt, ist der Gott, der sich als der Gott offenbart, der mit seinem Volk einen Bund schloß: Ich bin der Ich-bin für euch (Ex 3,14). Mit Abraham hat er einen Bund geschlossen, und seitdem ist er mit seinem Volk in der Geschichte unterwegs. So erhält die Geschichte der Juden einen eigenen sakramentalen Charakter: Sie enthüllt das Handeln JHWHs mit seinem Volk. Dies gilt vor allem für die großen Ereignisse in der jüdischen Geschichte. JHWH war es, der sein Volk aus der Knechtschaft Ägyptens ausziehen ließ; Er griff ein auf dem Sinai, begleitete sein Volk vierzig lange und schwere Jahre durch die Wüste, führte es ins Gelobte Land und befreite es später aus der Babylonischen Gefangenschaft. Daher ist unser Gott nicht der Gott der Philosophen, sondern der Gott Abrahams, Isaaks und Jakobs: der Gott, der mit Israel umgeht wie ein Bräutigam mit seiner Braut.

In der Fülle der Zeit hat dieser Gott einen neuen Bund geschlossen. Er hat seinen Sohn gesandt, geboren von einer Frau, geboren im jüdischen Volk: Jesus von Nazareth,[4]

---

4 *Mitten unter uns. Die schönsten Gebete von Huub Oosterhuis*, ausgewählt und übertragen von P. PAWLOWSKY (Wien-Freiburg-Basel 1982) 110 (ursprünglich H. OOSTERHUIS: *Zien – soms even. Fragmenten over God. Een voorlees-boek* (Bilthoven 1972) 114-115).

> der alles erlebt hat,
> was ein Mensch zu erleben bekommt,
> wenn er gut sein will:
> alles was unmenschlich und sinnlos
> und nicht auszuhalten ist,
> der Hunger, Durst und Einsamkeit gekannt hat,
> der verraten wurde,
> der trotzdem an dir festgehalten hat
> im Glauben...

Er wurde ermordet unter Pontius Pilatus; Er wurde gekreuzigt, ist gestorben und wurde begraben. Aber so wurde Er Gottes Sohn in Kraft und Herrlichkeit; denn wegen Seines Leidens und Todes hat Gott Ihn verherrlicht und Ihm einen Namen gegeben, der größer ist als alle Namen (Phil 2,9ff.). Jesus, der Gekreuzigte, wurde von Gott auferweckt von den Toten und zum Herrn und Messias gemacht (Apg 2,36). Er ist das Licht der Welt (Joh 8,12; 9,5). Wer die unendliche Tiefe des Lebens wahrnehmen will, kann von nun an nicht mehr an der Geschichte Jesu vorbei. Er erscheint am Horizont als das Ziel der Dinge, des Lebens, von der Geburt bis zum Tod, der ganzen Geschichte. Jede Sakramentalität – 'die sich verschiebende Perspektive' der Welt und der Geschichte – kommt in Ihm zusammen: Er ist das Ur-Sakrament. Dies hat weittragende Folgen. In der Geschichte gibt es noch andere Heilsfiguren, die Gott ans Licht bringen. Auch sie sind Sakramente Gottes. Aber die Sakramentalität Jesu reicht – für die, die an Ihn glauben – weiter. Mohammed und Jesus stehen für die Christen nicht auf einer Stufe, denn sie glauben, daß in Jesus von Nazareth das Heil endgültig ans Licht gekommen ist. Kurz gesagt, glauben die Christen, daß nur in und durch Jesus von Nazareth, der gekreuzigt wurde, den aber Gott von den Toten auferstehen ließ, Rettung möglich ist; kein anderer Name ist uns gegeben, in dem wir nach Gottes Heilsplan gerettet werden (vgl. Apg 4,10.12). Es ist der Glaube in dieses Ur-Sakrament, der die christlichen Kirchen verbindet.

4. DER CHRISTLICHE GLAUBE MUSS AUF SAKRAMENTALE WEISE ZUM AUSDRUCK KOMMEN

Daß der christliche Glaube auf sakramentale Weise zum Ausdruck kommen muß, hängt damit zusammen, daß die Menschen von Natur sakramentale Wesen sind. Durch ihre Leiblichkeit haben sie notwendig eine symbolische Natur. Sie können nicht zu sich selbst kommen, ohne sich auszudrücken. Was wir erfahren, erhält erst Gestalt, wenn wir es auch zum Ausdruck bringen. Wenn wir unsere Erlebnisse nur in unserm Inneren bewahren, werden sie nicht wirklich etwas von uns selbst. Sie bleiben vage, schwankend, suchend, eingeschlossen in sich selbst. Erst wenn wir unsere Erfahrungen und Erlebnisse ausdrücken, sind sie da, geschehen sie, werden wir uns ihrer klar bewußt. Das ist das Geheimnis jeder Beratung und Psychotherapie; und auch vieler menschlicher Gespräche. Bevor wir uns ausdrücken, wirbeln die Eindrücke in uns rund, und allerlei widersprüchliche Gefühle durchfahren uns. Wir wissen selbst nicht, wo wir dran sind. Indem wir uns aussprechen, werden wir frei und bestimmen über uns selbst. "Der Ausdruck bringt Konturen an in seinen (unseren) Beziehungen zu anderen und zur Welt; er vereint seine (unsere) verwirrten Gefühle und Eindrücke. Mit einem Wort, der Mensch wird er selbst, indem er sich selbst Form gibt",[5] und zwar: durch Wort und Gebärde. Wer liebt, kann dies durch Worte ausdrücken, aber er kann auch etwas oder sich selbst schenken. Erst wenn die Liebe zum Ausdruck gebracht wird, kommt sie zu sich selbst. Und hierbei geht es vor allem um sakramentale Äußerungen: das 'sprechende' Wort der Liebe, das kleine Geschenk, das mehr sein will als nur es selbst, die Umarmung, der Kuß.

Auch für den christlichen Glauben ist der sakramentale Ausdruck notwendig. Man kann von innerlichem Glaubensleben sprechen; dies gehört aber erst wirklich zu einem Menschen, wenn er seinem Erleben Gestalt gibt. Ohne diesen Ausdruck kann man wohl von Glaubenserfahrung sprechen; sie bleibt aber verschwommen, unsicher und suchend. Wenn der Glaube wirklich die ganze Person berührt, dann muß er auf sakramentale Weise zum Ausdruck gebracht werden. Ohne Worte, Gebärden, Handlungen, die die Tiefendimension der Glaubenserfahrung ausdrücken, kann sich der Glaube nicht wirklich vollziehen.

5. DER INNERSTE KREIS DER CHRISTLICHEN SAKRAMENTALITÄT

Der Glaube kann sich auf vielerlei Art ausdrücken. Die sakramentalen Ausdrucksmöglichkeiten sind gewissermaßen genauso unerschöpflich, wie dies bei der natürlichen Sakramentalität der Fall ist. So werden in den Schriften der Kirchenväter und in den alten Liturgietexten z.B. das Beten des Vaterunser, das Glaubensbekenntnis, Kirchweihe, Begräbnisfeierlichkeiten, liturgische Feste, Stundengebet, Fasten im Dezember, Weihwasser und Weihrauch als sakramentale Äußerungen genannt. Und man kann hinzufügen: das Segnen der Kinder, eine Kerze aufstellen, Blumen aufs Grab legen, ein Lied singen... Aber so wie man bei der natürlichen Sakramentalität einen innersten Kreis ziehen kann, so kann man dies auch bei der christlichen Sakramentalität. Es gibt sehr verdichtete Augenblicke, in

---

5 A. VERGOTE: *Het huis is nooit af. Gedachten over mens en religie* (Antwerpen-Utrecht 1974) 121.

denen die christliche Sakramentalität einen Höhepunkt erreicht. Dann sprechen wir von den Sakramenten im strengen Sinn.

Auf die ein oder andere Weise hängen diese sakramentalen Höhepunkte mit den existentiellen Wendepunkten des Lebens zusammen; darüber haben wir oben bereits gesprochen. Aber andererseits gehen sie in ihnen nicht auf; sie sind mehr als nur Schwellenriten für die Wendepunkte des Lebens. Denn die Taufe als Wiedergeburt aus Wasser und Geist ruft wohl auf die ein oder andere Weise die Geburt wach, aber sie braucht nicht per se im Augenblick der Geburt oder kurz danach vollzogen zu werden. Auch Erwachsene können getauft werden, und in den ersten Jahrhunderten war das sogar der Normalfall. Es ist daher auch zu wenig, wenn die Taufe nur als christliche Feier der menschlichen Geburt erlebt wird, wie das heute oft geschieht. Eine christliche Geburtsfeier ist wohl sinnvoll, aber als solche ist sie noch keine Taufe. Und ebensowenig kann man die Taufe vollkommen mit der natürlichen Initiation identifizieren. Denn die Taufe ist zwar ein Initiationssakrament, wie wir im nächsten Abschnitt darlegen werden, aber sie ist nicht per se an den Augenblick gebunden, in dem jemand als Erwachsener in die menschliche Gemeinschaft aufgenommen wird. Auch ein Kind und ein alter Mensch können getauft werden. Die christlichen Sakramente hängen also auf die ein oder andere Weise mit den Schwellenriten des menschlichen Lebens zusammen; sie nehmen auch einige sakramentale Ausdrucksweisen dieser Schwellenriten in ihre Gestaltung auf. Sie gehen jedoch in diesen Schwellenriten nicht auf. Wohl könnte man sagen: Die christlichen Sakramente nehmen auf eine eigene, neue, radikale Weise wieder auf, was in den Schwellenriten zum Ausdruck kommt. Es findet eine 'Entgrenzung' statt in Richtung auf eine neue Lebensgeschichte, die durch Jesus von Nazareth bestimmt wird. Bei der Taufe geht es dann nicht nur um die rein menschliche Geburt, sondern um die Wiedergeburt in und durch Jesus, wodurch der Mensch ausdrücklich in die christliche Heilsgeschichte eintritt. Er wird in die neue christliche Gemeinschaft eingeführt, in das neue Volk Gottes. So sind die christlichen Sakramente Wendepunkte dieser neuen Lebensgeschichte: die Augenblicke, in denen sich der Glaube an Jesus von Nazareth als das endgültige Heil auf sehr eindringliche Weise vollzieht und die Gläubigen auch auf ganz unentrinnbare Weise das Heil empfangen und die Verbundenheit mit dem Gott Jesu erfahren.

6. DIE TAUFE: EIN INITIATIONSSAKRAMENT

Initiation ist ein weiter Begriff, der nicht so einfach zu umschreiben ist. Jemanden initiieren heißt wörtlich: ihn einweihen, einführen, hineingeleiten. Im allgemeinen versteht man unter Initiation einen Komplex von Riten und mündlichen Unterweisungen, die auf eine fundamentale Veränderung im religiösen und sozialen Leben dessen zielt, der eingeweiht wird. Immer geht es um eine fundamentale Wende in der Krise des menschlichen Daseins: eine Bewegung aus Versuchung, Angst, Verlust, Niederlage, Tod hin zu Befreiung, zum Sich-selbst-Zurückfinden, zu Erneuerung, Freude, Aufstehen, Auferstehung. Eigentlich enthält jede tief-menschliche Krise, die wirklich durchstanden wird, Elemente der Initiation.[6]

Von Anfang an war die christliche Taufe ein Initiationssakrament. Man spricht vom Absterben des alten Daseins und von Wiedergeburt aus Wasser und Geist, wobei die Täuflinge in die christliche Gemeinschaft eintreten und aufgenommen werden. Das Untertauchen im Wasser war und ist wohl der deutlichste Ausdruck dieses Geschehens. Denn Wasser löst auf und läßt Formen verschwinden, es reinigt das Alte, es wäscht die Sünden ab und ist als Brunnen und Quelle ein Ort für neue Daseinsmöglichkeiten: für neues Leben und Wiedergeburt, neue Schöpfung und einen neuen Menschen. Durch Untertauchen im Wasser stirbt der alte Mensch, und es entsteht ein neues, wiedergeborenes Wesen. So schreibt Johannes Chrysostomus:[7]

> Die (Taufe) stellt Begräbnis, Sterben, Auferstehung und Leben dar (...) Wenn wir im Wasser gleichsam wie in einem Grab unser Haupt eintauchen, wird der alte Mensch gänzlich begraben und versenkt; wenn wir dann auftauchen, ersteht der neue Mensch.

Der Taufstein ist zugleich Grabstein und Mutterschoß. So wird das große Urbild des Wassers mit allen Gefühlskräften, die es hervorruft, in der christlichen Initiation in und durch Christus als dem neuen Ursprung evangelisiert. Es ist wohl deutlich, daß das Urbild viel von seiner gefühlsmäßigen Ausdruckskraft verliert, wenn vom Untertauchen nur noch ein Übergießen übrigbleibt.

Die Taufe ist ein sehr eingreifendes Geschehen, das sich einerseits am Täufling vollzieht: Der Herr selbst tauft, der Täufling erfährt die Taufe; er wird vom Täufer im Namen des Herrn untergetaucht. Andererseits handelt es sich um eine fundamentale Entscheidung des Täuflings selbst. Er bringt zum Ausdruck, daß er das alte Dasein ablegt – er schwört ihm ab – und bekennt Jesus als das endgültige Heil, indem er das Glaubensbekenntnis spricht und selbst in das Wasser hinabsteigt. So kommt der Glaube als christlicher Glaube zum ersten Mal ganz zu sich selbst. Damit will ich nicht sagen, daß man vor der Taufe noch nicht von Glauben sprechen konnte; ganz sicher kann er schon da sein. Aber er war wohl noch

---

[6] Wer sich in die wichtige Rolle, die die Initiationsriten in den Religionen und Kulturen spielen, vertiefen möchte, lese M. ELIADE: *Das Mysterium der Wiedergeburt. Ihre kulturelle und religiöse Bedeutung* (Zürich 1961).
[7] JOHANNES CHRYSOSTOMUS: *Homilia in Joannem* 25, 2, in J.-P. MIGNE: *Patrologia graeca* LIX (Paris 1862) 151.

auf der Suche, noch ohne definitive Entscheidung, bis der erste Schritt zum inneren Kreis der christlichen Sakramentalität getan war. In diesem Sinn ist die Taufe für den christlichen Glauben notwendig und ein unersetzbares Sakrament. Dies ist auch deshalb so, weil die, die diesen Schritt tun, auch wirklich an Jesus von Nazareth als dem endgültigen Heil teilhaben, womit ich keineswegs andere mögliche Wege ausschließen will. So sah die alte Kirche z.b. das Zeugnis Ablegen durch den Tod für das Evangelium als vollwertige Taufe an. In der alten Kirche wurde das Sakrament der Taufe auf besonders ausdrucksvolle Weise vollzogen. Nachdem der Täufling Satan und dem alten Dasein abgeschworen hatte, tauchte er unter, und während er im Wasser stand, legte er das Glaubensbekenntnis ab, im Dialog mit dem Täufer. Auf dessen dreimalige Frage: "Glaubst du an Gott, den allmächtigen Vater, glaubst du an Jesus Christus, den Sohn Gottes, der... und glaubst du an den Heiligen Geist", antwortete der Täufling jedesmal mit: "Ich glaube", wobei dreimal das Wasser über ihn ausgegossen wurde.[8]

Das 'Widersagst du dem Satan' ist für uns vielleicht schwer nachvollziehbar geworden. Es war ein konkreter Ausdruck der Bekehrung. Der Täufling wandte sich ab vom Westen, der Richtung von Untergang und Tod (die Sonne geht im Westen unter) und spieh aus zum Reich Satans. Die *pompa diaboli*, die Eitelkeiten des Teufels, denen er widersagte, deuteten auf eine konkrete Welt: auf den Götzenkult, der sich in den heidnischen Zeremonien zeigte, auf Schauspiele, öffentliche Ehrungen, Theater, kurz, auf das ganze heidnische Leben. Es ging um die Abwehr heidnischer Strukturen mit ihren Inhalten. So war der sakramentale Ausdruck der Bekehrung wirklich ein entscheidender Schritt, der auch gesellschaftliche Folgen hatte.

Man kann die Frage stellen, wie heute die Bekehrung des Teuflings auf eindringliche Weise Gestalt bekommen kann. Obwohl die Grundzüge der Bekehrung zu Christus immer wieder dieselben sind, soll sie doch zu jeder Zeit neu und ursprünglich erlebt werden. Dabei will ich noch darauf hinweisen, daß der sakramentale Ausdruck für dieses Element nicht unbedingt und ausschließlich im Augenblick des Abschwörens Gestalt erhalten muß. So kannte man in Mailand eine Zeitlang als Ritus nach der Taufe die Fußwaschung, die über Gallien auch nach Spanien kam. Die gallikanische Überlieferung sah diesen Ritus ausdrücklich als Zeichen dienender Liebe. Dies deutete man auf die folgende Weise: "Unser Herr und Retter Jesus Christus hat seinen Aposteln die Füße gewaschen. Ich wasche euch jetzt die Füße, damit auch ihr es tun sollt bei den Gästen und Freunden, die zu euch kommen".[9] Es scheint so, daß wir heutzutage schwerlich

---

8 HIPPOLYTUS: *Traditio Apostolica* 21.
9 L.C. MOHLBERG: *Missale Gallicanum Vetus (Cod. Vat. Palat. lat. 493)* (= Rerum Ecclesiasticarum Documenta. Series Maior. Fontes 3) (Roma 1958) Nr. 176.

von Bekehrung sprechen können, wenn wir keine Rechenschaft über die größeren Zusammenhänge, in denen wir leben, ablegen. Es hat in unserer Kultur eine Ausbreitung des Bösen, aus dem heraus wir uns bekehren müssen, stattgefunden. Erst wenn dieses Element mitspielt, kann man von wahrhaftiger Bekehrung zum Gott des Heils sprechen, der in Jesus von Nazareth in unsere Geschichte eingetreten ist. Und dies muß auch auf die ein oder andere Weise sakramental zum Ausdruck kommen; denn erst dann wird die Bekehrung zu etwas, das die ganze Person angeht. In verschiedenen alternativen Riten kommt etwas von der Bekehrung zu diesem 'neuen Lebensstil' zum Ausdruck.

Damit verbunden ist die Frage nach dem Glaubensbekenntnis. Der Täufling muß bei der Taufe entschlossener als vor der Taufe auf die Frage antworten: 'Ihr aber, für wen haltet ihr mich?' (Mk 8,29; Mt 16,15; Lk 9,20). Diese Frage trifft uns hier und jetzt. Daher soll auch der Glaube auf eine eigene, ursprüngliche Weise zum Ausdruck gebracht werden: Ist Jesus von Nazareth auch jetzt für den Täufling das endgültige Heil? Betrachtet man den sakramentalen Ausdruck aus dieser Perspektive, so wird deutlich, daß die Taufe ein erster Schritt ist. Denn einmal wird der sakramentale Vollzug des Glaubens ein ganzes Leben lang dauern und auch noch andere Konzentrationspunkte kennen. Zum andern hebt die Taufe für den Täufling die ethischen Konsequenzen keineswegs auf, im Gegenteil: Sie fordert ihn dazu heraus, sie auf sich zu nehmen.

Schließlich ist noch darauf hinzuweisen, daß die Taufe als Ausdruck der Bekehrung zum Glauben an den Gott des Jesus von Nazareth auch ein passives Moment in sich trägt. Im Vollzug der Taufe und durch sie wird der Täufling wirklich versöhnt, seine Sünden werden vergeben. Die Taufe ist auch eine Versöhnungsfeier. Der Täufling muß sich vom Bösen abwenden und es bis zum letzten bekämpfen; aber dieses Böse enthält auch die 'erbsündlichen' Abgründe des *mysterium iniquitatis*: das unergründliche Mysterium des Bösen; daraus kann der Mensch eigentlich nur in Jesu Namen gerettet werden. JHWHs Knecht wurde zum Märtyrer der Mächte der Finsternis, durch seinen Tod aber überwand Er diese Mächte. So hat Er die Welt versöhnt. Die Taufe ist also auch wirklich ein Bekenntnis des 'Sieh, das Lamm Gottes, das wegnimmt die Sünden der Welt'. Der Täufling muß daher auch das Kreuz des Herrn preisen. Hier haben die ethischen Konsequenzen der Taufe ihren tiefsten Grund, und von hierher erhalten sie ihren eigentlichen Antrieb. Der Täufling ist zu einem Leben des Dienens und der vollen Menschlichkeit, gegen die Mächte, aufgerufen; so ein Leben ist möglich im Namen dessen, der in diesem Leben unterging, aber aus dem Abgrund errettet wurde als Erstgeborener aus den Toten.

7. UND DIE KINDERTAUFE?

Nach dem Gesagten drängt sich die Frage auf: Welchen Sinn hat es, dieses Initiationssakrament an einem gerade geborenen Kind zu vollziehen?

7.1 Ein kurzer geschichtlicher Überblick

Im Neuen Testament wird die Kindertaufe nirgendwo ausdrücklich genannt. Wohl gibt es Stellen, die die Annahme rechtfertigen, daß ab und zu Kinder getauft wurden. In diesem Zusammenhang verweist man vor allem auf Texte aus der Apostelgeschichte und bei Paulus, wo erzählt wird, daß jemand mit seiner ganzen Familie (*oikos*) getauft wurde (vgl. Apg 10,1-2,24,44,47-48; 16,13-15,31,33; 18,8; 1Kor 1,16). Es liegt doch nahe, daß bei der Taufe einer ganzen Familie manchmal auch Kinder dabei waren.

Ab dem dritten Jahrhundert entsteht die allgemeine Praxis der Kindertaufe. Es gibt noch einige Mißverständnisse über die Frage, welche Motive beim Entstehen dieser Praxis eine Rolle gespielt haben. Manche meinen, daß die Kirche zu dieser Praxis aus dem Bewußtsein übergegangen ist, daß die Kinder von der Erbsünde befreit werden müssen. Das ist aber sicher nicht der Fall. Um das Jahr 200 findet man hauptsächlich zwei Argumente für die Notwendigkeit der Taufe. Das erste ist die persönliche Sündhaftigkeit der Erwachsenen. Das zweite ist Jh 3,5: "Wenn jemand nicht aus Wasser und Geist geboren wird, kann er nicht in das Reich Gottes kommen". Zweifellos hat das zweite Argument – zusammen mit der neuen sozialen Situation der Kirche, die an Umfang zunahm und schließlich Volkskirche wurde – dazu geführt, fortan alle Kinder zu taufen.

Interessant ist, daß sich mit dem Aufkommen dieser Praxis auch die Frage nach dem Sündigsein oder Nicht-Sündigsein des Kindes verschärfte. Immer häufiger wird man denn auch mit der Kindertaufe 'zur Vergebung der Sünden' konfrontiert. Tertullian (160-230) nimmt an, daß die Kinder von Beginn an von der Verderbnis beschmutzt sind; dennoch schließt er daraus nicht, daß dieser Zustand ein echter Sünden-Zustand ist. Im Zusammenhang mit der Kindertaufe stellt er daher auch die Frage, warum man sich so beeilt, unschuldige Kinder zu taufen.[10] Er verschiebt die Frage lieber auf später, wenn sich die Verderbnis in persönlichen Sünden manifestiert hat. Und Origenes (185-254) erzählt, daß zu seiner Zeit die Christen der alexandrinischen Kirche fragten, warum die Kinder getauft werden müßten, da sie doch nicht gesündigt hätten. Origenes' Antwort ist, daß niemand frei von Makeln ist, auch wenn er nur einen Tag auf der Erde lebt, und daß die Taufe diese 'Makel der Geburt'

---

10 TERTULLIAN: *Liber de Baptismo* 18, in J.-P. MIGNE: *Patrologia latina* I (Paris 1879) 1329-1331.

abwäscht.[11] So wächst u.a. gerade durch die faktische Praxis der Kindertaufe die Überzeugung, daß die Kinder durch die Erbsünde befleckt sind. Und so entsteht eine neue Argumentation für die Kindertaufe: Sie ist notwendig wegen der Erbsünde. Diese Argumentation erreicht ihren Höhepunkt bei Augustinus (354-430) und beeinflußt die westliche Tradition bis in unsere Zeit. Mit diesem Bewußtsein vollzog sich gleichzeitig eine Einengung. Die Taufe wird vor allem als Reinigung von der Erbsünde und als 'rettendes Mittel' – drückt nicht dieses Wort vor allem das Negative aus? – für den Himmel erfahren.

Im Lauf der Jahrhunderte wird der Zeitraum zwischen Geburt und Taufe immer kleiner. Dies geschah vor allem im 13. Jahrhundert. Aus 30 Tagen wurden allmählich 15, 8, 3 Tage, und schließlich entstand sogar die Neigung, am Tag der Geburt selbst zu taufen. Die Motive sind deutlich: Die Taufe ist für das Heil des Kindes absolut notwendig, und die Kindersterblichkeit war sehr hoch.

Ein erster Widerstand gegen die allgemeine Praxis der Kindertaufe kam im 16. Jahrhundert auf. Die sogenannten Wiedertäufer (Anabaptisten) erklärten jede Kindertaufe für ungültig und beriefen sich hierfür auf die Schrift. Sie gingen dazu über, auch Erwachsene noch einmal zu taufen, was auch bei den Protestanten scharfe Reaktionen hervorrief. Zwischen 1527 und 1540 wurden Tausende von Wiedertäufern zum Tod verurteilt und hingerichtet, mindestens so viele in protestantischen wie in katholischen Ländern. Der erste war Felix Mantz, der öffentlich im Zürichsee ertränkt wurde. Eine Chronik erzählt von ihm, daß er so mit Leib und Seele von der Wahrheit Zeugnis ablegte. Er selbst soll, als er das Urteil hörte, gesagt haben: 'Dies ist die wahre Taufe'.

Eine zweite Reaktion kam in unserem Jahrhundert auf. Sie hängt mit dem Faktum zusammen, daß sich die traditionellen Kirchen des Westens der bedeutenden Veränderungen bewußt wurden, die sich in der soziologischen Situation der Kirchen vollzogen hatten. War nicht die Taufe in bestimmten Ländern zu einem reinen Formalismus geworden? War nicht das Ende der Massen-Kirche angebrochen? Zunächst war es K. Barth, der 1939 in einem Vortrag in Utrecht scharfen Widerspruch anmeldete. Ab dieser Zeit bis zu seinem Lebensende wandte sich dieser protestantische Theologe stets heftiger gegen die allgemeine Praxis der Kindertaufe.[12] Er beruft sich dabei auf die Schrift, die die Taufe als eine persönliche und bewußte Tat des Glaubens betrachtet. Normalerweise darf man also die Taufe nur an Erwachsenen vollziehen. Zwar ist die Kindertaufe nicht un-

---

11 ORIGENES: *In Lucam homiliae* 14, in J.-P. MIGNE: *Patrologia latina* XXVI (Paris 1884) 298-299.
12 Vgl. K. BARTH: *Das christliche Leben (Fragment). Die Taufe als Begründung des christlichen Lebens* (= Die kirchliche Dogmatik IV/4) (Zürich 1967) 180-214.

gültig, aber sie ist "eine tief unordentliche Taufpraxis",[13] ein alter kirchlicher Irrtum, eine Wunde, an der die Kirche leidet.[14]

Beinahe 30 Jahre nach Barths erstem Widerstand drang die Diskussion über das Pro und Kontra der Kindertaufe auch in die katholische Kirche ein.

Eine erste Entwicklung im niederländischen Sprachraum begann 1957.[15] Beim liturgischen Kongreß in Tongerlo wurde dafür plädiert, mit der Kindertaufe ungefähr 10 Tage zu warten, um der Familie und den Freunden, vor allem aber der Mutter Gelegenheit zu geben, bei der Taufe dabei zu sein. Dieser Vorschlag stieß erst auf Widerspruch, wobei sich die Diskussionen auf die Frage der Kindersterblichkeit konzentrierten. Riskierte man es nicht, daß für manche Kinder die Pforten des Himmels verschlossen blieben?

Während sich – mit Zustimmung von Rom – die neue Praxis entwickelte, entstand bereits eine neue Entwicklung. In Frankreich war man darüber aufgebracht, daß ein Pfarrer sich weigerte, ein Kind nicht-praktizierender Eltern in einflußreicher gesellschaftlicher Stellung zu taufen. Die Diskussion führte zu einer Neubesinnung auf die Kindertaufe. Wurden nicht zu viele Kinder getauft, die nicht als Gläubige erzogen würden? Waren nicht die Motive, Kinder zur Taufe zu bringen, völlig nebensächlicher Art?

1965 erließen die französischen Bischöfe neue Richtlinien.[16] Die Eltern sollten katechetisch auf die Taufe ihres Kindes vorbereitet werden, so daß sie sich ihrer eigenen Verantwortung bewußt werden und sich frei für die Taufe ihres Kindes entscheiden könnten. Diese Praxis hatte selbstverständlich zur Folge, daß die Kindertaufe noch länger hinausgeschoben wurde und daß weniger Kinder getauft wurden als früher.

Kurze Zeit später erfolgte eine Entwicklung von sehr weittragender Art. Ab 1967 entstand in der katholischen Kirche eine Diskussion über die Taufe als solche. Während einige an der alten Praxis festhalten wollten, plädierten andere dafür, die Taufe auf das Erwachsenenalter zu verschieben. Diese Diskussion über das Für und Wider der Kindertaufe ist noch immer nicht zum Stillstand gekommen.

7.2. Das Für und Wider der Kindertaufe

Zunächst ist die Tatsache von Bedeutung, daß in unserer Kultur der christliche Glaube keine Selbstverständlichkeit mehr ist. Auch in den Nie-

---

13 BARTH: *Das christliche Leben* 213.
14 Vgl. BARTH: *Das christliche Leben* 214.
15 Vgl. *Tijdschrift voor liturgie* 42 (1958) 52-98; 268-270; für weitere Literatur siehe A. VERHEUL: De dooppraktijk in de jonge kerk. Bron van inspiratie voor de kerk van vandaag?, in *Tijdschrift voor liturgie* 52 (1968) 208.
16 J. BULCKENS: Nieuw licht op de pastoraal van het kinderdoopsel. Een belangrijke nota van het Frans episcopaat, in *Tijdschrift voor liturgie* 50 (1966) 325-330. Die Richtlinien sind erschienen in *Paroisse et liturgie* 48 (1966) 269-275.

derlanden geraten die Kirchen immer mehr in eine Diaspora-Situation, und zwar am stärksten in städtischen Gebieten. Aber wachsen nicht die Niederlande langsam zu einer einzigen großen Stadt zusammen? In dieser Diaspora-Situation ist mehr und mehr eine bewußte Entscheidung für den Glauben gefragt und wird der Glaube immer weniger durch das sozialkulturelle Milieu geschützt. Das führt dazu, daß die Zahl derer, die nur aus nebensächlichen Motiven gläubig sind, abnimmt und daß – damit zusammenhängend – die Zahl der Kindertaufen rückläufig ist. Man muß aber auch mit der Situation rechnen, daß doch auch aus nebensächlichen Gründen die Kindertaufe verlangt wird. Dann steht man vor der Wahl, entweder den Glauben der Eltern zu fördern oder die Kindertaufe nicht zu vollziehen. Wenn keine Garantien für den christlichen Glauben da sind, erscheint die Kindertaufe wenig sinnvoll. Kurz gesagt: Nur wenn die Eltern die für die Taufe nötigen Bedingungen erfüllen, hat es Sinn, in unserer Zeit Kinder zu taufen. Die Bedingungen für die Kindertaufe können keine anderen sein als für die Taufe Erwachsener, so daß bei der Taufe eines Kindes der Glaube der Eltern bestimmend ist.[17] Wenn sich die Eltern zwar mit dem christlichen Glauben verbunden fühlen, den entscheidenden Schritt innerhalb des konzentrischen Kreises der eigentlichen Sakramente aber nicht tun, wäre es dann nicht sinnvoller, an andere, mehr katechumenale Ausdrucksweisen des Glaubens zu denken, wie sie unter 8. beschrieben werden sollen?

Es gibt aber noch einen zweiten Faktor, der in pastoraler Hinsicht geklärt werden muß. Auch in einem gläubigen Milieu wird die Kindertaufe nicht immer als sinnvoll betrachtet. Es kann sein, daß die Eltern aus anderen Gründen die Taufe ihres Kindes nicht wollen. Man hört u.a. folgende Gründe:
- Das Kind muß neutral erzogen werden und später selbst wählen können.
- Solang die christlichen Kirchen gespalten sind, bewirkt die Aufnahme eines Kindes in eine bestimmte Kirche eine Verzögerung der Ökumene. Wenn es später selbst wählen muß, stößt es auf die tragische Spaltung der Christen, und die Herausforderung der Kirchen, zur Einheit zu gelangen, wird verstärkt.
- Das Kind kann noch nicht glauben; eine wahrhafte Taufe verlangt einen bewußten Akt des Glaubens.

Selbstverständlich muß man versuchen, jeweils die tieferen Hintergründe der Motive herauszufinden. Aber im allgemeinen erscheint es wichtig, den Kontra-Argumenten die Pro-Argumente gegenüberzustellen, wobei meines Erachtens letztere ausschlaggebend sind.

---

17 H. SCHMITZ: Taufaufschub und Recht auf Taufe, in Hj. AUF DER MAUR und B. KLEINHEYER (Hrsg.): *Zeichen des Glaubens, Studien zu Taufe und Firmung* (Zürich-Freiburg im Breisgau 1972) 265.

Das erste Argument ist sicher nicht stichhaltig. Kann man denn Kinder neutral erziehen? Übertragen nicht die Eltern von selbst ihre Lebensauffassung auf die Kinder? Eltern können in der Erziehung unmöglich die tieferen Gründe, aus denen sie leben, ausschalten. Sie geben immer, bewußt oder unbewußt, dem Kind bestimmte Maßstäbe und Überzeugungen mit. Natürlich wird das Kind die Werte und Überzeugungen seines Milieus um so kritischer betrachten, je mehr es den Weg zu seiner eigenen Identität hin beschreitet. Die Eltern dürfen nicht tyrannisch über den Glauben ihres Kindes, das in das Erwachsensein hineinwächst, herrschen. Wenn sie es doch tun, so müßte man vor der Kindertaufe zurückschrecken. Denn in diesem Fall kann man nicht von wahrhaft christlicher Lebenshaltung, die die menschliche Freiheit achtet, sprechen. Wenn die christliche Erziehung in aller Offenheit stattfindet und das Kind später andere Wege geht, sollte es seine Taufe doch schwerlich als eine Last betrachten können. Das Kind kann sein Suchen nach eigener Identität unmöglich von der Tatsache lösen, daß es in einem Milieu, das nicht wertfrei sein kann, aufgewachsen ist. Dies gilt in Bezug auf alles.

Auf diese Weise kann man auch das zweite Motiv behandeln. Gläubige Eltern können kaum ihre eigene christliche Tradition verleugnen. Sie übertragen sie auf das Kind, ob sie es wollen oder nicht. Selbstverständlich ist das Kind frei, später zu wählen, zu welcher Kirche es gehören will.

Seit der gegenseitigen Anerkennung der Taufe durch die christlichen Kirchen ist die Problematik in dieser Hinsicht deutlich einfacher geworden. Wohl muß angemerkt werden, daß die ökumenische Gesinnung der Eltern eine Rolle bei der Abwägung des Für und Wider spielen kann. Je geringer sie ist, desto stärker das ökumenische Argument gegen die Kindertaufe.

Am einschneidendsten ist das Motiv, daß das Kind noch nicht glauben kann. Normalerweise wird hiermit unmittelbar die Frage verbunden, ob die Kindertaufe nicht ein magischer Ritus ist, der im Widerspruch zum Evangelium steht.

Man kann die Frage stellen, ob es nicht ein typisch westliches Erbe ist, den Menschen ausschließlich als reines Bewußtsein zu betrachten. Eine solche Auffassung vom Menschen hat zur Folge, daß das Kind-Sein nicht in seiner Eigenart als vollwertige Phase betrachtet wird, sondern nur und ausschließlich als Vorstufe zum Erwachsen-Sein. Später wäre dann erst die Rede vom Mensch-Sein. Aber umfaßt das Mensch-Sein nicht ebenso das Gerade-Geboren-Sein und das Kind-Sein? Das Kind gehört im Vollsinn zur Familie, aber auf seine Weise. Genauso gehört es ganz und auf seine Weise zum Volk Gottes. Man braucht es nicht in einem 'Niemandsland' oder in einem Vor-Stadium stecken zu lassen. Eine solche Auffassung, die das Kind ausschließt, zeugt von einem verengten, rationalistischen Menschenbild. J. Klink bemerkt:[18]

> Es könnte doch sein, daß gerade der soeben beginnende Mensch durch Tiefen hindurchgeht, an die wir sogar jede Erinnerung verloren haben. Es beginnt schon bei der Geburt: aus dem Wasser in die Luft, aus der Finsternis ans Licht kommen, aus dem vollen Schutz herausgerissen werden und in einem unbekannten Raum anfangen, für sich zu sein. (...) Ein Mensch beginnt das Leben in dieser Welt mit Schreien. Und von diesem Augenblick an hört er nicht auf, nach Geborgenheit, Wärme und Sicherheit zu suchen, vielleicht sogar ein Leben lang. (...) Ein kleines Kind hat erst nur ein ganz kleines Fleckchen, auf dem es existieren kann: die Sicherheit und Geborgenheit, die die Eltern ihm geben. Rund um es herum ist das große Unbekannte. Es kann noch nicht alles überblicken, ist den Erfahrungen des Augenblicks ausgeliefert, kann deshalb Ängste erleben, gegen die die Erwachsenen sich gesichert haben. Es erlebt Momente aussichtsloser Verlorenheit, wenn sein Schutz ihm zu entfallen droht, aber auch die spontane Hingabe an den trostvollen Schutz der Menschen. (...) Es gibt vielleicht keine Lebensperiode, die so sehr auf den Glauben bezogen ist! Die Geschichte der Menschwerdung ist mit der Geschichte des Glaubens verwoben. Gerade diese Urerfahrungen des Lebens bilden die emotionale Grundlage, auf der Glaube wachsen kann. (...) Wer zum Glauben kommt, erfaßt, daß es die Geschichte seines ganzen Lebens ist.

Wenn also das Kind in seiner Eigenart gewürdigt wird, gehört es von Anfang an dazu. Genausowenig wie die Liebesäußerungen der Eltern dem Kind gegenüber leer und sinnlos sind, sind dies die Zeichen der Liebe Gottes. Sollte sich der Gott des Heils nicht auch des gerade geborenen Kindes erbarmen? Sein Name 'Ich bin der ich bin' gilt ebenso für das Kind. Das Kind wird in eine Welt geboren, in der Gut und Böse, Freude und Leid, Finsternis und Licht, Fallen und wieder Aufstehen vermischt sind. So ist die Welt von Geburt an, die Umgebung, zu der es gehört und die es von Anfang an am eigenen Leib erfährt. Das Kind wird nicht in ein Paradies hineingeboren. In der Taufe nun "wird sichtbar gemacht, daß dieses Kind nicht im Bösen und im Tod unterzugehen braucht".[19] Die Taufe ist das Zeichen, in dem der Gott des Heils in den Eltern und durch sie und die Kirchengemeinde zum Ausdruck bringt: Ich habe dich lieb, ich habe meinen eigenen Sohn in diese Welt gesandt, und Er hat die Mächte des Todes und der Finsternis besiegt; Er ist dein Bruder, Er lebt für immer; sein Geist ist für immer dein Lebensatem. Wenn das Kind im Wasser untergetaucht wird und das Volk Gottes den Glauben bekennt, dann vollzieht Gott in diesen Zeichen und durch sie auch wirklich eine neue Geburt an diesem

---

18 J. KLINK: *Kind und Glaube. Eine kleine Theologie für Eltern* (Zürich-Düsseldorf 1971) 31-33.
19 S. KONIJN: *Ter overbrugging, Een handreiking aan gelovige volwassenen* (Hilversum 1971) 71.

Kind, und Er macht seine Lebensgeschichte zu einer Heilsgeschichte. Das Kind wird hineingestellt "in die hoffnungsvolle Bewegung, in der Friede, Liebe und Versöhnung herrschen. In die Bewegung, in der das Gute über das Böse siegt, das Leben über den Tod".[20] Durch seine Eltern wird das Kind geboren, aber wie sollten sie es vor dem Tod retten können? Bei der Kindertaufe bekennen die gläubigen Eltern zusammen mit der Gemeinde, daß das Kind am Reich Gottes teilhat und ewig leben wird. So wird im gerade geborenen Kind der endgültige Sinn seines Lebens verwirklicht.

Es geht jedoch nicht nur um eine christliche Feier der Geburt. Natürlich wird bei der Initiation durch die Kindertaufe der Gedanke an die 'Krise' des Geborenwerdens mitspielen. Außerdem enthält auch die Geburt Initiationselemente. Aber eigentlich geht es nicht nur um eine christliche Deutung für all das, sondern um die Wiedergeburt aus Wasser und Geist: um die beeindruckende Feier der Initiation dieses Kindes in eine neue Gemeinschaft, die, so wie es, in Jesu Leben, Tod und Auferstehung eingetaucht ist.

Ich kann mir vorstellen, daß nicht jeder vom 'Pro' der Kindertaufe überzeugt ist. Auch wenn man davon ausgeht, daß die Eltern wie von selbst ihre Auffassung vom Leben übertragen und daß es nicht möglich ist, ein Kind neutral zu erziehen, kann es sein, daß gläubige Eltern einen anderen Weg gehen möchten. Wer stark die allmähliche Entwicklung des Kindes betont, wird auch als Gläubiger vielleicht eher mit einer christlichen Geburtsfeier, der evtl. noch andere Katechumenatsriten folgen, vorliebnehmen. Die Möglichkeit einer 'verteilten' Sakramentalität kann also für manche Gläubige, die ihre Taufe wirklich erleben, sehr wichtig sein. Man kann die Frage stellen, ob eine pluriforme Kirche nicht für das Entstehen einer vielfältigen Praxis offen sein muß.

8. DIE VORBEREITUNG AUF DIE TAUFE

8.1. Verschiedene Grade der Anteilnahme

Kürzlich wurde gesagt, man könnte bei den Getauften – grob gesagt – drei Kategorien unterscheiden: Katholiken, die irgendwann getauft wurden, für die aber der Glaube weiter keine Zukunft hat; dann suchende Gläubige, die sich zur Kirche gehörig fühlen und gerne am Leben und Zeugnis der Gemeinde teilnehmen, die aber die Sakramente nicht empfangen wollen oder können; und schließlich die, die ihrem Getauftsein positiv gegenüberstehen.[21]

---

20 KONIJN: *Ter overbrugging* 69.
21 J. HEYKE: Het ideaal van een gastvrije kerk, in *Kosmos en oekumene* 10 (1976) 138-139.

Die zweite Gruppe – die der suchenden Gläubigen – könnte man als Katechumenen beschreiben, obwohl sie getauft sind. Vor allem für diese Gruppe ist es schwierig, ihre Kirchlichkeit auf angemessene Weise auch in den Riten zum Ausdruck zu bringen. Wenn sie mit der Frage konfrontiert werden, ob sie ihr Kind taufen lassen sollen, so ist ihre ehrliche Antwort, daß sie so weit noch nicht sind. Und doch ist die Taufe das einzige liturgische Angebot bei der Zugehörigkeit zur Kirche. Die Taufe ist eine Art absolute Schwelle: Als Getaufter ist man in der Kirche, als Nicht-Getaufter draußen. Daher kann man die Frage stellen, ob das faktische liturgische Angebot wohl in ausreichendem Maße die verschiedenen Grade der Zugehörigkeit zur Kirche, so wie sie in unserer Zeit erlebt werden, respektiert. Auch bei denen, die ihr Kind nicht taufen lassen, gibt es solche, die auf die ein oder andere Weise eine Beziehung zur Kirche haben; ihnen ist es unmöglich, dies liturgisch zum Ausdruck zu bringen. Wenn sie trotzdem eine rituelle Form wünschen, wählen sie eben oft die Taufe, obwohl dieses Angebot über ihre Absichten hinausgeht. Diese Situation wird nicht immer als solche zur Sprache kommen. Weil das Angebot 'alles oder nichts' ist, bleiben die untergründigen Fragen oft verhüllt und verdeckt.

8.2. Vorsichtig mit dem Taufwasser umgehen

Meiner Ansicht nach ist dies keine gesunde Situation. Zunächst verlangt die Achtung denen gegenüber, die sich an die Kirche wenden, daß man aufmerksam auf ihre Fragen hört; es ist nicht recht, ihnen mehr anzubieten, als sie selbst wollen. Außerdem verliert auf diese Weise die Taufe und damit auch die Kirche auf die Dauer ihr 'eigenes' Gesicht; die Kirche wird 'farblos'. Denn bei der Taufe handelt es sich ganz ausdrücklich um ein konstitutives Element kirchlichen Geschehens. Wer sich taufen läßt, stößt auf den innersten Kreis, auf den Kern der Sakramentalität: Er schließt sich auf eindringliche Weise der Gemeinschaft derer an, die von Jesus das entscheidende Heil erwarten und in seinem Namen einen neuen Lebensstil führen wollen – wie verschiedenartig dieser Lebensstil auch sei. Wenn die Kirche in der Zukunft wirklich ein 'Gesicht' haben will, dann ist eine neue Strategie in Bezug auf die Taufe sicher nötig. In diesem Zusammenhang kann für uns die Praxis der alten Kirche erhellend sein. In der Traditio Apostolica von Hippolyt (um 200) liest man:[22]

> Wenn man dann die aussucht, die die Taufe empfangen werden, muß man ihr Leben untersuchen. Haben sie als Katechumenen auch angemessen gelebt? Haben sie Respekt vor den Witwen gehabt? Haben sie die Kranken besucht? Haben sie alle Arten von guten Werken getan? Wenn die, die sie

---

22 HIPPOLYTUS: *Traditio Apostolica* 20.

begleitet haben, positiv über sie aussagen, können sie das Evangelium hören ...

Die Täuflinge wurden auf Grund ihres Verhaltens 'ausgewählt' und auf Grund der Tatsache, daß es ihnen zukam, die Frohe Botschaft in sich aufzunehmen. Die alte Kirche ging vorsichtig mit dem Taufwasser um.

8.3. Die Bedeutung katechumenaler Feiern

War die alte Kirche nicht eigentlich sehr gastunfreundlich? Wer auf diese Frage eine Antwort sucht, müßte sich mit der Tatsache beschäftigen, daß in der alten Kirche auch die Katechumenen auf die ein oder andere Weise zur Kirche gehörten. Wer sich von der Kirche angezogen fühlte, konnte ins Katechumenat aufgenommen werden. Das Wort Katechumenat hängt mit dem Wort Katechese zusammen. Katechumenen waren die, die Katechese, d.h. eine Einführung in den Glauben, empfingen. Bei dieser Katechese ging es nicht rein um die Weitergabe von Lehrinhalten. Sie sollte den Glauben wecken und eine durch Jesus von Nazareth inspirierte Lebenspraxis wachsen lassen.

Zunächst waren mit der Zulassung zum Katechumenat schwere Forderungen verbunden. Motivation und religiöses Verlangen der Kandidaten wurden untersucht, und bestimmte Berufe (so z.B. der des Schwertfechters) waren ausgeschlossen. Später, nach dem Entstehen der Volkskirche, wurden die Forderungen milder. So klagt z.B. Augustinus (354-430) über die Tatsache, daß so viele Katechumenen da sind und es auch bleiben, weil sie vor den Forderungen, die die Taufe an sie stellt, zurückschrecken. Die Katechumenen gehörten jedoch dazu, und dies kam auch liturgisch in den Katechumenatsriten zum Ausdruck. Mit anderen Worten: Die Taufe war in der alten Kirche nicht das einzige Kriterium für die Zugehörigkeit zur Kirche.

Dieses Faktum ist sehr wichtig für unsere Zeit. Man sollte – auch in Bezug auf die Kindertaufe – kreativ hiermit umgehen. Hierbei kann man von der Frage ausgehen, wie die Kirche eine gastfreundliche Kirche sein kann, auch in dem Sinn, daß sie in ihrem liturgischen Angebot auf angemessene Weise auf die verschiedenen Grade der Zugehörigkeit zur Kirche reagiert. J. Straver weist darauf hin, daß die Geburt eines Kindes wahrscheinlich für viele junge Menschen ein Ereignis ist, das sie tief trifft. 'Die jungen Eltern werden durch ein Ereignis überwältigt, das ihnen den Verstand nimmt: "Es ist unbegreiflich", "Es ist ein Wunder", sagen sie'.[23] Viele junge Menschen machen bei der Geburt oder im Zusammenhang mit der Geburt vor allem des ersten Kindes religiöse Erfahrungen. 'Jemand sagte einmal am Morgen nach der Geburt: "Ihr (Pastöre) redet immer über Wunder; dies ist ein Wunder"'.[24]

---

23 J. STRAVER: *Dopen? wat een vraag... Pastorale ervaringen rond de kinderdoop* (Hilversum 1975) 43.
24 STRAVER: *Dopen? wat een vraag...* 43.

Jedoch ist diese religiöse Erfahrung noch nicht Grund genug für die Taufe. Wohl kann sie insofern eine wichtige Rolle spielen, als diese Erfahrung die Entscheidung zur Taufe beeinflussen kann. Es wäre also unrecht, wenn die Kirche rein auf Grund des religiösen Momentes beim Geburtserlebnis zur Taufe übergeht. Zu recht schreibt Straver:[25]

> Ist es nicht ziemlich dürftig, daß wir für das geheimnisvolle Geschehen der Geburt nur eine religiöse Feier kennen, nämlich die Aufnahme dieses Kindes in die Gemeinschaft der Kirche? Läßt diese Weise des Handelns die Unterschiede im Glauben, die in einer pluralistischen Gesellschaft wie der unsrigen so stark in Erscheinung treten, nicht unbeachtet? Geht es nicht zu weit, wenn jemand, der vielleicht zum ersten Mal in seinem Leben bewußt und persönlich mit dem Religiösen in Berührung kommt, jetzt über die Taufe so eng an die Kirche gebunden wird, daß sein Kind in die – für ihn – fremde Glaubensgemeinschaft aufgenommen wird? (...) Meinem Gefühl nach entsteht mehr Deutlichkeit und Freiraum, wenn ein Unterschied gemacht wird zwischen einer Feier der Geburt und einer Aufnahme in die Gemeinschaft der Kirche (...) Die Kirche müßte lernen, etwas mit den Gefühlen zu tun, die durch die Geburt eines Kindes wachgerufen werden (...) Dies bedeutet, daß sie nicht nur in einem bestimmten Sinn auf das Bedürfnis der Eltern, mit diesen Gefühlen etwas zu tun, reagieren kann. Einerseits wird man sehen müssen, daß die Geburtserfahrung die Augen für das Mysterium öffnen, den Glauben vertiefen und ein erster Ansatz sein kann für persönlichen Glauben; andererseits muß man sich vor Augen halten, daß nicht jedes persönliche Glaubenserlebnis eine Äußerung der Verbundenheit mit der Glaubensgemeinschaft Jesu Christi ist; Taufen ist wesentlich ein 'kirchliches' Geschehen ...!

Straver spricht mir mit dem, was er schreibt, aus der Seele! Eine wirklich gastfreundliche Kirche, die sowohl ihre eigene Identität achtet, als auch sie nicht verwässern lassen will, darf nicht auf jede religiöse oder christliche Frage mit dem Passepartout der Kindertaufe reagieren. Sie kann auch 'katechumenale' Feiern einführen: die neugeborenen Kinder willkommen heißen, die Kinder segnen, ihre Geburt feiern.

8.4. Die Taufgespräche

Das Gesagte hat wichtige Folgen für die Taufgespräche, die seit Vatikanum II in den Niederlanden und auch anderswo in der Kirche eingeführt sind.[26] Diese Taufgespräche richten sich im allgemeinen stark auf die Frage nach der Motivation für die Taufe. Sie gehen normalerweise von der Frage aus: Warum möchten Sie Ihr Kind taufen lassen? Wenn dies das Leitmotiv ist, stößt man auf allerlei Schwierigkeiten.

---

25 STRAVER: *Dopen? wat een vraag...* 46-47.
26 Einen ausgezeichneten Bericht über das Entstehen und die Art der Taufgespräche findet man in STRAVER: *Dopen? wat een vraag...*

Zunächst geht man davon aus, daß die Taufe das einzig mögliche Angebot ist. Wenn das liturgische Angebot breiter wäre, könnte man leichter von den Erfahrungen mit der Geburt ausgehen und von Fragen wie: Wo ist unser Platz im religiösen Erleben, in unserem Glauben? Wie ist unsere Lebensgeschichte? Erwarten wir von Buddha genausoviel Heil wie von Jesus von Nazareth? Wie stehen wir zu der Gemeinschaft, die wir Kirche nennen? Hiernach erst kann die Frage nach dem adäquaten Ritus beantwortet werden. Selbstverständlich verlaufen die Gespräche einfacher, wenn man vorher über ein vielfältiges Angebot informiert ist. Klar ist, daß Deutlichkeit hierüber nicht von heute auf morgen zu erreichen ist; dazu ist auch wohl eine Planung nötig.

Eine zweite Schwierigkeit besteht darin, daß die Frage: 'Warum möchten Sie Ihr Kind taufen lassen?' eigentlich genausoschwer zu beantworten ist wie die Frage: 'Was ist Theologie?' Solche Fragen richten sich nämlich stark an der Verstand, führen leicht zu Diskussionen und schrecken etwas einfältigere Menschen von den Vorbereitungsgesprächen ab. Die Gespräche sollten sich vielmehr auf die Lebensgeschichte und ihre Sinngebung beziehen. Dann berühren sie von selbst den ganzen Menschen. In dieser Hinsicht können wir immer noch viel lernen von der ältesten pastoralen Anleitung zum Taufgespräch, nämlich *Vom ersten katechetischen Unterricht* von Augustinus.[27] In diesem Büchlein, das wahrscheinlich im Jahre 405 entstanden ist, betont Augustinus, daß man einen Blick für das Zwischenmenschliche des Gesprächs haben muß, für die gegenseitigen Anschauungen, für den Fortgang des Gespräches, die Vorurteile und Vorbehalte, für die nicht-verbale Kommunikation und die emotionalen Voraussetzungen. Es geht ihm in erster Linie nicht um die Mitteilung verstandesmäßiger Inhalte, sondern um die Einübung in den Glauben als Lebensstil und in die Kirche als Lebensgemeinschaft. Und er weist darauf hin, daß dies nicht möglich ist, wenn sich der Begleiter selbst auf Abstand hält: Er ist selbst mit seiner ganzen Person mit einbezogen.

Offensichtlich sind pastoral-psychologische Zurückhaltung, Einfühlungsvermögen, Aufrichtigkeit und Respekt vor den Gesprächspartnern nicht erst in unserer Zeit Voraussetzung für eine fruchtbare Einführung in den Glauben.[28] Außerdem ist deutlich, daß Augustinus großen Wert auf das Erzählen legt. Der, der das Gespräch begleitet, muß die Frohe Botschaft so vortragen wie Philippus in der Kutsche des Höflings der Königin Kandake: erzählend (vgl. Apg 8,26-40). Es geht um den Roman der Liebe Gottes. Die Hauptsache ist die liebevolle und liebeweckende Erzählung von Gottes Umgang mit seinem Volk. Das ist der Kern, nicht allerlei – die

---

27 AUGUSTINUS: *De catechizandis rudibus*. Deutsche Übersetzung, *Vom ersten katechetischen Unterricht* (= Schriften der Kirchenväter 7) (München 1985).
28 R. ZERFASS: Die Last des Taufgesprächs. Nach Augustinus Büchlein 'De catechizandis rudibus', in AUF DER MAUR und KLEINHEYER (Hrsg.): *Zeichen des Glaubens* 219-232.

Lehre und Moral betreffende – Randfragen, die so leicht die Oberhand gewinnen, wenn beim Gesprächsbeginn ein falscher Start gemacht wurde. Die Art, wie Augustinus sich den Part des Katecheten im Taufgespräch vorstellt, könnte man als die primäre Weise von Sprechen bezeichnen, die auch der Liturgie eigen ist oder ihr jedenfalls eigen sein sollte.[29] In diesem Zusammenhang kann man fragen, ob nicht während der Gespräche Augenblicke des Feierns sinnvoll und (mit) Ausgangspunkt für ein Gespräch sein könnten. Wenn Eltern dem liturgischen Geschehen entfremdet sind, könnte dann nicht das Gespräch nach Teilnahme an einer Familienmesse oder Taufe nicht einfacher in Gang kommen? In dieser Richtung sollte man vielleicht mehr experimentieren.

Die Gespräche können schließlich zwischen Eltern und Pastor, aber auch in einer Gruppe stattfinden. Wir sollten – meine ich – die Gespräche in einer Gruppe vorziehen. Wenn sich mehrere Eltern zusammen auf ihren Glauben besinnen, kann schon bei diesen Zusammenkünften etwas von (Kirchen-) Gemeinschaft erfahren werden. Danach sollten sie vielleicht getrennt, per Elternpaar, mit dem Pastor über einen passenden Ritus sprechen können. Auch in der alten Kirche kannte man eine gemeinsame Taufvorbereitung, und ... Laien spielten dabei eine große Rolle als Begleiter.

9. DER RITUS DER KINDERTAUFE

Als die Kirche zur Praxis der Kindertaufe überging, übernahm sie den Ritus der Erwachsenentaufe für die Kinder. Jahrhundertelang hat die Kirche Kinder nach einem Ritus getauft, der eigentlich für Erwachsene bestimmt war. Das *Rituale Romanum* enthielt zwar einen eigenen Ritus für die Kindertaufe; dieser war aber nur eine gekürzte und angepasste Liturgie der Erwachsenen. Schon vor dem II. Vatikanischen Konzil waren viele mit dem Ritus der Kindertaufe unzufrieden. Die Liturgie-Konstitution (1963) plante eine Erneuerung der Kindertaufe, die die wirkliche Situation der Kinder berücksichtigen sollte. Dadurch wurde vielen ganz klar bewußt, warum der alte Ritus nicht verstanden wurde. Es ist durchaus möglich, daß bei der Frage nach dem Sinn der Kindertaufe auch der Engpaß, in dem sich die Liturgie der Kindertaufe befand, eine Rolle spielte. Ist nicht Liturgie vor allem eine Handlung, die ihren Sinn nicht erst von außen durch rationale Argumente empfängt? Der Sinn der Kindertaufe liegt zu allererst in der Taufhandlung selbst. Vorbereitende Katechese der Eltern ist wichtig; den tiefsten Sinn der Kindertaufe können sie aber erst in der Feier und durch sie erleben. Im alten Ritus nun bestand wenig Zusam-

---

29 F. VAN DER MEER: *Augustinus der Seelsorger. Leben und Wirken eines Kirchenvaters* (Köln 1958[3]) 477-479.

menhang zwischen den Texten und Riten der Taufe und dem faktischen, religiösen Bewußtsein der Gläubigen. Dieses Mißverständnis versuchte man durch das Einfügen meist historisierender Katechesen aufzufangen, so daß der Ritus sozusagen von außen seinen Sinn erhielt. Aus dieser Perspektive kann man die neuen Riten der Kindertaufe als wertvolle Versuche ansehen, die Kindertaufe wieder in ihrem eigentlichen Vollsinn erlebbar zu machen. Am 15. Mai 1969 erschien der neue römische Ritus für die Kindertaufe. Dieser Ritus hat die folgende Grundstruktur: Wortgottesdienst (Lesung, Homilie, Fürbitten), in dem und durch den die Eltern und die anwesende Gemeinde zur Bekehrung und zum Bekenntnis des Glaubens an Jesu Sterben und Auferstehung aufgefordert werden, wonach als Höhepunkt und Erfüllung die Taufe mit Wasser folgt. Charakteristisch ist der Zusammenhang mit dem Ostergeheimnis und die Betonung des Gemeinschaftscharakters der Taufe. Letzteres wird darin deutlich, daß das Taufen mehrerer Kinder in einer gemeinsamen Feier und bei aktiver Teilnahme der Gläubigen bevorzugt wird.

Die Grundstruktur des offiziellen Ritus findet man – mit Variationen – in den experimentellen Riten für die Kindertaufe wieder. Wie in der gesamten Liturgie, so ist auch bei den Taufriten eine zunehmende Pluralität zu beobachten. Einerseits hängt dies damit zusammen, daß die Taufe ein reiches, geheimnisvolles Geschehen ist, das in einem einzigen Ritus nicht ausgeschöpft werden kann. Andererseits ist es heutzutage ein Faktum, daß Riten und Gebete je nach Art, Umfang und Ort der konkreten Gemeinde angepaßt werden können müssen. Die neuen experimentellen Taufriten kann man als ein Suchen nach dem christlichen *way of life* verstehen. Ist es nicht ein Zeichen der Treue zur Tradition, daß man neu zu entdecken und zu erleben versucht, wie offenbarend und enthüllend das Taufgeschehen entsprechend der Absicht des Herrn ist?

10. NACH DER TAUFE

Es wäre gut, wenn der Pastor sich Zeit für eine kritische Nachbesinnung nähme, vielleicht zusammen mit denen, die an der Taufe beteiligt waren. Wenn man verantwortlich Liturgie feiern will, ist eine regelmäßige Evaluierung unverzichtbar. Außerdem muß gesagt werden, daß die 'Nachbehandlung' nach der Kindertaufe immer noch ein verwahrlostes Feld der Pastoral ist. Man kann die Frage stellen, ob die 'Nachbehandlung' nicht früher anfangen muß als erst zu dem Zeitpunkt, an dem das Kind am liturgischen Leben der Gemeinde teilnimmt oder in den Kindergarten oder in die Schule kommt. Die religiöse Erziehung des Kindes fängt nicht erst an, wenn es zu Verstand gekommen ist, sondern mit seiner Geburt. Gerade heute, da in den Familien viele religiöse Traditionen weggefallen sind, stößt man hier auf eine Lücke. Müßte nicht in dieser Hinsicht die Pfarrgemeinde den Eltern, die die Erstverantwortung für die religiöse Erziehung ihrer Kinder tragen, Hilfe anbieten? Man könnte an eine Fortsetzung der Gespräche denken, die vor der Taufe begonnen wurden. In Gruppengesprächen von Eltern können gerade im Zusammenhang mit der christlichen Erziehung allerlei Fragen zur Sprache kommen. Ab der Zeit, in der dem Kind Geschichten erzählt werden, sollte man die Geschichten aus der Bibel nicht vergessen; das Kind ist dafür ganz besonders empfänglich.

Im Direktorium für die niederländische Kirchenprovinz heißt es über die Familie:[30]

> Immer deutlicher erscheint die Wichtigkeit der religiösen Erziehung und des religiösen Erlebens in der Familie. Von alters her ist die Familie der Ort, an dem die christlichen Bräuche entstanden sind und lebendig erhalten werden. Viele dieser Bräuche befinden sich in einer Krise, z.B. Morgen- und Abendgebet, Beten vor und nach dem Essen usw. Aber es entstehen auch neue Sitten. Man will gerne als Familie auch die Glaubensgemeinschaft erfahren; man hat das Bedürfnis, den Glauben aktuell zu machen und sucht dabei immer nach Möglichkeiten, die Kinder miteinzubeziehen. Man liest in der Bibel und sucht nach neuen Gebetsformen, u.a. in der Hausliturgie. Eltern und Familie werden auch immer wieder dadurch aktiviert, daß sie bei der Vorbereitung auf die erste Eucharistiefeier, die Firmung der Kinder usw. um Hilfe gefragt werden.

Vielleicht zeugt dieser Text doch einigermaßen von *wishful thinking*: Man kann nur hoffen, daß das skizzierte Ideal mehr und mehr Realität wird und daß man nicht erst mit der religiösen Erziehung anfängt, wenn das Kind zu Verstand gekommen ist. Das wichtigste ist dann schon geschehen. Dies ist eine pastorale Aufgabe, die für ein gesundes Wachstum im Glauben nach der Kindertaufe lebenswichtig ist.

11. DIE TAUFE: EIN KIRCHLICHES GESCHEHEN

Wer den Schritt zum Wasser hin tut, seinen Glauben bekennt, tritt ein in die neue Gemeinschaft derer, die an Christus glauben. Sein Zuhause ist jetzt die christliche Gemeinde, wo es nicht mehr Juden und Griechen gibt, nicht Sklaven und Freie, nicht Mann und Frau, sondern wo alle 'Einer' sind in Christus (Gal 3,28). Die Taufe ist also kein rein individuelles Geschehen; denn wo getauft wird, geschieht Kirche. Gerade durch die Taufe wird Kirche konstituiert. Die Täuflinge treten ein in die Gemeinde der Getauften, und sie werden durch die Gemeinde aufgenommen. Es ist klar, daß diese Dimension in einer Haustaufe kaum zum Ausdruck kommen

---

30 *Directorium voor de Nederlandse Kerkprovincie in het jaar 1973* (Zeist 1972) 157-158.

kann. Die christliche Gemeinde könnte man zwar eine Familie nennen, aber die *familia Dei*, die Familie Gottes, ist beträchtlich größer als die eigene Familie. Es ist daher wichtig, daß die Taufe vor einer Ortsgemeinde und im Hinblick auf diese stattfindet. Dort können die Täuflinge – und im Fall der Kindertaufe können dies vor allem die Eltern – den Glauben in seiner kirchlichen Dimension auch wirklich vollziehen. Sie werden sich dessen bewußt, daß die Taufe mit Bezug auf die anderen Getauften notwendigerweise ein wechselseitiges Engagement mit sich bringt ('Seht, wie sie einander lieb haben') und ein Engagement der christlichen Gemeinde gegenüber der ganzen bewohnten Welt.

Ausdrücklich habe ich von der Ortskirche gesprochen. Denn die große universale Kirche wird hier konkret erfahren, erlebt und vollzogen. Oft wird die Kirche noch als reines Gegenüber, als ein universales Gegebenes gesehen, in dem die Sakramente als Heilsmittel an das Individuum ausgeteilt werden. Die Kirche wird dann leicht als 'etwas' erfahren, das sich zwischen Gott und den Menschen befindet: als ein fremder Faktor und eine nebensächliche Struktur. Und tatsächlich: Die universale Kirche als ein Gegebenes, losgelöst von der Ortskirche, ist ein abstrakter Begriff, eigentlich nur eine Idee. Daher verweist das Vatikanum II auch darauf, daß die universale Kirche gerade in der Ortskirche als Ortskirche erscheint. Dann aber ist die Kirche nicht als Hindernis aufzufassen. Von der Familie kann man doch auch nicht sagen, daß sie sich zwischen Eltern und Kind stellt; denn gerade ihre Zusammengehörigkeit und ihr Zusammenleben bilden die Familie. Die Kirche ist die Gegenwart des Herrn, sofern Er im konkreten Zusammenkommen der Ortskirchen, die sich einander unter dem Vorsitz des Nachfolgers Petri verbunden wissen, sichtbar wird. Ganz verdichtet spielt sich das Zusammenkommen im innersten Kreis der christlichen Sakramentalität ab, die mit der Taufe beginnt.

Leider ziehen sich durch die über die Welt verstreuten christlichen Gemeinden noch immer Trennungslinien. Sie erkennen sich nicht alle als vollwertige Gemeinden des Herrn an. Eins der größten Probleme der Christen ist die Frage, wie sie dem Ideal Ausdruck verleihen sollen, daß die Taufe eine Gemeinschaft der Christen der ganzen bewohnten Welt bewirkt. Es gibt doch nur einen Leib des Herrn Jesus. Die Kirchen suchen einen Ort, wo sie einander in Einheit und Geschwisterlichkeit begegnen können. Der erste wichtige Schritt ist durch die gegenseitige Anerkennung der Taufe getan. Die Kirchen erkennen gegenseitig die Taufe als vollwertig an. Aber die gegenseitige Anerkennung der Taufe bedeutet auch eine Herausforderung, nach weitergehender Einheit zu suchen und sie zu verwirklichen. Alle, die sich taufen lassen, erhalten diesen ökumenischen Auftrag; er ist ein wichtiges Element der kirchlichen Dimension des Glaubensvollzugs bei der Taufe, der eigentlich stärker im Ritus zum Ausdruck kommen müßte. Die Christen müßten sich eigentlich auf Grund ihrer Taufe darüber klar sein, daß sie einander und der ganzen

Welt und der Geschichte dienen müssen. Wahrhaftige Ökumene fängt dort an, wo die Getauften zusammen in Jesu Namen in die Welt gehen und so dem Reich Gottes Raum verschaffen. Vielleicht realisieren sich die Kirchen dies alles erst richtig, wenn sie vereint sind in der Eucharistie: im Brot und Wein dessen, der sich hingab für das Leben der Welt. In einem neuen Geist können sie dann das bekannte Lied von H. Oosterhuis singen:[31]

> Der Geist des Herrn hat uns
> den Anfang neu geschenkt,
> in alles, was da wächst,
> den Atem eingeschenkt.
> Der Gottesgeist beseelt,
> die kalt sind und versteint,
> Zerstörtes baut er auf,
> Zerstreutes wird geeint.
>
> Wir sind in ihn getauft
> und Glut ist seine Huld.
> Er spendet Hoffnung aus
> in Sehnsucht und Geduld.
> Wer weiß, woher er kommt,
> wer sieht schon seinen Schein?
> Er öffnet uns den Mund
> und läßt uns Brüder sein.
>
> Der Geist, der in uns wohnt,
> erhebt sein Flehn zu Gott,
> daß er in seinem Sohn
> uns auferweckt vom Tod;
> daß unser Leben nie
> zerbricht in Not und Hast,
> komm Schöpfergeist, mach ganz,
> was du begonnen hast.

---

31 *Du bist der Atem meiner Lieder. Gesänge von Huub Oosterhuis und Bernard Huijbers*, übertragen ins Deutsche von P. PAWLOWSKY (Freiburg-Wien-Gelnhausen 1976) 16-17 (ursprünglich H. OOSTERHUIS: *In het voorbijgaan* (Geheel herziene uitgave) (Baarn 1975) 96).

7. Theology of Baptism after Vatican II
Shifting Accents and Lacunae

Important shifts have taken place in the theology of baptism since Vatican II. In this article I will indicate where the new accents in contemporary baptismal theology are being placed. But I will also point out lacunae in that theology and, in that context, some recent initiatives toward further development. All of these involve the consequences and concretizing of the new baptismal theology in reference to liturgical practice. Because it is only possible for people to realize the radical nature of the shifts in accent against the background of baptismal theology prior to Vatican II, I will begin with a short, global sketch of the baptismal theology with which most of us grew up.

1. THEOLOGY OF BAPTISM PRIOR TO VATICAN II

Before Vatican II, baptismal theology revolved around the necessity of baptism for salvation. The lesson about baptism in the 1948 *Catechism of the Dioceses in The Netherlands*, which prior to Vatican II everyone learned by rote, began with the question, "What is the first and most essential sacrament?" The answer was, "The first and most essential sacrament is Holy Baptism".[1] In response to the question about why baptism is the most essential sacrament, comes the answer, "Holy Baptism is the most essential sacrament because through Holy Baptism original sin is forgiven and the right to life eternal is granted".[2] In other words, before all else baptism was seen as the means of forgiveness for original sin, and necessary, as it were, to get a sort of passport to heaven. This theme of original sin dominated baptismal theology. That had been the case since the fifth century, particularly under the influence of Augustine. Yet the positive sides of baptism also came into view in the old baptismal theology. In the catechisms before Vatican II, these were formulated in the scholastic terminology of the second millennium. To the question "What do we receive in Holy Baptism?", the 1948 *Catechism of the Dioceses in The Netherlands* answered, "In Holy Baptism we

---

* De theologie van het doopsel na Vaticanum II. Accentverschuivingen en lacunes, in *Tijdschrift voor liturgie* 73 (1989) 338-348. Translated by D. Mader, M.Div.
1 *Katechismus der Nederlandse bisdommen* (Sint-Michielsgestel 1948) 61.
2 *Katechismus der Nederlandse bisdommen* 61.

receive: 1. an everlasting character and the saving grace that make us into Christians, children of God and members of the Holy Church; 2. grace and assistance in order to lead a Christian life".[3]

2. THEOLOGY OF BAPTISM AFTER VATICAN II

It is obvious that baptismal theology did not simply change overnight after Vatican II. The new baptismal theology is the fruit of a much longer theological and liturgical movement that has taken place primarily in the twentieth century. It is not my intention to sketch the precise course of this historical development. Rather, I am interested in an overall picture of the new baptismal theology. What elements spring to the eye?[4]

2.1. General background: shifts in sacramental theology

It seems to me to be important to indicate a number of shifts in accent that baptismal theology shares with all the other sacraments. These involve the following:
– In contrast to the accent on the negative side, namely the sacrament as a remedy for sin, the positive side is stressed: the sacrament is incorporation in the mystery of Christ, in particular in the death and resurrection of Christ, and/or brings about a growing participation in that mystery.
– In contrast to the scholastic view of sacrament as remedy, the more personalistic and existential vision has arisen, of the sacrament as encounter with Christ and, in Him, with the Father, through and in the Holy Spirit.
– In contrast to the nearly exclusive relation of the officiant and the individual recipient the sacrament, it has become important that both the officiant and the recipients act within the context of the church as sacrament, which very concretely means that both the officiant and the recipi-

---

[3] *Katechismus der Nederlandse bisdommen* 62.
[4] Literature, B. NEUNHEUSER: *Taufe und Firmung* (= Handbuch der Dogmengeschichte IV/2) (Freiburg-Basel-Wien 1983²) 128-133; R. CABIÉ: L'initiation chrétienne, in A. MARTIMORT (ed.): *L'Eglise en prière* III. *Les sacrements* (Paris 1984); A. BLIJLEVENS a.o. (ed.): *Dopen met water en geest. Doopliturgieën, elementen voor vieringen en achtergrondbeschouwingen uit 20 jaar Werkmap voor liturgie (1966-1985)* (Hilversum 1988); A. HOUSSIAU: *Le baptême, entrée dans l'existence chrétienne* (Bruxelles 1983); M. LAWLER: *Symbol and sacrament. A contemporary sacramental theology* (New York 1987); M. SEARLE (ed.): *Alternative futures for worship* II. *Baptism and confirmation* (Collegeville 1987); Th. SCHNEIDER: *Zeichen der Nähe Gottes. Grundriss der Sakramententheologie* (Mainz 1979). For more literature, see also G. LUKKEN: Literatuur, in: De toekomst van de kinderdoop, in *Werkmap voor liturgie* 11 (1977) 238-241, and A. BLIJLEVENS and G. LUKKEN: Literatuur, in: De doop van volwassenen, in *Werkmap voor liturgie* 17 (1983) 196-200.

ent only act significantly within the ground plan and the interaction of relations within the church.

– In contrast to the accent on the efficacy (*opus operatum*), powerfully formulated in the minimal and juridical form of the very moment (*materia* and *forma*), it is now also stressed that belief (*opus operantis*) plays an important role.

– In contrast to understanding the sacrament primarily as an act of God, the emphasis is placed on the sacrament as a celebration of the community of the faithful: trans-des-cendence as opposed to trans-as-cendence.

– Consistent with this, in contrast to the sacrament as a sudden intervention from another world, the sacrament is seen as a manifestation of the gracious character of all human life and attention is given to the rich anthropological sides of the sacrament.

– And finally, in contrast to the rather isolated discussion of the sacraments, there is now a consciousness that all kinds of theological questions come together in a very concentrated manner in sacramental theology, including such questions as how we speak about God, the breadth of salvation, how freedom and grace are related, how we speak about Christ and the Holy Spirit, what the role of the church in the economy of salvation, how faith and experience are related.

2.2. Shifting accents in the theology of baptism

Contemporary baptismal theology is no longer dominated by the theme of original sin. Its central theme is the Easter mystery (Rom. 6). Baptism is the proclamation, celebration and representative performance of the death and resurrection of Christ.[5] The water is no longer purely seen as a means of cleansing – a tradition that is grounded in Scripture itself (I Cor. 6:9-11; Eph. 5:25-26; Heb. 10:22) – but as the complex symbol of chaos, death and dissolution, and of harmony, life and resurrection. Just as Jesus descended into the chaos of death and rose again, so the person receiving baptism descends into the water and rises again from it, thus entering into the mystery of Easter. This vision of baptism finds its most complete liturgical expression in immersion.

By recovering this central baptismal theme from Scripture, patristic sources and old liturgical usage, the scholastic and abstract doctrine of grace is personalized. Baptism is about constituting a relation between the person receiving the sacrament and the Lord Himself, who has suffered, died, risen and is coming again. It is about life in and through the Holy Spirit, in whom the person receiving baptism may henceforth call God Abba.

Thus the accent has shifted to the positive side of baptism. The remedy

5 LAWLER: *Symbol and sacrament* 74.

against sin now becomes the means of taking part in the intimacy of trinitarian life. This positive side of baptism also appears in all sorts of baptismal themes that, as it were, stand grouped around the central theme of the Easter mystery: baptism as new creation, new birth, second birth, rebirth, adoption as a child of God, deification, sanctification, indwelling, redemption, incorporation into the body of Christ, illumination, taking on the new, imperishable person, gifts of the Spirit, themes which are also all in line with the baptismal theology and baptismal liturgy of the Scripture and early church.

Can it then be said that there is a break with the old *original sin* theology that has determined baptismal theology for fifteen centuries? In a certain sense, yes. This is true particularly for the original sin theology which had become crystallized in the course of the centuries. This original sin theology posited a real state of sin, which was present in everyone from the first moment of human existence, and was not attributable to personal actions, but inherited from Adam. In a culture which places so strong an emphasis on personal responsibility and on the characteristic of human capacity, people have difficulty with such an individualistic formulation of original sin. The difficulty decreases considerably when original sin is seen as a solidarity shared by all in the *mysterium iniquitatis* that is present everywhere in our world. But it must be realized that this is not only a matter of evil in the world around us. It is also a matter of an intrinsic wound, an intrinsic inner void that all people share in common. Human beings appear insufficient in themselves. That is what Augustine wanted to bring establish in his argument against the Pelagians. People finally always stand in need of salvation, even at the deepest level of their being. In the end, it is only from God that salvation, the ultimate light, is possible: that new kingdom in which the lame walk, the blind see, righteousness flows like streams, well-bring reigns, creation and the environment come into their own, and death, chaos and dissolution are conquered. That is what is professed and celebrated in baptism.

The *salvific necessity* of baptism thus no longer exclusively depends on the self-sufficient negative side, but is 'illuminated' from the positive side. The bipolarity of baptism is no longer resolved to one pole, but is fully maintained. In the period in which the negative pole dominated exclusively, every child had to be baptized as soon after birth as possible in order that he or she would not be damned. That is what the old catechism wanted to emphasize above all else. The more charitable theologians prepared limbo for children who died before baptism, as a way out of hell. One can still speak of the salvific necessity of baptism, but now from another perspective, that of the performance of what, in the last analysis, is salutary for every person. Now that people are not fixated on the negative pole, they are much less obsessed with the question of how God fills the void for those who are not baptized. Theology before Vatican II spoke of the baptism of desire. Now people would appear to accentuate the Beatitudes: have they not seen how the way to salvation runs for those who are poor in spirit, those who mourn, the meek, those who hunger and thirst for righteousness, who are pure of heart, for the peacemakers or those who are persecuted for righteousness' sake (Matt. 5:1-10)?

Through this leap forward, baptism has again come to be seen as an *initiation* sacrament, an insight that is further borne out from the perspectives of both theology and social sciences.[6] Initiation involves a whole complex of rites and verbal instructions with an eye to fundamentally altering the initiate's social and religious life. Initiation is a lengthy process that touches upon a whole way of life. After Vatican II, this rediscovery of Christian initiation was made concrete in the new baptismal liturgy for adults.[7] In this, baptism is no longer limited to a momentary experience, but broadened out into a sacramental process consisting of various stages of conversion and growth in faith, marked by ritual celebrations and on Easter crowned by the climax of baptism, confirmation and the eucharist. In this baptismal liturgy, it becomes clear the extent to which being taken up into the community of faith is a process of socialization into the church, which does not involve only the cognitive/ intellectual side of life, but also the emotional. The Christian initiation process builds on the more general human pattern of initiation that is its anthropological foundation. It is in this general pattern, that people find the archetypical dialectic of human development in the field of tension between individual and broader sociocultural and religious values.[8] The process of growth in conversion and faith is also enacted within this field of tension. The person receiving baptism is gradually introduced into the community of faith, and the ecclesiastic dimension of faith is gradually realized. It reaches its climax in the three-fold initiation of baptism, confirmation and eucharist. Thus, in the new adult baptism, one can speak of baptismal theology made concrete, that underscores the importance of both conversion and faith, and the ecclesiastic dimension. It is not a matter of a sacramental performance that plays itself out between the officiant and the individual, but performing a rite of initiation in the field of tension of the individual and the community of faith, in which the officiant represents the local and universal church commu-

---

6 Cf. M. ELIADE: *Das Mysterium der Wiedergeburt. Initiationsriten, ihre kulturelle und religiöse Bedeutung* (Zürich-Stuttgart 1961); J. RIES: Les rites d'initiation à la lumière de l'histoire des religions, in HOUSSIAU a.o.: *Le baptême* 19-34; A. THOMPSON: Infant baptism in the light of the human sciences, in SEARLE (ed.): *Alternative futures* 55-102; H. ANDERSON: Pastoral care in the process of initiation, in SEARLE (ed.): *Alternative futures* 103-136.

7 *Rituale Romanum. Ordo initiationis christianae adultorum* ed. typica (Rome 1972).

8 Cf. THOMPSON: Infant baptism.

nity. In Thomistic theological terms, it could be said that in performing the initiation, the church is an *instrumentum conjunctum* of the Lord himself. Thus, the insight of the new baptismal theology is that it wishes to differentiate between a lifeless *instrumentum conjunctum* like the baptismal water, and a living *instrumentum conjunctum* like the church,[9] or, in other words, the actions of people entering a sacramental world. In every initiation, the church itself is conscious, or should become conscious, of the extent to which it is itself constituted on the ground of initiation, and has the responsibility of being 'continually initiate'. Only when this condition is fulfilled is the church plausibly an *instrumentum conjunctum*. When the tension between closed and open, past and future, giving and taking is implicit in initiation, then these implications are as valid for the church as they are for the instrumental milieu of the initiation. This means that the initiated church can not manifest itself as something static, but must be an *ecclesia semper reformanda*, all the more because 'continual initiation' is not only a Christian responsibility, but also an urgent demand of contemporary culture. In connection with the credibility and fruitfulness of the church as *instrumentum conjunctum*, there are obviously questions here regarding the openness of the church for the inculturation of faith, and preserving the balance between faith as the proper belief and as the right way of life.

The new baptismal theology strongly emphasizes the ethical consequences of baptism. Baptism is, as has already been noted, the beginning of a commission to 'continual initiation' in which the first and the second command are like unto each other, and in which love of one's neighbor is expressed both locally and globally. In the renewal and repetition of the baptismal vows, particularly on Easter Saturday night, ritual continually reiterates this dimension.

Like sacramental theology in general, the new baptismal theology devotes little or no attention to a rethinking of the theology of the everlasting character. On the one hand, this theology touches on the social/institutional side of baptism, and on the other, on the relation between the way humans deal with symbols and divine action. To enter into this discussion further at this point would take us too far from our topic.

One major and positive consequence for the credibility of the church is the mutual recognition of the validity of baptism that has arisen among denominations since the 1960's. The ecumenical meaning of baptism has been illuminated and concretized by this process. This in turn can have an exemplary effect on further ecumenism. The mutual recognition of the validity of baptism has taken place despite differing baptismal theologies and liturgies. This helps to establish a ground rule

---

9 Cf. S. HAPPEL: Speaking from experience. Worship and the social sciences, in SEARLE (ed.): *Alternative futures* 173-176.

2.3. Lacunae in the theology of baptism[11]

Anyone who steeps themselves in the shifts of accents in post-Vatican II baptismal theology, cannot escape the impression that adult baptism has functioned as the basic model for this new baptismal theology. Taking part in the Easter mystery is not seen so much as a reference to God who has spared the children of Israel or to the lamb by whose blood the Jews were saved, but rather as passing through the water. Of course this last image indicates that the recipient of baptism is the active adult who left the land of Egypt and passed through the Red Sea on the way to the promised land. From this it follows that the themes of baptism as new creation, new birth, rebirth, adoption as a child of God, illumination, putting on the new person, etc., while belonging to the tradition every bit as much as the death and resurrection theme, will be less central; they become, as it were, secondary themes woven around the central theme of the Easter mystery. The baptismal water accentuates the symbolism of death and resurrection more than that of the womb and creation. In the new baptismal theology the emphasis lies on the personal socialization to adult conversion and adult faith. This involves active participation in a prophetic church that is the successor to the national church. However strange it sounds, this conviction of the need for adulthood and autonomy of the initiate ultimately lies within the broad lines of the Catholic and protestant tradition of infant baptism. Thus it is not a matter of Anabaptist thought which rejects infant baptism, or even those protestant theologians like K. Barth and the Neo-Orthodox camp who are also opposed to infant baptism. Even within the tradition of infant baptism, theologians have had difficulty with baptizing infants. To an increasing degree, people have sought an escape route backwards, postponement to a later age. Thus Luther and Calvin maintained infant baptism, but reinterpreted confirmation into a rite of personal confession at a later age, and Catholics, who have always maintained infant baptism as a general practice, are in fact moving gradually toward the growing practice of underscoring the desirability of administering confirmation at a later age. In general, the point of departure in every case is the Council of Trent, at which it was determined that the initiation through confirmation and first communion should, at its earliest, be set at that age when a person has achieved intellectual and moral discrimination (i.e., seven or eight). Con-

---

10 NEUNHEUSER: *Taufe und Firmung* 129.
11 See for this part especially M. SEARLE: Infant baptism reconsidered, in IDEM (ed.): *Alternative futures* 15-54.

firmation theology itself had already long been developed as that of the *aetas perfecta*, the adult Christian age. The idea of a single initiation had already been broken, and a hidden problem involving infant baptism was driven into the open: the Christian life is apparently identified with the adult life. Childhood is only a period between birth and being a person, a sort of prelude to being an adult. In our own day, both confirmation theology and the liturgical practice of confirmation at later ages (with pleas for administering confirmation at the age of graduation from elementary school, or, by preference, at an even later age) are often a signal of a theology that is not entirely comfortable with infant baptism. Confirmation must, as it is, offer the final guarantee for the meaning of infant baptism. In this light, it is not surprising that some have developed baptismal theologies that draw out the consequences of post-Vatican II baptismal theology. For instance, Lawler proposes a Christian celebration of birth coupled with the postponement of baptism until the child makes a profession of faith for him or herself.[12] In support of this, among other things he calls upon the Declaration of the Freedom of Religion approved by Vatican II, which declares that no one should be forced into belief against their will.[13]

It should be noted that there have been some changes. While in the past children were always baptized with a baptismal ritual which was merely an abbreviation of that for adults, since 1969 the Catholic church for the first time has had a baptismal ritual which is geared for children. When, however, this ritual is compared with that for adults, it appears rather thin. It suggests that baptism is something that can be completed within the space of an hour. The new ritual for infant baptism does not reflect the progress from stage to stage that characterizes adult baptism. Moreover, in this ritual the initiation is only partly accomplished: unlike in the Eastern church, the newborn child is not anointed and taken into the eucharistic community. Further, the ritual makes little use of baptismal themes present in Scripture and tradition that are highly suited for the child. The new ritual for infant baptism does nothing to answer the questions regarding infant baptism which the new ritual for adult baptism has made even more pressing than before.

One can find an impetus to a more complete theology of infant baptism in Searle.[14] First of all, he directs our attention to the fact that attention for the child as child only arose in the seventeenth and eighteenth century. Before that time, children of less than seven or eight were not considered as persons. They were seen as irrational, subhuman beings or as defective adults. Only between four and seven, as children began to

---

12 LAWLER: *Symbol and sacrament* 80-81.
13 LAWLER: *Symbol and sacrament* 81.
14 SEARLE: Infant baptism reconsidered.

speak, comprehend and act more as adults, were they more or less admitted to adult life. In Augustine we find on the one hand the opinion that children are innocent, while on the other hand he sees the child as something negative. This darker side of the child, that can be found in Augustine's anti-Pelagian writings, came to dominate Western culture and was connected with the doctrine of original sin. The child knew only irrational desires that had to be reined in. This negative vision of the child as a sinner from inception thus supported the doctrine of the necessity of baptism. Only in our century have we broken through this negative view of the child, and attention to the individual, positive worth of the child has matured. Thus the theology of infant baptism must also be thought through anew.

A second step toward a full fledged theology of infant baptism is the question of whether there is a place for the child in the Christian sacred economy. It can be answered that Scripture itself places children in a very positive light in relation to salvation (Mk. 10:14-15; Lk. 9:47-48, 18:15-17; Matt. 18:1-5, 19:13-15).[15] In the perspective of the later Western negative view of the child, this Scriptural vision is all the more remarkable.

Intimately connected with this is the question of what soteriological value may be attributed to Jesus' being as a child. One can here cite the adage of the early church: what is not adopted is not saved. Well, the Lord certainly took the form of a newborn and growing child.[16] Most fundamentally, the child is made holy in the incarnation. Children can, from the very start, share in the Christian sacred economy.

People will have to discard the idea that in regard to faith the child is a purely passive being. This is particularly important because baptismal theology continually underscores the connection between baptism and faith. The view of Thomistic theology that the child receives the *habitus* of faith through baptism, which later is actualized, appears too much a makeshift solution. It originates from a view of the child as a purely passive being. But this conception reflects a constricted, rationalistic point of view, and a cognitive/intellectual view of faith.[17] Although children are pre-rational, they are active from the beginning. A child is not a blank slate, but has a characteristic human existence, as a child. A child is quite

---

15 G. RAMSHAW-SCHMIDT: Celebrating baptism in stages. A proposal, in SEARLE (ed.): *Alternative futures* 137-138. Searle also refers to numerous narratives in the Scriptures, from the saving of the children of Noah through that of Jairus's daughter, in which the theme of God's salvation for children comes to the fore.
16 Cf. AMBROSIUS: *Epistola* 48; ATHANASIUS: *Ad Epictitum* 7; BASILIUS: *Epistola* 261; CYRILLUS OF JERUSALEM: *Catecheses* 4, 9; GREGORIUS OF NAZIANZE: *Epistola* 101 ad Cledonium.
17 SEARLE: Infant baptism reconsidered 40-43. See also G. LUKKEN: De kinderdoop in de kerk van vandaag, in BLIJLEVENS a.o. (ed.): *Dopen met water en geest* 16-18, and G. LUKKEN: De doop. Een onvervangbaar sacrament, in BLIJLEVENS a.o. (ed.): *Dopen met water en geest* 105-107.

at home in a wholistic view, which considers people as more than purely transparent consciousness. A child has an individual life of faith, hope and love, precisely as a child. Faith is more than accepting truths. For everyone, it is also a way of life, entrusting oneself entirely to God. Children and the mentally handicapped can also, in their own manner, lead a life of complete dependence on God. A child also understands the continual movement of giving and taking, old and new, death and resurrection. In that sense, the Easter mystery can be lived out by every child, and in that sense one can also speak of the active participation of the child in the church community. One can even ask oneself if the child, as child, does not have a place in the prophetic witness of the church.

However, for the characteristic theology of infant baptism it is principally the stress on the sacramental form of the church that will be of importance. In contrast to the prophetic church, in the sacramental church the stress lies on the power of grace, at work beneath the level of consciousness. Just as is the case in parents' expressions of love toward their newborn children, so in the celebration of the sacraments more is happening than we can know.

The development of a theology of the family as *ecclesiola in ecclesia* is of great importance for a characteristic theology of infant baptism. The family is the first *locus* of socialization into faith. Therefore there is little sense in the baptism of a child who will grow up in a non-believing environment. In our culture the family (possibly the incomplete family) is more than ever the immediate environment of the *fides ecclesiae*. The family as *ecclesiola* is also a sort of living *instrumentum conjunctum* of sacramentality. In the Christian family it becomes a matter of the relation with the child in the light of sacred history, and that involves all the occurrences of the conception, carrying, birth and growth of the child as a unique being with his or her own name. Now, these experiences of the family as *ecclesiola* must be related to the great *ecclesia*. This is only possible if the *ecclesia* gives attention to the whole process by which the child enters into the sacred order. This means that the ritual translating the experience for the larger church could begin before birth, for after all the reception of the child into the sacred economy has already begun, and therefore also the sacramental celebration of the arrival of the child. Over a decade ago A. Scheer made a plea for an initiation-liturgy connected with the whole birth process, a ritual that would have to grow with the whole gestation process until that was fulfilled. In this proposal, Scheer made reference to the example of Eastern liturgy.[18] Within the framework of the new reflection on the theology of infant baptism, G. Ramshaw-Schmidt proposed dividing the whole initiation of the child into four

---

18 A. SCHEER: Zullen we ons kind alsnog laten dopen? Een pleidooi voor een aangepast pastoraat voor doopouders, in *Tijdschrift voor liturgie* 62 (1978) 163-173.

stages: 1) the pre-catechumenate, with a celebration before the birth and a celebration in which the intention to present the child for baptism is lifted up; 2) the catechumenate, which includes a celebration immediately after the birth[19] and a celebration of the enrollment of the child's name; 3) the purification and enlightenment, in which are included a ritual of preparation for baptism and, in a single ritual, the performance of baptism, confirmation and the eucharist; 4) the mystagogy, which includes two celebrations in memory of the initiate, one in the church and one in the family.[20] Thus child baptism would get its own fully developed ritual, and the original unity of initiation would be restored. It is the general conviction in contemporary baptismal theology that the sacraments of water, oil and table belong together, but how they are to be integrated in practice is a subject of controversy. The new initiatives given here for a theology of infant baptism are likewise a compelling argument for the restoration of the original unity of the initiation, as is still the case in the Eastern church. An additional advantage of this single initiation is that the scriptural symbolism of the water as the life-giving sign of the Spirit would again be developed.[21]

In the second section, above (2.2), I noted the central place of the Easter mystery and the more secondary baptismal themes. This involved such themes as new creation, new birth, second birth, rebirth, adoption as a child of God, incorporation into the body of Christ, deification, sanctification, indwelling, redemption, illumination, putting on the new, imperishable person, gifts of the Spirit, and sealing. It is precisely these themes, which equally go back to Scripture, the Fathers and early liturgies, that would have to receive a central place in a fully developed theology and liturgy of infant baptism. They would be able to give this theology and liturgy more anthropological foundation, because they are more suited for the situation of the child. Ramshaw-Schmidt has worked these themes into the rituals he has presented for trial.[22] In rituals of infant baptism the Easter mystery would be able to be expressed in the interpretation of the sparing of the children of Israel or the sparing of the

---

19 This would not be a matter of celebrating the birth as a threshold liturgy which indicates that a person is not yet ready for a real Christian initiation because the state of the parents' belief is not adequate for that initiation (cf. G. LUKKEN: *Geen leven zonder rituelen* (Baarn 1984) 83-91). Nor is it a celebration of the birth such as that proposed by M. Lawler as the first step toward baptism at a later age (cf. note 12).
20 RAMSHAW-SCHMIDT: Celebrating baptism in stages 137-155, has also worked out this proposal. In the second stage, the author has also included a ritual that could be performed in case of a miscarriage or stillbirth.
21 Cf. for this symbolism LAWLER: *Symbol and sacrament* 74-75 and 83.
22 RAMSHAW-SCHMIDT: Celebrating baptism in stages. It should be noted here that the anthropological basis of birth indeed deserves attention in rituals of infant baptism, but that infant baptism is more than a celebration of birth. Cf. G. LUKKEN: Liturgie van de kinderdoop tussen bevestiging en evangelische uitdaging, in *Praktische theologie* 11 (1984) 461.

firstborn of Israel thanks to the blood of the lamb. But one does not have to entirely exclude the dominant interpretation of the *pascha as transitus*; after all, the archetype of the growth of the child is that of giving and taking, falling and getting up again. On the other hand, it would be wrong to exclude the themes of infant baptism from adult baptism. It is a matter of a difference in accents and not of exclusively reserving the *pascha as transitus* for adult baptism and the other themes for infant baptism. An expansion of both themes would by no means have to make them mutually exclusive.

Whoever calls the old catechism to mind will be convinced that in a short time rather radical shifts have taken place in the theology and liturgy of baptism. One could speak of a new baptismal theology and baptismal liturgy that is more in line with the Scripture and early church, without falling into a literal repetition. The renewal of baptismal theology and baptismal liturgy after Vatican II has not yet reached its end, however. The prolegomena for a further extension of the theology of infant baptism are present, and these will not remain without their consequences for the liturgy of infant baptism.[23]

---

23 Further concentration on how these prolegomena are worked out in the Dutch experimental rituals for infant baptism would certainly be worth the effort. For these rituals, see L. GEUDENS and R. DE GRAVE: De eigen rituelen van het Nederlandse taalgebied, in BLIJLEVENS a.o. (ed.): *Dopen met water en geest* 44-79, and more elaborated L. GEUDENS and R. DE GRAVE: *Liturgieën voor de kinderdoop* (Westerlo 1975).

8. This is a Great Mystery
A Theological Reflection on the Sacrament of Marriage

Heidegger once said that we are repeatedly inclined "to define the essence of a fish up to the measure of his capability to live on dry land".[1] We often do the same with man. We imagine him as a Robinson Crusoë and then add his relations to the world and his fellow men. But the self is never without the world and without other people. The self and the things around it are always connected. P. Claudel has formulated this strikingly in one of his plays: "Heaven and earth touch each other, the body is related to the mind, everything ever created communicates with each other, all things are inevitably connected".[2] In particular this connection exists with other people. Nobody can be man without others. The self alone cannot decide on its destiny. It is all connected:[3]

> (...) there's not a skipping soul on the loneliest goat-path who is not hugged into this, the human shambles. And whatever happens on the farthest pitch, to the sand-man in the desert or the island-man in the sea, concerns us very soon.

H. Oosterhuis noted that this awareness belongs to the inalienable inheritance of the Jews and quotes M. Buber:[4]

> Every human being, with his whole being and doing, determines the world's destiny in a way which is unknowable for him and for others; for the causality that we can perceive is but a small sector out of the unthinkable multiple unseen influence from all to all.

However, not everyone is just as close to me. There seem to be, as it were, concentric circles which are getting smaller and smaller. As the circle gets smaller, the experience of fellow-men also becomes more tangible and more intense. That goes for the group of family and friends, of parents and children, of husband and wife.

---

* *In goede en kwade dagen. Beschouwingen over huwelijksliturgie en modellen van huwelijksvieringen uit 20 jaar werkmap Liturgie (1966-1985)* (Baarn 1991) 44-50, 115-118. Translated by W. M. Speelman, M.Div.
1 M. HEIDEGGER: *Über dem Humanismus* (Frankfurt am Main 1949) 6.
2 P. CLAUDEL, in *L'Annonce faite à Marie* (Paris 1912).
3 Chr. FRY: *A sleep of prisoners*, in IDEM: *Plays* (London-Oxford-New York 1971) 52.
4 H. OOSTERHUIS: *Mensen voor dag en dauw* (Baarn 1976) 20.

1. MARRIAGE: A NATURAL SACRAMENT

No doubt the alliances between man and woman for life are a high point of human forms of relationship. It is a very penetrating way of existing. It is therefore not surprising that at this junction of human life, life is experienced by us in its full mysterious depth and that the moment of solemnization of marriage is felt to be a participation in the great mystery of life. At the moment of solemnization everything that marriage is, is bonded together in a symbolization. A reference takes place: the alliance between man and woman is so penetrating that it touches the mystery of the divine Thou and that this mystery appears in marriage. There is a reference of the seen to the unseen, of an appearance of the invisible in the visible. And then the word sacrament is used.

> In marriage, both husband and wife feel called to transcend themselves and to unite in the deeper reality that lies above them, the answer to their latent quest and the principle of union between them. Religions have seen God as the supreme and ineffable mystery that penetrates everything and encompasses everything, in which everything is revealed and kept. (...) ultimately, man is married by and to God. The other person is the sacrament of God (...). One person becomes the sacrament for another when God is seen to be near because he is felt in the excellence of their love, and also felt to be distant, because he is veiled under the sacrament.[5]

Thus marriage evokes something beyond itself, which is the love of God for mankind: his love surrounds, encompasses so to speak, the love of husband and wife. This is so overwhelming that one could speak here of God's act of salvation. This is a transparency which marriage possesses by nature. By nature marriage refers to the mystery of God's love for us. Marriage is a natural sacrament.

2. NATURAL SACREMENTALITY: A FULL VALUE BASIS FOR THE CHRISTIAN SACREMENT

'Christians marry like everybody' is a saying of the early Church.[6] Indeed, the sacramental sign of the Christian marriage is nothing other than the earthly reality of marriage itself. To put it in a classical formulation: Christ established no sacramental sign of marriage, but took marriage the way it already existed. It is therefore no wonder that in the past Christian rituals of marriage were intensely and fundamentally influenced by the way in which marriage was celebrated in the different

---

5 L. BOFF: The sacrament of marriage, in *Concilium* 9 (1973) no. 7, 26.
6 NN: *Epistola ad Diognetum*, in J.-P. MIGNE: *Patrologia graeca* II (Paris 1886) 1173.

cultures. There have been periods, particularly since the Council of Trent, in which a gap grew between the Christian ritual of marriage and the existing culture. This was particularly true for the mission areas. Some years ago a missionary from Flores told me the following. He once assisted at a wedding service on Flores according to the classical Roman ritual. After the event it appeared that the bridal couple had not experienced this marriage rite as a real wedding service. This was because the girl had made her appearance without the usual festive clothes; she had not done her hair and at home the dowry had not been handed over. This had all been experienced as a sign that she actually did not want to marry. It is obvious that in that culture only a ritual of marriage in which the customs mentioned were respected would be satisfactory. And if I am well informed, it is not a custom of the Eskimos that husband and wife shake hands in public. How would it then be possible for a mutual handshake to express openly the words 'I do'? Fortunately, since Vatican II the Church realizes that in liturgy she must take into account the concrete earthly ritual reality of marriage. This is, as appears from the above, not only a matter of respect, but also of sound theology.

With regard to the Christian sacrament of marriage, a remarkable phenomenon is encountered. Marriage is one of those central 'border situations' in which life becomes more intense and more fierce, as is, for instance, also the case with birth, growing up or severe illness. All people surround these junctions of life with rites, in and through which they want to clarify the situation in front of God or the transcendental and make an appeal to him as a source of salvation. Christians too surround the central moments of life with rites. The general fact is that, for Christians, the given ritual expressions of these border situations do not suffice: baptism is more than a celebration of birth; confirmation is more than an initiation into adulthood. Only in marriage is this different. Marriage as earthly reality refers in a suggestive way to the real Christian mystery that a full value celebration of marriage between two baptized people – that is, between two people who are explicitly linked with Christ – can suffice as a sacramental sign itself.

Apart from that, it appears that precisely here new complicated questions are emerging. In Black Africa marriage is an act which proceeds step by step. The different steps of the taking as one's wife, thus of marriage, are generally speaking: the partner's choice; submission and acceptance of the official proposal of marriage; probation of the future husband and wife; acts through which, in the eye of the groups present, the boy and girl obtain the social status of husband and wife; taking the bride to the house of the bridegroom; festivities; cohabitation of husband and wife; the birth of the first child. Some questions may be posed here: do all these steps belong to the sacramental sign of marriage? Is not marriage in the

African view much *more* than the exchange of the words 'I do' between the partners only? Is it also the reaching of a mutual agreement between the different rightful claimants, that is to say, the tribes? And does having a baby belong to the sacramental sign? These are new and complicated questions. The African bishops have recently laid these questions before biblical exegetes, historians and theologians, including those from Europe.[7]

3. THE CHRISTIAN SACRAMENT

In marriage, therefore, there is no question of a sacramental sign proper to christianity. But there is a new spirit and a new vision on the earthly reality of marriage. According to St. Paul, this new spirit and vision are due to the fact that Christians 'marry in the Lord' (I Cor. 7:39). In the end Christian marriage refers to Christ and to the Church (Eph. 5:32). In other words, for Christians the worldly sign of marriage eventually refers implicitly to the relation between Christ and his Church.

Every marriage bears a deep symbolism: a reference takes place in it; the definitive alliance between husband and wife is experienced in such an intense way that marriage is lived through as touching the mystery of the transcendental. As people we try to name this mystery that goes beyond us. It has something to do with love, faithfulness, fullness, light, eternity. Religions point out this mystery with words such as 'higher power', 'God' or 'the divine Thou'. Today's Christians experience the most affinity with the way in which the Jews named this impenetrable mystery. Or rather: God himself has revealed the name of that mystery in a surprising way to the Jewish people. The One who, for the Jews, illuminates this world is the God who reveals himself as the God of the covenant with his people: I-will-be-there-for-you (Ex. 3:14). He is the One who – in terms of marriage – enlists the heart of Israel (Hos. 2:16-17) and who looks out for the day of the new covenant, the day on which a marriage is celebrated between JHWH and Israel for good (Hos. 2:18, 2:21-22). Hosea, Jeremiah (2: 2) and Ezekiel (23:3, 23:8, 23:19, 23:21) put the first phase of JHWH's early brideslove in the period of Israel's passage through the desert to the promised land. In the desert the marriage between JHWH and his people is solemnized and in the promised land the daily life of marriage begins,

---

7 Cf. *Naar een verinheemsing van het christelijk huwelijksritueel. Document van het symposion van de bisschoppenconferenties van Afrika en Madagascar, Acara 15 september 1976*, in *Archief van de kerken* 32 (1977) 725-729. See also P. ROUILLARD: Liturgies en Afrique, in *La maison Dieu* 130 (1977) 129-146, especially 141-143; Th. REY-MERMET: *Ce que Dieu a uni... Le mariage chrétien hier et aujourd'hui* (Paris 1974) 265-284.

with its ups and downs. Thus the relation of marriage between God and his people is one of the most striking images of the covenant. In this image JHWH appears as matrimonial faithfulness and love. He is and will be for his people as a bridegroom for his bride. It is therefore obvious that the Old Testament testifies to an intimate relationship between human marriage itself and the God of salvation.[8] In other words: for the faithful Jew the natural sacramentality of marriage offers a deep perspective on salvation. This is certainly the case in the light of the fulfillment of the covenant in the New Testament. For the faithful of the New Testament to marry means to dedicate oneself for life to the other *just as* Christ devoted his life to his Church.[9] The uniqueness of Jesus of Nazareth is that he gave himself up for his bride and that, at the cost of his own life, he made his people his bride. Thus a new community of salvation has been raised: his Church (Eph. 5:25). What Christians believe is formulated here in images of marriage, that is, salvation is possible in no one other than in and through Jesus of Nazareth, who was crucified, but whom God raised from the dead; and that no other name has been appointed to us, by which – according to God's intentions of salvation – we are saved (Acts 4:10, 4:12).

That unique name of Jesus, of that most beloved, is the ultimate reality that gives Christian marriage its identity. Thus human history, in its most intimate humanity, stands in a special way in the light of the death and resurrection of Jesus.

This should urge the Church to have a deep respect for marriage. True marriage refers to the ultimate ecclesiastical dimensions and also bears them within itself. It would be well if the Church was more prepared to listen and so to get to the bottom of its mystery in and through marriage. This could, for instance, lead to a less didactical Church, certainly in regard to marriage itself, and to a Church which is also affectively closer to the people. Perhaps in this way the Church could give up something of her too masculine character, giving to women their proper place. The great Church can learn from the *ecclesia domestica*, the domestic Church of the family, of which *Lumen gentium* (no 11) speaks.

Marriage between two baptized Christians is thus a symbol of the ultimate love between Christ and his Church: marriage evokes this love, but at the same time this love between Christ and the Church realizes itself in marriage. In that way the bride and bridegroom are themselves

---

8 A comprehensive treatment of this subject in the Old Testament can be found in E. SCHILLEBEECKX: *Het huwelijk* I. *Aardse werkelijkheid en heilsmysterie* (Bilthoven 1963) 28-75.
9 An elaborate discussion with regard to the New Testament can be found in SCHILLEBEECKX: *Het huwelijk* 89-159.

the ministers of this sacrament: it is they who fully administer this sacrament in its symbolic form at the solemnization. At the same time this sacrament has something lasting; that which is evoked and realized at the moment of celebration has to unfold in married life, in all the day-to-day worries, 'in good times and in bad, in sickness and in health'; husband and wife have to love each other mutually just as Christ loves his Church.[10]

4. THE CHRISTIAN MARRIAGE RITE

Medieval theologians often asked the question at which moment and through which sign the sacrament of marriage is being performed. After long discussions they reached the conclusion that the central moment of marriage is when two baptized persons say 'I do' to each other; and to this day this is the common view in the western Church. To this could be added: in whatever way this saying 'I do' finds expression in different cultures.

Strictly speaking, for Christians the exchange of the words 'I do' would suffice, and this for the sake of social legal acknowledgement. But it is obvious that Christians want to give expression to the real meaning of Christian marriage more explicitly. What we experience takes shape only when we also give expression to it. If we keep our ultimate experiences only within our inner selves, they do not really become a part of us. They remain insecure, unstable, searching, locked up in themselves. Only when we express our experiences and excitement are they real, then they happen and we become aware of them. Before we articulate them, the impressions within us flutter around and around, and all kinds of sometimes conflicting feelings run through us. A closer explicitation of faith with regard to marriage is therefore a far from incidental matter. An inner experience of faith in relation to marriage may well exist. But this will only really become something for those who want to marry when they give shape to that experience. That is what the marriage rite is focused on. This liturgy is an unfolding of the key moment against the horizon of Christian perspective. Besides, this unfolding of the central moment meets the inescapable human demand not to be satisfied with the central moment alone: one will not be content with the reading of the climax of a novel or with the performance of the dénouement of a play. The Christian marriage rite is thus the completely normal accompani-

---

10 From Eph. 5 some might tend to extrapolate the symbolic to the mutual relation between husband and wife, as if the husband represents Christ and as if the wife represents the church. However, one should not be misled by the culture-specific data of Eph 5. That is why I chose to use the word 'mutually' here.

ment of Christian marriage and within this liturgy the word 'I do' forms a key moment.

5. PREPARATION FOR THE MARRIAGE RITE

Those who understand the intention of the ecclesiastical marriage rite will automatically ask whether all who apply for ecclesiastical marriage have really reached that stage. The ecclesiastical celebration of marriage usually has a more festive and more penetrating character than the wedding ceremony in front of the registrar. It is possible that some are pulled towards the Church because of this element of celebration. Or is the intention more profound and do people want to express something of the transcendental of this moment in the wedding ceremony? If that is the case, people will look for a celebration which has a more religious character than the wedding ceremony at city hall, and try to find this in the ecclesiastical marriage rite. Since the state performs this rite of passage in a fully secularized way, people will turn to the Church. It will be obvious that in such a case the ecclesiastical marriage rite offers too much: those who recall the typical horizon of the Christian marriage, as described above, will naturally connect the current ecclesiastical celebration of marriage with the faith in Jesus of Nazareth as a unique way to salvation, no matter how (inadequate or wordless) that faith is expressed.

Considering the new Roman ritual of marriage, it must be observed that this expresses the Christian dimension of marriage in a maximalistic way.[11] Often, however, the situation of faith is more precarious and more insecure, but nevertheless sufficient for an ecclesiastical wedding service. Within the ecclesiastical ritual of marriage a greater differentiation is imaginable, which takes into account the various situations of faith of those who marry. I have not checked to what extent certain Dutch liturgies already contribute to that differentiation. In any case, this variety would still be a matter of a proper sacramental celebration of marriage, even if some formulations were stated more carefully or even if, for instance, the celebration of the Eucharist would be left out.

The pastor is confronted with new questions when couples are not up to the sacrament of marriage and yet ask for an ecclesiastical marriage. It is then very important that he listens very carefully to their questions. He ought to follow the principle that – also for the sake of the people who want to marry – it would be wrong to offer *more* than they ask for or choose. In the long run such a practice would only lead to the sacrament of marriage becoming colorless and devaluated; in that way the Church

---

11 F. BROVELI: La celebrazione del matrimonio. Analisi del nuovo rituale, in *Rivista liturgica* 43 (1976) 519.

would lose her own face, her own identity. Does this mean that in such cases nothing liturgical can be done? Not necessarily. It is of major concern to create the possibility of a celebration which ranges over a longer period.[12] A genuine celebration of the sacrament of marriage does not per se have to lead to an inhospitable Church. With regard to marriage, as with regard to baptism, catechuminal celebrations seem possible for those who feel related to the Church in one way or another.[13] It is thus not about – it should be said again and also clearly be proposed as such – the sacramental ecclesiastical celebration of marriage, but about a celebration on its way to it.

In the new Roman Ritual the necessity of cathechism *before* marriage is being stressed. The doctrinal and moral catechesis are brought up in connection with faith as a process. Rightly, the ritual starts from a well-considered preparation for the sacrament of marriage. This preparation can end in the sacramental celebration of marriage, but also in a more catechumenal celebration as a possible step to this sacramental celebration. Surely, this has nothing to do with constantly putting forward the question 'why' regarding the Christian marriage rite. This kind of question only aims at a rational understanding; it will easily lead to discussions back and forth and will make simple-hearted hesitant for preparatory talks. Conversely, it has everything to do with the life story of those who marry, which touches the integrity of the human being. These preparatory talks can take place between the couple and the pastor, but also in a group. The latter is preferable because it can lead to a richer exchange of experiences and also something can be experienced of the greater (Church) community wherein marriage has its place. After that, those who marry could talk separately with a pastor about adjusted rites, unless they want to confine themselves to a civil ceremony.

When a catechumenal celebration of marriage has been chosen, the question of a possible next step seems to arise again when the first child is expected: will the parents then decide for a more catechumenal rite again, a celebration of birth,[14] or will they at that moment ask that their child be baptized? In the latter case, they might also give expression to the deepest Christian dimension of their marriage. It would be ideal if this could be restricted to a nuptial blessing and not at this moment, a few years later, ask them to repeat the words 'I do'. In these cases the Catholic Church should, certainly for the future, dispense with the canonic form of marriage.[15]

12 BROVELI: La celebrazione del martrimonio 519. Cf. also P. PUAUD: Le 'mariage à l'église', mariage religieux ou sacrament?, in *Communautés et liturgies* 57 (1975) 226-244.
13 G. LUKKEN: De doopvoorbereiding, in *Werkmap voor liturgie* 11 (1977) 87-90 (= § 8.3 of no. 6 in this book, 'Die Taufe: ein unersetzbares Sakrament').
14 LUKKEN: De doopvoorbereiding 87-90.
15 K. RICHTER: The liturgical celebration of marriage. The problems raised by changing theological and legal views of marriage, in *Concilium* 9 (1973) no. 7, 72-87.

D. Power pleads for a more far-reaching practice with regard to the 'catechumenal' celebrations. He would want to consider these as a normal case. According to him, it is not right to coincide in time a legal and real marriage with a sacramental marriage. The sacramental marriage should only take place at the moment of the personal choice to 'marry in Christ'. Beforehand a celebration which is more an appeal of faith and an experience of marriage in faith is conceivable.[16]

Thus Power chooses an administration as adequate as possible of the sacrament and therefore a Church that leaves room for choices which are as clear as possible. I have my doubts about his position. Is it not conceivable that in *some* cases the rite *preceeds* faith? Must the balance between the *ex opere operato* and *ex opere operantis* always have to work out in perfect harmony? Will not sometimes, for the sake of the *sacramenta propter homines*, the *ex opere operato* be more accentuated?[17]

With the catechumenal as well as with the sacramental celebration of marriage, the question may arise that for an increasing number of couples marriage does not per se have to be the transition to a living together for the first time. The more a pastorally responsible preparation of marriage is undertaken, the more – as I see it – proper liturgical forms will be found and there will be further reflections on questions then arising.

---

16 D. POWER: The Odyssee of man in Christ, in *Concilium* 14 (1978) no. 2, 105-106.
17 See G. LUKKEN: *De onvervangbare weg van de liturgie* (Hilversum 1984²) 84-86.

9. Funérailles et marginalité

Dans la littérature allemande on range les funérailles parmi les *Kasualien*.[1] Le mot *Kasual* dérive du mot latin *casus*. Dans la liturgie casuelle il s'agit donc de cas spéciaux et de situations qui demandent une assistance liturgico-pastorale, comme par exemple le baptême, le mariage et les funérailles. En ce qui nous concerne il s'agit donc de cette situation spéciale où la communauté ecclésiale avec son président considèrent et célèbrent à partir de l'Evangile la mort et le départ d'un défunt en vue de mettre au clair cette mort et ce départ. Mais ainsi n'en suis-je pas encore à notre problème spécifique. Dans cette contribution nous nous occupons des rapports entre *Kasualien* et vie religieuse. Et c'est un problème fort complexe. C'est à bon droit que P. Born fait remarquer à ce sujet "Kasualien und Kirchlichkeit haben eine sehr komplexe und schwierige Relation".[2]

La liturgie des funérailles trouve ici tout naturellement sa place. A certains points de vue les problèmes qui la concernent sont plus simples que ceux du baptême et du mariage. En effet, pour ce qui est du défunt il ne s'agit pas ici d'un sacrement au sens strict. Mais d'un autre côté les problèmes sont plus compliqués. En effet dans le service des funérailles nous trouvons deux pôles: il s'adresse au mort et aux survivants. Il est question d'un double 'rite de passage'. D'une part la liturgie des funérailles est tournée vers le décès du défunt et d'autre part vers sa famille et ses connaissances. Et ces deux pôles peuvent avoir chacun sa propre relation avec la vie de l'Eglise. Ce n'est donc pas de la fausse casuistique – ou si l'on veut 'casualistique' – si, en première instance, nous simplifions le problème: comment approcher ceux qui sans avoir guère de rapport avec l'Eglise participent à un service de funérailles, ou bien demandent eux-mêmes un service religieux pour un défunt qui venait peu ou pas du tout à l'église. Nous sortons des cas limites; après nous pourrons parler de problèmes concrets et variés.

---

* *Questions liturgiques* 63 (1982) 143-160.
1 J. BOMMER: Der Verkündigungsaufgabe der Kasualien Taufe, Hochzeit und Beerdigung, dans F. FURGER e.a.: *Liturgie als Verkündigung* (= Theologische Berichte 6) (Zürich-Einsiedeln-Köln 1977) 167-199; R. ZERFASS: Kasualien, dans *Handbuch der Pastoraltheologie* V. *Lexikon der Pastoralliturgie* (Freiburg im Breisgau 1972) 235. Cfr. Kasualien, in *Lexikon für Theologie und Kirche* VI (Freiburg im Breisgau) 17-18.
2 P. BORN: Die Begräbnisliturgie: eine Verkündigungschance?, dans *Gottesdienst* 7 (1973) 164.

1. AVANT VATICAN II

Si nous voulons jeter quelque clarté sur les problèmes tels qu'ils se présentent aujourd'hui nous ferons bien de nous demander comment, avant le Concile, ces deux pôles fonctionnaient par rapport à la vie ecclésiale. Il ne s'agit pas pour autant de remonter à la pré-histoire, mais d'évoquer un passé récent.

1.1. Le rite de passage par rapport au défunt

Dans le *Codex Iuris Canonici* de 1918 diverses catégories de chrétiens sont exclus des funérailles religieuses (Cf. canon 1239-1242). Sont nommés: les non-baptisés, les apostats notoires, les hérésiarques, les schismatiques, les francs-maçons ou tous ceux qui se sont affiliés à une société de ce genre, ceux qui se sont suicidés avec préméditation, ceux qui ont péri dans un duel, ceux qui se font incinérer et les pêcheurs publics. Attention: il ne s'agit pas seulement ici de refuser des funérailles avec célébration eucharistique, mais d'enterrement religieux. Au canon 1241 il est spécifié que dans ces cas toute messe des défunts, ou messe d'anniversaire ou tout autre service de deuil doivent être refusés. Les catégories ainsi énumérées ne peuvent pas être inhumées en terre bénite et le canon 1242 ajoute que dans le cas d'un *excommunicatus vitandus* le corps inhumé par erreur en terre bénite doit être exhumé et transféré en terre profane. En fait la pratique pouvait parfois être moins rigoureuse, mais elle était très dure: de quoi peuvent témoigner ceux qui après le drame d'un enfant mort nouveau-né, étaient contraints par le rituel à un enterrement dans une terre non-bénite.

Il y avait donc des limites évidentes, mais devant la limite il n'était pas question d'autres nuances: les baptisés et les catéchumènes sérieux recevaient une sépulture religieuse (canon 1239) et pour des chrétiens saisonniers on était peu exigeant. La foi dans la résurrection était peu controversée, bien que je doive ajouter qu'il n'existe pas d'enquêtes pour cette époque. Peut-être y avait-il dans l'attachement à l'Eglise et dans la foi plus de degrés que nous ne pensons!

La signification théologique de ce rite de passage était que l'Eglise priait pour le défunt; elle faisait appel à la miséricorde de Dieu, à la clémence de son jugement, pour que le trépassé arrive à bon port. Elle célébrait sa mort comme une délivrance de l'esclavage et une entrée dans la terre promise, le paradis, une admission dans la communauté des anges et des saints. Et avant tout: la messe de funérailles était offerte pour le défunt. Cela signifiait que 'les mérites du sacrifice' (*fructus sacrificii missae*) étaient destinés au défunt qui par eux recevait rémission de ses peines temporelles (le purgatoire). La célébration de messes pour les défunts et les stipendia pour cette *applicatio* étaient une donnée essentielle.

1.2. Le rite de passage en rapport avec ceux qui restent

Il va de soi que la liturgie des obsèques dans un passé récent était aussi un rituel de passage pour les familiers et pour tous ceux qui se sentaient proches du défunt. Mais – et c'est ce que je veux souligner – cet élément n'était contenu que très implicitement dans le rituel. La liturgie était centrée exclusivement sur le mort; ainsi par exemple l'absoute n'était pas un adieu, comme c'est actuellement le cas, mais une prière pour le défunt pour la rémission de ses fautes et la clémence du jugement. Les assistants considéraient leur *transitus* comme une prière intense pour le défunt. Leur propre passage ne venait pour ainsi dire pas en question, sauf en ce qui concerne leur propre avenir: la messe de Requiem a depuis quelque temps été considérée comme un avertissement pour ceux qui sont présents et comme une préparation salutaire à leur propre mort.

Dans le bas moyen-âge et au temps de la contre-Réforme on soulignait même de façon poignante le caractère exclusif de la liturgie des obsèques comme 'rite de passage' réservé aux défunts. L'absence de certains éléments dans la célébration eucharistique lors des funérailles a été interprétée dans ce sens d'une manière historiquement inexacte. Ainsi dans la messe de Requiem la bénédiction finale est-elle omise: le motif en serait que le rituel est destiné uniquement au défunt.[3] Autre exemple: la communion des fidèles durant la messe de funérailles est tombée en désuétude. Ceci tenait à l'heure tardive des obsèques (au moyen-âge le plus souvent à la neuvième heure, c'est-à-dire après trois heures de l'après-midi) et aux strictes dispositions concernant le jeûne eucharistique. Mais on donnait comme explication le fait que la messe de Requiem était un sacrifice uniquement destiné au défunt. Même cette façon de voir avait conduit à l'interdiction de communier durant une messe de Requiem, interdiction qui a été définitivement supprimée en 1868.[4]

La liturgie des obsèques comme 'rite de passage' en rapport avec le défunt n'avait donc que peu ou pas de relief. Le rituel était toujours le même, compte non-tenu du fait qu'il s'agissait d'une foi faible ou douteuse ou controversée ou bien encore marginale. Tous, même les incroyants prenaient part à la même liturgie, à une seule exception près: à une période où il n'était pas question d'interdiction, certains ne pouvaient pas participer à la communion. La diversité des rapports avec l'Eglise n'apparait donc pas dans le rituel. Et, je le souligne encore une fois, nous savons peu de chose sur ce qui touchait réellement les présents et sur la diversité réelle des rapports avec l'Eglise. Qu'ont-ils compris? Qu'ont-ils entendu? Dans quelle mesure la relation du rituel avec la foi, du rituel

---

3 A. HOLLAARDT: Requiemmis, dans L. BRINKHOFF e.a. (éd.): *Liturgisch Woordenboek* II (Roermond 1965-1968) 2382-2389, spécialement 2385.
4 HOLLAARDT: Requiemmis 2386.

avec l'appartenance à l'Eglise était-elle adéquate ou inadéquate?

On peut conclure qu'avant Vatican II, en ce qui concerne les défunts, des limites strictes avaient été tracées. Mais devant ces limites il n'y avait aucune gradation en rapport avec la dimension ecclésiale. Et ceci vaut aussi pour les familiers: on ne faisait aucune différence en ce qui concerne leurs rapports avec l'Eglise. Le rituel même ne leur était qu'indirectement destiné.

2. APRÈS VATICAN II: NOUVEAUX PROBLÈMES

A la suite de l'effritement de l'Eglise populaire on a vu apparaître ce qui auparavant était caché: à savoir les différents degrés d'intérêt pour l'Eglise. Mais il y a plus: le nombre de baptisés qui n'ont avec l'Eglise que des rapports nuls ou marginaux a considérablement augmenté. Ce qui ne veut pas dire que le fait de ne pas pratiquer dénote le fait de ne pas être croyant. Il se peut agir – selon la note de la conférence belge de 1972 – de 'croyants non-pratiquants' aussi bien que de 'baptisés non-croyants'.[5] Les rapports entre la liturgie casuelle et la vie ecclésiastique sont devenus vraiment complexes. A quoi il faut encore ajouter que la foi dans la résurrection qui – plus encore qu'avant Vatican II – se trouve au centre même de la liturgie des funérailles est plus que jamais controversée.

Il est donc aussi certainement nécessaire de rechercher des formes adaptées de la liturgie des funérailles. En rapport avec celle-ci Lengeling fait remarquer: "Wären nicht 'Liturgien des Schwelle' wie man es genannt hat, und eine zeitgemässe Erneuerung einer Arkandisziplin richtiger als eine Feier der Eucharistie, die ihrer Würde nicht entspricht?"[6]

La question est cependant plus complexe que Lengeling ne le dit. Il y a, en effet, deux poles. Et en outre, la foi même de ceux qui peuvent participer vraiment à l'eucharistie, est dans certains cas une foi controversée.

2.1. Le rite de passage par rapport au défunt

Dans son article "Voelen met de Kerk" J. van Kilsdonk nous parle d'un prêtre-théologien septuagénaire qui à la fin de sa vie ne pouvait plus s'identifiér que partiellement avec l'Eglise. Une de ses dernières paroles était: l'Eglise est ce qu'il y a de meilleur et de pire au monde. Je cite Van Kilsdonk:[7]

---

5 Cité dans G. MATHON: Mariage-cérémonie ou mariage-sacrement?, dans *Questions liturgiques* 62 (1981) 23.
6 E. LENGELING: *Liturgie – Dialog zwischen Gott und Mensch* (Freiburg-Basel-Wien 1981) 61.
7 J. VAN KILSDONK: Voelen met de Kerk, dans A. BLOMMERDE e.a. (éd.): *Tussen gisteren en morgen. Feestboek voor een bisschop* (Breda 1981) 42.

De meilleur? lui demandai-je avec quelque curiosité. Alors il s'écria: Oui, elle est parfois ce qu'il y a de meilleur, par exemple lors des funérailles, lors de l'adieu au défunt. Personne ne comprend mieux que l'Eglise à laquelle j'appartiens l'art délicat d'un enterrement (...).

L'art délicat de l'enterrement: je pense que notre Eglise comprend encore toujours cet art de maîtresse façon. L'Eglise respecte encore toujours les rites de funérailles comme le faisait l'Eglise antique: comme des rites de piété et de bon voisinage.[8] Et parce que dans notre société les rites sont toujours davantage commercialisés et se délabrent, il est nécessaire de rester vigilant dans la pastorale.[9] Et, revenant à notre problème je dirai qu'une Eglise qui connait l'art de ces rites de piété et de bon voisinage ne peut qu'avoir le coeur très large dans la question des funérailles et de la marginalité. Quand il n'est uniquement question chez le défunt que d'une appartenance à l'Eglise ou d'une foi chrétienne, même controversée, l'Eglise ne peut pas tout simplement refuser ce 'rite de passage'.

Je plaide donc pour une pastorale large et compréhensive. Mais je veux bien y apporter une restriction. L'Eglise fait droit aussi bien à elle-même qu'au défunt en accomplissant ce 'rite de passage' de manière adéquate. Quand le défunt était tout à fait ou bien très éloigné de la célébration eucharistique – et je ne vise pas ici ceux qui, par exemple, viennent trois ou quatre fois par an à la messe – il ne me parait pas nécessaire d'insérer la célébration eucharistique dans le rite des funérailles. L'Eglise peut bien prier pour ce défunt au cours d'une célébration eucharistique, mais ce que je veux dire c'est que celle-ci ne doit pas faire partie du rite d'enterrement lui-même. On réalise bien qu'il y a une certaine fluidité dans les transitions. En cas de doute il m'est avis que la largeur de vue est plus adéquate que le rigorisme. Je plaide donc pour une liturgie de seuil où l'Eglise se recueille de façon adéquate devant ce défunt: un service de la Parole avec prière et ensuite accomplissement du rite des funérailles proprement dit.

On peut poser la question: où se trouve la limite? L'Eglise peut-elle étendre sa sollicitude à quelqu'un qui n'était pas croyant? Il se peut toujours que dans un tel cas les survivants demandent quand même un enterrement religieux. Je pense qu'intervient ici un facteur de complication du fait que la liturgie des morts est aussi un 'rite de passage' se rapportant aux survivants.

---

8 G. LUKKEN: Kernvragen rond de christelijke dodenliturgie, dans *Tijdschrift voor liturgie* 64 (1980) 146-148.
9 LUKKEN: Kernvragen 148-157.

2.2. Le rite de passage en rapport avec les proches parents

Le nouveau *Rituale Romanum* parle explicitement du rapport du rituel des funérailles avec les proches parents (no. 17 et no. 18): leur espérance doit être ranimée, leur foi dans la résurrection affermie, de telle sorte que leur douleur soit allégée. Il faut prêter attention à la tristesse et aux nécessités chrétiennes de la famille et des autres assistants. Par son contenu le rituel s'adresse expressément aux proches parents: j'ai déjà signalé le changement de l'absoute en un dernier adieu (cf. nos. 3, 10 et 46), mais cela s'exprime aussi dans les prières.

La traduction néerlandaise suit littéralement l'édition romaine.[10] Dans la traduction flamande, il apparaît que l'Introduction a été adaptée et que l'accent est porté plus fortement sur les obsèques comme rite de passage par rapport aux proches parents.[11]

La communauté qui se réunit autour du mort n'est généralement pas quelconque et anonyme. Elle est déterminée par rapport au défunt dont elle veut prendre congé. Il peut naturellement y avoir dans ce rapport différents degrés. Mais en général on peut considérer que l'attention de la grande communauté – qui, en tout cas, est toujours présente dans la personne du président et aussi, éventuellement, de la chorale et d'autres personnes ayant un rôle à remplir – se concentre sur la famille et les amis qui viennent prendre congé du défunt: à l'intérieur de cet ensemble, se trouve ce groupe central. On pourrait dire: le petit cercle formé par le président et le choeur supportent toute la liturgie des obsèques comme répresentants de la grande communauté ecclésiale.

J'ai expressément formulé avec prudence: le président et le choeur comme répresentants de la grande communauté ecclésiale. Naturellement l'idéal serait que la communauté locale soit présente de façon plus intense. A proprement parler la liturgie des obsèques est aussi pour toute la communauté locale un important rite de passage: en y participant chacun apprend à vivre à la limite de la mort, qui revient chaque fois que quelqu'un s'en va. Mais à mesure que l'urbanisation se développe, la participation de la communauté locale se réduit. Ainsi s'estompe inéluctablement cet aspect du rite de passage.[12]

Quoi qu'il en soit: quand les familiers demandent des funérailles religieuses c'est tout autant leur relation avec l'Eglise qui est en cause. Ici encore je plaide pour une large compréhension, mais avec des limites.

Prenons comme point de départ le cas où la famille demande des funé-

---

10 NATIONALE RAAD VOOR LITURGIE: *De uitvaartliturgie* (= Liturgie van de sacramenten en andere kerkelijke vieringen 8) (Hilversum 1982²).
11 INTERDIOCESANE COMMISSIE VOOR LITURGISCHE ZIELZORG: *De orde van dienst voor de uitvaartliturgie* (Brussel 1971) spécialement nos. 2-7.
12 Cf. à ce sujet l'article de A. POLSPOEL: De uitvaartdienst als moment in het proces van rouwverwerking, dans *Praktische theologie* 8 (1981) 371-384.

railles chrétiennes pour un incroyant.¹³ Que faire? J'incline à penser: si le défunt ne se comportait pas en ennemi de l'Eglise, pourquoi celle-ci ne lui appliquerait-elle pas ses rites de piété et de compassion, si les familiers plus ou moins attachés à l'Eglise le demandent. Pourquoi en un tel moment, une communauté ne pourrait-elle pas prier pour que la vie de ce défunt arrive à son plein épanouissement, pour que, derrière l'horizon il trouve enfin la grande lumière, ou mieux la Lumière qu'il avait recherchée? La communauté peut prier: Seigneur accorde à ce défunt le repos éternel et que l'éclaire la lumière éternelle. L'Eglise, sacrement du salut, est tournée vers le dehors, elle est universellement orientée vers l'avènement du Royaume de Dieu, ce royaume de paix, de justice et de lumière, pour tous, indistinctement. La mort lève toutes les frontières: c'est la croyance de la communauté et cela peut être celle de ceux qui dans ce cas demandent des funérailles religieuses. Mais il est compréhensible que dans ce cas extrême l'Eglise se contente d'une 'liturgie du seuil'.¹⁴

Je suis parti d'un cas limite extrême qui montre justement à quel point les rapports avec la famille peuvent entraîner des décalages du point de vue auquel on se placerait si l'on considérait le rituel uniquement comme rite de passage pour le défunt. Un tel décalage peut aussi se produire alors que considérant la liturgie des funérailles comme rite de passage pour le défunt on aurait opté pour une 'liturgie du seui'. Avant Vatican II on aurait dans ce cas certainement choisi la messe des défunts. Je pense qu'a présent le choix est devenu plus difficile et qu'en tout cas, on ne peut exclure la 'Liturgie du seuil'. Comme vous voyez, c'est un problème complexe. Il est nécessaire d'en arriver progressivement à une stratégie pastorale. Celle-ci est nécessaire pour ne pas tomber dans un cerle vicieux. En effet on entend souvent dire: On ne peut pas contrarier les gens car ils voient les coses tout autrement que nous ou bien encore: nous pouvons bien le faire , mais ailleurs on fait autrement. Je pense que seule une stratégie plus large, décanale, diocésaine et interdiocésaine peut briser ce genre de cercle vicieux.

Je soupçonne que nous aurions une vue plus claire du problème dans sa complexité si. dans la pratique, nous nous contentions de temps en temps d'une 'liturgie du seuil'. Il y a des cas où aucun doute n'est possible sur la question de savoir si la 'liturgie du seuil' n'est pas la forme la plus adéquate pour les obsèques. C'est par exemple le cas où tant du côté de la

---

13 Il ne s'agit donc pas pour moi du cas où l'on demande des funérailles religieuses parce que c'est tout de même mieux qu'un enterrement purement civil. W. NEIDEHART (éd.): *Die Rolle des Pfarrers beim Begräbnis: Wort und Gemeinde.* (Zürich 1968) 226-235, semble d'avis que même dans ce cas on doit agréer la demande; voir BOMMER: Der Verkündigungsaufgabe 173-185. Pour moi je n'ai à proprement parler en vue que des chrétiens croyants qui demandent des obsèques religieuses.

14 En dehors de la liturgie des funérailles proprement dite, l'Eglise peut naturellement prier pour ce défunt lors de la célébration eucharistique, par exemple durant la messe dominicale.

famille que du côté du défunt il n'est question que d'une appartenance à l'Eglise et d'une foi très marginales. Si nous pouvions dans ces cas en arriver à une pratique vraiment bonne – et c'est aussi par la force des choses une pratique affectueuse – tout ceci serait vivement clarifié.

3. IMPORTANCE D'UNE LITURGIE INDUCTIVE DES OBSÈQUES

Le nouveau *Rituale Romanum* contient trois modèles ou types de liturgie des obsèques (nos. 4-8). Mais ces trois modèles ne marquent aucune différence dans l'appartenance du défunt à l'Eglise. Ils sont destinés à tous les défunts sans exception. Si on trouvait un de ces modèles mieux en rapport avec ce qui nous occupe, on en ferait un usage abusif. En ce qui concerne le contenu des textes et des rites, ceux-ci non plus ne reconnaissent aucune variante en rapport avec l'appartenance du défunt à l'Eglise.

Dans la mesure où le rituel s'adresse à la famille notre question est bien à l'ordre du jour – l'introduction du rituel indique à ce sujet que les prêtres doivent tenir compte de manière toute spéciale de ceux qui sont présents à cette occasion, que ce soit des non-catholiques, ou des catholiques qui ne participent que rarement ou jamais à la célébration eucharistique ou qui semblent avoir perdu la foi (no. 18). Le rituel hollandais reprend ceci à la lettre tandis que le rituel belge accentue très fort cet élément.[15] Mais dans aucun des deux, nous ne trouvons indiqué qu'il soit possible de faire une différence dans les types de liturgie selon le degré d'attachement à l'Eglise. Les invitatoires se rapportent surtout au contenu de la liturgie et encore de façon très limitée. Car dans le texte liturgique même il est toujours question d'une foi massive dans la résurrection.[16] Le *Rituale Romanum* et aussi la traduction néerlandaise partent du principe que la foi dans la résurrection est déjà présente et doit seulement être confirmée. Il s'ensuit que l'espérance dans la résurrection sera vivifiée et fortifiée (no. 17).[17] Ceci ne correspond pas du tout à la réalité. Le rituel flamand emploie ici une formulation plus libérale: elle dit que c'est l'occasion de professer sa foi dans la vie éternelle mais ajoute aussitôt que l'on doit tenir compte d'autres convictions éventuelles (no. 2). Mais au surplus le rituel flamand devrait permettre une meilleure adaptation des textes et des rites: autrement ce rituel tient trop peu compte des réalités. Un bon exemple de créativité dans l'adaptation, c'est le rituel

---

15 INTERDIOCESANE COMMISSIE VOOR LITURGISCHE ZIELZORG: *De orde van dienst* nos. 2, 5 et 7.
16 A. BLIJLEVENS: Wie in de schaduw Gods mag wonen. Over de nieuwe uitvaartliturgie volgens de Romeinse ritus, dans *Werkmap voor liturgie* 11 (1977) 308.
17 A. GOUMANS: Hopen op verrijzenis. Grenzen en ruimte van deze thematiek in het vernieuwde Romeinse rituale van de uitvaartliturgie, dans *Tijdschrift voor liturgie* 64 (1980) 212-213.

français qui vaut pour tous les pays de langue française et donc aussi pour la Belgique wallonne.[18]

3.1. Foi controversée en la Résurrection

Dans notre société il est question d'un certain pluralisme dans l'attitude qu'ont les gens vis-à vis de la mort.[19] D'une enquête parmi les membres du syndicat chrétien de Flandre il résulte que 42,7 % seulement d'entre eux croient dans un au-delà, 39,3 % sont dans le doute et 18 % ne croit pas dans une autre vie après la mort.[20] D'une enquête parallèle faite en Hollande il apparait que 42 % des réponses sont positives à la question "Croyez-vous dans une autre vie après la mort?", 18 % ne sont pas très sûrs et 40 % n'y croit pas.[21] En ce qui concerne les Français les pourcentages sont les suivants: 37 % de croyants, 47 % de non-croyants et 16 % de sceptiques.[22] Il est donc question d'une grande diversité, de beaucoup de doute et d'incroyance par rapport à la résurrection. Et en même temps il se fait que presque tous les catholiques demandent des funérailles religieuses. En 1976 dans les diocèses flamands il y avait encore comme catholiques 90,7 % des défunts. Dans les diocèses wallons 79 % et dans l'archidiocèse de Malines-Bruxelles (bilingue) 78,9 %. Pour l'ensemble de la Belgique la moyenne était de 83,7 %.[23] Pour ce qui concerne la Hollande la moyenne des enterrements religieux enregistrés comme catholiques était de 79 %.[24]

Je veux encore attirer l'attention sur une autre donnée importante. Même chez eux qui croient à la résurrection cette croyance ne va pas de soi. Des incroyants – selon Vergote – font souvent remarquer, scandalisés, que ceux-là même qui croient en la résurrection prennent quand même difficilement congé de la vie. Mais cette remarque scandalisée est psychologiquement quelque peu naïve. "Elle méconnait le fait que la foi demande du travail, tout comme l'amour".[25] Même chez les croyants il peut donc être ici question de tensions et de conflits.

---

18 *Nouveau Rituel des Funérailles* I-II (Paris 1972).
19 A. BLIJLEVENS et E. HENAU: *Gelegenheidsverkondiging: uitvaart* (Averbode 1980) 9-21.
20 BLIJLEVENS et HENAU: *Gelegenheidsverkondiging* 19; cf. R. MASURE et M. MOLISSE: *Arbeider en godsdienst* (Brussel 1978) 48-51.
21 BLIJLEVENS et HENAU: *Gelegenheidsverkondiging* 20; cf. W. GODDIJN e.a.: *Opnieuw God in Nederland. Onderzoek naar godsdienst en kerkelijkheid ingesteld in opdracht van KRO en weekblad De Tijd* (Amsterdam 1979) 36-37.
22 BLIJLEVENS et HENAU: *Gelegenheidsverkondiging* 20 (aussi pour les chiffres concernant l'Autriche). Cf. *La Vie* numéro 1317.
23 BLIJLEVENS et HENAU: *Gelegenheidsverkondiging* 22.
24 BLIJLEVENS et HENAU: *Gelegenheidsverkondiging* 22.
25 A. VERGOTE: Godsdienstpsychologische notities, dans W. GODDIJN e.a.: *Hebben de kerken nog toekomst. Commentaar op het onderzoek 'Opnieuw God in Nederland'* (Baarn 1981) 141-142.

3.2. Pastorale inductive autour de la mort[26]

Se rendre compte de cette situation témoigne d'une grande sagesse pastorale. Le pasteur doit pouvoir s'approcher de ceux qui sont confrontés avec la mort, en commençant où ils en sont et non pas de l'autre côté. La pastorale doit pour ainsi dire chaque fois commencer par le bas, en tâtonnant à la recherche du mot juste, du geste juste et au juste moment. Aussi bien pour ceux qui ne croient pas ou presque pas, que pour ceux dont la foi est faible et branlante, mais aussi pour les vrais croyants il faut à ce moment – j'emploie ici l'expression de Vergote 'du travail'. Je plaide donc ici pour une pastorale inductive: pour une pastorale considérée comme 'maïeutique'.

Quand le pasteur se tient si près des gens il va constater que juste au moment où ils se trouvent en face de la mort beaucoup attendent une assistance et une explication de caractère religieux.[27] D'une part la mort d'un être aimé provoque un état de prostration chez ses proches[28] et dans ce sens le pasteur se présente *in tempore inopportuno* et d'autre part on s'attend à une assistance et une explication de caractère religieux et alors la visite du pasteur se fait *in tempore opportuno*. Une pastorale inductive répondra à cette situation.

3.3 Liturgie inductive des funérailles

Jusqu'ici j'ai parlé de la pastorale dans le sens large du mot. Et précisément la liturgie des funérailles ne peut pas être détachée de ce contexte plus large de la prise de contact et de l'aide pastorales. La liturgie des funérailles doit être elle aussi une maïeutique qui tienne compte du fait qu'il s'agit de ce défunt et de *cette* famille. Dans la liturgie des funérailles également le pasteur devra s'employer inductivement. Il doit pouvoir se faire comprendre par des questions. Quelquefois il doit pouvoir dire ce que les assistants voudraient dire sans pouvoir ou sans oser le faire.[29] Il doit leur être proche et formuler les sentiments qu'inspire ce dur

---

26 Inductive a ici la signification suivante: qui commence au particulier pour s'élever de là vers le plus général. Ceci est donc le contraire de déductive dont la signification: qui descend du général au particulier. Souvent la liturgie pastorale est comprise comme l'application d'une liturgie préétablie (en général) à une situation particulière, actuelle et présente. Ayant en vue la liturgie 'casuelle' nous proposons le contraire: en arriver à l'expression d'une liturgie d'en-bas, au départ de ce qui est particulier de manière à ce qu'elle soit mieux englobée dans la pastorale d'ensemble dans cette situation particulière.
27 BLIJLEVENS et HENAU: *Gelegenheidsverkondiging* 24-25.
28 Cf. les études sur le processus du deuil; voir A. POLSPOEL: *Wenen om het verloren ik* (Hilversum 1976).
29 W. BERGER: Uitvaart na zelfdoding. Een vraaggesprek met de voorganger, dans *Praktische theologie* 7 (1980) 351.

moment.³⁰ Il devra aider les familiers à aller plus loin, à s'ouvrir de telle sorte qu'ils soient éclairés dans leur nécessité présente. Il va de soi qu'il ne s'agit pas ici d'une simple assistance humaine, mais d'une assistance pastorale, dans la lumière de la foi chrétienne, au nom de l'Evangile. L'Evangile doit toutefois être servi avec authenticité et il ne faut donc pas que le pasteur se contente en de telles circonstances d'annoncer l'Evangile tout sec.³¹

Nous devons donc considérer qu'il s'agit de ce défunt et de *cette* famille dans le grand ensemble de *cette* communauté locale où ici et à cette heure la foi dans la résurrection doit être transmise et la prière pour les défunts prendre forme. C'est seulement ainsi que l'Eglise en ce moment – tout au moins dans nos régions de culture occidentale – apportera sa contribution à l'Eglise universelle et conservera vivante la foi dans la Résurrection et la prière pour les défunts qui ramène à la Sainte Ecriture elle-même.

In concreto
La préférence pour une liturgie inductive entraîne deux conséquences. La première, c'est que l'on choisisse le modèle ou le type de liturgie le plus adéquat. La seconde nous ramène au contenu de la liturgie.

Variété des modèles
J'ai déjà fait allusion précédemment à la diversité des modèles. Nous y revenons. Si je comprends bien on peut choisir entre trois modèles:
a) Un service de la Parole avec prière dans la cour d'honneur du cimetière ou du crematorium. En cas d'inhumation s'ajoute le rituel de l'enterrement.
b) Un service de la Parole avec prière dans l'église. A quoi s'ajoute le rituel de l'enterrement ou une courte liturgie dans le crematorium.
c) Service de communion ou célébration eucharistique dans l'église, après quoi le rituel d'enterrement ou un bref service au crematorium.

L'ordre de suite peut répondre à des degrés d'attachement à l'Eglise. Naturellement il ne s'agit pas ici d'imposer un certain choix: la pastorale inductive et la liturgie inductive veulent précisément répondre à des désirs et des questions en recherchant leur point de départ. Cela ne se peut que si un choix de rituel est possible.

En ce qui concerne le service de communion: je n'ai pas mentionné celui-ci comme un degré à part: au point de vue qui nous occupe il se trouve au même niveau que la célébration eucharistique. J'ai mentionné cette forme parce que elle peut parfois, en cas de nécessité, remplacer la célébration eucharistique et non pas comme forme de liturgie du seuil. Et

---

30 Une formulation de H. FORTMANN: *Hoogtijd. Gedachten over feesten en vasten* (Utrecht 1966) 103-104.
31 BOMMER: *Der Verkündigungsaufgabe* 195.

à ce sujet on doit prendre très au sérieux la critique exprimée par Lescrauwaet et Tillmans, à savoir qu'il faut être très prudent par rapport à l'institutionalisation des services de communion.[32] Néanmoins je puis imaginer qu'au point de vue de la pastorale inductive ils peuvent être irremplaçables précisément dans ces circonstances.

Le contenu
Donner une forme à une liturgie en y mettant certaines gradations n'est pas seulement une question de choix entre plusieurs modèles. Il s'agit aussi du contenu de la liturgie. Je vais successivement passer en revue le service de la Parole, la prière, les éléments non-oraux et la dimension sociale.

L'annonce de la Parole
La possibilité d'une liturgie inductive trouve sa première place dans le prêche. Henau plaide à juste titre pour un service de la Parole qui tienne compte de cette situation très concrète.[33] Ici le défunt se trouve à la place centrale lui qui est un souvenir commun mais aussi un mystère de la vie future. Selon moi, le *counselend preekmodel* concerne avant tout le défunt précisément en fonction de sa propre attitude de foi et de ses rapports avec l'Eglise et il s'adresse en même temps aux familiers pour les amener à une possible découverte de la foi dans la résurrection.[34] J'ajouterai ici un exemple que j'ai déjà eu l'occasion de citer.[35] Un pasteur avait eu un entretien avec un malade incurable, peu de temps avant sa mort. L'entretien s'était déroulé comme suit:

> P(asteur): Je lui ai demandé quels étaient ses rapports avec les autres malades.
> M(alade): Bah' ces contacts sont très superficiels. Je peux bien parler avec un docteur qui est ici. Mais celui-là, il a un inconvénient: Dieu, Dieu et encore Dieu.
> P.: Et ça vous embête?
> M.: Il faut être très prudent dans ces matières là (suit par fragments une histoire où à son travail il a eu parfois des querelles à propos de religion.)

---

32 J. LESCRAUWAET: Onze samenkomst op de dag des Heren, dans *Tijdschrift voor liturgie* 65 (1981) 207-218; De zondagsviering. Gedachten en suggesties vanuit de Commissie voor Liturgie in het Bisdom Breda, dans *Tijdschrift voor liturgie* 65 (1981) 202-206; W. TILLMANS: De liturgische viering o.l.v. een parochiaan, dans *Tijdschrift voor liturgie* 65 (1981) 248-253.
33 BLIJLEVENS et HENAU: *Gelegenheidsverkondiging* 53-62.
34 Au sujet de ce modèle de prédication pastorale, voir W. BERGER: Preken en counselen, dans *Tijdschrift voor pastorale psychologie* 4 (1972) 35-38; E. LINN: *Preaching and counseling. The unique method of Harry Emerson Fosdick* (Valley Forge 1966); T. ODEN: *Kerygma and counseling* (Philadelphia 1966).
35 LUKKEN: *Kernvragen* 160-161.

P.: Ne trouvez vous pas singulier que nous n'ayons pas encore dit un mot de Dieu, alors que c'est un peu mon job? Qu'est-ce que vous attendiez de moi?
M.: Ce n'est pas la même chose, vous ne venez rien me vendre.
P.: Je ne vois pas très bien ce que je pourrais venir vous vendre; vous n'avez besoin de rien...
M.: Non.
P.: Pas besoin de discussion. Parce que cela commence naturellement toujours ainsi?
M.: Oui, c'est bien ainsi...
P.: Vou vous trouvez tout à fait seul devant un mur et vous ne pouvez pas regarder de l'autre côté, mais vous devez le traverser.
M.: Non, on ne peut pas voir ce qu'il y a de l'autre côté. A cela il n'y a pas de réponse.
P.: Est-ce que cela vous intéresserait que j'aille avec vous vers ce mur – aussi loin qu'on peut?
M.: Oui..., oui, c'est bien.
P.: Ainsi nous aurons un peu un sujet de conversation, n'est-il pas vrai?
M.: Bon... (Silence).
P.: Vous êtes fatigué n'est-ce pas?
M.: Oui.
P.: Viendrais-je après-demain?
M.: Oui. Volontiers. Au revoir... Et merci bien.

Quelques jours plus tard le malade expirait. Le pasteur était encore une fois venu s'asseoir près de lui, alors qu'il était dans le coma. Dans son homélie le pasteur retraça à sa manière qui était très émouvante comment cet homme avait vécu et souffert. Mais au moment d'en venir à la religion il est passé directement à des formules comme "que Dieu est un Dieu des vivants et non des morts" etc. Il ne souffla pas un mot de son dernier entretien. Pourquoi ne pas dire que cet homme avait des difficultés avec Dieu, qu'il ne voyait pas Dieu comme un mot usé ou un sujet de discussion, qu'il voyait la mort devant lui comme un mur[36] et qu'il aimait bien avoir un prêtre auprès de lui pour l'accompagner le plus loin possible. Après quoi le pasteur aurait pu exprimer sa propre foi vécue: cet homme ne serait-il pas étonné maintenant qu'il est derrière le mur et qu'il a combattu le bon combat?... Et il demanderait aux familiers s'ils peuvent le suivre dans cette foi... Ce sont là seulement des suggestions fragmentaires par lesquelles je veux rendre évidente la manière de donner un sens à cette mort et de le suggérer aux personnes présentes.

---

36 Dans des situations de crise, les gens emploient souvent des symboles pour s'exprimer. "C'est ainsi qu'ils disent: se sentir vidés, se trouver dans un désert, devant un mur; se sentir en cage, liés, prisonniers". C'est aussi le cas dans des dialogues avec des moribonds. Les pasteurs doivent apprendre à utiliser ces images pour arriver à communiquer à ce niveau de profondeur. Cf. P. ZUIDGEEST: Mensen leven van beelden, dans *Praktische theologie* 8 (1981) 302.

Le service de la Parole ne se limite pas au prêche. A vrai dire il commence dès le mot d'accueil. Comprenez-moi bien. Il ne s'agit pas de commencer directement par des allusions à des sentiments profondément chrétiens, en recherchant les grands mots.[37] Le pasteur doit commencer où en sont les assistants, les prendre par la main, les conduire. Mais c'est précisément à partir de ce commencement qu'il peut se produire bon nombre de choses au point de vue de l'évangélisation. On en trouve un exemple frappant dans les funérailles d'une jeune femme qui s'était suicidée.[38] Le service se déroula dans l'église des étudiants de Nimègue. Tout le spectre de notre société s'y trouvait représenté: des gens désolés, d'autres choqués, des croyants, des incroyants, des sceptiques, avec tous les degrés d'amour ou d'attachement envers la disparue. Dans son accueil le président interpréta pastoralement comme suit les sentiments des assistants:[39]

> C'est parce que nous nous sentons liés à elle que nous nous rassemblons ici. Nous sommes rassemblés ici ce matin pour accomplir la dernière chose que nous puissions faire. Nous sommes réunis dans cette église. Pour certains d'entre nous ceci est un lieu connu, de toute confiance, parlant par lui-même. Et c'est un très bon sentiment. Pour d'autres il rappelle un passé qui se trouve loin en arrière, les années d'enfance. Tout cela était jadis plein d'ambiance et de chaleur, mais maintenant cela ne vous convient plus, cela ne vous intéresse plus. Un tel sentiment peut aussi exister. Et peut-être en est-il parmi nous qui sont pleins d'amertume et de rancune et de peine pour tout ce que l'Eglise et la foi leur ont fait. Laissons cela de côté. En ce moment tout cela se fond ensemble car avant tout nous sommes ici de sa part, pour tout ce qu'elle a fait pour nous, pour ce qu'elle a signifié pour chacun d'entre nous personnellement. Car depuis que nous le savons nous sommes intensément mis en présence de la vie et de la mort: contradictions qui vont la main dans la main. Son choix à elle choque, émeut, chagrine, fâche. Nous sommes impuissants devant cet évènement irrévocable.
>
> Pourquoi? Que cherchait-elle? Quelque chose que nous n'étions pas en état de lui donner? Comment nous témoigner les uns aux autres que nous

---

37 G. VAN HEMERT: Elementen die soms vergeten worden, dans *Werkmap voor liturgie* 12 (1978) 92: "Cela me parait une règle essentielle qu'a l'ouverture de chaque service, mais surtout d'un mariage ou de funérailles, qu'il ne soit d'abord rien dit de pieux, de profond, de nourrissant. Le mot de bienvenue, c'est un *atrium*, et non pas une église. Il aide les gens à s'accommoder de la situation et à s'accommoder entre eux. Un bon thème est la simple constatation du fait qu'on est venu ici d'un peu partout. Ou d'autres choses que les gens ont vécues peu auparavant. Cela repose aussi de constater qu'on s'est rassemblé ici spécialement pour le défunt et que l'on va pouvoir passer une petite heure en dehors du brouhaha de la vie pour pouvoir un peu écouter et se souvenir. Ne pas oublier de souhaiter spécialement dans ces paroles d'ouverture la bienvenue aux enfants. Pas d'exhortation, de monition, de condoléance à ce moment. Le service doit encore commencer".
38 BERGER: Uitvaart na zelfdoding 347-353.
39 BERGER: Uitvaart na zelfdoding 348-349.

avons fait tout ce que nous avons pu? Autant de questions et d'émotions qui se mêlent entre elles. Nous réunir ici ne donne pas de réponse. Je pense aussi que personne d'entre nous n'attend une réponse.

En tout premier lieu nous sommes ici pour elle. Aussi de notre part. Pour nous consoler et nous encourager les uns les autres en chantant, en écoutant et selon toutes présomptions, dire peut-être quelque chose qui ressemble à une prière.

Cette heure concentrée autour de son souvenir va nourrir notre espoir que la vie est indestructible. Irrésistible comme un enfant qui vient de naître. De cette attente témoignent ces fleurs, ces cierges, l'encens que nous brûlons. Elle les aimait. Elle est passée candidement à l'invisible. Puissions-nous nous aussi passer candidement cette heure.

Sur l'importance des éléments non-verbaux auxquels le président fait allusion à la fin de son discours d'accueil, je reviendrai dans la suite. Par la suite dans son homélie, le président cherche encore en tâtonnant à exprimer sa foi et à éveiller la foi chez les autres; je cite seulement un passage:[40]

Sa mort, la mort qu'elle a choisie, est un fait inéluctable dans ma vie. Inévitablement la mort est quelque chose qui nous arrive. Si nous pouvions choisir, nous choisirions tout de même plutôt quelques années de plus à vivre, même difficilement. Sa mort n'a-t-elle pas été un choix extrême en vue d'une prise de conscience de soi-même? Une expression d'effrayante bravoure, un désir passionné de vie? Sa mort me met en face du choix que je fais: mon choix pour la vie. Bientôt le choeur va chanter "Cent fois je dois croire en un nom sans visage et alors je puis seulement espérer que vous *êtes*, que *Vous* êtes, lumière invisible". Le chant du centurion. Il est écrit de lui dans l'Evangile. Je vous en lis le passage (suit le récit).

Je parlais de découverte, de révélation (*disclosure*) à propos de la foi dans la résurrection, dans et par la prédication. Je veux faire à ce propos une remarque de caractère théologique. Quand quelqu'un vient à la foi il n'est pas question d'un passage logique des *praeambula fidei* à la foi elle-même. Entre les deux, il y a un moment insaisissable. Il y a dans la perspective un saut dû à la *lumen fidei*. Et bien, dans cette situation le prédicateur s'efforce d'exprimer le plus possible les *praeambula fidei*, dans l'espoir que grâce à la *lumen fidei* la perspective éclate en effet dans le sens d'un acte de foi. La conduite pastorale et ce qu'elle demande d'engagement chez les auditeurs, c'est pour ainsi dire le travail qui doit préparer à la foi. C'est un travail dont nous devons nous acquitter. Le véritable déclanchement de perspective, c'est quelque chose qui vient de plus haut que nous, c'est un moment de grâce.

En rapport avec ce qui précède, je voudrais faire une seconde observa-

---

40 BERGER: Uitvaart na zelfdoding 350.

tion. Un théologien contemporain a fait remarquer à ce sujet que dans notre société la structure de crédibilité par rapport à la foi dans la résurrection n'est pas très heureuse. Dans un certain sens on peut comparer notre situation à celle des Grecs païens du temps de Jésus: ils ne connaissaient pas comme les Juifs l'attente d'une résurrection générale de tous les hommes. Cette pensée leur était totalement étrangère et les désorientait. J'ai dit: dans un certain cas, car les Grecs croyaient en tout cas encore en l'immortalité de l'âme. Pourtant il y a un *praeambulum fidei* qui, de notre temps, peut-être compris par beaucoup. C'est que Dieu qualifie de non-échec ce qui apparemment est un échec. Ceci apparaît de façon éminente dans la vie de Jésus. Ce Jésus de Nazareth, ce juste, criait suspendu à la Croix: une vie manquée. Et Dieu n'intervint pas près de Jésus pas plus qu'il ne le fit à Dachau et à Auschwitz. L'annonce de la résurrection de Jésus veut dire qu'il n'est pas du tout question de fiasco, au contraire. Sa vie a été marquée comme celle d'un juste et elle s'est accomplie en Dieu.[41]

L'évangélisation par la liturgie ne se limite pas aux mots d'accueil et au prêche. Elle touche aussi le choix des lectures et des antiennes. Ce choix doit aussi se faire de manière inductive. Le nouveau *Rituale Romanum* présente une grande variété de lectures.

La prière
La liturgie inductive touche aussi la façon de prier. Mutatis mutandis ce qui a été dit pour l'évangélisation vaut aussi pour la prière. On doit tenir compte de ce défunt et de cette famille dans cette communauté. Je pense à ce sujet que les prières qui se trouvent dans le rituel ne peuvent pas toujours convenir parce qu'elles sont trop massives. Il faudrait plus de variété, comme cela se trouve dans le rituel français;[42] à mon avis ils faudrait laisser plus de liberté au président.

Précisément dans la liturgie des funérailles, un moment de prière adéquat est de grande importance. Ceci vaut pour la famille. Mais cela vaut d'autant plus encore au point de vue de la prière pour le défunt. Maintenant que l'on a découvert la liturgie des funérailles comme 'rite de passage' pour les familiers, on a parfois tendance à oublier que la prière pour le défunt est un élément essentiel et indispensable de la liturgie chrétienne de la mort. L'habitude de prier pour les défunts est une pratique séculaire de l'Eglise à l'Ouest comme à l'Est. Elle est l'expression de notre solidarité avec les morts, de notre confiance en la miséricorde de Dieu et de notre espérance en un accomplissement final. La question des images concrètes et des hypothèses concernant les situations intermédiaires est à ce sujet

---

41 E. SCHILLEBEECKX: "Ik geloof in de verrijzenis van het lichaam", dans *Tijdschrift voor geestelijk leven* 28 (1972) 435-451.
42 Voir note 18.

secondaire.[43] Une formulation adéquate de la prière pour les défunts est d'importance aux moments explicites de prière; je dis les moments explicites parce que toute la liturgie des obsèques dans son sens le plus large est une prière pour le défunt, précisément comme 'rite de passage' pour le défunt: c'est ou ce doit être le leit-motif de tout l'ensemble.

Les éléments non-verbaux
En liturgie il ne s'agit pas seulement de paroles. C'est surtout à propos de liturgie des défunts qu'il est nécessaire de s'en rendre compte. C'est en effet le langage des attitudes symboliques qui dans un temps de mutisme comme le deuil a la propriété de parler aux gens.[44] L'enchâssement des éléments non-verbaux donne la vie à la parole dans la liturgie. Quand il fait défaut la liturgie devient moins efficace. Les éléments non-verbaux sont encore plus importants quand on se contente d'un service de la Parole avec prière.

Que l'on pense à ce propos à la valeur propre de la musique et de la parole chantée. Mais le non-verbal touche aussi: la disposition des lieux, l'éclairage, l'ambiance, le repos, l'emplacement du cercueil, celui de la croix, et du cierge pascal, et des autres cierges, des fleurs, etc. Il touche aussi l'emploi de l'eau bénite et de l'encens; on peut encenser le cercueil mais on peut aussi, par exemple, faire brûler de l'encens auprès du cercueil pendant la prière pour le défunt. Et encore: se pencher devant le cercueil: un geste qui peut exprimer le respect devant ce que cet être humain avait d'unique et son mystère. D'importance est aussi la distribution des rôles: quand l'implication des assistants s'exprime aussi dans la distribution des rôles, le caractère inductif de la liturgie s'en trouve augmenté.

Enfin j'attire encore l'attention sur des rites comme par exemple la fermeture du cercueil,[45] le transport du cercueil par la famille ou les amis, la distribution d'images souvenir, etc.

La dimension sociale
Dans une liturgie occasionnelle on est tenté d'accentuer l'élément consolateur. Mais la question est de savoir si l'on fait droit au mort, aux proches et à l'Evangile en en restant là. Dans la liturgie inductive la dimension sociale peut également trouver sa place; elle peut même faciliter la révélation de la foi dans la résurrection. A l'heure actuelle beaucoup de gens sont préoccupés par l'injustice qui règne dans le monde. Il se peut même

---

43 H. MERTENS: De relativiteit van de traditionele beelden, dans *Tijdschrift voor theologie* 10 (1970) 384. Cf. G. LUKKEN: Een dodenliturgie van Huub Oosterhuis. Theologische analyse en toetsing, in *Tijdschrift voor liturgie* 59 (1975) 347-349.
44 R. RIESS: Die Krisen des Lebens und die Kasualien der Kirche, dans *Evangelische Theologie* 35 (1975) 77-78.
45 Cf. LUKKEN: Kernvragen 10. Le rituel français a donné forme de façon remarquable à ce rite: *Nouveau rituel des funérailles* II, no. 240.

que le défunt en ait été la victime. L'anamnèse de la souffrance qui s'est accumulée dans l'histoire et l'attente et l'espoir qu'un jour viendra le règne de la justice et de la paix est un thème cher à beaucoup. C'est dans cette paix que vont les défunts et c'est aussi notre avenir. La dimension sociale prise en soi peut prendre place à tous les degrés de la liturgie des funérailles et elle peut rendre reconnaissable le thème de la résurrection. Elle peut surtout être un stimulant pour aller plus loin et pour s'engager à la rencontre du royaume de Dieu.

4. LITURGIE INDUCTIVE ET RAPPEL

Peut-être mon plaidoyer pour une liturgie inductive des funérailles appelle-t-il la question de savoir si j'ai prêté suffisamment attention à la nécessité de rappel et de reprise de connaissance que comporte toute bonne liturgie.

Hélas je ne puis m'étendre ici là-dessus. Peut-être puis-je encore donner deux explications à titre d'éclaircissement. Tout d'abord: une liturgie des funérailles peut être si singulière qu'elle en devient méconnaissable à l'intérieur d'un ensemble plus grand. L'induction s'est alors développée aux dépens de la plus grande communauté qui – tout au moins dans le rôle du ministre – est intéressée à cette liturgie et qui précisément doit veiller à l'identité de la communauté locale à l'intérieur de l'ensemble plus vaste des autres communautés de maintenant et de jadis (tradition). La liturgie ne doit jamais tomber dans l'excès d'une émotivité ultra individuelle, même si elle est l'expression d'un groupe. Ce que je veux dire c'est que précisément comme événement social elle ne peut rien d'autre que d'emprunter ce qui est l'essentiel de la célébration et ceci dans sa forme même; c'est pourquoi l'Ecriture elle-même est la première source, sans oublier les autres richesses du passé de l'Eglise.

Ensuite: il se peut que précisément au nom de l'inductivité le chant grégorien et les formulations massives de la résurrection soient nécessaires. Certains peuvent mieux exprimer leur foi de cette façon-là. Il vous est évident, j'en suis sûr, que mon plaidoyer se situe entre ceux deux extrêmes: il s'agit d'un emprunt créatif et d'une inductivité dirigée.

Conclusion

A l'heure actuelle, pour beaucoup de gens, l'Eglise locale, la communauté paroissiale sont quelque chose d'anonyme. Il s'y heurtent, par exemple, à l'occasion d'un enterrement. Celui-ci peut être un moment très intense où l'on peut expérimenter quelque chose de l'Eglise. Quand elles s'accomplissent de manière adéquate les funérailles peuvent à leur façon contribuer à la construction de l'Eglise.

L'intensité de ce moment exige aussi par conséquent une pastorale du deuil mais aussi d'autres formes liturgiques adéquates. Et ceci aboutit à l'exigence d'une liturgie du seuil en général, mais, dans notre cas, surtout aussi des formes adéquates pour le service anniversaire et pour le Jour des Morts.

10. Liturgiewissenschaft und 'Musik der christlichen Liturgie'

Was ist der Ort der Kirchenmusik innerhalb der Liturgiewissenschaft? Während der vergangenen Jahre habe ich verschiedene Male dafür plädiert, daß die Kirchenmusik ein unverzichtbarer Teil der Liturgiewissenschaft sein sollte und daß sie daher einen Platz an den katholisch-theologischen Fakultäten und Hochschulen erhalten müßte. Dabei wäre es natürlich ein zu großer Luxus, wenn alle katholisch-theologischen Fakultäten und Hochschulen einen Musikdozenten hätten. Aber man sollte wenigstens über ein gemeinsames Vorgehen nachdenken. Nur so könnten Liturgie- und Kirchenmusikwissenschaft aus ihrer wechselseitigen Isolierung herausgeführt werden. In diesem Artikel gehe ich aus von der Beziehung zwischen Liturgie und Kultur und komme dann zum Verhältnis von Liturgie und Kirchenmusik.

1. DIE VERBINDUNG ZWISCHEN LITURGIE UND KULTUR

Es ist schwierig, christliche Liturgie zu studieren, ohne die verschiedenen Kulturen und Kulturperioden, in denen sie entstanden ist, zu kennen. Liturgie und Kultur sind miteinander verbunden. Dies gilt für die Vergangenheit; dies gilt ebenso für die Gegenwart. Ich denke, daß ich diese Behauptung nicht näher erklären muß. Für die Vergangenheit verweise ich auf das Handbuch von H. Wegman über die Geschichte der Liturgie.[1] Vor der Behandlung der Liturgie in den verschiedenen Perioden der Geschichte geht er jeweils auf den kulturellen Kontext ein. Was die heutige Liturgie betrifft: Da nun, nach Vaticanum II, die Lokalkirchen wieder sie selbst werden, wird es überdeutlich, wie sehr die Liturgie durch die eigene Kultur bestimmt wird oder bestimmt werden muß; man denke an Europa, aber z.B. auch an Afrika oder Indien.

Mit dieser Behauptung ist jedoch mehr gemeint. Eigentlich ist es zu wenig, wenn man sagt, daß Liturgie und Kultur miteinander verbunden sind. Man könnte nämlich annehmen, die Kultur sei eine eigene Wirklich-

---

* Liturgiewetenschap en "muziek van de christelijke liturgie", in *Tijdschrift voor liturgie* 66 (1982) 111-122. Übersetzt von G. Merks-Leinen, M.A.
1 H. WEGMAN: *Geschiedenis van de christelijke eredienst in het westen en in het oosten. Een wegwijzer* (Hilversum 1983²) (= IDEM: *Geschichte der Liturgie im Westen und Osten* (Regensburg 1979); IDEM: *Riten en mythen. Liturgie in de geschiedenis van het christendom* (Kampen 1991).

keit und die Liturgie ebenfalls. Dies ist aber nicht der Fall. Es ist zweifellos die Absicht von H. Wegman zu zeigen, daß in jeder Periode unserer Kulturgeschichte auch die Liturgie ein Teil einer bestimmten Kultur ist. Mit anderen Worten: Die christliche Liturgie gehört immer zu einer bestimmten Kultur. Sie ist in sie – innerhalb ihrer – integriert. So ist die Liturgie der Alten Kirche in die griechisch-römische Kultur integriert. Und genauso ist die Liturgie des frühen Mittelalters unlöslich verbunden mit dem kulturellen Ganzen dieser Periode oder besser noch: Sie ist in das kulturelle Ganze integriert und ein Teil von ihm.[2]

Wenn die christliche Liturgie ein Teil einer bestimmtem Kultur ist, so heißt dies nicht, daß man sie völlig mit dieser bestimmten Kultur identifizieren kann. Dies hätte zur Folge, daß sie zusammen mit dieser bestimmten Kultur untergehen könnte. Die christliche Liturgie ist aber in der Lage, sich in die verschiedenen Kulturen zu integrieren. Auf die Frage, inwiefern die christliche Liturgie auch mehr ist als eine bestimmte Kultur, gehe ich nicht ein. Es ist die Frage nach den universellen Möglichkeiten der christlichen Liturgie. Eigentlich führt das noch weiter: Es berührt die Frage nach der Universalität und dem eschatologischen Charakter des Christentums.

Wenn die christliche Liturgie faktisch immer ein Teil einer bestimmten Kultur ist, dann ist es selbstverständlich, daß sie auch mit den verschiedenen Schichten, mit den verschiedenen Niveaus und Kodes dieser Kultur verbunden ist. Und dies gilt dann für alle Niveaus: für das ökonomische (d.h.: die Art, in der der Gütertausch geregelt ist), das ethische, das politische, das ästhetische Niveau usw. Diese Niveaus stehen nicht unverbunden nebeneinander, sondern sind miteinander verknüpft. Das heißt nicht, daß man immer bzgl. aller Niveaus von kultureller Gleichzeitigkeit sprechen könnte. Wohl muß man sich klar machen, daß auch kulturelle Ungleichzeitigkeit eine bestimmte Relation zur Folge hat. So kann es sein, daß sich die Liturgie von einer bestimmten Kultur gelöst hat, weil sie sich bestimmten Niveaus oder sogar allen Niveaus verschließt. Dann befindet sich die Liturgie in einer Ghetto-Situation, was faktisch in den Jahrhunderten zwischen Trienter Konzil und Vaticanum II der Fall war. Interessant ist, daß die Gläubigen in dieser Periode über ihr eigenes Umfeld und auf ihre eigene Weise die Verbindung zwischen feststehender Liturgie und anderen Niveaus zu erhalten suchten.

Innerhalb der verschiedenen Niveaus einer Kultur gibt es einzelne, die die Liturgie unmittelbar berühren: Sie haben mehr oder weniger unmittelbar mit dem liturgischen Ausdruck selbst zu tun. Ich denke hierbei an den Raum, die Bilder, die Dramaturgie, die Musik. Hier geht es mir um letztere. Um aber die Verbindung zwischen Musik und Liturgie zu verdeutli-

---

2 Vgl. A. ANGENENDT: Religiosität und Theologie. Ein spannungsreiches Verhältnis im Mittelalter, in *Archiv für Liturgiewissenschaft* 20-21 (1978-1979) 28-55.

chen, muß ich erst etwas sagen, das mehr den Raum und die Dramaturgie betrifft.

Wir alle kennen die Erklärungen der Liturgiker über das Entstehen der Elevation bei der Konsekration im Mittelalter. In Studien zur Geschichte der Liturgie steht unverändert immer wieder, daß sie mit dem Verlangen zusammenhängt, die Hostie zu sehen. Es gibt aber noch eine Erklärung, die wenigstens eine Ergänzung zur klassischen sein kann: Sie stammt von J. van den Berg.[3] Van den Berg weist darauf hin, daß die Elevation in einer hohen Kirche entstanden ist: Die Höhe der gotischen Kirche und die Elevation gehören zusammen. In Kirchen wie Ronchamp und in Kirchen im Fabrikhallenstil mußte die große Elevation bei der Konsekration wohl verschwinden. Jetzt, wo das Dach so platt ist, ist sie unmöglich geworden. So bestimmt der Raum die expressive liturgische Gebärde, und die liturgische Gebärde ist mit dem Raum verwoben. Beide, Kirchenraum und Elevation, sind unlöslich mit der Gotik verbunden. Das grenzenlose Linienspiel des gotischen Kirchengebäudes und der gotischen Dramaturgie spiegelt sich wider und inkarniert sich sozusagen im Zentrum der Eucharistie. Und dasselbe gilt natürlich für die Musik: Man kann sich die mittelalterliche Liturgie nicht vorstellen ohne das Linienspiel der Polyphonie und der ausgearbeiteten Tropen, die zu Sequenzen werden. Wohl gibt es, wie mir scheint, einen Unterschied zwischen den Bereichen Raum, Dramaturgie und Musik. Der Raum bildet mehr die Atmosphäre der christlichen Liturgie, während Dramaturgie und Musik wohl mehr ein innerliches Band zum liturgischen Ausdruck selbst haben. Auf das Band zwischen Musik und Liturgie möchte ich näher eingehen.

2. DIE VERBINDUNG VON LITURGIE UND KIRCHENMUSIK

Im folgenden bespreche ich erst die Tatsache, daß zwischen Liturgie und Kirchenmusik ein intrinsisches Band besteht. Dann gehe ich auf die Bedeutung der Kirchenmusik für die liturgische Hermeneutik ein.

2.1. Ein intrinsisches Band

Die Musik ist so mit der Liturgie verbunden, daß man sie nicht als etwas betrachten kann, das von außen hinzugefügt wird. Die Musik ist mehr als ein Appendix der Liturgie oder als etwas nur Hinzukommendes. Beide sind so miteinander verbunden, daß man von einem intrinsischen Band sprechen muß. Das wechselseitige Verhältnis ist das der Inhärenz.

Gehen wir vom *Ordo Missae* aus. Innerhalb des Ordo finden sich Teile, die aus sich selbst nach Musik verlangen: Akklamationen, Hymnen,

---

3 J. VAN DEN BERG: *Metabletica van de materie* (Nijkerk 1969) 282-284.

Psalmen, die nach einer Antwort verlangen (beim Einzug, bei der Opferung und der Kommunion), Psalmen, die als Zwischengesänge zwischen zwei Lesungen einen eigenen Platz einnehmen, Texte, die danach verlangen, rezitiert oder kantilliert zu werden, so daß sie an Aussagekraft gewinnen; auch gibt es die Augenblicke 'gefüllter Stille', in denen eine Motette oder instrumentale Musik erklingen kann. Im *Ordo Missae* gibt es also eine Reihe Texte, eine Anzahl Augenblicke, die nach einer eigenen Vertonung verlangen. Ohne diese Vertonung sind sie nicht gut denkbar. Es ist sogar die Frage, ob manche Texte nicht besser wegfallen könnten, wenn keine Musik da ist. In dem Fall bleibt ein 'ausgedünnter' Ordo übrig: ein Ordo, den man sicher einmal auf diese Weise vollziehen kann, aber nicht immer. Man stelle sich die Liturgie des Ostens einmal ohne Gesang vor: Das geht gar nicht. Aber im Westen geht das genausowenig!

Was für den *Ordo Missae* gilt, gilt eigentlich auch für den Ordo des Offiziums. Und es gilt natürlich auch für den Ordo der Sakramente und Sakramentalien, wenigstens dann, wenn sie nicht auf private Weise vollzogen werden, sondern innerhalb der Gemeinde: Hier sind sie zu Hause, und nur hier können sie gesellschaftlich relevant sein und werden.

Ohne Musik verlieren demnach einige Grundelemente des Ordo ihren eigenen Wert. Aber es ist noch mehr zu sagen. Ohne Musik kann man auch nicht gut den strukturellen Platz bestimmter Teile des Ordo erkennen. Ich meine damit folgendes: Innerhalb eines guten Ordo hat jedes Element einen eigenen strukturellen und in gewissem Sinn unersetzlichen Platz; nun erhalten bestimmte Elemente im Ordo diesen eigenen unersetzlichen Platz erst, wenn sie und weil sie aus dem Wort (oder/und dem Ritus), verbunden mit Musik bestehen oder umgekehrt: aus Musik, verbunden mit dem Wort (oder/und dem Ritus). Erst so sind sie als eigene Gattungen zu unterscheiden. Wenn man sich dessen nicht bewußt ist, verwischen sich die Gattungen leicht. Es geschieht z.B. ziemlich oft, daß jeweils die geschlossene Form des Strophenliedes gewählt wird;[4] das hat einen schlaffen, faden, leblosen Ordo zur Folge, in dem alles nebeneinander steht und die fließenden, aber zugleich spannungsreichen Übergangslinien verschwunden sind. Man findet nur noch lose Bruchstücke. Dann werden die liturgischen Zusammenkünfte langweilig und träge. Natürlich gibt es eigenständige und abschließende Elemente in einem Ordo, aber man darf die anderen, die gerade verbindend sind und andere Elemente wachrufen, nicht verwahrlosen. Schließlich ist noch die Frage zu stellen: Darf man Musik, sofern sie für einen bestimmten Platz im Ordo gemacht ist, einfach versetzen?

---

4 Ein Strophenlied wird u.a. durch ein Reimschema, durch einen in jeder Strophe wiederkehrenden Rhythmus und ein gleichbleibendes Metrum charakterisiert. Daher kann jede Strophe auf dieselbe Melodie gesungen werden. Die offene Form dagegen, wie z.B. der Wechselgesang, hat einen unregelmäßigen Textaufbau.

Die Folge kann also sein, daß einige Grundelemente eines guten Ordo nicht ohne Musik funktionieren können und dies hat evtl. auch wieder Folgen für die Grundelemente, die keine Musik brauchen oder für die Musik weniger nötig ist (z.B. bei den Lesungen). Dann: Musik ist nötig, damit die Elemente innerhalb eines Ordo ihre jeweilige Verschiedenheit zum Ausdruck bringen können. Nur so erhalten sie ihre Bedeutung. Denn entsteht Bedeutung nicht gerade durch Verschiedenheit? Wie könnten wir die Farben unterscheiden, wenn sie nicht voneinander verschieden wären. Es geht hier um eine Grunderkenntnis der Semiotik oder Semiologie. Seit kurzem ist der Begriff Semiologie auch Kirchenmusikern nicht mehr fremd: Er hat nämlich bei der Neuinterpretation der Gregorianik, ausgehend von den alten Handschriften, seinen Einzug gehalten. Auch hier gilt die Grunderkenntnis, daß Unterschied und Bedeutung sehr eng zusammenhängen:[5]

> L'on recherche la raison (*logos*) de la diversité des signes (*semeion*) afin d'en déduire les principes fondamentaux pour une interprétation authentique et objective (...). Cette interprétation (...) doit (...) se laisser guider par les faits que nous révèle l'étude *comparative* de *divers* signes: seule base réelle pour l'exécution pratique.

Zum Schluß dieses Abschnitts ein Zitat aus dem Dokument von *Universa Laus* über die Musik im Gottesdienst, das 1980 veröffentlicht wurde:[6]

> Singen heißt nicht: einem Text Musik hinzufügen. Ebensowenig ist es die zufällige Begegnung von reiner Musik und Poesie. Nein, Singen ist eine menschliche Urgebärde, in der Wort und Ton ein Ganzes bilden. (...) Gesang und Musik sind strukturell ein Teil der christlichen Liturgie.

2.2. Liturgische Hermeneutik

Wenn Musik und Liturgie so eng miteinander verbunden sind, so folgt daraus unmittelbar, daß die Bedeutung der Musik in der Liturgie nicht von Wort und Ritus getrennt ist, und ebenso, daß die Bedeutung von Wort und Ritus nicht von der Musik getrennt ist. Die intrinsische Verbundenheit hat weittragende Folgen. Es ist nicht meine Absicht, diese Folgen hier für die Seite der Kirchenmusik auszuführen. Das bereits genannte Dokument von *Universa Laus* bedeutet einen großen Schritt in die rich-

---

5 E. CARDINE: in *Sémiologie Grégorienne* (Solesmes 1970) 1. Vgl. A. KURRIS: Het Graduale Triplex. Wetenschappelijk naslagwerk of praktisch zangboek?, in *Gregoriusblad* 104 (1980) 241-254; A. HOLLAARDT: Gregoriaans nu en in de toekomst. Studiedag N.S.G.V. 1979, in *Gregoriusblad* 103 (1979) 247-251.
6 UNIVERSA LAUS: De la musique dans les liturgies chrétiennes, in *La Maison-Dieu* Nr. 145 (1981) 14 (sub 5) und 20 (sub 1). Vgl. zu diesem Dokument *La Maison-Dieu* Nr. 145 (1981) 7-48 und *Rivista Liturgica* 68 (1981) 10-73.

tige Richtung: einen Schritt, den die *Consociatio Internationalis Musicae Sacrae* (CIMS) nicht so ohne weiteres als nicht getan betrachten kann und darf. Zu Recht spricht das Dokument von *Universa Laus* nicht mehr über 'Kirchenmusik' oder 'geistliche Musik' (*musica sacra*), als ob es um eine selbständige Größe ginge, sondern über 'Musik der christlichen Liturgien': Immerhin geht es in der Kirchenmusik um eine echte liturgische Handlung.[7] Da der Ausdruck 'Musik der christlichen Liturgien' oft schwierig im Kontext zu gebrauchen ist, wähle ich die Bezeichnung in der Einzahl: 'Musik der christlichen Liturgie'. Diese Bezeichnung habe ich auch für den Titel meines Artikels benutzt, und ich werde sie ab jetzt immer gebrauchen: Sie bringt nämlich die intrinsische Relation ausgezeichnet zum Ausdruck.

Welche Konsequenzen hat dies für die Liturgiewissenschaft? Man kann sie so zusammenfassen, daß Liturgiewissenschaftler bei der Interpretation der Liturgie die Musik nicht außer acht lassen können, sonst kommen sie zu unvollständigen, falschen oder verzeichneten Interpretationen. Kurz gesagt: Die Konsequenzen berühren unmittelbar die liturgische Hermeneutik. Der Liturgiewissenschaftler darf also die liturgischen Texte und Riten nicht als ein selbständiges Ganzes betrachten und daneben die Musik als ein anderes selbständiges Ganzes. Denn die Musik hat Einfluß auf die Bedeutung der Liturgie. Im folgenden möchte ich dies *in concreto* zeigen, zunächst auf eine mehr primäre Weise von der Praxiserfahrung her, dann an Hand einiger exakter Beispiele und schließlich an Hand einer mehr allgemeinen Erkenntnis, die mir von einem Einleitungskursus in die Kirchenmusik von A. Kurris noch in Erinnerung ist.

2.3. Ein erstes Beispiel aus der Praxis

1971 war ich bei einem Wettbewerb für Jugendchöre. Die Chöre, die mitmachen wollten, mußten vorher den Text der ganzen Liturgiefeier und eine Tonbandaufnahme der Lieder einsenden. Mit Hilfe dieses Materials sollte eine Jury eine Vorauswahl treffen. H. Jongerius und ich gehörten zur Jury: Wir beide sollten vor allem die liturgischen Aspekte in die Beurteilung miteinbeziehen, während anderen die musikalischen Aspekte zugeteilt waren. Wir stellten einige Kriterien auf, an Hand derer wir das ein-

---

7 Vgl. UNIVERSA LAUS: De la musique 9 (sub 3). Zu den zwei Richtungen in der Kirchenmusik nach Vaticanum II, nämlich *Universa Laus* und CIMS, vgl. G. KOCK: *Tussen altaar en oksaal. Stromingen in de kerkmuziek na Vaticanum II* (nicht veröffentlichte Diplomarbeit, Tilburg 1980). Die CIMS steht noch immer auf dem Standpunkt der 'geistlichen Musik' als eines eigenen, abgerundeten Ganzen. Vgl. zur Abgrenzung der Begriffe religiöse Musik, Kirchenmusik und liturgische Musik, M. ROSEEUW, P. SCHOLLAERT und J. DE WIT: Religieuze muziek. Expressie van het onzegbare, in J. HEMELS und H. HOEKSTRA (Hrsg.): *Media en religieuze communicatie. Een uitdaging aan de christelijke geloofsgemeenschap* (Hilversum 1985) 341-355.

gesandte Textmaterial beurteilten. So kamen wir zu einer ersten Sondierung und vorläufigen Rangfolge der Chöre. Danach war eine Zusammenkunft mit den Musikern aus der Jury geplant. Wir hörten die Tonbänder, die die Chöre eingeschickt hatten. Die Zusammenkunft war sowohl für die Musiker als auch für die Liturgiewissenschaftler eine Entdeckung. Die Musiker bekamen mehr Gefühl für die liturgischen Kriterien und die Liturgiewissenschaftler entwickelten ein Bewußtsein für den eigenen Anteil der Musik an der Liturgie. Texte, die uns zunächst kaum annehmbar schienen, erhielten durch die Musik ein anderes Profil. Und auch das Umgekehrte geschah: Ein guter Text wurde schlechter, durch die Musik. Also traten Veränderungen in unserer vorläufigen Rangfolge auf. Im nachhinein erwies es sich als unrichtig, einen Liedtext losgelöst von der Musik zu beurteilen. Die Bedeutung, die Kraft und die Schwäche eines solchen Textes, wird mitbestimmt und beeinflußt durch die Musik. Dies ist doch eine Selbstverständlichkeit, aber wie oft beschäftigen sich Liturgiewissenschaftler ausschließlich mit Texten?

2.4. Erklärung an Hand einiger konkreter Beispiele

Zunächst führe ich ein Beispiel aus der Gregorianik an. Die *Antiphona ad introitum* des ersten Adventssonntags ist im Graduale *Ad te levavi animam meam* enthalten. Text und Musik gebe ich so wieder, wie sie im *Graduale Triplex* (S.15) zu finden sind, in dem sich, nach der erneuerten Ausgabe des *Graduale Romanum*, die genaue Wiedergabe der Zeichen der wichtigsten Quellen befindet, und zwar die Notation des Scriptorium von Metz und von St. Gallen aus dem 9. und 10. Jahrhundert.[8]

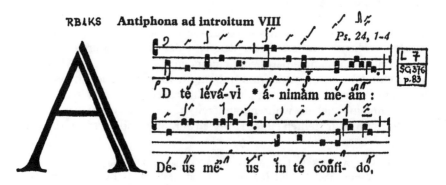

Das Offertorium derselben Messe hat einen etwas anderen Text, und zwar: *Ad te Domine levavi animam meam*. Auch vom Offertorium gebe ich Text und Musik wieder, so wie sie im *Graduale Triplex* (S.17) zu finden sind:

---

8 Vgl. KURRIS: Het Graduale Triplex.

Man könnte nun sagen, daß es doch nicht viel ausmacht, ob das Wort *Domine* im Text steht oder nicht. Es könnte wegfallen, ohne daß sich dadurch der Text wesentlich verändert. Wenn man aber die Musik zum Text hinzunimmt, wird doch ganz deutlich, daß zwischen beiden Gesängen ein großer Unterschied ist. Die Akzente in der Musik sind deutlich verschieden; die Fachleute könnten außerdem die Notation der alten Handschrift hinzuziehen.[9] In der *Antiphona ad introitum* haben wir es mit einem kurzen Text zu tun, in dem die Aufmerksamkeit sofort auf das Wort *animam meam* gezogen wird. Im Offertorium dagegen ist der Satz in zwei Teile geteilt, nämlich in: *Ad te Domine* und: *levavi animam meam*. *Domine* erhält hier einen ganz besonderen Akzent. Es spielt die Rolle einer Kadenz: eines eigenen vorläufigen Schlusses des Halbsatzes. So wird durch die Melodie deutlich gemacht, daß das Wort *Domine* im Text keineswegs unwichtig ist. In der Zeit, in der die Komposition zu diesen Texten entstand, wollte man den Text offensichtlich auf zwei verschiedene Weisen singen und damit auch auf zwei verschiedene Weisen interpretieren.[10] Verschiedene Interpretationen also, durch die Musik entstanden, wie dies z.B. auch der Fall ist, wenn in Handschriften Psalmentexte für eine Pause auf verschiedene Arten unterbrochen werden. Mit Recht verweist daher Visentin darauf, daß der alte Gesang oft der beste Interpret alter Liturgietexte ist. Dies gilt umso mehr, als die Komponisten früher im Hinblick auf ihre Musik im allgemeinen völlig frei waren in der Wahl, der Komposition und der Anpassung der Texte.[11]

Man kann auch Beispiele aus der heutigen niederländischen Liturgie anführen. Bei der Analyse niederländischer eucharistischer Hochgebete hat

---

9 Ich lasse sie außer Betracht; ein Beispiel ist zu finden bei HOLLAARDT: Gregoriaans nu 249.
10 E. CARDINE: Psautiers anciens et chant grégorien, in *Richesses et déficiences des anciens psautiers latins* (= Collectanea Biblica Latina 13) (Città del Vaticano 1959) 249-258.
11 P. VISENTIN: Lo studio della teologia nella liturgia, in *Introduzione agli studi liturgici* (= Liturgica 1) (Roma 1962) 197.

H.J. Auf der Maur ausdrücklich die Musik in seine Analyse miteinbezogen. Dann wird deutlich, daß die Musik zu einem eigenen Akzent im Text oder zu einer anderen Texteinteilung führen kann; und das heißt: zu einer eigenen oder anderen Interpretation. Einige Beispiele:
– Das eucharistische Hochgebet von H. Oosterhuis "Dann hast du, Gott, der du lebst"[12] endet mit den Worten: "Also nehmen wir dieses Brot und diesen Becher und suchen wir einander, um Mensch zu sein". Auf der Maur schreibt hierüber:[13]

> Auffallend ist, daß dieser letzte Teil (...) durch seine musikalische Formung auf besondere Weise, durch einen zweistimmigen Kanon, betont wird. Außerdem wird er wiederholt, wodurch deutlich werden soll, daß dieser Teil, sowohl strukturell als auch inhaltlich, der Höhepunkt des Hochgebetes ist.

– Zum Hochgebet "Um in Menschen Mensch zu werden" von H. Oosterhuis[14] bemerkt Auf der Maur, daß es unbedingt gesungen werden muß und daß die musikalische Komposition seinen Bekenntnischarakter unterstreicht.[15] Außerdem wird deutlich, daß die Textstruktur durch die musikalische Struktur verstärkt wird. Er verweist hierfür vor allem auf die auffallende Verwendung der Gregorianik inmitten anderer Musik am Ende der beiden Hauptteile: "wie ein Sklave starb" und "empfehl ihn deiner Obhut als lebendiger Geliebten, als den Menschen, der dir nah ist". Diese beiden Schlüsse erhalten so einen starken Akzent.[16]
– Beim Hochgebet "Der du weißt" von H. Oosterhuis[17] folgt der Komponist offensichtlich einer anderen Texteinteilung, was eine kleine Bedeutungsverschiebung zur Folge hat.[18] Mit Bezug auf dasselbe Hochgebet

---

12 "Toen hebt gij, God die leeft", in *Liturgische Gezangen voor de viering van de eucharistie* (Hilversum 1975) Nr. 190. Deutsche Übersetzung in *Mitten unter uns. Die schönsten Gebete von Huub Oosterhuis*, ausgewählt und übertragen von P. PAWLOWSKY (Wien-Freiburg-Basel 1982) 207-208.
13 H.J. AUF DER MAUR: Vier tafelgebeden van Huub Oosterhuis, in H. WEGMAN (Hrsg.): *Goed of niet goed? Het eucharistisch gebed in Nederland* 2 (Hilversum 1978) 13.
14 "Die naar mens'lijke gewoonte", in *Liturgische Gezangen* Nr. 202. Deutsche Übersetzung in H. OOSTERHUIS: *Auf halbem Weg* (Wien-Freiburg-Basel 1975) 50ss.
15 AUF DER MAUR: Vier tafelgebeden 19.
16 AUF DER MAUR: Vier tafelgebeden 19-21; vgl. auch S. BELLEMAKERS: *Lees: het zinsverband van woord en vlees. Het belang van de 'close reading' methode bij het bestuderen en beoordelen van liturgische teksten, aan de hand van een onderzoek naar de christologie in enkele tafelgebeden van Huub Oosterhuis* I (nicht veröffentlichte Diplomarbeit, Tilburg 1985) 34-53; L. VAN TONGEREN: Het liturgisch gezang als theologische vindplaats, in A. BLIJLEVENS (Hrsg.): *Liturgiewetenschap* 3 (Kampen 1991) 96.
17 "Gij die weet", in *Liturgische Gezangen* Nr. 170. Deutsche Übersetzung in *Mitten unter uns* 92-94.
18 AUF DER MAUR: Eucharistisch gebed 16, in H. WEGMAN (Hrsg.): *Goed of niet goed? Het eucharistisch gebed in Nederland* (Hilversum 1976) 97-98.

kann man darauf hinweisen, daß in der vertonten Version in zwei Passagen mitten im Gebet das Wort 'ein' mit Bezug auf Jesus von Nazareth weggefallen ist: "einer der nicht aus Eigennutz gelebt" und "Einer der in der letzten Nacht die er noch lebte".[19] Der Komponist B. Huijbers hat hiermit die Betonung der Einzigartigkeit Jesu von Nazareth abgeschwächt.

– Ein letztes Beispiel entnehme ich der Vorlesung *Einleitung in die Musik des christlichen Gottesdienstes*, die A. Kurris im Studienjahr 1980-1981 an der Theologischen Fakultät in Tilburg gehalten hat. Es bezieht sich auf Psalm 25,1. In der Übersetzung von Ida Gerhardt und Marie van der Zeyde heißt Vers 1:[20]

Tot U, Heer, stijgt mijn verlangen.	Zu dir, Herr, steigt mein Verlangen empor.
Op U, mijn God, is mijn vertrouwen.	Auf dich, mein Gott, will ich vertrauen.

Diesen Vers verwendet Oosterhuis als Antiphon, als Refrain für den Psalm; außerdem strahlt Vers 1 durch Oosterhuis' Übersetzung viel mehr Sicherheit aus:

Naar U gaat mijn verlangen, Heer,	Nach Dir verlange ich, Herr,
Heer, mijn God, ik ben zeker van U.	Herr, mein Gott, ich vertraue auf Dich.

So wird Psalm 25 bei Oosterhuis ein Psalm ohne Zweifel. Und diese Interpretation wird auch durch die Melodie von Huijbers noch um einiges verstärkt.[21]

---

19 VAN TONGEREN: *Het liturgisch gezang* 95.
20 I. GERHARDT, M. VAN DER ZEYDE: *Het Boek der Psalmen* (Boxtel 1974) 25.
21 *Liturgische Gezangen* Nr. 18.

2.5. Eine allgemeine Einsicht

Im Zusammenhang mit der liturgischen Hermeneutik möchte ich zum Schluß eine allgemeine Einsicht wiedergeben, die mir aus der genannten Vorlesung von A. Kurris im Gedächtnis geblieben ist. In der romantischen Musikauffassung spielt der Künstler eine große Rolle. Er ist der Artist (möglichst mit wehendem Schopf), der versucht, mit seiner Musik das Publikum zu überwältigen. Die Musik steht der Äußerung seiner Emotionen zu Diensten. Der Künstler selbst steht zentral. Etwas von dieser romantischen Musikauffassung scheint in der Popmusik zurückzukehren. Der Popstar steht, evtl. zusammen mit der Combo, zentral. Sie versuchen, das Publikum mitzuziehen und zu überwältigen. Das Schlagzeug spielt dabei eine große Rolle. Außerdem weiß die moderne Technik mit allerlei Mitteln und indem sie einen bestimmten *sound* hervorbringt, die Emotionen wachzurufen. Und schließlich gibt es noch die bekannten musik-technischen Mittel: Wenn man viele Synkopen (Verschiebungen der Betonung) gebraucht, dann wirkt die Musik umso eindringlicher; dann zwingt und überwältigt sie noch mehr. Der Körper reagiert darauf unmittelbar, indem er gegen das feste Metrum – stoßend – sich zu bewegen beginnt.

Wendet man dieses Vorgehen auf die Liturgie an, dann wirkt der Text viel zwingender. Thetische Texte werden noch thetischer und offene Texte werden in eine bestimmte Richtung gezwungen. So kann die Mehrdeutigkeit eines Textes in die Richtung der Eindeutigkeit, der ersten Sprache gedrängt werden. Die Wörter verlieren ihre Symbolkraft und Tiefe. Aus liturgischer Sicht ist das nicht gut. Und liturgisch-hermeneutisch hat das wichtige Folgen: Eine Interpretation, die auf Grund des Textes offen sein müßte, wird in eine bestimmte Richtung gelenkt.

In der Liturgie muß die Musik der Liturgie dienen und nicht nur den Interpreten oder der Combo. Es geht um 'Musik der christlichen Liturgie'. In der christlichen Liturgie nun können Wort und Musik auf verschiedene Weisen zusammenhängen. Dabei darf die Musik ruhig einmal thetisch sein oder das Wort in einer bestimmten Richtung interpretieren. Dies darf aber nicht der einzige Weg sein. Im Dokument von *Universa Laus* von 1980 wird hierzu folgendes gesagt:[22]

> Entsprechend dem jeweiligen literarischen Genre und vor allem der Beziehung zwischen denen, die sprechen, steht in der Feier einmal die Vermittlung einer Botschaft im Vordergrund, dann wieder das auf angenehme Weise Aufnehmen der vorgetragenen Worte, dann wieder die einstimmige Handlung des Singens, dann wieder der selbstlose Lobpreis. Jedem dieser Sprachtypen entspricht eine eigene Beziehung zwischen Text und Musik.

---

22 UNIVERSA LAUS: De la musique 13.

In jedem dieser Fälle eignet sich die Gruppe das Wort auf eine je eigene Art an.

Es sind also verschiedene Beziehungen zwischen Wort und Musik denkbar. Man kann sich sozusagen eine Waage vorstellen: Auf der einen Seite überwiegt das Wort, hier gibt es nur Sprechgesang und Kantillation, während auf der anderen Seite die Musik das Übergewicht hat, hier geht es vor allem ums Jubilieren (Alleluja und Glossolalie); zwischen beiden liegen viele Möglichkeiten. Wie dem auch sei: Für die liturgische Hermeneutik ist es wichtig, die Beziehungen zwischen Text und Musik genau zu erkennen, da sie auf die Bedeutung des Textes Einfluß haben.

3. KONKLUSIONEN

Mit dem Vorhergehenden möchte ich folgende Konklusionen verknüpfen.
1. "Es ist nicht möglich, sich mit Liturgie zu befassen, ohne die Musik zu beachten: Dies gilt sowohl für die praktische als auch fur die theoretische Seite der Liturgie".[23]
2. Die Liturgiewissenschaft darf die Musik nicht als ein Gebiet betrachten, das außerhalb ihrer Kompetenz liegt. Sie muß sich damit beschäftigen. Dann ist es nicht so wichtig, ob die Musik der christlichen Liturgie einen Teil der Liturgiewissenschaft ausmacht oder ob sie ein unverzichtbares Nebenfach ist. Es geht darum, daß sie nicht ohne einander auskommen können. Interdisziplinäre Zusammenarbeit wäre vorläufig schon ein großer Fortschritt.
3. Alle, die Liturgie als Spezialfach studieren, müßten über die fundamentalen Prinzipien der Musik der christlichen Liturgie Bescheid wissen. Dies verlangt auch einiges an musik-technischem Wissen. Man muß sich darüber klar sein, daß auch früher schon die Kenntnis der fundamentalen Prinzipien der Gregorianik eine selbstverständliche Forderung war.
4. Es ist von großer Bedeutung, daß sich Liturgiewissenschaftler in der Musik der christlichen Liturgie noch weiterbilden und umgekehrt: daß sich Kirchenmusikwissenschaftler in der Liturgiewissenschaft weiterbilden. Nur dann wird die Integration auch auf wissenschaftlichem Niveau Früchte tragen können.
5. An den katholisch-theologischen Fakultäten oder Hochschulen ist, wenigstens für die, die Liturgie als Spezialfach studieren, eine Einleitung in die Musik der christlichen Liturgie notwendig. Hierbei müßte man zur Zusammenarbeit miteinander kommen. Die Anwesenheit eines Dozenten für Musik der christlichen Liturgie innerhalb der theologischen Fakultäten und Hochschulen erscheint außerdem notwedig, um auf wissenschaftlichem Niveau zu wirklicher Integration zu kommen.

---

23 UNIVERSA LAUS: De la musique 20.

6. Indirekt berührt unsere Frage eine viel tiefer reichende Frage, nämlich die nach dem Verhältnis zwischen Theologie und *artes*. Die Theologie hat sich den *artes* weitgehend entfremdet. Die Aufhebung dieser Verfremdung erscheint mir für die Theologie lebenswichtig; wohl bin ich davon überzeugt, daß noch ein langer Weg vor uns liegt.

PART II

Semiotics & Liturgy

11. La liturgie comme lieu théologique irremplaçable
Méthodes d'analyse et de vérification théologiques

En 1926, dom F. Cabrol écrivait que la plupart des théologiens des 17ᵉ et 18ᵉ siècles avaient mieux compris que les théologiens modernes l'importance de la liturgie dans la théologie.[1] Ils lui accordaient une place dans la théologie scolastique et s'efforçaient d'intégrer les données de la science liturgique dans la dogmatique. En 1957, C. Vagaggini déplaça l'accent de la remarque de dom Cabrol en affirmant que la science liturgique dépasserait le stade d'un intérêt purement ou exclusivement historique pour accéder à une étude scientifique du contenu théologique de la liturgie, grâce aux acquisitions historiques.[2] Et, en 1970, A. Häußling écrit: "La science liturgique ressort du domaine théologique (...) Je suppose que cette thèse ne rencontrera pas d'opposition de principe dans nos milieux".[3]

La bibliographie des rapports entre liturgie et théologie s'est considérablement développée depuis 1957 et surtout depuis la Constitution sur la Liturgie (1963).[4] Un coup d'oeil sur cette bibliographie montre que la

---

* *Questions liturgiques* 56 (1975) 317-332. Epilogue traduit par F. Hoppenbrouwers.
1 F. CABROL: Liturgie, dans *Dictionnaire de théologie catholique* IX/1 (Paris 1926) 789.
2 C. VAGAGGINI: *Initiation théologique à la liturgie* I (Bruges-Paris 1959) 7-9.
3 A. HÄUSSLING: Die kritische Funktion der Liturgiewissenschaft, dans H.B. MEYER: *Liturgie und Gesellschaft* (Innsbruck 1970) 106.
4 Je donne la bibliographie la plus importante depuis 1957, dans l'ordre chronologique: E. SCHILLEBEECKX: Lex orandi lex credendi, dans H. BRINK e.a. (éd.): *Theologisch woordenboek* II (Roermond 1957) 2926-2928; C. VAGAGGINI: *Initiation théologique à la liturgie* I-II (Bruges-Paris 1959-1963); J. MULDERS: Geloof, dans L. BRINKHOFF e.a. (éd.): *Liturgisch woordenboek* I (Roermond 1958-1962) 819-826; H. SCHMIDT: Lex orandi, lex credendi, dans H. SCHMIDT: *Introductio in liturgiam occidentalem* (Rome 1960) 131-139; I. DALMAIS: La liturgie et le dépôt de la foi, dans A. MARTIMORT e.a.: *L'Eglise en prière* (Paris 1961) 220-228; J. MULDERS: Liturgie en geloof, dans *Jaarboek Werkgenootschap van katholieke theologen in Nederland* (Hilversum 1961) 167-182; C. VAGAGGINI: *Liturgia e pensiero teologico recente* (Leçon inaugurale à San Anselmo, Rome) (Roma 1961); Y. CONGAR: *La foi et la théologie* (Tournai 1962) 137-148; J. PASCHER: Theologische Erkentnis aus der Liturgie, dans J. RATZINGER et H. FRIES: *Einsicht und Glaube* (Freiburg im Breisgau 1962) 243-258; P. VISENTIN: Lo studio della teologia nella liturgia, dans *Introduzione agli studi liturgici* (= Liturgica 1) (Roma 1962) 189-223; Y. CONGAR: *La Tradition et les traditions* II *Essai théologique* (Paris 1963) 117-123, 183-191; H. HENKEY: Liturgical theology, dans J. MILLER: *Yearbook of liturgical studies* (1963) no. 4, 77-107; I. DALMAIS: La liturgie comme lieu théologique, dans *La Maison-Dieu* 78 (1964) 97-105; H.B. MEYER: Liturgische Theologie oder Theologie des Gottesdienstes, dans *Zeitschrift für katholische Theologie* 86 (1964) 327-331 (critique de H. Henkey, cité plus haut); B. NEUNHEUSER: Liturgie in Gesamtzusammenhang der Theologie, dans *Archiv für Litur-*

giewissenschaft 8 (1964) 86-160; E. SCHILLEBEECKX: La liturgie comme lieu théologique, dans *Approches théologiques* I *Révélation et théologie* (Bruxelles-Paris 1965) 187-190 (même texte que dans l'article de 1957 cité plus haut); J. MULDERS: Lex orandi, lex credendi, dans L. BRINKHOFF e.a. (éd.): *Liturgisch woordenboek* II (Roermond 1965-1968) 1486-1488; J. MULDERS: Theologie, dans L. BRINKHOFF e.a. (éd.): *Liturgisch woordenboek* II (Roermond 1965-1968) 2665-2668; A. STENZEL: Liturgie als theologischer Ort, dans *Mysterium salutis*. *Grundriß heilsgeschichtlicher Dogmatik* I (Einsiedeln 1965) 606-621 (= La liturgie, lieu théologique, dans *Mysterium salutis*. *Dogmatique de l'histoire du salut* III (Paris 1969) 161-181); E. BARTSCH: Liturgiewissenschaft, dans E. NEUHÄUSLER et E. GÖSSMANN: *Was ist Theologie?* (München 1966) 310-349; J. LECLERCQ: *Chances de la spiritualité occidentale* (Paris 1966) 179-224; H.B. MEYER: Liturgie als Hauptfach, dans *Zeitschrift für katholische Theologie* 88 (1966) 315-335; E. VILLANOVA: Cinquanta anys de teologia de la liturgia, dans *II. Congréss litúrgic de Montserrat* I (Montserrat 1966) 195-214; R. SWAELES: Liturgie et théologie, dans E. DEKKERS e.a.: *La formation liturgique dans les monastères* (= Liturgie et monastères, études 2) (Bruges 1967) 75-92; A. MARTIMORT: L'enseignement de la liturgie dans les séminaires, dans *Seminarium* 19 (1967) 107-129; A. ALSTEENS: Liturgie, théologie et sens d'aujourd'hui, dans *Paroisse et liturgie* 50 (1968) 387-400; R. CALLEWAERT: Pour situer le renouveau liturgique dans son contexte: l'apport de la théologie, de la philosophie et des sciences humaines, dans *Paroisse et liturgie* 50 (1968) 135-146; K. RAHNER: Problèmes de théologie pratique, dans *Ecrits théologiques* XI (Paris 1970) 109ss. (éd. allemande: Die praktische Theologie im Ganzen der theologischen Disziplinen, dans *Schriften zur Theologie* VIII (Einsiedeln etc. 1967) 133-149; E. GRIESE: Perspektiven einer liturgischen Theologie, dans *Una Sancta* 24 (1969) 102-113; B. NEUNHEUSER: Der Beitrag der Liturgie zur theologischen Erneuerung, dans *Gregorianum* 50 (1969) 589-615; H. RENNINGS: Objectifs et tâches de la liturgie, dans *Concilium* 42 (1969) 107-121; D. von ALLMEN: Die Geburt der Theologie. Das Problem einer 'einheimischen' Theologie im Lichte des Neuen Testaments, dans *Evangelische Missionszeitschrift* 28 (1970) 50-71, 160-175; R. AUBERT: La théologie catholique, A. Durant la première moitié du XXe siècle, § III, 2, Théologie et Liturgie, dans *Bilan de la théologie au XXe siècle* I (Tournai-Paris 1970) 455-457; H.-W. BARTSCH: Zur Hermeneutik der Sakramente, dans *Ermeneutica e tradizione* (Roma 1970); A. HÄUSSLING: Die kritische Funktion der Liturgiewissenschaft, dans H.B. MEYER: *Liturgie und Gesellschaft* (Innsbruck 1970) 103-130; M. KOVALEWSKI: Le rôle de la liturgie dans le renouveau de la théologie et de l'anthropologie chrétienne, dans *Présence orthodoxe* 2 (1970) 215-228; F. VANDENBROUCKE: Sur la théologie de la liturgie, dans *Nouvelle revue théologique* 92 (1970) 135-164; K. WARE: The theology of worship, dans *Sobornost* 5 (1970) 729-737; B. HÄRING: Rapporti fra teologia morale e liturgia, dans *Rivista liturgica* 57 (1971) 212-218; P. FERNANDEZ: La Liturgia, disciplina principal o nueva dimension de la teologia, dans *Ciencia Tomista* 62 (1971) 581-610; S. MARSILI: La liturgia nella strutturazione della teologia, dans *Rivista liturgica* 57 (1971) 153-162; F. NAKAGAKI: Metodo integrale. Discorso sulla metodologia nell'interpretazione dei testi eucologici, dans *Fons vivus*. *Miscellanea liturgica in memoria di don Eusebio Maria Vismara* (= Bibliotheca Teologica Salesiana, Sez. I, Fontes 6) (Zürich 1971) 269-286; J. PINELL: Per uno studio scientifico della liturgia, dans *Rivista liturgica* 57 (1971) 248-260; W. SWIERZAWSKI: Hermeneutyka wliturgii, dans *Ruch biblijny i liturgiczny* 24 (1971) 131-147; P. VISENTIN: L'insegnamento della dogmatica in rapporto alla liturgia, dans *Rivista liturgica* 57 (1971) 186-211; P. FERNANDEZ: Liturgia y teologia. La historia de une problema metodologico, dans *Ciencia Tomista* 63 (1972) 135-179; G. LAPOINTE: La liturgie, lieu privilégié d'intégration de la foi, dans *Liturgie et vie chrétienne* 82 (1972) 229-239; S. MARSILI: Liturgia e teologia, dans *Rivista liturgica* 58 (1972) 455-473; Una Tavola rotonda sul tema 'liturgia e teologia', dans *Rivista liturgica* 58 (1972) 474-478; A. HOUSSIAU: La liturgie, lieu privilégié de la théologie sacramentaire, dans *Questions Liturgiques* 54 (1973) 7-12; G. LUKKEN: La liturgie, moyen d'expression irremplaçable de la foi, dans *Concilium* 82 (1973) 11-23; D. POWER: Deux expressions de la foi: culte et théologie, dans *Concilium* 82 (1973) 95-101.

thèse de Häußling rencontre de plus en plus de partisans, surtout ces dernières années. Il devient évident aussi que la science liturgique, par son insertion dans la théologie, est confrontée à de nouvelles questions de méthodologie scientifique; de plus, les avis diffèrent sur la place que doit recevoir la liturgie dans l'ensemble de la théologie.[5]

Le développement de la science liturgique esquissé plus haut me porte à croire qu'elle se trouve devant une double question: celle de la valeur de la liturgie comme lieu théologique et celle des méthodes d'analyse et de vérification théologiques qu'elle peut appliquer aux sources liturgiques, y compris le matériel actuellement disponible des sources.

1. LE CONCEPT CLASSIQUE: *LOCUS THEOLOGICUS*

Reconnaître la valeur de la liturgie comme lieu théologique implique d'abord de situer, de manière précise, ce dernier concept dans sa signification habituelle.[6] Dans la philosophie d'Aristote le concept *locus* (*topos*, lieu) renvoie aux prémisses d'un syllogisme dialectique. Mais les humanistes introduisirent un autre emploi du concept *locus*. Inspiré par Cicéron, Rodolphe Agricola lui donna la signification de 'lieu d'origine'. Des mots-clés aide-mémoire, des thèmes majeurs, des schémas généraux et des résumés servirent de *loci*, surtout pour les orateurs. Cel conduisit ensuite à l'expression 'lieu commun' (*locus communis*). Le concept humaniste de *locus* s'employa très vite dans toutes les sciences. Chaque science posséda ses propres *loci*, de sorte que dans l'étude d'un problème scientifique on pouvait directement disposer de notions, de points de vue, de schémas avec lesquels on pouvait étudier la science concernée. Ainsi naquirent les topiques juridiques, médicaux, historiques, etc.

Le dominicain Melchior Cano († 1560) reprit le concept *locus* en théologie dans sa signification humaniste. On connaît son ouvrage *De locis theologicis libri XII*; ce dernier allait devenir un traité de théologie en lui-même. Le topique théologique sera dès lors l'endroit où la théologie peut puiser ses arguments pour éclairer le mystère de la foi, tirer des conclusions théologiques, réfuter des théories, etc. Melchior Cano ne plaçait pas la liturgie dans les lieux théologiques, alors qu'il aurait pu y justifier son insertion.[7] C'est seulement au milieu du 17ᵉ siècle que la liturgie fut employée comme lieu théologique. L'intérêt porté aux lieux théologiques signifiait sans conteste un développement important dans la théologie.

---

5 Cf. note 4, surtout HENKEY: Liturgical theology (1963); MEYER: Liturgische Theologie (1964); MARSILI: Liturgia e teologia (1972); Una Tavola rotonda (1972).
6 H. BRINK: Cano, Melchior, dans H. BRINK e.a. (éd.): *Theologisch woordenboek* I (Roermond 1952) 697-701; E. SCHILLEBEECKX: Loci theologici, dans H. BRINK e.a. (éd.): *Theologisch woordenboek* II (Roermond 1957) 3003-3006.
7 J. RANFT: *Der Ursprung des katholischen Traditionsprinzips* (Paderborn 1931) 24 ss.

On aboutit à la théologie positive, la recherche historique des sources fut l'objet d'une étude intensive. Pour la liturgie, ce furent la recherche historique des sources orientales et occidentales de celle-ci et leur édition. La science liturgique dans son aspect historique naquit et se développa surtout aux 17ᵉ et 18ᵉ siècles.

Cependant l'influence de la recherche des sources sur la théologie fut moins considérable qu'on ne l'aurait sans doute attendu. La raison en est que les lieux étaient surtout utilisés comme preuves d'affirmations théologiques. On les considérait comme un arsenal de données pour la construction théologique et la défense de vérités déterminées. En outre l'attention se concentrait plus sur le lieu du magistère explicite, celui du magistère romain pour lequel les autres lieux allaient servir.[8] L'emploi des lieux acquit souvent un caractère dialectique, juridique et presque casuistique; à la place d'organes vitaux de communications où Dieu parle à son Eglise et l'édifie, les lieux devinrent des références scientifiques avec diverses qualifications au service du magistère. Il n'est donc pas tellement étonnant qu'un lieu aussi concret et compliqué que la liturgie disparut pratiquement de la théologie au 19ᵉ siècle.[9] Théologie et liturgie s'ignorèrent l'une l'autre.

2. LIEU THÉOLOGIQUE COMME ENDROIT DE L'EXPRESSION DE LA FOI

Nous sommes familiarisés avec l'affirmation que la révélation de Dieu en Jésus-Christ est la source de la théologie. "Mais la révélation ne nous est pas accessible autrement qu'exprimée dans la foi".[10] On peut donc dire que la source de la théologie se trouve dans la foi de l'Eglise. L'Eglise en interprète le contenu, elle justifie cette foi autant qu'elle le peut pour la pensée humaine et l'existence, elle en montre les exigences morales, elle essaye d'y ouvrir des voies d'accès, etc. De plus, avec P. Schoonenberg, il est préférable de parler de la foi comme source de la théologie, "parce que alors, plus clairement encore, la foi d'une époque où la théologie est étudiée reflète aussi la foi de tous les croyants de ce temps".[11] Schoonenberg pense tout autant au passé qu'au présent. La pastorale actuelle, la praxis de l'Eglise sont aussi des lieux théologiques.

Approcher les lieux théologiques de cette façon entraîne des conséquences très importantes pour la théologie. Cela signifie que celle-ci doit

---

8 Cf. note 4, CONGAR: *La foi et la théologie* (1962) 143.
9 Cf. note 4, VAGAGGINI: *Initiation théologique à la liturgie* II (1963) 70-81. Il en donne une large description.
10 P. SCHOONENBERG: Het avontuur der christologie, dans *Tijdschrift voor theologie* 12 (1972) 324.
11 SCHOONENBERG: Het avontuur der christologie 324.

accorder son attention à des lieux très concrets et vitaux: aussi concrets et vitaux que la foi même dans les différentes périodes de l'Eglise d'hier jusqu'à aujourd'hui. Dans ce sens la remarque de Congar est importante lorsqu'il déclare que la théologie serait réduite à un minimum si elle consistait seulement dans le catéchisme complété par Denzinger; car la théologie doit étudier toute la richesse de l'Ecriture et la tradition écrite et orale de l'Eglise: la théologie est une 'science des mystères' et elle doit scruter de manière scientifique l'*auditus fidei* de l'Eglise.[12]

La théologie ne peut donc se contenter d'une étude des formulations explicites du mystère, parce que ce lieu n'exprime pas tout. Par rapport aux autres lieux, le magistère est en effet un lieu déclaratif et non un lieu constitutif.[13] La recherche de l'*auditus fidei* est un travail considérable, d'autant plus que l'on a conscience que depuis peu les historiens sont attirés par l'étude du passé tel qu'il était, c'est-à-dire de la vie dans sa forme la plus concrète, la plus vivante et la plus parlante pour nous. Cela signifie pour l'histoire de l'Eglise qu'elle ne peut se contenter d'une simple description du passé à l'aide des papes, des rois et des grandes figures, mais qu'elle doit accorder de l'importance à la vie quotidienne de foi des chrétiens. Il s'agit donc tout autant de l'étude de la vie concrète de la communauté dans son dynamisme plénier. De la même manière la théologie devra garder le contact ou retrouver ce contact avec l'expérience vivante de foi du passé. Elle ne pourra pas employer, par exemple, des expressions du magistère en les coupant de la situation concrète de foi où celles-ci furent formulées. Cela s'applique aussi à l'époque actuelle comme lieu pour la théologie: la réponse contemporaine des communautés chrétiennes à la question de Jésus "Mais pour vous, qui suis-je?" (Mc. 8,29; Mt. 16,15; Lc. 9,20) a une valeur propre comme lieu théologique.[14] Pour Schoonenberg la révélation ne nous est pas autrement accessible qu'exprimée dans la foi en sorte que la foi exprimée est source de la théologie. Je voudrais nuancer quelque peu cette formulation. La foi s'exprime dans les oeuvres et s'accomplit aussi dans le symbole et le rite. On pourrait donc dire: la révélation ne nous est pas autrement accessible qu'explicitée dans la foi. En d'autres mots, les lieux théologiques sont des lieux de révélation, parce que, et en tant que la foi apparaît explicitement dans ces lieux.

---

12 Cf. note 4, CONGAR: *La foi et la théologie* (1962) 137-138.
13 Cf. note 4, FERNANDEZ: Liturgia y teologia (1972) 171.
14 E. SCHILLEBEECKX: De toegang tot Jesus van Nazareth, dans *Tijdschrift voor theologie* 13 (1973) 44. Plus en détail, dans IDEM: *Jesus, het verhaal van een levende* (Bloemendaal 1974) 469-549.

3. LIEUX THÉOLOGIQUES PREMIERS ET SECONDS

Le terme second ne doit pas être compris de manière péjorative. Il est employé ici dans la ligne de distinction qui existait déjà dans l'Eglise orientale primitive, celle entre théologie première et théologie seconde, et analogiquement ici, entre orthodoxie première et orthodoxie seconde.[15]

Théologie première signifie la première réflexion sur Dieu (théo-logie); son lieu est l'expression de foi première se trouvant dans la praxis de la foi de l'Eglise, dans le passé, comme aujourd'hui. On pense ici à la praxis de l'autenthique vie chrétienne: "La vie des saints est aussi une parole de Dieu" (Pie IX),[16] mais il s'agit aussi de la praxis de l'acte rituel de l'Eglise, de la liturgie. Théologie seconde indique la réflexion sur Dieu 'en seconde instance'; son lieu est l'expression de la foi s'exprimant dans la pensée des théologiens et du magistère.

Analogue à la distinction entre théologie première et théologie seconde est celle entre orthodoxie première et orthodoxie seconde. Le mot orthodoxie a tout d'abord la signification de 'juste louange' et dans un sens dérivé celle d'"enseignement vrai'.

Les lieux premiers ne sont pas moins importants que les lieux seconds en théologie. Lorsque celle-ci néglige les premiers, elle perd son *Sitz im Leben* et aussi la voie la plus sûre pour pénétrer dans les mystères de la foi. Elle risque alors de devenir un procédé sec et étrange, qui ne voit plus la relativité des conceptualisations dans la vie chrétienne, qui de soi sont inadéquates. L'attention portée aux sources premières garde la théologie vivante et donne au théologien la modestie d'une docte ignorance et l'indispensable attitude doxologique.[17]

4. CARACTÈRE IRREMPLAÇABLE DE LA LITURGIE COMME LIEU THÉOLOGIQUE

Parmi les lieux théologiques premiers, la liturgie a une valeur inamissible. Cela tient au fait que l'expérience chrétienne commence vraiment à faire partie de l'homme, lorsque celui-ci lui donne forme. Lorsque la foi arrive à s'exprimer, elle devient alors partie vitale de toute la personne et l'homme peut réellement participer à l'événement du salut sur lequel est centré l'acte de croire. La foi chrétienne peut être traduite en un comportement chrétien authentique. Quelle que soit l'importance de ce comportement, il n'est pas suffisant pour porter à sa pleine stature l'expérience de

---

15 Cf. note 4, LUKKEN: La liturgie (1973) 22-23 (et la bibliographie mentionnée); POWER: Deux expressions de la foi (1973).
16 A. COMBES: *Sainte Thérèse de Lisieux et sa mission* (Paris 1954) 212, note 4.
17 Cf. note 4, POWER: Deux expressions de la foi (1973) 100.

foi. Toute expérience humaine prend sa pleine stature par la voie de l'expression symbolique qui confère aux sentiments et aux dispositions intimes stature et forme, de sorte que l'homme les prenne à son compte et les actualise. Cette expression qui engage l'homme avec toutes ses facultés réalise la communication la plus plénière. Il en va de même pour la foi: si elle est un acte de la personne totale qui entre en contact avec le Dieu du salut, il faut qu'elle s'exprime en mots, en symboles, en actions et rites symboliques. C'est précisément ce qui s'opère dans la liturgie. C'est seulement dans et par la liturgie que la foi peut se réaliser comme foi personelle, comme foi de cette communauté. L'expression de la foi dans la liturgie est d'une importance capitale pour que la foi puisse passer en acte. Dans l'expression de la liturgie la foi préalable acquiert sa pleine stature et devient une véritable remise de soi.[18] On peut affirmer à juste titre que la liturgie est une expression de la foi, qu'aucune autre expression ne peut remplacer sans plus, comme la prose ne remplace pas la poésie, ni les mots la musique.[19]

La valeur irremplaçable de l'expression liturgique ne présente pas seulement une base anthropologique, elle est aussi en rapport avec la condition sacramentelle de l'Eglise. Le rapport entre la base anthropologique donnée et la condition sacramentelle de l'Eglise fait que celle-ci se construit de la manière la plus existentielle, là où la communauté célèbre la liturgie. La réalité ecclésiale apparaît le plus visiblement dans la liturgie, celle-ci est ainsi *culmen* et *fons* de l'agir de l'Eglise, suivant la Constitution sur la Liturgie (no. 10). Si la liturgie est la forme d'expression la plus existentielle de l'être ecclésial, il s'ensuit que la réflexion théologique trouvera dans la forme liturgique une matière enrichissante pour sa recherche. Le lieu théologique de la liturgie présente une richesse propre et l'étude de ce lieu conduit la théologie à saisir des aspects précis de la réalité du salut qu'elle n'avait pas encore – ou insuffisamment – incorporés.

Dans ce sens on peut parler avec B. Neunheuser de "la contribution de la liturgie au renouveau théologique" ou avec Häußling de "la fonction critique de la science liturgique" par rapport à la théologie.[20]

5. MÉTHODES D'ANALYSE EN LITURGIE, COMME LIEU THÉOLOGIQUE

Lorsque le théologien s'est familiarisé avec la vive lumière de la théologie seconde, il doit, selon A. Houssiau, accomplir une profonde conversion,

---

18 Cf. note 4, LUKKEN: La liturgie (1973) 14-15 (et la bibliographie mentionnée).
19 Cf. note 4, WARE: The theology of worship (1970) 734.
20 Cf. note 4, NEUNHEUSER: Der Beitrag der Liturgie (1969); HÄUSSLING: Die kritische Funktion (1970).

afin de pouvoir saisir et enregistrer la réalité complexe de la liturgie dans sa pleine valeur.[21] La liturgie a bien un contenu de notions conceptualisables, mais ce contenu n'est pas l'essentiel, et il se trouve enfoui dans toute l'expérience vitale. La recherche du contenu théologique de la liturgie doit toujours tenir compte du contexte assez élaboré où celle-ci se trouve.

5.1. La liturgie dans le passé

Les dernières décennies, la recherche théologique sur la liturgie s'est intéressée de plus en plus à la liturgie du passé. Il est impossible de présenter une bibliographie complète dans le cadre de cet article. Je me contenterai de signaler que beaucoup d'études ne sont hélas pas encore publiées.[22] Une grande unanimité paraît exister sur la méthode d'investigation, et celle-ci perfectionne de plus en plus. Cela ressort des monographies et des publications qui décrivent explicitement la méthode.[23]

Elle se présente de la manière suivante. Textes et rites sont replacés dans leur contexte historique et l'on s'interroge sur la signification qu'ils avaient dans le milieu où ils sont nés. On recherche la place que les textes et rites concernés occupaient dans la liturgie et l'année liturgique, leurs rapports avec la mentalité d'alors et le milieu doctrinal. Si c'est possible, on identifie l'auteur, ce qui sera ordinairement une supposition ou une hypothèse. Dans l'interprétation des textes, on tient compte de leur structure propre, du rythme, du style et du genre littéraire. Eventuellement on examine l'histoire des textes et rites étudiés dans les différentes sources grâce auxquelles peuvent surgir de petites, mais fort significatives, variations. On comparera en outre ces textes et rites aux parallèles existant dans d'autres liturgies, les liturgies orientales notamment. La question de

---

21 Cf. note 4, HOUSSIAU: La liturgie (1973) 8-9.
22 Les dissertations suivantes, par exemple, H. BÜSSE: *Salus in der römischen Liturgie. Ein Beitrag zur Sprache und Theologie liturgischen Gebetstexte* (Pontificia Università Gregoriana) (Roma 1959); E. ALBERICH: *El misterio de Navidad en el Sacramentario Leóniano. Ensayo de teologia liturgica* (Pontificio Ateneo Salesiano) (Torino 1962); A. PERNIGOTTO-CEGO: *Il concetto di 'sollemnitas' nel Sacramentario Veronese. Un contributo alla teologia della solemnità liturgica* (San Anselmo) (Roma 1965); M. AUGÉ: *La oración 'super populum' en el Sacramentario Veronese. Estudio de su forma y contenido* (San Anselmo) (Roma 1967); V. GROSSI: *Liturgia battesimale e peccato originale in relazione alla controversia pelagiana* (San Anselmo) (Roma 1967); P. PUTHANANGADY: *The theological elements in the Christmas liturgy of the Gelasian Sacramentary (Cod. Reg. 316)* (San Anselmo) (Roma 1967); F. NAKAGAKI: *Participazione attiva dei fideli secondo il Sacramentario Veronese. Un importante aspetto dell' ecclesiologia in prospettiva liturgica* (San Anselmo) (Roma 1969); voir aussi: Dieci anni di studi liturgici. Tesi doctorali (1962-1971), dans *Rivista liturgica* 82 (1972) 547-552; G. LUKKEN: *Original Sin in the Roman liturgy. Research into the theology of Original Sin in the Roman Sacramentaria and the early baptismal liturgy* (Leiden 1973).
23 Cf. note 4, VISENTIN: Lo studio della teologia (1962); NAKAGAKI: Metodo integrale (1971).

leur place dans les grands ensembles où ils s'intègrent doit être posée: les formules sont souvent reprises dans l'unité plus grande de formulaires et ceux-ci dans des sections. On peut ainsi distinguer les *Leitmotive* centraux des pensées secondaires, aussi bien dans les formules, que dans les formulaires et sections.

Cette étude s'accompagne aussi d'une recherche sur la terminologie. De même qu'une étude biblique qui se veut scientifique est précédée d'une étude des termes, ainsi la découverte du contenu théologique de la liturgie est liée à une recherche de la signification exacte des mots et concepts qui sont employés dans la langue cultuelle, ici le latin liturgique. Dans ce domaine, la science liturgique est défavorisée par rapport aux études bibliques qui, elles, disposent de nombreuses monographies et d'un ouvrage monumental comme le *Theologisches Wörterbuch zum Neuen Testament*, alors que la recherche sur la terminologie de la liturgie en est encore au premier stade.[24] L'interprétation des textes et rites recevra l'aide des disciplines auxiliaires, comme l'épigraphie, l'archéologie chrétienne, l'iconographie, l'histoire de la spiritualité, l'histoire de l'herméneutique biblique et les sciences religieuses.

L'analyse terminée, il faut lier les données en une synthèse. La conclusion sera que l'étude de la liturgie d'une période déterminée ne représente pas *la* théologie, mais *une* théologie bien définie, dont on montrera qu'elle a reçu une signification plus ou moins universelle. Il faut compléter la méthode sur un point. La science liturgique est trop peu consciente du lien étroit qui existe entre musique et liturgie. Visentin a montré que le chant ancien est souvent le meilleur interprète des textes liturgiques.[25] Ainsi, une analyse du texte de l'Introit de Pâques ne peut suffire, il faut y ajouter la mélodie grégorienne.[26] Le grégorien peut donner un accent particulier à un mot déterminé.[27] Hélas, la collaboration interdisciplinaire entre la science liturgique et la musique d'église n'existe pratiquement pas.

5.2. La liturgie officielle aujourd'hui

Maintenant que tous les livres de la liturgie romaine sont renouvelés, la recherche théologique sur la liturgie se trouve devant une tâche assez considérable. Quelle méthode employer pour la liturgie romaine officielle d'aujourd'hui? A mon avis, il faudra accorder une place aux éléments suivants:

24 W. DÜRIG: *Imago. Ein Beitrag zur Terminologie und Theologie der römischen Liturgie* (Münchener theologische Studien 2/5) (München 1952) v-vi.
25 Cf. note 4, VISENTIN: Lo studio della teologia (1962) 197.
26 Cf. J. GAJARD: *Les mélodies de la Semaine Sainte et de Pâques* (Paris-Rome 1952) 53-59.
27 E. CARDINE: Psautiers anciens et chant grégorien, dans *Richesses et déficiences des anciens psautiers latins* (Collectanea biblica latina 13) (Rome 1959) 249-258.

a) Etude de la préhistoire du renouveau liturgique, comme elle apparaît dans le mouvement liturgique.

b) Etude de la préhistoire précédant immédiatement le renouveau liturgique: la genèse de la Constitution sur la Liturgie, la Constitution elle-même et l'interprétation de celle-ci dans les documents et commentaires officiels.

c) Etude de la genèse des nouveaux textes liturgiques: étude des avant-projets, des amendements et des critères appliqués. On trouve des renseignements partiels en ce domaine dans la revue *Notitiae*, publiée par la Congrégation pour le Culte divin et dans les grandes revues liturgiques. La recherche théologique disposerait ainsi d'une étude complète et documentée sur le sujet.

d) Etude des nouveaux livres liturgiques, tant les textes et rites que les *praenotanda*. Il faut distinguer dans l'étude des textes:
– les textes repris intégralement de sources liturgiques existants;
– les textes repris de sources liturgiques existantes, mais qui ont été adaptés;
– les nouveaux textes, que l'on peut diviser en créations complètes (une petite partie), centonisations[28] de textes liturgiques existants et transpositions liturgiques de textes bibliques, patristiques et conciliaires (Vatican II).

Les publications sur les sources directes des nouveaux livres sont encore fragmentaires. L'existence d'une revue de synthèse avec tables de concordance est d'une grande importance pour cette étude.

Pour l'étude de la signification originelle des textes et rites, la méthode décrite plus haut pour la liturgie du passé est applicable ici. Beaucoup d'éléments de cette méthode s'appliquent aussi à l'étude de la signification actuelle des textes et rites; on tiendra compte surtout du nouveau contexte, des modifications apportées et des critères qui ont guidés les rédacteurs des nouveaux livres.

e) Etude des traductions approuvées. Dans cette étude, la traduction originale servira de base, avec les remarques présentées par la Congrégation pour le Culte Divin et la Congrégation pour la Doctrine de la Foi, et les transformations apportées à la suite de ces remarques. Enfin, une comparaison des traductions de différents pays peut être significative pour la recherche théologique.

5.3. La liturgie expérimentale aujourd'hui

La liturgie expérimentale dans plusieurs pays présente un lieu théologique assez particulier. Une étude systématique de cette liturgie pose dès l'abord

---

28 Centonisation: texte composé de fragments empruntés à diverses sources; c'est un genre littéraire assez employé en liturgie.

la question des sources à consulter comme point de départ. H. Schmidt remarque que la meilleure source se trouve dans les communautés de prière elles-mêmes et dans les feuilles stencylées.[29] C'est une tâche particulièrement difficile de rassembler ces sources de manière représentative et il faudra trouver des critères. Habituellement le point de départ idéal sera difficilement réalisable et on sera obligé de se limiter à ce qui en a été imprimé. On rencontre déjà ainsi une quantité considérable de matériel. Il faudra constituer une étude documentaire par domaine linguistique, comme celle que Schmidt a entrepris sur un plan général.[30]

Comment étudier ces sources de la manière qui s'accorde le mieux à leur contenu théologique? La méthode de recherche doit encore prendre forme. Si j'essaie d'avancer quelques éléments, je me rends compte qu'ils ne forment qu'une ébauche et qu'ils doivent se développer et apporter leurs preuves.

a) Avant chaque analyse, il foudrait participer sans préjugés à la liturgie qu'on veut étudier, soit sur le vif, soit au moyen d'enregistrements, disques etc., afin que cette liturgie pénètre dans l'existence. Ce sera souvent impossible et on en sera réduit à des possibilités qui se présentent.

b) Pour une participation sans préjugés on peut faire appel à la psychologie pratique (supervision) qui nous conduit à abandonner nos propres projections et libère en nous la source de la 'parole personelle'.

c) Avant de passer à une analyse détaillée, il faut situer le mieux possible la liturgie à étudier: poser la question de sa genèse, le lieu de son origine, l'auteur, essayer éventuellement d'atteindre les critères appliqués.

d) Le plus difficile est l'analyse elle-même. La littérature pourra peut-être aider les liturgistes dans la recherche d'une méthode. E. Krzywon a posé la question de la possibilité d'une étude systématique de la relation entre la littérature et la théologie.[31] Il considère la théologie de la littérature comme une branche possible de la science littéraire, ce qu'il précise comme suit: théorie attentive à l'influence réciproque entre littérature et théologie. Cette théologie de la littérature prendrait comme point de départ la littérature elle-même et travaillerait suivant les méthodes de la science littéraire. On peut considérer les créations liturgiques sous l'angle littéraire, en sorte que surgisse la question de la possibilité d'appliquer les méthodes d'analyse littéraire à l'analyse de la liturgie expérimentale. N'est-il pas frappant que les liturgies d'Oosterhuis sont l'objet d'un jugement de la part des critiques littéraires?[32] Par leurs critiques on en découvre le contenu théologique.

---

29 H. SCHMIDT: *Bidden onderweg van 1960-1970. Documentaire studie, met bibliografie en citaten-selectie* (Haarlem 1971) 10.
30 Cf. SCHMIDT: *Bidden onderweg* 10.
31 E. KRZYWON: Literaturwissenschaft und Theologie. Elemente einer hypothetischen Literaturtheologie, dans *Stimmen der Zeit* 99 (1974) 108-116.
32 K. FENS: De realiteit van de menswording. *Bid om vrede* van Oosterhuis, dans journal

Je pense que pour la liturgie expérimentale la méthode d'analyse la plus féconde est celle répandue aux Pays-Bas par la revue *Merlijn*.[33] Cette méthode peut se caractériser comme une méthode de *close-reading* (lecture littérale, mot à mot), décrite ainsi par Oversteegen: "une lecture critique partant du fait que chaque partie d'un texte occupe (doit occuper) une place dans une structure pleinement cohérente".[34] C'est la méthode d'une lecture d'observation, pour ainsi dire le nez sur le texte. Il faut écarter autant que possible les arrières-pensées et les préjugés et essayer d'observer simplement et concrètement. On tâche de découvrir l'architecture structurale du tout, on dissèque les textes, on les subdivise et on en découvre ainsi les motifs et les thèmes à travers les détails. C'est alors qu'on essaye d'élaborer une formulation générale. Il n'y a pas unanimité sur cette méthode dans la science littéraire: certains doutent de la possibilité d'une telle analyse sans a-priori et se demandent si des jugements et ordres de valeur ne s'y glissent pas inconsciemment. L'analyse donne une appréciation de la littérature et la personne du critique y est nécessairement tout entière engagée.[35] Nonobstant, je pense que la méthode de *close-reading* est très fructueuse pour l'analyse de la liturgie expérimentale dans son contenu théologique, d'autant qu'il ne sagit pas tellement ici d'une critique de cette liturgie comme littérature, mais plutôt d'une découverte aussi justifiée que possible du contenu théologique, sans poser encore la question de vérification théologique. La méthode de *close-reading* vise surtout le mot, mais je crois qu'elle peut-être une base valable pour l'intelligence (*intus-legere*) et l'interprétation des rites indiqués et suggérés par des mots dans cette liturgie.

e) La collaboration inter-disciplinaire entre la science liturgique et la science musicale sera indispensable dans l'élaboration d'une méthode scientifique de la recherche.

f) Il serait aussi important d'envisager si les méthodes de science du théâtre peuvent être d'une aide quelconque dans l'analyse théologique de la liturgie expérimentale.

De Tijd (3 septembre 1966); IDEM: *In het voorbijgaan* van Huub Oosterhuis. Tastend schrijven over God, bidden en de hemel, dans journal *De Tijd* (14 décembre 1968) ; W. DE MOOR: Oosterhuis' voorleesboek: Israels verhaal doorvertellen, dans journal *De Tijd* (26 août 1972); IDEM: De grote en verheven dingen van Huub Oosterhuis. *Hoever is de nacht*: imponerende Godslyriek, dans journal *De Tijd* (20 septembre 1974).

33 *Merlijn*, rédaction de K. FENS, H. JESSURUN D'OLIVEIRA et J. OVERSTEEGEN, volumes 1 (1963) – 4 (1966).

34 J. OVERSTEEGEN: Analyse en oordeel (1), dans *Merlijn* 3 (1965) 178.

35 H. GOMPERTS: *De twee wegen van de kritiek* (discours inaugural à Leiden) (Amsterdam 1966); J. OVERSTEEGEN: Leiden ontzet (en Amsterdam niet minder). Notities bij de ontgroening van H.A. Gomperts, dans *Merlijn* 4 (1966) 149-178; H. JESSURUN D'OLIVEIRA: Heldhaftige literatuurbeschouwing, dans *Merlijn* 4 (1966) 235-242; T. ANBEEK: De literatuurwetenschap en de lezers, dans *De Gids* 137 (1974) 159-176.

6. VÉRIFICATION COMPARATIVE

L'analyse seule ne peut suffire dans l'étude théologique de la liturgie. Le contrôle de la liturgie doit suivre le travail analytique. Le fait que la liturgie est un lieu théologique inamissible ne signifie nullement que tout ce qui s'y rencontre est justifié au plan théologique. Les études sur l'adage de Prosper d'Aquitaine *legem credendi lex statuat supplicandi* ont assez prouvé les limites de celui-ci.[36] Il serait injuste de considérer la liturgie comme source absolue de la foi et d'affirmer, comme les modernistes, que la liturgie crée le dogme.[37]

Mais comment vérifier la valeur théologique de la liturgie? E. Schillebeeckx répond que la liturgie a une valeur théologique pour autant qu'elle soit soutenue dans une confession de foi permanente par toute la communauté croyante, aussi bien l'Eglise enseignante que l'Eglise confessante.[38] D'autres auteurs ont essayé d'établir des normes plus concrètes en rapport avec la valeur normative de la liturgie en théologie. Je pense à M. Pinto, C. Vagaggini, I. Dalmais, Y. Congar, A. Alcala et A. Stenzel.[39] On peut conclure généralement que ces normes fondent la valeur théologique dans un autre lieu théologique, celui de l'autorité que l'Eglise a donnée aux différents éléments de la liturgie. Je ne voudrais pas déprécier la légitimité de ces normes, mais celles-ci appellent deux questions. Premièrement, ces normes ne sont-elles pas établies à partir du concept de lieu dans le sens d'argument pour la théologie? Ne conduisent-elles pas facilement à abandonner le lieu compliqué de la liturgie, puisque l'argumentation à l'aide de la théologie seconde est une voie plus simple qu'il faut de toute façon emprunter? Deuxièmement, comment employer ces normes lorsqu'il s'agit de vérifier la liturgie expérimentale où la référence à l'autorité de l'Eglise est impossible?

On avancera peut-être le critère de la nécessaire unité de tous les lieux théologiques pour laquelle plaide Schoonenberg, tenant compte de la vie actuelle de foi et de l'expérience pastorale. Il écrit:[40]

---

36 K. FEDERER: *Liturgie und Glaube. Eine theologiegeschichtliche Untersuchung* (= Paradosis 4) (Freiburg 1950). Les études de la note 4 se retrouvent ici, mais c'est surtout l'adage *lex orandi, lex credendi* qui fait l'objet de la bibliographie.
37 G. TYRELL: *Lex orandi; or, prayer and creed* (London 1903); cf. H. DENZINGER et A. SCHÖNMETZER: *Enchiridion symbolorum, definitionum et declarationum de rebus fidei et morum* (Rome etc. 1963[32]) 3440, 3442, 3449.
38 Cf. note 4, SCHILLEBEECKX: Lex orandi (1957) 2927; SCHILLEBEECKX: Liturgie (1964) 157.
39 M. PINTO: *O valor teologico da liturgia* (Braga 1952) 323; A. ALCALA: *La Iglesia. Misterio y mission* (Madrid 1963) 64, cf. 131-139. Cf. note 4, DALMAIS: La liturgie et le dépôt de la foi (1961) 225; IDEM: La liturgie comme lieu théologique (1964); CONGAR: *La foi et la théologie* (1962) 144-145; STENZEL: Liturgie als theologischer Ort (1965), surtout 609-614.
40 SCHOONENBERG: Het avontuur der christologie 325.

> La foi entière est source de théologie et ainsi aucune de ses expressions – la Bible, les écrits des Pères de l'Eglise, les déclarations conciliaires – n'est source de la théologie sans toutes les autres: l'Ecriture Sainte avec la tradition, et inversement pas de tradition, pas de dogme sans leur fondement scriptuaire. Les lieux s'éclairent et se critiquent mutuellement. Il en va de même avec l'existence contemporaine de foi et l'expérience pastorale. Quel que soit son niveau scientifique, l'existence de foi doit être éclairée et vérifiée par les autres lieux théologiques. C'est par cet accord avec les autres lieux théologiques que l'existence d'aujourd'hui se trouvera être une existence de foi. Je dis accord et non identité. Il ne suffit pas à l'expérience d'aujourd'hui de répéter ce qui fut dit autrefois ou ce qui a toujours été dit. (...) L'Esprit parle un langage toujours nouveau aux églises; il peut nous expliquer ce que nous ne pouvions comprendre jadis – ou ne voulions pas accepter. Formulations, rapports et points difficiles peuvent se déplacer, des surprises apparaître de manière heureuse, mais pas de contradiction. La théologie devra non seulement accepter le lieu de l'existence contemporaine de foi, mais aussi le vérifier.

Je caractérisais volontiers la méthode décrite par Schoonenberg comme celle de vérification théologique comparative. J'emploie à dessein ce terme qui évoque le livre de A. Baumstark *Liturgie comparée*.[41] Baumstark explique ainsi le fondement de la méthode de la liturgie comparée: une méthode qui ne diffère en rien de la méthode comparative des sciences positives; son objet seul ressort de la théologie.[42] Baumstark craignait à juste titre que des *a-priori* théologiques nuisent aux données empiriques de la science liturgique historique. Maintenant que la science liturgique occupe en théologie la place qui lui revient, un complément important à Baumstark se révèle nécessaire. Sa méthode doit être complétée par celle de la vérification théologique comparative, qui doit suivre l'analyse. En accordant par cette méthode une attention explicite à la problématique des lieux théologiques premiers et seconds, on peut situer dans son champ d'investigation le dialogue entre théologie première – et donc la liturgie – et théologie seconde: les lieux théologiques premiers et seconds s'éclairent mutuellement. Dans cette perspective, on pourrait présenter le schéma suivant:

---

[41] A. BAUMSTARK: *Liturgie comparée. Principes et méthodes pour l'étude historique des liturgies chrétiennnes* (Chevetogne 1953³). A partir de 1923 Baumstark enseigna à l'Université catholique de Nimègue, et aussi depuis 1926 à l'Université d'Etat d'Utrecht.

[42] BAUMSTARK: *Liturgie comparée* 3: "Par ce rapprochement, on entend délimiter nettement la place occupée par l'histoire de la liturgie dans l'ensemble des sciences. Seul son objet appartient à la théologie. Mais le travail à faire sur lui ne diffère pas du travail comparatif des sciences exactes".

Autrefois   *Aujourd'hui*

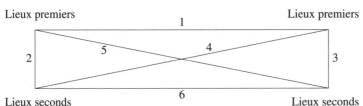

D'après l'étude de la liturgie comme lieu théologique, on peut indiquer les lignes de direction suivantes:

1) Les lieux théologiques premiers du passé et d'aujourd'hui se vérifient les uns par les autres, c'est-à-dire la liturgie d'aujourd'hui est comparée à celle du passé et inversement.

2) Les lieux théologiques premiers et seconds du passé se vérifient réciproquement; par exemple la célébration eucharistique du Moyen-Age et la doctrine de la transsubstantiation.

3) Les lieux théologiques premiers et seconds d'aujourd'hui se vérifient réciproquement; par exemple, la célébration eucharistique actuelle et les enseignements de la théologie sur l'eucharistie.

4) Les lieux théologiques premiers d'aujourd'hui et les lieux théologiques seconds du passé se vérifient réciproquement; par exemple la liturgie baptismale actuelle et la théologie du baptême dans le passé.

5) Les lieux théologiques premiers du passé et les lieux théologiques seconds du présent se vérifient réciproquement; par exemple, la liturgie baptismale dans le passé et les enseignements théologiques sur le baptême aujourd'hui.

Une sixième voie existe, celle qui touche la vérification de la liturgie comme lieu théologique, le rapport entre les lieux théologiques seconds du passé et du présent; par exemple, l'enseignement sur la transsubstantiation et celui sur la transfinalisation. Pour un processus complet de vérification de la liturgie comme lieu théologique, cette voie servira aussi. Cela démontre combien les lieux théologiques sont liés entre eux, et la liturgie à la théologie.

Par la méthode de vérification comparative, la théologie devient une réalité complexe et ample: tâche qui ne doit pas l'effrayer car la théologie sera fidèle à elle-même, en gardant tous les lieux dans son champ d'étude. Une réponse est ainsi possible à la question de savoir si ce que nous faisons aujourd'hui en liturgie est digne de confiance. La méthode de vérification permet à la science liturgique de se développer sous son aspect théologique comme science critico-normative au service de la *liturgia condenda*.

7. EPILOGUE

En ce qui concerne sa méthode d'analyse cet article qui date de 1975 demande quelques éclaircissements supplémentaires. En même temps ces remarques faciliteront le passage aux articles suivants.

Selon l'article en question il faudrait étudier la liturgie d'autrefois et la liturgie officielle en employant la méthode historique, tandis que l'étude de la liturgie expérimentale contemporaine employerait mieux la méthode de *close-reading*. Depuis il est devenu clair, que toute liturgie – actuelle et historique – peut être étudiée à l'aide des deux approches. L'analyse sera désormais accomplie tant diachroniquement par le moyen de la méthode historique que synchroniquement (c'est-à-dire achroniquement) en se servant de la méthode de *close-reading*. En rapport avec la méthode de *close-reading* il faut ajouter quelques renseignements bibliographiques. Elles concernent non seulement la méthode elle-même mais son application aussi.[43] A la méthode de *close-reading* de la liturgie on pourrait ajouter la méthode de *close-listening* et de *close-seeing*.

Il est évident de par son nom que la méthode de *close-reading* est originaire des pays anglophones. Là elle est née dans le sein du mouvement *New Criticism*, qui défendait l'autonomie du texte.[44] Ce mouvement a pris son essor indépendamment d'une initiative parallèle en Russie, ce qui était dû aux frontières linguistiques. Sous l'influence de T.S. Eliot et I.

---

[43] En ce qui concerne la méthode elle-même, voir A. STOCK: *Umgang mit theologischen Texten* (Zürich-Einsiedeln-Köln 1974); A.-M. MUSSCHOOT: Le *New Criticism*, dans M. DELCROIX et F. HALLYN (éd): *Méthodes du texte. Introduction aux études littéraires* (Paris-Gembloux 1987) 16-18; K. FENS et H. VERDAASDONK (éd.): *Op eigen gronden* (Utrecht 1989); O. HEYNDERS: *De verbeelding van betekenis* (Leuven-Apeldoorn 1991). En ce qui concerne l'application de la méthode à la liturgie, voir STOCK: *Umgang mit theologischen Texten* 75-155; G. LUKKEN: Een dodenliturgie van Huub Oosterhuis, dans *Tijdschrift voor liturgie* 59 (1975) 310-350; A. SCHEER: Peilingen in de hedendaagse huwelijksliturgie. Een oriënterend onderzoek, dans *Tijdschrift voor liturgie* 62 (1978) 259-317; A. STOCK: *Veni Sancte Spiritus* frei übersetzt. Eine poetologische Analyse, dans H. BECKER et R. KACZYNSKI (éd.): *Liturgie und Dichtung. Ein interdisziplinäres Kompendium* II (= Pietas liturgica 2) (St. Ottilien 1983) 41-66; A. STOCK: Een Hymne, een verheven lied, dans *Werkschrift voor leerhuis en liturgie* 4 (1984) 78-83; S. BELLEMAKERS: *Lees: het zinsverband van woord en vlees. het belang van de 'close-reading' methode bij het bestuderen en beoordelen van liturgische teksten, aan de hand van een onderzoek naar de christologie in enkele tafelgebeden van Huub Oosterhuis* I-II (thèse de deuxième cycle de la Faculté de Théologie de Tilburg non éditée, Tilburg 1985); S. BELLEMAKERS: De *close-reading* methode beschreven en toegepast op de tekst 'Die naar menselijke gewoonte' van Huub Oosterhuis, dans *Jaarboek voor liturgie-onderzoek* 2 (1986) 49-85; L. VAN OORSCHOT: *... enkel de dood... De dood in de liederen van Huub Oosterhuis en het spreken over de dood door Edward Schillebeeckx* (thèse de deuxième cycle de la Faculté de Théologie de Tilburg non éditée, Tilburg 1988); L. VAN TONGEREN: Het liturgisch gezang als theologische vindplaats, dans A. BLIJLEVENS (éd.): *Liturgiewetenschap* III (Kampen 1991) 83-107.

[44] Cf. MUSSCHOOT: Le *New Criticism* 16-18.

Richards ce groupe s'est développé en Angleterre pendant les années vingt et trente. Dès lors les États-Unis ont pris l'avantage, où ce courant de pensée s'est épanoui pendant les années trente et quarante. Le mouvement s'est groupé autour de J. Ranson et son assistent A. Tate. Le groupe *New Criticism* peut être caractérisé par son retour au texte. La méthode de *close-reading* est une lecture microscopique du texte, qui est considéré comme une unité indépendante et organique, c'est-à-dire un ensemble construit de parallèles, contrastes et paradoxes. Le but de cette analyse immanente est de montrer que tout texte a son unicité propre. Le mouvement *New Criticism* exerce toujours son influence. Si l'on compare cependant la méthode de *close-reading* à celle de la sémiotique d'A. Greimas et son école de Paris, on peut constater des traits communs ainsi que des différences. La sémiotique de Greimas insiste sur l'autonomie du texte, mais en même temps elle se rend compte des structures sous-jacentes aussi. Pour cette raison sa sémiotique permet de réaliser une étude approfondie du texte. Elle explore de différentes manières les réseaux des différences, qui se trouvent sous la structure de surface, et elle a su développer une métalangue systématique pour valoriser ces réseaux des différences. Finalement la métalangue de Greimas peut-être appliquée à des objets non-liguistiques. La sémiotique de Greimas et son école de Paris sera traité dans les contributions suivantes.

12. Plaidoyer pour une approche intégrale de la liturgie comme lieu théologique
Un défi à toute la théologie

En 1975, je publiais un article consacré à la liturgie comme lieu irremplaçable de la théologie et aux méthodes d'analyse convenant à ce lieu.[1] Durant les douze années qui ont eu cours depuis lors, il a paru nombre d'études nouvelles sur les rapports entre la théologie et la liturgie.[2] Il en ressort qu'il existe un consensus au sujet de l'irremplaçabilité du *locus theologicus* liturgique. Et un nombre croissant de théologiens vont même jusqu'à prétendre qu'il faut considérer la liturgie comme étant davantage encore qu'un lieu irremplaçable pour la théologie. En effet, la liturgie chrétienne est une manière d'être de la révélation chrétienne et, à ce titre, une 'théologie primaire' qui doit donner son orientation à toute la théologie. Dans sa réflexion à propos de Dieu, la théologie devrait davantage se faire éclairer par cette théologie primaire, considérée comme un dialogue avec Dieu.

---

* *Questions liturgiques* 68 (1987) 242-255.
1 G. LUKKEN: La Liturgie comme lieu théologique irremplaçable. Méthodes d'analyse et de vérification théologiques, dans *Questions liturgiques* 56 (1985) 97-112 (= no. *11* dans ce livre; bibliographie en note 4). Pour quelque complément d'information voir S. MARSILI: Teologia liturgica, dans D. SARTORE et A. TRIACCA (éd.): *Nuovo dizionario di liturgia* (Roma 1983) 1525.
2 Contentons-nous de citer les plus importants, A. CAPRIOLI: Linee di recerca per uno statuto teologico della liturgia, dans *Communio* 41 (1978) 35-44; P. DE CLERCK: 'Lex orandi, lex credendi'. Sens original et avatars historiques d'un adage équivoque, dans *Questions liturgiques* 54 (1978) 193-212; A. TRIACCA et A. PISTOIA (éd.): *La liturgie, expression de la foi. Conférences Saint Serge, XXVe Semaine d'études liturgiques, Paris 1978* (Roma 1979); K. LEHMANN: Gottesdienst als Ausdruck des Glaubens. Plädoyer für ein neues Gespräch zwischen Liturgiewissenschaft und dogmatischen Theologie, dans *Liturgisches Jahrbuch* 30 (1980) 197-214 (Bibliographie en note 28-30); G. WAINWRIGHT: *Doxology. The praise of God in worship, doctrine and life. A systematic theology* (New York 1980); M. SODI: Liturgia. Pienezza e momento della storia della salvezza, dans *Mysterion. Miscellanea liturgica in occasione dei 70 anni dell'Abate Salvatore Marsili* (Torino 1981, Roma 1982); H. GARTNER et M. MERZ: Prolegomena für eine integrative Methode in der Liturgiewissenschaft. Zugleich ein Versuch zur Gewinnung der empirischen Dimension, dans *Archiv für Liturgiewissenschaft* 24 (1982) 165-189; A. HOUSSIAU: La redécouverte de la liturgie par la théologie sacramentaire (1950-1980), dans *La maison Dieu* no. 149 (1982) 27-55; S. MARSILI: Teologia liturgica, dans SARTORE et TRIACCA (éd.): *Nuovo dizionario di liturgia* 1508-1525; I. DALMAIS: Le Mysterion. Contribution à une théologie de la liturgie, dans *La maison Dieu* no. 158 (1984) 14-50; T. BERGER: Lex orandi – lex credendi – lex agendi. Auf dem Weg zu einer ökumenisch konsensfähigen Verhältnisbestimmung von Liturgie, Theologie und Ethik, dans *Archiv für Liturgiewissenschaft* 27 (1985) 425-432; A. KAVANAGH: *On liturgical theology* (New York 1985); T. BERGER: 'Doxology' – 'Jubilate' – 'Liturgical Theology'. Zum Verhältnis von Liturgie und Theologie. Publikationen aus dem englischsprachigen Raum, dans *Archiv für Liturgiewissenschaft* 28 (1986) 247-255.

En ce qui concerne les rapports entre liturgie et théologie, le présent article, à vrai dire, poursuit un objectif plus limité. Nous nous en tiendrons seulement à considérer la liturgie comme lieu théologique. Je commencerai par montrer que l'influence de la liturgie comme lieu théologique ne progresse que lentement et difficilement. Ensuite, je plaiderai néanmoins en faveur d'une progression plus avancée dans l'exploration de la liturgie comme lieu théologique et ceci à un double point de vue: 1. l'objectif comme tel doit être élargi de manière à ce que la source liturgico-théologique apparaisse plus intégralement; 2. on doit pouvoir en arriver à des méthodes de recherche mieux intégrées au regard de cette source théologique.

1. INFLUENCE DIFFICILE

Ceci va peut-être susciter de l'étonnement, mais la difficulté d'influence de la liturgie comme *locus theologicus* commence en toute proximité, dans la théologie sacramentelle. En 1957, le théologien néo-thomiste Ch. Journet critiquait le liturgiste J. Jungmann parce que celui-ci concluait de son analyse de la prière eucharistique romaine et d'autres liturgies, que l'assemblée réunie sur place est la première intéressée à la célébration de l'eucharistie. Il caractérisait l'argumentation de Jungmann comme purement externe et non-théologique.[3] En cette année 1957, alors que C. Vagaggini faisait encore figure de pionnier avec son étude *Il senso teologico della liturgia*, ce point de vue de Journet pouvait encore se comprendre, surtout si l'on tient compte de l'évolution des derniers siècles. On pensait pouvoir fonder l'univers sacramentel en dehors des rituels dans lesquels et par lesquels il s'accomplit. Mais cet idéalisme n'a pas encore disparu le moins du monde. Ainsi F. Durwell, très apprécié des théologiens, écrivait-il, en 1980, que dans la réflexion théologique à propos de l'eucharistie, on ne doit pas sortir de l'eucharistie elle-même. Cela reviendrait à tourner autour du mystère au lieu d'y pénétrer![4] C'est incidemment seulement que Durwell cite ensuite les sources liturgiques. A. Houssiau constate à ce propos que l'influence de la liturgie sur la théologie sacramentelle se développe plus lentement et plus difficilement que ce n'était le cas avec la théologie positive qui trouvait son inspiration dans la Bible et chez les Pères. Et cette constatation se confirme quand, par exemple, on parcourt les fascicules récemment parus du *Handbuch der Dogmengeschichte* concernant la théologie sacramentelle en général et les sacrements en particulier.[5] Les sources liturgiques y jouent, il est

---

3 HOUSSIAU: La redécouverte (1982) 31.
4 F. DURWELL: *L'Eucharistie, sacrement pascal* (Paris 1983) 9-34.
5 M. SCHMAUS e.a. (éd.): *Handbuch der Dogmengeschichte* (Freibourg 1951-).

vrai, un plus grand rôle que par le passé, mais elles se présentent encore beaucoup trop peu comme un véritable *locus theologicus*. Ne doit-on pas dire qu'il est vraiment grand temps que les manuels de science liturgique et de théologie sacramentelle s'interpénètrent? On pourrait alors parler d'un progrès réel dans le rapport entre la liturgie et la théologie sacramentelle. Le premier essai dans ce sens, se rencontre dans le manuel italien *Anàmnesis*.[6]

Si la liturgie exerce encore si peu d'influence dans la théologie sacramentelle même, on peut bien deviner que ce sera certainement le cas dans tout le reste de la théologie. En théologie systématique les études liturgico-théologiques qui justifient des sources liturgiques, ne sont pratiquement jamais citées et encore moins utilisées.[7] S. Bellemakers attire l'attention sur ce problème en menant une enquête sur la christologie dans les prières eucharistiques de H. Oosterhuis. La liturgie actuelle donne à la nouvelle christologie un fondement primaire solide. Mais précisément là où dans cette christologie on pourrait s'attendre à une allusion à la liturgie, il semble que celle-ci soit tout à fait en dehors du champ visuel des dogmaticiens.

> En ceci les théologiens sont trop souvent assimilables à ces experts en relations humaines qui écoutent bien et analysent les entretiens entre amoureux (...), mais se tiennent bien à distance des jeux concrets de l'amour.[8]

2. UNE APPROCHE PLUS INTÉGRALE

Nonobstant la lenteur et la difficulté des progrès dans les rapports entre liturgie et théologie, cet article a pour but de plaider en faveur d'une progression pénétrante dans la recherche du *locus theologicus* liturgique. Il

---

6 Ceci vaut notamment pour l'eucharistie, voir S. MARSILI e.a. (éd.): *Anàmnesis* III/2 *La liturgia, eucaristia* (Toronto 1983). Rien de tout cela n'est à trouver dans le récent manuel français, A. MARTIMORT: *L'Eglise en prière. Introduction à la liturgie* I-IV (Paris 1983-1984, édition nouvelle) et trop peu dans le manuel allemand également récent, H. MEYER e.a. (éd.): *Gottesdienst der Kirche. Handbuch der Liturgiewissenschaft* I-VIII (Regensburg 1983-). Cf. B. CARDINALI: La nuova edizione di "Eglise en prière", dans *Rivista liturgica* 73 (1986) 704-712.
7 Que l'on pense à des études comme A. COPPO: Vita cristiana e terminologia liturgica a Cartagine verso la metà dell III secolo, dans *Ephemerides liturgicae* 85 (1971) 70-86; W. DÜRIG: *Pietas liturgica. Studien zum Frömmigkeitsbegriff und zur Gottesvorstellung der abendländischen Liturgie* (Regensburg 1958); G. LUKKEN: *Original Sin in the Roman liturgy. Research into the theology of Original Sin in the Roman sacramentaria and the early baptismal liturgy* (Leiden 1973).
8 S. BELLEMAKERS: *Lees: het zinsverband van woord en vlees. Het belang van de 'close-reading' methode bij het bestuderen en beoordelen van liturgische teksten, aan de hand van een onderzoek naar de christologie in enkele tafelgebeden van Huub Oosterhuis* I (thèse de deuxième cycle de la Faculté de Théologie de Tilburg non éditée, Tilburg 1985) 271.

va falloir se résoudre à une approche plus intégrale de ce domaine de la recherche. Une telle approche plus intégrale postule avant tout un élargissement de l'objectif lui-même de telle sorte que le *locus theologicus* liturgique soit employé, moins sélectivement. Ensuite il y va également d'une méthode de recherche plus intégrale vis-à-vis de ce domaine liturgico-théologique élargi.

2.1 Elargissement de l'objectif

L'histoire est une discipline orientée vers la totalité du sens du passé. Elle dirige ses efforts vers la pénétration de cette totalité. Si l'on prend en considération une limitation plus serrée du domaine envisagé, ceci vaut tout autant pour l'histoire de la liturgie et l'étude historico-théologique des sacrements. Au fait, si l'on prend en mains les monographies qui traitent du sujet – et les manuels récents qui en traitent semblent refléter correctement l'état de la question – il apparaît que pratiquement il n'est fait usage que de sources exclusivement littéraires.[9] Il est toujours question de l'Ecriture, des Pères de l'Eglise, des théologiens, des décisions de l'autorité doctrinale, de témoignages à propos de liturgie et des *ordines* et scénarios écrits de la liturgie. Les sources non-littéraires ne remplissent qu'un rôle très marginal: que l'on pense à l'architecture (construction et orientation de l'église), aux images dans l'espace liturgique (iconographie et sculpture), à son ornementation, aux couleurs, aux ustensiles et à leur modelé, à la musique, au recours à des estampes dans les livres de piété et en toutes sortes d'occurences à caractères liturgique (première communion, ordination sacerdotale, funérailles, fêtes de dévotion) etc. Et même dans les sources liturgiques strictement littéraires (les *ordines*), on procède encore à une sélection. On laisse tomber de nombreuses références non-littéraires comme les descriptions détaillées de l'espace liturgique, les indications concernant les mouvements et les positions des acteurs dans cet espace, l'habillement, les couleurs etc. Aussi est-il significatif que dans le manuel italien, le paragraphe consacré à l'herméneutique liturgique se rapporte exclusivement aux principes d'interprétation des textes liturgiques. Tout ceci est d'autant plus remarquable que règne parmi les liturgistes la conviction que précisément la symbolique non-verbale et non-littéraire (appelée 'symbolique présentative' ou 'code restreint') est essentielle pour toute liturgie et que c'est précisément elle qui est prégnante au plus haut point. En ce qui concerne le passé il est donc question d'une observation très sélective de l'ensemble de la signification liturgique. Et ceci vaut également pour l'époque actuelle. Dans le *ordo* de la liturgie on étudie avant tout les textes liturgiques. Dans la littérature liturgique il est toujours et toujours constaté que c'est la *célébration* liturgique elle-même

---

9 Pour les manuels récents voir notes 5 et 6.

qui est la source primaire, mais il apparaît chaque fois que fait pour ainsi dire défaut, toute recherche de liturgie *in actu* comme lieu théologique.[10] Un élargissement d'objectif dans la recherche liturgique est nécessaire si on veut réellement faire droit à la liturgie et tant que site de recherche pour la théologie. A ce propos il est intéressant d'attirer l'attention sur le plaidoyer permanent de P. Post en faveur d'une étude de la 'bande visuelle' dans le contexte de la liturgie.[11] On plaide également en faveur d'un approfondissement de la recherche en fait de musique liturgique dans la science liturgique.[12] Il faut voir sans nul doute un développement favorable dans l'attention croissante envers l'histoire des mentalités (Annales) ce qui conduit à un élargissement des sources en matière de liturgie.[13] Toutefois, il se passera encore bien du temps avant que dans les manuels on puisse mettre en oeuvre l'objet intégral du *locus theologicus* liturgique.

2.2 Une méthode plus intégrale de recherche

Il ne suffit pas d'avoir en vue un objectif plus intégral. Les méthodes de recherche sur cet objectif doivent également être plus intégrales. Je ne puis mieux expliciter ma pensée que par l'exemple suivant. Voici quelque temps, un de mes étudiants dont l'étude s'attache au rituel néerlandais de la crémation, me demandait en quel endroit de son mémoire il devait porter son attention sur l'architecture et l'aménagement des crématoires. Il considérait comme une difficulté le fait que son mémoire se limitait aux *rituels* de la crémation. Il ne se pouvait donc agir que d'un appendice à son mémoire. Je lui ai répondu qu'il pouvait franchement traiter ces choses comme faisant partie du rituel. Il n'existe en effet aucun rituel que

---

10 On peut, par exemple, citer P. VAN HOOIJDONK et H. WEGMAN: *Zij breken hetzelfde brood. Een kritische wegwijzer bij de viering van de eucharistie op basis van een liturgie-historische en -sociologische analyse* (= De kerk van morgen 9) (Amersfoort 1972); A. GOVAART: *Zijn wij geworden deze wereld* (thèse de deuxième cycle non éditée, Nijmegen 1981); A. SCHEER: De beleving van liturgische riten en symbolen, dans J. VAN DER VEN (éd.): *Pastoraal tussen ideaal en werkelijkheid* (= Theologie en empirie 1) (Kampen 1985) 105-120; G. LUKKEN: *Semiotische analyse en comparatieve theologische verificatie van twee huwelijksliturgieën*, projet de recherche dans le programme "Studie, toepassing en ontwikkeling van de semiotiek van Greimas in relatie tot christelijke expressie" (Faculté Théologique, Tilburg 1984-1989).
11 Par exemple P. POST: Ruimte voor het beeld. Enige notities over de beeldband in de liturgiewetenschap, dans *Tijdschrift voor liturgie* 66 (1982) 98-110.
12 LUKKEN: La liturgie comme lieu irremplaçable 326, et IDEM: Liturgiewetenschap en 'muziek van de christelijke liturgie', dans *Tijdschrift voor liturgie* 66 (1982) 111-122 (= no. 10 dans ce livre)
13 Cf. P. POST, G. LUKKEN et H. WEGMAN: Bidprentjes als liturgische bron, dans *Jaarboek voor liturgie-onderzoek* 2 (1986) 1-31; et "Heortologische bijdragen: theologie en vroomheid in de viering van de christelijke feesten", programme de recherche à l'Université Catholique d'Utrecht.

se déroule ou se soit déroulé en dehors de dimensions spatiales concrètes. Encore ceci vaut-il pour les autres dimensions: iconographiques, musicales, ornementales, etc. Il est question d'un objet unique et intégral. Dès lors on se demande si au cours de la recherche méthodique elle-même, tous les aspects ne doivent pas être imbriqués l'un dans l'autre.

Un excellent essai dans cette direction a été opéré par la théologie dite empirique, qui porte également sur la recherche en matière de liturgie.[14] On rassemble les méthodes de la science liturgique et des sciences empiriques et on s'applique à étudier l'objet de manière plus intégrée interdisciplinairement et même intradisciplinairement (Dans ce dernier cas, c'est la même personne qui maîtrise les deux méthodes). Dans ce cas, il existe bien, à mon avis deux problèmes. a) En fin de compte les méthodes littéraires continuent à jouer un grand rôle, de sorte que l'approche des dimensions non-littéraires de l'objet se fait par des méthodes littéraires. b) Le recours simultané à des méthodes interdisciplinaires et intradisciplinaires a pour effet de rassembler des instruments très variés de diverses disciplines. Qu'on se représente dès lors à quel point il est souvent difficile de rassembler différentes directions en une seule et même discipline. A mon avis le sémiotique de l'Ecole parisienne (A. Greimas) peut venir à point. Elle dispose, en effet, d'une instrumentation homogène applicable aussi bien aux dimensions verbales et littéraires de la liturgie qu'aux autres dimensions. Dès lors il ne me paraît pas impossible qu'à la longue cette approche sémiotique plus intégrale puisse éclairer certaines questions de méthode dans la théologie empirique et qu'elle puisse à tout le moins prendre place dans cette théologie. Ceci touche en effet l'analyse du contenu du rituel.[15]

Dans ce qui suit je vais d'abord introduire très sommairement au métalangage sémiotique de l'Ecole de Paris. J'indiquerai ensuite, très sommairement aussi, comment in concreto ce métalangage permet une recherche plus intégrale en matière de liturgie.

2.2.1. *Le métalangage de l'Ecole de Paris*

La sémiotique est la science des signes. Mais il ne s'agit pas seulement des signes verbaux mais également des nombreux signes qui existent dans notre monde en dehors de tout verbalisme. On trouve dans la sémiotique deux directions différentes: d'une part la sémiotique de Peirce, du nom de Charles Sanders Peirce (1839-1914) et d'autre part la sémiotique de Ferdinand de Saussure (1857-1913) et qui porte son nom. A. Greimas (1917-1992) et l'école de Paris qui s'est formée autour de lui sont dans la tradition de la sémiotique saussurienne. Greimas a développé un métalangage

---

14 SCHEER: De beleving.
15 Cf. SCHEER: De beleving 113-114.

sémiotique, c'est-à-dire un langage au delà du langage. Ce métalangage n'est pas lié exclusivement à des expressions linguistiques, mais s'applique également à des expressions non-linguistiques. La vertu de ce métalangage consiste dans le fait qu'il est applicable à tous les énoncés, en sorte que par son truchement l'étude d'objets divers est mieux interchangeable et qu'il est ainsi fait droit au caractère propre des énoncés non-linguistiques qui, à vrai dire, sont généralement étudiés par des méthodes littéraires. Qu'on pense à l'architecture, à la peinture, au film, aux bandes dessinées, au théâtre, à la musique, aux rituels, etc. En tant que tel ce métalangage est également applicable à la liturgie qui est à la fois un objet linguistique et très largement non-linguistique. Ce metalangage peut fort bien être mis en oeuvre en vue de l'analyse de tous ces objets. On doit toutefois faire observer qu'en ce qui concerne les objectifs non-linguistiques, la phase opérationelle n'en est, à bien des points de vue, qu'à ses débuts.[16]

Au cours des ans, Greimas a effectivement mis au point un instrument conceptuel qui permette d'analyser selon leur signification toutes sortes d'ensembles significatifs. Cet instrument est encore toujours en cours de developpement et sera dans l'avenir toujours mieux élaboré. Il est destiné à l'analyse des *ensembles* significatifs, ce qui veut dire, par exemple que dans l'analyse d'un discours littéraire il ne s'agit pas d'analyser des phrases séparées, mais de rechercher l'architecture significative de l'ensemble de ce discours considéré comme un tout. En outre, cet instrument est destiné analyser synchroniquement les discours. Donc il s'agit d'une approche immanente du discours. En général nous avons l'habitude d'étudier les ensembles significatifs selon des méthodes historico-littéraires. Nous nous demandons, par exemple qui est l'écrivain ou l'auteur de l'ensemble significatif et comment celui-ci a été produit, quel milieu a pu exercer sur lui une influence, etc, etc. Les méthodes appropriées qui président à l'approche de nombreuses sources liturgiques sont également très sophistiquées. Au vrai, la sémiotique de Greimas ne s'intéresse guère à l'histoire précis de l'apparition d'un ensemble significatif, mais à cet ensemble tel qu'il se trouve sous nos yeux. Le discours tel qu'il se présente est un ensemble de signification et il s'agit de dégager celle-ci du discours même. Il n'est d'ailleurs pas du tout question de dénier l'intérêt des approches historiques ni l'influence des contextes socio-culturels. Mais la sémiotique de Greimas concentre son attention sur l'ensemble significatif comme tel; l'instance qui l'a produit, de même que le contexte ne viennent qu'en second ordre, dans la mesure où l'on en retrouve des traces dans le discours même. Au surplus la diachronie peut effectivement jouer un rôle

---

16 En ce qui concerne l'instrumentarium d'A. Greimas, le mieux est de consulter A. GREIMAS et J. COURTÉS: *Sémiotique. Dictionnaire raisonné de la théorie du langage* I-II (Paris 1979 et 1986).

ici, en ce sens qu'il est question de diachronie quand on peut situer dans un système sémiotique une transformation entre deux états structurels dont l'un représente un état initial et l'autre un état final.

Un concept important dans la sémiotique de Greimas est celui de parcours génératif. Greimas essaie de mettre à nu la texture de signification qui se cache sous le discours tel que nous l'appréhendons dans l'immédiat. Le discours, tel qu'il se présente à nous, se trouve à ce niveau de perception immédiate, qu'on appelle niveau de manifestation. En ce qui concerne le réseau des rapports qui se dissimulent, en quelque sorte, sous ce niveau, Greimas distingue trois niveaux qui révèlent, chacun à sa manière, la signification ainsi le canevas significatif gagne en abstraction à mesure que le niveau est plus profond. Autrement dit: le parcours génératif d'un discours donné suit un certain trajet qui va du plus abstrait au plus concret. Si nous allons du plus concret au plus abstrait les trois niveaux sont les suivants: le niveau des structures discursives, le niveau de surface et le niveau profond, avec à chacun de ces niveaux deux composantes qui s'imbriquent: la composante syntactique et la composante sémantique. Cela nous entraînerait trop loin d'entrer dans le détail de ces divers niveaux. Il est néanmoins important de noter que selon Greimas, les réseaux significatifs des trois niveaux dont nous venons de parler peuvent trouver forme concrètement en divers langages appelés langages de manifestation, soit aussi bien des langues littéraires-verbales que non-verbales, comme l'architecture, la peinture, la danse, le théâtre, l'opéra, le film, etc.

2.2.2. La liturgie en tant qu'objet de plusieurs langages de manifestation: concrétisation

Dans la suite notre attention va se concentrer sur deux sujets liturgiques concrets, soit le Rituel du mariage du *Rituale Romanum* (1614) et le nouveau rituel romain du mariage de Vatican II.[17] Ces rituels présentent tous deux un objet syncrétique ce qui veut dire qu'ils contiennent divers langages de manifestation. Il n'est pas possible de traiter tous. Je m'en tiendrai à trois langages de manifestation soit l'architectonique, la proxémique et la verbale littéraire. Etant donné la portée limitée de cet article l'analyse méthodique ne peut être que très sommaire. En vue de sa lisibilité, il est surtout nécessaire d'éviter les terminologies trop techniques. Ce qui m'importe, c'est de monter qu'il s'agit ici d'une approche méthodique réellement intégrale.

a. Le Langage de manifestation architectonique
Pour avoir une vue exacte sur les deux rituels on devrait pouvoir disposer d'une analyse sémiotique de l'architecture dans laquelle il sont ou ont été

---

17 *Ordo Celebrandi Matrimonium* editio typica (Città del Vaticano 1969).

exécutés. Les espaces peuvent être très variables. Mais en première instance on devrait pouvoir partir des espaces tels qu'on les rencontre aux périodes durant lesquelles on doit situer ces rituels.

Or donc la sémiotique de l'architecture s'occupe de l'espace bâti: un espace conçu par la voie de toutes sortes de représentations telles que dessins, maquettes, descriptions de matériaux, décomptes, etc. Le bâtiment est la résultante de toute une chaîne d'activités qui va de conception, de la programmation des activités jusqu'à sa construction et, aussi, sa mise en exploitation. Cette dernière, y compris les qualifications ultérieures ajoutées par l'utilisateur (mobilier, aménagement, décoration, etc.) appartient également à la sémiotique de l'architecture.

Ainsi donc, dans l'espace ecclésial où doit se situer le rituel romain du mariage, il est question, au niveau profond, d'un rapport très particulier entre les différents espaces.[18] Tout d'abord doit-on attirer l'attention sur la démarcation très nette entre le bâtiment comme tel et l'espace qui l'environne. Qui veut pénétrer dans le bâtiment doit de toute évidence franchir un seuil; ainsi le bâtiment s'oppose-t-il comme lieu sacré à l'espace extérieur. Une fois qu'on pénètre à l'intérieur, l'espace apparaît topologiquement comme strictement articulé. Il y est question d'un espace moins sacral, soit le vaisseau et d'un espace extrêmement sacré: le choeur sacerdotal. Celui-ci n'est accessible qu'au clergé. Pour le commun des fidèles, il est tabou. A l'intérieur de ce choeur sacerdotal, il y a aussi un espace, le plus élevé et le plus sacré, où se trouve l'autel. Ces deux espaces que sont la nef et le choeur se situent, au point de vue de la communauté, dans le rapport de l'accessible versus l'interdit, de l'horizontal versus le vertical. A un niveau plus concret (soit celui de surface) cette topologie profonde se traduit en formes géométriques où la préférence va, semble-t-il, aux formes en longueur. Et en passant par ce niveau de surface se produit finalement la signification du bâtiment concret.

Tout autre est la topologie profonde du bâtiment dans lequel se doit situer le nouveau rite romain du mariage. La démarcation entre l'espace intérieur et extérieur est beaucoup moins accentuée. On ne peut plus tellement parler d'opposition entre profane et sacré. La fonction de l'immeuble apparaît davantage comme devant servir le lieu de réunion de la communauté. L'opposition se marque plutôt entre privé et public, entre espace naturel et lieu réservé au jeu liturgique. Le rapport entre la nef et le choeur sacerdotal est également différent. Il n'est plus question d'une démarcation nette ou de l'opposition de haut versus bas. L'opposition topologique est plutôt celle de la périphérie versus le centre. Topologiquement parlant il est plutôt question de cercles concentriques où les

---

18 Cf. A. LÉVY: *Sémiotique de l'espace: architecture classique sacrale* (Thèse de troisième cycle EHSS, Paris 1979); IDEM: Les différents niveaux de signification dans la construction de l'espace architectural, dans *Degrés* 11 (1983) no. 35-36, 1-18.

cercles plus larges participent d'une manière ou d'une autre au cercle central. Cette topologie peut aussi se concrétiser géométriquement de manières diverses (éventuellement aussi dans des formes en longueur) et se traduire ainsi via le niveau de surface, en langage architectonique concret.

b. Le langage de manifestation proxémique
La proxémique est une partie de la sémiotique qui vise à analyser les dispositions des sujets et des objets dans l'espace et, plus particulièrement, l'usage que les sujets font de l'espace aux fins de signification.

Ainsi donc, si on observe la manière dont les sujets utilisent l'espace décrit, il apparaît que dans chacun des rituels le passage de l'extérieur vers l'intérieur s'effectue différemment. Dans l'espace où il convient de placer le *Rituale Romanum* lors du passage de l'extérieur à l'intérieur, il est question de se détacher de l'espace extérieur. Le sujet doit traverser plusieurs espaces pour arriver à la nef de l'église. En franchissant le seuil il marque à l'évidence son passage d'un monde à un autre monde (ce qui s'exprime également en langage de manifestation de la gestique: il y a, par exemple, un rite de purification: le signe de croix avec de l'eau bénite; à comparer avec le fait de se déchausser au seuil d'une mosquée, de se couvrir la tête au seuil de la synagogue, etc.). A propos de la position des sujets dans l'espace intérieur le *Rituale Romanum* du mariage fournit une indication intéressante. Durant la conclusion du mariage, le couple se trouve "in aliquanta ab altari distantia seu ante presbyterium", ce qui veut dire une certaine distance à partir de l'autel et à partir de la nef, juste devant la limite du choeur. Cette proxémique correspond exactement à la topologie de l'espace. Le couple demeure, tout comme l'assemblée des fidèles, en dehors du choeur mais se tient le plus près possible de cet espace sacral durant l'accomplissement du sacrement de mariage. L'espace sacral est ici également défini à partir du point central le plus sacré: l'autel.

Dans le rituel du mariage d'après Vatican II on trouve une autre proxémique. En ce qui concerne le passage de l'extérieur à l'intérieur: le couple est accueilli au seuil de l'église par le ministre en habit liturgique officiel (no. 33). J'ai montré dans une analyse précédente que s'accomplit ici le passage de l'informel et privé à l'officiel et public et donc d'un pouvoir-faire informel et privé à un pouvoir-faire officiel et public.[19] Ensuite, le parcours spatial est accompli depuis la porte de l'église vers l'autel en une procession solennelle bien ordonnée à laquelle prennent part les assistants, le prêtre, le couple lui-même, et, éventuellement, les parents, témoins et autres. De manière non-verbale, le couple est alors conduit vers le lieu central du faire officiel et ministériel et installé comme prota-

---

19 G. LUKKEN: Het binnengaan in de kerk in de Romeinse huwelijksliturgie: een semiotische analyse, dans *Jaarboek voor liturgie-onderzoek* 1 (1985) 69-89.

goniste de la célébration. Il est installé dans la position du pouvoir-faire ministériel. Théologiquement parlant, il n'est donc pas sans importance qu'il soit ici question d'une entrée officielle du couple ou qu'on laisse tout simplement tomber cette entrée – une alternative considérée comme possible par le rituel même. L'assemblée se trouve dans l'espace où se célèbre le mariage, non pas séparément de l'autel mais comme une périphérie autour d'un centre. De cette manière aussi, la participation active, qui est soulignée dans le texte du rituel, est proxémiquement exprimée. Il y est, en effet, continuellement fait allusion au rôle de témoin et de vérification rempli par la communauté locale ici présente.

c. Le langage de manifestation littéraire-verbale

Il n'est pas pensable de fournir ici une analyse complète des textes dans lesquels et par lesquels l'accomplissement du mariage s'effectue dans chacun des deux rituels. Je me contenterai donc de ce qui suit. Greimas distingue, en ce qui concerne la narrativité dans les discours (aussi bien littéraires-verbaux que d'autre sorte) quatre phases structurelles, soit: 1. la phase de la manipulation (= influence exercée) d'un destinataire par un destinateur; 2. la phase de compétence (= équipement) du destinataire par rapport à l'action à accomplir; 3. la performance (= l'action proprement dite) qui produit une transformation; et, 4. la sanction (= appréciation) de l'action accomplie et de l'état qui en résulte par le destinateur ou par son délégué.

Dans le *Rituale Romanum*, le couple accomplit, il est vrai, une performance en prononçant le 'oui' sacramentel, mais cette performance n'est que le côté extérieur, formel et juridique, de la conclusion du mariage. Elle est plutôt une condition en vertu de laquelle le couple est équipé (compétence) pour la performance proprement dite qui concerne le côté interne, définitif et existentiel du sacrement en dont le prêtre lui-même est le sujet opérateur. Il accomplit, en effet, la performance proprement dite en tant que sujet instrumental de l'instance divine en disant: "Ego conjungo vos in matrimonium. In nomine Patris et Filii et Spiritus Sancti. Amen". En ce qui concerne le côté interne du sacrement, c'est donc, dans le *Rituale Romanum*, le prêtre qui administre le sacrement et les époux ne font que le recevoir. Ce cours des choses répond exactement aux dimensions architectoniques et proxémiques du rituel. Le prêtre se trouve dans l'espace sacral d'où se fait la véritable prise de contact avec le sacré; et le couple se trouve juste devant cet espace pour recevoir le sacrement. Le caractère exclusif de l'espace sacré demeure intact tandis que les fiancés s'en rapprochent au plus près.

Dans le rituel de Vatican II, il apparaît que les fiancés assurent eux-mêmes la performance de la conclusion du mariage. Ils échangent entre eux le 'oui' sacramentel. Le rôle du prêtre se limite à être un destinateur de l'événement et ceci également au nom de la communauté. Il suscite la performance en exerçant son influence (manipulation) et la vérifie (= sanction), au nom de la communauté également, quand elle est accomplie. Et, au moment même où les fiancés accomplissent la performance, il s'agit d'une performance divine. Le couple est aussi uni par Dieu lui-même, par le Christ, par la Trinité. Dans ce rituel ce sont donc les fiancés eux-mêmes qui sont les ministres du sacrement. Ici également le cours des choses correspond exactement aux dimensions architectoniques et proxémiques du rituel. Le couple est conduit à l'autel et ainsi il est équipé (compétence) d'un pouvoir-faire ministériel ordonné de telle sorte qu'il soit réellement sujet opérateur en rapport avec la performance matrimoniale proprement dite.

C'est ainsi que dans chacun des deux rituels trois langages de manifestation agissent entre eux et se renforcent l'un l'autre. Il apparaît possible, avec une instrumentation homogène de rassembler dans un même champ visuel et de manière intégrante, plusieurs langages de manifestation du rituel. Ainsi apparaît-il dans notre analyse que les trois langages de manifestation se renforcent mutuellement et en outre peut-on, une fois de plus, constater la réalité de l'influence de la symbolique non-verbale. Pour le lecteur il sera toutefois évident que le renforcement réciproque ne se vérifie pas toujours. Ainsi, par exemple, peut-on se demander ce qui se produirait si on devait appliquer le *Rituale Romanum* dans une église bâtie et ordonnancée après Vatican II. Mais même alors reste valable l'analyse, d'une manière homogène et intégrée, de divers langages de manifestation dans leurs rapports réciproques, par le truchement du métalangage sémiotique. Des questions analogues à celles qui concernent la liturgie se posent en science du théâtre quand on joue un drame de Shakespeare sur une scène moderne.

3. DÉFI POUR TOUTE LA THÉOLOGIE

L'approche intégrale du *locus theologicus* liturgique peut être exemplative en ce qu'elle nous montre ce qui est possible au regard des *loci theologici* de la théologie en général. En pratique, ceux-ci se limitent de manière quasi exclusive aux sources littéraires et délaissent la plupart des sources non-littéraires.[20] En ce qui concerne le passé, H. Mertens cite expressément l'enseignement par l'image aux fidèles qui ne savaient ni lire, ni écrire. La foi *ex auditu* était également une foi *ex visu* par les mosaïques, les fresques, les peintures, les sculptures, les tapisseries, les vitraux, les

---

20 Cf. les divers programmes d'enseignement et de recherche des facultés et hautes écoles de théologie.

céramiques.[21] Et il y a beaucoup plus encore... Et que penser de l'engouement actuel pour le visuel? En général, en ce qui concerne le passé et le présent, la théologie ne se montre-t-elle pas trop sélective et ainsi n'y a-t-il pas énormément de significations chrétiennes qui restent cachées? Une mise en oeuvre plus intégrale du *locus theologicus* liturgique peut être un défi pour l'ensemble de la théologie, bien que, personnellement, je sois persuadé que l'influence de la liturgie sur la théologie également ne se développera que lentement et difficultueusement.

---

21 H. MERTENS: 'In illo tempore'. Verhalend verkondigen en belijden, dans D. DE GEEST et J. BULCKENS: *De verborgen rijkdom van bijbelverhalen. Theorie en praktijk van de structurele bijbellezing* (Leuven 1986) 178-179, 187.

13. Semiotics of the Ritual
Signification in Rituals as a Specific Mediation of Meaning

In *De onvervangbare weg van de liturgie* and *Geen leven zonder rituelen* the central question was the meaning of ritual.[1] In these two works the approach to liturgy was an anthropological one. The new and quite recent discipline of semiotics as the science of signs and systems of signs was not considered. Nevertheless it is exactly along this road, that a new approach of the question is possible. Since 1976 I have pursued this discipline, and especially the semiotics of A. Greimas and his Paris school. This was detailed research of many different objects and it remained rather inaccessible because of its complexity. It was then not yet possible to go into the question of the meaning of ritual from semiotics in a somewhat synthetic way. In this article I would like to try this, as intelligibly as is possible. I base it mainly on semiotic analyses of details of the ritual as this has been given shape in the christian liturgy.

According to Greimas 'meaning' (*sens*) is only attainable through the discourses which people create. These discourses mediate 'meaning' through the process of signification which is behind it. Therefore the question of the meaning of the ritual is translated in this article into the semiotic question to the process of signification of the ritual. How do rituals give meaning? Is it possible to describe the characteristics of their system of signification? What do the threads of the ritual web look like? In this the question to what is specific for the ritual as such is central. In theory it should be possible to tackle from semiotics the question to the fundamental shifts which have taken place through the ages regarding ritual in our culture.[2] An answer to this question, however, will not be possible until we have much more semiotic analyses of rituals than are available at the moment. Although I will draw attention to developments occasionally in this article, it is limited in scope to the fundamental question into the specific creation of sense in and through ritual as such.

---

* Semiotiek van het ritueel. De betekenisvormgeving in rituelen als een eigen bemiddeling van zin, in B. VEDDER a.o. (ed.): *Zin tussen vraag en aanbod* (= TFT-Studies 18) 142-156. Translated by M. Schneiders, M.Div.

1 G. LUKKEN: *De onvervangbare weg van de liturgie* (Hilversum 1984²); IDEM: *Geen leven zonder rituelen. Antropologische beschouwingen met het oog op de christelijke liturgie* (Hilversum 1988³).

2 G. LUKKEN: Les transformations du rôle liturgique du peuple. La contribution de la sémiotique à l'histoire de la liturgie, in C. CASPERS and M. SCHNEIDERS (ed.): *Omnes circumadstantes. Contributions towards a history of the role of the people in the liturgy* (Kampen 1990) 15-30.

1. PERCEPTION AS A STARTING POINT

Greimas himself mentioned that he was inspired by the phenomenology of perception. His reading of the French philosopher Merleau-Ponty and the German phenomenologist Husserl were of great importance for the way in which he related perception and signification with each other.[3] The first step towards a semiotics of ritual is therefore its perception (*aisthèsis*). This perception is closely related with our corporality and its manifold sensority. He who participates in the christian liturgy, perceives a directed totality which is rather complex. Many 'languages' act upon our senses at one and the same time: the architecture of the church building with its images, windows, incidence of light, furnishing, the attire of the different liturgical roles, the sound of the word, spoken or sung, and of the music, the innumerable movements, the liturgical utensils and elements, the colours, the scents (of incense, ointment), etcetera. It is not a singular perception of a text in a book, but perception of all the senses together: a synaesthesia (*sun-aisthèsis*) which, so it seems, is essential for the christian liturgy and for the liturgical religious experience.

This liturgical perception then we experience as being meaningful, because we perceive manifold differences, or at least shadows of differences. The colours 'say' something to us, because we recognize them in their mutual differences. Without the perception of these differences there would be one obscure mass. The same is true for sounds, shapes, etcetera. We therefore only perceive meaning by discovering differences gradually. In his recent works Greimas returned to this starting point and he elaborated it further.[4] He mentioned there that the problem of the elementary structure of signification was the one over which he had to rack his brains the most.[5] Regarding the discovering of the elementary structures of meaning he uses the image of a child which begins to perceive shadows of differences and similarities in the variegated world and thus comes to the conclusion that the one is not the same as the other: e.g. 'black' is not the same as 'non-black'. This is the beginning of the coming into being of the so-called semiotic square, which shapes the elementary structure of meaning. Greimas mentions explicitly that he does not remain stuck at the mere observation that the one is not the same as the other (as does in his opinion J. Derrida with his ideas about the deconstruction of meaning).[6] On the con-

---

3 H. PARRET: Inleiding, in W. VAN BELLE a.o. (ed.): *Algirdas Julien Greimas. De betekenis als verhaal. Semiotische opstellen* (= Semiotisch perspectief 1) (Amsterdam 1991) 11.
4 A. GREIMAS: *De l'imperfection* (Périgueux 1987); A. GREIMAS and J. FONTANILLE: *Des états de choses aux états d'âmes. Essais de sémiotique des passions* (Paris 1991).
5 M. ARRIVÉ and J. COQUET: *Sémiotique en jeu. A partir et autour de l'oeuvre d'A.J. Greimas* (Paris-Amsterdam-Phildelphia 1987) 312.
6 ARRIVÉ and COQUET: *Sémiotique en jeu* 312. See also R. SCHLEIFER: *A.J. Greimas and the nature of meaning. Linguistics, semiotics and discourse theory* (London-Sidney 1987).

trary, essential for the elementary structure of meaning is the fact that the negative term is a turning point to a positive contrary term: from 'non-black' one comes to the conclusion that one has to do with the colour 'white'. In a semiotic square:

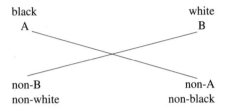

Essential therefore is that one does not remain stuck to the absence ('non-black'), but that an absence calls a presence ('white') into being. "I am not a philosopher, but it is this type of aporias which I, as a semiotician [for whom 'signification' is therefore the central issue (G.L.)], had to solve and which I had to face in my way".[7] In this most elementary system of differences (A – non-A – B – non-B – A and the motion between these poles) Greimas classifies the fundamental axiologies which lie behind human objects on the deep level. And on the basis of this elementary system of signification an extensive system of differences is established at the higher levels: at the so-called surface level we find the elementary narrative structures and at the so-called level of discoursive structure this narrative web is further enhanced with time, places, actors, themes and references to the natural world. Thus from the depth, through the surface level and the discoursive level meaning is formed at the so-called level of manifestation, i.e. the level which we perceive immediately. In a diagram:

level of manifestation: the text as a whole, or the ritual
discoursive level
surface level
deep level

If one wants to have any 'understanding' of the meaning as it gets shape in rituals, one should not come to a standstill at the first perception. One has to map its systems of signification.

---

7 ARRIVÉ and COQUET: *Sémiotique en jeu* 314.

2. THE FUNDAMENTAL NARRATIVE SCHEME OF THE RITUAL

Rituals have a development in which one usually is able to recognize the elementary narrative scheme which Greimas has brought to light especially for textual discourses. In this it not only concerns stories, but also many other textual discourses, such as scientific or legal treatises. It is important to sketch briefly the narrative scheme. As the length of this article has a limit, I will present this scheme by illustrating it at the same time with a ritual. Here and elsewhere in this article I will refer especially to the post-Vatican II Roman marriage ritual as it was published in Dutch.[8] The first phase of the narrative scheme is the manipulation by a destinator of a destinatee with an act which has to be performed in view. The marriage ritual begins which such a manipulation by the priest as destinator regarding the bridal couple as destinatee. In an introductory speech he invites bride and groom to marry and he prepares a second elementary phase, viz. that of competence. The competence may consist of a wanting, a knowing how, a having to and a being able to. In the marriage ceremony we find this phase of competence in the three questions asked to the couple regarding their freedom, their faithfulness and their willingness to accept children and raise them in the faith. Thus the couple is made competent for the performance of the ceremony: the giving of the vows (the 'I want to'). In this act the bridal couple is joined with the so-called object of value, in this case the matrimonial union. Finally in a fourth phase a sanction upon the performance is provided by the priest as destinator: also on behalf of the community present, which is in fact co-destinator, he evaluates the performance positively: 'From now on the community of the Church will see you as married people...' In human discourses we do not always find a 'neat' succession of the four phases of the narrative scheme as in the ritual which we have seen, neither are all four phases always expressed. While in the prayer of supplication the phase of manipulation has a dominant role (compare the marriage blessing, which follows upon the contracting of the marriage), in a prayer of praise the phase of sanction is emphasized (we praise and give thanks to God) and in the sacraments the act to be performed receives the main accent. However, if the other phases may not be present explicitly, they

---

8 NATIONALE RAAD VOOR LITURGIE: *Het huwelijk* (= Liturgie van de sacramenten en andere kerkelijke vieringen 7) (Hilversum 1977). See for analyses G. LUKKEN: Het binnengaan in de kerk in de Romeinse huwelijksliturgie. Een semiotische analyse, in *Jaarboek voor liturgie-onderzoek* 1 (1985) 69-89; IDEM: De nieuwe Romeinse huwelijksliturgie, in SEMANET (G. LUKKEN (ed.)): *Semiotiek en christelijke uitingsvormen. De semiotiek van A.J. Greimas en de Parijse school toegepast op Bijbel en liturgie* (Hilversum 1987) 155-208; IDEM: De plaats van de vrouw in het huwelijksritueel van het Rituale Romanum en van Vaticanum II. Van ondergeschiktheid van de vrouw naar een zekere evenwaardigheid van man en vrouw, in *Jaarboek voor liturgie-onderzoek* 4 (1988) 67-89 (= no. 16 in this book).

are always logically implied. Thus the prayer of supplication presupposes that God is competent to perform the act asked for, and the prayer is directed at the execution of what is being asked and often a thanksgiving for the granting of what is prayed for is pronounced beforehand. The web of ritual acting is thus characterized by different distinguishable phases. In this context we may mention that the christian ritual is rather often described as *actio sacra*. With this people indicate that it is an 'acting'. Through semiotics a more specific characterization is possible. It can indicate what kind of acting is involved and which phase of the narrative scheme is predominant in the different rituals.

The narrative scheme is, so to speak, a diagram in which the elementary course within the discourse comes to light in its successive stages. This 'skeleton' is always completed further with specific values. Now, in the analysis of the marriage ritual mentioned before, it emerges that in the joining with the marriage the transition is performed from the values /informal/, /private/, /initial/, /provisional/, /open/, /inclusive/, /fusion without differentiation/ to the values /official/, /public/, /complete/, /permanent/, /enduring/, /closed/, /exclusive/ and /unity of two without separation/.[9] These values may be represented at the deep level in an elementary square as follows:

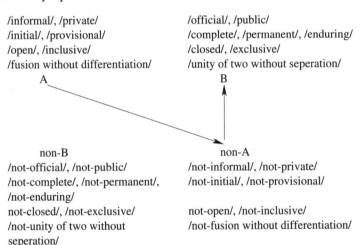

/informal/, /private/ /initial/, /provisional/ /open/, /inclusive/ /fusion without differentiation/
A

/official/, /public/ /complete/, /permanent/, /enduring/ /closed/, /exclusive/ /unity of two without seperation/
B

non-B
/not-official/, /not-public/
/not-complete/, /not-permanent/, /not-enduring/
not-closed/, /not-exclusive/
/not-unity of two without seperation/

non-A
/not-informal/, /not-private/
/not-initial/, /not-provisional/

not-open/, /not-inclusive/
/not-fusion without differentiation/

In the square it becomes clear what the system of fundamental values looks like and how the fundamental movements in the marriage ritual under consideration develop: from A via non-A to B. In the 'story' of the ritual event as it is started by the destinator, a certain fundamental pattern of values plays an important role. The destinator tries in his mani-

---

9 For the analysis see LUKKEN: *De nieuwe Romeinse huwelijksliturgie*.

pulation to bring round (to persuade, to tempt, to force, etcetera: there are many possibilities) the destinatee to acceptance of this pattern of values. And in the sanction the main issue is whether the pattern of values has been realized by the subject of doing: 'From now on the community of the Church will see you as married people... What God has united, let no man separate.'

In rituals then one recognizes the narrative scheme. But the narrative scheme of the ritual goes further. It is also valid for the – if I may call it that – broader horizontal line of the ritual: for what precedes the ritual and with which the ritual is united inseparably, as the institution narrative, the scenario and the script. It is important to look into these elements and to return then to the system of the ritual *in actu* as a complex discourse with many 'languages'.

3. INSTITUTION NARRATIVES

When analyzing christian rituals one often comes upon institution narratives. These can occur at many different places in the ritual: in the readings from Scripture in the liturgy of the Word, in the sermon, in the prayers, in the central act. The last mentioned is the case when in the middle of the Eucharistic prayer the institution narrative is recited: 'On the night he was betrayed, he took bread...', with the related 'do this in memory of me'. But elsewhere as well an institution narrative can play a large part. Thus in the rite of the blessing of the baptismal water after Vatican II reference is made to the command of Jesus to baptize. And as regards our ritual of marriage: in the nuptial blessing it is remembered, how God created human beings as man and wife and how he united them: on this basis God is asked to bless this marriage. And among the readings we find the Old Testament texts about the institution of marriage 'in the beginning' and the institution narratives regarding marriage from the New Testament. It is here that we again come upon the elementary narrative scheme. In fact it is about the first phase of the narrative scheme: the institution narratives constitute the phase of manipulation of the ritual. The main actors who play a role in these narratives, have *vis-à-vis* the actors of the ritual the role of destinators, who also give competence to these actors for its performance. These destinators also determine the pattern of values of the act which the actors of the ritual have to perform. The whole set of values that is involved in the ritual, is traced back to its original divine destinator through the institution narrative. We could say that the institution narratives constitute the fundamental framework of values of the ritual. References are often made to the institution narratives in the more reflexive introductions to the ritual in the service books. And they have a fixed position in the theological treatises of sacramental theology. In all this the issue is to keep the link between origin and ritual. Does the christian ritual comply with the original pattern of values or does it deviate from it? Secondary deviations of the pattern of values appear to be possible here, but fundamental deviations are judged negatively. Semiotic analysis of rituals does probably reveal, that fundamental deviations do always involve a disturbance in the pattern of relation of the values on the deep level. In this context semiotics may have an important part to play in sacramental theology. The question to the part of the divine destinator (God, Christ), the apostolic Church and the post-apostolic Church in the determination of the 'direction of meaning' of the sacraments[10] may undoubtedly be clarified in a new way with the use of semiotics.

4. SCENARIO AND SCRIPT

As in theatre we can distinguish scenario and script in the christian liturgy. With scenario we may indicate the liturgical service book as it is officially published. The script is the same textual corpus as it is edited and amplified with details in view of the celebration of the liturgy by the ceremoniarius or the liturgical committee. The unedited scenario functions from a narrative point of view for the detailed script as destinator and as the agency which provides competence. And scenario and script together are the destinators and agencies which provide competence to the actual performing of the liturgy (the liturgy *in actu*). Often the scenario is preceded by an introduction, in which a link is made between the ritual which is described and the institution narrative of this ritual. Earlier ritual shapes of the ritual through the ages are often also mentioned here. These may be very multiform as is e.g. the case with the christian marriage rituals in the West, which preceded the post-Vatican marriage ritual. The comparative study of this in liturgical studies (*liturgie comparée*) is of importance here to determine the extent to which variants in the pattern of values and in its expression occur. Thus one tries to determine to what extent the rituals of the past are normative narratively speaking as destinators for the service book of today and for adaptations of the ritual to a new culture. In this way it becomes clear that between the institution narrative and the liturgy *in actu* there are many intermediate destinators, who act as the same number of agencies providing competence, which regard the knowing how, the being able to and also the having to of the ritual performance. Here one encounters the repetitive character of the ritual, which does not preclude creativity at all, but does restrict it.

10 E. SCHILLEBEECKX: *Christ, the sacrament of encounter with God* (London-New York 1963) 142-155.

The scenario and the script are text-books in the literal sense of the word. In these text-books one may semiotically speaking distinguish two types of texts. One finds the language of the rubrics in them: the indications as to how the ritual has to be performed. This language is close to scientific language, which is cognitive and intended at a making known, and through this making known to an acting. It is much more impersonal and as clear and unambiguous as is possible. Next to this one finds in the scenario the liturgical texts themselves, which have to be pronounced. Some of these are rubrical in nature, as e.g. 'Let us pray', 'Let us stand up', 'Let us kneel down'. Most of them are, however, more literary or poetical texts, in a language which liturgists quite often call the 'second language' in opposition with the unequivocal scientific language, which is described as 'first language'. Semiotically speaking we are dealing here with texts which on the level of content contain a far greater wealth of meaning. Often at the actual level of discoursive structures there is a network of different thematic lines (so-called thematic isotopies), which means that the perspective can move from one line to another and vice versa. And emotions (of joy, sadness, awe, honour, modesty, etcetera) play a larger role in these texts as well. To this must be added that the system of the texts as regards content is much supported and motivated by the form of the expression. Because of this these texts not only have a cognitive dimension, they are also pathematic in character: intended at the generation of emotions which are linked with corporality and the senses. Moreover, one often finds in the scenario texts which are combined with music, which usually strengthens their pathematic character.

I just mentioned the operation of the expression form. In this context it is necessary to go in more detail into the Greimassian view of the sign, as it is not familiar for most of us. Until now we were discussing the content form of the signification, which creates meaning. We have to realize that we were talking all the time about one plane of the sign, i.e. the signified. Semiotics does distinguish in the sign two planes: the signifier (the expression) and the signified. Just as with the signified we are concerned with the discovery of the content form, in the same way with the signifier we are concerned with the expression form Thus:

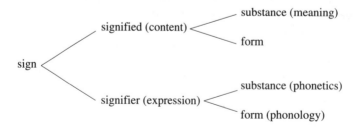

To determine the signification in an object it is of great importance to understand the relation between the form of expression and the form of content. This relation is most limited in prose texts. In these it is more or less arbitrary. In a theological paper the same contents may be articulated in different ways without it affecting these contents. It does not make much difference whether I say that according to Scripture God has a better eye for the poor than for the rich, or that God discriminates against the rich for the poor. In the following text from a song by W. Barnard[11] the same is said, but in a way which makes the form of the expression far less arbitrary and therefore much more difficult to replace.

De Heer vervult met goed The Lord replenishes with good(s)
uit 's hemels overvloed from heaven's abundance
der hongerigen monden. the mouths of the hungry.
Hij ziet geen rijken aan, He does not regard the rich,
maar heeft met al hun waan but them with all their delusion
hen ledig weggezonden. he has sent away empty-handed.

In one way or another the expression form touches here upon the content form. We may e.g. note that we are dealing here with two sets of three lines with the same rhyme scheme. And we may ask: does the order of the two equal parts of the stanza (lines 1-3 and 4-6) as the first and last part respectively interfere with the signification on the content plane as the relation between Gods preference for the poor and his scorn for the arrogant rich? We cannot in any way shift the order and put lines 4-6 in front and let them be followed by lines 1-3. It seems that in one way or another there is a relation between patterns of relation on the expression plane and patterns of relation on the content plane. Such a relation is technically called a semi-symbolic system.

Beside the linguistic form of the expression another form of the expression may interfere in the signification in a scenario and script. Every text is also a visual entity. It has its own graphic design, its own lay-out. Texts are printed bold or thin, in italics or roman, in small or large type, in red or black, with consecutive lines or arranged exactly, with line spacing, centred, etcetera. This visual form of expression may strengthen and support the textual forms of meaning, and thus make them more persuasive, but they may also change the contents and disturb it. Thus in the post-Vatican II service books the relation red-black points to the relation of contents: rubrics (i.e. indications for acting) – text. And it is possible that one emphasizes the import of a biblical text *vis-à-vis* the other texts by printing it in italics, while the other texts are in roman type. For the signification on the content plane it is therefore not at all the same, whether a

---

11 *Liedboek voor de Kerken* ('s-Gravenhage-Leeuwarden 1973) 101.

prayer is printed on a narrowly folded sheet of the A4 format with all the lines set consecutively, or that a lay-out is provided which correlates with the content form of the prayer. An incorrect arrangement of the lines may change or obscure the contents.

A special place in the scenario is occupied by the texts which are set to music. It is the strength of the Greimassian metalanguage that it with one and the same set of instruments can analyze both text and music as regards expression form and content form. In this way it is possible in a refined way to study the signification of text and music in their mutual interaction in the various genres of liturgical songs as one web. This is something new, because until now the analysis of text and music were done according to different methods and it was therefore very difficult to tune these analyses to each other.

Finally we may point to the fact that the scenario and the script, especially in the so-called rubrics, contain many destinators which give indications for the furnishing of the space, its use and the acts which have to be performed. As these indications usually are brief, and as the performances give a better view, it is better to describe the indications when we discuss the liturgy *in actu*.

5. THE LITURGY *IN ACTU*

A special connection between the scenario/script and the liturgy *in actu* is constituted by the destinators in the celebration of the liturgy. Usually the role of destinator is played by the president, but in more elaborate liturgical celebrations this role is often represented by the ceremoniarius and the conductor of the choir (or, as it may be, the organ player), who lead as a kind of directors the course of the celebration from the background. These destinators may or may not have the scenario or script as destinator in their hand and apply it as such. In view of the celebration these books therefore often have a fine design.

From the above it is clear that scenario and script have no purpose in themselves. They belong to the horizontal narrative structure of the ritual and function as very nearby destinators and agencies which provide competence of the liturgy *in actu*. They are printed linguistic textual entities which are intended as 'pace-setters' for the performance of the ritual. As such they are semiotically speaking a very limited and reduced object. It is therefore remarkable that liturgical scholars concentrate mainly on scenario and script and in this moreover often only on their texts, and that the far more extensive object of the liturgy *in actu* is so little studied. We may ask whether this attitude is not characteristic for our culture, which from the invention of the printing press, highlights printed texts as the proper entities of meaning. The result of this way of looking at things is that people easily see the liturgy *in actu* as a mere 'decoration' of the written scenario and script. For a long time this has been the point of view of theatrical studies. The performance (the *mise en scène*) was seen as the translation of the published text. The actual performance was in a way of secondary importance for the play. The interpretation of the printed text was put first and the performance was considered merely as the support of a linguistic discourse by a non-linguistic discourse.[12] But today's semiotics of the theatre have a different view. The performance is a completely separate and new discourse, in which many 'languages' come together. The systems of signification of this entity are much more complicated and richer than those of the printed or written object. And this complicated object is what matters ultimately. The same is true for the liturgy. A script is merely the destinator which provides competence of the liturgy *in actu*, in which there is not written but spoken language and in which the systems of signification of this spoken language are also influenced by various other languages: the language of architecture and the space, the spatial relations between different objects and actors, the movements in the space, the gestures, the music, the scents, the climatological circumstances, the materials which are used, which have everything to do with the tactile sense, etcetera. To this very day there exist cultures for which this new view of semiotics is only natural. One of my students, Jean Pierre Niati, is from Zaire. He wants to study the enculturation of certain elements of the renewed Zairean liturgy. When we suggested him to start from the new service book approved by Rome for the Zairean liturgy, he objected. The service book is no more than a tool, the Zairean rite itself is something different. Therefore we decided to take a video tape of an actual performed liturgy as the primary source for the research project. For a culture which is oriented towards oral communication this is self-evident. Emphasis in such a culture is on oral tradition and oral communication. When something of the ritual is put into writing, the manuscript will be seen as a deposit of the oral performance of the culture, much more so than vice versa.[13] In oral cultures it is rather the liturgy *in actu*, handed down by tradition, which is the destinator and the agency providing competence, more so than the written scenario! In contemporary theatre we may note attempts to return to this tradition. An example of this in my country is the *werktheater*, which is given shape in the actual performances. And we may also think of the farmers' theatre as it took shape when Ernesto Cardenal was minister for culture in Nicaragua.[14] This attitude and

12 P. PAVIS: *Problèmes de sémiologie théâtrale* (Montréal 1976).
13 P. ZUMTHOR: Le texte médiéval entre oralité et écriture, in H. PARRET and H.-G. RUPRECHT (ed.): *Exigences et perspectives de la sémiotique* II (Amsterdam 1985) 826-843.
14 J. VAN LIESHOUT and M. MERCX: *Spelenderwijs revolutie maken. Volkstheater in Nicaragua* (Nijmegen 1986).

approach seems to be of importance for a living liturgy in our part of the world. At least we might wish for an interaction between scenario and liturgy *in actu*. This a certainly another way of looking at things than that of present-day Roman authorities, who consider the printed standard edition of the Roman service books (the *editio typica*) to be the only destinator and who presume that this standard edition in its turn is translated into a vernacular version, which they must approve and which has to be followed strictly. From the notion that the liturgy *in actu* is normative it is also possible to account better for the fact that the study of old liturgical manuscripts is not the same as studying printed texts. Manuscripts stem from an oral culture, they represent texts which were first spoken and heard. With manuscripts it is not only a matter of visual reading, but just as much a matter of recognizing the sounds which are represented. For the destinators of manuscripts are not other written (and 'seen') texts, but spoken texts *in actu*. To see things in such a way may have consequences for the interpretation of the semiotic form in these texts. To put it briefly: for the interpretation of an old Roman prayer an attempt to hear it once again is relevant: the study of the form of its expression, of form, rhythm, construction, etcetera, with the interpretation in view, is not at all of minor importance.

The liturgy *in actu* is therefore an extremely complicated discourse in which many 'languages' come together. Just as with the perception of liturgy we may see a perception of various senses at the same time (*synaesthesis*), in the same way we have to realize when analyzing the signification that we are dealing with various languages at the same time, which interfere in the signification. What has been said regarding the analysis of music in the liturgy, is true in a wider sense for the complicated discourse of the liturgy. Greimassian semiotics offers the possibility to unravel this complicated discourse with its many languages with one and the same set of instruments. We have to understand this properly. Especially with a view to the development and the operationalizing of the Greimassian metalanguage a lot of research is still necessary.

It seems important to go in some detail into the importance of including speech, space and acts in the analysis of the liturgical signification.

In the liturgy *in actu* the text becomes a spoken word. This means that the intonation, the timbre of the voice, the volume of the sound, etcetera, play a part in the signification. Regarding the intonation people rightly note the difference between a protestant and a catholic service. The connection between the reading of a text at a reciting tone and at a vivid tone could point to a distinction between a more sacred and a more secular use of the text. In the liturgy of the period before Vatican II there was a refined distinction between speaking aloud, speaking half-loudly, speaking under breath and the inaudible whispering of the priest when reciting the words of the consecration. Thus there was as regards the sound a form of expression which probably corresponded to a content form of, on the one hand laical speaking addressed to the community and on the other hand exclusively priestly, sacred speaking addressed to God. Only a precise analysis within the context of the ritual itself could reveal whether or not my interpretation is correct. Anyhow, various elements in this matter deserve in a celebration a closer analysis and they are semiotically of relevance.

Then there is the language of architecture. In liturgical scholarship it is usual to discuss ecclesiastical architecture and the furnishing of the liturgical space detached from the ritual. Semiotics makes clear that the interrelation between ritual and architecture is so fundamental, that we may speak of the architectonic dimensions of the ritual.[15] In this way the meaning of the church building is strongly determined by the way in which the relation inside-outside has received shape and is it possible to consider various elements of the furnishing, such as the nave, the altar, the ambo, as destinators and competence providing agencies of the ritual. The narrative course of the ritual is strongly determined by the architecture. It is important to bring to mind in this context that the acquisition of certain powers (the competence of being able to) is linked to certain demarcated places. The altar is the place of the one who is competent to preside, the ambo is intended for the one who has the competence to read (perhaps just this one time), etcetera. In this context the entrance procession of the bridal couple, which was introduced as an option in the post-Vatican marriage ritual, is interesting. The couple is greeted at the door (on the threshold) of the church by the priest, who is dressed in his official vestments and is accompanied by his assistants. Semiotic analysis shows that here a transition is performed from informal and private to official and public acting.[16] Then a spatial trajectory is followed from the door of the church through the nave to the altar. This is done in a solemn, organized procession, in which the assistants, the priest, the bridal couple itself and sometimes also the witnesses, the parents and even others participate. The bridal couple is lead to the altar: the central place for official acts. Thus it is established as the proper subject of doing in the marriage service and is made competent to act publicly and officially. Then, during the contracting of the marriage the priest as official destinator has his place opposite the bridal couple, which as the proper subject of doing is surrounded by the witnesses, family, friends and the community as official co-destinator of the performance. Thus fundamental values which play a decisive role in the marriage ritual, are expressed clearly in a non

---

15 G. LUKKEN: Die architektonischen Dimensionen des Rituals, in *Liturgisches Jahrbuch* 39 (1989) 19-36.
16 LUKKEN: Het binnengaan in de kerk.

verbal way by the furnishing of the architectonic space, by movements and positions in space and by the connection of actors with specific places in the space.

We may also point out that in practice there are rather large differences between what I simply call modern and older churches. In older churches the threshold between inside and outside is usually considerably higher than in modern churches. One is going through different portals before one is inside. And at the same time it is true in most cases that the altar in older churches is considerably higher than the nave. This difference in architecture interferes in the signification of the aforementioned entrance ritual. In the old architecture the expression of official competence of the bridal couple comes across much more sacredly than in a modern church.

Finally I would like to mention the 'language' of gestures. Just before the exchanging of the marriage vows bride and groom give each other mutually their right hand and they hold them together during the pronunciation of the marriage vows. In this performance the transition from open, inclusive and fusion without differentiation to closed, exclusive and unity of two without separation is expressed. And after the exchange of the vows follows the performance with the rings. Mutually bride and groom put the ring to each other's finger as a enduring material sign in which the values of faithfulness and permanence lay hidden. This expresses the transition from a relation between a man and a woman which was open, inclusive, initial and temporary to one which is closed, exclusive (i.e. excluding all others), final and enduring.

6. ANALYSIS OF THE SIGNIFICATION AS A WAY TO SENSE

Greimas saw his semiotics as a project with a scientific vocation. It is directed at insight in and understanding of the process of signification in order to gain access to the sense which can only be discovered in and through this process. Therefore the production of meaning in rituals has not been considered here as a unique and individual event, but as a process which can be generalized.[17] This is in a way an impoverishment, which is inevitable in every scientific approach. The rituals themselves are richer and the primary open-minded perception may penetrate deeper into the ritual. What we intended was to give a reflexive and adequate description of the signification in rituals in order to discover in what way rituals are creators of sense. It turns out that they do this in their own typical way, which differs from that of e.g. a philosophical text, of a novel, of a poem, etcetera.[18] The distinctive features are to be found

---

17 PARRET: Inleiding 8-9.
18 The length of this contribution makes it impossible to deal with the differences between

especially in the specific formation of the narrative structures and in the syncretism of many 'languages' which come together in various ways (each time differently) in the ritual. For this reason rituals make an appeal to the integral human being and can be salutary in a holistic way. The refined semiotic description of the process of creating sense through rituals has undoubtedly a practical (and 'pastoral') importance. A better knowledge of the signification in rituals may gain us a perception on the criteria which are important for the evaluation and creation of authentic rituals.

---

the ritual and the other performing arts (theatre, ballet, opera, etcetera). Fundamental differences include: the absence of an institution narrative and the fact that in the performing arts there are actors and public, while the ritual has only participants. From a discussion with my colleague L. van Tongeren it emerged that with the performing arts we are normally dealing with a larger freedom on the part of the director and actors regarding the *mise-en-scène* than in rituals, and that the destinators of the ritual (the tradition, the ecclesiastical authorities) do usually exercize a stronger sanctioning influence on the ritual *in actu*.

14. Zur theologischen Rezeption der Semiotik von Greimas
Widerstände und Mißverständnisse

Während der vergangenen 15 Jahre hat Nico Tromp in der Exegese einen neuen Weg beschritten. 1976 gehörte er zu den Initiatoren der STREX (Strukturelle Exegese) – Gruppe, die 1978 ihren Namen in SEMANET (Semiotische Analyse durch niederländische Theologen) veränderte: eine interfakultäre Arbeitsgruppe der Katholisch – Theologischen Universität Utrecht und der Theologischen Fakultät Tilburg. Mit der Zeit fiel die Wahl auf die Semiotik von A. Greimas.

Diesen neuen Weg zu betreten, ist nicht einfach. Zunächst muß man sich in die semiotische Metasprache (eine Sprache über die Sprache) vertiefen, die ihre eigene Widerspenstigkeit hat und die einige literaturwissenschaftliche Schulung voraussetzt. Dann muß man sich eine Art des Lesens aneignen, die wirklich anders als die erlernte Art ist. Es geht um eine neue Praxis des Lesens. Sie zu lernen, verlangt Zeit und Durchhaltevermögen. Wer aber einmal in das neue Paradigma eingedrungen ist, stößt auf neue Schwierigkeiten. Er muß sich mit einer ziemlich 'ungläubigen' Umgebung beschäftigen. Er bekommt allerlei Beschwerden zu hören über den Weg, den er eingeschlagen hat.[1] Die Semiotik arbeitet mit einem Begriffsapparat, der unnötig kompliziert ist. Sie ist intolerant und schließt andere Methoden aus. Sie verwirft die Diachronie (Aufeinanderfolge in der Zeit) und damit die geschichtliche Dimension des Objektes. Der Strukturalismus ist inzwischen schon wieder überholt. Die Semiotik von Greimas ist nur für streng narrative Texte zu gebrauchen. Die semiotische Vorgehensweise bringt selten etwas Neues hervor; sie ist nur Rekonstruktion des Textes und führt nicht zu seiner Interpretation. Sie glaubt zu Unrecht, daß eine objektive Analyse möglich sei. Die Semiotik von Greimas schenkt weder dem Autor, noch dem Leser auch nur die geringste Aufmerksamkeit. Und vielleicht besteht darin der größte Widerstand, daß man ihre Publikationen von Zeit zu Zeit einfach verschweigt.[2]

---

* De receptie van de Greimassiaanse semiotiek bij theologen. Weerstanden en misverstanden, in P. BEENTJES, J. MAAS und T. WEVER (Hrsg.): 'Gelukkig de mens' (Kampen 1991) 121-135. Übersetzt von G. Merks-Leinen, M.A.

1 G. BOUWMAN: De wonderbare visvangst (Lc. 5,1-11). Een proeve van integrale exegese, in W. WEREN und N. POULSSEN (Hrsg.): *Bij de put van Jakob. Exegetische opstellen* (= TFT-Studies 5) (Tilburg 1986) 109-129; M. MENKEN: Narratieve prediking en exegetische methoden, in *Praktische theologie* 14 (1987) Nr. 2, 80-92; siehe auch *Kohelet. Faculteitsblad van de Theologische Faculteit Tilburg* 4 (1987) Nr. 5, 17-18.

2 Vgl. in diesem Zusammenhang M. VERVENNE: 'Do we use them as a form, or as the voice of our hearts?' Exegetical reflections on the Psalms of Israël, in *Questions liturgiques* 71

Man kann nicht leugnen, daß die theologische Rezeption der Semiotik von Greimas besonders mühsam verläuft. Es gibt viele Widerstände und Mißverständnisse. Auf sie möchte ich in diesem Artikel eingehen. Dabei ist mir klar, daß Zurückweisungen und Beschwerden verschiedene Destinatoren (Bestimmer) haben können: von Mißtrauen und Angst vor dem Unbekannten bis zu Lücken im Wissen. Was ich, wie auch immer, im Auge habe, ist das, worum es in der Wissenschaft u.a. geht: eine Erweiterung ihrer kognitiven Kompetenz in Bezug auf die Semiotik von Greimas. Eine solche erweiterte Kompetenz ermöglicht ein abgewogeneres Urteil als wir es bei SEMANET, und dann gewöhnlich eher beiläufig, zu hören bekommen.

Vielleicht ruft es Verwunderung hervor, daß ich in diesem Artikel von 'theologischer' Rezeption spreche. Ich will hierzu zwei Dinge bemerken. Zunächst ist dieser Beitrag auf Exegeten zugespitzt; aber er ist auch breiter zu verwenden. In Bezug auf die verschiedenen theologischen Disziplinen sind nur wenige Ergänzungen nötig. Dann soll am Ende dieses Artikels deutlich werden, daß bei semiotischem Vorgehen Exegese und Theologie auf tiefgehende Weise ineinander integriert werden.

Zur allgemeinen Einleitung verweise ich noch auf das Folgende. Obwohl die Semiotik eine lange Vorgeschichte hat, hat sie sich doch erst in den letzten Jahrzehnten zu einer international anerkannten und richtig gefestigten Disziplin entwickelt. Sie wird praktisch von allen und innerhalb aller Disziplinen studiert: von der Biologie und Physik bis zur Philosophie und Theologie. Im letzten Jahrzehnt erschienen jährlich sicher 1000 streng semiotische Publikationen.[3]

Das breite Gebiet der Semiotik kennt hauptsächlich zwei Richtungen: die sogenannte Semiotik nach Peirce, die auf Ch. Peirce (1839-1914) zurückgeht und die Semiotik nach de Saussure, die auf den Schweizer F. de Saussure (1857-1913) zurückgeht. Es ist nicht möglich, beide Richtungen als solche miteinander in Übereinstimmung zu bringen.[4] Der Unterschied zwi-

---

(1990) 162-190. Der Artikel gibt eine Übersicht über die verschiedenen Zugänge zu den Psalmen, erwähnt jedoch keine einzige Veröffentlichung von CADIR (Centre pour l'Analyse du Discours Religieux, Lyon) oder SEMANET.
3 Vgl. *Sema. Semiotic abstracts edited by the members of the Institute for Semiotic and Communication Research* (Essen-Amsterdam-Philadelphia, seit 1988).
4 Einen Versuch hierzu machte E. VAN WOLDE: *A semiotic analysis of Genesis 2-3. A semiotic theory and method of analysis applied to the story of the Garden of Eden* (= Studia Semitica Neerlandica 25) (Assen 1989). Sie entwickelt ein Analyse-Instrumentarium, wobei sie die Semiotik von Greimas der Semiotik von Peirce unterordnet, auf Kosten wesentlicher Elemente der Semiotik von Greimas. Vgl. auch die Besprechung von N. Tromp in *Nederlands theologisch tijdschrift* 45 (1991) 244-245. Es ist also immer wichtig zu sagen, aus welcher Richtung der Semiotik man spricht. So meint E. van Wolde in ihrem Beitrag 'Uitdagingen aan de theologie. Exegese en de semiotische methode', in *Verslag Stegon-symposium. Uitdagingen aan de theologie* (Kampen 1990) 8-18, mit 'die Semiotik' jeweils vor allem die Semiotik von Peirce. Wenn ich in diesem Artikel über 'die Semiotik' spreche, ist stets die Semiotik von Greimas gemeint.

schen beiden Richtungen hängt mit dem Faktum zusammen, daß Peirce ein Philosoph war und de Saussure ein Sprachwissenschaftler: Letzterer ist der Begründer der allgemeinen Sprachwissenschaft. Peirce nimmt das Zeichen in das Ganze eines dynamischen Prozesses auf, mit der Wirklichkeit als Motor und Quelle. Es geht ihm in dauernden Interpretationsprozessen um den Gebrauch von Zeichen durch Menschen. Bei diesem breiten Ansatz von Peirce ist es nicht leicht, seine Semiotik zu operationalisieren. In dieser Hinsicht muß noch sehr viel geschehen. Die Zielsetzung der Semiotik von de Saussure ist beschränkter. Sie beschäftigt sich eher mit dem Resultat der Bedeutungsbildung durch Zeichen mit Bezug auf die Wirklichkeit. Es geht also um faktische Diskurse und ihre mögliche Relation untereinander, deren Bedeutungsbildung man zu analysieren versucht. Dabei geht es um die Analyse verschiedener Diskurse mit Hilfe ein und derselben Metasprache: Texte, aber auch Fotos, Filme, Bildgeschichten, Gemälde, Bilder, Theater, Tanz, Riten, Architektur usw. Die Semiotik von de Saussure verfügt über viel mehr operationelle Analysemodelle als die Semiotik von Peirce. Über den Dänen L. Hjelmslev als Zwischenglied hat A. Greimas (der aus Litauen stammt, aber vor allem in Frankreich arbeitet) diese Semiotik entwickelt; sie wird auch oft als die Semiotik der Pariser Schule bezeichnet.[5]

1. EIN WIDERSPENSTIGER UND NEUER BEGRIFFSAPPARAT

Seit den zwanziger Jahren fassen die Exegeten, aus der Schule der Formgeschichte kommend, die später unterschieden wurde in die überlieferungsgeschichtliche und die redaktionsgeschichtliche Methode, ihr Fach als Literaturwissenschaft auf. J. Delorme und P. Geoltrain stellen nun fest, daß hiermit etwas Merkwürdiges geschah. Man legte sich nämlich keine Rechenschaft darüber ab, daß man mit veralteten linguistischen Instrumenten aus dem 19. Jahrhundert arbeitete.[6] Es ist erstaunlich, daß K. Schmidt, M. Dibelius und R. Bultmann ihre Werke schrieben, ohne sich zu informieren, was z.B. gleichzeitig von den russischen Formalisten geschrieben wurde.

Wenn sich die Exegese selbst so sehr von der Literaturwissenschaft her versteht, dann kann sie selbstverständlich nicht an den Entwicklungen in dieser Literaturwissenschaft vorbeigehen.[7] Eine sehr wichtige Ent-

---

5 Vgl. J. COQUET (Hrsg.): *Sémiotique. L'école de Paris* (Paris 1982), und weiter (auch für Literatur) SEMANET (G. LUKKEN, Hrsg.): *Semiotiek en christelijke uitingsvormen. De semiotiek van A.J. Greimas en de Parijse school toegepast op Bijbel en liturgie* (Hilversum 1987). Vor allem sind wichtig die beiden Teile, A. GREIMAS und J. COURTÉS: *Sémiotique. Dictionnaire raisonné de la théorie du langage* I-II (Paris 1979-1986).
6 J. DELORME und P. GEOLTRAIN: Le discours religieux, in COQUET: *Sémiotique. L'école de Paris* 104.
7 Vgl. C. GRIVEL: *Methoden in de literatuurwetenschap* (Muiderberg 1978); M. DELCROIX und F. HALLYN: *Méthodes du texte. Introduction aux études littéraires* (Paris-Gembloux 1987).

wicklung ist zweifellos die der Semiotik von A. Greimas. Die Semiotik von Greimas zielt darauf ab, das rein intuitive Lesen von Diskursen (Texten, aber auch nicht-linguistischen Objekten) zu vermeiden. Eine solche Lesart manifestiert oft viel stärker die Stellungnahme des Lesers als die des Textes. Die Semiotik von Greimas möchte den Text selbst zum Sprechen bringen. Im Hinblick darauf konstruiert sie eine Metasprache, die in Bedeutungsschichten des Objektes vordringen will, die nicht unmittelbar, 'mit bloßem Auge', wahrzunehmen sind. Diese Metasprache muß ein bestimmtes Maß an Komplexität, logischer Integrität und Stabilität haben. Nur dann kann sie der Anforderung entsprechen, einerseits als Repräsentation des Textes als Erkenntnisobjekt adäquat zu sein und andererseits eine Vermittlerrolle bei der Analyse von Texten zu spielen.[8] Eine solche Metasprache muß präzis sein. Ihre Bedeutung muß genau bestimmt sein. Aus diesem Grund findet man im Diktionär von Greimas allerlei nähere semiotische Präzisierungen von Termini aus der Literaturwissenschaft und außerdem viele Neologismen.[9] Die natürliche Sprache, die wir sprechen, ist zu sehr mit sekundären Bedeutungen, Konnotationen und Assoziationen beladen, um als Analyse-Instrument funktionieren zu können. Die Metasprache von Greimas ist einerseits deduktiv, andererseits wird sie aber ständig angefüllt und angepaßt durch den Kontakt mit Analysen konkreter Diskurse.[10] Wer im Diktionär von Greimas blättert, findet tatsächlich einen ganz eigenen Jargon. Vor allem wenn man in der allgemeinen Literaturwissenschaft nicht zu Hause ist, ist es nicht einfach, einen Einstieg zu finden. Hierfür war das Übersetzen des Diktionär von Greimas für SEMANET damals ein sehr geeigneter Weg.[11] Der Diktionär ist ein sehr konsistentes Ganzes und selbst ganz und gar 'semiotisch': Die Begriffe verweisen dauernd aufeinander, wodurch seine Lektüre nicht einfach ist. Aus Anlaß der Übersetzung des Diktionär bemerkt der Filmsemiotiker E. de Kuyper:[12]

> Sehr glücklich (...) bin ich mit der Übersetzung eines so fundamentalen Werkes (...) durch eine kleine Gruppe von Eifrigen der Tilburger Fakultät für Theologie (!). Das Analytische Wörterbuch der Semiotik (...) ist für mich genauso wichtig wie der van Dale oder der Petit Robert, jedoch viel reizvoller und vergnüglicher zu lesen. Es ist eine Art Labyrinth: Man erfährt durch die Lektüre sozusagen am eigenen Leib, was das bedeutet,

---

8 P. HAIDU: Text and history. The semiosis of twelfth-century lyric as sociohistorical phenomenon (Chrétien de Troyes: D'Amors qui m'a tolu), in *Semiotica* 33 (1981) Nr. 1-2, 190.
9 GREIMAS und COURTÉS: *Sémiotique. Dictionnaire*.
10 GREIMAS und COURTÉS: *Sémiotique. Dictionnaire* I, 395; HAIDU: Text and history 190-191.
11 A. GREIMAS und J. COURTÉS: *Analytisch woordenboek van de semiotiek* I (= TFT-Studies 6), übersetzt von K. JOOSSE und P. DE MAAT (Tilburg 1987).
12 E. DE KUYPER: Waar is de oorspronkelijke sierlijkheid, zinnelijkheid, scherpte van Roland Barthes in het Nederlands!, in *Vrij Nederland* (8. Sept. 1990).

ein 'semiotisches System'. Eine unerschöpfliche Leseerfahrung.

Es ist also nicht richtig zu sagen, diese Metasprache sei einfacher als z.B. die Sprache der historisch-kritischen Methode. Daß man trotzdem gerade der Semiotik vorwirft, zu viel mit einem Jargon zu arbeiten,[13] hat meiner Meinung nach drei Gründe. Erstens handelt es sich um eine neue Sprache, die uns überhaupt nicht vertraut ist. Viele Begriffe, die in der Sprachwissenschaft gar nicht als Jargon aufgefaßt werden, müssen vertraut gemacht werden. Dann weisen die Semiotiker darauf hin, daß die Methode für den pastoralen Gebrauch sehr geeignet ist, weil man keine historisch-kritischen Vorkenntnisse und nicht verschiedene Nachschlagewerke braucht. Wohl muß man hinzufügen, daß dies nur dann wahr ist, wenn man mit einem vereinfachten, der Praxis angepaßten Instrumentarium arbeitet.[14] Schließlich ist es auch nicht unmöglich, daß eine gewisse defensive Einstellung mitspielt, in der die Angst vor dem Neuen eine Rolle spielt oder, um es Greimasianisch auszudrücken, in der der semantische Wert 'altbewährt' (vs 'neu') das Anti-Programm bestimmt.

2. INTOLERANT?

Durch das Paradigma einer neuen Methode fällt auch ein gewisses Licht auf andere Methoden. Es bleibt nicht aus, daß der, der neue Wege geht, die neuen Wege mit den alten Wegen vergleicht. Hinzu kommt normalerweise auch Kritik. So habe ich schon auf den Vorwurf von J. Delorme und P. Geoltrain hingewiesen, daß die Exegeten faktisch mit veralteten linguistischen Instrumenten arbeiten. Im selben Zusammenhang bemerken sie, daß die Exegeten nach 100 Jahren philologischer und exegetischer Arbeit eine beachtliche Menge an Information und Randdokumenten zu verarbeiten haben, wodurch sie gezwungen sind zu sagen, was sie über den Text denken und nicht, was der Text selbst sagt.[15] Und W. Vogels kritisiert die vorhandenen Methoden im Hinblick auf ihre Verwendbarkeit für Pfarrer (eine Kritik, die ich bereits einigermaßen relativiert habe).[16] Es

---

13 MENKEN: Narratieve prediking 88-89.
14 Vgl. J. MAAS und N. TROMP: *Constructief bijbellezen. Zelfstandig en actief in de Bijbel lezen: een semiotische methode* (Hilversum 1987). Vgl. auch die vielen Versuche von CADIR in seiner Zeitschrift *Sémiotique et Bible*. Man vereinfachte die Metasprache sogar im Hinblick auf ihre Verwendung durch Kinder; siehe *Sémiotique et Bible* 5 (1981) Nr. 21. Interessant ist auch das Interesse für die Semiotik von Greimas in Korea, wo man diese Methode für die Einführung in die Bibel gebraucht, weil – bei so vielen Bekehrungen – die klassischen Methoden zu arbeitsintensiv sind; vgl. J. DELORME: Sémiotique au pays du matin calme, in *Sémiotique et Bible* 12 (1988) Nr. 51, 1-7.
15 DELORME und GEOLTRAIN: Le discours religieux 104.
16 W. VOGELS: *En Hij ontsloot de schriften. Een doe-het-zelf methode voor bijbellezing en verkondiging. De semiotiek. Theorie en praktijk* (Mechelen 1985) 12-20.

ist auch nicht unmöglich, daß das Aha-Erlebnis der Entdeckung auf manche den Eindruck einer Neigung zu methodischer Exklusivität macht. SEMANET und auch die meisten anderen, die den neuen Weg gegangen sind, sind allerdings von Anfang an davon überzeugt gewesen, daß auch andere Wege möglich sind und daß diese Wege wissenschaftlich gesehen ihre eigene Begehbarkeit haben. Wie dem auch sei: Wir sehen die Semiotik von Greimas vielmehr als eine Herausforderung und mögliche Bereicherung des methodischen Arsenals.[17] Das Wort 'Methode' bedeutet etymologisch 'der Weg (*hodos*) an dem entlang (*meta*)'. Da jede Methode eine gewisse Reduktion impliziert, kann es unserer Ansicht nach nie um die Alleinherrschaft einer Methode gehen.[18]

3. SYNCHRONIE – DIACHRONIE

Es ist ein weitverbreitetes Mißverständnis, daß die Semiotik der Pariser Schule nur an der 'Synchronie' (Gleichzeitigkeit) interessiert wäre und daß sie die Diachronie (die Aufeinanderfolge in der Zeit) ausschließe. In diesem Zusammenhang ist es wichtig, sich zuallererst klarzumachen, daß der Begriff Synchronie bei F. de Saussure nie die Bedeutung hatte, alle Wörter und Taten verschiedener Subjekte in ein und demselben Augenblick zu registrieren.[19] Der Begriff bezieht sich bei ihm auf alle Elemente und Faktoren, die zu ein und demselben Moment einer und derselben Sprache gehören; anders ausgedrückt: zu einem Zustand dieser Sprache.[20] Als solcher steht der Begriff Synchronie gegenüber dem Begriff Diachronie, der sich auf die Entwicklung innerhalb der Sprache vom einen Zustand zum andern bezieht.[21] Dann: Greimas ist der Meinung, daß der Begriff Synchronie nur operational war, sofern er imstande war, den Begriff 'linguistisches System' (= interne relationale Sprach-Organisation) zu begründen. Seiner Auffassung nach ist der Begriff jedoch genauso ungenau wie der dehnbare Begriff 'heute'.[22] Nach P. Haidu geht es beim Begriff Synchronie darum zu versuchen, die Bedeutung aufeinander folgender Ereignisse zu erfassen.[23] Die Synchronie bezieht sich auf die Gleichzeitigkeit der Relationen, die die Unterschiede (z.B. weiß vs

---

17 N. TROMP: Oud en nieuw, in *Kohelet. Faculteitsblad van de Theologische Faculteit Tilburg* 4 (1987) Nr. 3, 13.
18 G. LUKKEN, P. DE MAAT, M. RIJKHOFF und N. TROMP: Een methode van semiotische analyse, in *Bijdragen. Tijdschrift voor filosofie en theologie* 44 (1983) 118-119.
19 A. GREIMAS: Structure et histoire, in IDEM: *Du sens. Essais sémiotiques* (Paris 1970) 107.
20 GREIMAS und COURTÉS: *Sémiotique. Dictionnaire* I, 97-98, 374; O. DUCROT und T. TODOROV: *Dictionnaire encyclopédique des sciences du langage* (Paris 1972) 178.
21 DUCROT und TODOROV: *Dictionnaire encyclopédique* 189-190.
22 GREIMAS und COURTÉS: *Sémiotique. Dictionnaire* 97-98, 374.
23 P. HAIDU: Semiotics and history, in *Semiotica* 40 (1982) Nr. 3-4, 189.

schwarz) bezeichnen und so Bedeutung konstituieren. Es ist die Rede von einer gleichzeitigen Anwesenheit der Elemente, die Bedeutung haben: 'any grasp of meaning per se is a shift of the sequential, the temporal, into a synchronic and atemporal mode of understanding'.[24] So führt Haidu neben dem terminus synchron den terminus achron (= nicht-zeitlich) ein. Greimas nun ist der Meinung, daß es auf jeden Fall besser ist, den Terminus synchron durch den Terminus achron zu ersetzen. Die semiotischen Strukturen auf der Ebene der Tiefenstruktur kann man zunächst als achron charakterisieren. Im semiotischen Viereck findet man eine nicht-zeitliche Repräsentation der verschiedenen Werte in der Relation der Kontrarietät (A ↔ B), Subkontrarietät (nicht-B ↔ nicht-A), Kontradiktion (A ↔ nicht-A und B ↔ nicht-B) und Implikation (B ← nicht-A und A ← nicht-B):

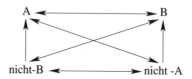

Im semiotischen Viereck wird jedoch nicht nur die Achronie, sondern auch die Diachronie repräsentiert.[25] Im semiotischen Viereck kann man wahrnehmen, wie sowohl von statisch-achronen Werten als auch von ihren diachronen Aufeinanderfolgen die Rede ist. Das semiotische Viereck läßt also auch die elementaren Strukturen der narrativen Transformationen vom einen Wert zum andern erkennen. So schließt das semiotische Viereck den Begriff 'Geschichte' ein.[26] Die Semiotik hat also ganz sicher einen Blick für die Geschichte. Für die Exegese bedeutet dies, daß man mit Hilfe der Semiotik von Greimas innerhalb eines Corpus von Texten die wesentlichen Transformationen der Bedeutung angeben kann.[27] Es wäre jedoch ein neues Mißverständnis, wenn man aus dem Vorhergehenden schließen würde, die Semiotik von Greimas bestimme die Bedeutung eines Textes vom referentiellen Rahmen ihres historischen Settings aus, von der Frage her, was die ursprüngliche Bedeutung des Textes gewesen sein könnte oder von der Genese des Textes her. Diese Elemente sind für die Semiotik nicht von entscheidendem Interesse für die Bedeutung eines Textes. Sie enthalten höchstens Lese-Hypothesen, die am Text selbst erprobt werden müssen. Ich komme hierauf unter 6. zurück.

24 HAIDU: Semiotics and history 189.
25 P. HAIDU: La sémiotique socio-historique, in H. PARRET und H.-G. RUPRECHT (Hrsg.): *Exigences et perspectives de la sémiotique* I (Amsterdam 1985) 224-225.
26 Für eine Ausarbeitung hiervon im Hinblick auf die Liturgiegeschichte vgl. G. LUKKEN: Les transformations du rôle liturgique du peuple. La contribution de la sémiotique à l'histoire de la liturgie, in C. CASPERS und M. SCHNEIDERS (Hrsg.): *Omnes circumadstantes. Contributions towards a history of the role of the people in the liturgy* (Kampen 1990) 15-30.
27 Hierzu könnten sich die Exegeten bei P. Haidu erkundigen, HAIDU: Text and history.

4. VERALTET ODER VOLLAUF IN ENTWICKLUNG?

Die Semiotik von Greimas wird von vielen als 'strukturalistische' Semiotik charakterisiert. Und man fügt manchmal hinzu, daß der Strukturalismus schon wieder im Rückzug ist.[28] Mit anderen Worten: Lohnt sich denn dann noch die Mühe, sich in die Semiotik zu vertiefen? Ist sie nicht nur eine Mode? Diese Bemerkungen klingen mir ziemlich defensiv in den Ohren. Außerdem kann man die Frage stellen, ob nicht vor allem auf dem Gebiet der Methoden eher eine inklusive Auffassung gerechtfertigt ist. Wenn neue Wege möglich sind, so braucht man deshalb doch noch nicht die alten Wege aufzugeben. Es ist jedoch notwendig, auf die gemachte Bemerkung näher einzugehen.

Zuerst: Die Charakterisierung der Semiotik von Greimas als 'strukturalistische Semiotik' ist zu begrenzt. R. Schleifer hat überzeugend gezeigt, daß das Projekt von Greimas sowohl zum Strukturalismus als auch zum Poststrukturalismus gerechnet werden muß. Dies gilt vor allem von seiner Auffassung über die Art der 'Bedeutung'. Es würde zu weit führen, die Frage hier zu vertiefen. Ich muß mich mit der Empfehlung begnügen, das schwierige, aber auch klärende Buch von Schleifer zu lesen.[29]

Dann: In den letzten Jahren geschahen in der Semiotik der Pariser Schule wichtige neue Entwicklungen. Die Kenntnis des Instrumentariums der Pariser Schule beschränkt sich bei den Exegeten durchgängig auf die sogenannte Ebene der Tiefenstruktur mit ihrem semiotischen Viereck und die Ebene der Oberflächenstruktur, wie dies in den frühen siebziger Jahren entwickelt wurde: die vier Phasen der narrativen Reihe und die Wertobjekte mit ihren semantischen Investierungen.[30] Seit diesen Jahren hat sich aber die Metasprache weiter entwickelt. Dies betrifft vor allem die nähere Ausarbeitung der Modalitäten der Oberflächenstruktur, was die Frage der 'Passionen' berührt.[31] Es geht nicht nur um Subjekte mit der Kompetenz des Wollens, Könnens und Wissens; vielmehr werden diese Modalitäten verfeinert wahrgenommen. So erhalten die Subjekte ihren Charakter und ihr Temperament. Außerdem hat sich die Aufmerksamkeit auf die viel konkretere Ebene der diskursiven Strukturen konzentriert. Dies betrifft die relationellen Modelle der Zeit, des Ortes, der Ak-

---

28 BOUWMAN: De wonderbare visvangst 109; D. GREENWOOD: *Structuralism and the biblical text* (Berlin 1985) 119.
29 R. SCHLEIFER: *A.J. Greimas and the nature of meaning. Linguistics, semiotics and discourse theory* (Beckenham 1987).
30 Vgl. z.B. die – übrigens richtige – Darlegung von MENKEN: Narratieve prediking.
31 Vgl. A. GREIMAS: *Du sens II. Essais sémiotiques* (Paris 1983); A. GREIMAS und J. FONTANILLE: *Des états de choses aux états d'âmes. Essais de sémiotique des passions* (Paris 1990). Auf eine eigene Weise hat H. Parret die Metasprache in Bezug auf die Passionen ausgearbeitet in H. PARRET: *Les passions* (Bruxelles 1986). Ein erster Versuch, Parrets Theorie zu operationalisieren, ist zu finden in M. DECKERS-DIJS: *Begeerte in bijbelse liefdespoëzie. Een semiotische analyse van het Hooglied* (Kampen 1991).

teure und Begriffe wie Thematisierung, Figurativisierung und Ikonisierung.[32] Neu ist auf dieser Ebene auch, was Greimas mit 'aspektueller Syntax' bezeichnet: Es geht nicht mehr nur um den Anfangs- und Endzustand in einem Diskurs, sondern auch um den 'Prozeß des Werdens' in Bezug auf Zeiten, Orte und Akteure.[33] Und hinsichtlich der Wertsysteme (Axiologien) auf der Ebene der Tiefenstruktur bekommt Greimas einen Blick für die Intensitätsgrade von Werten, die das Absolute der semiotischen Oppositionen nuancieren. Es geht nicht einfach mehr nur um weiß oder schwarz, sondern um das Schwarz-Werden und das Zum-Schwarzen-hin-Tendieren.[34] Und am überraschendsten ist seine Entwicklung in Bezug auf die ästhetische Wahrnehmung.[35]

Die weitere Entwicklung der diskursiven Strukturen hat zu einer größeren Beachtung dessen geführt, was man die Enunziation nennt (=Versprachlichung, Äußerung; dieses letzte Wort zeigt, daß es sich auch um ein nicht-linguistisches Geschehen handeln kann) und die Instanz der Enunziation mit ihren zwei Polen: dem Enunziator als der vorausgesetzten 'Quelle' des Diskurses (was mehr umfaßt als nur den Autor) und dem Enunziatär als dessen Ziel und Orientierung, evtl. zu konkretisieren als der gemeinte Leser.

Schließlich will ich in diesem Zusammenhang noch anmerken, daß es ein Mißverständnis ist, die Semiotik nur mit erzählenden Texten in Verbindung zu bringen. Die Metasprache ist für die Analyse aller Arten von Diskursen geeignet, auch poetischer und rein wissenschaftlicher Diskurse.

5. NUR EINE REFLEXIVE VERTIEFUNG DES LESEPROZESSES, DIE WENIG NEUES HERVORBRINGT?

Menken sagt: 'Ich kann mich oft nicht des Eindrucks erwehren, daß eine strukturell-analytische Behandlung einer Bibelerzählung nicht mehr hervorbringt, als was man mit 'bloßem Auge' auch schon herausfindet. Das ist bis zu einem gewissen Grade logisch, wenn meine Charakterisierung dieser Methode als 'reflexive Vertiefung des Lernprozesses' richtig ist'.[36] Tatsächlich versucht die Semiotik herauszufinden, wie in konkreten Dis-

---

32 Vgl. SEMANET: *Semiotiek en christelijke uitingsvormen* 25-37.
33 A. GREIMAS: On meaning, in *New literary history. A journal of theory and interpretation* 20 (1989) Nr. 3, 544.
34 GREIMAS: On meaning 545.
35 A. GREIMAS: *De l'imperfection* (Périgueux 1987); vgl. auch W. KRYSINSKI: Toward defining aesthetic perception. Semiotics and utopian reflection, in *New literary history* 20 (1989) Nr. 3, 693-706; H. PARRET: *Le sublime du quotidien* (Paris-Amsterdam-Philadelphia 1988).
36 MENKEN: Narratieve prediking 89.

kursen die Bedeutungsbildung zustandekommt. Dies bedeutet jedoch nicht, daß von Interpretation keine Rede wäre. Die Grenze zwischen dem Wie und Was ist nicht absolut zu ziehen. 'Die Frage des *Wie* berührt das *Was* der Bedeutung'.[37] Es ist ganz sicher auch die Rede von einer Arbeitsweise, durch die die Bedeutung gefunden wird.[38] Und auf die Frage, ob die Methode etwas Neues lehrt, kann man antworten:[39]

> Es wäre schon viel gewonnen, wenn wir einen anderen Weg gegangen wären. Vielleicht erkennen wir die bekannte Landschaft von einem anderen Weg aus wieder. Aber wir erkennen sie doch nicht ganz wieder, wenn wir den zweiten Weg nicht gegangen wären. Wenn man meint, daß nichts Neues dabei herauskommt, dann hat man nichts davon verstanden. Man hat dann nicht die Reise unternommen, die wir vorschlagen (...) Wer die Reise nicht unternimmt, sieht nichts Neues.

Übrigens ist es nicht schwer zu zeigen, daß der semiotische Weg zu wirklich neuen oder erneuernden Interpretationen führen kann: Ich begnüge mich damit, auf zwei überdeutliche Beispiele hinzuweisen: die Analyse von Psalm 139 von J. Holman und meine eigene Analyse des römischen Trauungsritus.[40] Daher ist die Bemerkung, die komplizierte Metasprache stehe in keinem Verhältnis zum Ergebnis und es handele sich um Mäuse gebärende Berge, nicht gerechtfertigt.[41]

6. EINE THEOLOGISCHE LESEPRAXIS

Im Vorhergehenden ging es um die Semiotik von Greimas als Instrumentarium und Methode. Panier weist darauf hin, daß man besser von einer

---

37 D. LOOSE: Betekenis is de vertaling van de betekenis. Dat wil zeggen: er is geen antwoord (interview met J. Delorme), in *Kohelet. Faculteitsblad van de Theologische Faculteit Tilburg* 4 (1987) Nr. 5, 22.
38 TROMP: Oud en nieuw 13.
39 LOOSE: Betekenis is de vertaling van de betekenis 22.
40 J. HOLMAN: Psalm 139 een palimpsest?, in *Schrift* (1989) Nr. 124, 148-157; IDEM: A semiotic analysis of Psalm CXXXVIII (LXX), in A. VAN DER WOUDE (Hrsg.): *In Quest of the past. Studies on Israelite religion, literature and prophetism. Papers read at the Joint British-Dutch Old Testament Conference, held at Elspeet 1988* (= Oudtestamentische Studiën 26) (Leiden 1990) 84-100; IDEM: Psalm 139 (TM) and Psalm 138 (LXX). A semiotic comparison, in K.-D. SCHUNCK und M. AUGUSTIN (Hrsg.): *Goldene Äpfel in silbernen Schalen. Collected communications to the XIIIth Congress of the International Organization for the Study of the Old Testament, Leuven 1989* (Frankfurt am Main-Berlin-Bern 1992) 113-121; G. LUKKEN: Relevantie van de semiotische methode voor de liturgiewetenschap, in *Jaarboek voor liturgie-onderzoek* 2 (1986) 32-48 (= Nr. 15 in diesem Buch); IDEM: De nieuwe Romeinse huwelijksliturgie, in SEMANET: *Semiotiek en christelijke uitingsvormen* 155-226.
41 Vgl. MENKEN: Narratieve prediking 89.

Lesepraxis spricht.⁴² Wie dem auch sei, es wäre ein Mißverständnis, aus dem Vorhergehenden den Schluß zu ziehen, daß es darum gehe, über den Diskurs eine Art Raster zu legen, sodaß der Diskurs dann ganz leicht seine Geheimnisse preisgibt. Vielleicht haben wir selbst manchmal diesen Eindruck gemacht, vor allem in der Periode, in der die narrative Logik der Erzählung besonders betont wurde. Die semiotische Leseweise hat jedoch nichts Mechanisches. Es ist sicher nicht so, daß man – wie zuweilen suggeriert wird – mal gerade an einem Abend ein semiotisches Viereck konstruieren könnte, noch ganz abgesehen von dem Faktum, daß das semiotische Viereck nur ein Teil einer reichen und komplizierten Metasprache ist. Bei der semiotischen Leseweise wird immer wieder deutlich, daß die Texte selbst widerspenstig sind und ihre Bedeutung sicher nicht 'obendrauf' liegt. Die semiotische Leseweise verlangt viel Einsatzvermögen und Kreativität vom Leser (dies gilt auch und manchmal noch mehr für uns schon lange vertraute Texte!). Das Besondere der Semiotik von Greimas besteht ja darin, daß sie sich nicht auf der unmittelbar wahrnehmbaren Ebene des Textes abspielt. Es geht ihr nicht um den Text, den man 'mit bloßem Auge' wahrnimmt: um die sogenannte Ebene der Manifestation. Die semiotische Lesepraxis geht davon aus, daß die Bedeutungsbildung nicht in den Zeichen unmittelbar (wie z.B. die Sprachzeichen eines Textes) wahrzunehmen und zu erfassen ist. Vielmehr muß die Bedeutungsbildung durch den Leser mit Hilfe der semiotischen Metasprache konstruiert werden. Der Leser ist also keineswegs ein passiver Empfänger einer vorgegebenen Botschaft. Im Gegenteil: Er oder sie ist als Subjekt in eine Lesepraxis eingebunden, die auf eine eigene Weise die Frage des Lesens und der Rezeption aufwirft. Der größte Unterschied zu anderen Leseweisen ist, daß diese Leseweise nicht von der Ebene der Expression, den Worten, Sätzen usw., ausgeht. Darin unterscheidet sie sich gerade von der Stilistik und der rhetorischen Lesemethode. Es ist sehr wichtig, sich diesen Unterschied klar zu machen. Der Leser richtet sich in erster Linie auf die spezifischen Strukturen des Inhalts, technisch gesprochen auf die Form des Inhalts. Es geht, in concreto, um die spezifischen Strukturen des Inhalts auf drei Ebenen, die sozusagen unter der Ebene der Manifestation liegen: die Ebene der diskursiven Strukturen, die Ebene der Oberflächenstruktur und die Ebene der Tiefenstruktur. Diese Formen des Inhalts werden auf der Ebene der wahrnehmbaren Manifestation mit Formen des Ausdrucks verbunden. Die Bedeutung eines Textes wird also nicht dadurch kon-

---

42 L. PANIER: Lecture sémiotique et projet théologique, in *Recherches de science religieuse* 78 (1990) 202-203. Im Zusammenhang hiermit und mit dem Folgenden vgl. auch IDEM: Une lecture sémiotique des textes. Questions de théologie biblique, in *Sémiotique et Bible* 13 (1989) Nr. 56, 19-36; IDEM: La nomination de fils de Dieu, in *Sémiotique et Bible* 13 (1990) Nr. 59, 35-41; IDEM: *La naissance du fils de Dieu. Sémiotique et théologie discursive. Lecture de Luc 1-2* (= Cogitatio fidei 164) (Paris 1991); P. BEAUDE: Compte rendu soutenance de thèse, in *Sémiotique et Bible* 13 (1990) Nr. 59, 30-34.

struiert, daß man die Bedeutung der verschiedenen Wörter und Sätze bestimmt. Die Arbeitsweise besteht nicht darin, daß man die Bedeutung von einer philologischen und historischen Bestimmung der Wörter her bestimmt. Nein, man versucht mit Hilfe der Metasprache, Strukturen des Inhalts zu finden. Ein Beispiel: Eine bestimmte Form des Inhalts auf der Ebene der Oberflächenstruktur ist die narrative Semantik. Im postvatikanischen römischen Trauungsritus nun wird die narrative Semantik u.a. bestimmt durch die Oppositionen /offen/ und /inklusiv/ vs /geschlossen/ und /exklusiv/. Nun verbindet sich die narrative Semantik auf der Ebene des Ausdrucks mit allerlei Wörtern, Sätzen, Redensarten durch den ganzen Diskurs hindurch. In diesem Diskurs ist dauernd die Rede von einem Wechselverhältnis, das jeden anderen als Ehepartner ausschließt.[43] In poetischen Texten kann dabei die Rede von einer weiteren Wechselwirkung zwischen der Form des Ausdrucks und der Form des Inhalts sein. Diese vollzieht sich dann allerdings nicht direkt zwischen Elementen des Ausdrucks und Elementen des Inhalts. Vielmehr geht es um ein sogenanntes semi-symbolisches Bedeutungssystem, in dem bestimmte *Relationen* auf der Ebene des Ausdrucks in Wechselwirkung stehen mit bestimmten *Relationen* auf der Ebene des Inhalts, wodurch die Bedeutungsbildung voller und persuasiver wird.

Diese Leseweise nun ist keineswegs vertraut. Wir sind vielmehr gewöhnt, den Text von der direkten Bedeutung der Wörter her zu begreifen: Dies bedeutet oder bedeutete das. Wir konzentrieren uns dann auf den Text als Verweisung auf die Welt außerhalb des Textes, wobei wir besonders auf Verweisungen achten, die sich auf historische Fakten beziehen. Man beobachtet dann z.B. im römischen Trauungsritus, daß sich in diesem Diskurs widerspiegelt, was die alte Kirche unter dem Ehebund verstand. Hier nun liegt sicher nicht das vorrangige Interesse der semiotischen Lektüre von Greimas. Sie stellt die Frage: In wessen Namen ist diese ganze auf unsere vergangene und heutige Welt verweisende Figurativität – in wessen Namen sind alle diese Verweisungen – zusammengebracht? Der Text der römischen Trauliturgie verweist auf das Schließen eines christlichen Ehebundes nach christlicher Tradition; die Frage ist aber: In wessen Namen sind in diesem Textganzen alle diese Verweisungen auf den christlichen Ehebund zusammengebracht? Was ist nun das Spezifische dieses Textes? Was ist die ihn tragende Bedeutungsstruktur? Ist auf Grund einer Konstruktion durch den Leser eine Lesehypothese über die tragende Bedeutungsstruktur möglich, sodaß dieser Text in seiner Bedeutungsbildung sozusagen zu neuem Leben gelangt?

Nach der Semiotik von Greimas verläuft der Kommunikationsprozeß zwischen Text und Leser sicher anders als dies in den uns vertrauten klassischen Kommunikationstheorien beschrieben ist. Hier ist die Rede von drei Elementen: der Sender (der Autor) – die Botschaft – und der Empfän-

---

43 Vgl. LUKKEN: De nieuwe Romeinse huwelijksliturgie 191-208.

ger (der Leser). Man geht also davon aus, daß es zuerst einen Sender gibt, dann eine Botschaft und schließlich einen Empfänger. Weil der Sender dem Text vorausgeht, ist man bei der Interpretation der Botschaft stark an der Vorstellungswelt und Biographie des Autors und der Entstehungsgeschichte des Textes interessiert. Diese sind für die Interpretation mit-bestimmend.

Nach der Semiotik von Greimas sind die drei genannten Elemente – Sender, Botschaft und Empfänger – viel mehr ineinander verwoben. Man stößt hier in der Semiotik auf die unter 4. schon genannten Begriffe: Enunziation (Versprachlichung, Äußerung) und Instanz der Enunziation, zu der sowohl der Enunziator (der Sender) als auch der Enunziatär (der Empfänger) gehören. Nach der Semiotik von Greimas nun konstituiert sich der Sender als Sender nur in der Enunziation und durch die Enunziation dieser konkreten Botschaft. Und der Empfänger als Empfänger dieser Botschaft konstituiert sich als solcher nur durch das so gut wie mögliche Interpretieren dieser Botschaft. Der Leser kann außerdem nur etwas vom Sender – der Quelle – dieser Botschaft gewahr werden durch das Lesen und Interpretieren dieses Textes. Er muß eine Hypothese formulieren über die Bedeutungsbildung, die sich in diesem Text verbirgt, seitdem sie durch den Sender als strukturierende Instanz auf diese Weise in einen Diskurs gefaßt ist. Der Leser muß sozusagen die Undurchsichtigkeit des Diskurses, in dem sich die Enunziation verfestigt hat, durchdringen und versuchen, den Text als einen Akt der Bedeutungsbildung ans Licht zu bringen. Nur so kann sich der Leser als Leser konstituieren. Ich spreche ausdrücklich von 'versuchen' und von 'Hypothese'. Denn der Text behält immer seine Widerspenstigkeit, seine Dichte. Dadurch ist ein solcher Text immer wieder für andere Lektüren und neue Leser disponibel. Wohl kann man sagen: Je mehr meine Lesehypothese der Bedeutungsbildung dieses Textes gerecht wird, desto mehr nähert sie sich auch dem 'Ursprung' dieses Textes. So versucht der Leser durch seine Konstruktion der Bedeutung der 'Quelle', die ursprünglich diese Bedeutung in diesem Diskurs zustandegebracht hat, so nahe wie möglich zu kommen. So versucht er, den Text sozusagen neu zum 'act' zu bringen und zu enunzieren. Wer sich klar macht, wie stark Bibeltexte als 'Wort Gottes' betrachtet werden, kann schwerlich das Interesse dieser aktiven semiotischen Leseweise verkennen. Und was für die Bibel gilt, gilt *mutatis mutandis* auch für die christliche Tradition. Die semiotische Leseweise versucht aufzuspüren, was die Tradition auf der Suche nach der Offenbarung in ihrem Ursprung bewegt. So betrachtet wird Bibellesen und auch das Lesen der christlichen Tradition wieder zu einer *lectio divina*: ein echt theologisches Geschehen. Lesend wird der Leser bei dieser Leseweise außerdem auch sozusagen selbst durch den Diskurs interpretiert, insofern der Diskurs auch über ihn selbst geht: Wie oft ist dies nicht in der Schrift und der christlichen Tradition der Fall? So ist diese semiotische Lesart auch ein Versuch, das Subjekt von seinem christlichen Ursprung her zu interpretieren.

Dies alles führt zu Konsequenzen für das Verhältnis von Exegese und systematischer Theologie. Seit dem 17. Jahrhundert wird in der Exegese sehr stark die Schrift als Dokument der ursprünglichen Heilsgeschichte betont. Die Exegese beschäftigt sich mit dem kritischen Studium der Bibeltexte und ihrer historischen Verankerung. So will die Exegese die ursprünglichen Ereignisse aus der Vergangenheit, die Fundament des Glaubens sind, ans Licht bringen. Sie will sozusagen die Realität des christlichen Glaubens garantieren. Die systematische Theologie muß dann versuchen, das biblische Material in die heutige Kultur und die heutige Glaubenssituation hinein zu aktualisieren. Dies ist auch das Anliegen der heutigen Christologie, z.B. von E. Schillebeeckx. Exegese und systematische Theologie haben sich also auseinander entwickelt.

Bei der semiotischen Leseweise von Greimas sieht die Sache wirklich anders aus. Hier geht es nicht um den Text als Studientext wie in der heutigen Exegese. Es geht auch nicht um den Text als Dokumentation der Heilsgeschehnisse. Sie betrachtet die Bibeltexte vielmehr als ein *oeuvre de signification*: als ein Werk mit Bedeutungsbildung, in dem das ursprüngliche Wort bewahrt wird und sozusagen untergetaucht ist und das dort auf einen Leser wartet, der interpretiert und interpretierend als Leser konstituiert wird. So wird in dieser semiotischen Leseweise das Lesen der Schrift selbst wieder ein theologisches Geschehen, das versucht, den Ursprung des Wortes zu berühren.

Beim Stegon-Symposion 'Herausforderungen an die Theologie' hat E. van Wolde über 'Exegese und die semiotische Methode' gesprochen.[44] Der Titel ihres Vortrags war zweifellos zu global. Sie behandelte die Frage der Relation zwischen Exegese und Semiotik von einer bestimmten Richtung der Semiotik aus: der Semiotik von Peirce.[45] Dies ist ein sinnvolles Vorgehen, das auf die wechselseitige Relation sicher ein eigenes Licht fallen läßt. Gleichzeitig ist aber zu sagen, daß dieses Vorgehen sich weiterhin im klassischen Spannungsfeld der Hermeneutik bewegt, wie man sie z.B. bei Schillebeeckx finden kann.[46] Die Semiotik von Greimas macht noch ein anderes, nach meiner Meinung sehr innovatives Vorgehen möglich. Hier können Exegese und Theologie wieder gegenseitig integriert werden, ohne daß dabei etwas vom wissenschaftlichen Gehalt beider verloren gehen müßte. Außerdem ist dieses Vorgehen ganz eng mit dem der alten Kirche verbunden, die sicher wußte, daß die Theologie schließlich und endlich eine semiotische Disziplin ist. Für Theologen, die die Semiotik betreiben, geht es also um mehr als nur um eine flüchtige Beziehung zu einer 'fremden' Disziplin. Beide Disziplinen sind bereits ein 'älteres Paar'.[47] Die

---

44 VAN WOLDE: Uitdagingen aan de theologie. N.B.: Stegon ist eine durch den niederländischen Staat finanzierte Stiftung die die theologische und religionswissenschaftliche Forschung koordinieren und fördern will.
45 Vgl. meine Bemerkung in Fußnote 4.
46 Vgl. die zitierte Literatur in VAN WOLDE: Uitdagingen aan de theologie 15.
47 PANIER: Lecture sémiotique 200.

Semiotik berührt auf die ein oder andere Weise die Theologie selbst, weil das Offenbarwerden Gottes für die Menschen, sein Erscheinen in der Geschichte, in der Schrift und im Menschen Jesus eigentlich und wesentlich zu tun haben mit den Fragen nach den Zeichen und ihrer Interpretation.[48]

---

48 PANIER: Lecture sémiotique 200.

15. Relevance of Semiotic Analysis to the Liturgical Sciences
Illustrated in the Light of the Rite of Marriage

In the last few decades, researchers have become increasingly interested in the theological content of liturgy. There is unanimity on the method used in these investigations, and this method is regularly being improved. This can be observed from the studies that treat certain theological contents of liturgy[1] and from the methodological publications.[2] It can be characterized as a literary-historical method.[3] In recent years, this method has brought much of the theological content of liturgy to light. However, if the results of these studies are compared with, for example, the well-known German *Handbuch der Dogmengeschichte*, it becomes clear that these results have scarcely been integrated into systematic theology.[4] Moreover, it is clear that much more research is still to be done. In this respect, it is important to note that the historical approach to liturgy has been innovated by the so-called history of mentalities (Annales), which investigates new sources and makes use of other disciplines. But, it appears that this new approach also follows the literary-historical method.

Recently a new method has been applied in the investigation of liturgy as an object of theological research: semiotics. As a new field, semiotics is not always easily accepted. The method has to prove itself to the established order. As a result, several difficulties arise. First of all, semiotics is a science with many different views. The research group SEMANET (Semiotic Analysis by Dutch Theologians) has chosen to follow the

---

* Relevantie van de semiotische analyse-methode voor de liturgiewetenschap, in *Jaarboek voor liturgie-onderzoek* 2 (1986) 32-48. Translated by W.M. Speelman, M.Div.

1 See for example: F. NAKAGAKI: *Participazione attiva dei fedeli secondo il Sacramentario Veronense. Un importante aspetto dell ecclesiologia in prospettiva liturgica* (Roma 1969); G. LUKKEN: *Original Sin in the Roman liturgy. Research into the theology of Original Sin in the Roman sacramentaria and the early baptismal liturgy* (Leiden 1973); J. FRENDO: *The post-secreta of the "Missale gothicum" and the eucharistic theology of the gallican anaphora* (Maltha 1977).

2 Good examples of this are: P. VISENTIN: Lo studio della teologia nella liturgia, in *Introduzione agli studi liturgici* (= Liturgica 1) (Roma 1962) 189-233, and F. NAKAGAKI: Metodo integrale. Discorso sulla metodologia nell interpretazione dei testi eucologici, in *Fons Vivus* (= Bibliotheca theologica Salesiana I/6) (Zürich 1971) 279-286.

3 A short description is given in G. LUKKEN: De liturgie als onvervangbare vindplaats van de theologie. Methoden van theologische analyse en verificatie, in H. BERGER a.o. (ed.): *Tussentijds. Theologische Faculteit Tilburg. Bundel opstellen bij gelegenheid van haar erkenning* (Tilburg 1975) 325-327 (cf. no. 11 in this book).

4 M. SCHMAUS a.o. (ed.): *Handbuch der Dogmengeschichte* (Freiburg-Basel-Wien 1951-).

semiotics of A. Greimas (Paris School), which, via L. Hjelmslev, goes back to F. de Saussure. In the second place, semiotics is a very difficult matter. It takes a great deal of energy and time to get used to the semiotic set of devices. A third complication is that mastering a theory is one thing, but applying this theory in the semiotic analysis of an object is another. This demands much practice and, as it were, a new attitude. Finally, when semiotics is applied to the analysis of a new object, such as liturgy, new questions will be encountered. This is all the more true because liturgy is a very complex object, which encompasses much more than texts alone.

This means that much innovating work has to be done, which takes time. And at the same time, the question repeatedly asked is: what relevance does the semiotic method have in the study of liturgy? This article deals with this question of relevance by performing a semiotic analysis of the Roman liturgy of marriage in the Dutch translation.[5] Although something will be said about the entrance rite of the bridal couple at the beginning of the ritual,[6] the analysis will concentrate on the section concerning the solemnization of marriage as such (nos. 43-46).[7] But there is also a further limitation: a total analysis of this section would take too many pages.[8] Therefore, a somewhat simplified analysis will be performed here. This simplification, however, has its advantages. The final intention of this article is to introduce the method to the reader, to show the reader what the method is about and, therefore, to formulate the analysis in as readable a form as possible. By thus breaking down some barriers, it may become clear that semiotic analysis can be used to disclose liturgy as a *locus theologicus* and to contribute to the liturgical sciences as a theological discipline.

---

[5] NATIONALE RAAD VOOR LITURGIE: *Het huwelijk* (= Liturgie van de sacramenten en andere kerkelijke vieringen 7) (Hilversum 1977). The object of analysis is the official Dutch translation of the ritual of the liturgy of marriage. This translation has been rendered into English as accurately as possible. In the semiotic view, every translation of the *editio typica* is a new discourse with its own signification. This means that if the official English translation were chosen as the object of analysis, a new analysis would have to be performed. Only then, after this new analysis, would it be possible to compare the English and Dutch translations and to evaluate their differences with reference to the *editio typica*. Such a comparison would not focus on similarities and differences between individual words, but rather on similarities and differences in the significations of the three discourses concerned in their integrity.

[6] See G. LUKKEN: Het binnengaan in de kerk in de Romeinse huwelijksliturgie, in *Jaarboek voor liturgie-onderzoek* 1 (1985) 69-89.

[7] The members of SEMANET P. de Maat, M. Rijkhoff and N. Tromp have contributed to the analysis of this section.

[8] An elaborate analysis of no. 43-46 is given in G. LUKKEN: De nieuwe romeinse huwelijksliturgie, in SEMANET (G. LUKKEN ed.): *Semiotiek en christelijke uitingsvormen. De semiotiek van A.J. Greimas en de Parijse school toegepast op Bijbel en liturgie* (Hilversum 1987) 155-208.

An English translation of the Dutch text of the solemnization of marriage (nos. 43-46) will be given. It is important for the reader to examine this text closely before considering the different points concerning the relevance.

THE RITE OF MARRIAGE

1   43. *All rise, including the bridal couple. The priest addresses the bridal couple in these or similar words:*
N. and N., you have come to the church
in order to – before the community, present here,
5   and the Church's minister –
let confirm and seal your love by the Lord.
In baptism Christ has already consecrated you.
Now he blesses your love
and strengthens it in the sacrament of marriage,
10   so that you can be faithful to each other
and can assume the duties of marriage.
Answer therefore before the Church community, present here,
to the questions that I am going to ask:

1   44. *The priest then questions the bride and bridegroom about their freedom, their faithfulness and their willingness to accept and bring up their children:*

priest	N. and N.,
5	have you by free will
	band with the full consent of your heart
	come here
	in order to marry with each other?
bridal couple	Yes.
10 *priest*	Are you willing
	as married people
	to love and to honor each other
	all the days of your life?
bridal couple	Yes.

15   *The following question may be omitted if this is advisable because of circumstances, for example, if the couple is advanced in years.*

priest	Are you willing
	to accept children as a gift from Gods hand,
	to let them share in your love
20	and to bring them up in the spirit of Christ and his Church?

bridal couple   Yes.

THE MARRIAGE VOWS

1   45. *The priest invites the bridal couple to declare the marriage vows:*
    priest   Together you want to conclude the covenant of mar-
                       riage.
                       May I then ask you
5   to give each other the right hand
                       and here in this community
                       before your relatives and friends
                       before God and before his Church,
                       to make known your will
10   to marry with each other.

    Bride and bridegroom give each other the right hand
    bridegroom   N., I accept you as my wife,
                       and I promise you
                       to remain true
15   in good and bad days,
                       in poverty and wealth,
                       in sickness and health.
                       I want to love and honor you
                       all the days of our life.

20 *bride*   N., I accept you as my husband,
                       and I promise you
                       to remain true
                       in good and bad days,
                       in poverty and wealth,
25   in sickness and health.
                       I want to love and honor you
                       all the days of our life.

    If it seems preferable for pastoral reasons, the bridal couple may make the marriage vows by answering questions from the priest.
30 *First he asks the bridegroom:*
    priest   N., do you want to accept N. as your wife,
                       and do you promise her
                       to remain true
                       in good and bad days,
35   in poverty and wealth,
                       in sickness and health?
                       Do you want to love and honor her
                       all the days of your life?

    bridegroom   Yes, I want to.

40 *Immediately after this, the priest asks the bride:*
    priest   N., do you want to accept N. as your husband,
                          and do you promise him
                          to remain true
                          in good and bad days,
45   in poverty and wealth,
                          in sickness and health?
                          Do you want to love and honor him
                          all the days of your life?

    bride   Yes, I want to.

50 *For pastoral reasons the conference of bishops may decree, in virtue of the faculty in no. 17, that the bridal couple always makes the marriage vows by answering the questions from the priest .*

1   46. *The priest confirms the marriage vows and says:*
    priest   From now on the Church community
                          will consider you as married (people).
                          May the Lord
5   confirm and bless your marriage.
                          What God has joined,
                          men shall not divide.

    all   Amen.

1. Before I go more deeply into the numbers just quoted, I would like to say something about the beginning of this nuptial mass. The rubrics of nos. 39-40 concern the entrance of the bridal couple into the church.[9] A semiotic analysis of this entrance rite focusses on a broader object then we would expect following a literary-historical method. In a semiotic analysis the positions and movements of the actors within the spatiality of the church building are being focussed. The analysis reveals a theological signification at the very beginning of the celebration, without many words being used. By crossing the treshold of the church building and by solemnly walking in procession towards the altar, the bridal couple is equipped with an official, public and ordained 'being able to do'. In a non-verbal way the bridal couple is being installed as protagonists of the celebration. Therefore, whether the bridal couple enters the church officially or this entrance is cancelled is not an unimportant matter – by the way, cancelling this entrance rite is an alternative made possible by the rubrics themselves. In any case, the entrance of the bridal couple into the church and the way in which this is done is a determining factor in the constitution of the actual subject of doing in the solemniza-

---

9 See for an analysis of this entrance, LUKKEN: Het binnengaan in de kerk.

tion and this touches the question who is the minister of the sacrament. The analyis of the non-verbal aspects of liturgy is made possible by the semiotic method. In contrast to the literary-historical method, the semiotic method is not merely focussed upon the literary. The aim of using semiotics is the perception and analysis of all objects in which significance is being formed. This is true for architecture, but also for dance, movies and music. In this respect the method opens many perspectives in the analysis of liturgy. However, for the most part these perspectives are still in the future, as they have scarcely been realized in analyses.

2. During a discussion of the new Roman rite of marriage, one of my students said: it is very remarkable that in the ritual of exchanging marriage vows in no. 45, no connection whatsoever is made with God or with Christ, while the theology of marriage considers christian marriage to be an image of the relationship between Christ and his Church. At the *moment suprême* of the solemnization, marriage appears as a purely interhuman relationship. I remember having pointed out other sections of the ritual of marriage to that student. This concerned two sections, namely, no. 46, in which the priest confirms that God has joined the married couple, and no. 33, where in the blessing of the bride and bridegroom the following is said: "God, You have made the covenant between man and wife / to be a sacred mystery, / as great as the love of Christ for his bride, the Church". The answer, however, remained unsatisfactory, for it is true that the supreme moment does not express anything of the actual theology of marriage. I believe that semiotic analysis makes it possible to formulate a satisfactory answer to this question.

In the development of a grammar for the analysis of sense, Greimas did not focus on separate sentences, but on the text as a totality, the discourse as a whole. It concerns a grammar of the story, a narrative grammar, which can also be applied to non-verbal discourses. This narrative grammar has four phases:
1) The manipulation by a destinator of a destinatee with regard to an intended performance.[10]
2) The phase in which the destinatee is equiped with competence, so that he becomes a virtual and actual subject of doing. This phase can be articulated with the help of the modalities of having to, wanting to, being able to and knowing how to act.
3) The phase in which a subject of doing carries out a performance.
4) The judgement of the carried out performance by the destinator or in

---

[10] Note of the translator: in the English translation of A. GREIMAS and J. COURTÉS: *Sémiotique. Dictionnaire raisonné de la théorie du langage* I (Paris 1979) 'destinateur' and 'destinataire' have been translated as 'sender' and 'receiver'; see A. GREIMAS and J. COURTÉS: *Semiotics and language: an analytical dictionary* (Bloomington 1982) 378.

the name of the destinator, whereby the subject of doing becomes a recognized subject.

In a semiotic analysis of nos. 43-48, three of these four phases of the narrative grammar can be recognized explicitly:
1) The phase of manipulation can be found in the introductory speech (no. 43) and in the introduction to the actual solemnization (no. 45, 1-10). As destinator, the priest manipulates the bridal couple as destinatee. The local Church community is closely connected with the priest as destinator (cf. no. 43, 4 and no. 45, 6-8).
2) The phase of equipment remains implicit and is not dramatized as such.
3) The manipulation is directed toward the performance carried out in no. 44 and no. 45. In no. 44 there is a performance which concerns the open and public confirmation by the bridal couple before the priest of the freedom, faithfulness and, eventually, the acceptance and upbringing of children. If that performance has been carried out, it will be judged positively in no. 45, 2-3: "Together you want to conclude the covenant of marriage". As destinator, the priest judges the situation just created, in which the conditions for a wedding have been fulfilled. Then, logically connected with this judgement, the priest proceeds to the manipulation with regard to the next performance. This concerns the exchanging of the marriage vows, which indeed has its place in no. 45, 11-27 (resp. 28-52).

It is also possible to describe the relation between the performances in no. 44 and no. 45. The performance in no. 44 is a condition for the performance in no. 45. The first performance can be indicated as an auxiliary program in relation to the base program of no. 45. This auxiliary program can also be described in terms of equipment (second phase of the narrative scheme): the performance of this program is the acquisition of the ability with respect to the base program.
4) If the performance of no. 45 (the exchanging of marriage vows) has been carried out, it is followed by the fourth and last phase of the narrative scheme with respect to the base program: the judgement in no. 46: "From now on the Church community will consider you as married ...". The priest connects the Church community with himself as judging destinator of the base program in no. 45.

In the light of the consistency of the narrative grammar mentioned, it is possible to formulate a satisfactory answer to the question asked by the student.
a) First of all, it appears that in the phase of judgement the destinator judges not only the marriage vows, but also and very explicitly another base performance as having been carried out. In no. 46, 6-7 he says: "What God has joined, men shall not divide". On the one hand he establishes that the bride and bridegroom are now to be considered as joined in

marriage, but on the other hand he also establishes that it is God who has made them inseparable. Obviously, at the *moment suprême* another performance has also been carried out, in which God is the subject of doing. The actual solemnization of marriage, therefore, can be articulated in two simultaneous base performances: the exchanging of marriage vows by the bride and bridegroom as mutual subjects of doing, and the joining of them both by God.

b) Secondly, in the light of the narrative grammar it becomes clear that Christ is involved in the base program too. In the manipulation in no. 43, 6 and 8-9, there is an allusion to a base performance, which is indicated as a confirming, sealing, blessing and strengthening of the love of the bridal couple by Christ. This base performance can be no other than the mutual exchanging of the marriage vows in no. 45. The reason for this is that by the indication "therefore" in no. 43, 12, no. 43, 8-9 is explicitly connected with no. 44, which in turn is connected with no. 45 by the indication "may I *then* ask" (no. 45, 4).

This base performance, which has Christ as its subject of doing, returns in the judgement in no. 46, 4-5: "May the Lord confirm and bless your marriage". As in no. 43, 6 Christ is mentioned as the subject of doing in the performance of sealing and confirming the marriage, "the Lord" in no. 46, 4 can be said to indicate Christ. As such, no. 46, 4-5 can also refer to a second base performance, which takes place later, that is, the blessing of the bride and bridegroom. This performance, then, would be begged for here, by a manipulation directed to God as destinatee. However, because of the close connection with no. 43, 6 and 8-9, this invocative speaking can *also* and *simultaneously* be explained as a modest way of speaking. The priest avoids saying: I confirm that Christ has blessed this marriage.

Our interpretation is, therefore, that the priest alludes to no. 45 and at the same time suggests that the narrative program of the blessing will be developed later in the ritual. In defence of a co-referring to no. 45, it can be noted that the rubrics of no. 46, 1 speak about a "confirming" of the marriage vows and that no. 46 as a whole is connected with this "confirming" as well as the formula of 46, 4-5, which speaks about a "confirming and blessing" of the marriage by the Lord. In this connection "confirming by the Lord" must mean something like: approving, saying "yes".

The *moment suprême*, therefore, contains three performances:
1) The performance of the exchanging of marriage vows, which has the bride and bridegroom, each individually, as its subject of doing.
2) The performance by God, who makes them inseparable.
3) The performance by Christ, who confirms, seals, blesses and strengthens.[11]

---

11 Looking at no. 48 (the exchange of the rings), a fourth performance can be distinguished, which has the trinity as subject of doing. I will not examine that performance.

This analysis shows that several events come together in the solemnization of marriage; they are, as it were, bound together in no. 45: at the actual moment of the solemnization. With regard to no. 45, one could speak about marriage, in the words of E. Schillebeeckx, as "human reality and saving mystery".[12] Semiotic analysis sheds light upon this *locus theologicus* and makes it possible to formulate an integrated answer to the question posed.

3. In connection with the preceding, three matters can be clarified.
a) Since 1973 Rome has taken over the translation of the kernel formulas of the sacraments.[13] Liturgists correctly note that such conduct is in fact a return to the magic of the kernel formula, which in this way is divorced form its context. Semiotic analysis, however, throws yet another light upon this matter. The translation of the kernel formula appears not to be a matter of only translating the kernel formula! A translation of the rest of the discourse can immediately refer back to the climax of the sacramental event. If Rome wishes to reserve the right of translation of the kernel formula to itself, it should actually reserve this right with respect to the entire discourse. Translation is by no means a matter of individual sentences, let alone of individual words, as is suggested in the document concerning the reservation of the kernel formula to Rome.[14] Translation is a matter of rendering one text-*whole* into another text-*whole*. In order to be able to really take control of a translation, a semiotic analysis should be performed upon the text concerned.
b) At the entrance into the church the bridal couple is being installed as protagonists of the celebration. As we have seen, the couple is equipped with an official, public and ordained 'being able to do'. This equipment (second phase of the narrative scheme) is also displayed in the solemnization. The bridal couple appears to be the actual subject of doing (minister) and the priest – together with the Church community – appears to act as destinator: he manipulates the performance, he announces the competence of wanting or knowing how, and he judges the performance. In this respect it is remarkable that the witnesses, who occupy their own place in the procession at the entrance into the church, are not mentioned in the solemnization of marriage.
c) The ritual has an explicit ecclesiastical dimension. The role of the local Church community, present in the church concerned ("present here" in no. 43, 4.12), and in this community the circle of family and friends (cf.

---

12 E. SCHILLEBEECKX: *Marriage. Human reality and saving mystery* (London 1976²).
13 See R. KACZYNSKI: *Enchiridion documentorum instaurationis liturgicae (1963-1973)* I (Torino 1976) nos. 3110-3114. It concerns a letter to the presidents of the conferences of bishops, dated October 25, 1973 'de normis servandis quoad liturgicos libros in vulgus edendos, illorum translatione in linguas hodiernas peracta'.
14 See KACZYNSKI: *Enchiridion* especially no. 3112 and 3113.

no. 43, 3-4.12; no. 45, 6-7), is being stressed. The Church community is co-destinator and as such also co-verifyer of the event. The minister represents the Church community. The broader Church community comes up only as an extension of the local community present (no. 45, 8). No. 46, 2 may refer to the broader as well as the local Church community, but the local community, present as destinator, undoubtedly forms the basis and is emphasized more forcefully.

4. Actually, the narrative grammar is little more than a kind of syntagmatic skeleton. In every discourse this skeleton is, as it were, dressed up with the semantic component. With respect to the signification, the semantic component has its very own value. An analysis of the semantic component of the discourse can reveal much of its theological content.

It is clear that this discourse is about the covenant of marriage and that it takes place in a given, ritual and institutional frame, sometimes mitigated by alternatives (no. 44, 15ff.; no. 45, 28ff.) This is a sort of décor, a background. It is the world to which the discourse is referring. Technically speaking, the covenant of marriage and the given, institutional – somewhat mitigated – frame are called the figurative isotopy of the discourse. In theological terms, I would translate it as its framing, its presentation.

More important, however, is the question: what is finally being thematicized against this background? What does the discourse want to say about marriage within this ritual frame? This question concerns the so-called thematic isotopies: a question that can hardly be said to be irrelevant in theology, as it immediately touches the theological thematic of the discourse.

Thematic isotopies can be indicated in oppositions. These thematic oppositions are related to the semiotic axiom, according to which all meaning is based on difference. How could we ever know what is black if we did not know the opposition black-white? Besides, the semantic oppositions, which can be found in the discourse, are also the starting points and the ending points of the main transitions in the discourse. With the help of these oppositions, therefore, the way in which the transformations (performances) from one value to the other take place can be indicated.

After a detailed and accurate analysis, we traced four thematic isotopies in our discourse. The following transformations take place in this solemnization:

1) From /informal/ and /private/ to /official/ and /public/. In other words: before the performance of the ritual the bridal couple is, as far as their mutual love and their marriage are concerned, not yet connected with the values /official/ and /public/. It may be that they have felt connected with each other for a long time and/or that they have already

lived together for a long time, but only by this ritual are they connected with this love of marriage in an official and public way. Such a view may be criticized (for example, because the civil marriage has already taken place), but the only thing that matters now is that this is the view of the discourse.
2) A second redundant opposition is: /initially/ or /temporary/ versus /definitive/ and /permanent/. In other words: by the performance of marriage the bridal couple is connected with values as the /definiteness/ and /permanentness/ of marriage.
3) A third redundant opposition seems to be /open/ and /inclusive/ versus /closed/ and /exclusive/. Continually, this discourse speaks of a reciprocity, which excludes any other as a partner in this marriage. Bride and bridegroom conclude an exclusive covenant with each other. This opposition is very strong in the exchange of marriage vows. As an example, I think it is important to give more details of the analysis here.

In no. 45, 2-3 the priest introduces the marriage vows with the observation: "Together you want to conclude the covenant of marriage". "Together" is emphasized by its initial position in the phrase. In this manner, the priest stresses the fact, that these two (each one of them) exclude any other as a possible partner in the covenant. The priest says, as it were: with each other, not with another or others. It is exactly this which they publicly declare. In a plastic way, this exclusive reciprocity is expressed in the closed circle resulting from giving each other the right hand. Within this circle of the *iunctio manuum*, husband and wife promise each other exclusive faithfulness (cf. "my wife", "my husband") in all circumstances. Concerning these circumstances, three areas are being referred to: the temporal reality ("in good and bad days"), the economic reality ("in poverty and wealth") and the physical reality ("in sickness and health"). This threefold concretization has the form of a climax: reality becomes more and more physical. It is truly about all circumstances. This effect of totality is also caused by mentioning each time a positive and a negative aspect ("poverty and wealth", etc.). These aspects are pairs of totalities: by mentioning the extremes, everything that is in between them is included. A well-known totality pair is 'heaven and earth'.

The exclusive reciprocity is also indicated in another way. In no. 45, 12 a transformation is indicated, in which the bridegroom is the subject of doing in an acceptance of his bride as someone who gives herself. He connects himself with the bride as the one who gives herself to him as his wife. Nota bene: this is not an activity in which the man alone is the actor; it does not say "I take you as or to be my wife", but "I accept you as my wife".[15] In other words, the activity of the man implies the activity

---

15 Note of the translator: unhappily, in the English ritual the phrases are indeed "I, N., take you, N., to be my wife" and "I, N., take you, N., to be my husband".

of the woman. The word "accept" indicates that the woman's giving of herself is presupposed. It implies a preceding judgement by the man that at this moment the woman explicitly wants to give herself to him. This judgement is based upon several preceding elements, such as the coming to the church (no. 43, 3), the answer by the woman (no. 44, 9) and especially (chronologically nearest) the giving of the right hand by the bride to the bridegroom. The gesture of giving the right hand expresses even more than the text "I accept you" does: it is the activity by the bride with regard to the man who accepts her as his wife. The man accepts the hand which the woman has actively put in his hand, while he pronounces the words: "I accept you as my wife". In this way it is verbally and somatically expressed that the activity of the bridegroom is also a reaction to the same offer by the woman. The rite of the *iunctio manuum* and the accompanying text pronounced by the bridegroom, therefore, appear to contain a strong exclusive reciprocity. This exclusive reciprocity is still being emphasized by the bride's words in no. 45, 20: words that also go together with the giving of the right hand, this time by the man.

4) A fourth opposition seems to be: /mixture without differentiation/ vs. /duality without separation/. This opposition means that, at the beginning of the ritual, the bridal couple comes forward in an undifferentiated manner: not as bride and bridegroom separately, but as bridal couple. In the actual solemnization of marriage they are, as it were, separated and addressed as bride and bridegroom, each in their own individuality (strongly emphasized in no. 45, 11-49). Only after this are they considered as inseparably joined (no. 46). And that which can disturb this inseparable duality is the undifferentiated: the (forbidden) anti-program of the separation has the undifferentiated "men" as subject of doing: "What God has joined, men shall not divide" (no. 46, 6-7). It is interesting that the process of differentiation also remains important after the solemnization: from the nuptial blessing (no. 33) it appears that marriage as a duality is also in its endurance realized through differentiation of husband and wife. This, however, will not be elaborated here.

I hope to have demonstrated that the Greimassian method of semiotic analysis is of great relevance to the opening up of liturgy as *locus theologicus*. The importance of it will increase even more if it turns out that with the help of this method it is not only possible to open up liturgy as a mere literary *locus*, but as a *locus* in its integrity. There is still much to do ...

16. Die Stellung der Frau im Trauungsritus des *Rituale Romanum* und nach Vatikanum II.

Von der Unterordnung der Frau zu einer gewissen Gleichwertigkeit von Mann und Frau

Die heutige Theologie interessiert sich für die Frage, wie in der Liturgie das Verhältnis zwischen Mann und Frau zum Ausdruck kommt. Das ist eine umfangreiche Frage, und zwar aus zwei Gründen. Zunächst umfaßt die Liturgie eine unübersehbare Fülle liturgischen Materials aus Vergangenheit und Gegenwart, aus Ost und West. Außerdem ist die wissenschaftlich-methodische Untersuchung der Liturgie auf eine bestimmte Thematik hin eine zeitraubende Sache. Denn es geht ja nicht einfach darum, die bestimmte Thematik aus bestimmten Riten herauszuziehen. Wenn man den Quellen als solchen gerecht werden will, muß man sie zuerst genau analysieren. Erst vom ganzen Kontext her und im Kontext kann die untersuchte Thematik richtig eingeschätzt werden.

Im Hinblick auf die zu untersuchende Thematik sind Trauungsriten sicher ein interessantes Objekt. In diesem Artikel beschränke ich mich auf das Szenarium zweier maßgebender und einflußreicher Trauungsriten der römischen Liturgie: den Trauungsritus des *Rituale Romanum* von 1614 und den postvatikanischen Trauungsritus von 1969. Dabei möchte ich die Quellen soweit wie möglich innerhalb der niederländischen Situation behandeln. Aus diesem Grund habe ich den Trauungsritus des *Rituale Romanum* in der Version gewählt, in der er vor dem Vatikanum II in den Niederlanden praktiziert wurde.[1] Er weicht insofern vom Ritus von 1614 ab, als der Trauung eine kurze Ansprache vorausgeht und einzelne Teile ins Niederländische übersetzt sind. Für den postvatikanischen Trauungsritus benutze ich die niederländische Übersetzung der 1979 erschienenen *Editio typica*.[2] Die Untersuchung beschränkt sich auf beide

---

* De plaats van de vrouw in het huwelijksritueel van het *Rituale Romanum* en van Vaticanum II. Van ondergeschiktheid van de vrouw naar een zekere evenwaardigheid van man en vrouw, in *Jaarboek voor liturgie-onderzoek* 4 (1988) 67-89. Übersetzt von G. Merks-Leinen, M.A.
1 *Promptuarium Sacerdotum*, editio III augmentata (Hilversum 1947) 112-128.
2 NATIONALE RAAD VOOR LITURGIE: *Het huwelijk* (= Liturgie van de sacramenten en andere kerkelijke vieringen 7) (Hilversum 1977). Wie im vorhergehenden Beitrag "Relevance of semiotic analysis to the liturgical sciences" ist die offizielle niederländische Übersetzung des Ritus Objekt der Analyse (vgl. für die Argumentation Fußnote 5 des vorhergehenden Beitrags). Die für diesen Beitrag wichtigen Abschnitte dieser Übersetzung sind so genau wie möglich ins Deutsche übersetzt.

Trauungsriten als solche, d.h. auf den Ritus der Eheschließung und der Segnung der Neuvermählten. Ein Vergleich beider Riten mit Bezug auf die genannte Thematik liegt natürlich nahe.

Auch im Hinblick auf die Untersuchungsmethode ist eine Entscheidung zu treffen. Erstens ist zwischen diachronen und synchronen Methoden zu wählen. Beide sind möglich. Ich beschränke mich auf die synchronen Methoden. Sie sind vor allem dann sehr geeignet, wenn man soviel wie möglich die Quellen selbst zu Wort kommen lassen will. Außerdem ist zu wählen zwischen der Methode des *close-reading* und der der Semiotik.[3] Ich wähle die letztere, und zwar die von A. Greimas und der Pariser Schule, weil sie über ein sehr ausgewogenes und kontrollierbares Analyse-Instrumentarium verfügt. Dabei entsteht wohl das Problem, daß die semiotische Analyse sehr zeitraubend ist und die vollständige Wiedergabe der Analyse viel Raum einnimmt. Aus diesem Grund wird es nötig sein, nicht die Analyse selbst, sondern die Resultate der Analyse wiederzugeben. Im folgenden behandele ich mit Bezug auf die Thematik zuerst die Eheschließung in beiden Riten (1), dann die Segnung und Überreichung der Ringe (2), dann den Segen der Neuvermählten (3). Am Schluß gehe ich auf die Resultate ein, die sich ergeben, wenn man beide Riten als Ganze miteinander vergleicht (4).

1. DIE EHESCHLIESSUNG

1.1. Das *Rituale Romanum*

Wenn man die semiotische Analyse der Eheschließung nach dem *Rituale Romanum* mit Bezug auf das Verhältnis von Mann und Frau zu einander näher betrachtet,[4] so fällt auf, daß es hier um den Abschluß eines bilateralen juristischen Vertrages zwischen beiden geht. Das 'Nehmen' der Frau durch den Mann geschieht im Tausch gegen das 'Nehmen' des Mannes durch die Frau. Es geht um einen Tauschvertrag, bei dem Bräutigam und Braut als gleichwertige und deutlich unterschiedene Subjekte des Handelns auftreten. Sie vollziehen eine formale und äußere Performanz, die als das äußere Zeichen des Sakramentes fungiert. Sofern man von einer passiven Rolle bezüglich der eigentlichen Innenseite des Sakramentes sprechen kann, so betrifft diese sowohl den Mann als die Frau. Der Abschluß des bilateralen juristischen Kontraktes kommt vor allem in der

---

3 Vgl. zur Literatur über die *close-reading* Methode, Fußnote 43 des Beitrags "La liturgie comme lieu théologique irremplaçable" (= Nr. *11* in diesem Buch).

4 Für die vollständige Analyse der Eheschließung nach dem *Rituale Romanum* vgl. G. LUKKEN: Semiotische analyse van de huwelijkssluiting in het post-tridentijnse Rituale Romanum, in *Jaarboek voor liturgie-onderzoek* 3 (1987) 41-85.

Formel des 'Nehmens' des anderen zum rechtmäßigen Mann, (der anderen zur rechtmäßigen Hausfrau) zum Ausdruck. Ihr folgt die *iunctio manuum* auf Ersuchen des Priesters. Es ist nicht unmöglich, daß bei dieser Performanz die Betonung weniger auf den streng juristischen Werten /formal/ und /äußerlich/ mit Bezug auf die Ehe liegt als bei der vorhergehenden Performanz. Denn man kann schließlich die Performanz des Sich-die-rechte-Hand-Gebens nicht nur als eine vertragliche und formalleibliche Gebärde ansehen, sondern auch als Ausdruck existentieller Verbundenheit von Mann und Frau. Die Hand ist dabei ein Zeichen für die ganze Person. Daher sollte in dieser Performanz nicht so sehr das juristische 'Nehmen zu', sondern mehr das 'Sich-selbst-als-Person-Geben' betont werden. So wird diese Performanz in ihrer gleichwertigen Wechselseitigkeit auch weiter reichen als die vorhergehende.

Angesichts der Thematik richtet sich die Aufmerksamkeit selbstverständlich auf die Bezeichnung der Frau – im Gegensatz zum Mann – als Hausfrau. Diese Bezeichnung ruft im diskursiven Gedächtnis Mikro-Geschichten wach, in denen die Frau ans Haus gebunden ist und der Mann derjenige ist, der draußen auftritt. Es wäre unrichtig zu sagen, der Ritus thematisiere in diesem Teil diese Rolle der Frau. Anders gesagt: Es geht in diesem Teil sicher nicht darum, diese Rolle zu betonen; vielmehr wird sie als Selbstverständlichkeit vorausgesetzt. Man kann vielleicht von einer figurativen und nicht von einer thematischen Isotopie sprechen.

1.2. Der postvatikanische Ritus

DIE FEIER DER TRAUUNG

1 43. *Alle, auch das Brautpaar, stehen auf. Der Priester wendet sich an das Brautpaar mit folgenden oder ähnlichen Worten:*
N. und N., Sie sind zur Kirche gekommen,
um vor der hier anwesenden Gemeinde
5 und ihrem kirchlichen Diener
Ihre Liebe durch den Herrn bestätigen und besiegeln zu lassen.
Schon durch die Taufe hat Christus Sie geheiligt.
Jetzt segnet er Ihre Liebe
und stärkt sie im Sakrament der Ehe,
10 sodaß Sie einander treu sein
und die Pflichten der Ehe auf sich nehmen können.
Antworten Sie daher vor der hier anwesenden Gemeinde auf
die Fragen, die ich Ihnen jetzt stelle:

1 44. *Der Priester stellt jetzt Fragen bezüglich der Freiheit von Braut und Bräutigam, bezüglich ihrer Treue und ihrer Bereitschaft, ihre Kinder anzunehmen und zu erziehen:*
Priester   N. und N.,
5   sind Sie aus freiem Willen

		und mit der vollen Zustimmung Ihres Herzens
		hierhin gekommen,
		um einander zu heiraten?
	Brautpaar	Ja.
10	*Priester*	Sind Sie bereit,
		als Vermählte
		einander zu lieben und zu achten
		alle Tage Ihres Lebens?
	Brautpaar	Ja.

15 *Die folgende Frage unterbleibt, wenn die Umstände, z.B. das hohe Alter der Brautleute, es nahelegen.*
      Priester   Sind Sie bereit,
                      Kinder als Geschenk aus Gottes Hand anzunehmen,
                      sie an Ihrer Liebe teilnehmen zu lassen
20   und sie im Geiste Christi und seiner Kirche zu erziehen?
      Brautpaar   Ja.

Die Vermählung

1 45. *Der Priester lädt das Brautpaar ein, den Vermählungsspruch zu sprechen:*
      Priester   Darf ich Sie also fragen,
                      einander die rechte Hand zu geben
5   und hier in dieser Gemeinschaft,
                      vor Ihrer Familie und Ihren Freunden,
                      vor Gott und seiner Kirche,
                      Ihren Willen, einander zu heiraten, bekannt zu machen.

10 *Braut und Bräutigam geben einander die rechte Hand.*
      Bräutigam   N., ich nehme dich an als meine Frau,
                      und ich verspreche dir,
                      treu zu bleiben
                      in guten und bösen Tagen,
15   in Armut und Reichtum,
                      in Krankheit und Gesundheit.
                      Ich will dich lieben und achten
                      alle Tage unseres Lebens.
      Braut   N., ich nehme dich an als meinen Mann,
20   und ich verspreche dir,
                      treu zu bleiben
                      in guten und bösen Tagen,
                      in Armut und Reichtum,
                      in Krankheit und Gesundheit.
25   Ich will dich lieben und achten
                      alle Tage unseres Lebens.

1   46. *Der Priester bestätigt den Vermählungsspruch und sagt:*
    Priester   Von nun an soll die Kirchengemeinde
                    Sie als Vermählte betrachten.
                    Der Herr festige und segne
5   Ihren Ehebund.
                    Was Gott verbunden hat,
                    das darf der Mensch nicht trennen.
    Alle   Amen.

Auch im postvatikanischen Trauungsritus treten Braut und Bräutigam bei der Eheschließung als gleichwertige Subjekte des Handelns auf.[5] Es fällt auf, daß die Differenziertheit und auch die existentielle Wechselbeziehung beider hier viel stärker betont werden. Im Vermählungsspruch wird über ein "Annehmen" des anderen als Mann, bzw. der anderen als Frau gesprochen. Man findet hier eine Transformation, in der beide einander als sich Gebende annehmen. Der Bräutigam, bzw. die Braut, bringt sich selbst in Verbindung mit der Braut, bzw. dem Bräutigam, als jemand, der sich, bzw. die sich, ihm, bzw. ihr, anbietet. Es heißt nicht: "ich nehme dich zu meiner Frau", bzw. "zu meinem Mann", sondern: "ich nehme dich an als meine Frau", bzw. "als meinen Mann". Mit anderen Worten: Die Aktivität des einen schließt die der anderen ein. Das Wort 'annehmen' drückt aus, daß das Sich-einander-Anbieten vorausgesetzt wird. Es impliziert eine vorhergehende Beurteilung (Sanktion), daß beide sich ausdrücklich geben wollen. Diese Sanktion beruht im Ritus selbst auf mehreren vorhergehenden Elementen, wie z.B. das Zur-Kirche-Kommen (Nr. 43,3), die Antwort auf die vorhergehenden Fragen (Nr. 44) und vor allem – chronologisch am nächsten – das Reichen der rechten Hand, das als Handlung in der Rubrik unter Nr. 45,10 angegeben wird. Diese Gebärde des Gebens der rechten Hand drückt sogar explizit mehr aus als der Text "ich nehme dich an als meine Frau", bzw. "als meinen Mann", nämlich die Aktivität der beiden, die einander annehmen. Der Mann nimmt die Hand der Frau an, die sie in seine Hand legt und die in seiner Hand liegt, während er die Worte ausspricht: "ich nehme dich an als meine Frau". Und ihrerseits vollzieht die Frau auf korrelative Weise dieselben Performanzen. So wird die gleichwertige Wechselbeziehung, die in der ausgesprochenen Formel schon da ist, bedeutend verstärkt.

Nach dem "ich nehme dich an als meine Frau", bzw. "als meinen Mann" folgt: "und ich verspreche dir, treu zu bleiben in guten und in

---

5 Für die vollständige und detaillierte semiotische Analyse des postvatikanischen Trauungsritus vgl. G. LUKKEN: Relevantie van de semiotische analyse-methode voor de liturgiewetenschap, in *Jaarboek voor liturgie-onderzoek* 2 (1986) 32-48 (= Nr. 15 in diesem Buch); IDEM: De nieuwe Romeinse huwelijksliturgie, in SEMANET (G. LUKKEN Hrsg.): *Semiotiek en christelijke uitingsvormen. De semiotiek van A.J. Greimas en de Parijse school toegepast op Bijbel en liturgie* (Hilversum 1987) 155-208.

bösen Tagen, in Armut und Reichtum, in Krankheit und Gesundheit. Ich will dich lieben und achten alle Tage unseres Lebens". Vor allem durch die Bezeichnung 'versprechen' wird die gleichwertige Wechselbeziehung beider Parteien bedeutend verstärkt. Der Ausdruck 'ich verspreche dir' impliziert nämlich die Voraussetzung, daß der andere oder die andere mich um etwas bittet.[6] Und das geht sogar noch weiter: Der Ausdruck 'ich verspreche dir' impliziert einen Wunsch meinerseits, der darauf gerichtet ist, daß du mich um etwas bittest. Nun, diese starke Wechselseitigkeit, die bereits die Formel 'ich verspreche dir' enthält, wird noch dadurch verstärkt, daß der andere, bzw. die andere entsprechend dieselbe Formel ausspricht. Das Versprechen kann außer der Form 'Ich verspreche dir' auch die Form haben 'Ich will' mit Infinitiv.[7] Parallel zum 'Ich verspreche dir' findet sich nun bei der Eheschließung der Satz: "Ich will dich lieben und achten alle Tage unseres Lebens". 'Ich will' ist hier also nicht einfach der Ausdruck der modalen Kompetenz des Wollens, sondern einer echten Performanz, die dem 'ich verspreche' gleichwertig ist. Das Wollen verweist auf die vorausgesetzte Frage des anderen oder der anderen und ist eigentlich eine Frage des Ich, die auf beständige Treue des Du gerichtet ist, im Tausch für die beständige Treue des Ich. Das 'Ich will' verweist auch auf den von mir vorausgesetzten Glauben des Du, daß ich mein Versprechen halten werde und auf meinen Glauben, daß das Du seinerseits treu bleiben wird. Hier geht es um ein wechselseitiges Glauben: um ein gegenseitiges Vertrauen, das gewissermaßen zwischen Ich und Du zirkuliert. Diese tiefe Wechselseitigkeit, die sich hinter der Formel "ich will dich lieben und achten" verbirgt, wird noch dadurch verstärkt, daß Braut und Bräutigam diese Formel jeweils allein aussprechen.

Außerdem kann man folgendes feststellen: Während zunächst Braut und Bräutigam ohne Differenzierung als Brautpaar bezeichnet werden (Nr. 43,1; Nr. 44,9.14.21), wird diese Undifferenziertheit dann allmählich durchbrochen. So wird in Nr. 43,3, in der Einleitung, das Brautpaar wohl entsprechend der eigenen individuellen Differenziertheit als Mann und Frau mit dem eigenen Namen genannt: "N. und N.", aber doch gilt noch, daß beide gleichzeitig angesprochen werden. In Nr. 44, bei den die Freiheit betreffenden Fragen, scheint dann eine zunehmende Differenziertheit aufzutreten. Es wird zwar einerseits dreimal vom Brautpaar (Nr. 44,9.14.21) gesprochen, andererseits findet man aber auch die Bezeichnung "Braut und Bräutigam" (Nr. 44,1-2) und die Individualisierung durch "N. und N." (Nr. 44,4). In Nr. 45, bei der eigentlichen Vermählung, kann man dann, mit Bezug auf die Differenzierung von Braut und Bräutigam, von einer Klimax sprechen. Wie bereits gesagt, wird hier sehr deutlich,

---

6 P. BRANDT: Promettre. Note de travail, in *Actes Sémiotiques. Bulletin* 7 (1984) Nr.32, 15-22.
7 BRANDT: Promettre 18ff.

daß es um zwei in einem Wechselverhältnis geht. Gerade in diesem Augenblick werden Braut und Bräutigam beide sozusagen auf ihre eigenen Füße gestellt, um sich von daher einander zuzuwenden und bleibender ehelicher Treue zu versichern. Die beiden eigene Identität wird betont. Man könnte auch sagen: Die Gleichwertigkeit von Mann und Frau als differenzierte Individuen wird auf besonders eindringliche Weise zum Ausdruck gebracht. Erst von dieser eindringlichen Gleichwertigkeit her wird in Nr. 46 die undifferenzierte Bezeichnung "Vermählte" (Nr. 46,3) gebraucht.

Obwohl im Ritus des *Rituale Romanum* bei der Eheschließung sicher von Gleichwertigkeit von Mann und Frau die Rede ist, so kann man doch sagen, daß im postvatikanischen Ritus die Gleichwertigkeit auf eine viel eindringlichere Weise zum Ausdruck kommt. Die diesbezügliche Glaubwürdigkeit des postvatikanischen Ritus wird noch dadurch verstärkt, daß nicht mehr von 'Hausfrau' gesprochen wird.

2. DIE SEGNUNG UND ÜBERREICHUNG DER RINGE

2.1. Das *Rituale Romanum*

Es fällt auf, daß im *Rituale Romanum* nur von einem Ring die Rede ist, und zwar von dem der Braut. Dieser Ring wird vom Priester gesegnet und vom Bräutigam der Braut überreicht, während der Priester noch einmal eine Gebärde des Segnens macht im Namen des Vaters und des Sohnes und des Hl. Geistes. Man kann also von einem überflüssigen Segen sprechen: Erst wird der Ring selbst gesegnet, dann empfängt ihn der Bräutigam aus der Hand des Priesters (*Sacerdos* groß geschrieben), und schließlich noch ein neuer Segen, während der Bräutigam der Braut den Ring überreicht. Dies alles betont sehr den sakralen Charakter des Geschehens, das ganz auf die Braut gerichtet ist.

Der Text bei der Segnung des Ringes spricht von diesem Ring als Zeichen der *fidelitas integra* der Braut zu ihrem Bräutigam. Auch bei der einleitenden Ansprache des Priesters am Anfang des Ritus ist die Rede vom Ring der Braut, und zwar als Zeichen "edler Liebe und bleibender Treue". In dieser Ansprache erhält der Ring auch einen juristischen Anstrich. Es ist die Rede vom Ring als "Unterpfand Ihrer edlen Liebe und bleibenden Treue". Ein Pfand wird beim Vertragsabschluß über eine Hypothek abgegeben. Wie ein Haus das Pfand ist für geliehenes Geld, so ist der Ring das Pfand für geschuldete Liebe und Treue. Man könnte sagen: Wenn die edle Liebe und die bleibende Treue aufhören, dann müßte der Ring zurückgegeben werden. In dem Fall wird der Ring 'beschlagnahmt'. Den Ring als Garantie zu betrachten, paßt deutlich zum juristischen Vertrag der eigentlichen Eheschließung. Dies drückt vor allem die Garantie des integralen, dauerhaften, definitiven Charakters dieses Vertrages aus. Dabei geht es dann nicht um den Ring selbst, sondern, dem Segensgebet entsprechend, um den getragenen Ring (*quae eum gestaverit*). Als von der Frau getragener ist er ein solches Symbol. Dieser Ring kann, entsprechend dem Segensgebet, nur dank dem Segen der Trinität als Symbol der *fidelitas integra* funktionieren. Über den Weg der *fidelitas integra* werden dann im Segensgebet zwei Ziele verfolgt: das tatsächliche Verbleiben der Braut *in pace, et voluntate tua* und das Leben der Braut für immer in wechselseitiger Liebe. Mit anderen Worten: Die *fidelitas integra*, die durch das Tragen des gesegneten Ringes symbolisiert wird, behütet sowohl die Beziehung zu Gott als auch die zum Bräutigam. Die Braut wird also deutlich als die untergeordnete gesehen: Sie empfängt vom Bräutigam den von Gott gesegneten Ring; dann wird die Braut als das Zentrum aller Aktivität aufgefaßt, einschließlich der wechselseitigen Liebe! Von der Wechselseitigkeit des gerade geschlossenen Vertrages ist hier nicht mehr viel zu finden!

Nach dem Überreichen des Ringes wird um göttlichen Schutz gebetet, wobei das Leben als ein Kampfschauplatz gesehen wird. Das Brautpaar wird auf hinterlistige Weise bedroht, und der Priester bittet um Hilfe und Schutz. Hier geht es um beide, Braut und Bräutigam. In einer abschließenden Oration wird das Gebet um Schutz und Hilfe fortgesetzt und zugespitzt. Gott wird gebeten, auf seine Diener herabzusehen. Die Ehe erscheint dabei als göttliche Institution, die auf Fortpflanzung des menschlichen Geschlechts gerichtet ist. Auch dieses Gebet bezieht sich nicht nur auf die Frau, sondern auf das Brautpaar als solches.

2.2. Der postvatikanische Ritus

Im postvatikanischen Ritus findet man unter Nr. 47 die Segnung und unter Nr. 48 die Überreichung der Ringe.[8] Der Text lautet folgendermaßen:

```
1   47. Priester    Allmächtiger Gott,
                    segne + die Ringe,
                    die sie einander geben.
                    Diese Ringe mögen ein bleibendes Zeichen
5                   ihrer gegenseitigen Liebe und Treue sein.
        Alle        Amen.

1   48. Der Bräutigam steckt den Ring an den Finger seiner Braut und
    kann dabei sagen:
```

---

[8] Für die vollständige Analyse der Ringzeremonie des postvatikanischen Trauungsritus vgl. LUKKEN: De nieuwe Romeinse huwelijksliturgie 155-208.

	Bräutigam	N., empfange diesen Ring
		als Zeichen meiner Liebe und Treue.
5		(Im Namen des Vaters und des Sohnes und des Hl.
		Geistes.)

Die Braut steckt ebenso den Ring an den Finger des Bräutigams und kann dabei sagen:

	Braut	N., empfange diesen Ring
		als Zeichen meiner Liebe und Treue.
10		(Im Namen des Vaters und des Sohnes und des Hl.
		Geistes.)

Hier geht es um zwei Ringe, einen für die Braut und einen für den Bräutigam. In Nr. 47,4-6 findet eine Evaluierung (Sanktion) der beiden gesegneten Ringe statt. Sie werden als bleibendes Zeichen der gegenseitigen Liebe und Treue dieses Mannes und dieser Frau betrachtet. Diese Sanktion ist zugleich eine Manipulation: Sie wird ausdrücklich in der Form eines Wunsches ausgesprochen: "Diese Ringe mögen ein bleibendes Zeichen ihrer gegenseitigen Liebe und Treue sein". Als solche impliziert diese Sanktion also auch ein zukünftiges Programm gegenseitiger Liebe und Treue. Weil das Gebet sich an Gott richtet, wird vorausgesetzt, daß Er das handelnde Subjekt in diesem Programm ist. Nur indirekt richtet sich die Manipulation an das Brautpaar selbst als handelndes Subjekt. Deutlich ist, daß hier, wie auch im *Rituale Romanum*, im Zusammenhang mit dem Ring ein Wert wie der der Ausdauer eine große Rolle spielt. Gleichzeitig aber zeigt sich, daß mit dem Gebrauch von zwei Ringen auch ein Sprechen über Gegenseitigkeit in Treue und Liebe verbunden ist.

In Nr. 48 geht es dann um die Überreichung der Ringe: Der Bräutigam steckt den Ring an den Finger seiner Braut, und die Braut steckt den Ring an den Finger des Bräutigams. So wird auf non-verbale Weise etwas zum Ausdruck gebracht. Der Hand, die bei der Eheschließung in der Hand des anderen/der anderen liegt, wird jetzt etwas, nämlich der Ring, hinzugefügt. So wird etwas ausgedrückt, das in der *iunctio manuum* als solcher nicht zum Ausdruck kam und nur verbal formuliert wurde: der bleibende Charakter der Performanz. Der Mann befestigt an der Hand der Braut das bleibende Zeichen ihrer Treue zu ihm. Und die Frau befestigt an der Hand des Mannes das bleibende Zeichen seiner Treue zu ihr. Es geht also bei der Frau um das Tragen des Ringes als Zeichen ihrer Liebe und Treue zum Mann und korrelativ beim Mann um das Tragen des Ringes als Zeichen seiner Liebe und Treue zur Frau. Beim Überreichen des Ringes kann ein Text gesprochen werden. Der Mann kann bei der Überreichung zur Frau sagen: "N., empfange diesen Ring als Zeichen meiner Liebe und Treue". Das Programm, das durch den Mann beabsichtigt wird, ist dann, daß die Frau den für sie bestimmten Ring empfängt als Zeichen der Liebe und Treue ihres Mannes. Und umgekehrt bittet die Frau den Mann, den für ihn bestimmten Ring zu empfangen als Zeichen der Liebe und Treue seiner Frau.

Es ist deutlich, daß bei der Überreichung der Ringe eine doppelte, wechselseitige Transformation der nicht-sichtbaren-beständigen Liebe und Treue in sichtbare-beständige Liebe und Treue stattfindet. Was in der Performanz bei der Eheschließung hörbar war, wird hier auf non-verbale Weise auch sichtbar. Man kann auch anmerken, daß bei der Überreichung der Ringe Text und Gebärde nicht miteinander korrespondieren. Bei der Gebärde ist der Ring ein Wertobjekt, das bleibende Konjunktion mit Liebe und Treue zum andern ausdrückt. Bei der gesprochenen Formel ist der Ring ein Wertobjekt, das bleibende Konjunktion mit Liebe und Treue des anderen ausdrückt. Dies nun scheint die Differenziertheit von Mann und Frau stark zu akzentuieren. Während die Ringe gerade die wechselseitige und ausschließliche Verbundenheit von Braut und Bräutigam symbolisieren, so kommt gleichzeitig in diesen Symbolen auch eine differenzierte Wechselseitigkeit zur Sprache, sowohl meine Treue zum anderen/zur anderen, als auch die Treue des anderen/der anderen zu mir. So schließt die Performanz der Überreichung der Ringe an die Performanz der Eheschließung an. Beim Abschluß des Ehebundes verfließt die Identität von Mann und Frau keineswegs, im Gegenteil: Der Ehebund ist nur ausgehend von der unersetzlichen Identität eines jeden möglich. Es geht um eine Verbundenheit in Zwei-Einheit. Nur auf Grund hiervon können Braut und Bräutigam als Verheiratete betrachtet werden.

So wird deutlich, daß, was diesen Abschnitt betrifft, ein großer Unterschied zwischen dem *Rituale Romanum* und dem postvatikanischen Ritus besteht. Während das *Rituale Romanum* bei der Ringzeremonie sozusagen einen Strich macht durch die Gleichwertigkeit von Mann und Frau, so wie sie bei der Eheschließung zum Ausdruck kam, wird sie im postvatikanischen Ritus konsequent durchgehalten. So bedeutet die Ringzeremonie eine weitere Akzentuierung der vollkommen gleichwertigen Rolle der Frau in der Ehe.

3. DIE SEGNUNG DER NEUVERMÄHLTEN

3.1. Das *Rituale Romanum*

Das *Rituale Romanum* spricht von einer *benedictio nuptialis*: von einem Ehesegen.[9] Diese Bezeichnung läßt erwarten, daß sowohl der Bräutigam

---

9 Anmerkung der Übersetzerin: Im Deutschen wurde dieses Segensgebet aus dem *Rituale Romanum* immer 'Brautsegen' genannt. Der lateinische Begriff *benedictio nuptialis* ist jedoch umfassender; er verweist nicht auf eine Person, sondern auf die Ehe. *Benedictio nuptialis* wird hier, dem Niederländischen entsprechend, mit 'Ehesegen' übersetzt.

als auch die Braut gesegnet werden. Diese Erwartung wird auch noch durch den Abschnitt in der Einleitung verstärkt, in dem zu lesen ist: "Nach dem 'Vaterunser' vor dem 'Erlöse uns, Herr' geht der Priester auf die Epistelseite, wendet sich Bräutigam und Braut zu, die vor dem Altar niederknien. Er spricht über sie die folgenden Gebete". Faktisch wird dann deutlich, daß, nach einem Gebet über die Ehe als göttliche Institution (*Propitare, Domine*), ein Segen folgt, bei dem die Segnung der Braut stark betont wird. Wenn man das Ganze überschaut, wird deutlich, daß der Bräutigam als Objekt der Segnung praktisch nicht vorkommt. Dies ist eigentlich erst am Ende der Segnung der Fall, wo die Bitte ausgesprochen wird 'daß beide die Kinder ihrer Kinder sehen mögen bis ins dritte und vierte Geschlecht und daß sie das gewünschte Alter erreichen mögen', eine Bitte, die übrigens in einer kurzen Segensformel am Ende der Feier, nach dem *Benedicamus Domino* oder *Ite, missa est* wiederholt wird. Anscheinend ist es möglich, von einem Ehesegen und von Gebeten über beide zu sprechen, auch wenn sich alle Aufmerksamkeit auf die Braut konzentriert. Nachdem zum Ausdruck gebracht ist, daß die Ehe in jeder Hinsicht eine Institution ist, die in Gottes Initiative ihren Ursprung hat, wird Gott gefragt, wohlwollend auf diese seine Dienerin herabzusehen (*respice propitius super hanc famulam tuam*). Die deiktische Bezeichnung "diese", zusammen mit der Verbindung von Braut und Gott als dem Akteur der Enunziation (*tuam*), lenkt die volle Aufmerksamkeit auf die Braut. Es ist die Rede von "herabsehen": eine Bewegung von oben nach unten, und von einem Dienstverhältnis ("Dienerin"). Das wohlwollende Herabsehen wird im folgenden ausführlich mit Bezug auf die Braut spezifiziert. So wird innerhalb dieses figurativen Trajektes des Dienstverhältnisses vor allem die Abhängigkeit und Unterordnung der Braut betont. Auf der Linie dieser Betonung liegt auch die Metapher, in der die Bitte ausgesprochen wird, daß die Ehe für sie ein *jugum dilectionis et pacis* sein möge: Liebe und Friede müssen durch die Frau in die Ehe getragen werden, so wie Tiere ein Joch auf ihrer Schulter tragen. Als Dienerin ist die Frau auch immer an den Glauben und die Gebote gebunden (*nexa fidei mandatisque*). Es geht um ein Gebundensein an die kognitive Dimension (Glaube) und an die pragmatische Dimension (Gebote). Die Abhängigkeit der Braut wird weiter betont durch die Bitte um Schutz (*tua se expetit protectione muniri*) und Stärkung für ihre Schwachheit mit der Kraft der Zucht (*muniat infirmitatem suam robore disciplinae*). Man kann sagen, daß die Abhängigkeit und Unterordnung der Braut mit Bezug auf Gott und die durch Ihn eingesetzte Ehe den Rahmen bilden für das, worum im Segen gebetet wird. Es handelt sich hier um eine figurative Isotopie. Es würde jedoch zu weit führen, wenn man sagt, daß es sich hier auch um eine thematische Isotopie handle. Mit anderen Worten: Es ist nicht so, daß die Abhängigkeit und Unterordnung der Braut das eigentliche Thema des Segens bilden. Bei dem Segen als solchem geht es vielmehr um die thematische Isotopie einer

Bestärkung der Braut in ihrem Ehebund. Abstrakter und auf semio-narrativem Niveau formuliert: Es geht darum, daß die Braut dank dem Segen Gottes ihre Ehe transformiert und immer wieder transformiert von /vorläufig/ in /definitiv/ und /dauerhaft/, von /anfänglich/ in /Erfüllung/ und /Vollheit/, von /Unterbrochenheit/ in /Kontinuität/ und von /institutionell/ in /existentiell/.

Es fällt auf, daß beim Ehesegen sehr oft von der Ehe als einer göttlichen Institution gesprochen wird. Dies berührt auch unmittelbar die Rolle der Frau. In diesem Zusammenhang ist vor allem die folgende Passage wichtig:

> Deus, qui potestate virtutis tuae de nihilo cuncta fecisti: qui dispositis universitatis exordiis, homini, ad imaginem Dei facto, ideo inseparabile mulieris adjutorium condidisti, ut femineo corpori de virili dares carne principium, docens, quod ex uno placuisset institui, numquam licere disjungi.

In dieser Passage ist von sechs Performanzen die Rede, die alle Gott als handelndes Subjekt haben:
- Gott hat alles aus dem Nichts gemacht;
- Er hat den Ursprung des Weltalls bestimmt;
- Er hat den Menschen nach dem Bild Gottes gemacht;
- Er hat für den Menschen die Frau als unabtrennbare Hilfe eingesetzt;
- Er hat dem weiblichen Körper von der männlichen Leiblichkeit her seinen Ursprung gegeben;
- So lehrte Er, daß nie getrennt werden darf, was nach seinem Willen aus Einem eingerichtet wurde.

Nachdem also gesagt ist, daß Gott alles aus dem Nichts gemacht hat (erste Performanz) und daß Er den Ursprung des Weltalls bestimmt hat (zweite Performanz), wird gesagt, daß Er den Menschen nach dem Bild Gottes gemacht hat (dritte Performanz). In dieser letzten Performanz ist die Rede von unabtrennbarer Verbundenheit des Menschen mit seinem Ursprung durch Ähnlichkeit. Man kann von einer Art Gleichwertigkeit sprechen, die unterschieden ist in Ursprung und Bild. Wenn diese göttliche Performanz erwähnt ist, wird in der vierten Performanz über das Einsetzen der für den Menschen unabtrennbaren Hilfe der Frau gesprochen. Der, der zuerst undifferenziert als 'Mensch' bezeichnet wird, wird jetzt näher differenziert als 'Mensch' und 'Frau': Dem Menschen wird durch Gott eine Frau gegeben. Dabei geht es dann nicht rein und ausschließlich um die Differenzierung als solche, sondern um die Differenzierung im Hinblick auf die Frau als unabtrennbare Hilfe für den 'Menschen'. Die Rolle der Frau wird bestimmt als die einer 'Hilfe', wodurch suggeriert wird, daß der Mensch der 'erste' ist. Diese differenzierte Verbundenheit der Frau ist kraft der Schöpfung da und wird daher als definitiv und unlösbar angesehen.

Dann wird gesagt, daß Gott dem weiblichen Körper von der männlichen Leiblichkeit her (fünfte Performanz) seinen Ursprung gegeben hat. Aufs neue wird die Differenzierung angegeben. Jetzt wird freilich nicht mehr über die Differenzierung in 'Mensch' und Frau gesprochen, sondern in Mann und Frau. Die unabtrennbare Hilfe, die dem Menschen institutionell gegeben ist, ist derart (*ideo*), daß dem weiblichen Körper sein Ursprung durch Gott vom männlichen Körper her gegeben ist. Mit anderen Worten: Die Unabtrennbarkeit der Hilfe von der Frau hängt mit der Abkunft aus dem Mann zusammen. Man kann fragen, ob diese nähere Spezifizierung der Unabtrennbarkeit nicht insofern auf die dritte und vierte Performanz zurückwirkt, als man *homo* eher mehr spezifisch als 'Mann' betrachten muß als mehr generisch als 'Mensch'. Das würde allerdings bedeuten, daß nur der Mann nach dem Bild Gottes gemacht wäre und daß die Frau ihr Bild-Sein vom Mann ableiten würde: eine Auffassung, die man tatsächlich in der Tradition findet. Es führte allerdings zu weit, diese Auffassung in diesen Diskurs hineinzulesen. Man kann lediglich sagen, daß ein Vergleich zwischen der vierten und fünften Performanz diesbezüglich zu einer gewissen Ambiguität führt. Einerseits geht es bei der vierten Performanz offensichtlich um den Menschen, andererseits wird bei der fünften Performanz nicht deutlich gesagt, daß der 'Mensch' differenziert wird in Mann und Frau, wohl aber daß die Frau aus dem Mann entstanden ist. An sich könnte man noch zu einem intertextuellen Vergleich mit dem Buch Genesis übergehen; denn wahrscheinlich bezieht sich der Text darauf. Ich verzichte jedoch auf den intertextuellen Vergleich, weil dies zu weit führen würde.

Schließlich folgt noch die sechste Performanz, nach der Er lehrte, daß nie getrennt werden darf, was nach seinem Willen als Eins eingesetzt ist. Diese Performanz hat die Form einer Beurteilung (Sanktion)-Beeinflussung (Manipulation). Durch die genannte Schöpfungsordnung tritt Gott auf als Destinator, der 'tut wissen', wie nach seinem Willen die Institution der Ehe strukturiert ist. Nach diesem Willen ist die Ehe zwischen Mann und Frau aus einer Einheit zusammengefügt. Mit anderen Worten: Gott hat die Ehe vom Ursprung her als Eins bestimmt. Und dieses Faktum ist seinerseits wieder Destinator für das Verbot der Scheidung. Die von Gott gewünschte Sache selbst, nämlich *quod ex uno placuisset institui*, ist ein institutioneller Destinator. Anders gesagt: Das Müssen nicht-zu-tun (*devoir ne pas faire*) wird durch die ursprüngliche Einheit von Mann und Frau, die der Unterschiedenheit voneinander vorausgeht, geboten. In diesem Teil des Diskurses wird also die Einheit von Mann und Frau vom einen menschlichen, bzw. männlichen Ursprung her institutionalisiert; von der noch undifferenzierten Einheit des Menschen, bzw. des Mannes her (*de virili carne – ex uno*).

Aus diesem Abschnitt über die Institution der Ehe kann man schließen, daß in diesem Diskurs auf die ein oder andere Weise der Unterschied zwischen Mann und Frau thematisiert wird. Dabei würde es zu weit führen, aus dem Diskurs herauszulesen, daß der Mann direkt ein Abbild Gottes wäre und die Frau ihr Abbild-Sein vom Mann ableite. Wohl könnte man die Gegenüberstellung von Mann und Frau, wie sie hier zum Ausdruck kommt, am besten bezeichnen mit Werten wie /ursprünglich/ und /stark/ vs. /abgeleitet/ und /schwach/. Diese Gegenüberstellung schien sich schon im Ritus der Segnung und Überreichung der Ringe anzukündigen. Und sie wird durch weitere Fakten in diesem Diskurs, auf die ich näher eingehen will, bestätigt.

Der Segen ist darauf gerichtet, daß Gott den Ehebund, so wie er von Anfang an strukturiert und geordnet ist (*societas principaliter ordinata*), instand hält. Gott sorgt für die Beständigkeit seines Segens, der seit der Schöpfung bestand und der trotz der Strafe der Erbsünde und Sintflut bestehen bleibt. Erbsünde und Sintflut funktionieren dabei als handelnde Subjekte in einem Anti-Programm, das die Werte, auf die der Segen hinzielt, bedroht. Dabei richtet sich alle Aufmerksamkeit auf die Braut. Der Segen ist vor allem ein Herabsehen auf diese Dienerin. Im Hinblick auf sie wird das Anti-Subjekt näherhin personifiziert: Es wird darum gebeten, daß der bekannte Anstifter allen Übels (*ille auctor praevaricationis*) auf gar keine Weise widerrechtlich auf bestimmte Handlungen der Braut Anspruch erhebt. Dies würde eine Unterbrechung der Werte der /Definitivität/, /Ausdauer/, /Erfüllung/, /Fülle/ und /Kontinuität/ bedeuten, auf die der Segen vor allem oder eigentlich praktisch ausschließlich im Hinblick auf die Braut gerichtet ist. Es ist wirklich auffallend, daß sich der Segen mit Bezug auf den Bräutigam nur auf die Werte der /Erfüllung/ und /Fülle/ durch das Erreichen eines hohen Alters und das Erlangen des ewigen Lebens richtet. Nur hier kommt der Mann – und dann zusammen mit der Frau – in den Blick. Diese exklusive Gerichtetheit des Segens auf die Frau in jeder Hinsicht ist dann auch sicher ein diesen Diskurs mitbestimmender Wert. Hier wird der Unterschied zwischen Mann und Frau thematisiert. In Bezug auf die Ehe als solche wird der Mann nicht gesegnet und dies, obwohl er, ebenso wie die Frau, nach dem letzten Segen am Ende der Hochzeitsmesse durch den Priester angespornt wird, die Pflichten der Ehe zu erfüllen. Der Mann befindet sich also in Bezug auf den Segen in einer anderen Position als die Frau, und dies scheint mit der göttlichen Performanz zusammenzuhängen, die in Verbindung mit der Ehe als Institution genannt wird. Die Gegensätzlichkeit zwischen Mann und Frau ist tatsächlich die von /ursprünglich/ und /stark/ vs. /abgeleitet/ und /schwach/.

Bei dem Ehesegen wird nach den Performanzen in Bezug auf die Schöpfung eine christologische Performanz ausgesprochen: *Deus, qui tam excellenti mysterio conjugalem copulam consecrasti, ut Christi et Ecclesiae sacramentum praesignares in foedere nuptiarum*. Weil diese Performanz möglicherweise auf eindringliche Weise die Stellung der Frau gegenüber dem Mann berührt, gehe ich tiefer darauf ein. Es geht hier um die Performanz des 'Konsekrierens' der *conjugalis copula*, das heißt: der Verbindung oder Vereinigung von Mann und Frau als Vermählte. Die Konsekration findet statt durch ein herausragendes 'Mysterium'. Mysterium verweist hier auf eine sichtbare Wirklichkeit, die auf die ein oder andere Weise an einer nicht-wahrnehmbaren Wirklichkeit partizipiert und auf sie verweist. Mit anderen Worten: Gott hat den Ehebund zwischen Mann und Frau konsekriert, das heißt geheiligt und auf eine höhere Ebene gebracht, indem er ihn zu einer herausragenden sichtbaren Wirklichkeit gemacht hat, die auf eine unsichtbare Wirklichkeit verweist. Der Text enthält eine ziemlich pleonastische Formulierung. Nachdem gesagt ist, daß Gott den Ehebund durch ein herausragendes 'Mysterium' geheiligt hat, wird als Folge angegeben, daß der Ehebund ein Abbild ist (*praesignares*) und eine sichtbare-unsichtbare Wirklichkeit (*sacramentum*) in Bezug auf die Relation Christus – Kirche.

Es ist also die Rede von einer neuen Wirklichkeit, die eine andere Wirklichkeit in sich trägt, diese andere Wirklichkeit jedoch nicht erscheinen läßt. Semiotisch betrachtet ist hier die Rede von einem 'Sein' und zugleich 'nicht-Erscheinen'. Die Transformation bezieht sich auf das 'Sein', auf der Ebene des 'Erscheinens' aber wird diese Transformation kognitiv nicht wahrgenommen. In diesem Sinn ist es semiotisch richtig, von 'verborgen' zu sprechen. Doch ist damit nicht alles gesagt, weil gleichzeitig auf die ein oder andere Weise von Sichtbarkeit die Rede ist: von Erscheinen also. In diesem Sinn kann man, semiotisch betrachtet, von 'wahr' sprechen. Es ist dann wohl auch nicht ganz richtig, *mysterium* und *sacramentum* mit 'verborgen' oder mit Geheimnis zu übersetzen. Der Grund dafür ist, daß diese Begriffe zu sehr das 'nicht-Erscheinen' betonen und zu wenig die Tatsache unterstreichen, daß auf die ein oder andere Weise auch etwas von der wirklichen Performanz im 'Sein' ans Licht kommt. Eine Bezeichnung wie 'Heilsmysterium' wird dem Text wohl noch am ehesten gerecht. Gott hat den Bund zwischen Mann und Frau dadurch geheiligt, daß er ihn zu einem Heilsmysterium gemacht hat, in dem die Beziehung zwischen Christus und der Kirche auf geheimnisvolle Weise abgebildet wird.

Man stößt hier im Grunde auf die Ehetheologie, nach der der Ehebund zwischen Mann und Frau ein Abbild des Bundes zwischen Christus und seiner Braut, der Kirche, ist. Nach dieser Ehetheologie kommt in der christlichen Ehe und durch sie diese Relation zustande. Es ist möglich, diese Theologie so zu lesen, daß der Mann Christus repräsentiert und die Frau die Kirche. In diesem Fall könnte in dieser Ehetheologie auch die Unterordnung der Frau unter den Mann ein Faktum sein. Aber es ist doch immer wieder die Frage, ob der Diskurs selbst diese Bedeutung in sich trägt. Im Abbild geht es zunächst um die Beziehung zwischen dem Ehebund und dem Bund zwischen Christus und seiner Kirche. Ob auch thematisiert wird, daß der Mann die Rolle Christi hat und die Frau die der Kirche, ist jeweils im konkreten Diskurs zu untersuchen. Nun, im Ehesegen nach dem *Rituale Romanum* könnte für eine 'untertänige' Lesart der Ehetheologie mit Bezug auf die Frau ein Hinweis darin zu finden sein, daß die Frau dort als /abgeleitet/ und /schwach/ gegenüber dem Mann als /ursprünglich/ und /stark/ erscheint. Gegen eine solche Lesart spricht allerdings, daß die Figur 'Braut' als solche bei der Kirche fehlt und daß im Hinblick auf die Ehe nicht von Mann und Frau gesprochen wird, sondern von einer *conjugalis copula* ohne nähere Differenzierung. Diese letzten Hinweise scheinen mir entscheidend zu sein. Meiner Ansicht nach wäre es daher unrichtig, in diesem Abschnitt die Unterordnung der Frau unter den Mann thematisiert zu sehen.

3.2. Der postvatikanische Ritus

Der postvatikanische Trauungsritus kennt drei Möglichkeiten für die Segnung der Brautleute, und zwar eine lange Segnung (Nr. 33) und zwei kurze Segnungen (Nr. 120 und 121). Die lange Segnung (Nr. 33) ist in den Trauungsritus selbst aufgenommen. In diesem Sinn ist ihr im Vergleich zu den Alternativen in Nr. 120 und 121 der Vorzug zu geben. Diese lange Segnung ist eine Bearbeitung des Ehesegens aus dem *Rituale Romanum*. Man neigt dann dazu, diese Segnung an Hand der Analyse des Ehesegens aus dem *Rituale Romanum* zu analysieren und jeweils die Unterschiede anzugeben. Die geänderte Segnung ist aber ein eigener Diskurs mit seinem eigenen Kontext. Erst wenn dieser Diskurs als Ganzer und als solcher analysiert ist, kann man ihn mit dem aus dem *Rituale Romanum* vergleichen. Nach der Übersetzung von Nr. 33 gebe ich hier die Resultate der Gesamtanalyse mit Rücksicht auf das Thema der Rolle der Frau wieder.

1   33. *Nach dem Vaterunser wird das 'Erlöse uns ...' weggelassen. Der Priester wendet sich an das Brautpaar und sagt, mit gefalteten Händen:*
    Brüder und Schwestern,
    laßt uns mit einem demütigen Gebet an den Herrn wenden
5   und bitten,
    daß Er wohlwollend seinen Segen herabsende auf seine Dienerin N.,
    die sich in Christus mit ihrem Bräutigam verbunden hat,
    und daß Er sie beide, die in einem heiligen Bund vereinigt sind,
    (durch das Sakrament des Leibes und Blutes Christi)
10 in Liebe und Einmütigkeit vereinigt erhalte.

    Alle beten eine Zeitlang in der Stille. Danach breitet der Zelebrant die Hände aus und spricht:
    – Gott, Du hast durch die Fülle Deiner Kraft
    alles aus dem Nichts geschaffen,
15 und die Entstehung der Welt bestimmt;

Du hast den Menschen gemacht nach dem Bild seines Gottes
und dem Mann eine Frau als unabtrennbare Hilfe gegeben;
es ist Dein Wille,
daß beide nicht mehr zwei sind, sondern ein Fleisch,
20 und was Du zu einer Einheit gemacht hast,
das darf der Mensch nicht trennen.

– Gott, Du hast den Bund zwischen Mann und Frau
zu einem heiligen Geheimnis gemacht,
so groß, wie die Liebe Christi zu seiner Braut, der Kirche.

25 – Gott, durch Dich wird die Frau mit ihrem Mann verbunden:
diesem Bund,
der seit der Schöpfung besteht,
schenkst Du Deinen Segen,
einen Segen, der auch nach der Strafe der Erbsünde und Sintflut
30 bei uns geblieben ist.
Gott, schaue doch gnädig herab auf Deine Dienerin (N.);
sie bittet für ihre Ehe um die Hilfe Deines Segens:
laß Liebe und Frieden von ihr ausstrahlen,
und mache sie zum Ebenbild der großen Frauen,
35 die die Heilige Schrift uns als Beispiel vorstellt.

Gib,
daß sie das volle Vertrauen ihres Mannes besitze,
daß er sie achte als einen gleichwertigen Lebensgefährten,
daß er ihr die Ehre erweise, die ihr zukommt,
40 und sie liebe wie Christus
seine Braut, die Kirche, liebgehabt hat.

Und nun bitten wir Dich, Herr:
hilf, daß Deine Diener N. und N.
im Glauben treu sind und an Deinen Geboten hängen,
45 ihrem Versprechen treu sind
und untadelig in ihrem Lebenswandel;
gib, daß sie durch die Kraft der Frohen Botschaft
vor allen gute Zeugen Christi seien.
(Gib, daß ihre Ehe fruchtbar werde,
50 daß sie ihren Kindern gute Eltern sein
und daß sie beide einst die Kinder ihrer Kinder sehen mögen.)

Gib, daß sie am Ende in hohem Alter
zu einem Leben der Seligen gelangen in Deinem himmlischen Königreich.
55 Durch Christus unsern Herrn.

Alle   Amen.

In der einleitenden Rubrik wird gesagt, daß der Priester sich dem Brautpaar zuwendet, was bedeutet, daß er ein Programm ausführen will. Dieses Programm besteht anscheinend zunächst in einer Beeinflussung der anwesenden Brüder und Schwestern. Sie werden dazu aufgefordert, sich mit einem demütigen Gebet an den Herrn zu wenden (Z. 3-5). Dieses Gebet seinerseits zielt darauf ab, den Herrn in Bezug auf seinen Segen im Hinblick auf das Brautpaar zu beeinflussen. Es ist eigentlich unrichtig, ohne weiteres zu sagen, daß das Brautpaar als solches Zustandssubjekt ist, das mit dem göttlichen Segen verbunden werden muß. Es geht nämlich um "seine Dienerin N." als Subjekt der Sache seines "wohlwollenden Segens" und um beide als Zustandssubjekte der Werte wie "Liebe und Einmütigkeit", auf die sich der Segen richtet (Z. 6-10). Nach dieser Einleitung spricht der Priester dann ein Segensgebet aus, in dem dieselbe Gliederung wiederkehrt: Der Segen richtet sich zuerst an die Braut und erst danach an Braut und Bräutigam. Im Segensgebet kommt zuerst die Ehe als göttliche Institution zur Sprache. Es werden vier Performanzen genannt, die Gott als handelndes Subjekt haben:
- Gott hat alles aus dem Nichts geschaffen;
- Er hat die Entstehung der Welt bestimmt;
- Er hat den Menschen nach dem Bild Gottes gemacht;
- Er hat dem Mann eine Frau als unabtrennbare Hilfe gegeben.

Es fällt auf, daß im Hinblick auf den Menschen bei der dritten Performanz nicht von schaffen, sondern von 'machen' gesprochen wird:[10] Anscheinend geht es um ein Handeln Gottes, das Ihm sozusagen näher liegt und weniger von seiner Kompetenz verlangt. Etwas Ähnliches wird wohl auch durch die Wendung "nach dem Bild seines Gottes" ausgedrückt (Z. 16). Es ist die Rede von Verbundenheit mit dem Ursprung durch Gleichnis. Der Mensch ist unabtrennbar mit Gott verbunden. Es besteht eine bestimmte Gleichwertigkeit, die unterschieden wird in Ursprung und Bild. Und diese unterschiedene Einheit hat gleichzeitig etwas Institutionelles und Objektives: Sie ist ein in der Menschheit vom Ursprung her anwesendes Gegebenes.

Bei der vierten Performanz erscheint eine neue Differenzierung. Der, der bei der dritten Performanz undifferenziert als 'Mensch' bezeichnet wird, wird jetzt in Mann und Frau unterschieden: Dem Mann wird eine Frau gegeben (Z. 17). Dabei geht es nicht nur einfach um die Differenzierung als solche, sondern im Hinblick auf die Frau als unabtrennbare Hilfe. Es ist also die Rede von einer differenzierten Verbundenheit, die kraft der Schöpfung anwesend ist. Dabei scheint die Wendung 'Hilfe' auf den Mann als 'ersten' zu weisen.

Wenn die vierte Performanz formuliert ist, beginnt der Priester mit

---

10 Dieser Unterschied besteht im Ehesegen nach dem *Rituale Romanum*, wo beide Male *facere* verwendet wird, nicht.

einer Sanktion mit Bezug auf diese Performanz. Er sagt: "Es ist Dein Wille, daß beide nicht mehr zwei sind, sondern ein Fleisch" (Z. 18-19). Gott wird demnach durch den Priester als Destinator eines Programms betrachtet und beurteilt, das sich auf das "nicht mehr zwei, sondern ein Fleisch Sein" von Mann und Frau richtet. So wird noch einmal das Institutionelle, Definitive und Dauerhafte der Ehe betont. Wohl besteht ein Unterschied zur vierten Performanz. Da wird die Einheit auf die Frau hin ('unabtrennbare Hilfe') zum Ausdruck gebracht, während dies hier auf beide hin, Mann und Frau, geschieht. Außerdem wird hier, deutlicher als bei der vierten Performanz, der bleibende Auftrag zur Transformation der Differenzierung in zwei in eine untrennbare Einheit ausgedrückt. Es ist also die Rede von einem gleichwertigeren institutionellen Platz der Frau. Der Priester sagt dann: "und was Du zu einer Einheit gemacht hast, das darf der Mensch nicht trennen" (Z. 20-21). Hier geht es um ein Verbot eines Anti-Programms, mit dem 'Menschen' als handelndes Subjekt.[11] Jetzt ist also nicht mehr Gott der Destinator, wie gerade noch ("es ist Dein Wille"), sondern die durch Gott bewirkte Sache selbst ("was Du zu einer Einheit gemacht hast"). Ausgangspunkt für das Verbot des Anti-Programms ist dieser institutionelle Destinator. Mit anderen Worten: Das Müssen nicht-zu-tun (*devoir ne pas faire*) wird durch die Eheeinheit aufgetragen, so wie sie kraft der Schöpfung durch Gott zustandegekommen ist. Außerdem wird klar, daß die Scheidung vom undifferenzierten 'Menschen' ausgeht: Die Einheit könnte durch das, was nicht getrennt, aber vermischt und ungeordnet ist, geschieden werden.

Nachdem im Text die christologische Dimension der Eheinstitution zur Sprache gebracht ist – auf die entsprechende Analyse komme ich noch zurück – wird im Segensgebet zur eigentlichen Segensbitte übergeleitet (Z. 25-30). Der Segen besteht von Anfang an, und die Anti-Programme der Strafe der Erbsünde und Sintflut haben ihn nicht aufhören lassen. Die Strafe der Erbsünde und Sintflut bestand aus Disharmonie, Trennung und Vernichtung. Es war die Rede von Konfusion, Unordnung und Trennung dessen, was zusammengehört. So sind die Wendungen "Strafe der Erbsünde und Sintflut" da, wo auch der 'Mensch' ist, der 'trennt'. Dank dem Segen jedoch konnte die Ehe als geordnete Einheit standhalten. Zunächst spitzt sich das Segensgebet auf die Braut zu (Z. 31-35). Als Dienerin, auf die Gott gnädig herabsieht, befindet sie sich auf dem figurativen Trajekt des Dienstverhältnisses und der Abhängigkeit. Im Hinblick auf die Braut wird gebetet um Werte wie /Beständigkeit der Zwei-Einheit/, /Fülle/ und /Kontinuität/. Dann kommt der Mann in den Blick,

---

11 In der Aussage 'was Du zu einer Einheit gemacht hast' wird einerseits das Objekt deutlich, das nicht getrennt werden darf. Andererseits verbirgt sich in diesem Ausdruck die Eheeinheit selbst als ein Destinator: Als das, was Gott zu einer Einheit gemacht hat, darf es der Mensch nicht scheiden.

während die Frau einen zentralen Platz behält: "Gib, daß sie das volle Vertrauen ihres Mannes besitze, daß er sie achte als einen gleichwertigen Lebensgefährten, daß er ihr die Ehre erweise, die ihr zukommt, und sie liebe wie Christus seine Braut, die Kirche, liebgehabt hat" (Z. 36-41). Die Frau ist hier also das rezeptive Subjekt. Die Aktivität geht vom Mann aus, aber er ist hier nicht derjenige, um den es geht; der Segen richtet sich über den Mann an die Frau und noch nicht an den Mann als solchen. Interessant ist dabei das folgende: Obschon das Handeln der Frau hier zwar weniger explizit zum Ausdruck kommt, ist es doch auf die ein oder andere Weise da, und zwar gerade in den Wendungen "das volle Vertrauen", "achte" und "die Ehre erweise, die ihr zukommt". Durch diese Wendungen soll der Eindruck entstehen, daß die Bewegung vom Mann her im Sein und Verhalten der Frau begründet ist. Es besteht eine Aktivität, die vom Mann ausgeht, auf Grund vorausgesetzter Aktivitäten seitens der Frau. So wird in diesem Abschnitt betont, daß Einheit und Verbundenheit sich ständig in und durch Differenzierung und durch exklusive Wechselseitigkeit vollziehen. Außerdem fällt auf, daß in diesem Abschnitt ausdrücklich die Gleichwertigkeit von Frau und Mann zum Ausdruck gebracht wird: Es wird darum gebeten, daß der Mann seine Frau als gleichwertige Lebensgefährtin anerkenne.

Die Reihe der Segensgebete über die Braut wird folgendermaßen eingeleitet: "Gott, schaue doch gnädig herab auf Deine Dienerin" (Z. 31). Entsprechend ist der Übergang zu den Segensgebeten über Braut und Bräutigam zusammen: "Und nun bitten wir Dich, Herr" (Z. 42). Offensichtlich handelt es sich um eine Klimax: "doch" geht über in die enunziative Ablösung "nun"; auf dieses "nun" scheint sich das Segensgebet zu konzentrieren. Die Enunziation gibt ihm, wie auch immer, einen eigenen Akzent. Erneut erscheint in dieser Reihe von Segensgebeten das Dienstverhältnis, jetzt aber von beiden: von Braut und Bräutigam. Sie werden als "Diener" des "Herrn" beschaut (Z. 43). Im Hinblick auf beide wird um Treue sowohl in Bezug auf die kognitive als die pragmatische Dimension gebeten. Es geht um Werte wie /Ausdauer/ und /Fülle/. Es wird die Wirkung der Ehe nach außen hin erfleht, da, wo gebetet wird, "daß sie durch die Kraft der Frohen Botschaft vor allen gute Zeugen Christi seien" (Z. 47-48). Schließlich wird gebetet um /Fülle/ und /Ausdauer/ durch die Fruchtbarkeit der Ehe, liebevolle Beziehung zu den Kindern, durch das Erreichen eines hohen Alters und die endgültige Vollendung in der himmlischen /Fülle/ (Z. 49-54).

Auch in diesem Ehesegen kommt eine christliche Performanz der Ehe zum Ausdruck. Im Zusammenhang mit der Rolle der Frau ist es wichtig, hierauf näher einzugehen. Der Text heißt: "Gott, Du hast den Bund zwischen Mann und Frau zu einem heiligen Geheimnis gemacht, so groß, wie die Liebe Christi zu seiner Braut, der Kirche" (Z. 22-24). Es ist die Rede von einer Relation zwischen dem Bund von Mann und Frau und der Liebe

Christi zu seiner Braut, der Kirche, die auf der Ebene des Geheimnisses liegt. Geheimnis, oder 'verborgen', bedeutet semiotisch betrachtet: 'Sein' und gleichzeitig 'nicht-Erscheinen'. Es ist also, narrativ gesehen, die Rede von einer Transformation in Bezug auf das 'Sein', die auf der Ebene des 'Erscheinens' nicht wahrgenommen wird. Nun fällt auf, daß der Text nicht über den Bund von Mann und Frau spricht als Geheimnis der Liebe Christi zu seiner Braut, der Kirche, sondern von "einem Geheimnis, so groß wie die Liebe Christi zu seiner Braut, der Kirche". Mit anderen Worten: Auf der Ebene des 'Seins' ist nicht die Rede von einer Relation zwischen dem Bund von Mann und Frau als solchem und der Liebe Christi zu seiner Kirche als solcher, vielmehr geht es um die Relation zwischen der Heiligkeit des Bundes und dem Umfang der Liebe Christi zu seiner Braut, der Kirche. Die Heiligkeit des Bundes zwischen Mann und Frau hat einen so großen Umfang, daß sie der Liebe Christi zu seiner Kirche ähnlich ist. Die Qualität der Heiligkeit wird quantitativ ausgedrückt. Es geht um einen Vergleich des Maßes der Heiligkeit des Bundes auf dem Niveau des Seins mit der übergroßen, übermenschlichen Liebe Christi. Dieser Abschnitt ist also, christologisch gesehen, sicher 'schwächer' als der im Ehesegen des *Rituale Romanum*, wo die Rede ist von einer Relation zwischen dem Ehebund als solchem und dem Bund Christi mit seiner Kirche. Außerdem ist der Text insofern begrenzter, als er nur die Relation von 'Sein' und 'nicht-Erscheinen' und also 'Geheimnis' zum Ausdruck bringt und daher allen Nachdruck auf die Unsichtbarkeit des 'Seins' legt. Daß es auch, wie bei jedem Symbol, um Sichtbarkeit und also um 'Erscheinen' geht, kommt hier nicht zum Ausdruck.[12] Die Frage ist jetzt, ob hier denn nicht die unterschiedenen Rollen von Mann und Frau thematisiert und sozusagen christologisiert werden. Man könnte darauf hinweisen, daß hier doch keine Rede ist von einer undifferenzierten Bezeichnung wie *conjugalis copula*, sondern daß hier ausdrücklich vom "Bund zwischen Mann und Frau" gesprochen wird. Doch erscheint es unrichtig, hier die Relation zur Rolle von Mann und Frau so durchzuziehen, als ob der Mann Christus und die Frau die Kirche repräsentieren würden. Was hier nämlich thematisiert wird, ist die Quantität der Heiligkeit des Bundes. Deshalb wäre es meines Erachtens unrecht, in diesen Abschnitt eine Unterordnung der Frau unter den Mann hineinzulesen, die dann christologisch legitimiert würde. Eine solche Auffassung würde dem Diskurs Unrecht tun. Anders ist es bei dem bereits genannten Abschnitt, wo beim Segen der Mann in den Blick kommt und gebetet wird: "Gib, daß (...) er sie liebe wie Christus seine Braut, die Kirche, liebgehabt hat" (Z. 36-41).

---

12 Übrigens ist meines Erachtens die niederländische Übersetzung dieses Abschnitts unrichtig: In der lateinischen *Editio typica* steht hier nämlich genau derselbe Text wie im *Rituale Romanum*. Ich begnüge mich mit dem Hinweis auf die gerade gemachte Analyse des betreffenden Abschnitts bei der Behandlung des Ehesegens nach dem *Rituale Romanum*.

In diesem Abschnitt wird eine Christusrepräsentation des Mannes und eine ekklesiale Repräsentation der Frau suggeriert. So scheint hier die Unterordnung der Frau christologisch legitimiert zu werden. Merkwürdigerweise muß man dann aber feststellen, daß dieser Abschnitt als solcher nicht im Ehesegen des *Rituale Romanum* vorkommt.

Es ist deutlich, daß der postvatikanische Ehesegen in Bezug auf die Rolle der Frau einen Fortschritt gegenüber dem Ehesegen im *Rituale Romanum* bedeutet. Dieser Segen konzentriert sich ja nicht ausschließlich auf die Braut, und die Opposition Mann – Frau wird nicht thematisiert als die von /ursprünglich/ und /stark/ vs. /abgeleitet/ und /schwach/. Im Gegenteil: Die Betonung der Unterschiedenheit, d.h. der jeweils eigenen Individualität, um der Einheit willen, wird in diesem Segen deutlich thematisiert. In diesem Segen kommt zum Ausdruck, daß die Zwei-Einheit von Mann und Frau bewahrt bleibt durch den wohlwollenden Vollzug des Segens Gottes, durch den Gott ständig bewirkt, daß durch wechselseitige Differenzierung von Mann und Frau die Einheit von Mann und Frau zustandekommt. Man kann sagen, daß der Ehesegen des postvatikanischen Ritus in dieser Hinsicht konsequent an die Eheschließung selbst und an den Ritus der Segnung und Überreichung der Ringe anschließt. Auch der postvatikanische Ehesegen unterscheidet sich in dieser Hinsicht stark vom Ehesegen des *Rituale Romanum*, in dem wohl von Differenzierung die Rede ist, jedoch auf einseitige Weise: Es geht dort um eine Einheit ohne Trennung, die ausschließlich von der Frau her thematisiert wird. Die Betonung der jeweiligen Eigenart und Wechselwirkung fehlt. Auch beim Ehesegen des *Rituale Romanum* liegt dies auf der Linie des Vorhergehenden, insofern nämlich auch die Ringzeremonie einseitig auf die Frau abgestimmt ist. Jedoch führt der postvatikanische Ehesegen die Linie, die bei der Eheschließung und bei der Segnung und Überreichung der Ringe beginnt, nicht in jeder Hinsicht durch. Man kann auf den Abschnitt hinweisen, in dem der Mann als Repräsentant Christi und die Frau als Repräsentantin der Kirche vorgestellt werden. Außerdem klingt in Bezug auf die Rolle der Frau das alte *Rituale Romanum* dort noch durch, wo beim eigentlichen Segen die Aufmerksamkeit doch zuerst wieder auf die Braut gerichtet ist und der Bräutigam erst von hierher in den Blick kommt.

Aus literar-historischen Betrachtungen ist näher zu erklären, was hierfür der Grund ist. Bei der Erneuerung des Ritus nach dem Vatikanum II wollte man – unter starkem Einfluß einer Veröffentlichung des Niederländers J. de Jong[13] – den klassischen Ehesegen des *Rituale Romanum* als

---

13 J. DE JONG: Brautsegen und Jungfrauenweihe. Eine Rekonstruktion des altrömischen Trauungsritus als Basis für theologische Besinnung, in *Zeitschrift für Katholische Theologie* 84 (1962) 300-322; vgl. auch IDEM: Reconstructie van de oud-romeinse huwelijksliturgie als basis voor theologische bezinning, in *Tijdschrift voor liturgie* 46 (1962) 341-363.

herausragenden Segen soweit wie möglich erhalten, ihn aber gleichzeitig der neuen Vorschrift von Vatikanum II, nach der die Segnung sich in Zukunft auf Braut und Bräutigam zu richten hat, anpassen.[14] Dies führte in Nr. 33,36-41 zu einem ziemlich gewundenen Übergang zur Segnung von Braut und Bräutigam. Aus der Sicht der synchronen Methode ist diese Erklärung nicht möglich und auch nicht relevant. Die synchrone Methode gibt genau an, worin die Verdienste des Textes, so wie er jetzt vor uns liegt, bestehen. Dabei wird deutlich, daß der Text wohl auf den ersten Blick durch die Betonung der Frau und den Eindruck der Christusrepräsentation des Mannes ein einseitiges patriarchales Bild von der Frau zu bezeugen scheint, daß er aber andererseits gerade die Unterschiedenheit von Mann und Frau in ihrer Gleichwertigkeit stark betont und daher gut in die heutige Zeit paßt.

Der postvatikanische Ritus bietet in Nr. 120 und 121 noch zwei alternative Weisen für den Segen über Braut und Bräutigam an. Die Segnung nach Nr. 120 bedeutet einen Fortschritt im Vergleich zum Ehesegen, der in den Ritus selbst aufgenommen ist (vgl. Nr. 33). Der Segen wird über Braut und Bräutigam gleichermaßen ausgesprochen. Die Zwei-Einheit der beiden und die Wechselseitigkeit ihrer Beziehung werden betont. Am Ende dieses Segens wird jedoch ein besonderes Segensgebet formuliert, sowohl im Hinblick auf den Mann als die Frau. In dieser Segensbitte wird die Rolle der Frau als Mutter und als diejenige, die "ihr Haus durch liebevolle Hingabe und Herzlichkeit erstrahlen läßt" deutlich, während der Mann als derjenige betrachtet wird, der "seine Aufgabe erfüllt als treuer Ehemann und sorgsamer Vater". Da bei der Frau so ausdrücklich auf ihre herzliche Hingabe in Bezug auf ihr Haus verwiesen wird, wird der Eindruck des Gegensatzes erweckt zwischen /nach innen gerichtet/ und /privat/ in Bezug auf die Frau vs. /nach draußen gerichtet/ und /öffentlich/ in Bezug auf den Mann. Bei aller Gleichwertigkeit zeigt dieser Segen doch gleichzeitig ständig ein bestimmtes Rollenverständnis bezüglich der Frau, das gerade in unserer Kultur durchbrochen wird. Dies geschieht allerdings nicht in der zweiten Alternative: beim Segen nach Nr. 121. Das Segensgebet wird gleichzeitig über Braut und Bräutigam ausgesprochen, und ihre Rollen werden nicht weiter differenziert. Nur noch ein schwaches Echo von der besonderen Rolle der Braut klingt nach beim Gebet "für diese Braut und für den Mann, dem sie sich heute durch das Sakrament der Ehe vermählt". Der Segen geht dann aber unmittelbar über in ein Gebet über Braut und Bräutigam zusammen. Man kann daraus schließen, daß dieser Segen die Gleichwertigkeit von Mann und Frau auf sehr offene Weise deutlich werden läßt.

---

14 Konstitution über die heilige Liturgie, Art. 78.

4. KONKLUSIONEN

Am Ende dieser Analysen des Trauungsritus nach dem *Rituale Romanum* und des postvatikanischen Trauungsritus kann man folgendes konkludieren. Erstens: Bei der Eheschließung selbst nach dem *Rituale Romanum* kann man von Gleichwertigkeit von Mann und Frau sprechen. Dies ist jedoch keineswegs der Fall beim Ritus der Segnung und Überreichung der Ringe und beim Ehesegen. Im Gegenteil: In diesen Teilen des Ritus wird die Stellung der Frau als der des Mannes vollkommen untergeordnet angesehen. Die Ring-Zeremonie als Ganze macht sozusagen einen Strich durch die Gleichwertigkeit von Mann und Frau, wie sie bei der Eheschließung zum Ausdruck kommt. Und im Ehesegen wird die Frau als 'schwacher' und bei der Schöpfung sozusagen 'abgetrennter' Mensch betrachtet, der – im Gegensatz zum Mann – den besonderen Segen Gottes nötig hat. Zweitens: Der postvatikanische Trauungsritus bedeutet einen wichtigen Fortschritt. Dies gilt zunächst für die Eheschließung selbst, in der Mann und Frau als sehr gleichwertige und eigenständige Individuen in Erscheinung treten, die gerade in ihrer Unterschiedenheit und durch sie zum Bund einer Zwei-Einheit fähig sind. Dieselbe Betonung kehrt auf eindrucksvolle Weise bei der Überreichung der Ringe wieder, wobei die dauerhafte und ausschließliche Verbundenheit von Braut und Bräutigam in differenzierter Wechselseitigkeit sichtbar gemacht wird. Der Ehesegen schließlich betont, daß auch im Eheleben selbst die Zwei-Einheit nur in der Unterschiedenheit und durch sie immer wieder zustandekommen kann. Der Ritus als Ganzer ist also ein wichtiger Fortschritt gegenüber dem des *Rituale Romanum*. Doch legt der Ehesegen noch einen eigenen Akzent auf die Frau, als ob sie zu allererst den Segen nötig hätte und der Mann erst an zweiter Stelle. Außerdem erweckt der Ehesegen den Eindruck, daß die Frau in der Ehe die untergeordnete Rolle der Kirche zu repräsentieren habe gegenüber dem Mann als Repräsentanten Christi. Von einem weiteren Durchbruch kann man in den alternativen Segensgebeten sprechen, bei denen Braut und Bräutigam zusammen gesegnet werden. In der ersten Alternative klingt wohl noch das klassische Rollenverständnis von der Frau durch. Dies fehlt allerdings vollständig im zweiten alternativen Segen.

17. Semiotic Analysis of the Confession at the Beginning of the Eucharist

In the Roman Missal a confession can be found at the beginning of the Eucharist.[1] This confession has a long tradition; the first onsets are to be found in the ninth century in the Sacramentary of Amiens: the present *confiteor* is already recognizable.[2] A possible way to reflect on this confession is to describe its history. This would be a reflexion along the line of diachrony (through time). On the other hand it is also possible to consider this confession without the help of external, historical data: as a self-reliant, synchronic (simultaneous) whole. In my analysis the last track is followed: the path of semiotics, in case a specific semiotics, that of Greimas, sometimes called the semiotics of the Paris School. The text of the confession goes as follows:[3]

1   *Then the confession of guilt[4] follows. The priest invites the faithful to this:*

    Brothers and sisters,
    Let us confess our sins, let us convert ourselves to God
5   in order to celebrate the sacred eucharist properly.

    A short silence follows. Then all confess together:
    I confess to almighty God,
    and to all of you,
    that I have sinned
10 in words and thoughts,
    in doing and failing to do,

---

* Semiotische analyse van de schuldbelijdenis aan het begin van de eucharistieviering, in *Bijdragen. Tijdschrift voor filosofie en theologie* 47 (1986) 290-317. Translated by W.M. Speelman, M.Div.
1 *The Roman Missal* (Collegeville (Minn.) 1974) 406-410.
2 V. LEROQUAIS (ed.): L'*Ordo Missae* du sacramentaire d'Amiens (IXe s.), in *Ephemerides liturgicae* 41 (1927) 440. Cf. H. WEGMAN: Schuldbelijdenis, in L. BRINKHOFF a.o. (ed.): *Liturgisch Woordenboek* II (Roermond 1965-1968) 2532.
3 *Altaarmissaal voor de Nederlandse kerkprovincie* (Utrecht 1979) 600-601. The object of analysis is the confirmed Dutch translation of the *Confiteor*. This translation has been rendered into English as accurately as possible. For the motivation of this method, see footnote 5 in the contribution "Relevance of Semiotic Analysis to the Liturgical Sciences" (= no. 15 in this book).
4 Note of the translator: where the English language uses the word 'confession', in Dutch it is common to say 'confession of guilt'.

> *striking their breasts they say:*
> through my fault, through my fault,
> through my great fault.

15 *Then all continue:*
   Therefore I beg blessed Mary, ever virgin,
   all the angels and saints,
   and you, brothers and sisters,
   to pray for me to the Lord, our God.

20 *After this follows the absolution by the priest:*
   May almighty God have mercy on us,
   forgive us our sins
   and bring us to everlasting life.
   all   Amen.

A semiotic analysis of a discourse is usually a lengthy process which goes forward, as it were, gropingly. This process resulted in two hypotheses which I wish to present to the readers.[5] Perhaps they will be incited to go and look for a third, more decisive hypothesis themselves.

THE FIRST HYPOTHESIS

Semiotic analysis concentrates on the web that lies hidden under the perceivable manifestation level. With that the sense pattern increases in abstraction as the level lies deeper. With increasing degree of abstraction the level of discoursive structures, the surface level and the deep level come up successively.

1. THE LEVEL OF DISCOURSIVE STRUCTURES

With respect to the discoursive structures[6] two components are relevant: the discoursive syntax and the discoursive semantics.

---

5 First I have performed an analysis individually and presented this to J. Joosse, P. de Maat and L. van Tongeren. This led to some more or less inessential corrections that I incorporated in hypothesis 1. The more basic questions resulted in hypothesis 2, which was introduced notably by P. de Maat. However, I incline to think that a still more specific reading of this discourse must be possible.
6 Especially in recent years, the level of discoursive structures has seen marked development.

1.1. Discoursive syntax

This component is about the question how the discourse is given form with regard to the actors, times and places.

Discoursive situations

In our text there is a certain succession in time (temporalization). Apart from the designation 'Then' in line 1, which indicates that this discourse is preceded by another discourse, *temporal designations* can be found in:
line 5: in order to celebrate the sacred Eucharist properly;
line 6a: A short silence follows;
line 6b: Then all confess together;
line 15: Then all continue;
line 20: After this follows the absolution.
In lines 6a and 6b, 15 and 20 strict temporal designations are given. Line 5 shows a temporal programming: the program of celebration is to follow the program of confession. It is possible that these temporal designations indicate a certain articulation in the text. They might indicate several scenes such as can be found, so to speak, in the theatre. In technical terms these scenes are called discoursive situations. Discoursive situations, however, are also indicated by designations of space (spatialization) and designations of actors (actorialization).

This discourse does not give *designations of space*. Everything happens at one and the same spot.

As far as the *actors* are concerned: in lines 1-5 the actors are the priest and the faithful as 'brothers and sisters'. In lines 6b-14 the actor 'all' is indicated as the subject of the confession; this actor is being individualized in the text as 'I'; another actor seems to be 'all' in front of whom the confession is made. Furthermore there is the actor God. In lines 15-19 also the actor 'all' is to be found, which is individualized in the text as 'I'. Moreover, one can find as actors: Maria, angels, saints, brothers and sisters and God. In lines 20-24 the actors are the priest, God, we and 'all'.

There is a certain change of actors in the scenes of lines 1-5, 6b-14, 15-19 and 20-24. These scenes respond to the scenes that can be distinguished from the temporalization. There might be some doubt with regard to line 6a: in theory this can be a separate scene, which stands between lines 1-5 and 6b-14. As far as lines 6b-14 and 15-19 are concerned: these scenes are bound by the same actor as subject, that is the 'I'. As a working hypothesis this text can be articulated in the following scenes or discoursive situations: lines 1-5; 6a; 6b-14; 15-19; 20-24.

Actors of the enunciation and actors of the utterance

The question may be asked in what way the actants are brought into discourse. This is the question of the *mise en discours* of the actants.[7] An answer to this question can only be given departing from the text itself, the so-called utterance (French: *énoncé*). This utterance *presupposes* an enunciation (French: *énonciation*), also known as the bringing into discourse (French: *mise en discours*). It is therefore not possible to consider the domain of enunciation without taking the utterance into account. The utterance is, indeed, the result of the enunciation, but in the text-whole itself this enunciation is only presupposed. It is possible to look for indicia of the enunciation in the text itself, where they can be found in a certain sense as traces and semblances.

There are usually several actors within the utterance. These actors are, as it were, in the utterance disengaged (French: *débrayés*) from the domain of enunciation: as representatives of the not-I. The universe of the utterance is always a universe of the not-I. By definition the I is outside the utterance. For instance, if there is an actor in the utterance called Peter, this is an actor of the utterance which is related to other actors of the utterance (John, Mary, Paul, Janet). All these actors have in common that they can be situated in relation to a position of enunciation, which can be indicated as an 'I' and which is outside the enunciation as such. The actors of the utterance are therefore without exception a not-I. This will be clear immediately when the utterance speaks about the actors in the third person. But even in case the utterance speaks about I, we, my, our, your, this is about a not-I with respect to the domain of the enunciation. Still one has to admit that these actors are somehow nearer to the domain of enunciation. They are, to be sure, disengaged (French: *débrayé*), but at the same time they are semblances of the enunciation (French: *énonciation*) within the utterance (French: *énoncé*): what we have here is an enunciated enunciation (French: *énonciation énoncée*). In this way it is possible to mark the articulation between actors in a discourse, who appear in a more objectifying way, and actors who are connected with the domain of enunciation.

If the above-mentioned is applied to our discourse an additional complication will come up. As it happens, the utterance of our text shows two strata: a) the rubrics; b) the texts to be pronounced and the acts to be performed. With regard to both layers we will examine how the actors function.

---

7 A. GREIMAS and J. COURTÉS: *Sémiotique. Dictionnaire raisonné de la théorie du langage* (Paris 1979) s.v. 'Discursivisation', 'Actorialisation', 'Acteur', 'Actant'; GROUPE d'ENTREVERNES (= CADIR): Eléments d'analyse. L'analyse de la composante discursive, in *Sémiotique et Bible* (1984) no. 33, 1-7. The term actor indicates the concrete personage, as the term actant indicates the position within the syntactic structure of the surface level, such as sender and receiver, subject of doing, subject of state and object of value.

Semiotic Analysis of the Confession   339

The first stratum, that of the rubrics, speaks in a very objectifying manner about the actors as 'the priest' (l. 1, 20), 'the faithful' (l. 2), 'all' (l. 6, 15, 24), 'they' (l. 12). As far as the actors are concerned the rubrics do not contain traces of the domain of enunciation. The rubrics have not been formulated in dialogue. They do not say: 'you have to confess now' or 'I command you to do this'. The objectifying character of the rubrics is still being strengthened by the use of the present tense. Apparently it goes without saying that the texts are indeed pronounced by the actors concerned and that the acts are performed by them. This means that the rubrics are prescriptive.

The second stratum of the scenario concerns the texts to be pronounced and the acts to be performed. In this stratum there are again utterances in which actors appear. This second stratum concerns as it were utterances in second degree: they are disengaged from the domains of enunciation as represented in the rubrics: the priest and all. As for these utterances in the second degree the question can again be asked, whether a more detailed articulation of the actors is possible. This is indeed the case. Some actors appear in the text in a very objectifying way: as actors of the utterance. This is true for 'God' (l. 4, 7, 21), 'Mary' (l. 16), 'angels and saints' (l. 17), 'the Lord' (l. 19). But there are also actors which show traces of the domain of enunciation, such as 'brothers and sisters' (l. 3), 'us' (l. 4, 21, 22, 23), 'our sins' (l. 4, 22), 'I' (l. 7, 9, 16), 'all of you' (l. 8), 'my fault' (l. 13, 14), 'you, brothers and sisters' (l. 18), 'our God' (l. 19). Here the actors of the enunciation are concerned.

This articulation in actors of the utterance and actors of the enunciation gives us insight into a shift which takes place in the discourse. Lines 4 and 7 speak in an objectifying manner about God: there he is an actor of the utterance. In line 18 this manner of speaking appears to have changed. On the one hand God still appears as an actor of the utterance: he is 'the Lord'; on the other hand he appears as an actor of the enunciation: he is 'our God'. This connection between God as actor of the utterance and as actor of the enunciation is made via the indication 'our' which refers to the collective actor of the enunciation in lines 16 and 18: 'you, brothers and sisters' as the addressee (French: *interlocutaire*) and 'I' as the one who speaks (French: *interlocuteur*). Thus God is, as it were, involved in the dialogue which takes place between the brothers and sisters and the I, and thus he comes closer to the domain of enunciation. This happens just at the end of the confession, just before the prayer for mercy and forgiveness (l. 21-22). By connecting God as an actor of the utterance and as an actor of the enunciation accordingly, undoubtedly the effect will be that the persuasiveness of the prayer to God is strengthened.

It is striking that the rubrics in line 20 do not proceed with 'Then' as in lines 6 and 15, but with 'After this'. Just as actors of the utterance can be distinguished from those of the enunciation, in the same way temporal indications of the utterance can be distinguished from those of the enunciation. Thus indications such as 'now', 'today', 'at present', are temporal indications of the enunciation. They are traces of the present of the domain of enunciation. On the other hand, indications such as 'yesterday', 'in the year 1983', etc. are temporal indications of the utterance. As far as our discourse is concerned it can be noted that in the indication 'After this', in the rubrics just before the absolution, there is a trace of the domain of the enunciation of the rubrics. The objectifying character of the rubrics is to some extent broken here. I have the impression that in this way in this discourse the absolution is assuming an accent of its own.

1.2. Discoursive semantics

In discoursive semantics an important distinction is made between the figurative and the thematic functions of the discourse. With the figurative function it is possible to describe how the discourse speaks about our world. Precisely in its reference to our world the discourse is organized and structured in a specific way. It should be realized that the figurative function is not about the words of the discourse, but about the organization of the content (the 'form' of the content) as far as it refers to our world. The so-called figurative trajectories are specifications of this organization. The thematic function, on the other hand, is focused on the question in what respect this concrete text speaks about our world. The question is then *what* the discourse wants to say about this world. In the analysis of the confession I will try to describe the figures as much as possible in their relation to the concrete actors. This way it will become clear which is the thematic role of the different actors.

God

God is addressed as 'almighty God' (l. 7). It is about someone, who in every respect is competent with regard to being able: an almighty and sovereign lord who is superior to his subjects. This evokes oppositions as /ruler/ vs. /subject/, and /distance/ vs. /proximity/.

The subjects who come under this lord, are not only opposed to the almighty God as subjects, but also as sinners, that is, as subjects who have not responded to the prescribed axiology (system of values). These sinners stand *before* the almighty God and confess that they have sinned. In this way the sovereign lord is characterized as a powerful judge, before whom each individual subject ('I confess', l. 7; 'that I', l. 9, etc.) stands as offender. There is a large distance between this lord-judge and the individual, sinful subjects. This distance is accentuated by the begging and by the sinner's appeal to many mediators (l. 16-18): the almighty God is not approached directly, but through others. Therefore it is the more noticeable that the mediators are asked 'to pray to the Lord, *our* God' (l. 19). To be sure, the sovereignty of the Lord and Judge over his subjects and offenders is maintained, but at the same time solidarity and relation are suggested. Here it is noticeable that no reference is made to 'the Lord, *my* God', which would have been expected after the individual begging, but to 'the Lord, *our* God'. This has to do with the mediation of the 'brothers and sisters' which is called in. In this way the mutual solidarity is stressed between the individual I who is begging and the brothers and sisters who, as congregation, mediate with God. And, as we have seen, through the indication 'our', God is also more involved in the dialogue between the I and the congregation.

When the priest announces the wish for mercy and forgiveness, the discourse again speaks of the 'almighty God' (l. 21). Here too the figure of the almighty God seems to refer to a sovereign lord and judge, but at the same time it can be noted that after the mediation with 'the Lord, our God' this figure is coloured differently. The almighty God is more dynamic, he comes closer. Considering the previous accentuation of the distance between God and the sinner, perhaps this coming closer may also be interpreted spatially. Having mercy is a bowing down toward the sinners, who appear as a collectivity this time ('us', 'our', l. 21-23). After this movement the discourse speaks about forgiving: the judge pardons the sinners. And even more, he will bring us to everlasting life: again a spatial movement. The almighty God accompanies us *as* almighty God in order to show us the way to everlasting life, protectingly he leads us there, he takes us by the hand, towards the conjunction with him to share in the life in which also angels and saints, called on as mediators, share.

The *thematic role* of God seems to be one of a sovereign lord and judge at distance who does not condemn his sinful subjects, but who after mediation comes nearer, pardoning them and taking them by the hand to everlasting life. In the figures around God *oppositions* are being thematicized as:
/lord/ vs. /subject/
/judge/ vs. /offender/
/distance/ vs. /proximity/
/rift/ vs. /conjunction/
/condemnation/ vs. /forgiveness/, /grace/.[8]

---

[8] The word 'grace' is not to be interpreted in a theological sense; it is used as a neutral term in the sense of the pardoning judge. The opposition is between /grace/ vs. /justice/.

I, we

As has been mentioned, 'I' and 'we' are subjects of a sovereign and almighty lord. There is a distance between the subjects and their lord, which is enlarged because I/we have not responded to the prescribed axiology: as sinners we stand before the almighty lord and judge. And everyone individually confesses that he has performed an anti-program, in thoughts and speech, or with respect to the human mind, in the inner and the outward (l. 10). Everyone has also performed an anti-program in acts: in doing and in failing to do (l. 11), in other words in doing what is not allowed and in failing to do what should be done. There is talk of sinning with regard to thinking in all respects and with regard to acting in all respects. The I recognizes its complete sinfulness. This is even stressed by the repeated 'through my fault, through my fault, through my great fault' (l. 13-14), whereby everybody strikes his breast: the guilt is expressed verbally and somatically. The figure of confession seems to imply a change of direction. The confession of sins is also a turning towards God, a conversion to him: in line 4 confession and conversion are juxtaposed almost as synonyms. This is opposed to the turning away from God by sinning. It is possible that here too are spatial dimensions: people turn towards the almighty God, the judge before whom they now stand.

As subject, sinful and guilty in all respects, the I stands at a great distance and threatened before his almighty judge. And from this position the I turns towards this judge. Conscious of an absolute condemnation the I begs the entire heavenly court ('blessed Mary, ever virgin, all the angels and saints', l. 16-17) to plead with the Lord, our God (l. 19).

About the figure Lord, our God, enough has been said already. The mediators stand as blessed in front of the sinful and guilty individuals; note that the confession is done in order to celebrate the *sacred* eucharist properly (l. 5). As such the human representatives among them (Mary and all the saints) stand close to God. This is also true for the non-human beings (the angels), who belong to the divine world. It is remarkable that blessed Mary as a human being is mentioned *before* the angels: she is considered as the one who stands nearest to the Lord, our God and as the first mediator. It is also remarkable that she is not mentioned as the mother of Christ, but as 'ever virgin'. It might be that because of this she is placed *before* the angels. Undoubtedly the temporal indication 'ever' suggests something which starts here and continues in eternity. It is a qualification assigned to Mary by the I as an observing actant. This so-called temporal aspectualization is also involved in the mediation. It strengthens the bridging function of Mary. Those who are close to the Lord, – or perhaps one should say: those who are in conjunction with him – are called upon as mediators. The begging intends to bridge the distance between the almighty God and the sinners. And in this bridging the congregation present ('you, brothers and sisters', l. 18) also plays a role. Clearly there is a gradation: Mary is closest to God, then come the angels and saints, and then – closest to us – the brothers and sisters.

Finally the priest asks God to have mercy on the sinners, to come closer to them (also spatially), to convert a possible condemnation into grace and forgiveness and to protectingly bring them to everlasting life. The almighty God is asked to definitively bridge the distance; it is a wish for a conjunction with him for ever: eternal life, in which also the mediators share. Thus, there is a movement from absolute distance and condemnation towards forgiveness, grace, conjunction and acceptance.

The *thematic role* of I/we seems to be one of an in all respects sinful and guilty human, who is to be condemned by God as an almighty and sovereign lord and judge, but who calls in the mediation of the heavenly court and the congregation and for whom, finally, the priest asks for God to come to him, to have mercy on him and to take him by the hand towards a definitive conjunction. In the figures around I/we *oppositions* are being thematicized as:
/lord/ vs. /subject/
/judge/ vs. /offender/
/sinful/, /guilty/ vs. /saint/
/mediated/ vs. /direct/
/turn away/ vs. /turn towards/
/distance/ vs. /proximity/, /approach/
/rift/ vs. /conjunction/
/condemnation/ vs. /forgiveness/, /grace/.

Brothers and sisters, all of you

To a certain extent the 'all of you' in line 8 is juxtaposed to the almighty God in line 7. Both figures are addressed as a judicial instance before which the individual makes a confession. The 'all of you' is not the sum of the individual sinners, but the congregation present as a community which performs a judging function, while all individually confess their sins at the same time. The figure 'to' (in 'I confess to') is ambiguous. On the one hand it means 'before', which, as has been mentioned, evokes the judicial instance before which the confession is made. But on the other hand the figure 'to' seems to suggest publicity: it is a public and official confession; 'to' then indicates in presence of all as an official instance. Note that 'all of you' sounds less personal than 'brothers and sisters' as used in lines 3 and 18. There is a certain distance to an official judicial instance, before which the individual confesses himself as sinful and guilty in all respects.

In line 18 the congregation is addressed in another way. It is not considered as the judicial and judging instance anymore, but as mediator together with the heavenly court. This means that the congregation present is considered as a bridge towards the almighty God, as a bridging instance. The bridging, however, is not only towards God, but also towards the individuals: the impersonal 'all of you' is changed into 'brothers and sisters'. After this mediation the lord is addressed by the begging sinner as 'Lord, our God'.

In line 3, in the exhortation by the priest to a confession of sins, the congregation is also addressed as 'brothers and sisters': there the congregation is addressed in its close association with the priest.

The *thematic role* of the congregation is first of all one of a judicial instance before which the individual members of the congregation confess their sins and one of a mediating instance, upon which the individual members of the congregation call for an intercession with the almighty God. In the figures around brothers and sisters and all of you, *oppositions* are being thematicized as:
/judicial instance/ vs. /offender/ and /sinful/
/public/ and /official/ vs. /private/
/institutional/ vs. /individual/
/rift/ vs. /bridging/.

Priest

The priest directs the congregation towards a confession of sins and a conversion (l. 1-5). Here the confession of *guilt* and the confession of *sins* are used as synonyms. In the confession itself, however, there is a clear distinction between sin and guilt: there is sin through guilt (l. 9-14). And this being guilty is strongly emphasized in a threefold repetition together with a somatic expression. Moreover, by using white spaces this section is set apart between the beginning and the end of the confession. And finally, in the rubrics of line 1-2 the word confession of guilt is used as a technical term.

As a minister the priest has an institutional role regarding the congregation. But by speaking of 'brothers and sisters' (l. 3) and by including himself in the summons to a confession of sins and a conversion ('let *us* confess *our* sins, let *us* convert *ourselves*', l. 4) the priest constitutes a very close link with the congregation. In the actual confession he, as it were, steps out of his institutional role and, like the others, he too individually confesses his sins and guilt. And even if his institutional role remains accentuated by his position in front of the congregation, at the moment of confession this role is not being thematicized. After the confession of guilt the priest takes up his institutional role again. He ordains the almighty God to come closer, to forgive and to assist in establishing a definitive conjunction (l. 21-23), which is affirmed by the congregation (l.

24). Actually, the role of the priest is doubled here: on the one hand he stands, institutionally, in front of the congregation, on the other hand he connects himself with the congregation as receiving subject ('... mercy on *us*, ... forgive *us* our sins, ... bring *us*', l. 21-23).

The priest addresses God in a begging form: 'May almighty God ...'. He utters a wish of which the fulfilment depends on God. It is a so-called deprecative formula. This *deprecatio* is indicated in the rubrics (l. 20) as 'the absolution'. Apparently this is a known fixed formula. Absolution means to release, to discharge. The rubrics seem to suggest more than the absolution formula itself, insofar as the term 'absolution' has a more indicative content and stresses the fact that the priest utters the deprecative formula with authority. Thus, the institutional role of the priest is accentuated by the rubrics.

The *thematic role* of the priest *as* priest is to incite the congregation to confession and conversion and to incite the almighty God to forgiving and this by virtue of his institutional office. In the figures around the priest *oppositions* are being thematicized as:
/institutional/ vs. /individual/
/official/ vs. /private/.

Blessed Mary, all the angels and saints

In the foregoing enough has been said regarding the figures around these actors. I shall confine myself to the formulation of the thematic role and the thematicized oppositions. The *thematic role* is that of mediators nearby God for those who *hic et nunc* confess sins and guilt. In the figures around these actors *oppositions* are being thematicized as:
/distance/ vs. /proximity/
/guilty/ vs. /saint/
/sinful/ vs. /saint/
/rift/ vs. /bridging/.

Isotopies

Until now I have found some oppositions thematicized in the figures of the text. I will now list these oppositions:
/lord/ vs. /subject/
/judicial instance/ vs. /offender/ and /sinner/
/distance/ vs. /proximity/
/condemnation/ vs. /forgiveness/, /grace/
/guilty/ vs. /saint/
/sinful/ vs. /saint/
/turn away/ vs. /turn towards/
/mediated/ vs. /direct/

/rift/ vs. /bridging/, /conjunction/
/institutional/ vs. /individual/
/official/ vs. /private/
/public/ vs. /private/

The question is which of these oppositions are prevalent in the text. This is the question for the thematic isotopies, which are distinguished from the figurative isotopies, the abounding smallest units of meaning that refer to our world. The figurative isotopies are a kind of décor against the background of which the thematic isotopies can be situated. The décor of our text seems to be one of a judicial instance before which the guilty sinner stands. The figurative isotopy seems to be /jurisdiction/. The thematic isotopies seem to be the following:
/distance/ vs. /proximity/, /approach/
/condemnation/ vs. /forgiveness/, /grace/
/rift/, (/separation/ or /removal/) vs. /bridging/, /conjunction/.

2. THE SURFACE LEVEL

Like the discoursive level, the surface level also consists of two components: the syntactical and the semantical. I shall consider the semantical component first and then the syntactical.

2.1. The narrative semantics

The narrative semantics is more abstract than the discoursive semantics. In analytical practice, however, it is not easy to distinguish the thematic isotopies of the discoursive level from the more abstract values of the surface level. This is also true for our analysis. The conclusion can therefore be drawn that the surface level of our discourse selects the following values:
/distance/ vs. /proximity/, /approach/
/condemnation/ vs. /forgiveness/, /grace/
/rift/, (/separation/ or /removal/) vs. /bridging/, /conjunction/.

2.2. The narrative syntactics

In analysing the discoursive structures concerning the components of temporalization and actorialization I have distinguished the following scenes or discoursive situations: lines 1-5; 6a; 6b-14; 15-19; 20-24. I have mentioned that this is a working hypothesis concerning a possible syntactical articulation of the discourse. There was some doubt with regard to 6a (the short silence): this may be a discoursive situation in itself, but it is also possible that this situation is narrowly connected to l. 1-5. And concerning l. 6b-14 and 15-19 it has been mentioned that these situations more or less belong to one another as far as they contain the same actor, that is the 'I'.[9] The discoursive syntactics is as it were a first onset for a more profound syntactical analysis on the surface level. As it turns out, the given articulation plays a role in the narrative syntactics.

lines 1-5

The discourse starts with an invitation by the priest (l. 1-2). The invitation can be described as the first phase of the narrative scheme: the phase of manipulation. The destinator provides the destinatee with the modalities of wanting and/or having to. In our discourse the figure 'invites ... to this' (l. 1-2) is not so much invested with the modality of having to as it is with the modality of wanting of a certain program. In the rubrics this program is indicated as confession of guilt and in the text, to be uttered by the priest, as a program of a confession of sins and conversion to God (l. 4). Also in this text to be uttered by the minister the phase of manipulation can be recognized. The destinator manipulates the destinatees in their modality of wanting ('let us') in order that they will indeed carry out the intended program.

Regarding the role of the destinator: this is also directed towards himself. In the twice repeated 'we' the destinator himself is included. Therefore, the destinator has a double actantial role: he is destinator and also destinatee together with the faithful. I will return to the description of line 5.

line 6a

The second phase of the narrative scheme is the phase of competence. If the destinatee wants to or has to carry out a program he needs more than only a wanting to and a having to do. In order to become a subject of doing (French: *sujet opérateur*) of a program also the modalities of being able to and knowing how to are necessary. At the manifestation level of our discourse this phase is not expressed. But the phase is presupposed. This appears from the fact that everyone indeed proceeds to the confession that he has sinned. Still we may ask ourselves whether nothing more can be said about the being able to and knowing how to. First, there is a short silence (l. 6a), and only after this silence all confess together. The silence is undoubtedly directed towards a positive reaction with respect to the modality of wanting. But the silence can also be the space within which the subject of doing provides himself with the modalities of being

---

[9] This is even more so if during the confession the priest adopts a bending posture. However, we confine ourselves to the discourse as scenario.

able to and knowing how to. This is the characteristic feature of scene 6a. Regarding the phase of competence it can be mentioned that the text which is to be uttered as a confession, is a given ritual text: a formula, which, moreover, is recited together. As such this text is an aid to the confession of sins, which touches the modalities of being able to and knowing how to.

lines 6b-14

The third phase of the narrative scheme is the phase of the performance: the subject of doing is going to do something. This performance leads to a certain transformation in which a subject (the so-called situated subject or subject of state, which may or may not be the same as the subject of doing) is transformed from one state into another. At first sight it seems that the performance in our text concerns the confession of guilt. All (or I) cause themselves (myself) to be transformed from one state, in which they are (I am) not connected with the confession of guilt, into another state, in which they are (I am) connected with the confession of guilt. This, however, is a false presupposition. In our text, the performance to which the priest invites is a very typical one, which belongs to the fourth phase of the narrative scheme.

The fourth phase of the narrative scheme is the phase of sanction. In this phase the destinator judges the situation or state caused by the transformation. This concerns an interpretative doing. Our text concerns a sanctioning conclusion of a foregoing program, or rather, several foregoing programs. It turns out that the judgement, although belonging to the fourth phase of the narrative scheme, does not necessarily form the conclusion of a text: the judgement may even form the heart of a text as is the case in our confession of guilt.[10] The performance to which the priest invites has a very typical quality. It is not a performance in the proper sense of the word. Perhaps it can be described as a modal performance, that is, a performance concerning the judgement upon a foregoing program or foregoing programs. The 'I' confesses to have sinned. This confession is a judgement upon one or several preceding programs as not complying with what the destinator in those programs proposed. In the preceding programs there must have been anti-programs not complying with the demanded axiology. In our text we meet with a so-called reflexive judgement, that is, a judgement in which the judging destinator and the subject of doing are one and the same actor. The actor judges his own anti-programs: both roles are being performed by the 'I'.[11]

---

10 L. PANIER: La sanction. Remarques de grammaire narrative, in *Actes Sémiotiques. Le Bulletin* 6 (1982) no. 21, 5.
11 PANIER: La sanction 11.

The anti-programs are being judged by the 'I' with respect to the performance (to sin: third phase of the narrative scheme) and with respect to the competence: 'through my fault' (second phase of the narrative scheme). The operations of judgement are cognitive operations which relate to pragmatic operations, that is, operations concerning the doing, characteristic for the phases of competence and performance.[12]

In the confession of guilt the negative judgement upon the competence is very strongly emphasized: 'through my fault, through my fault, through my great fault' (l. 13-14). This is being emphasized by a gesture of striking the breast (I will return to this). Finally, it can be noted that in the text of the confession this part is set apart by white spaces and forms the centre. The Dutch technical term 'confession of guilt' is therefore only natural.

Semiotically speaking, guilt implies the following: a certain program is modalized by a having to, either by a commandment (French: *préscription*) or by an interdiction; the destinatee is able to perform this program and knows how to do this, but he does not want to do it. The text speaks about a great fault, in other words, the 'I' was easily able to and knew very well how to, but definitely did not want to and chose for the contrary. There was a very definite active resistance, contrary to the active obedience.[13] To sin is to perform an anti-program which is contrary to the program that is to be performed. According to the confession there are several anti-programs involved: 'I have sinned in words and thoughts, in doing and failing to do' (l. 9-11).

- In words, that is, by speaking: it concerns a verbal performance by which a narrative program has been performed contrary to the intended program.
- In thoughts, that is, by thinking: it concerns a performance of the mind by which a narrative program has been performed contrary to the intended program.
- In doing: it concerns a performance by which a forbidden narrative program has been performed actively. A forbidden narrative program (interdiction) is modalized by a having not to do.[14]
- In failing to do: it concerns a performance by which a prescribed narrative program has not been performed actively.[15]

Thus, the text accentuates that many and many sorts of anti-programs have been performed: cognitive (in words and thoughts) and pragmatic (in what I have done and failed to do). The enumeration gives the impres-

---

12 PANIER: La sanction 13.
13 A. GREIMAS: *Du Sens II. Essais sémiotiques* (Paris 1983) 86-87.
14 GREIMAS and COURTÉS: *Dictionnaire* 96 and 190-191, the 'interdiction' concerns a 'devoir ne pas faire'. See also s.v. 'Injonction'.
15 GREIMAS and COURTÉS: *Dictionnaire* s.v. 'Préscription' and 'Injonction'.

sion that it concerns a totality: everything is included. The 'I' sinned in all respects.

The judgement is made before two instances: 'the almighty God' (l. 7) and 'all of you' (l. 8). They are the ones to whom the confession is addressed. The 'I' assumes that they are the final instances of the judgement. The judgement is therefore split. The 'I' shares the judging instances with his own judgement. The almighty God and all form a kind of judges, a court, before whom the confession is made as a public confession. The 'I' considers them as having the competence to judge whether the programs of the 'I', with respect to the competence as well as the performance, are in conformity with the demanded axiology. The 'I' assumes that the judgement of both instances will be negative, that is, will be a condemnation.

Until now the judgements of the 'I' as well as the judicial instances have been described as a pragmatic sanction: it is a judgement about the conformity between the pragmatic operations (*opérations pragmatiques*) of competence and performance of the 'I' with respect to the demanded axiology.[16] But beside the pragmatic judgement a cognitive judgement can be distinguished.[17] In a cognitive judgement the destinatee comes to the so-called veridiction.[18] He verifies the relation between what is real (*immanence, être*) and what appears on the outside (*manifestation, paraître*).[19] The relation between the being (*être*) and the appearing (*paraître*) can assume many forms: it can be a secret or a lie, a falsehood or a truth. Compare the following scheme:

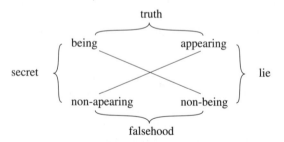

In judicial instances the cognitive judgement with its veridiction plays an important role.[20] The court verifies if the crime indeed has been committed; it tries to unearth what has not appeared into the open, etc. One

---

16 GREIMAS and COURTÉS: *Dictionnaire* s.v. 'Sanction'.
17 GREIMAS and COURTÉS: *Dictionnaire* s.v. 'Sanction'.
18 GREIMAS and COURTÉS: *Dictionnaire* s.v. 'Véridiction'.
19 Manifestation is used here in a different sense than in the term manifestation level.
20 A. GREIMAS: *Sémiotique et sciences sociales* (Paris 1976) 90 ff.

of the elements of veridiction for a court is the confession. Such a confession is at stake here. The 'I' affirms a positive relation between the being and the appearing and assumes that this allows the court to make an adequate pragmatic judgement, in case a condemnation. It is true that in our text the judicial instances are arranged in coordination ('and', l. 8), but the final and most authoritative instance is beyond any doubt the one who is called the almighty, God. Greimas points out that the court is as it were a substitute for an original destinator of judicial messages.[21] The court represents the legislator and as such it is only a substitute destinator (*destinateur suppléant*), who regains the law and verifies the conformity with the axiology prescribed by the law via veridiction. The question can be asked whether in our text both instances are considered as substitute destinators. It is obvious that at least God has also the actantial role of the ultimate destinator. Perhaps a trace of this can be found in the discourse itself where it speaks of God as the almighty.

A negative pragmatic judgement complies with a negative retribution: the punishment of the condemned.[22] An offender can be punished in two ways: by an individual destinator, or by a social destinator. In the first case the punishment is a revenge, in the second it is an administration of justice.[23] In our confession we have a social destinator. The 'I' assumes the judicial instances, God and the congregation, to confirm that there is sin and guilt and to impose and execute or cause to execute an adequate punishment. The social destinator is always invested with the modality of the absolute being able to do: this destinator is charged with the judgement and everything that is implied by the judgement, including the punishment. 'All of you', therefore, means the congregation present as a social entity with the competences due to it. At the same time all present confess their sins and guilt individually, including the priest. This affirms the oppositions found in the discursive semantics: /public/ and /official/ vs. /private/, and /institutional/ vs. /individual/. These oppositions appear in every administration of justice.

Whether the judge himself sometimes also violates the prescribed programs is not under discussion in the administration of justice. He just is the competent social instance that judges and imposes the penalty. This is also true for the congregation. As social destinator it has the competent authority to judge and impose the penalty, and as such there is no question whether or not the individual members of the congregation also violate the prescribed programs. It is typical that our text *at the same time* speaks of collective individuals who make a confession *and* of the social entity of the congregation present as judging instance.[24]

21 GREIMAS: *Sémiotique et sciences sociales* 91.
22 GREIMAS and COURTÉS: *Dictionnaire* s.v. 'Punition' and 'Justice'.
23 GREIMAS: *Sémiotique et sciences sociales* 95 and 201; GREIMAS: *Du Sens II* 243-244.
24 In essence this touches the theological questions regarding the Donatism in the fourth and fifth century. See f.i. B. NEUNHEUSER: *Taufe und Firmung* (= Handbuch der Dogmengeschichte IV/2) (Freiburg-Basel-Wien 1983) 60-73.

The confession of guilt is accompanied by the gesture of striking the breast (l. 12). From the text it is not clear whether this gesture is performed one time or three times. The gesture can have a double function: it can be an expression of the confession and at the same time it can stimulate the confession. As expression this gesture is the somatic expression of the modal performance of confessing guilt. By the gesture of striking the breast the verbal negative judgement is accompanied by a somatic judgement which completes and supplements it. Because of this, the negative judgement becomes a totality: the 'I' in its totality is involved. By the gesture of striking the breast as expression the special accent upon the negative judgement of the self is increased.[25] Striking the breast also has the function of activating the confession. As such this rite is a destinator who manipulated the 'I' to the performance of the confession.

The invitation by the priest concerns not only a confession but also a conversion to God. In the analysis of the discursive semantics I mentioned that both performances are juxtaposed as near synonyms. In that case the confession of guilt implies a conversion to God: a change of direction. This would mean that the confession of guilt is not only a modal performance (belonging to the phase of manipulation), but also a performance as the third phase of the narrative scheme. In theory, however, the conversion can also be considered as a performance which logically follows the performance of the confession. Anyhow, a performance is concerned in which the 'I' as subject of doing connects itself as situated subject with the change of direction in conversion and conciliation.

lines 15-19

The figure 'therefore' connects l. 15-19 with l. 7-14, and thus relates this part with the preceding. This relating includes three possibilities: a) it may concern the confession itself of sin and guilt; b) it may concern the negative judgement of the self by the 'I'. This very negative self-judgement of the anti-programs and the connected assumed condemnation and adequate punishment by the almighty God and the congregation then influence the 'I' to a new performance, a begging; c) finally, it is possible that it concerns the confession as well as the negative self-judgement.

To beg means: to ask insistently and earnestly. As performance it is a manipulation. This manipulation is done from a subordinate position of the 'I' as destinator, namely the position of one who confesses guilt and sins, of one who judges himself as guilty, or both, of one who confesses *and* who judges himself. The distance to the one who the 'I' wants to manipulate (God) is so large that the begging is not directed to him

---

25 See page 342.

directly, but through mediators.[26] The 'I' asks these mediators to become destinator in a manipulation directed to God. This manipulation is indicated as 'praying to the Lord, our God', which means something like pleading with God. It thus concerns a manipulation of God with respect to a modal program, that is, a program which is to be performed by God as subject of doing. Our discourse does not reveal what this program precisely implies. But it is clear that it at least concerns a non-performance of the adequate punishment connected with the negative judgement.[27]

It is remarkable that the congregation, which had a function of judicial instance and from which as such a negative judgement with all its consequences is to be expected, is now called in as fellow mediator. Apparently, the 'I' assumes that the congregation can also play the role of positive mediator next to its role of judicial instance. Therefore, next to the opposition /institutional/ vs. /individual/ also the opposition /condemnation/ vs. /grace/ appears.

lines 20-24

After the begging of the 'I' the wish of the priest follows (l. 21-23). It thus becomes clear that not only the just mentioned (D_1 and D_2) act as destinator with respect to God (D_1 only indirectly), but also the priest (D_3). While in the preceding the modal program in which God is manipulated has been indicated only as a non-negative program with regard to the 'I', we now find a more specific interpretation. It concerns a manipulation of God by the priest regarding the wanting of programs in which God as subject of doing will have mercy on us (including the priest), will forgive us our sins and will bring us to everlasting life. Within the discourse this manipulation receives a typical accent from the indication in l. 20: 'After this'.[28]

It seems to me that the program of God contains three operations. First, he is being asked to have mercy on us. In the description of the discoursive structures this operation has been analysed as a movement of

---

26 Manipulation is a neutral term which should not be immediately interpreted theologically, as A. HÄUSSLING does in a review of R. VOLP: *Zeichen. Semiotik in Theologie und Gottesdienst*, in *Archiv für Liturgiewissenschaft* 25 (1983) esp. 246.
27 This program of the 'I' can be more clearly described in the following formula:
$D_1 \Rightarrow D_2 \Rightarrow [(S \vee Om) \rightarrow (S \wedge Om)]$,
in which: D_1 = I as destinator (D = destinator)
D_2 = Mary, angels and saints, brothers and sisters as destinators
S = God as subject of doing
$\vee$ = disjunction
$\wedge$ = conjunction
Om = the at least non-negative program with regard to the 'I' (Om = modal object).
28 As has been mentioned at page 339-340.

the almighty God towards us: an approaching, which perhaps may be interpreted also spatially. Then there is the operation of forgiving sins: the judge pardons the sinner. Greimas notes that, when the balance of a legal order has been disturbed, this balance can be restored by punishment, but also by forgiveness: forgiveness too can absolve the narrative tension.[29] Finally, there is the operation of the bringing us to everlasting life. This is a spatial movement in which God protectingly leads us to the conjunction with him and with the mediators who already share in his everlasting life. The question might be asked whether the gift of everlasting life cannot be considered as a reward, opposed to the punishment that was expected. Normally, a reward follows the performance of a program that complies with the intended axiology. In this case it would be a reward 'for nothing' which follows the forgiveness of sins. It seems to me, however, that the third operation should not be considered as such. On the contrary, it seems to be a third operation of its own, by which God enables us to perform the narrative programs necessary to reach everlasting life, the conjunction with him. The program contrary to this is the program of sin, which can be assumed to lead to a lasting rift and eternal death. The operations mentioned realize values as respectively 1) /proximity/, /conciliation/; 2) /forgiveness/ and /grace/; 3) /conjunction/, in case /help towards conjunction/. In the text these operations cannot be found as performative program, but as modal program: it is a program that is hoped for and in which the priest as destinator manipulates God as destinatee.

Interesting is, that the rubrics (l. 20) speak about '*the* absolution' by the priest. In the description of the discursive semantics I mentioned that it, apparently, is a known, fixed rite and that absolution means to release and to discharge. The rubrics might suggest more than the absolution formula itself, insofar as in the West the term absolution has a more indicative content.[30] If indeed an indicative discharge is intended in terms of 'I discharge you from your sins ...', this would be a performative program in which the priest acts as subject of doing in the name of God. But it is obvious that in our text as such 'the absolution' cannot be interpreted indicatively. On the contrary, it is an absolution in deprecative form. It is true that the indication 'the absolution' strengthens the institutional, authoritative role of the priest. This would mean that the deprecative formula is enunciated with authority by the competent instance and therefore has more validity.

After the absolution all answer 'Amen' (l. 24). In this way the congre-

---

29 GREIMAS: *Du Sens II* 243. Cf. also PANIER: La sanction 5. When it concerns a non-social destinator the balance can be restored by revenge. See GREIMAS: *Du Sens II* 240-245.
30 Compare page 345 above.

gation enunciates a positive judgement upon the manipulation by the priest. Thus, the congregation takes up the position of co-destinator in the hoped for program of God.

line 5

The invitation by the priest to a confession and conversion ends with the words: 'in order to celebrate the sacred eucharist properly' (l. 5). The program of the confession of sins and of conversion, therefore, is not isolated, but is directed towards the competence (to be able to celebrate properly) of another program, the celebration of the eucharist. This is a so-called instrumental program directed towards a base program. The absolution by the priest is not stated expressly in this instrumental program. But the absolution seems so inextricably bound up with the instrumental program mentioned, that it can be presupposed as implied by the instrumental program.

Regarding the competence it says 'in order to celebrate *properly*'.[31] The conclusion could be drawn that without the instrumental program the eucharist can be celebrated, but that in such a case something would be lacking in the quality of the competence with regard to the being able to. The deficiency then can have two sorts of qualifications: it can be a /non-well/ or a /poor/ competence:

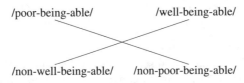

Transformation

Finally, we can try to point out which transformation is at stake in the totality of our discourse. This is a transformation which can be described in the following formula:
$Sd \Rightarrow [(Ov_1 \wedge S \vee Ov_2) \rightarrow (Ov_1 \wedge S \vee Ov_2)]$,
in which: Sd = God (Sd = subject of doing)
　　　　　S = I, we (S = subject of state)
　　　　　Ov_1 = /distance/ (Ov = object of value)
　　　　　　　　/condemnation/
　　　　　　　　/rift/
　　　　　Ov_2 = /proximity/, /conciliation/
　　　　　　　　/forgiveness/, /grace/
　　　　　　　　/conjunction/

---

31 Note of the translator: literally, the Dutch text says: 'in order to be able to celebrate the sacred eucharist *well*'.

356 SEMIOTICS AND LITURGY

It is this transformation which in our discourse appears as a modal program.

3. THE DEEP LEVEL: FUNDAMENTAL SEMANTICS AND SYNTACTICS

At the deep level the question comes up which is the final elementary architecture of the signification in our discourse. This elementary structure is described in the so-called fundamental semantics and syntactics. These can be outlined as follows in a semiotic square:

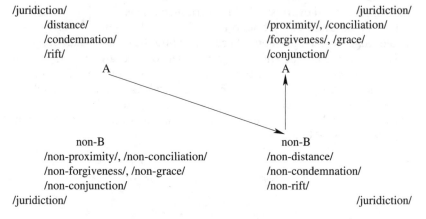

Concerning the fundamental semantics: in the square the smallest redundant contextual meaning-units can be found. These thematic isotopies are, with their negations, indicated as A, non-A, B and non-B. The figurative isotopy, /juridiction/, is placed in the four corners of the square: this isotopy is as it were the décor against the background of which the thematic isotopies have their differentiating meaning.

Beside the *relations*, also the *operations* have been visualized in the semiotic square: they concern the fundamental syntactics of our discourse. The following operations have been visualized: a) There is a conversion, implied in the confession of guilt. This is an operation from A to non-A. b) The begging of the 'I' is directed to an operation by God, which we have indicated as a non-performance of the punishment connected with the negative judgement. This operation too runs from A to non-A. c) The manipulation by the priest in the absolution is directed towards an operation that goes from A via non-A to B.

THE SECOND HYPOTHESIS

In the first hypothesis some questions remain unanswered:
a. According to the first hypothesis the opposition /distance/ vs. /proximity/ is a thematic isotopy.[32] This opposition, therefore, plays a determining role in our discourse. The question was asked whether it is true that in the confession of guilt the distance between the almighty God, as lord and judge, and the sinners is so determining. Is not exactly the relational aspect being accentuated in this discourse? Apparently, there is a disturbed relationship with God which is being restored. We have turned away from God and must convert ourselves to God (l. 4). That is the reason why we confess our sins and guilt before him and beg him as the Lord, our God (l. 7-19); finally, God is asked to have mercy on us, to forgive us our sins and to bring us to everlasting life (l. 21-24).
b. As figurative isotopy the jurisdiction is proposed and against that background the thematic isotopy /condemnation/ vs. /forgiveness/, /grace/ is placed. But if in this discourse God is considered a judge, is he not a very special judge then? After all, usually a judge does not forgive. Although one could answer that an absolute ruler can judge as well as forgive, it remains true that the judge in our confession of guilt is a very mild judge. And moreover, an essential phase in jurisdiction is the act of establishing that the crime has been committed. But here there is only a self-confession. The essential phase of the establishment is lacking. Should we not say, that this self-confession, exactly as a means of informing God about a self-judgement, is a phase of turning towards God? In this way a beginning of a turning towards God would be present within the confession of sins and guilt itself. Then again the relational comes out.
c. In line 8 'all of you' is being interpreted as a judicial instance.[33] The parallelism between 'to all of you' and 'to almighty God' (l. 7) counts in favour of this. The question is, however, if not this discourse from the start stresses the relational with respect to the congregation present: it says 'brothers and sisters' (l. 3) and this is repeated in the part of the begging (l. 18): so there is a relationship. Also in figures as 'our' and 'us' (l. 4, 19, 21, 22, 23) solidarity is expressed. Should we not interpret the figure 'to all of you' of line 8 in a relational sense, next to the opposition /public/ vs. /private/, which is undoubtedly present? In other words: here too the opposition /judicial instance/ vs. /offender and sinner/ might have to be cancelled.
d. Semiotically speaking, the striking of the breast (l. 12) has been analysed insufficiently. A symbolic meaning has been attached to it. This is true. But if this gesture is also analysed as such, it can be considered as

---

[32] Page 346 above.
[33] Page 343-344 above.

a spatial movement. The 'I' points at himself, fixes the attention on himself. Spatially a connection is made with the 'I'.

e. With reference to the thematic isotopy /condemnation/ vs. /forgiveness/, /grace/ in the first hypothesis assumptions are made several times. It says: 'The 'I' assumes that the judgement of both instances will be negative, that is, will be a condemnation'; and: 'The 'I' assumes the judicial instances, God and the congregation, to confirm that there is sin and guilt and to impose and execute or cause to execute an adequate punishment'; and finally: 'This very negative self-judgement of the anti-programs and the connected assumed condemnation and adequate punishment by the almighty God and the congregation then influence the 'I' to a new performance, a begging'.[34] This means that the condemnation and the adequate punishment have not been manifested as such in the discourse. This causes a doubt concerning the thematic isotopy /condemnation/ vs. /forgiveness/, /grace/ and the figurative isotopy /jurisdiction/.

From the preceding the question arises whether it is not another isotopy which is determinative in this discourse: an isotopy connected with the relational which has been regularly observed. It is remarkable that a directionality is spotted several times: 'let us convert ourselves to God' (l. 4), 'to pray ... to the Lord, our God' (l. 19) and – spatially – 'May almighty God ... bring us to everlasting life' (l. 21-23). The spatial directionality and orientation also plays a role where there is a confession 'to almighty God' and 'to all of you' (l. 7-8). The striking of the breast in line 12 is a spatial movement towards the self, which is forcefully accentuated by the accompanying text 'through my fault, through my fault, through my great fault' (l. 13-14). This being-directed-towards can also be found in the begging for mediation of blessed Mary, all the angels and saints and the brothers and sisters (l. 16-18), and in God's mercy on us and his forgiving us (l. 21-22). The many repetitions or series strengthen this stress upon orientation: to God and to all of you (l. 7-8), in words and thoughts, in what I have done and failed to do (l. 10-11), through my fault, through my fault, through my great fault (l. 13-14), angels and saints, brothers and sisters (l. 17-18). Finally, the totality of confession and conversion is directed towards a proper celebration of the eucharist (l. 5).

As a result of these observations the following thematic isotopy can be proposed: /self-oriented/ vs. /goal-oriented/. This last term is preferred to the term /directed towards another or the other/, because the orientation also concerns 'matters', such as the sacred eucharist and the bringing to everlasting life. As figurative isotopy /relationality/ might be formulated. The relations and operations can be spotted in the next semiotic square:

---

[34] Page 350, 351, 352.

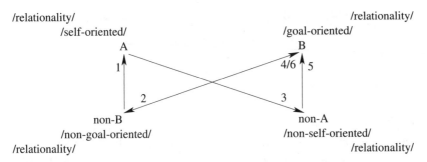

Against the background of /relationality/ the following operations can be distinguished:
1. There is an invitation to turn to the confession of sins. This operation runs from non-B to A.
2. The confession concerns the operation of sinning. This operation of sinning runs from B to non-B.
3. The operation of silence, of confession, begging and conversion runs from A to non-A.
4. The operation of mercy, forgiveness and the bringing to everlasting life runs from non-B to B. If the bringing to everlasting life is considered to be an operation in its own right, the trajectory would be: mercy and forgiveness from A to non-A and bringing to everlasting life from non-A to B.
5. The absolution as such leads the 'I'/'us' from /non-self-oriented/ to /goal-oriented/, that is, from non-A to B.
6. Finally, the proper celebration of the eucharist is an operation from non-B to B.

SUMMING-UP

Every now and then semiotic analysis is reproached for the pretence of a totally objective interpretation of an object. This is a misunderstanding. An objective interpretation is only possible in as much as semiotic analysis considers itself to be bound to the object. Whenever there is discussion about some interpretation or other, then – at least within this method – only those arguments are valuable which depart from the object itself, and not those which are based on data outside the object. For the rest an object is considered to bear more than one meaning and it is therefore obvious that several interpretations are possible. The fact that we could formulate two hypotheses is perhaps connected with this. And if these two hypotheses are compared, the one that is the more loyal to the object and at the same time produces an as consistent as possible reading is the best. Personally, I keep wondering, after this analysis of the confession of guilt, whether an even more consistent and specific (that is, closer to the object) reading is not conceivable.

18. Die architektonischen Dimensionen des Rituals

Vor kurzem fertigte einer meiner Studenten eine Examensarbeit über die niederländischen Feuerbestattungsrituale an. Bei seinen Untersuchungen über die Vorgänge in Krematorien sammelte er auch Informationen über den Bau und die Einrichtung von Krematorien. Bei der Abfassung seiner Arbeit kämpfte er mit der Frage, wo er diese Informationen unterbringen sollte. Gehörten sie überhaupt zu seiner Arbeit? Diese beschränkte sich doch nur auf die Rituale. Sie könnten also höchstens in einem 'Anhang' untergebracht werden. Ich habe ihm geantwortet, daß die Architektur und die Einrichtung von Krematorien wie ein Bestandteil des Rituals selbst behandelt werden können und daß er damit anfangen kann, weil sie auf fundamentale Weise den Ritus selbst bestimmen. Diese Antwort ist in der Liturgiewissenschaft keineswegs selbstverständlich. Man erforscht das christliche Ritual normalerweise, ohne den Raum, in dem es vollzogen wird, einzubeziehen. Und wenn man über das Kirchengebäude und seine Einrichtung spricht, dann geschieht das durchweg ohne Zusammenhang mit dem Ritual.

Mir geht es in dieser Einführung darum, nachzuweisen, daß Ritual und Raum untrennbar miteinander verbunden sind. Der Raum, und in unserem Fall besonders der architektonische Raum des Kirchengebäudes, ist ein integrierender Bestandteil des Rituals. Es spielt darin eine viel fundamentalere Rolle, als man es sich normalerweise vorstellt. Diese enge, fundamentale Beziehung werde ich mit Hilfe der Semiotik des Raums, beziehungsweise mit Hilfe der Semiotik der Architektur, deutlich machen.

1. DIE BEZIEHUNG ZWISCHEN RAUM UND RITUAL; DIE SACHLAGE IN DER LITURGIEWISSENSCHAFT

Wenn man die Sachlage mit dem Blick auf die Beziehung zwischen Liturgie und Raum in der heutigen Liturgiewissenschaft umreißen will, dann bieten die neueren Handbücher der Liturgiewissenschaft einen guten Anknüpfungspunkt. Das italienische Handbuch *Anàmnesis* spricht nirgends über die Beziehung zwischen Raum und Ritual.[1] Das Kirchenge-

---

* *Liturgisches Jahrbuch* 39 (1989) 19-36.
1 S. MARSILI (Hrsg.): *Anàmnesis. Introduzione storico-teologica alla liturgia* I-V (Torino 1974-).

bäude und seine Einrichtung werden überhaupt nicht behandelt. Es ist sogar so, daß es in dem Paragraphen über die 'liturgische Hermeneutik' ausschließlich um die Interpretationsregeln liturgischer Texte geht.[2] Auch andere non-verbale Äußerungen kommen nicht in den Blick. Das französische Handbuch *L'Eglise en prière* enthält im Band I, der von den 'Principes de la Liturgie' handelt, ein Kapitel mit dem Titel 'Les signes'; darin wird im Rahmen von 10 Seiten in einem über das Kirchengebäude, den Altar, das Baptisterium und den Friedhof gesprochen.[3] Im Rest des Werkes kommt der liturgische Raum nur sehr beiläufig zur Sprache.[4] Im deutschen *Handbuch der Liturgiewissenschaft* findet man erneuernde Erkenntnisse in Bezug auf die non-verbalen Elemente der Liturgie, insbesondere in dem kürzlich erschienenen Band über die 'Gestalt des Gottesdienstes'.[5] Darin schreibt R. Sequeira über den 'Gottesdienst als menschliche Ausdruckshandlung'. Er bemerkt, daß das Interesse der Liturgiewissenschaft sich bis heute vor allem auf zwei Ausdrucksformen richtete: die verbale und die musikalische; das Gebiet der kinetischen Ausdrucksformen fand praktisch kein Interesse.[6] Er umreißt den Stand der Wissenschaft und stellt fest, daß auch nach dem Konzil wenig liturgiewissenschaftliche Arbeiten erschienen sind, "die sich um eine übergreifende systematische Darstellung der Bewegungsdimension und um entsprechende begriffliche Klärungen bemühen".[7] Sequeira unterbreitet dann einen Vorschlag für die Systematik und die Terminologie in Bezug auf die Bewegungsdimension. Dabei zeigt sich allerdings, daß er es versäumt, eine ganz wichtige Grundform liturgischen handelns in seine Systematisierung hineinzunehmen, nämlich die räumliche Dimension. Es ist sogar so, daß er die Dimensionen des Raumes (und auch der Bilder, des Altargeräts und der Kleidung) vollkommen loslöst von den Dimensionen des Wortes, der Musik und der Bewegung. Er schreibt:[8]

---

2 Vgl. M. AUGÉ und R. CIVIL: Ermeneutica liturgica, in MARSILI (Hrsg.): *Anàmnesis I. La liturgia, momento nella storia della salvezza* (Casale Monferrato 1979²) 159-207.
3 A. MARTIMORT (Hrsg.): *L'Eglise en prière. Introduction à la liturgie*, édition nouvelle, I. Principes de la liturgie (Paris 1983) 210-220.
4 A. MARTIMORT (Hrsg.): *L'Eglise en prière. Introduction à la liturgie*, édition nouvelle, I-IV (Paris 1983-1984).
5 R. SEQUEIRA: Gottesdienst als menschliche Ausdruckshandlung, in R. BERGER u.a.: *Gestalt des Gottesdienstes. Sprachliche und nicht-sprachliche Ausdrucksformen* (= Gottesdienst der Kirche. Handbuch der Liturgiewissenschaft 3) (Regensburg 1987) 7-39.
6 SEQUEIRA: Gottesdienst 24-26. Siehe auch IDEM: Liturgy and dance. On the need for an adequate terminology, in W. VOS und G. WAINWRIGHT (Hrsg.): *Gratias Agamus. An ecumenical collection of essays on the liturgy and its implications on the occasion of the twenty fifth anniversary of Studia liturgica (1962-1987)* (= Studia liturgica 17) (Rotterdam 1987) 157-165.
7 SEQUEIRA: Gottesdienst 25.
8 SEQUEIRA: Gottesdienst 19.

> Da der liturgische Raum eigens behandelt wird (s. u. 6 und Teil 8, 543 B: Kirchweihe), können wir uns hier mit einigen Hinweisen begnügen. Der liturgische Ausdruck sowohl der Heiligung des Menschen als auch der Gottesverehrung entfaltet sich notwendigerweise im Raum. Die räumlichen Bedingungen sind daher eine wesentliche, wenngleich sekundäre Ausdrucksdimension, insofern sie den primären Ausdruck in Wort-, Klang- und Handlungssymbolen ermöglichen und mitprägen (...) Was soeben vom Raum gesagt wurde, gilt – mutatis mutandis – auch von all jenen Dingen, welche wie jener das räumliche Umfeld der liturgischen Feier mitbestimmen (...).

Man kann daraus schließen, daß Sequeira einerseits zwar Wert legt auf die räumliche Manifestationssprache, daß er diese aber andererseits als wesentlich sekundäre Dimension nach den eigentlichen Grundformen kultischen Handelns ansieht. Sie wird nicht in die 'übergreifende systematische Darstellung' aufgenommen.

Bei seiner eingehenderen Systematisierung der Bewegungsdimension spricht Sequeira auch über die Semiotik. Er sagt:[9]

> Man muß allerdings darauf hinweisen, daß auch die Semiotik bisher selten auf andere als sprachliche Ausdrucksformen einging und ihre Methoden nur ansatzweise für die Untersuchung non-verbaler Ausdrucksformen in Anspruch genommen worden sind.

Wenn Sequeira hier auf die Semiotik im allgemeinen hinweist, scheint mir seine Bemerkung nicht richtig zu sein. In der heutigen Semiotik geht es ja gewiß nicht nur um die verbalen Manifestationssprachen, sondern ebensosehr um die non-verbalen. Wenn sich seine Bemerkung jedoch an die Liturgiewissenschaft wendet, dann besteht sie zweifellos zu Recht. Diese hat sich auch in Bezug auf die Semiotik bisher in der Hauptsache mit der Analyse der verbalen Manifestationssprache beschäftigt. Es ist denn auch wichtig, daß die Liturgiewissenschaft die Semiotik näher auf die non-verbalen Manifestationssprachen hin operationalisiert. Liturgie ist nun einmal mehr als ein Textszenario oder ein Text-Drehbuch, das bei der Feier mit anderen, non-verbalen Manifestationssprachen dekoriert wird. Ebenso wie in der Theaterwissenschaft wächst in der Liturgiewissenschaft die Einsicht, daß es bei der Liturgie schließlich um ein komplexes synkretisches Objekt geht; darin sind allerlei Manifestationssprachen ineinander verwoben, die zusammen zu der Bedeutungsbildung des Objekts beitragen.[10]

---

9 SEQUEIRA: Gottesdienst 26.
10 Für die Theaterwissenschaft vergleiche beispielsweise P. PAVIS: *Problèmes de sémiotique théâtrale* (Montreal 1976).

2. SEMIOTIK DER ARCHITEKTUR

Die Semiotik der Architektur ist ein Bestandteil der Semiotik des Raumes, die viel umfassender ist. So kann der Terminus Raum zum Beispiel auf die konstruierten Räume einer Landschaft oder eines Parks, einer Stadt oder eines Dorfes, eines Gemäldes, eines Fotos, einer Skulptur usw. hindeuten. Es geht mir hier um ganz bestimmte Räume, nämlich erbaute Räume, oder, wenn Sie so wollen, Gebäude. Auch der Terminus Architektur wird im weitem Sinne gebraucht. So spricht man zum Beispiel von Garten- und Landschaftsarchitektur. Wenn ich den Terminus Architektur gebrauche, dann beschränke ich mich ebenfalls auf den erbauten Raum.

Die Semiotik der Architektur entstand in der Pariser Schule in den siebziger Jahren. 1973 wurde in Paris ein erstes Kolloquium über die Semiotik des Raumes gehalten, wobei auch die Architektur zur Sprache kam. Die Semiotik der Architektur betrifft nun nicht allein den Raum als vorgegebenes Produkt, sondern auch den Raum als Produkt, das gebraucht wird. Es handelt sich also sowohl um ein *ouvrage réalisé* als auch um ein *oeuvre incessante*, das ständig durch faktischen Gebrauch im täglichen Leben transformiert wird.[11] Es geht sowohl um einen Raum, der von einem Subjekt produziert worden ist oder produziert wird, als auch um einen Raum, der von einem Subjekt gebraucht worden ist oder gebraucht wird. Das Subjekt ist also bei Bedeutungsbildung des Raumes als Produzent und Konsument des Raumes einbezogen.

Vor dem Produzieren erbauten Raumes sind viele vermittelnde Produktionen nötig: man denke an Maquetten und Arbeitsvorlagen, an die Aufmachung des Objekt für Bauunternehmer und Auftraggeber, an die Kostenberechnungen, die Gebrauchsanweisungen für das Gebäude, die Organisationsschemata usw. Hinzu kommt, daß es sich um einen wohnlichen Raum handelt, in dem sich menschliche soziale Verbindungen vollziehen können. Dies erfordert Maßnahmen für das Klima, das Licht, die Geräusche usw. Gerade wegen der vielen vermittelnden Ausdrücke, ist so das Gebäude das Resultat einer ganzen Kette von Handlungen, die man als ebensoviele narrative Programme ansehen kann. Bei diesen narrativen Programmen sind viele Destinatoren und Handlungssubjekte beteiligt: der Architekt selbst, der Bauunternehmer, der Auftraggeber, die Fabrikanten der Materialien, die Geldgeber, die Politiker, die die Vorschriften bestimmen, usw. Das Gebäude ist letztendlich ein Produkt aus vielen Programmen und Gegenprogrammen. Mit Hilfe dieses Bestandteils der Semiotik der Architektur sollte man bei der Konstruktion eines konkreten Gebäudes umreißen können, wie die verschiedenen narrativen Pro-

---

11 A. RENIER: Espace. Représentation et sémiotique de l'architecture, in *Espace et Représentation* (Paris 1982) 11. Vergleiche auch IDEM: Domaines actuels de la recherche sémiotique à la conception architecturale, in *Sémiotique et Bible 9* (1983) Nr. 32, 12-18.

gramme mit ihren Phasen von Manipulation, Kompetenz, Performanz und Sanktion und mit ihren eigenen Destinatoren, Handlungssubjekten und semantischen Wertemustern verlaufen sind, und wie sie sich zueinander verhalten. Eine solche Analyse kann einen deutlicheren Blick auf die Entstehungsgeschichte des Gebäudes geben. Und wenn es darum geht, ein Gebäude zu konstruieren, könnten eine gute Planung und vorhergehende Abstimmung der verschiedenen narrativen Programme und des Verhältnisses zwischen den verschiedenen Aktanten dem architekturalen Konzept des Ganzen wichtige Dienste leisten.[12] Wenn es sich um die Konstruktion eines Kirchengebäudes handelt, werden sicherlich auch die Vermittlungen liturgischer Studien und kirchlich-liturgischer Regelungen in die Programmierung einbezogen werden müssen. Es kommt dann darauf an, zuvor den Ort der Programme und der semantischen Werte, die von der liturgischen Perspektive her beabsichtigt werden, richtig zu bestimmen und diese mit anderen Programmen in Verbindung zu bringen. Dasselbe gilt natürlich, wenn das Gebäude als *oeuvre incessante* gemeint ist. Namentlich bei der Renovierung und Wiedereinrichtung monumentaler Gebäude können Programme einander im Wege stehen: ein Schulbeispiel ist die Renovierung der Servatiuskirche in Maastricht, wo das Programm der Neugotiksachverständigen und das der Liturgiesachverständigen einander in die Quere kamen. Wichtig ist es dann, daß man exakt prüft, welche semantischen Werte in den diesbezüglichen Programmen im Spiele sind und wie sie sich zueinander verhalten. Eine solche Analyse kann verhindern, daß in der Verwirrung der Diskussion semantische Werte ins Spiel gebracht werden, die eigentlich nicht dran sind, wie im Fall der Servatiuskirche die Werte der Orthodoxie der liturgischen Einrichtungsprogramme. Mindestens kann die Semiotik der Architektur mit ihren genauen Analysemethoden dann viel klären und darlegen, was durcheinander geraten ist.

In der Semiotik der Architektur ist die Tatsache grundlegend, daß das Gebäude eine große Rolle spielt bei der Bestimmung der Weise, wie die Kommunikation der Menschen untereinander und der Menschen mit der Außenwelt verläuft.[13] Anders gesagt: die Architektur bestimmt für diejenigen, die von der Architektur Gebrauch machen, in hohem Maße die Kommunikation untereinander und mit der Umgebung. Das konkrete Gebäude spielt eigentlich die Rolle eines delegierten Destinators, der die Relationen derjenigen, die von dem Gebäude Gebrauch machen, manipuliert, beeinflußt. Es handelt sich um einen delegierten architektonischen

---

12 A. RENIER: L'apport de la sémiotique à la conception architecturale, in M. ARRIVÉ und J. COQUET: *Sémiotique en jeu. A partir et autour de l'oeuvre d'A.J. Greimas* (Paris-Amsterdam-Philadelphia 1987) 157-174.
13 M. HAMMAD: Primauté heuristique du contenu, in H. PARRET und H. RUPRECHT (Hrsg.): *Exigences et perspectives de la sémiotique* I (Amsterdam-Paris 1985) 229-240.

Destinator in Bezug auf die narrativen Programme der Benutzer des Gebäudes. Dabei spreche ich von einem delegierten Destinator, weil der eigentliche Destinator der – gemeinhin kollektive – Aktant ist, der das Gebäude konstruiert und organisiert: der Architekt, der Auftraggeber, der Bauunternehmer usw. Sie konstruieren und organisieren das Gebäude so, daß dieses die Relationen der Menschen untereinander und ihre Relationen mit der Umgebung näher bestimmt. Fangen wir mit den Relationen zwischen dem Menschen und den Umgebungsfaktoren an. Die Architektur reguliert als Destinator, wie die menschlichen Aktanten mit den Aktanten, die durch das Licht, die Luft, die Wärme, die Straße, die Stadt, die Landschaft usw. gebildet werden, verbunden sind, oder auch nicht. Fenster sind gleichsam delegierte Destinatoren in Bezug auf das natürliche Licht und die Weise, wie diejenigen, die sich in dem Gebäude bewegen, mit dem natürlichen Licht verbunden oder davon isoliert werden. Und so gibt es auch architektonische Destinatoren in Bezug auf die Relation zwischen dem Menschen und dem Geräusch, der Temperatur, der Landschaft usw. Ich will mich aber auf die Regulierung der Relationen zwischen den Menschen untereinander konzentrieren. Man stelle sich ein Parlamentsgebäude vor: der Plenarsaal ist normalerweise so gelegen, daß er nicht unmittelbar für jedermann zugänglich ist. Er ist keine öffentliche Tribüne. Letztere hat oft einen separaten, eigenen Eingang. Im Plenarsaal sind die Stühle oder Bänke so arrangiert, daß der Unterschied zwischen dem Sessel des Vorsitzenden und den Bänken der politischen Parteien unmittelbar deutlich ist. Die Relationen zwischen öffentlicher Tribüne, Abgeordneten und Vorsitzendem des Parlaments werden durch die Architektur selbst reguliert. Die Architektur bestimmt, daß und wie jene handeln müssen und können, und damit ihre Kompetenz. Ein Abgeordneter hat nicht die Kompetenz, auf dem Sessel des Vorsitzenden Platz zu nehmen usw. Und wohlgemerkt, wenn ich von Kompetenz spreche, geht es um die zweite Phase der narrativen Reihe. Die Kompetenz von Vorsitzendem und Abgeordneten wird also narrativ gesprochen in grundlegender Weise von der Architektur bestimmt und reguliert. Und dieses trifft ebensogut für allerlei andere Gebäude zu. Man denke an ein Schulgebäude, wo die Lage des Zimmers des Direktors, der Lehrer und die der Klassenräume die modalen Relationen untereinander reguliert, ebenso wie dieses im Klassenraum selbst durch die Stellung des Pults und der Stühle und der Bänke der Schüler der Fall ist. Nur der Lehrer ist befugt, kompetent, hinter dem Pult Platz zu nehmen; weiterhin ist es so, daß die modalen Beziehungen zwischen Lehrer und Schülern mit verschiedenen semantischen Werten belegt werden, je nach der Einrichtung des Klassenraums. So wird ein Pult, das höher und den Schülern gegenüber steht, eher auf autoritäre modale Beziehungen weisen, und ein Pult, das auf gleicher Ebene mit Stühlen drumherum gruppiert steht, auf modale Beziehungen, die eine gewisse 'herrschaftsfreie Kommunikation' bezwecken. Es wird bereits jetzt deutlich sein, daß auch in Kirchengebäuden die Architektur die Rolle eines delegierten Destinators in bezug auf die modalen Verhältnisse spielen kann und damit der Kompetenzen der verschiedenen Akteure, und daß verschiedene semantische Werte im Spiel sein können. Man denke nur an den Unterschied zwischen Schiff und Priesterchor und an die Cathedra des Bischofs. Auf die spezifische Anwendung der Semiotik der Architektur bezüglich des Kirchengebäudes und der christlichen Liturgie gehe ich im letzten Teil meines Referats näher ein. Zuvor möchte ich noch auf einige andere allgemeine Erkenntnisse der Semiotik der Architektur hinweisen.

1. Zunächst: die Architektur als delegierter Destinator bindet die Aktanten in ziemlich stabile modale Beziehungen ein. Die Veränderung dieser modalen Beziehungen erweist sich als nicht einfach. Sie ist oft nur möglich durch einen Verstoß gegen die Konventionen und die Regel von Ethik und Etikette. Ein einfacher Bürger kann sich bei einer Führung durch den Thronsaal gegebenenfalls einen Augenblick auf den Thron des Königs oder der Königin setzen, wenn er das aber bei der Eröffnung der Generalstaaten tut, ist das ein gewaltiger Verstoß gegen die wechselseitigen Beziehungen.

2. Sodann: nach Hammad ist es verwunderlich zu entdecken, daß es eigentlich nur eine sehr kleine Zahl topischer Konstellationen oder, mehr technisch semiotisch formuliert, topischer Konfigurationen gibt.[14] Das ist für sehr verschiedene Zivilisationen der Fall, wie die japanische, die syrische und die europäische, aber das trifft auch für verschiedenartige Gebäude zu, wie die Wohnung, die Universität, das Theater, die Börse und, mann könnte hinzufügen, das Kirchengebäude.

3. Eine dritte Bemerkung schließt sich dem an, was ich über die Kompliziertheit und Feinabstimmung der narrativen Programme gesagt habe: Man kann im Hinblick auf ein Gebäude eine Aufeinanderfolge von Destinatoren entdecken und damit eine Aufeinanderfolge von Manipulationen. So kann man folgendermaßen an eine Aufeinanderfolge denken:

a) der kollektive Destinator Architekt, Bauunternehmer, Auftraggeber usw.;

b) das Gebäude selbst als delegierter Destinator mit allen seinen Subdestinatoren wie die Einteilung, die Einrichtung, die Fenster, die Mauern usw.;

c) derjenige, der das Gebäude benutzt und/oder verwaltet und als ein zweiter Destinator Änderungen oder Ergänzungen anbringt, zum Beispiel eine Umsetzung von Mobiliar, einen Rolladen an das Fenster oder eine besondere Beleuchtung, die ihrerseits wieder, als durch den zweiten Destinator delegierte Destinatoren, ihren Einfluß auf die Relationen ausüben.

4. Eine vierte wichtige Erkenntnis ist die folgende: Die Regulierung der Relationen zwischen Personen hängt oft nicht sosehr von dem ab, was ge-

---

14 HAMMAD: Primauté heuristique du contenu 236.

sagt wird, als vielmehr von dem, was getan wird, und von dem Ort, wo es getan wird.[15] Dabei spielen die Grenzen zwischen dem architektonischen Raum und dem Raum draußen und die Grenzen zwischen den Räumen innerhalb des Gebäudes eine große Rolle. Es geht dann um die Frage, ob von wirklichen Grenzen die Rede ist, die nur bedingt überschritten werden können. Eine Grenze, die man beliebig überschreiten kann, ist ja keine Grenze im eigentlichen Sinne des Wortes. Bei der semiotischen Analyse eines Gebäudes ist es also wichtig, zu prüfen, ob es spatiale Grenzen gibt die bedingt überschritten werden können, und unter welchen Bedingungen sie überschritten werden können.[16] Die Grenzen deuten darauf hin, daß die betreffenden 'getrennten' Räume mit verschiedenen Kompetenzen verbunden sind, und daß sie mit verschiedenen semantischen Werten belegt sind. So kann nicht jedermann ohne weiteres ein Privathaus betreten.[17] Die Schwelle zwischen drinnen und draußen kann nur bedingt überschritten werden. Die Bedingung für die Kompetenz des Überschreitenkönnens der Schwelle kann zum Beispiel sein, daß man Eigentümer oder Mieter dieses Hauses ist. So bedeudet die Tür die Abgrenzung zwischen dem, was bleibend (im Falle von Eigentum) oder zeitweilig (im Falle von Miete) als eigene Domäne betrachtet wird, und demjenigen, was gemeinsames Terrain ist. Die Tür ist also die Trennwand zwischen zwei Räumen, in denen die Kompetenzen unterschiedlich sind und in denen verschiedene semantische Werte im Spiel sind: der Raum außerhalb des Hauses ist nämlich mit dem semantischen Wert 'öffentlich' und der Raum innerhalb des Hauses mit dem semantischen Wert 'privat' belegt. Ein Gast wird von dem Herrn des Hauses hineingelassen, daß heißt: der Herr des Hauses verleiht ihm als Destinator die Kompetenz, in das Haus hineingehen zu können. Wenn der Gast dann einmal drinnen ist, bleibt ein Unterschied zwischen den verschiedenen Räumen des Hauses. Es kann sein, daß der Gast nicht weiter als bis zum Flur kommt; es kann auch sein, daß der Gastgeber seinen Gast in das Wohnzimmer hineinläßt, oder ihm sogar das ganze Haus zeigt. Das bedeutet, daß es auch innerhalb des Hauses allerlei Grenzen gibt, die auf eine Abstufung hinsichtlich der Kompetenzen und des Privatcharakters der Räume hinweisen. Erst wenn es jemandem zugestanden wird, alle Räume frei zu betreten, ist er ganz zu Hause, weil er sich als Subjekt mit allen Räumen verbinden kann. Das Programm des Diebes, der widerrechtlich alle Zimmer betritt, wird denn auch als vollkommen im Widerstreit zu dem Programm des Gastgebers empfunden. Nach dem Diebstahl werden dann auch oft die Grenzen

---

15 M. HAMMAD: L'architecture du thé, in *Actes Sémiotiques. Documents* 9 (1987) Nr. 84-85, 6.
16 HAMMAD: L'architecture du thé 14-23.
17 Vgl. M. HAMMAD: Définition syntaxique du topos, in *Actes Sémiotiques. Le Bulletin* 3 (1979) Nr. 10, 25-27.

verschärft. Man manipuliert den eventuellen Dieb durch eine Alarmanlage und erschwert seine Kompetenz, eindringen zu können, durch zusätzliche Schlösser, Laden usw. So wird bestätigt, wie die räumlich-architektonischen Gliederungen eine Grundlegende Rolle in der Strategie der menschlichen Kommunikation und damit in den menschlichen narrativen Programmen spielen.

In diesem Zusammenhang will ich noch auf eine weitere Nuancierung hinweisen, die in der Semiotik der Architektur wichtig sein kann. Die Regulierung der Beziehungen auf dem Wege der Architektur kennt zwei Dimensionen: die somatische Dimension und die kognitive Dimension. Die somatische Dimension betrifft den physischen Zugang zu einem Raum und die kognitive Dimension den mentalen Zugang. So ist eine hohe Mauer eine Begrenzung, die sowohl die somatische Dimension als auch die kognitive Dimension betrifft: man kann, physisch gesehen, nicht in den anderen Raum eindringen, aber man kann den Raum auch nicht wahrnehmen. Das kann darauf hindeuten, daß der Raum hinter der Mauer in jeder Hinsicht verbotenes Gebiet ist. Aber das modale Verhältnis ändert sich, wenn es sich um eine Umzäunung mit Gitterstäben handelt. In diesem Fall stößt man zwar auf eine somatische Unzugänglichkeit, aber nicht auf eine kognitive: man kann den anderen Raum wahrnehmen. Außerdem kann es noch einen Unterschied ausmachen, ob es sich um einen Zaun handelt, der ja geöffnet werden kann, oder um eine bloße Umfriedung. So können über die Architektur die sozialen Relationen in differenzierter Weise geregelt werden. Anders gesagt: die genannten delegierten Destinatoren beeinflussen jeder in seiner Weise die Kompetenzen der Aktanten und damit ihre narrativen Programme.

5. Ein letzter allgemeiner Punkt ist dieser: Wie schon bemerkt, werden durch den – normalerweise kollektiven – Aktant, der den Raum baut, die sozialen Relationen auf allerlei Weisen spatial reguliert. Nun kann es sein, daß die Benutzer sich faktisch nichts von diesen 'eingebauten' Destinatoren ihrer Relationen zu Herzen nehmen oder sich dagegen wehren. Sie werden dann, wie von selbst, Destinatoren negieren, entfernen oder verändern. So kann es sein, daß eine Garderobe an der Haustür niemals funktioniert, weil man immer durch den rückwärtigen Eingang hereinkommt. Man wird sich dan entscheiden, die Garderobe zu entfernen und eventuell umzustellen. Und wenn man sie beibehält dann bekommt sie eine andere Funktion, zum Beispiel die eines historischen Relikts, eines Denkmals oder einer Zierde. Aber auch dann kann sie ein räumlicher Destinator bleiben, zum Beispiel eines Programms der Erinnerung an die Vergangenheit oder der ästhetischen Bewunderung.

3. SEMIOTIK DER ARCHITEKTUR UND CHRISTLICHES RITUAL

Ich habe den Eindruck, daß in strikt rituellen Räumen die gegenseitigen Relationen und die des Menschen mit der Umgebung noch viel eindringlicher und fundamentaler durch den Raum selbst reguliert werden. Im Ritual werden die Relationen auf eine sehr stabile Weise über die räumlichen Destinatoren reguliert. Das gilt für alle Rituale. Wenn es also stimmt, daß die räumlichen und insbesondere die architektonischen Dimensionen ein integrierender und grundlegender Bestandteil in den menschlichen Kommunikationsstrategien sind, dann gilt dieses in verstärktem Maße für die Kommunikationsmuster des Rituals. Der Raum selbst mit seinen Gliederungen und seiner Einrichtung gehören zu dem narrativen Programm des Rituals. Anders gesagt: die räumlichen Destinatoren beeinflussen die Akteure des Rituals; sie bestimmen ihre wechselseitigen Kompetenzen und bringen bestimmte semantische Investionen des Rituals mit sich. Das bedeutet, daß die räumlich-architektonische Dimension in höchstem Maß integrierender Bestandteil des Rituals ist. Wenn man die Dimension nicht in differenzierter Weise in die Analyse des Rituals einbezieht, bekommt man ein unvollständiges Bild von diesem Ritual. Mehr noch: man vernachlässigt ein grundlegendes Element. Die räumlich-architektonische Dimension des Rituals ist sogar so fundamental, daß man bei der Betrachtung und Analyse des Rituals eigentlich immer mit ihr Anfangen müßte. Meiner Meinung nach weisen dies einige konkrete Ritualanalysen in überzeugender Weise aus. Ich denke namentlich an M. Hammads Analyse des Empfangs eines Gastes in einem japanischen Haus und der japanischen Teezeremonie.[18] Wir verfügen noch nicht über semiotische Analysen nach dem Begriffsapparat der Pariser Schule, die sich auf die räumlich-architektonischen Dimensionen des christlichen Rituals beziehen. Ich bin damit momentan noch vollauf beschäftigt. Im Vorangehenden habe ich einige allgemeine Operationalisierungen der Semiotik nach Art der Pariser Schule gezeigt. Ich will diese nun im letzten Teil meines Referats stärker auf die räumlich-architektonischen Dimensionen des christlichen Rituals hin konkretisieren. Weil detaillierte Analysen noch fehlen, muß ich notgedrungen einigermaßen global sein. Aber das kann doch genügen, um Ihnen einen Einblick in die Sache zu geben, um die es hier geht.

Ich wähle als Ausgangspunkt das Kirchengebäude, wie es sich gemeinhin zwischen Trient und Vaticanum II darstellte. Bei diesem Gebäude gibt es im allgemeinen eine starke Trennung zwischen dem Gebäude als solchem und dem Raum außerhalb des Kirchengebäudes. Wer das Gebäude betritt, muß eine sehr deutliche Schwelle überschreiten. Oft muß das Subjekt durch mehrere kleinere Räume hindurchgehen, um in das Gebäu-

---

18 Vgl. HAMMAD: Définition syntaxique du topos; IDEM: L'architecture du thé.

de zu gelangen. Und beim Eingang des eigentlichen Kirchenraumes findet man zu beiden Seiten Weihwasserbecken, die das Subjekt zum Vollzug eines Purifikationsritus manipulieren: das Kreuzschlagen mit geweihtem Wasser. Der Raum innerhalb des Gebäudes steht in deutlichem Gegensatz zum Raum außerhalb des Gebäudes. Der Innenraum scheint in Anbetracht der Bedingung der Purifikation, die an die Schwellenüberschreitung gestellt wird, mit sakralen Werten verbunden zu sein. Wenn man danach den Innenraum überblickt, erscheint dieser topologisch scharf gegliedert. Es gibt ein Kirchenschiff, das durch eine deutliche Grenze vom Priesterchor getrennt ist. Die Abtrennung betrifft nicht die physische Dimension: man kann ja bis in den äußersten Punkt der Apsis blicken. Es geht um eine Abtrennung, die die somatische Dimension betrifft. Zwischen Priesterchor und Schiff befindet sich die Kommunionbank, die als ganze durchläuft, oder die bei einer Unterbrechung in der Mitte durch ein Gitter abgeschlossen ist. Die Grenze wird außerdem dadurch gekennzeichnet, daß der Priesterchor höher liegt. Darinnen bildet dann der Altar seinerseits den zentralen und höchsten Punkt. Die Grenze zwischen Schiff und Chor kann nur unter der Bedingung der Weihe überschritten werden: die räumliche Einteilung manipuliert so die Akteure und bestimmt ihre Kompetenzen innerhalb des zu vollziehenden Rituals. Der Klerus hat die Kompetenz, innerhalb des Priesterchorraums handeln zu können, die Laien haben nicht die Kompetenz, diese Grenze zu überschreiten. Die sakralen Handlungen als solche werden innerhalb des Priesterchorraums verrichtet, und die Laien können darin nicht das eigentliche Handlungssubjekt sein. Das Kirchengebäude selbst ist also weiter in einen weniger sakralen oder sakral-profanen Raum, nämlich das Schiff, gegliedert und in einen ausschließlich sakralen Raum, den Priesterchor.[19] Die Gläubigen kommen der Grenze am nächsten, wenn sie kommunizieren. Die Kommunionbank ist dabei so eingerichtet, daß sie die Gläubigen außerhalb des Priesterchores hält, und daß sie die Gläubigen zum Knienmüssen destiniert. Der Priester befindet sich bei der Kommunionausteilung auf der anderen Seite: er steht, und zwar innerhalb des sakralen Raumes. Von diesen Kompetenzen her vollzieht sich die Performanz der Übertragung des eigentlichen Wertobjektes, der Eucharistie, wobei der Laie der Empfänger ist und der Priester das Handlungssubjekt. So funktioniert die Kommunionbank als ein Destinator, der exakt die Kompetenzen der Akteure im *moment suprême* der Kommunion bleibend bestimmt.

In diesem Zusammenhang ist auch die Anweisung in den Rubriken des Trauungsrituals des *Rituale Romanum* von 1614 interessant: das Brautpaar befindet sich nach dieser Anweisung bei der Eheschließung "in aliquanta ab altari distantia seu ante presbyterium" (in einiger Entfernung

---

19 Interessant ist, daß eine ähnliche Gliederung von 'mehr und weniger' auch in dem Raum der japanischen Teezeremonie vorkommt; HAMMAD: L'architecture du thé 23-27.

vom Altar oder vor dem Priesterchor), das heißt: vom Altar her gibt es einigen Abstand und vom Kirchenschiff her befindet sich das Brautpaar vor der Priesterchorschranke. Diese Anordnung entspricht genau der räumlichen Gliederung. Das Brautpaar bleibt, ebenso wie die Gemeinde, außerhalb des Priesterchores, aber es nähert sich diesem exklusiv sakralen Raum wohl so dicht wie möglich. Der sakrale Raum wird dabei auch vom zentralsten Punkt her angezeigt. Dieses räumliche narrative Programm ist die fundamentale Basis dessen, was sich in Wort und Handlung vollzieht. Die detaillierte semiotische Analyse des Eheschließungsszenarios im *Rituale Romanum* zeigt, daß das Brautpaar zwar eine Performanz dadurch vollzieht, daß es das Ja-Wort spricht, aber diese Performanz berührt nur die juristische, gleichsam profane Außenseite der Eheschließung. Sie ist eher ein bedingtes Programm, durch das das Brautpaar für die eigentliche Performanz ausgerüstet (Kompetenz) wird, die die endgültige und existentielle Innenseite des Sakraments bildet und deren Handlungssubjekt der Priester selber ist. An der Seite des Priesterchores oder innerhalb seiner Umzäunung stehend vollzieht er als ein instrumentales Subjekt der göttlichen Instanz die eigentliche Performanz, wenn er sagt: "Ich verbinde euch zur Ehe. Im Namen des Vaters und des Sohnes und des Heiligen Geistes. Amen". Braut und Bräutigam sind so ganz allein Empfänger des sakralen Wertobjekts christlichen Ehebundes, das ihnen vom Priester übertragen wird. So sind die räumlich-architektonische Manifestationssprache und die Manifestationssprachen von Handlung und Wort auf das engste miteinander verbunden.[20]

Im Raum des Kirchengebäudes gibt es noch andere von dem Erbauer delegierte Destinatoren, die die Programmierung des Rituals beeinflussen. Wenn die Gläubigen hineinkommen, beugen sie ihr Knie. Destinatoren, die zu dieser Kniebeuge einladen, sind das Tabernakel und das brennende Ewige Licht, das auf die – übrigens unsichtbare – Anwesenheit der Eucharistie hinweist. Einen anderen Destinator bilden die Bänke, die zum Knien und Sitzen eingerichtet sind. Ferner gibt es ziemlich viele Handlungen im Ritual, die von räumlichen Destinatoren beeinflußt werden: man denke an die Kniebeugen des Priesters vor dem Tabernakel, an das Altarküssen, an das Sich-Hinbewegen zur Epistel- und Evangelienseite, sowie zum Ambo oder zu den Ambonen, an die Verkündigung von der Kanzel, an den Ort des Priestersitzes und die Cathedra des Bischofs. Namentlich die Verbindung mit dem Altar, den Ambonen, der Cathedra und der Kanzel drücken modale Kompetenzen aus. Und ihre konkrete Gestaltung kann diese Kompetenzen mit semantischen Werten wie Exklusivität und

---

20 Vgl. G. LUKKEN: Plaidoyer pour une approche intégrale de la liturgie comme lieu théologique. Un défi à toute la théologie, in *Questions liturgiques* 68 (1987) 249-254 (= Nr. *12* in diesem Buch); IDEM: Semiotics and the study of liturgy, in VOS und WAINWRIGHT (Hrsg.): *Gratias Agamus* 114-116.

Autorität besonders betonen. Hier liegt entschieden ein Unterschied vor zwischen einer hohen Cathedra und einem einfachen Stuhl, zwischen einem hohen und geschlossenen Rednerpult und einer einfachen Kanzel. Wenn sich im Raum ein Lettner befindet, ist von der Semiotik her eine verfeinerte Analyse der rituellen räumlichen Programmierung möglich. Ein Lettner zieht eine Grenze somatischer Unzugänglichkeit, aber zugleich kognitiver Zugänglichkeit. Er ruft auch eine bestimmte Tensität in Bezug auf das sakrale Geschehen hervor, dem man ja nur aus der Distanz folgen kann. So könnte man auch nachprüfen, wie in der östlichen Liturgie über die Ikonostase die göttliche Liturgie in hohem Maße programmiert wird, wobei allerlei Differenzierungen mit aufgenommen werden können, wie die der verschiedenen Türen in der Ikonostase und auch das Schließen der Vorhänge, wodurch Unzugänglichkeit für das Auge, aber nicht für das Ohr gegeben ist.

Wie schon bemerkt, kann es vorkommen, daß die faktischen Benutzer des Raums bestimmte im Raum vorhandene Destinatoren negieren. In diesem Fall wird das Ritual selbstverständlich nicht mehr durch diese Destinatoren in ihrer ursprünglichen programmatischen Funktion beeinflußt. So kann es zum Beispiel geschehen, daß die Weihwasserbecken hinten in der Kirche keine Funktion mehr haben, daß Nebenaltäre nicht mehr verwendet werden, oder daß eine Kanzel mitten im Kirchenschiff vernachlässigt wird. In diesem Fall werden die betreffenden Destinatoren zu historischen Relikten früherer ritueller Programme. Mann kann sie als solche beibehalten, als historisches Relikt, das zu einem auf die Vergangenheit gerichteten Programm destiniert, oder als Denkmal, das zu einem ästhetischen programm destiniert. Es kann auch sein, daß man sie entfernt. Hier spielt dann das ganze Problem der Wiedereinrichtung monumentaler Kirchengebäude hinein, wobei die Programme von Liturgikern und Kunsthistorikern mit ihren jeweils eigenen Werten miteinander in Dialog treten müssen.

Nach dem Vaticanum II ist der Kirchenraum erheblich verändert worden. Die Grenzen, die das Gebäude von außen abschirmen, sind verschoben, ebenso wie die semantischen Investitionen, die damit einhergehen. Das gilt auch für Artikulationen innerhalb des Gebäudes. Es ist keine so deutlich markierte Grenze zwischen Priesterchor und Schiff mehr da, was auf Verschiebungen in der Kompetenz von Gemeinde und Priester weist. Zwischen Trient und Vaticanum II gab es eine Opposition zwischen Priesterchor und Schiff. Es war ein Verhältnis von Dominanz des Topos des Priesterchores in Bezug auf das Schiff. In der Semiotik der Pariser Schule spricht man in diesem Fall von einer polemischen, topischen Konfiguration.[21] Dem steht die sogenannte kontrahierende, topische Konfigu-

---

21 Vgl. M. HAMMAD: Rituels sacrés / rituels profanes. Usages significants de l'espace, in A. RENIER (Hrsg.): *Espace. Construction et signification* (Paris 1984) 228.

ration gegenüber, wobei die Subjekte rund um einen zentralen, leeren Punkt sitzen. Diese topische Konfiguration deutet auf Gleichheit und Offenheit im Verhältnis hin.[22] Nun, ich habe den Eindruck, daß in den meisten Kirchen aus der Zeit nach dem Vaticanum II eine topische Konfiguration vorliegt, die sich zwischen der polemischen und der kontrahierenden topischen Konfiguration befindet. Die Subjekte sitzen oder stehen um ein Zentrum, das nicht leer, sondern gefüllt ist und zugleich als dominierender und destinierender Pol funktioniert. Dabei wird die kontrahierend-polemische Konfiguration bisweilen eher zur kontrahierenden Seite, ein anderes Mal zur polemischen Seite neigen. Eine Neigung zur polemischen Seite liegt vor, wenn der Priester auch dann im Zentrum bleibt, wenn andere ihre Rollen erfüllen. Eine Neigung zur kontrahierenden Seite aber liegt vor, wenn er vorne in der Gemeinde sitzt und nur dann ins Zentrum geht, wenn er auch tatsächlich *in actu* auftritt. Und es wird Ihnen klar sein, daß in diesen Fällen entsprechend Nuancierungen in den Kompetenzen von Priester und Gemeinde angebracht werden müssen.

Ich sprach über den Altar als zentralen Destinator. Wenn er in der Tat im Zentrum steht, wird damit die Eucharistiefeier als das eigentliche Hauptprogramm markiert. Wenn aber der Altar etwas zur einen Seite und der Ambo etwas zur anderen Seite aufgestellt werden, werden der Wortgottesdienst und die Eucharistiefeier als gleiche rituelle Programme reguliert.

Bis jetzt ging ich von der Posititon nach dem Vaticanum II aus, die H. Muck als "die Mühe um eine angemessene Verteilung der liturgischen Orte" typisiert hat.[23] Muck nun ist der Meinung, daß man in dieser Option in unserer Kultur zuviel festlegt. Er lehnt in bezug auf das Kirchengebäude diese fixierten räumlichen Destinatoren des Rituals ab und plädiert für einen Raum, der vielmehr "die Vorgänge und Darstellungsbemühungen umfaßt, als daß er sie artikuliert und symbolisiert".[24] Er ist gegen eine totale Festgelegtheit und plädiert für handlungsoffene und bedeutungsoffene Räume mit einer offenen Mitte.[25] Man kann sich dann fragen, ob man bei einem solch kreativen Gebrauch des Raumes noch sagen kann, daß der Raum das Ritual grundlegend bestimmt. Kann man in diesem Fall noch von räumlichen Destinatoren und namentlich von räumlichen Subdestinatoren sprechen? Liegen dann noch wohl bestimmte Kompetenzen vor, die mit verschiedenen Topoi verbunden sind? Gilt dann noch, daß es immer nur eine kleine Zahl topischer Konfigurationen gibt?

Ich meine, daß man diese Fragen bejahen muß. In diesem Zusammen-

---

22 HAMMAD: *Rituels sacrés / rituels profanes* 228.
23 H. MUCK: *Stadt-, Wohn- und Kirchenraum. Zur Strukturierung ihrer Beziehungen* (Arbeitspapier zu Studientagen der AKL in Rolduc. September 1988) 5.
24 MUCK: *Stadt-, Wohn- und Kirchenraum* 5.
25 MUCK: *Stadt-, Wohn- und Kirchenraum* 2-3.

hang verweise ich auf einen interessanten Aufsatz von I. Darrault mit dem Titel "L'espace de la thérapie".[26] Er spricht dort über eine stark nichtverbal ausgerichtete Therapie, die auch die räumlichen Dimensionen verwendet, und die sich seit etwa 10 Jahren in Europa entwickelt hat. Man benutzt dabei als therapeutischen Raum einen Saal, der viel offenläßt. Selbstverständlich ist dieser Raum als ganzer in seiner Gestaltung ein Destinator der narrativen Programme, die sich dort vollziehen können. Aber die Subjekte können den Raum sehr kreativ gebrauchen. Es gibt allerlei Mittel, mit denen sie Räume innerhalb des größeren Raumes kreieren können. Sie können also selbst die räumlichen Subdestinatoren bestimmen. So kann es sein, daß das Kind von dem Therapeuten gerufen wird und sich hinter Kissen verbirgt. Es schirmt dann einen eigenen Topos von Unzugänglichkeit ab und verweigert jede Konjunktion mit dem Topos des Therapeuten. Semiotisch gesprochen liegt ein Versuch sowohl somatischer wie auch kognitiver Unzugänglichkeit vor. Wenn dann eine räumliche Annäherung des Kindes zum Therapeuten stattfindet, spielt eine bestimmte fiktive Grenze eine große Rolle. Das Kind kann zum wiederholten Male vor dieser Grenze stehen bleiben und zurückziehende Bewegungen machen. Diese Grenze trennt den Topos des Therapeuten von dem des Kindes. Erst wenn es diese Grenze überschritten hat und sich mit dem Topos des Therapeuten verbunden hat, ist der Kontakt offenbar gelungen. So stellt sich heraus, daß fiktive oder nicht-fiktive Grenzen und damit fiktiv oder nicht-fiktiv näher artikulierte Räume die Programme der Handlungssubjekte destinieren und manipulieren. Die Handlungssubjekte können also selbst die Subdestinatoren des Raumes anbringen: sie stellen sich in Opposition auf oder stellen beziehungsweise setzen sich im Kreis, wodurch auch die mit diesen topischen Konfigurationen verbundenen Kompetenzen bestimmt werden. Auch so wird klar, daß es eigentlich nur eine kleine Zahl topischer Konfigurationen gibt. Man kann also sagen, daß die gleichen räumlichen Gesetzmäßigkeiten sich wiederholen, daß aber nun die Handlungssubjekte selbst gleichsam Architekt des Raumes sind und somit auch Architekt der rituellen narrativen Programme. Auch das kreative Ritual wird also vom architektonischen Raum aus eingreifend und grundlegend manipuliert.

Hiermit hoffe ich, ausreichend gezeigt zu haben, daß die architektonische Dimension des Rituals jede Aufmerksamkeit verdient, daß sie weit mehr als bisher in das Studium des Rituals als ein integrierender und grundlegender Bestandteil einbezogen werden muß und daß das semiotische Instrumentarium der Pariser Schule dabei große Dienste leisten kann, namentlich weil es ein semiotisches Instrumentarium betrifft, womit nicht nur verbale, sondern auch non-verbale Manifestationssprachen auf nachprüfbare Weise analysiert werden können.

---

26 I. DARRAULT: L'espace de la thérapie, in RENIER (Hrsg.): *Espace* 129-138.

19. La sémiotique de l'architecture de l'église en tant que sémiotique du visuel

La sémiotique de l'architecture de l'église peut être considérée comme une partie de la sémiotique de l'architecture, qui elle-même fait partie de la sémiotique de l'espace. La sémiotique de l'architecture, qui naquit au début des années soixante-dix au sein de l'école de Paris d'A. Greimas, fonctionnera dans notre article comme le point de départ. Le premier colloque concernant la sémiotique de l'espace a eu lieu à Paris en 1972, où l'on a parlé de l'architecture aussi. Cette sémiotique de l'architecture de l'école de Paris se rend non seulement compte de son objet, l'espace construit en tant que tel, mais de l'espace comme objet d'usage courant aussi. Il s'agit donc de l'espace construit, c'est-à-dire d'un ouvrage réalisé, de même qu'il s'agit d'une oeuvre incessante, qui est continuellement transformée par l'emploi de cet espace.[1] Il s'agit là en même temps d'un espace qui est produit par le sujet et d'un espace qui est employé par le sujet. Le sujet comme producteur et comme consommateur font partie du processus d'attribution du sens à l'espace architectural.

Afin de réaliser de l'espace construit on a besoin de nombreuses réalisations intermédiaires, par exemple des maquettes, des épures, des calculs des frais, de la présentation de l'objet aux constructeurs et aux adjudicateurs, des plans de travail et des mesures à prendre pour obtenir un climat de travail favorable. Un bâtiment est donc le résultat d'une chaîne d'opérations et chaque anneau de cette chaîne peut être considéré comme un programme narratif à soi. En outre il y a un bon nombre de destinataires et de sujets de faire, qui sont impliqués dans la réalisation d'un bâtiment: les adjudicateurs, l'architecte, le bâtisseur, la loi en vigueur, les fabricants des matériaux, les financiers, les politiciens, la presse, l'opinion publique, et caetera. Les bâtiments sont donc le résultat d'un processus compliqué. La sémiotique pourrait expliquer sans doute les relations entre les différents programmes et anti-programmes qui jouent un rôle dans ce pro-

---

* De semiotiek van de kerkruimte als semiotiek van het visuele, in *Jaarboek voor liturgieonderzoek* 5 (1989) 275-299. Traduction par F. Hoppenbrouwers.
1 A. GREIMAS et J. COURTÉS: *Sémiotique. Dictionnaire raisonné de la théorie du langage* I-II (Paris 1979-1986); A. RENIER: *Espace, représentation et sémiotique de l'architecture* (Paris 1982); IDEM: Domaines actuels de la recherche sémiotique à la conception architecturale, dans *Sémiotique et Bible* 9 (1983) no. 32, 12-18; IDEM: L'apport de la sémiotique à la conception architecturale, dans M. ARRIVÉ et J. COQUET: *Sémiotique en jeu. A partir et autour de l'oeuvre d'A.J. Greimas* (Paris-Amsterdam-Philadelphia 1987) 157-174.

cessus. Ainsi elle pourrait éclaircir les problèmes, qui se produisent durant la conception et la construction d'un bâtiment. Pour cette raison il serait avantageux d'engager la sémiotique de l'architecture au cours de la réalisation d'un projet.[2] Ceci vaut aussi pour la construction d'une église ou de l'espace liturgique, où, outre les programmes mentionnés ci-dessus, ceux du droit canonique et des rituels à accomplir entrent en jeu aussi. La génèse d'une église, qui est pourtant très intéressante, ne fera cependant pas partie de notre exposé.[3] Ici nous nous restreindrons à l'église ou l'espace liturgique en tant qu'espace construit. Cela est une première restriction.

Une deuxième restriction concerne notre analyse de l'espace liturgique par moyen de la sémiotique du visuel. Dans sa thèse de troisième cycle sur l'architecture classique sacrée qui date de 1979 et dont A. Greimas fut le directeur, A. Lévy fit remarquer qu'il dut se limiter à la manifestation visuelle de la perception de l'architecture.[4] Pourtant l'espace architectural consiste en d'autres éléments qui ne se limitent pas à l'isotopie visuelle. Ils existent en effet d'autres formes de perception, par exemple le toucher, l'odorat et l'ouïe. Notre article implique donc une imperfection. Cela est dû au fait que l'école de Paris a élaboré une sémiotique de l'architecture qui insiste sur l'isotopie visuelle. Ainsi en 1986 dans le deuxième tome du *Dictionnaire* A. Renier a défini l'architecture comme une discipline d'expression *plastique* à l'instar de la peinture et de la sculpture.[5] Dans le même *Dictionnaire* J. Floch a précisé que tous les discours plastiques ont pour matériau premier le monde des qualités visuelles.[6]

L'avantage de l'approche de la sémiotique de l'architecture comme une sémiotique du visuel est la possibilité de la rendre opérationnelle. Car en vue de la sémiotique plastique l'école de Paris a élaboré une instrumentation, qui a été appliquée déjà à des objets plastiques, surtout à des peintures et des photos.[7] Afin d'analyser un image mortuaire, nous avons rendu opérationnelle cette instrumentation nous-même.[8]

---

2 V. surtout RENIER: L'apport de la sémiotique.
3 V. en particulier G. LUKKEN: Die architektonischen Dimensionen des Rituals, dans *Liturgisches Jahrbuch* 39 (1989) 19-36 (= no. *18* dans ce livre).
4 A. LÉVY: *Sémiotique de l'espace. Architecture classique sacrée* (Thèse de troisième cycle, dir. A.J. Greimas, EHSS) (Paris 1979, polycopiée).
5 A. RENIER: Architecturale (sémiotique-), dans GREIMAS et COURTÉS: *Sémiotique* II, 16-17.
6 J. FLOCH: Plastique (sémiotique-), dans GREIMAS et COURTÉS: *Sémiotique* II, 169-170.
7 Cf. GREIMAS et COURTÉS: *Sémiotique* II, 42-43; 53-54; 73; 104; 168-170; 203-206; A. GREIMAS: Sémiotique figurative et sémiotique plastique, dans *Actes sémiotiques. Documents* 6 (1984) no. 60; F. THÜRLEMANN: *Paul Klee. Analyse sémiotique de trois peintures* (Lausanne 1982); J. FLOCH: *Les formes de l'empreinte* (Périgueux 1986).
8 G. LUKKEN: Een bidprentje, dans SEMANET (G. LUKKEN éd.): *Semiotiek en christelijke uitingsvormen. De semiotiek van A.J. Greimas en de Parijse school toegepast op Bijbel en liturgie* (Hilversum 1987) 255-276.

En ce qui concerne l'analyse du signifiant plastique, c'est-à-dire de l'expression plastique, il y a deux catégories importantes: les catégories topologiques et les catégories plastiques.

Les *catégories topologiques* peuvent être divisées en deux groupes: la position et l'orientation.

La notion de *position* marque des oppositions comme:
haut/bas/du côté de
sur/sous
droite/gauche
à côté de (l'opposition contractuelle)/opposé à (l'opposition polémique).

La notion d'*orientation* vise la direction topologique ou le dynamique, par exemple:
orienté en haut *vs* orienté en bas
orienté en avant *vs* orienté en arrière
orienté avec *vs* orienté contre.

Le deuxième groupe est celui des *catégories plastiques*, qu'on peut diviser en deux:
les catégories *chromatiques*, qui concernent les couleurs et les contrastes, et les catégories *eidétiques*, qui marquent les formes ouvertes ou fermées; le carré, le triangle, le cercle.

L'analyse de la forme de l'expression (le signifiant) à l'aide de ces catégories est un instrument important pour découvrir la forme du contenu (le signifié), car du point de vue de la sémiotique du visuel l'architecture est un système semi-symbolique. Cela veut dire que les deux plans du signe, notamment celui de l'expression et celui du contenu, se rapportent l'un à l'autre. Tandis que dans un système symbolique chaque élément de l'expression renvoie à un seul élément du contenu (comparez l'algèbre et les signaux routiers), dans un système semi-symbolique il s'agit de la conformité des *relations* sur le plan de l'expression avec certaines *relations* sur le plan du contenu. Nous pouvons nous demander par exemple, ce que signifient les relations entre le dedans et le dehors ou entre le nef et le sanctuaire sur le plan de l'expression pour la relation entre ces éléments sur le plan du contenu.

Pour notre analyse nous employerons des photos. On pourrait nous objecter qu'il s'agit là plutôt d'une analyse de photos d'un objet architectural que d'une analyse de l'objet lui-même. En effet il valait mieux d'aller visiter les lieux eux-mêmes pour y effectuer l'analyse. Mais afin de remédier à cette objection nous avons ajouté la coupe et le plan nécessaires à notre analyse. Une maquette serait encore plus convenable pour imiter la réalité, mais comme nous ne voulons proposer au lecteur qu'une vue générale cela ne semble pas nécessaire.

En premier lieu nous voudrions porter notre attention sur l'église de Sainte-Bernadette à Nevers (France), qui a été construite de 1963 à 1964 par C. Parent et P. Virilio (photo 1). Si nous regardons l'extérieur de ce bâtiment, nous sommes frappés par la construction peu commune. Pour cette raison nous croyons que ce bâtiment est assez convenable pour notre analyse.

Du point de vue de la catégorie de *position* nous pouvons diviser la façade en une partie supérieure et en une partie inférieure. Nous remarquons aussi que cette partie supérieure est placée plus en avant, tandis que la partie inférieure est placée en retraite. La plus grande partie de la façade est positionnée horizontalement, mais le côté droite par contre verticalement.

En ce qui concerne l'*orientation* la partie supérieure est orientée horizontalement en avant vers l'extérieur, alors que la partie inférieure est orientée horizontalement en arrière vers l'intérieur. Cette orientation vers l'intérieur est renforcée par la forme oblique du mur à l'intérieur sur le côté droite près de l'entrée. L'élément à droite s'élève à la verticale.

Du point de vue *chromatique* nous apercevons que la partie supérieure est exposée au jour, pendant que la partie inférieure est à l'ombre.

Quant aux catégories *eidétiques* nous signalons que la partie supérieure est massive et qu'elle a des formes rondes, tandis que la partie inférieure est rectangulaire et qu'elle est interrompue par la porte d'entrée qui consiste en trois segments.

Il y a donc un bon nombre de constituants de la forme de l'expression de cette façade. De prime abord il paraît, que la partie inférieure se rapporte plutôt à l'intérieur et la partie supérieure plutôt à l'extérieur. Les formes rondes de la partie supérieure ont l'air de repousser celui qui veut entrer. La partie inférieure a l'air de l'inviter. Finalement il semble que l'élément vertical unit la partie inférieure et supérieure.

En insistant sur la figurativisation de ce bâtiment, il nous semble que cette analyse peut être poussée encore plus loin. En ce qui concerne la figurativisation, la sémiotique de Greimas se pose la question suivante: à quel monde connu se réfert-il ce bâtiment? ou en d'autres termes: se réfert-il à un autre discours architectural? Nous pourrions répondre, qu'il se réfert à un bâtiment avec des formes closes et massives en béton. Il existe cependant une référence très concrète à un monde connu. Ce bâtiment a été figurativisé de telle façon, qu'il s'agit – selon l'école de Paris – d'une iconisation: le bâtiment nous fait penser à un bunker sur la côte atlantique (photo 2). Nous y signalons la figurativisation des formes closes, du béton épais, de la force, de l'épaisseur, de l'hostilité, de la sécurité, de quelque chose d'impénétrable. Ce sont tous des éléments des parcours figuratifs d'un bunker.

Notre bâtiment a pourtant un discours architectural à soi. Nous ne connaissons aucun bunker, qui a une entrée aussi visible. Dans le cas d'un bunker l'entrée est cachée et souterraine. L'entrée de notre bâtiment par contre se trouve en plein jour et elle est assez large. Il y a une porte, qui invite quelqu'un à entrer. En ce qui concerne la figurativisation de ce bâtiment il existe une thématisation individuelle, qui peut être déduite de l'expression de la forme propre au bâtiment. Afin de découvrir la thématique nous devons déceler les relations d'opposition dans la figurativisation. Ainsi nous trouverons les valeurs thématiques, qui déterminent la place des figures dans ce discours. En ce qui concerne la partie supérieure et inférieure du bâtiment, les relations semi-symboliques de la forme de l'expression semblent correspondre à une relation d'opposition entre hostile et invitant. Ainsi la façade est la frontière entre deux espaces topiques, qui forment une relation d'opposition, à savoir l'espace topique d'intérieur et celui d'extérieur. Nous employons cette notion d'espace topique' pour désigner un espace qui peut contenir des hommes et des objets et qui correspond à un certain programme narratif.[9]

L'espace topique d'extérieur se rapporte à des programmes narratifs qui menacent l'homme, et l'espace topique d'intérieur à des programmes narratifs qui sauvent l'homme. Autrement dit, l'intérieur et l'extérieur sont des objets de valeur avec un investissement sémantique à soi. Cet investissement n'est pas celui de /sacrale/ vs /profane/, mais plutôt celui de /sécurité/, /sauvegarde/, /vie/ vs /danger/, /menace/, /mort/. La partie supérieure destine le bâtiment à se défendre contre des programmes menaçants provenants de l'extérieur, tandis que la partie inférieure destine ceux qui se trouvent à l'extérieur à y entrer.

Nous voudrions insister un peu sur la partie inférieure de la façade (photo 3). Elle est divisée en deux murs en béton par une porte composée de trois segments. Cette porte est couverte et placée en arrière. Un mur destine quelqu'un à ne pas pouvoir passer. Il est pragmatiquement impénétrable. Du point de vue cognitif un mur forme la clôture pour ceux qui se trouvent dedans. Dans le cas présent les deux murs s'orientent vers la porte. Ils mènent le visiteur au lieu, où il peut entrer dans le bâtiment. Si la porte est fermée, le bâtiment est pragmatiquement impénétrable. En outre elle exprime une interdiction en ce qui concerne la compétence de celui qui veut y pénétrer. Et encore, la porte est opaque, de manière qu'elle exprime l'impénétrabilité cognitive aussi. Dans le cas de l'espace liturgique il est évident, qu'il fait une grande différence si la porte d'entrée est en verre et transparente ou qu'il y a un mur en verre ou non. Quoi qu'il en soit, quand la porte de notre église est ouverte, elle manipule le vouloir, le devoir, le pouvoir et le savoir de ceux qui entrent dans l'espace liturgique pour y réaliser les programmes de l'espace topique d'intérieur. En vue de

9 Cf. M. HAMMAD, S. ARANGO, E. DE KUYPER et E. POPPE: L'espace du séminaire, dans Communications 27 (1977) 29; M. HAMMAD: Définition syntaxique du topos, dans Actes sémiotiques. Bulletin 3 (1980) no. 10, 25-27.

la largeur de la porte elle semble exprimer une invitation à de nombreuses gens.

Nous avons déjà fait remarquer l'élément vertical, qui unit la partie inférieure et supérieure (photo 1). Dans cette partie se trouve une fenêtre étroite et longue. Elle montre la relation entre deux étages. Si nous entrons dans le bâtiment nous y voyons en effet qu'il est divisé en deux étages et que dans l'élément vertical il y a une escalier qui unit le rez-de-chaussé à l'étage supérieur. Au rez-de-chaussé du côté droite de la porte se trouve le baptistère (photo 4). Là se trouvent une chapelle et les locales paroissiales aussi. L'espace liturgique proprement dit se trouve à l'étage supérieur ou – selon l'expression de la forme: la partie la plus protégée et le meilleur refuge. Nous nous restreindrons à cet espace-là. Sur le plan de l'espace liturgique (photo 5) nous voyons en bas l'escalier, qui se trouve dans l'élément vertical, et au milieu encore un autre escalier. Nous y apercevons encore la nef et le sanctuaire. La photo suivante (photo 6) montre l'arrière de cet espace, où les bancs sont mis dans le sens de la largeur et orientés vers l'avant. Remarquons aussi la lumière qui vient d'en haut. Les autres bancs sont orientés vers l'avant aussi (photo 7). Nous voyons une lumière raffinée sur le mur derrière l'autel, qui monte d'en bas. La coupe de l'église montre nettement l'éclairage (photo 8). Au milieu de l'espace la lumière tombe d'en haut et, en avant; derrière l'autel elle monte d'en bas. Nous n'insistons pas sur les formes eidétiques et chromatiques de cette église. Il nous suffit de constater que notre intuition première a été confirmée: cet espace liturgique est un refuge sûr.

De prime abord il est évident, que cet espace liturgique forme un seul espace topique. Celui qui y entre se trouve dans un espace d'un faire liturgique collective. Il doit être disposé à accomplir les programmes, qui en premier lieu sont destinés par cet espace de faire liturgique et dans cet espace de faire liturgique. Ces programmes sont déterminés par la segmentation de cet espace de faire liturgique, qui est divisé en deux espaces topiques. Il y a un espace de faire (topos 1) qui est plus ou moins séparé de celui de la nef (topos 2) (photo 7). Les deux espaces topiques sont disposés de telle façon que l'un serre contre l'autre, mais l'espace topique 1 est plus haut de trois marches. L'orientation de la nef (topos 2) est assez remarquable. D'un côté elle est divisée en deux par l'escalier central et, dans la mesure où les deux parties descendent vers cet escalier, elle s'y oriente (photo 8). De l'autre côté la nef (topos 2) s'oriente vers l'espace topique 1, puisque tous les bancs sont orientés en avant et la lumière mystérieuse sur le mur derrière l'autel attire l'attention. La descente de l'arrière de la nef renforce cette orientation en avant. Cela vaut aussi pour l'autre partie de cet espace, qui monte en avant. Ici l'orientation est renforcée par les marches sur lesquelles ont été posés les bancs (photo 7). Il paraît que l'on sort d'une vallée et que l'on monte jusqu'au sommet d'une coline. Il paraît que l'orientation de la nef en avant est plus forte que celle des deux parties de la nef vers l'escalier. La deuxième orientation est donc subordonnée à la première.

Les espaces topiques 1 et 2 ne sont pas simplement juxtaposés, puisqu'ils s'opposent l'un à l'autre. L'espace topique 1 est orienté vers l'espace topique 2, ce que prouve la disposition de l'autel et du pulpitre (l'ambon), et l'espace topique 2 est orienté vers l'espace topique 1, ce que prouve la disposition des bancs. Cette opposition est encore soulignée par le fait que l'espace topique 1 est un peu plus élevé que l'espace topique 2. L'éclairage peu commun de l'espace topique 1 y attribue aussi. L'espace en tant que tel ne nous fournit pas l'argumentation nécessaire pour délimiter la frontière entre les deux espaces topiques. L'opposition des deux espaces topiques donne cependant lieu à la supposition, qu'ils existent des conditions qui déterminent la transgression de la frontière entre l'espace topique 1 et 2, et que ces conditions-là se rapportent à la compétence qui est liée aux programmes narratifs, qui se déroulent dans les espaces topiques. Les différents espaces topiques – et cela vaut pour l'architecture en général aussi – jouent le rôle de destinateur en ce qui concerne les relations modales et par conséquent en ce qui concerne les compétences de ceux, qui figurent dans les espaces topiques en question.

Alors, les espaces topiques de cet espace liturgique ne sont pas juxtaposés mais plutôt opposés. Quand les espaces topiques s'opposent l'un à l'autre, M. Hammad parle d'une *configuration topique polémique* (figure 1), où la compétence qui est liée à l'espace topique 1 est opposée à celle de l'espace topique 2.[10] Ceux qui se trouvent dans l'espace topique 2 n'ont pas de compétence pour figurer dans l'espace topique 1. En d'autres termes, puisqu'il s'agit là d'une configuration polémique, la compétence de l'espace topique 1 est exclusive. Nous pourrions établir une comparaison entre cette configuration polémique et un exemple de la vie politique. Comparez par exemple l'espace topique des ministres dans l'Assemblée nationale qui s'oppose à l'espace topique des représentants.

L'espace topique 1 destine à plusieurs programmes narratifs. Néanmoins il y a un programme narratif central, qui est destiné par l'autel qui se trouve au milieu de l'espace topique 1. Les programmes narratifs, qui sont destinés par le pulpitre et la chaire, ont l'air d'y être subordonnés. La compétence de l'espace topique 1 concerne le devoir, le vouloir, le pouvoir et le savoir faire en ce qui concerne ces programmes. L'opposition plus ou moins nette de la nef (topos 2) manipule les gens, afin qu'ils participent aux rituels qui s'y accomplissent: leur compétence consiste en une réceptivité à ce qui se passe dans l'espace topique 1 et en une action affirmative en ce qui concerne de ces événements. Ceux-là ne sont pas les

---

10 M. HAMMAD: L'architecture du thé, dans *Actes sémiotiques. Documents* 9 (1987) no. 84-85, 30-31.

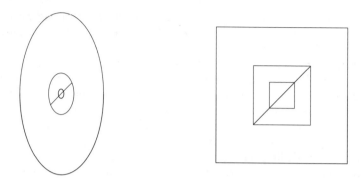

figure 2. la configuration topique contractuelle

sujets opérateurs des programmes rituels mais plutôt les sujets d'état. C'est semble-t-il la conclusion inévitable, que nous devons tirer à propos de l'opposition spatiale absolue des deux espaces topiques. Cela n'exclut cependant pas qu'au niveau de la langue de manifestation textuelle ceux, qui se trouvent dans l'espace topique 2, sont en même temps les sujets opérateurs. Rappelons-nous par exemple le texte du canon romain, qui pendant des siècles exprimait cette idée. Si les deux langues de manifestation se contredisent, il se pose nécessairement la question suivante: quelle langue a dominé l'autre ou la domine toujours en ce qui concerne la signification. En général l'étude de la liturgie ne se rend compte que des textes et elle tend à négliger le fait, que la langue de manifestation spatiale peut jouer un rôle particulier dans le discours liturgique.

La configuration topique polémique se retrouve assez souvent dans les églises catholiques, mais dans les temples aussi (photo 9). Il est évident, que dans un temple le programme rituel principal est destiné par la chaire et que le rituel qui est destiné par la table de la Cène y est subordonnée.

La frontière entre les deux espaces topiques d'une configuration topique polémique peut varier considérablement. Nous allons vous donner quelques exemples. A la photo 10 cette frontière est peu accentuée. Elle ressemble celle de la Sainte-Bernadette à Nevers. A la photo 11 le contraste entre les deux espaces topiques est nettement marqué par le sanctuaire élevé et la table de communion. Cette opposition était encore plus grande au Moyen-Age, où dans la plupart des églises la nef était séparée du sanctuaire par une barrière, qui rendait le sanctuaire pragmatiquement impénétrable. Pourtant le sanctuaire n'était pas impénétrable sur le plan cognitif (photo 12). Nous pouvons établir une parallèle entre ces exemples-là et l'iconostase dans les églises d'Orient. En ce qui concerne l'iconostase elles ont réussi d'exploiter un bon nombre des aspectualisations possibles, qui ont d'ailleurs une portée plus large que la sémiotique du visuel. Les portes fermées causent une impénétrabilité visuelle et cognitive, tandis que l'accessibilité auditive reste intacte. Mais dans l'ouest aussi nous rencontrons des exemples pareils. Rappelons-nous la prière du canon de la liturgie romaine, que l'on priait avant le concile de Vatican II. Au moment suprême de l'eucharistie le sanctuaire était inaccessible. Le faire rituel y avait lieu de manière somato-pragmatique, audible et tangible, mais il existait quand-même une impénétrabilité visuelle et cognitive. L'élévation succédait à la consécration du pain et une sonnette avertissait les croyants qu'ils devaient fixer leur regard sur l'hostie (*Augenkommunion*). Cette aspectualisation était suivie de la communion, qui fut une conjonction très tangible et tensitive à l'objet de valeur. Sur la langue on recevait une hostie, qu'on n'était pas permi de toucher des mains. L'intimité de cette conjonction était dû à la tangibilité et moins au goût (en réalité l'hostie n'avait aucun goût particulier). Quant à l'espace liturgique la communion consistait en une approche du lieu saint. Les croyants s'agenouillaient devant la table de communion, qui marquait la frontière entre la nef et le sanctuaire. Là ils recevaient l'hostie du prêtre, qui s'était posé sur la frontière même du lieu saint. L'exposition de l'hostie dans l'ostensoir dans le sanctuaire provoquait une grande tension en ce qui concerne l'aspectualisation. L'hostie était visible, mais comme l'ostensoir était vitré l'hostie n'était point accessible aux croyants du point de vue de la tangibilité. Cela valait pour les reliques aussi, mais ils furent cependant accesibles d'une voie intermédiaire, car le peuple croyant était permis de baiser le vitre des reliquaires. D'ailleurs au Moyen-Age les croyants pouvaient baiser de telle manière la 'relique' du saint sacrement de l'autel aussi.

Mais retournons à la sémiotique du visuel proprement dite. Il est évident que l'opposition polémique entre les deux espaces topiques peut varier considérablement et que sur le plan discursif elle peut avoir plusieurs expressions, si bien syntaxiques (l'aspectualisation) que sémantiques (la figurativisation, par exemple la différence entre la chaire et le simple pulpitre).

La configuration topique polémique s'oppose à la *configuration topique contractuelle* (figure 2). Celle-ci a la forme expressive d'un cercle ou d'un carré, qui contourne un espace vide. C'est une configuration qui exprime une position équivalente voisine, et qui est liée aux compétences équivalentes de ceux, qui se sont réunis de cette manière. Elle peut se produire dans le cas des rituels, qui s'accomplissent autour d'un espace vide. En même temps il nous faut nous rendre compte, que cette configuration topique contractuelle est peu commune dans la liturgie. Certaines liturgies féministes tendent à réaliser cette configuration, mais elle se transforme assez rapidement en une troisième configuration topique.

384 La sémiotique de l'architecture de l'église

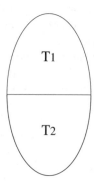
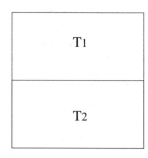

figure 1. la configuration topique polémique

Cette configuration se réalise entre autres, dès que l'on remplit le vide par un objet (par exemple une bougie, un pulpitre ou un autel) ou par quelqu'un qui créent alors l'opposition entre eux et le cercle. Il est possible aussi qu'en maintenant le vide, quelqu'un dans le cercle représente une certaine contrariété et forme un espace topique particulier en tant qu'hôte ou officiant (figure 3). Là nous voyons un cercle ou un carré, qui peuvent être ouverts. A cette place ouverte se trouve un espace topique bien défini, qui représente une certaine contrariété.[11] C'est une opposition relative. Dans ces cas-là nous rencontrons une configuration, qui se place entre la configuration topique polémique et la configuration topique contractuelle. D'un part elle exprime l'opposition et de l'autre la juxtaposition. Il s'agit d'une *configuration topique polémo-contractuelle*. A la photo 13 nous voyons une famille de nomades dans le désert arabe, qui fête la Pâque. Nous pourrions croire qu'il s'agit là d'une configuration contractuelle, mais c'est le père de la famille qui remplit pourtant le rôle d'hôte. Cet élément polémique n'est pas nettement visualisé, ce qui est dû à la démarcation assez floue de son espace topique. Cependant nous constatons une certaine opposition, dans la mesure où le père en tant qu'hôte occupe l'espace topique qui se trouve au milieu. Le rituel qui s'y accomplit (les mots, les gestes) prouve la particularité de cet espace topique. Les églises et les temples contemporains eux aussi sont marqués par la configuration topique polémo-contractuelle (photos 14 et 15). Comparés aux configurations topiques polémiques ces exemples montrent que les compétences ont été distribuées de manière différente. D'un côté nous remarquons l'équivalence ou la participation réciproque aux compétences et de l'autre l'opposition, mais l'accent peut porter soit sur l'équivalence soit sur l'opposition. Nous n'insisterons pas sur les différentes modalités de ces deux aspects.[12] D'ailleurs, sur le plan discursif il y a des nuances particulières possibles en ce qui concerne l'aspectualisation et la figurativisation.

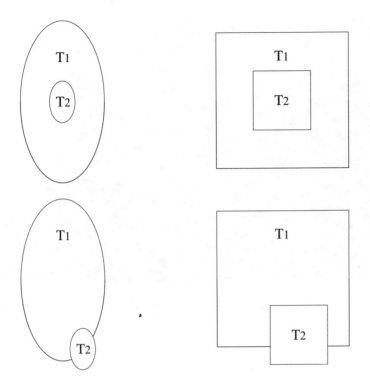

figure 3. la configuration topique polémo-contractuelle

Nous espérons que nous avons réussi à indiquer l'avantage de la sémiotique du visuel de l'école de Paris pour éclaircir la signification d'une église et les programmes qui s'y accomplissent. Surtout en ce qui concerne l'espace nous espérons d'avoir montré que cette sémiotique du visuel peut être complétée par moyen des sémiotiques non-visuelles. Enfin nous voudrions souligner l'importance de cette élucidation sémiotique pour la théologie de la liturgie. La théologie se rend trop peu compte de la mesure, dans laquelle elle se manifeste dans la construction de l'espace liturgique en tant que tel.

---

11 Cf. HAMMAD, ARANGO, DE KUYPER et POPPE: L'espace du séminaire.
12 Cf. LUKKEN: Die architektonischen Dimensionen.

1: R. GIESELMANN: *Neue Kirchen* (Stuttgart 1972) 103

2: R. GIESELMANN: *Neue Kirchen* (Stuttgart 1972) 103

3: R. GIESELMANN: *Neue Kirchen* (Stuttgart 1972) 104

4: R. GIESELMANN: *Neue Kirchen* (Stuttgart 1972) 104

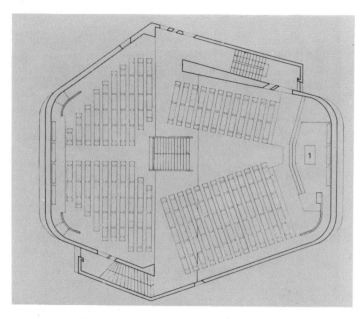

5: R. GIESELMANN: *Neue Kirchen* (Stuttgart 1972) 105

6: R. GIESELMANN: *Neue Kirchen* (Stuttgart 1972) 105

7: R. GIESELMANN: *Neue Kirchen* (Stuttgart 1972) 105

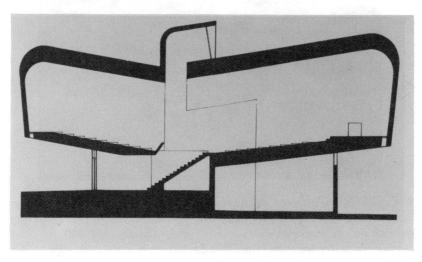

8: R. GIESELMANN: *Neue Kirchen* (Stuttgart 1972) 105

9: R. STEENSMA: *Opdat de ruimten meevieren. Een studie over de spanning tussen liturgie en monumentenzorg bij de herinrichting en het gebruik van monumentale hervormde kerken* (Baarn 1982) 190
(Le temple de Bodegraven (aux Pays-Bas) après la restauration de 1968 à 1971)

10: R. GIESELMANN: *Neue Kirchen* (Stuttgart 1972) 97
(La St. Etienne de Bernhausen (Baden-Würtemberg en Allemagne) de 1964 à 1968)

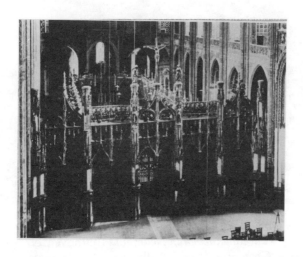

12: L. BRINKHOFF e.a. (éd.): *Liturgisch woordenboek* I (Roermond 1958-1962) xxxv
(Le jubé de la cathédrale St. Cécile (Albi en France) 16e siècle)

11: M. VAN DER PLAS et J. ROES: *De kerk gaat uit. Familiealbum van een halve eeuw katholiek leven in Nederland* (Bilthoven 1973) 15 (La St. Joseph, Groningen (aux Pays-Bas))

13: J. ZINK: *Vijf broden en twee vissen* (Hilversum 1973) 175

14: R. GIESELMANN: *Neue Kirchen* (Stuttgart 1972) 140
(Die Konzilsgedächtniskirche (Wien-Lainz en Autriche) de 1965 à 1968)

15: R. STEENSMA: *Opdat de ruimten meevieren. Een studie over de spanning tussen liturgie en monumentenzorg bij de herinrichting en het gebruik van monumentale hervormde kerken* (Baarn 1982) 139
(L'église gothique de Noordwijk-Binnen (aux Pays-Bas) après le réaménagement de 1970 à 1975)

Index of Names

Abraham, 161
Adam, A., 32, 38, 152, 153, 187
Aegidius Romanus, 144
Aesculapius, 115, 116
Agricola, Radulphus, 241
Ahlers, R., 42
Alberich, E., 246
Alcala, A., 251
Alexander VII, 49
Alfaro, J., 151
Alfrink B., 73
Allmen, D. von, 240
Alsteens, A., 240
Altizer, T., 54, 69
Aman, E., 38
Ambaum, J., 32
Ambrosius, 192
Amougou-Atangana, J., 29
Anbeek, T., 250
Anderson, H., 188
Andrieu, M., 154
Angenendt, A., 225
Aquinas, Thomas, 144
Arango, S., 379, 385
Aristoteles, 241
Arrivé, M., 270, 271, 364, 375
Athanasius, 125, 192
Aubert, R., 240
Auf der Maur, Hj., 32, 171, 178, 232
Augé, M., 246, 361
Augustin, M., 130, 293
Augustinus, 116, 131, 138, 143, 169, 176, 178, 187, 192
Baaren, Th. van, 50, 56
Bachelard, G., 91
Bahr, H., 110
Barnard, W., 39, 277
Barth, K., 169, 170, 190
Barthes, R., 99
Bartholomäus, W., 150

Bartsch, E., 240
Bartsch, H.-W., 240
Basilius, 192
Baumstark, A., 252
Beatrix (Queen), 85
Beaude, P., 294
Becker, H., 254
Beelaerts, M., 36
Beentjes, P., 40, 284
Bekaert, G., 62, 63
Bellarminus, see Robertus Bellarminus
Belle, W. van, 270
Bellemakers, S., 232, 254, 258
Berg, J. van den, 226
Berger, H., 11, 28, 152, 299
Berger, R., 32, 37, 361
Berger, T., 256
Berger, W., 214, 216, 218, 219
Bergkamp, N., 103
Berkelmans, J., 70
Berti, C., 61
Bertsch, L., 42
Blankesteijn, H., 63
Blommerde, A., 88, 208
Blond, G., 29
Blijlevens, A., 31-34, 36-39, 42, 185, 192, 195, 212-214, 216, 232, 254
Bode, F.-J., 36
Böcker, B., 41
Boelens, W., 36-38
Boeracker, H., 35
Boff, L., 90, 91, 143, 145, 150, 151, 158, 159, 197
Bogers, H., 52
Bommer, J., 78, 205, 211, 215
Bonifatius VIII, 144
Boom, A.L., see K. Fens
Boon-Schilling, H., 40
Born, P., 205
Bornewasser, J., 25, 26, 45

Index of Names

Boudewijnse, H., 41
Bouwman, G., 284, 291
Bouyer, L., 49
Braeckmans, L., 26
Brandt, P., 316
Brink, H., 239, 241
Brinkhoff, L., 24, 154, 207, 239, 240, 335, 391
Bro, B., 60
Broveli, F., 202, 203
Brugman, A., 37
Buber, M., 196
Buddha, 178
Büße, H., 246
Bugnini, A., 55, 73, 74
Buitendijk, F., 113, 160
Bulckens, J., 170, 268
Bultmann, R., 118, 286
Cabié, R., 185
Cabrol, F., 239
Calabuig, I., 61
Callewaert, R., 56, 240
Calvin, Johannes, 190
Candace (Queen), 178
Cano, Melchior, 241
Cantalamessa, R., 33
Caprioli, A., 256
Cardenal, E., 279
Cardinali, B., 258
Cardine, E., 228, 231, 247
Caspers, Ch., 21, 38, 41, 269, 290
Cataneo, E., 49
Chauvet, L., 96
Chrysostomus, see Johannes Chrysostomus
Cicero, 241
Civil, R., 361
Claudel, P., 141, 196
Clerck, P. de, 256
Combes, A., 244
Congar, Y., 143, 144, 146, 147, 150, 151, 239, 242, 243, 251
Coppo, A., 258
Coquet, J., 270, 271, 286, 364, 375
Courtés, J., 262, 286, 287, 289, 304, 338, 349-351, 375, 376
Cyrillus of Jerusalem, 192
Dalmais, I., 239, 251, 256

Damen, L., 74
Darrault, I., 374
Debuyst, F., 63
Deckers-Dijs, M., 291
Degen, H., 15, 40
Dekkers, E., 240
Delcroix, M., 254, 286
Delorme, J., 20, 36, 41, 286, 288
Denzinger, H., 243, 251
Derrida, J., 270
Dibelius, M., 286
Döring, H., 143
Drijvers, P., 24, 25
Ducrot, O., 289
Dürig, W., 247, 258
Duffhues, T., 68
Duin, J., 24, 25
Dullaart, L., 70
Durwell, F., 257
Ebbers, J., 102
Eliade, M., 64, 165, 188
Eliot, T.S., 254
Ellebracht, M., 116
Engemann, W., 41
Erharter, H., 41
Eupen, Th. van, 27
Eyden, R. van, 46
Eykenboom, P., 116
Ezekiel, 199
Federer, K., 251
Feiner, J., 118, 143
Felling, A., 68
Fens, K., 132, 249, 250, 254
Fernandez, P., 240, 243
Finkenzeller, J., 31, 33
Floch, J., 376
Fontanille, J., 270, 291
Fortmann, H., 91, 95, 116, 121, 215
Frendo, J., 299
Fries, H., 239
Fry, Chr., 196
Furger, J., 78
Furger, F., 205
Gajard, J., 247
Galland, C., 17
Gartner, H., 256
Geest, D. de, 268
Gennep, A. van, 81, 108, 109

Geoltrain, P., 286, 288
Gerhardt, I., 233
Gerosa, L., 42
Geudens, L., 195
Gieselmann, R., 386-389, 391, 393
Goddijn, W., 28, 68, 213
Gößmann, E., 240
Goethe, J.W., 90, 145
Gomperts, H., 250
Goumans, A., 212
Govaart, T., 72
Govaart, A., 260
Grave, R. de, 195
Greeley, A., 103
Greenwood, D., 291
Gregorius of Nazianze, 192
Greimas, A., 14, 18, 20, 41, 255, 261-263, 266, 269-298, 300, 304, 310, 312, 338, 349-351, 354, 375, 376, 378
Griese, E., 240
Grivel, C., 286
Groen, B., 41
Groot, M. de, 77, 78
Grossi, V., 246
Guardini, R., 24, 141
Günther, A., 145
Gusdorf, G., 94
Gy, P.-M., 15
Habermas, J., 110
Härdelin, A., 28
Häring, B., 240
Häußling, A., 239-241, 245, 353
Hahn, A., 100, 101, 104, 109
Haidu, P., 287, 289, 290
Hallyn, F., 254, 286
Hals, Frans, 72
Hameline, J., 81, 108
Hamilton, W., 54, 69
Hammad, M., 364, 366, 367, 369, 370, 372, 373, 379, 381, 385
Happel, S., 189
Harnack, A., 116
Hart, O. van der, 66, 137
Heidegger, M., 196
Heidt, A., 24
Heilmann, A., 120
Heimbrock, G., 41

Hellenberg Hubar, R. van, 23
Hemels, J., 229
Hemert, G. van, 218
Hempelmann, R., 42
Henau, E., 42, 213, 214, 216
Henkey, H., 239, 241
Henrix, H., 31
Herlyn, O., 37
Hermans, J., 31, 84
Hes, B., 32
Heuvel, P. van den, 132
Heyke, J., 174
Heynders, O., 254
Hilgenfeld, H., 27
Hilhorst, H., 68, 75
Hilten, W. van, 77
Hippolytus, 166, 175
Hjelmslev, L., 286, 300
Hobsbawm, E., 86
Hoekstra, H., 229
Hof, O., 24, 25
Hollaardt, A., 25, 207, 228, 231
Holman, J., 130, 293
Hoogbergen, G., 9, 17, 23
Hoogeveen, P., 111
Hooijdonk, P. van, 27, 28, 60, 260
Hoppenbrouwers, F., 329, 375
Hosea, 199
Hoste-Van Bockel, R., 31
Houssiau, A., 33, 185, 188, 240, 245, 246, 256, 257
Huizing, P., 144, 147
Huizinga, J., 89
Husserl, E., 270
Hutschemaekers, G., 86
Huijbers, B., 72, 233
Isaac, 161
Jacob, 161
Jeremiah, 199
Jespers, F., 42
Jessurun d'Oliveira, H., 250
Jetter, W., 90, 101, 102, 104, 110
Joel, 153
Johannes Chrysostomus, 165
Johnson, M., 17
Jong, J. de, 332
Jongerius, H., 229
Joosse, J., 12, 35, 42, 287, 336

Index of Names

Journet, Ch., 257
Jungmann, J., 27, 257
Kaczynski, R., 42, 254, 307
Kasper, W., 152, 153
Kavanagh, A., 256
Keiren, H., 29
Keller, Helen, 121, 122
Kilsdonk, J. van, 208
King, Martin Luther, 61
Klee, H., 145
Kleinheyer, B., 39, 171, 178
Klink, J., 173
Kloppenburg, W., 83
Knaapen, H., 27
Kock, G., 229
Kok, K., 74
Kolakowski, L., 113
Konijn, S., 173, 174
Koster, Koos, 76
Kovalevski, M., 240
Kraft, H., 120
Kranemann, B., 40
Krekhovetsky, Y., 156
Krysinski, W., 292
Krzywon, E., 249
Küng, H., 147
Kuhn, J., 145
Kuiper, Jan, 76
Kurris, A., 228-230, 233, 234
Kuyper, E. de, 287, 379, 385
Laag, Hans ter, 76
Laan, H. van der, 34
Lambot, C., 131
Lans, J. van der, 75
Lapointe, G., 240
Lawler, M., 37, 185, 186, 191, 194
Leclercq, J., 240
Légaut, M., 142
Lehmann, K., 256
Lengeling, E., 208
Leo I, 125
Leroquais, V., 335
Lescrauwaet, J., 32, 48, 152, 153, 155, 216
Lévy, A., 264, 376
Leijssen, L., 35, 37, 39, 41
Lieshout, J. van, 279
Linn, E., 216

Löhrer, M., 118, 143
Logister, W., 35
Loor, H. de, 68
Loose, D., 293
Lorenzer, A., 32, 134, 136, 138
Lukken-Spieringhs, M., 9, 11
Luther, Martin, 190
Luijpen, W., 95
Maas, J., 40, 42, 284, 288
Maas-Ewerd, Th., 25, 38
Maat, P. de, 16, 17, 31, 32, 35, 287, 289, 300, 336
Mader, D., 45, 88, 140, 184
Maertens, J., 99
Manders, H., 46
Mann, F., 27
Mantz, Felix, 169
Marche, Olivier de La, 89
Marsili, S., 240, 241, 256, 258, 360, 361
Martimort, A., 185, 239, 240, 258, 361
Martin, G., 53
Martin, M., 112, 115
Mast, F. de, 23
Masure, R., 213
Mathon, G., 208
Meer, F. van der, 45, 46, 179
Menken, M., 284, 288, 291-293
Mercx, M., 279
Merks-Leinen, G., 118, 158, 224, 284, 311
Merleau-Ponty, M.-J.-J., 270
Mertens, E., 75
Mertens, H., 221, 267
Merz, M., 256
Meßner, R., 42
Metz, J.-B., 69
Meyer, H.-B., 239-241, 258
Meijer, J., 30, 40, 156
Meyer zu Schlochtern, J., 42
Migne, J.-P., 120, 125, 138, 155, 165, 168, 169, 197
Miller, J., 239
Möhler, J., 145
Mohammed, 162
Mohlberg, L.C., 131, 143, 166
Moingt, J., 40
Molisse, M., 213

Index of Names 399

Moor, W. de, 250
Moreton, B., 29
Muck, H., 373
Müller, K., 27
Müller, L., 42
Mulders, J., 154, 155, 239, 240
Musschoot, A.-M., 254
Mutsaerts, W., 9
Nakagaki, F., 240, 246, 299
Neidehart, W., 211
Neuhäusler, E., 240
Neunheuser, B., 33, 185, 190, 239, 240, 245, 351
Niati, J.P., 279
Nieuwkoop, R., 82, 83
Nocent, A., 83, 84
Nocke, F., 34
Nübold, E., 36
Nijk, A., 50, 51, 53, 58, 98
Oden, T., 216
Onna, B. von, 70
Oñatibia, I., 156
Oorschot, L. van, 254
Oosterhuis, H., 16, 29, 38, 52, 61, 72, 76, 77, 80, 95, 103, 111, 116, 127, 161, 183, 196, 232, 233, 249, 258
Origenes, 168, 169
Overbosch, W., 63
Oversteegen, J., 16, 250
Panier, L., 42, 293, 294, 297, 298, 348, 349, 354
Pannenberg, W., 39
Parent, C., 378
Parret, H., 270, 279, 282, 290-292, 364
Pascher, J., 239
Paulus, 152, 168, 199
Paulus VI, 46, 53
Pavis, P., 279, 361
Pawlowsky, P., 161, 183, 232
Peirce, Ch., 261, 285, 286, 297
Pellisson, P., 49
Pernigotto-Cego, A., 246
Peters, J., 68
Petrus, 148
Philippus, 178
Pilgram, F., 145
Pinell, J., 240
Pinto, M., 251

Pistoia, A., 256
Pius IX, 49, 244
Pius XII, 154
Plas, M. van der, 392
Plato, 53
Plattel, M., 70
Polspoel, A., 210, 214
Pontius Pilatus, 80, 162
Poppe, E., 379, 385
Post, P., 86, 260
Poulssen, N., 284
Power, D., 42, 203, 204, 240, 244
Probst, F., 145
Prosper d'Aquitane, 251
Puaud, P., 203
Puthanangady, P., 246
Quispel, G., 154
Rahner, K., 118, 145, 149, 152, 240
Ramshaw-Schmidt, G., 192-194
Ranft, J., 241
Ranger, T., 86
Ranson, J., 255
Ratzinger, J., 239
Rauter, H.-M., 41
Reckman, W., 24-26, 36, 40
Reifenberg, H., 28
Rembrandt, 72
Renier, A., 363, 364, 372, 374-376
Rennings, H., 240
Reve, G.K. van het, 92
Rey-Mermet, Th., 199
Richards, I.A., 254, 255
Richter, K., 203
Ries, J., 188
Rieß, R., 221
Riet, P. van t', 39
Robertus Bellarminus, 144
Robinson, J., 69
Roeck, B. de, 24,25
Roes, J., 68, 392
Roguet, A., 25
Romero, O., 34
Rordorf, W., 28
Roseeuw, M., 229
Rouillard, P., 199
Ruhbach, G., 39
Ruprecht, H.-G., 279, 290, 364
Ruijter, A. de, 36, 85

400 INDEX OF NAMES

Rijen, A. van, 29
Rijk, C., 70
Rijkhoff, M., 16, 17, 31, 32, 289, 300
Sara, 77, 78
Sartore, D., 256
Saussure, F. de, 261, 285, 286, 289, 300
Sauter, G., 152
Schaeffler, R., 113
Scheeben, M., 125, 145, 149
Scheer, A., 26, 193, 254, 260, 261
Schillebeeckx, E., 46, 52, 111, 142, 145, 151, 200, 220, 239-241, 243, 251, 275, 297, 307
Schleifer, R., 270, 291
Schlemmer, K., 39
Schlette, H., 52, 53, 59
Schmaus, M., 257, 299
Schmid-Kaiser, S., 34
Schmidt, H., 10, 94, 239, 249
Schmidt, K., 286
Schmitz, H., 171
Schneider, Th., 185
Schneiders, M., 9, 38, 269, 290
Schönmetzer, A., 251
Schollaert, P., 229
Schoonenberg, P., 242, 251, 252
Schreuder, O., 68, 69
Schunck, K.-D., 130, 293
Schupp, Fr., 29
Searle, M., 20, 41, 185, 188-192
Semmelroth, O., 143, 145
Senn, F., 38
Sequeira, R., 361, 362
Shakespeare, William, 267
Sierksma, F., 107
Smeulders, C., 23
Smits, A., 28
Smulders, P., 145
Snippenburg, L. van,
Sodi, M., 256
Sölle, D., 80, 91
Speelman, W.M., 196, 299, 335
Steeg, L. ter, 142
Steensma, R., 390, 394
Steggink, O., 75
Stein, Ph., 24, 25, 36
Steiner, J., 29

Stenzel, A., 240, 251
Stock, A., 254
Stouthard, P., 65, 68
Straver, J., 176, 177
Sullivan, Miss, 121
Swaeles, R.,
Swierzawski, W., 240
Tate, A., 255
Taylor, M., 69
Tenbruck, F., 101
Terstegge, A., 132
Tertullianus, 120, 168
Thatcher, M., 132
Thomassinus, 145
Thompson, A., 188
Thürlemann, F., 376
Thurlings, J., 68
Tillmans, W., 216
Tillo, G. van, 65, 68
Todorov, T., 90, 289
Tongeren, L. van, 21, 42, 232, 233, 254, 283, 336
Tourneux, N. Le, 49
Traets, C., 32
Triacca, A., 256
Tromp, N., 16, 17, 31, 32, 35, 285, 288, 289, 293, 300
Tsirpantis, C., 153
Tyrell, G., 251
Uleyn, A., 104
Vagaggini, C., 145, 239, 242, 251, 257, 284
Vallemont, P. de, 50
Vanbergen, P., 46
Vandenbroucke, F., 240
Vedder, B., 41, 269
Veldhuis, W., 60, 75
Ven, J. van der, 260
Verdaasdonk, H., 254
Vergote, A., 75, 104, 122, 127-129, 139, 163, 213, 214
Verheul, A., 170
Verhoeven, C., 92
Vermeer, Jan, 72
Vervenne, M., 284
Villanova, E., 240
Virilio, P., 378
Visentin, P., 231, 239, 240, 246, 247, 299

Vismans, Th., 10
Vogels, W., 288
Voisin, J. de, 49
Volp, R., 33, 41, 353
Vorgrimler, H., 30
Vos, W., 35, 361, 371
Vries, S. de, 83
Vrijdag, H., 37, 84
Vuijst, J., 29
Wainwright, G., 35, 256, 361, 371
Ware, K., 240, 245
Wegman, H., 25-29, 34, 40, 60, 156, 224, 225, 232, 260, 335
Weiler, A., 144
Weiß, B., 30
Weren, W., 20, 284
Werner, H., 99
Westerhoff, J., 83
Wever, T., 40, 284

Willemon, W., 83
Willems, B., 144, 145, 147
Willemsen, Joop, 76
Winkeler, L., 11
Winkelhofer, A., 145
Winter, G., 56, 57
Winterswyl, L., 125
Wit, J. de, 42, 229
Wolde, E. van, 285, 297
Wolf, J. de, 30, 40
Woude, A. van der, 130, 293
Wijngaards, J., 129
Zahn, E., 72
Zerfaß, R., 178, 205
Zeijde, M. van der, 233
Zink, J., 393
Zuidgeest, P., 217
Zumthor, P., 279
Zijderveld, A.C., 66

Tabula gratulatoria

Abdij Sint-Benedictusberg, Lemiers
Dick and Perla Akerboom, Nijmegen
Ds. N.K. van den Akker, 's-Hertogenbosch
Dr. P. Al O.Praem., Heeswijk-Dinther
Alt-Katholisches Seminar der Universität Bonn, Bonn, Germany
Prof. Dr. J. Ambaum, Kerkrade
Ambrose Swasey Library, Rochester, U.S.A.
M.T. van Amsterdam, Kudelstaart
Mgr. R. Philippe Bär O.S.B., Chevetogne, Belgium
Abt A. Baeten O.Praem., Abdij van Berne, Heeswijk-Dinther
H.L. Beck, Tilburg
Servaas Bellemakers, Tilburg
Chr. A. Paul Berbers, Bottrop, Germany
J.C. van den Berg, Heerenveen
Prof. Dr. H.H. Berger, Tilburg
Prof. Dr. Teresa Berger, Duke University, Durham, U.S.A.
Prof. Dr. W.J. Berger, Nijmegen
Biblioteca Pont. Univ. Urbaniana, Roma, Italy
Biblioteca del Seminario Arcivescovile di Milano, Italy
Bibliotheek Abdij O.L. Vrouw van Koningshoeven, Tilburg
Bibliotheek Bisdom Breda, Breda
Bibliotheek Diocesaan Seminarie, Antwerpen, Belgium
Bibliotheek Sint-Janscentrum, 's-Hertogenbosch
Bibliotheek Theologische Faculteit KU Nijmegen, Nijmegen
Bibliotheek U.T.P., Heerlen
Bibliothek der Theologischen Hochschule, Vallendar, Germany
Bibliothek Deutsches Liturgisches Institut, Trier, Germany
Bibliothek der Phil.-Theol. Hochschule der Salesianer Don Boscos, Benediktbeuern, Germany
Bibliothèque du Centre National de Pastorale Liturgique, Paris, France
Rev. Paul G. Bieber, Chicago, U.S.A.
Paul B. van den Biggelaar, Amsterdam
J. Bluyssen, 's-Hertogenbosch
A.J.M. Blijlevens, Heerlen
Antoine Bodar, Amsterdam
Dr. Wim L. Boelens S.J., Groningen
J.P. Boendermaker, Hilversum
Hans Bornewasser, H. Landstichting
Prof. Dr. H.W.J. Bosman, Tilburg
R.E.O.A. Bot, Voorburg
Heinzgerd Brakmann, Bonn, Germany
A.H. Bredero, Dongen
Bridwell Library, Dallas, U.S.A.
Gerard Broekhuijsen, Breda
Frans Brouwer, Utrecht
F.S.M. Bult-Lukken, Drunen
Gabriella M. Bult, Drunen
Stephan A.G.M. Bult, Amsterdam
G. van de Camp, 's-Hertogenbosch
Charles Caspers, Tilburg
Paul Christiaens, St. Agatha-Rode, Belgium
Th. Clemens, Zeist
Paul De Clerck, directeur Institut Supérieur de Liturgie (Paris), Brussel, Belgium
Marion Corvers, Oisterwijk
Robert J. Daly S.J., Boston College (Theological Studies), Chestnut Hill, U.S.A.

Lucien Deiss, Vaucresson, France
Karin en Peter Derks-Hanff, Oss
Diocesaan Pastoraal Centrum, 's-Hertogenbosch
Rev. Dr. Arlo Duba, Hot Springs, U.S.A.
Drs. S.A.L. van Dijk, Tilburg
Prof. Dr. H.F.J.M. van den Eerenbeemt, Tilburg
J.P.R.M. Eggermont, Sas van Gent
J.H.M. Ettema, Groningen
Dr. H. Faber, Maarn
Drs. P.B. Feenstra and A.C.H. Berlis, Arnhem
Ds. Drs. G.H. Fredrikze, Woerden
Dr. Albert Gerhards, Bonn, Germany
Marcel Gielis, Turnhout, Belgium
Winfried Glade, Mödling, Austria
Dr. André Goossens, Boechout, Belgium
M. de Haardt, Tilburg
Benno Haeseldonckx, Brussel, Belgium
Prof. Dr. Philipp Harnoncourt, Graz, Austria
E. Henau, Wezembeek-Oppem, Belgium
Luc van Hilst, Tremelo, Belgium
A.H. Hollaardt O.P., Nijmegen
J.C.M. Holman, Tilburg
Drs. P.M.J. Hoogstrate, Mijdrecht
Drs. Frans Hoppenbrouwers, Tilburg
A.A.J. Huijben, Delft
Dr. Kevin W. Irwin, Catholic University Theology Dept., Washington DC, U.S.A.
J.Y.H.A. Jacobs, Tilburg
Jan Jans, Oud-Turnhout, Belgium
C.H.A. Janssens, Gilze
Gustaaf Janssens, Leuven, Belgium
Frans Jespers, Voerendaal
Jezuïtengemeenschap Mechelen, Mechelen, Belgium
Johannes Gutenberg-Universität Mainz, Germany
St. John's Seminary Library, Brighton (MA), U.S.A.
Evert and Emmy de Jong, Driebergen

Ko Joosse, Rotterdam
Rev. J.M.C.M. van Kemenade, Casteren (N.Br.)
Mr. and Mrs. Kemme, Lanaken, Belgium
Rev. John H. McKenna C.M., St. John's University, Jamaica (NY), U.S.A.
P.E.R. Keizer, Kandersteg, Switzerland
J. de Kesel, Gent, Belgium
Ad de Keyzer, Nijmegen
Dr. Martin Klöckener, Trier, Germany
Drs. G.L.N. Kock, Heesch
Dr. A. Kurris, Eys-Wittem
Drs. R.G.A. Kurvers, Naaldwijk
J.A.A. van Laarhoven, 's-Hertogenbosch
Prof. Dr. Jozef Lamberts, Hombeek-Mechelen, Belgium
Gordon Lathrop, Philadelphia (PA), U.S.A.
Cyriel M.J. Laudy, Sittard
A.S. Laurier S.M.M., Berg en Dal
C.J.N. Lavaleije, IJsselmuiden
Martin van der Leeden, Berlicum
Ir. H.H.J. Lelieveldt, Rotterdam
G. Leloux, Etten-Leur
Lambert Leijssen, Leuven, Belgium
H. Loevendie, Oisterwijk
W. Logister, Tilburg
Dr. J.J.C. Maas and P.A.M. Maas-Post, Dussen
Paul de Maat, Dorst
D. Mader, Amsterdam
Henk Manders CSSR, Wittem
Ben Mathis, Bunnik
Gabriele and Karl Merks, Tilburg
Gemma Mertens, Oosterhout
L. Meurders, Nuth
Dr. J.A.J. Meijer CSSR, Tilburg
Tijs Michels, Tilburg
Dr. J. Mulders S.J., Den Haag
Fr. De Muynck, Brugge, Belgium
R. Nauta, Eelde
Nederlandse Sint-Gregoriusvereniging, Utrecht

Nederlandse Vereniging voor
   Semiotiek, Uithoorn
G. van Nistelrooij, Breda
E.H. van Olst, 's-Hertogenbosch
Ignacio Oñatibia, Facultad de
   Teología, Gasteiz-Vitoria, Spain
Onze Lieve Vrouweabdij, Oosterhout
C. van Ooijen, Goes
P. Oskamp, Doorn
Johan M.J. van Parijs, Notre Dame,
   U.S.A.
Prof. W. de Pater, Leuven, Belgium
St. Paulusabdij, Oosterhout
G.W. Pieterse, Nijmegen
Prof. Jean Paul M.F. Pinxten, Haacht,
   Belgium
Albert Pirenne, Goirle
Emile Poppe, Nijmegen
Jack Post, Maastricht
Dr. P.G.J. Post, Naarden
Dr. James F. Puglisi S.A., Centro pro
   Unione, Roma, Italy
Prof. Dr. Heinrich Rennings,
   Lampaden, Germany
Dr. Susan K. Roll, Faculteit der
   Godgeleerdheid, KU Leuven,
   Belgium
Gerard Rouwhorst, Nieuwegein
H. Richard Rutherford C.S.C.,
   Portland (Oregon), U.S.A.
Dr. John Barry Ryan, Manhattan
   College, Bronx (NY), U.S.A.
M. Rijkhoff, Goirle
Anton H.M. Scheer, Rosmalen
Marc Schneiders, Alphen a.d. Rijn
Prof. Dr. N. Schreurs, Heumen
Ds. G. van Schuppen, Wierden
I.A.M. Seeboldt, Egmond-Binnen
A. Smeets, Tilburg
Silveer de Smet, Leuven, Belgium
Prof. Dr. A.H. Smits, Oosterhout
   (N.Br.)
Dr. G.J.C. Snoek, Aalsmeer
Willem Marie Speelman, Tilburg
P. Stevens, Heerlen
B.L.J. Stockmann, Utrecht
Rev. Dr. Gianfranco Tellini,
   Dunblane, Great Britain

Rev. Dr. Jacob Thekkeparampil,
   Kottayam, India
Theologisch Seminarium Hydepark,
   Doorn
Theologische Faculteit Tilburg –
   Bibliotheek, Tilburg
Gérard P.P. van Tillo, Amsterdam
Louis van Tongeren, Tilburg
Nico Tromp M.S.C., Echt
Kristin De Troyer, Kampen
Prof. David Truemper, Valparaiso
   University, Valparaiso (IN), U.S.A.
Uitgeverij Gooi en Sticht, Baarn
Uitgeverij Kok Pharos, Kampen
Universitätsbibliothek Tübingen,
   Tübingen, Germany
Veronica van Valkenhoef,
   Driebergen-Rijsenburg
Drs. Jeroen M.M. van der Ven, Boxtel
C.M.L. Verdegaal, Breda
Ambroos Verheul O.S.B., Affligem,
   Belgium
Dr. A.C. Vernooij, Zeist
R.L.M. Visser, Purmerend
Wiebe and Cornelia E. Vos, Grave
Nico Vreeswijk, Veghel
Drs. J.P.F. Waegemakers, 's-
   Hertogenbosch
Prof. Dr. Geoffrey Wainwright, The
   Divinity School, Duke University,
   Durham (NC), U.S.A.
J.R. van der Wal, Balk
Prof. Dr. Knut Walf, Nijmegen
Marcel Weemaes, Abdij van Male,
   Brugge, Belgium
Prof. Dr. H.A.J. Wegman, Utrecht
J. Weitjens, Rotterdam
Prof. Dr. W.J.C. Weren, Oisterwijk
Werkgroep voor Liturgie Heeswijk,
   Heeswijk-Dinther
T. Wever, Amsterdam
Drs. Jeroen de Wit, Borne
M.G.M. de Wit, Eindhoven
Henk and Willemien Witte, Goirle
M.J. Zuijderhoff, 's-Hertogenbosch
Drs. M.A. van Zutphen, Waalwijk